The undersigned are engaged in raising a Regiment for the

Defence of the State !

A camp has been established near Charleston, where Companies joining us will be equipped and furnished with a

COMPLETE UNIFORM,

including shoes and overcoats. We earnestly invite our fellow-citizens to join us in our effort to

DEFEND OUR HOMES AND OUR LIBERTIES!

and to drive our enemies from the soil they have invaded.

Information can be had of Col. Stevens, at Charleston, or of Lieut. Col. Capers, at Columbia.

C. H. STEVENS,
ELLISON CAPERS.

The recruiting poster distributed to all districts of the State of South Carolina seeking recruits for the new regiment.
(Courtesy The Citadel Archives, The Citadel, Charleston, S.C.)

ENLISTED
FOR THE WAR

The Struggles of the Gallant
24th Regiment, South Carolina
Volunteers, Infantry, 1861-1865

EUGENE W. JONES JR.

Longstreet House
Hightstown, NJ
New Book No. 134
1997

Permission has been secured to quote from the following:

Ellison Capers Papers, J.D. Padgett Papers, photos of B.B Smith and Ellison Capers and
recruiting poster, from The Citadel Archives, Charleston, S.C.

James Tillman Diaries, from Special Collections, Clemson University Libraries, Clemson,
S.C.

Braxton Bragg Papers, Ellison Capers Papers, C.S.A. Archives, W.H.T. Walker Papers,
Charles Edgeworth Jones Papers, from Special Collections Library, Duke University,
Durham, N.C.

Augustine T. Smythe, J.H. Steinmeyer, Stevens Family, and Teague Papers, from the South
Carolina Historical Society, Charleston, S.C.

Beckwick Family Papers, Braxton Bragg Papers, Ellison Capers Papers, J.B. Cummings
Papers, Joseph Espey Papers, Gale & Polk Family Papers, Daniel Goran Papers, R.M. Gray
Papers, Janus I. Hall Papers, William Makall Papers, Marcus J. Wright Papers, and W.T.
Watson Diary, from Southern Historical Collection, Library of the University of North
Carolina at Chapel Hill, N.C.

Ellison Capers Papers, Gale/Polk Papers, University of the South Archives, Swanee, Tenn.

Papers and photographs, South Caroliniana Library, University of South Carolina, Columbia,
S.C.

First edition.

Please direct all correspondence and book orders to:
LONGSTREET HOUSE
PO Box 730
Hightstown, NJ 08520

ISBN Number 0-944413-43-9

Printed in the United States of America

TO
ANN DOLORES JONES,
JULY 27, 1933-JANUARY 28, 1995
My lovely, lovely wife.
Because she lived,
This manuscript lives.

Ellison Capers in general officer's uniform
(*Courtesy Perkins Library, Duke University*)

CONTENTS

v

MAPS

ILLUSTRATIONS

PREFACE

This book offers the reader an opportunity to trace the struggles of a South Carolina regiment which served during the great American Civil War. The regiment, officially known as the 24th Regiment, South Carolina Volunteers, Infantry, was generally known to its soldiers as "The Gallant Twenty-Fourth."

The men were fairly homogeneous notwithstanding that they hailed from nine separate South Carolina communities. The majority of the men were farmers, though the one company from Charleston consisted primarily of blue collar workers and skilled artisans.

The roster of the regiment (Appendix I) lists 1,520 men who served in the regiment. The roster of the Consolidated 16th and 24th Regiment South Carolina Volunteers Infantry (Appendix II), which was established on April 10, 1865, lists the names of 425 soldiers. There were 201 soldiers previously assigned to the 24th Regiment, and 224 from the 16th Regiment.

In its history the 24th proudly claimed to have been "first" several times. This was the first South Carolina regiment which enlisted to serve for the duration of "the war." Afterwards, it was accepted for Confederate service, and the governor designated the new organization, "The first regiment under recent acquisition."

The 24th participated in several skirmishes on James Island in early 1862, albeit its first real taste of combat was at the Battle of Secessionville on June 16, 1862, where it suffered its first combat fatality. Defending the coast, the regiment drew assignments at Wilmington and Pocotaligo, in addition to James Island. However, the next severe battle after Secessionville was at Jackson, Mississippi, May 14, 1863.

After spending the hot, dry summer in Mississippi, the South Carolinians joined the Army of Tennessee at Chattanooga in August 1863. It became one of four South Carolina regiments permanently assigned to the western army, and it remained there until General Johnston surrendered in North Carolina on April 26, 1865.

The 24th suffered more than 1,000 casualties during the war. The roster in Appendix I lists the following deaths: killed in action: 148; died of disease or some unknown fate: 189; died of Wounds: 46; died while a prisoner of war: 47; died as a result of an accident: 6.

Some of the actions were especially devastating. At Jackson, the regiment counted 105 soldiers killed, wounded and captured. At Chickamauga, it lost 169 men in 40 bloody minutes, and during the Atlanta Campaign it lost one half its strength. At Franklin, the 24th was in the front line of attack and suffered mightily; the lieutenant colonel was killed, and the regimental commander seriously wounded. At the same time, the brigade commander was killed and the division commander wounded. At Nashville, a large number of the men were captured.

The 24th participated in numerous battles. At Missionary Ridge, it performed admirably as rear guard for Breckenridge's Corps. The 24th fought in every battle of the Atlanta Campaign except Ezra Church. At Kennesaw, it was posted as the advanced skirmish line for the brigade. At Jonesboro, the 24th was cited for repulsing numerous attacks and holding a critical spot in the defensive line. Even though badly used up at Franklin, the regiment captured one of the few Union colors taken by the Confederate army that day. During the retreat from Nashville, General Cheatham cited Brigadier General States Rights Gist's Brigade, of which the 24th was a part, as the only brigade in his corps which was under arms and following the orders of its leaders.

The men stood by the colors of the regiment until the surrender. In North Carolina, due to its reduced strength, the 24th was consolidated with the 16th Regiment and became the Consolidated 16th and 24th Regiment, South Carolina Volunteers, Infantry. On April 26, 1865, the new consolidated regiment was inspected and pronounced "ready for the fray," an honor awarded few regiments then with the Army of Tennessee.

From a wide range of resources, I have garnered the information that recounts the deeds of the 24th. This study examines the details of mundane events as well as the more fascinating actions of the regiment with particular emphasis on the daily hardships borne by the individual soldiers.

An extensive reservoir of information is found in the writings of General (later Bishop) Ellison Capers, who was appointed lieutenant colonel of the 24th and ended the War as the brigade commander. Capers was seriously wounded three times and received minor injuries twice. The regiment was the brainchild of Brigadier General Clement Hoffman Stevens, who was killed leading his brigade during the battle of Peachtree Creek.

The colors of the 24th were never captured. At the unhappy surrender, the men started removing the stars and other adornments from the flag as souvenirs. Colonel Benjamin Burg Smith, commander of the new consolidated regiment, saved the flag from total desecration, and today the original colors are on permanent display in the Confederate Relic Room, Columbia, South Carolina.

During the War, the men suffered numerous deprivations and misery, and through it all never lost the will to fight or shirked a required duty. The toughest obstacle the men confronted was the challenge to endure the hardships of surviving until the time for battle. Even in the face of the most serious adversity, the soldiers never doubted they would emerge victorious.

This writer's primary objective has been to document the experiences of the men of the 24th Regiment. Ellison Capers considered writing this history more than 100 years ago. Such a manuscript would have provided unequaled insight into the experience of the regiment, but, sadly, he did not. I am hopeful this record will provide a clearer understanding of the values cherished by a population which could not or would not compromise them.

ACKNOWLEDGEMENTS

Only a few of the people who have contributed to this project may be mentioned here. Those not mentioned are entitled to full recognition that this project could not have been completed without their aid. For that, everyone has my eternal gratitude. I hope the few individuals and archives' staffs that are mentioned here will be demonstrative of my appreciation to each person or group that provided the aid necessary to bring this project to fruition.

Otto Warren of Orangeburg, South Carolina, was a source of inspiration for the project. In addition to providing the pictures of his ancestor, Captain Joseph K. Risher, Otto made available his personal set of the *Official Records*, which saved untold hours of labor in the library.

John Bigham of the Confederate Relic Room, Columbia, South Carolina, made the unusual contribution of assisting in acquiring photos of the soldiers, and also serving as a source of inspiration and encouragement. John is a descendant of Private James Bigham, a member of the regiment who distinguished himself during the war, especially at Franklin. John read and adjusted the final manuscript and from its pages developed some statistics that are mentioned.

Jane Yates, Archivist at the Citadel, threw open the records held at that facility, and in the early days provided insight and inspiration necessary for one to take on such a project as this. The staff of Allen Stokes at the Caroliniana Library, University of South Carolina, in addition to exercising incredible patience, offered suggestions for researching and locating sources of material related to the project.

Richard McMurry spent his valuable time reading my manuscript and offering a critique that, no doubt, led to its publication. In this regard, the efforts of David Martin, of Longstreet House, are of special significance.

Invaluable assistance was provided by the staffs of every archives visited either in person or by mail: the South Carolina Historical Society; the National Archives; Emory University Library; University of Georgia Library; the Atlanta Historical Society; the Georgia Historical Society; the Tennessee State Library and Archives; Perkins Library, Duke University; the University of the South Library; the Southern Historical Collection at the University of North Carolina at Chapel Hill; the South Carolina State Archives; Clemson University Libraries; Rice University Archives; the historians at the Kennesaw Mountain National Military Park, and at the Chickamauga-Chattanooga National Military Park.

Numerous other individuals and institutions made contributions. They include Dianne Timmerman, Archivist, Edgefield Archives, Edgefield, South Carolina, who provided access to records of two companies that hailed from Edgefield; the library staffs in Beaufort, Charleston, Chester, Colleton, Hampton, and Marlboro counties; and the historian's office in

Pendleton, S.C. Those staffs were always courteous and forever went that extra step to assist me in my quest for information.

There are many individuals who deserve my appreciation for contributing photos and information about ancestors. My neighbor, Cal Lambert, used his expertise with a computer to draw several of the maps. Another neighbor, Bruce Swanger, used his years of experience as a professional proofreader. Carl McIntyre and Parker Hills, of Jackson, Mississippi, provided me with photographs and key information about the regiment's battles there. Ray Cooper, of Early Branch, S.C., George Bailey, of Wilson, N. C., and Jacob F. Strait, of Georgetown, SC, and J. R. Fisher, Jr., located pictures of ancestors who served in the regiment.

Cynthia Moseley, of Spartanburg, South Carolina, a descendant of both General Stevens and the Capers families, provided information. Tim Burgess, the preeminent researcher and writer, of Nashville, Tennessee, provided information about the battles at Franklin and Nashville. Barry J. Crompton offered needed encouragement. Hurley Badders, a Stevens family buff and historian at Pendleton, S.C., gave me a boost in doing the research.

The motivational support for the entire project came from my lovely wife, Ann Jones, who never once complained about vacations spent visiting archives or many, many other inconveniences. Without her care, encouragement, and tolerance, it is unlikely this project could have been contemplated, much less completed.

There are still many others. To those mentioned and to those not mentioned, I thank you and hope you will find that, within these pages, your efforts were worthwhile.

ENLISTED
FOR THE WAR

General Clement Hoffman Stevens
(Courtesy South Caroliniana Library, University of South Carolina, Columbia, S.C.)

CHAPTER 1

"First Regiment of Infantry of Recent Acquisition"

At the Battle of Peachtree Creek on July 20, 1864, General John Bell Hood's Army of Tennessee charged an already entrenched enemy in a vicious onslaught. Seeing that his brigade could not maintain its advanced position in the face of the strong Union counterattack, Brigadier General Clement Hoffman Stevens fearlessly spurred his horse into the middle of the leaden hail that flew around his men and personally barked the command to withdraw. As Stevens' clarion voice rang out, the horse underneath the general fell to the ground, mortally wounded by a well-placed enemy minié ball. Stevens nimbly extricated himself from the falling animal and turned his right side toward the direction of the enemy fire. All in the same movement, another enemy minié ball struck the old fellow behind his right ear. Without a murmur, the former commander of the 24th Regiment, fell unconscious.[1]

Stevens' aides, without regard for their own safety, sprang to his side and exclaimed happily, "He is still alive." They gathered the unconscious general in their arms and hurried to the nearest hospital. Both aides were severely wounded as they performed the task. At the hospital, the surgeons skillfully removed the ball from the head and brain of the fallen general and exuded confidence that Stevens would make a full recovery. The general displayed the same energy fighting for his life as he did in his life's activities and battles. On the morning of July 25, 1864, however, General Stevens' condition suddenly worsened and he died without regaining consciousness. His aides accompanied his remains until they were laid to rest in a private lot at Magnolia Cemetery in Charleston, South Carolina. Sadness prevailed throughout the entire state as the citizens mourned the loss of a brave general and contemplated that the prime leadership of the beloved Southern Confederacy was rapidly waning.[2]

Three years earlier, Stevens had returned, severely wounded, from the Battle of First Manassas, where he served as a volunteer aide to his brother-in-law, Brigadier General Bernard E. Bee. Recovering rapidly, Governor F. W. Pickens appointed Stevens as the commander of the 16th Regiment, South Carolina Militia. Even the most casual observer realized that the regiment did not possess essential equipment or sufficient manpower to satisfy its commitments. Therefore, on October 6, 1861, Stevens decided on

3

a higher goal and tendered his resignation as commander of the militia regiment. Simultaneously, he gained the Governor's authority to raise a regiment of infantry for 12 months' service with the Confederacy. Stevens eagerly applied his enormous energy seeking volunteers throughout the state.[3] Thus, the group of men who formed the regiment that became the 24th began assembling.

Even before the War, Stevens lived an interesting, danger-laden and adventure-filled life. He was born in Connecticut, a son of a United States Naval Officer who hailed from Montego Bay, Jamaica. His mother was a member of the French Huguenot "Faysoux" family of Charleston. Clement's father resigned from the Navy and became a rancher in Florida, but he was killed leading a regiment of infantry during the Seminole wars. Mrs. Stevens moved with her children to Pendleton, South Carolina, and resided with her sister, Ann Faysoux Bee, the mother of General Bernard E. Bee. The house was generally known as the "Bee Hive."

Clement responded to his inner urging for a life of adventure and left home at an early age. He signed on as secretary to near kinsmen, Commodores William Bee Shubrick and Edward Shubrick, as they sailed the seven seas. In 1842, he left the sea and settled in Charleston, where he became a successful Broad Street banker and businessman.[4] He soon married his first cousin, Ann Bee, and when the War started, Colonel and Mrs. Stevens were the proud parents of three sons.

Stevens was a champion of states rights and a strong supporter of the Southern political philosophy, and fully realized that the threat of war was real. He designed an "ironclad battery" which guarded the entrance to Charleston Harbor, and used his political influence to gain funds for the project even before the secession proclamation was adopted. Afterwards, Stevens supervised construction of the new guardian of Charleston Harbor. Local newspapers pronounced it as the first "ironclad fortification ever erected" and claimed that it served as the forerunner or model for the first armor-plated ship.[5]

The future general was actively involved in many other political decisions and preparations for the defense of the city of Charleston. Stevens' presence or influence could be found at such "hot spots" around Charleston as Cummings Point, Coles Island and Fort Moultrie, during the early days after secession as the state moved toward War.

In addition to General Bee, Stevens had two brothers who served in the Confederate military service; however, his highly respected near kinsmen, the Shubricks, remained with the Union. A brother, Peter Faysoux Stevens, Superintendent of the Citadel, commanded the artillery battery which fired on the *Star of the West* when she attempted to relieve Fort Sumter on January 9, 1861. Peter later raised the Holcomb Legion, which served in Virginia. His other brother, Lieutenant Henry K. Stevens, was a member of the U. S. Navy, but he resigned his commission with the U. S. Navy to enter the Confederate Navy. Subsequently, Henry was killed in battle while serving aboard the Confederate gunboat *Cotton* on the Red River in 1863. Peter was the only one of the three brothers who survived the War.[6]

As Stevens began recruiting the new regiment, the strong war fervor that existed in South Carolina intensified when the Union Navy established a base at Hilton Head, on the coast near Beaufort. South Carolina citizens were eager to drive the invaders from the soil of their homeland, and, as a result, numerous militia units were springing up in communities throughout the state. Several of those units became part of the new regiment.

The first company to volunteer for duty with the regiment was Company A, 16th S.C.M., The Marion Rifles, which marched to Stevens' headquarters and tendered its services on October 16, 1861.[7] Stevens immediately accepted the offer, and, on the spot, designated the company as the right-guard company of the new regiment, a designation the company retained for the duration of the war. The Marion Rifles were already a veteran organization. They had entered active military service soon after the state seceded and manned positions in several critical assignments around Charleston, such as Sullivans and Coles Islands.[8]

Soon afterwards, the Pee Dee Rifles, from Marlboro District, also joined the new regiment. This company was in a camp of instruction at Camp Magnolia, near the Charleston city limits. Stevens accepted the company for service in the new regiment on December 4, 1861.[9]

Stevens searched for the best talent available for assistance in recruiting the new regiment. His attention was immediately attracted to Ellison Capers, a youthful officer who was serving in the 1st Regiment, South Carolina Militia. Capers' sister had married Stevens' brother, Peter. Thinking Ellison might prefer service with a regiment of "Volunteers," Stevens offered the young Citadel associate professor of mathematics the position of lieutenant colonel.[10]

Capers considered the offer tempting. He agonized about the dilemma and discussed it with his wife, Charlotte (Lottie) Rebecca Palmer. The young man had recently settled in his employment with the Citadel and was already the father of two adorable children, Kate and Frank. Capers enjoyed his employment, and he was deeply in love with his family and completely happy with his life. Military service did not enter into his career planning, but he possessed a strong desire to perform his duty for the country.

Capers received a promotion to lieutenant colonel in the First Militia and considered remaining with that regiment. Many thought the Citadel Corps of Cadets might volunteer and enter the Confederate Army as a separate unit. Thus Capers would have another highly desirable option. In addition, several of the young professor's friends urged that he raise yet another regiment. However, he felt that he did not possess that level of energy.

Ellison Capers wearing his State Militia uniform
(Courtesy of The Citadel Archives, The Citadel, Charleston, S.C.)

6

In the meantime, during Capers' absence, the men of the First Militia Regiment were remanded to their homes and the regiment was disbanded. The soldiers who desired further service joined other Confederate units. Service with the First Militia was no longer an option. The Corps of Cadets did not volunteer as a separate unit, and it was no longer a choice.

Finally, Capers accepted Stevens' offer, deciding that he would serve under the guidance of a "Real Man," a decision that he never regretted. On November 25, 1861, Capers notified the college, "Having determined to devote my services to the cause of our country in the active Army of our State, I hereby tender my resignation as an officer of the Citadel Academy."[11] Thus, the Stevens/Capers Regiment began forming, although the two new officers did not envision the hardships and perils the regiment would face in the years ahead.[12]

The new lieutenant colonel was the son of a Methodist minister. He was reared in a devoutly religious family that traveled the state, residing in Charleston and as far away as Pendleton. The family eventually settled in the "Box House" near Pendleton. Ellison graduated from the Citadel in 1856 with the dubious honor of standing last in his class. During his cadet days he was known as a "young hellion," constantly engaging in boyish pranks and scraps. Even at a young age, Ellison Capers possessed a quality of leadership that inspired others. His natural ingenuity and strong leadership talent served the new regiment well.[13]

Few units in the Confederate Army could boast the quality of leadership destined for the new regiment. Both Stevens' and Capers' leadership qualifications were impeccable. Indeed, time would prove that they both performed well. The legislative bodies of South Carolina considered them among the "best officers" of the state.

Stevens and Capers instituted an intense recruiting program for soldiers from all sections of South Carolina. They placed advertisements in the *Charleston Mercury* and *Daily Courier* in addition to other state newspapers. Handbills were distributed statewide. Several recruiting offices were opened in Charleston, and Stevens and Capers constantly traveled throughout the State seeking volunteers. The recruiting theme was simple: "Defend Our Homes and Our Liberties."[14]

Recruiting efforts were also enhanced by a call from President Jefferson Davis for South Carolina to muster five additional infantry regiments. That call, supported by an appeal from the State Adjutant and Inspector General, Brigadier General States Rights Gist, motivated many individuals to volunteer. Actually, after the Federal landing on Hilton Head on November 7, 1861, citizens needed little additional encouragement as they volunteered by families, clans and communities.

Individual companies arrived in Charleston from every part of the state. On January 16, 1862, the first six companies destined for the Stevens/Capers

STATE OF SOUTH CAROLINA.
Adj't & Insp. Gen'ls Office.

January 13 1862

Special Order
No 6.

A Camp of Instruction
and organization having been established
near Charleston S.C. Ellison Capers
is herewith appointed Commandant of
the Post with the rank of Lieut Colonel
and will be obeyed and respected accordingly

Lieut Col Capers will report for further instructions to these Head Quarters.

By Order

S. R. Gist
Adj & Insp Genl
of S.C.

Lt Col
Ellison Capers

562

8

Regiment entered a camp of instruction. The new regiment reached a full complement of 10 companies and entered Confederate Service on April 20, 1862.[15]

The Governor established the camp of instruction, Camp Gist, four miles from the new bridge spanning the Ashley River in St. Andrews Township. The camp was located adjacent to the main Savannah highway near the Savannah and Charleston Railroad. The James Island Ferry crossed Wappoo Creek near where the Wappoo Cut joined the Stono River.[16]

These were busy times for the two leaders. Stevens remained in Charleston and continued recruiting for the additional companies. He also acted as mustering officer for other regiments as additional militia or volunteer companies arrived in Charleston.

The Governor's order that established the camp of instruction appointed Capers commander of Camp Gist. During the next couple of months, the new commander toiled tirelessly. At times he regarded as almost insurmountable the task of teaching raw talent the essentials of military service. He lamented, "500 men encamped and nearly all are perfectly ignorant of military duties! Captains, lieutenants & privates, all to be taught, and I am perfectly alone."[17] The men received rigorous training in military drill, discipline, and tactics often requiring long difficult days and sometimes even longer nights.

A determined Capers struggled desperately to complete his mission without becoming frustrated when confronted with more work than one could hope to accomplish. He wished that Lottie were nearby so she could visit him frequently. "The work before me is so great," he wrote, "And I have no one to help me that it makes me feel quite blue." Even so, totally enmeshed in the task, the astute young leader noticed the broader aspects of the conflict and worried about the unusual number of Federal vessels off the bar.[18]

The regiment desperately needed an experienced soldier to assist with the regimental drill. Finally, a noncommissioned officer, Sergeant Alfred Holmes, Company F, indicated that he had attended a military school and was experienced in military drill. Capers immediately appointed Holmes as the new regimental drill-master. The sergeant proved highly capable and provided invaluable service by assuming a large share of the workload. Later in the war, Holmes became adjutant of the regiment.

Almost before the training began, storms and bad weather interrupted the schedule at Camp Gist. Neither barns nor animal shelters were available, so the soldiers sent the horses to the city after the first night of the inclement weather. Protected from the elements only by tents, the men fared little better than the animals. The soldiers did little else than fulfil the duties of the regiment during the rain and winds. Despite the terrible weather conditions, only a few became ill. On January 25, 1862, the dawn broke with clear skies

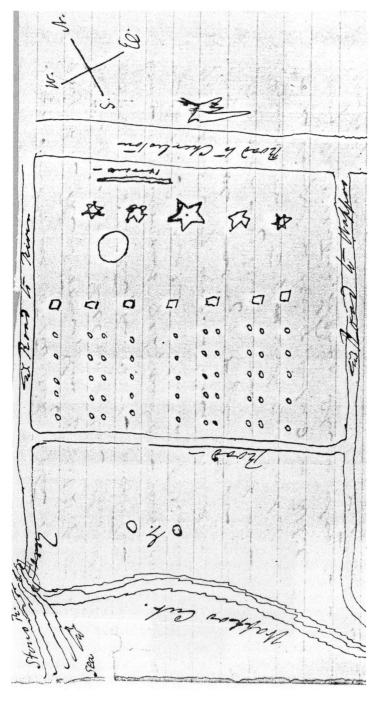

Map drawn by Ellison Capers showing location of Camp Gist and layout of the tents. The camp was located in St. Andrews parish along the main road to Charleston, four miles from the bridge across the Ashley River.
(Courtesy The Citadel Archives, Capers Papers)

10

and bright sunlight. Smiles appeared on every face, and the morale of the regiment increased perceptibly. Already, the indomitable spirit of the men was apparent, and the leaders confidently predicted they would become the core of a fine regiment.[19]

The men were recruited for 12 months' service with the Confederate Army. In the meantime, the Confederate Government began accepting the prospect of a long war and forbade the recruitment of additional troops for the standard period of service. Governor Pickens proposed that the six companies undergoing training at Camp Gist become a full regiment, contingent upon the soldiers extending their enlistment commitments to serve for the duration of the war. The men thoroughly discussed the proposition among themselves. Finally, on March 18, 1862, the Colleton Guards, led by Captain Jesse S. Jones and Lieutenant Joseph K. Risher, became the first company to extend its enlistment period. The five remaining companies soon agreed to the change, and the Governor and the Council approved the formation of the new regiment on April 1, 1862. Within three weeks, the Governor assigned four additional companies to the original six to form a full regiment of infantry designated "1st Regiment of Infantry of Recent Acquisition."[20]

The Governor presented Stevens and Capers with their commissions April 3, 1862, as well as the necessary directives formalizing the new regiment as the 24th Regiment, South Carolina Volunteers, Infantry. Stevens read the orders at dress parade the next day and assumed command. The new commander also presented the regiment "a fine stand of colors," sewn by Mrs. Stevens.[21]

In the meantime, the training of the troops at Camp Gist continued at full bore with days that began early and ended late. Immediately after breakfast, at 6:45 a.m., the officers attended drill, which was repeated at 2 p.m. Stevens and Capers reviewed the regiment at dress parade daily at sunset. Between times, officers gave instructions in close-order drill and tactics.[22] Little time remained for frivolity during those long, difficult days. Yet, the very thought of meeting the hated foe on the field of battle created in the men a sort of contentment. No soldier deserted during the camp of instruction.

Finally, the troops completed the difficult and often boring mustering and training process. The men were eager for battle and did not wait long before receiving an assignment. On April 16, 1862, Brigadier General Roswell Sabine Ripley, commander at Charleston, posted the 24th at Coles Island, a barrier island located on the coast at the mouth of the Stono River, near Folly Island.[23] Several batteries of artillery supported by infantry units occupied the island, which was a critical first line of defense for Charleston. This first assignment would challenge the new regiment's mettle.

General Roswell S. Ripley
(Courtesy South Caroliniana Library, University of South Carolina, Columbia, S.C.)

The leaders of the 24th admired the quality of men assembled and concluded that it would become a fine Confederate Army unit. Older men as well as young boys left their families, many for the first time. Other South Carolinians delayed entering chosen occupations and professions until after they served the country in the army. Ellison Capers promised to dedicate his life to the service of God, but not until the contest between the states ended.[24]

Few records exist that identify the origin of most companies in the new regiment.[25] Some companies were named, while others assumed the name of the commander. No commander would lead the same company throughout the war.[26] Some received promotions, resigned, or became either prisoners of war or casualties.

Company A, The Marion Rifles, hailed from Charleston. Its members were firemen who manned the Marion Fire Station located on Columbus Street in Charleston. Members were assigned to a militia company for state service with the 16th South Carolina Militia Regiment. Later, the men entered the Confederate States Army as members of Company A, 24th Regiment. During the war, the company commanders, Captains C. B. Sigwald and John Henry Steinmeyer, were from Charleston. Officially mustered into the regiment on December 31, 1861, the company was the first to volunteer for service with the new regiment. Since the state did not send the 16th Militia Regiment to Virginia for the Battle of Manassas, many members of the Marion Rifles volunteered for assignment to other South Carolina units that did. Most of those men remained with the other units. Many were skilled artisans in a variety of crafts. Company A was the only infantry company from Charleston permanently assigned to the Army of Tennessee. After the war, the survivors returned to the fire engine station on Columbus Street and again served the local community in that capacity.[27]

Company B, The Pee Dee Rifles, hailed from Marlboro District. Company commanders were Captains Edwin Spears and later Robert Johnson, both from Marlboro District. The company organized for state service in the summer of 1861. It offered its services to the Confederate States Army and mustered into the regiment December 4, 1861. Until joining the new regiment, the company attended a camp of instruction at Camp Magnolia, near Charleston. Most of the soldiers were farmers, and many naively expected to continue their farming business after entering military service.[28]

Company C, Captain M. T. Appleby's Company, was from Colleton District, now Dorchester County, near St. George, South Carolina. Captains Appleby, W. C. Griffith and A. C. Appleby, all from Dorchester County, successively commanded the company during the war. Captain M. T. Appleby was Captain A. C. Appleby's father. The original muster point for this company was Appleby's Church Grounds, originally known as the

Methodist Meeting House, near Grover, South Carolina. The soldiers were predominantly farmers.[29]

Company D, The Evans Guard, claimed Beaufort District or the area that is now Hampton County. Many were from the Whippy Swamp area. Captains W. I. Gooding, A. B. Addison and A. E. Bowers commanded the company during the war. Apparently, the Whippy Swamp Guard provided the nucleus for the company. The soldiers were mostly farmers.[30]

Company E, the Colleton Guards or Captain Jones' company and later Captain Risher's company, hailed from Colleton District. The area is known as "upper Colleton County and lower Bamberg County." Captain Risher retained command longer under combat conditions than any other company commander who served in the regiment. The original muster point of the unit was at the Salkehatchie River Bridge near Yammassee. In 1861, the company, organized for state service, was stationed near the Edisto River at Jacksonboro. New officers were elected at a reorganization meeting held December 26, 1861, at Green Pond. Early in January 1862, the unit boarded the train at Salkehatchie bound for Charleston to offer its services to the Confederacy. The soldiers of this company were farmers, including the two commanders.[31] Company E was the first in the 24th to extend its enlistment period from one year to the duration of the war.

Company F, Captain D. F. Hill's Company, was from the Anderson/Abbeville Districts. The company commanders were Captains Hill, S. W. Sherard and C. S. Beaty. The mustering place was directly across the road from Carswell Baptist Church, located in Hall Township, Anderson County. Most of the soldiers came from the farm.[32]

Company G, Captain John H. Pearson's Company, hailed from Columbia or Richland District. Captains Pearson, D. H. Hamiter and William Beckham commanded the company during the war. The original muster point was Camp Johnston, located at Lightwood Knot Springs near Columbia, where the men attended a camp of instruction in December 1861. The state assigned the company to the 24th Regiment when the men changed their enlistment period from 12 months to the duration of the war. Historical information about the background of this company is sparse. Some of the men served with the Richland Volunteers before forming a separate company.[33]

Company H, Captain J. A. Thomas' company, hailed from Chester District, primarily in the Richbourg Community. Captains Thomas and W. Lyle Roddey commanded the company. The state assigned this company to the regiment when it accepted a period of service for the duration of the war. The men were mostly farmers, including Captain Thomas, who continued to look after farm business after entering service.[34]

Company I, the Edgefield Light Infantry or Captain A. J. Hammond's company, came from Edgefield District near the town of Edgefield. Its commanders were Captains Hammond, L. B. Wever and James Tillman. The company attended a camp of instruction at Lightwood Knot Springs near Columbia early in 1862. The state assigned the unit to the 24th Regiment when the men extended the enlistment period to the duration of the war. Colonel Stevens selected Captain Hammond as regimental major of infantry as soon as the company arrived for duty with the regiment. The soldiers were primarily farmers.[35]

Company K, Captain Samuel S. Tompkins' company, came from Edgefield District near the community of Hamburg. Captains Tompkins and J. C. Morgan commanded the company during the war. The men arrived in Charleston dressed in homespun uniforms and were very boastful that no Yankee threads adorned their backs. The women of Edgefield District worked hard and proudly used their spinning wheels for a good cause. The men were mostly farmers.[36]

As the companies assembled as a regiment, Colonel Stevens selected and organized the staff for the new regiment and requested approval from Judah P. Benjamin, Secretary of War:

> Submit the following names for your approval as the Regimental staff...these officers have been for two months past rendering gratuitous but very efficient service in their several capacities in the Camp of Instruction where six of these companies have been under drill:
> St. Julian Ravenel, Surgeon, with rank of Major; Thomas S. Ogier, Jr., Asst. Surgeon, Captain; Robert H. Kingman, Quarter Master, Captain; John A. Bowie, Asst. Commissary, Captain; J. Clarence Palmer, Adjutant, First Lieutenant. The Surgeon and assistant surgeon have both passed satisfactory examinations before the Medical Board. The Quarter Master and Commissary are prepared to execute requisite Bonds so soon as the proper forms are furnished.[37]

Stevens also selected noncommissioned officers for key positions. He appointed Sergeant M. Triest, of Charleston, to be regimental sergeant major, Thomas Addison, of Beaufort, to be quartermaster sergeant, and David Bozeman, of Anderson, to be hospital steward. In every instance, these individuals performed their duties in an exemplary manner.[38] Sadly, most of the original appointees did not survive the war.

The men readily adapted to camp life. They engaged in repeating rumors, discussing the news about the war and political activity in the new Confederacy, and exchanging information about home life. Debates often raged about whether the news was reliable.

The men were naturally curious and constantly heard reports that the Union army was moving further into the South. They kept a watchful eye on the activities of the Federals at nearby Hilton Head. In April, dispatches

General Pierre G. T. Beauregard
(Courtesy South Caroliniana Library, University of South Carolina, Columbia, S. C.)

from Shiloh gladdened and saddened the hearts of the men of the regiment as the Confederate Army attempted to halt the Federal advance into Tennessee. The news of a great Confederate victory came at a cost of the life of General Albert Sidney Johnston, whom many Southern soldiers considered one of the better Southern generals. Reports of the battle at Shiloh on April 7, 1862, did not reach the men of the regiment as promptly as did the news of the victory of April 6. Another report circulated that Mr. Robert Barnwell Rhett, editor of the radical Charleston Mercury, had declared "that by April, England & France would acknowledge the Confederacy & break the blockade, then the North would be like a chicken with his head cut off." One senior officer stated that he did "not believe one word of it."[39]

Indeed, the blockade of the Southern ports was already a source of excessive anxiety and consternation among Southerners. The men noticed that General Pierre G. T. Beauregard was becoming increasingly grey, "probably from his inability to get hair dye through the blockade." Beauregard's defenders thought it was because of the stress and worry of his job. Others worried about the conduct of South Carolina political activity. One reported, "The convention is holding secret sessions, & it is hard to tell what they are at."[40] Obviously, the leadership of the state propagated the rumor mill, albeit unintentionally.

Finally, the camp of instruction ended. The regiment was needed to replace another regiment which had completed its tour of outpost duty on one of the many sea islands near Charleston. Early in the morning of April 16, 1862, the soldiers packed haversacks, removed tents, and eagerly anticipated a welcome exit from Camp Gist.[41] At 9 a.m., the regiment began the 12-mile hike to Coles Island, the new assignment. En route they stopped for only two short breaks or rest periods and reached the island at 5 p.m.

There the regiment relieved Colonel Johnson Hagood's 1st Regiment of six-month volunteers and Lucas' Battery of heavy artillery, which immediately departed for Fort Johnson. The Eutaw Battalion and a squadron of cavalry remained on duty at the island with the 24th.[42]

Four days later, amid cold, rainy, and disagreeable weather, the final company joined the regiment. At 6 p.m., Company K, Captain Tompkins' company, which had completed a camp of instruction at Lightwood Knot Springs near Columbia, joined the regiment. The company formed on the beach for review, and afterwards the men checked into quarters. En route from Columbia, the train was derailed near Ridgeville, South Carolina. The accident claimed the lives of two of the men and crushed the legs of a third. The survivors thought the accident scene was dreadful and arrived at camp still shaken.[43]

At Coles Island, additional responsibilities were given the two principal officers of the 24th. Colonel Stevens became commander of all army units stationed there and retained Adjutant Palmer as his administrative support. As he frequently did, Capers became commander of the 24th; he named Lieutenant John Henry Steinmeyer, acting adjutant. This organization remained in effect until the regiment began its withdrawal from the island.[44]

The key position of commander of the Department of South Carolina, Georgia, and Florida was soon changed. Early in March 1862, President Davis recalled the highly popular General Robert E. Lee to Richmond. When Lee departed, his second in command, Major General John Clifford Pemberton, became the commander. Pemberton, a devoted and loyal Confederate soldier, was a native of Philadelphia with marital ties to the South. However, the new commander was often abrupt and short tempered. He did not communicate effectively with the local citizens or politicians as had his predecessors, Beauregard and Lee. Pemberton exacerbated the situation when he implemented a strategy, first proposed by General Lee, to evacuate Coles Island because of its exposed position. Colonel Stevens strongly disagreed with the move and rode his horse into Charleston to remonstrate against the withdrawal.[45] However, Pemberton stuck by his decision.

Pemberton introduced a new position, the West Line, which he thought would provide a better defense. He established the new line across James Island, anchored on the east at Secessionville, and on the west at Fort

Pemberton. Here he was confident that the Confederate forces could successfully defend themselves from any Union ground attack. Even Ellison Capers thought the Confederate infantry "could whip them every time."

Considering the situation at Charleston critical, Pemberton, with Governor Pickens' and President Davis' approval, declared martial law on May 5, 1862.[46] General Ripley, Pemberton's second in command, appointed a military governor for the city. Ripley visited Coles Island and related that he had considered three officers for the position: Colonels Stevens, Johnson Hagood (Commander of the 1st Regiment), and Capers. The position did not interest Stevens, however, but Capers, always eager for a challenge, would have liked to receive the appointment.[47] For unknown reasons, Ripley selected Colonel Hagood.

The citizens of Charleston objected to martial law. For their own safety, Pemberton urged the civilian population, especially the women and children, to seek a safer environ further inland.[48] Slowly and regretfully, most of the civilian population packed up and departed the city. Heeding Pemberton's exhortations, Colonel Stevens rented a house in Pendleton and moved his family there.[49] Few of the 24th's family members were in Charleston, including Mrs. Capers, who was already residing at Cherry Grove Plantation, a safe distance from Charleston.

As the Confederates started the evacuation of Coles Island, the men dismantled the heavy artillery batteries. The longshoreman loaded the precious cargo aboard the deck of a small, light draft, side-wheel steamer, the *Planter*, for transfer to Fort Ripley, a new harbor defensive position.[50] That night the boat's slave crew made a successful bid for freedom and surrendered the *Planter* to the Federal fleet intact with its valuable cargo of cannons.[51] Even more critical than the loss of the boat and its cargo, the crew provided the Federals with intelligence about the evacuation of Coles Island. The Northerners, no doubt, realized that this move opened the Stono River for the passage of Union gunboats, largely unmolested, as far inland as Fort Pemberton.

The proximity of the heavy guns aboard the Union gunboats was a constant worry for members of the regiment. If the Federals sailed up the Stono River and used those guns properly, they could place Fort Pemberton in peril. If the fort capitulated, the Northern blue-coats would find Charleston's back door, just as the British red-coats had done during the War of 1812.[52] However, the Federals failed to capture the well-armed fort, and the fears of the Confederates were for naught.

Despite orders for eventual evacuation, the regiment continued to establish strong defensive positions on Coles Island. The 24th occupied a Revolutionary War fort, Fort Palmetto, which local historians believed had been constructed by the Spaniards. The men reinforced the fort with logs and sand, and it became a formidable defensive structure. In all likelihood, the fort could withstand an attack by the heaviest guns of the Union fleet. As if challenging the enemy, the regimental colors of the 24th furled proudly from the flag staff at Fort Palmetto's highest point. However, the safety of the men in such an exposed and unprotected position gravely concerned both Stevens and Capers.[53]

The men liked the assignment at Coles Island, which was a considerable improvement over Camp Gist. The island was a more healthful place with airy and comfortable quarters, and as the spring weather arrived the days were extremely pleasant. The duty at Coles Island was good despite the confinement and the constant threat of the enemy's big guns.

The men were well fed at Coles Island. Although meat was scarce, they enjoyed an excellent diet of oysters, clams, and other fresh seafood.[54] Foragers purchased beef, flour, and other foodstuffs from the local farmers and citizens. On one expedition, Corporal Benjamin Moore, of Company A, was killed on Folly Island as a result of an accident.[55]

In addition to military duties, the soldiers busied themselves with personal projects for the homefolk. Private James D. Padgett's brother wanted a pony, and it was rumored that a wild species of the animal inhabited the area near James' duty station. However, James was doubtful whether he could obtain a pony for his brother on Coles Island:

> I don't believe...there is a pony on this Island that can be caught at any price, but I have been credibly informed, by our pickets, ...there are...some...of them on Folly Island. Some two or three miles off, and almost in the woods for order. We have been talking about going over sometime soon and catch some of them and if we succeed in doing so, I will send you one...if I do not get a wild one...I will see if I can buy one cheap, if you can wait a while.

James did not record whether he captured or purchased a pony for his brother.[56]

The escape route from Coles Island concerned Stevens. The causeway, the only route of retreat, traversed the marsh along the Stono River and across Battery Island, which the enemy gunboats could easily bombard from the Stono River. A retreat, if one became necessary, would place the men in an extremely exposed and hazardous position. Colonel Stevens' concern for the island's escape route prompted a decision to construct an inland bridge or causeway over the marsh. The proposed causeway was sufficiently distant from the Stono River to provide a safe route to James Island.

The men worked very hard constructing the new causeway, and it was rapidly completed. The bridges spanned several streams, including one with a depth of 12 feet which the gunboats could navigate. The creek was obstructed with logs and timbers to foil the gunboats. Even this early in the war, Stevens' perspicacity showed.[57]

19

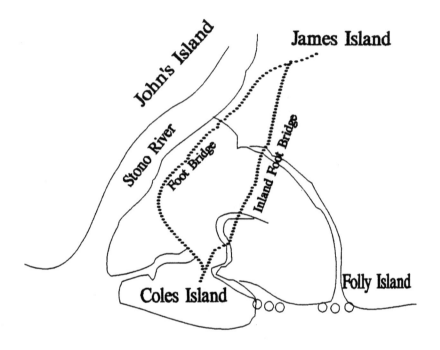

**First Duty Station with Evacuation Routes.
Drawn by the author from a sketch located at The Citadel Archives,
Charleston, S.C. Coles Island is now underwater.**

While they were engaged in the project, the men sometimes doubted the need for the causeway. Some thought they were working excessively hard and one soldier griped that they were on duty nearly every day "owing to so many of the damn rascals" pretending sickness. Another complained because he thought they were "throwing up a road" that would span more than two miles of the extremely boggy marsh. He frequently sank waist deep in the mire and could get out only with help. Still, the soldiers realized that the colonel was constructing the bridge or causeway so the regiment could reach safety if attacked.[58] The men grumbled, but they worked hard and soon completed the task.

Officers of the regiment were selected by elections as positions became vacant. At Coles Island, the men of Company I elected a third lieutenant. Private Padgett politicked very hard for the position and informed the folks at home about the election:

> The election for third lieutenant comes off this evening. I
> am in hopes that it will result favorably for me. I will lose
> one vote by K. S. Key being absent...two in the hospital
> unable to go to the polls.[59]

Padgett, an astute politician, delayed asking for a furlough or leave of absence until after the election. Although he did not get elected, he was promoted to lieutenant approximately two years later.[60]

Much of the personal activity of soldiers in the regiment involved personal health or business at home. Most of the men were in excellent health and rarely experienced illness, unless the "sickness" was an escape from an unpleasant work detail such as constructing the new causeway. A few soldiers attempted to conduct their homefront business by mail, such as managing the farm, selling produce, and settling accounts.[61]

General Pemberton began a slow withdrawal of the troops from Coles Island, and on May 7, 1862, the Eutaw Battalion departed the island. Less than a week later, May 13, Colonel Stevens and all but 130 men of the 24th Regiment withdrew to the safer confines of James Island.

Lieutenant Colonel Capers commanded the 130 troops remaining at Coles Island. With the protection of the big guns gone, the anxiety of the men increased perceptively as they awaited departure. The men, constantly on alert for Union gun boats crossing the bar, used ploys to lead Federal observers to believe that the island was still fully occupied. Dummy guns were installed in conspicuous places, and the regimental colors continued to wave proudly and defiantly from their lofty staff.[62]

From Secessionville on May 15, Colonel Stevens regretted that he could not share the exposed position at Coles Island with his men:

> I wish I could come to you...I cannot leave the Regi-
> ment....The enemy has moved a little more cautiously than
> I expected. They will be in on the tide tomorrow. I send

21

you provisions and some more ammunition. I feel very anxious about tomorrow. Tell your men...they must keep cool and bear themselves bravely. Be careful...they do not cut you off. The landing force may be large, as the large ship outside will probably send some of her men in with the others.[63]

Colonel Stevens never assigned his men a mission in which he himself was unwilling to participate.

At James Island, the regiment entered a bivouac about two miles from Fort Johnson, where quarters were nonexistent, and the men braved the elements unprotected.[64] They yearned for the airy and comfortable accommodations of Coles Island. Colonel Stevens was concerned about the men's suffering, and he was soon able to find a new bivouac with quarters at Royal's Place. There, the regiment's camp was nearer Fort Johnson and only two miles from Secessionville.

Picket duty was the regiment's principal activity. From the latest bivouac, the 24th was assigned the duty in front of the main Confederate line. The regiment also maintained a picket outpost on Battery Island and one at Rivers' and Grimballs' Plantations.[65]

General Ripley, Pemberton's second in command, appointed General Gist commander of James Island and St. Andrews Parish, which included responsibility for Coles Island and vicinity. Gist made an official visit to the small detachment on Coles Island and found the military affairs at the outpost in excellent condition. He also echoed Colonel Stevens' concern for the safety of the detachment. Gist asked that Capers keep him advised "immediately & fully" as the situation developed and authorized direct communication between the detachment and the headquarters in Charleston.[66] The new commander reassured an anxious Capers that he "relied upon his judgement to do the right thing" during the pending crisis and advised the detachment to keep "a bright lookout." At the end of his official report, the visitor added a note that suggested turning over the causeway planks broad side up so one could traverse the new bridge more safely.[67]

As Stevens predicted, the Federals made an appearance on May 17, 1862, at 8 a.m., anchoring four vessels behind Folly Island.[68] Capers held the small detachment in readiness and awaited the enemy's move. Since the gunboats could cross the bar only on high tide, the times of danger this day were at 10 a.m. and again twelve hours later.[69] Soon after the ships arrived, the sailors lowered six small boats that moved about the channel "sounding as they went," determining depths.

The appearance of the boats created both excitement and apprehension in the men. As the Federal sailors surveyed the channel, one of the small boats sailed very near the coast line. Capers placed ten of the 24th's riflemen, ready for action, in a position as near the boat as possible under cover of the sand dunes and breast works. Finally, the riflemen fired their weapons into the approaching small boat. Ellison boastfully wrote Lottie the outcome of the maneuver:

> It was well done. And by MY orders the first Yankee fell...One man was brought down, whether killed or wounded I can't say. My officers all saw the man fall. The boat promptly turned back.[70]

Future information revealed that the man actually had slipped and fallen and was not struck by the Confederate minié balls.[71] At that moment, however, the report was good for the morale of the Southerners and, even better, the small boat advanced no further. Still, the boat left several channel markers in the water.[72] The boats returned on the high tide the next day, but they did not come within range of the detachment's small arms fire again.

For the men, the final tour of duty at Coles Island was long and dreary. Exposed duty assignments normally lasted only three days, but by May 17 the assignment had already extended to four days. Stevens reassured the detachment that two companies from another regiment would soon provide relief.[73] In the meantime, the men of the 24th willingly worked hard and expected to encounter danger as they maintained the appearance of a fully armed garrison. The detachment was the only force between the Federals and the Stono, and daily the men became more anxious about the exposed position. However, completion of the inland causeway escape route somewhat alleviated the soldiers' fears.

Some of the men tended to their own health during the assignment at Coles Island. Capers quit smoking his pipe and cigar, and although he found the task difficult, he conquered his longing for tobacco. Ellison, a highly religious individual, opined as he suffered the effects of nicotine withdrawal, that "abstinence from tobacco had strengthened my religious beliefs."

If and when the Federal fleet entered the harbor and opened fire, the garrison would begin immediate evacuation of the island. The lowering of the flag would signal the men to fire the buildings and commence the withdrawal.[74] Lieutenant William G. Hawkins' fire detail prepared the buildings for destruction, each soldier trained for a particular task as all eyes watched anxiously for the signal. The detachment was under explicit instructions:

> Do not take unnecessary chances. If the Federals land a small detail, they are to be driven off with rifles. If they land a force too large to be driven off with rifles, then the retreat may be ordered.[75]

The increase in the number of Union ships that waited on the other side of the bar increased the men's uneasiness. The soldiers expected an imminent enemy assault and remained constantly alert. Finally, a large barge

23

sailed into the harbor cautiously sounding the channel. The pickets were eager and could barely restrain their impatience as they held their aimed and ready rifles to their shoulders. However, the soldiers waited and waited and finally the barge turned. At long range, the Confederates could restrain their impatience no longer and opened fire, which only hastened the barge to withdraw.[76]

The activity of enemy vessels on the other side of the bar increased on May 20, 1862. Doubtless, the Yankees had digested the intelligence provided by the crew of the *Planter* that the Confederates minimally occupied Coles Island.[77] As the long expected advance finally began, the soldiers actually felt relieved. Capers, Steinmeyer, and Sergeant B. E. Robinson of Company A, quietly watched the enemy's actions from their vantage point atop the bombproof.

Finally, a small armada of five Federal gunboats eased into the harbor. The first vessel missed the channel and went aground off Folly Island. In a single file, the other four moved southward and crossed the bar. The grounded vessel struggled free and followed behind the others as they sailed into the harbor. Immediately, the gunboats began shelling.[78] One boat continued up the Stono River as far as Battery Island, firing "with impunity" as it went. As a result, the men appreciated the significance of Stevens' acumen at building the inland causeway.

Braving the artillery blasts, Sergeant Robinson clambered about halfway up the flagpole and acted as an observer, remaining there until called down. Later, Lieutenant Colonel Capers paid Robinson a most deserved compliment for his cool courage under fire. He titled the noncommissioned officer, "The Sergeant Jasper of the 2nd Revolution."[79]

The detachment evacuated the island safely. With the buildings ablaze from the enemy artillery blasts and large bombs bursting all around, it rapidly became a hazardous place. The Union gunboats bombarded with an impressive display of firepower that indicated the strength of the Union's large naval guns. Without hesitation, Capers decided it was time for the evacuation, and the men lowered the flag, cut down the flag pole, and fired the remaining buildings. Under cover of the smoke from the flames, the men traversed the new inland causeway and foot bridges and gained the safety of James Island without a single serious injury. The detachment retired with its colors proudly unfurled leading the way. The pleasant, albeit anxious, days of duty at Coles Island ended as the detachment joined the remainder of the regiment at Royals Place.

The inland causeway escape route from Coles Island proved the soldiers' salvation and had, no doubt, saved the entire detachment. The old causeway was also under a heavy bombardment under which no one could have survived.[80]

While firing the buildings, Lieutenant William G. Hawkins lost his prized sword. He did not miss the sword until the detachment was across the causeway, and it was too late to return and search for it.

During this withdrawal, the men displayed the mettle and gallantry that became the prime characteristics of the regiment. Many experienced the fire of enemy guns for the first time, but each accepted the challenge and performed his duty with calmness and fortitude, remaining cool and composed as veterans. Afterwards, Colonel Stevens recognized the entire detachment for its coolness and bravery.[81]

With Union gunboats entering the Stono, picket duty along the river became hazardous. On the day following the evacuation of Coles Island, the Colleton Guards, Company E, performed picket duty on Battery Island with a 60-man detail. Captain Jones established the advanced post at the old magazine located on the northernmost point of the Island. Sergeant Samuel White, Corporal Calvin Wilson, Privates Adam Carter, Isaac Carter, B. C. Hudson, and Andrew Hudson manned the post. Jones placed the second post in a thicket some 250 yards nearer the causeway between Battery Island and James Island. He positioned the main support of 20 men in the James Island woods near the Battery Island road. The relief force of 30 men waited near the Old Legare Settlement.[82]

The men at the advanced post noticed the Union gunboats sailing the Stono River shelling the shore line on both sides. One boat, an enemy steamship, stopped near the obstructions the Confederates had placed in the Stono River. About 11:00 a.m., Sergeant White notified the detail commander that a small boat, launched from the steamer, was approaching the shoreline of the Island carrying a landing party. Before Jones could dispatch support for the advanced picket, another of the enemy's gunboats arrived, established a position near Battery Island, and commenced a second imposing artillery barrage in as many days. Shelling with grape and shrapnel, the gunboat enfiladed the Battery Island bridge and causeway and obliterated the picket detail's line of retreat. When the shelling began, the members of the second picket line safely crossed the causeway. However, the barrage interrupted communication with the advanced detail. Thinking they had not been seen, the advanced detail entered the old abandoned ammunition bunker for shelter. The Federals sent ashore a small landing party, who spotted the place where the pickets sought shelter, surrounded the bunker, and captured the entire detail.[83]

The Union gunboat fire made exposed positions hazardous for the pickets. The severe artillery fire from the enemy's gunboat penetrated the cover of the detachment in every direction, and Jones prudently withdrew his men. After the firing subsided, the picket detail resumed all previous positions except the advanced post, which Jones wisely decided not to continue.

Late that afternoon the men noticed that one of the enemy vessels departed in the direction of Coles Island, and two others moved toward the pilings located in the river. Sensing a measure of relief, Stevens withdrew the entire picket line to a position nearer Legare's Place.

The men captured by the Federals were the first members of the regiment to become prisoners of war. The next day, a concerned Stevens urged Pemberton to arrange an exchange for the captured men saying, "I would be much gratified to have them returned to the regiment."[84]

At first, the Federals imprisoned the captured men at Hilton Head. In August 1862 the Union Navy transported the prisoners aboard the steamer *Arago* to Fort Columbus, located on Governor's Island near New York City. After the men languished there for several weeks, the Yankees transferred the prisoners to the hideous Fort Delaware prisoner of war camp. Private B. C. Hudson died there on September 4, 1862. In November, 1862, the Federals exchanged the surviving prisoners at Aiken's Wharf, on the James River near Richmond. Private Isaac Carter developed typhoid fever, and immediately after the exchange the Confederate surgeons hospitalized the ill man. He recovered and returned for additional service with the regiment.[85] The remaining men, although not completely well when exchanged, also rejoined the regiment after a well-deserved furlough.

As the Union forces neared Charleston, the population as well as the soldiers became anxious and expected an attack at any moment. Confederate intelligence reported that 25 or 30 thousand Federal troops would invade James and Johns Islands. General Nathan George "Shanks" Evans, new commander on James Island, estimated a Union force of 10,000 men, "judging by the number of enemy camps," on nearby Johns Island alone.[86] The constant activity of the Federal gunboats intensified the apprehension. The boats traveled the Stono, blasting shells at everything that moved or looked Confederate.[87] General Pemberton prepared for an invasion supported by a sizable Union fleet through Charleston Harbor.

The Federals now established the "Department of the South," which included the states of South Carolina, Georgia, and Florida.[88] Major General David Hunter, a senior political general, commanded the department. Second in command was Brigadier General Henry Washington Benham, a West Point graduate who had been first in his graduating class.[89] Brigadier General I. I. Stevens, a rising star in the ranks of the Northern leadership, commanded one of the divisions, and Brigadier General Horatio G. Wright the other. General Stevens held little esteem for either Hunter or Benham.[90]

Stevens' Division, accompanied by Benham, made an uncontested landing on Battery Island on June 2, 1862. At the same time, Wright's Division crossed John's Island.[91] Strangely, the Confederates did not challenge the advance of the Union forces. Possibly, it was because of the Confederate's respect for the Union gunboats' large guns. Also, Pemberton

26

believed the line across James Island was strong enough to assure the safety of the Confederate positions. Even Capers saw little danger from an infantry attack.[92] On Battery Island, the Federals felt secure under the protection of the fleet's heavy guns, which were strategically positioned in the Stono and Folly Rivers. Advanced Federal pickets signaled the gunboats and directed the fire of the big guns.[93]

General Pemberton's revisionist strategy for defense of Charleston so near its boundaries distressed the Governor and his Council as well as the Charleston City Council and citizens. General Ripley also disagreed with Pemberton and thought that the new line was too close to the city. Ripley also considered the evacuation of Coles Island such a mistake that he volunteered for duty in Virginia and departed the city on May 28, 1862.[94] The policy provoked extensive consternation among the citizens and other governing officials, and General Pemberton's unpopularity increased.[95] As a result of the implementation of the new policy, city and state officials petitioned Richmond for the general's removal.

The idea that Pemberton's strategy was faulty became the popular viewpoint throughout the city. Captain John Johnson, the Charleston Harbor engineer, agreed with Ripley, Stevens, and the citizens. He termed the evacuation of Coles Island "an unwise order," and as a consequence of the abandonment of Coles Island, the Union Army landed safely on James Island. The engineer officer rationalized that the move presented the Federals an open invitation into Charleston via James Island.[96] Thus, the evacuation of Coles Island, in the opinion of many, precipitated the Battle of Secessionville.

After the capture of the pickets on Battery Island, the action on James Island was relatively quiet until June 2, 1862. During the interim, the enemy gunboats randomly shelled the island during their frequent excursions up the Stono River. The Confederates attempted several unsuccessful feints to draw the gunboats within the range of the batteries mounted at Fort Pemberton. On May 25, a Federal gunboat was damaged severely when it attacked the floating battery near Dixon's Island. The activity of the enemy gunboats, which fired at everyone, military or civilian, whether afoot, on horseback, or in a vehicle, was very annoying. On May 31, several residents riding a horse-drawn buggy were crossing Newton's Cut Bridge when a shell landed nearby. The soldiers thought the startled citizens looked very humorous when they abandoned the buggy and fled across an open field to gain safety.[97]

On the same day, another gunboat fired several shells that landed near the camp of the 24th as Brigadier General Gist and his staff honored the regiment with an official visit.[98] A camp rumor, reliably repeated but never validated, indicated that some dust smudged General Gist's uniform.

On June 2, 1862, the gunboats dueled with Captain Chichester's Battery

27

at Legare's Point and Captain Warley's Secessionville Battery. After firing for about an hour, the Union gunboats withdrew. One horse suffered a broken leg and was the only injury.[99] However, the barrage drove the 24th's pickets from the point nearest Battery Island to a safer position on James Island. Confederate intelligence later learned that during the firing, the Federals landed another large body of troops on Battery Island.[100]

Because of the landing, General Gist withdrew Captain Chichester's artillery battery across the causeway from Legare's. However, three invaluable seacoast 24-pounder howitzers became mired so badly that the soldiers left the guns on the causeway overnight. Stevens asked that Lieutenant Colonel Capers retrieve the guns and determine the enemy's strength, if possible. Capers selected four companies for the mission:

The Marion Rifles, (Company A), Captain Sigwald's Company;
The Pee Dee Rifles, (Company B), Captain Spears' Company;
The Evans Guard, (Company D), Captain Goodings' Company; and
The Colleton Guards, (Company E), Captain Jones' Company.

Early the next morning, with the men still rubbing the cobwebs of sleep from their eyes, the detail eagerly departed the camp hoping the enemy would challenge for the guns. In addition, Capers informed the detail, that they "were to kill, capture or drive the enemy into the river."[101] Now the men were wide awake and alert.

The men soon arrived at Rivers' place and discovered that soldiers assigned to the 100th Pennsylvania Regiment were already covering the three guns with small arms fire.[102] Two companies of Confederate pickets, the Charleston Riflemen and the Beauregard Light Infantry, Lieutenant F. R. Lynch and Captain E. B. White's companies, were on duty at the outpost. The two companies warmly engaged the Pennsylvanians, but the mired guns were in danger of falling into the hands of the enemy. Taking command of all six companies, Capers charged the Northerners, who slowly gave way. The Confederates pursued the Pennsylvanians through the woods and high grass until the Yankees occupied several slave houses at Legare Place. At times, the fighting became hand-to-hand. When the Federals reached the protection of the houses, they poured a severe fire into the advancing Southerners. That fight continued for about three quarters of an hour until Capers charged again.[103]

As the men reformed, Lieutenant Colonel P. C. Gaillard arrived in relief with the remainder of the Charleston Battalion, doubling the Confederate forces. As the senior officer, Capers mobilized the entire force. Mounting his little horse, "Hardtimes," the young colonel, poised and confident, rode in front of the men and asked, "Who will follow me on an attack of the Yankees?" Every company volunteered, but only six were selected, one from the 24th Regiment and the remainder from the Charleston Battalion:

The Evans Guard, Company D, 24th Regiment;

The Charleston Riflemen, Lieutenant Lynch;

The Irish Volunteers, Captain W. H. Ryan;

The Beauregard Light Infantry, Captain White;

The Sumter Guard, Lieutenant Ward Hopkins; and

The Calhoun Guard, Captain F. T. Miles.

Capers first threw out Captain Sigwald's company, the Marion Rifles, as skirmishers. The Marions eagerly pushed forward, drawing the fire of the enemy as they occupied some pines and maintained pressure on the flank of the enemy skirmishers.[104] Gaillard took charge of the remainder of the force and also maintained a steady fire that diverted considerable enemy rifle fire from the attacking companies.

The battle was fought with intensity as the Confederates led by Capers, charged the flank of the Pennsylvanians. The Confederates drove the Yankees from the slave houses to a position nearer the river and the safety of the enfilading fire of the big guns aboard the Union gunboats. During the melee, several minié balls struck the ground between the feet of Capers' horse, Hardtimes.

The Federals noticed that the Pennsylvanians were suffering serious difficulty. They hurriedly dispatched a relief column composed of the 28th Massachusetts and 8th Michigan Regiments. As the Union regiments advanced, the shelling from the gunboats intensified and reached the advanced position of the Confederate force. Capers ordered a withdrawal to consolidate his entire force on the line held by Gaillard.[105] The Federals moved forward but did not advance past Legare Place as the enemy gunboats lobbed artillery shells for the remainder of the day. The Union infantry remained, keeping up a steady small arms fire until after dark. However, the battle was over, and the 24th became a veteran regiment, bloodied in battle.

Considering the amount of musket fire, casualties were light. The Confederates suffered nine wounded from the Charleston Battalion, and eight more from the 24th. The adjutant of the Charleston Battalion was severely wounded and captured. News soon arrived that the wound was less severe than originally thought and the adjutant would survive.[106]

It was here that the 24th captured its first prisoners. The attack on the slave houses resulted in the capture of one Federal officer and 21 enlisted men. The prisoners were well armed, neatly dressed in blue uniforms, and in the opinion of the observers, were fine looking soldiers. Among the prisoners were Union Captain James Cline, Sergeants Robert F. Moffatt and David I. Gilfillan and 19 privates, all members of the 100th Pennsylvania.[107] One prisoner related that they were treated poorly, everyone addressing the Federals as "goddamned sons of bitches." However, Cline reported that Southerners, both citizens and soldiers, treated the prisoners with respect.

After the skirmish, Capers commended the Marions for splendid duty performance. Drawing the fire of the Yankees from their advanced position was largely responsible for the success of the Confederate charge. He later wrote, "It was well and promptly done, the Marions soon occupying the pines and had the enemy's skirmishers retiring."

That afternoon Colonel Stevens placed a detail of volunteers from the Marion Rifles in a skirmish line under Lieutenants Steinmeyer and Hawkins. The Marions took possession of an area of woods between their defensive line and the Stono River. The company accomplished that action while under heavy shelling from the Union gunboats in the Stono River. Late in the afternoon, a Union force from Battery Island began advancing on the woods occupied by the Marions. Simultaneously, another Union force began an attack from the direction of the Grimball Plantation. The appearance of the additional enemy troops forced the Marion Rifles from their advanced position in the woods to the line held by Capers' men.[108] The exhausted, yet exhilarated, troops departed the battlefield and rested at the regimental area that night. With more experience, the troops would never think of quitting the battlefield to sleep.

The capture of 22 enemy soldiers that day made the men feel especially triumphant. The news was equally good for the morale of the citizens of Charleston. However, Capers agonized because the Confederates did not accomplish the primary objective, which was to recover the three invaluable pieces of artillery. He believed someone should have retrieved the artillery while his detachment hotly engaged the Pennsylvanians at the slave houses. Because that was not done, the guns fell into the hands of the enemy.

The Pennsylvanians related stirring tales about how they captured the three large artillery pieces. Colonel Daniel Leasure, the commander of the 100th Pennsylvania, claimed, "About fifty [men of the 100th Pennsylvania]...charged right smack up to a battery of siege guns and actually hauled off two of the guns by hand while the enemy from another battery just rained shells amongst them, hitting everything but them [men of the 100th Pennsylvania]. They [the guns] are enormous 8-inch siege howitzers. In all this, they never lost a man or received a scratch."[109] Afterwards, Sergeant Moffat claimed that the Confederates contested the Union force with five battalions or 2,000 men. The Confederate artillery did not participate and the only artillery shells hurled into the area were Federal, possibly from the gunboats. Leasure also mentions a bayonet attack "that carried everything in front of it." However, there is no other existing record of a bayonet attack by either side. The Southerners' attack on the slave houses became hand-to-hand at times, which could account for the report. However, the results of the battle were clear. The Confederates captured twenty-two Union soldiers at a cost of three invaluable pieces of Confederate artillery.[110]

It rained that night and the men of the 24th spent a wet, weary, hungry, and anxious night as they slept on their arms, ready for battle the next morning. One observer described the night as tempestuous.[111] At daylight, the men eagerly reoccupied the positions they held the day before. In the meantime, as Capers feared, the Pennsylvanians had already hauled off the artillery pieces.

The next morning the Federals did not honor the presence of the Confederates even with an artillery shell. Obviously, with the Confederate guns in hand, the enemy was no longer interested in continuing the battle. The Federal shield of enfilade artillery fire prevented pursuit, and the Confederates withdrew with feelings of disappointment. The melee of June 3, 1862, ended with both sides claiming victory.

In the following days, the proximity of the picket line to the Federal picket line created significant anxiety and became the primary campfire topic of the soldiers. The pickets on either side did not converse, though neither thought they were in danger from the other. Capers continued to worry that Fort Pemberton might fall. Two days later, he shared his concern with Lottie about leaving the Stono River open for passage by the Federal gunboats:

> They may not take the fort for their artillery practice is so
> fine, their guns so heavy & numerous that I fear they will.
> Charleston is...in some danger.[112]

Routine duties lasted only for a short time. Stevens' picket detail skirmished with the enemy at the Presbyterian Church on June 7. Although the 24th suffered no loss, the 7th Regiment, Connecticut Volunteers, left a soldier dead on the ground and Lieutenant Colonel Capers personally captured another soldier.[113] The Confederates questioned the prisoner and learned that most of the Port Royal troops were on James Island and the main enemy force was at Grimball's Plantation. Gist deduced from the intelligence that the enemy planned a heavy expedition against the City.[114] The men anxiously watched and waited.

The Northern soldier Capers captured was a gallant fellow who reluctantly surrendered and at first communicated hesitantly. The prisoner was an intelligent man who served for the defense of the Union and said that his home was at Hartford, Connecticut. However, after a time, the prisoner exchanged names with the Confederates and agreed to correspond after the war. Later, the Confederates lodged the prisoner in the county jail at Columbia.[115]

Capers followed up on his promise to correspond after the war and wrote the man several times, but he never received a reply. In 1904, then a bishop, Capers met Bishop Brewster from Connecticut, related the story and informed the Connecticut Bishop that he still possessed the soldier's rifle and would happily return the weapon. Bishop Capers had forgotten the given name of the soldier and was somewhat confused about his last name, recalling it as Woodward. Bishop Brewster enlisted the aid of the *Hartford*

31

Courant, and the soldier was soon identified as Private (later Corporal) Milton Woodford, and his family was contacted. On James Island, Woodford had acted as a scout for his regiment, the 7th Connecticut, as his unit made a reconnaissance through thick woods away from Grimball's Plantation. The colonel of the regiment instructed Private Woodford, "Go way out." He did so and became separated or lost in the thicket when Capers happened along.[116]

Corporal Woodford died on June 11, 1887, leaving a wife and five children, who were residing at Bristol, Connecticut. Woodford's daughter, the wife of Dr. Louis L. Beach, graciously accepted the rifle on behalf of the family and highly prized the weapon. She notified all surviving members of Company A, Seventh Connecticut Volunteers, that Bishop Capers had returned her father's weapon. Mrs. Beach invited her father's old comrades to visit her home and view the gun.[117] The *Hartford Courant* published several articles praising the kindness and generosity of Bishop Capers, "the fighting Bishop of South Carolina." The War sometimes made friends of those in strange places and circumstances.

Following the June 2 melee, the Confederates kept a watchful eye on the Federals as they settled into occupying James Island. On June 10, 1862, the 47th Georgia Regiment, as a result of a reconnaissance in front of Grimball's place near the Union line, verified the strength of the Federal forces already there.[118] The Union threat became so intimidating that General Pemberton personally directed the strengthening of the defensive line across James Island, concentrating his troops near Secessionville.

By June 15, the two opposing armies occupying James Island were thought to be approximately equal in strength. The Confederates counted 6500 effectives available on the island.[119] The Federal Intelligence estimated the Confederate strength at 11,000. The Northern intelligence habit of overestimating Confederate strength held at James Island.

In May, 1862, the Confederates felt secure behind the strong defensive line across James Island, although they were apprehensive because of the strength of the Federal landing force.

CHAPTER 2

DEFENDING THE COAST

James Island and Secessionville

The Federal generals watched through binoculars and spy glasses as the Confederates worked feverishly at strengthening the defensive line. The generals were especially apprehensive about the artillery battery at Secessionville. They named it the "Tower Battery" because of a 200-foot-tall observation tower the Southerners raised behind the breastworks. General Benham monitored the activity and decided that an attack should be launched before the opposition could become better prepared for battle. Benham testily made his views known to his superior, General Hunter, who disagreed. Although he recognized the menace from The Tower Battery, Hunter held the view that he did not have sufficient strength to advance toward Charleston until he received adequate reinforcements.[1]

Compared with the strength of the Union Forces, Fort Lamar was lightly manned. The commander at the fort mustered only two battalions of infantry, two companies of artillery and seven artillery pieces already emplaced. At 1:00 a.m. on June 16, General Evans sent 100 men from the 22nd Regiment to reinforce the fort's work detail. On the right flank of Fort Lamar, across Lighthouse Creek, stood Battery Reed, armed with two 24-pounders.[2]

General Pemberton maintained a strong picket force in front of both the fort and the main defensive line. The troops at Fort Lamar supported the picket detail in front of the fort and served Battery Reed. Responsibility for the picket detail on the right flank of the fort and along the river rested with Johnson Hagood's Special Brigade, which Pemberton organized for the purpose. The brigade included the 1st, 24th and 25th South Carolina Regiments, the 46th Georgia Regiment, and McEnery's 4th Louisiana Battalion. In addition, the brigade mustered a battery of field artillery and a detail of ten or twelve cavalrymen designated for courier duty. Hagood divided the brigade and alternately assigned one half to picket duty and held the other half in reserve.[3] On the night of June 15, 1962, seven companies of the 24th Regiment performed picket duty along the line between Secessionville and Fort Pemberton.

General Hunter, through his binoculars, continued to study the strong Confederate defensive line. In spite of Benham's intercessions, the general maintained a belief that his forces were not strong enough for a successful advance on Charleston. Therefore, Hunter decided to hold his present position. On June 11, 1862, he returned to Hilton Head to petition Washington for the necessary reinforcements. As he departed, Hunter instructed General Benham not to attack Charleston or Fort Johnson until the Union troops were "largely reinforced."[4]

After Hunter's departure, Benham constantly observed the defenders reinforcing the defenses of the Tower Battery. His apprehension increased as the Confederate artillery shells found the range of the Union camp. After several days of observations, General Benham decided that a reconnaissance in force would eliminate the Tower Battery and secure the safety of the camp and still comply with Hunter's prohibition against an attack on Charleston. Although every Union general objected to the attack, Benham, an aggressive officer, gave orders for the operation.

On Monday, June 16, 1862, between 3:00 and 4:00 a.m., the Federals silently marched out of camp, every Union soldier eager for the assault.[5] In compliance with his superior's plan, General Stevens directed his division of 3500 men, supported by Rockwell's Battery, in a frontal assault on the fort itself. Accompanied by General Benham, General Wright's Division of 3100 men, supported by Hamilton's Battery, initiated a flank attack on the fort. Wright held one brigade in reserve.[6]

Benham readied his gunboats, the *Hale* and the *Ellen*, to move forward and "remain out of sight until after the action... started."[7] The two gunboats would only serve as a convoy for the army's signal corps in the day's battle.

Stevens surprised the Confederate pickets and captured four men and one officer. The Federals gave a "loud huzzah" when they captured the pickets, and the remaining Confederates fired a few rifle shots, wounding two men. However, the noise from the incident did not alarm the soldiers at the fort nor those on the line manned by the 24th. The remaining Confederate pickets ran for the safety of the fort. Pursued closely by the Yankees, they breathlessly arrived at Fort Lamar as dawn was breaking.[8]

The roar of Fort Lamar's exploding guns broke the quiet stillness of the morning and announced the beginning of the battle. Signaled by the artillery and musketry, the Union gunboats steered a course up the river in the direction of the Tower Battery until the crews gained a clear view of the battlefield. The sailors desperately coveted a share of the battle, and disappointment showed as the Confederates mowed down many of their friends.[9]

On the night of the attack, Colonel Stevens commanded the Hagood's Brigade picket detail, and Colonel Hagood the reserve. Stevens had at his disposal the seven companies of the 24th Regiment, one company of the 47th Georgia, six companies of the 1st Regiment and Boyer's field artillery battery.[10] The reserve consisted of the Eutaw Battalion, the 4th Louisiana

Battalion, four companies of the 1st Regiment and three companies of the 24th.

While Stevens' Division assaulted Fort Lamar, Wright's Division advanced over the Battery Island Road and along the western side of Lighthouse Creek. General Wright did not arrive at his place on the flank until well after General Stevens made the initial assault.[11]

General Williams held his reserve brigade of 1,600 troops near the Crossroads. Williams' troops were in close support of Hamilton's guns on the Battery Island Road.

The 1st Brigade of Wright's Division included the 3rd New Hampshire, 3rd Rhode Island, and the 97th Pennsylvania. Wright's 2nd Brigade, held in reserve, mustered the 6th Connecticut, 47th New York, 45th Pennsylvania, and 1st New York Engineers.[12] The 1st Brigade, which counted a strength of about 1,500 effectives, advanced slowly and cautiously along the western side of Lighthouse Creek.

Colonel Stevens was near the Cross Roads when he learned that Fort Lamar was under attack. Always cool and resourceful, Stevens notified Colonel Hagood by messenger and placed the picket detail reserve in positions to provide flank support for the fort. He placed the men of the 1st Regiment behind a good breastwork of felled timber on the eastern side of the road. Most units of the 24th maintained vigilance at the picket position, which was critical for a warning of an alternate Federal attack. Portions of four companies, about 100 men, of the 24th were available to Stevens:

Company D, The Evans Guard, Lieutenant Beckham, commanding;

Company G, Captain Pearson's company, Lieutenant Hamiter, commanding;

Company I, The Edgefield Light Infantry, Captain Morgan, commanding;

Company K, Captain Tompkins company, Captain Tompkins, commanding.

Stevens situated these men still farther to the left of the 1st Regiment in a prone position behind some felled trees and thick bushes that formed a reasonably good abatis. He placed Company I, The Edgefield Light Infantry, inside some bushes, at a crucial position. The men of the 24th were directly across the path of Wright's advancing regiments.[13]

Stevens placed Lieutenant Jeter's artillery piece on the right side of the regiment. Without hesitation Jeter opened fire on the Federal troops, who were in full view near the Hill Place.[14] The Yankee return fire fell near the position occupied by the 24th.

Shortly after 4:30 a.m., Stevens' message reached Colonel Hagood, who immediately ordered the bugler to sound "fall-in." The men hastily assembled, swiftly started toward the battlefield and soon caught the sight and sound of the artillery shells bursting at Secessionville.[15] The panorama increased the intensity of each man's excitement to the point that the soldiers could barely restrain themselves from individually charging into the thick of the battle.[16]

Lieutenant Colonel J. McEnery's 4th Louisiana Battalion approached the fort directly across the causeway or footbridge. The Louisianians arrived at the fort at a run yelling at the top of their lungs, "Remember Butler," recalling Union General Butler's actions during the occupation of New Orleans. The Louisianians stopped the advance of the enemy force that approached the fort along the marsh under cover of the myrtle bushes.[17] Battle participants considered the arrival of the Louisiana Battalion as the turning point of the battle.

Hagood responded rapidly and dispatched the reserve. As the men neared the battlefield, their eagerness and excitement intensified and they vociferously charged forward. When the soldiers caught sight of the battlefield they turned off the road and ran through a field, a creek, and yet another field, all the time with artillery shells falling all around.[18]

Colonel Stevens placed the new arrivals behind a hedge that offered only minimal protection. The men had hardly taken the position when volley after volley of Union musketry poured forth. One observer described the sound of the minié balls as, "Zit! Zit! Zit!"[19] The Federal rifle fire wounded two men within five minutes. Under fire for the first time, no one knew whom or where the next bullet would strike, yet, the leaders noticed that the raw men acted with the coolness of veterans. Someone passed word of an enemy advance and the defenders fixed bayonets, prepared for a charge. Strangers approached the Confederate position, and when challenged answered that they were friends.

> One Yankee officer cried out, "Don't fire, we are friends
> ...you will kill our own men, etc." A Confederate soldier
> called out, "Where from?" Answer, "Rhode Island."

In response, the Confederates shot the man dead, and one of his companions quickly joined him. Some still thought the men were friends until a Southerner removed a belt from one of the dead men. He held it up and asked if they could see "the U.S.?" At this, the defenders opened an intense fire on the remaining enemy soldiers hiding behind some trees.[20]

As soon as Hagood arrived on the field, he realized that the guns at Battery Reed were silent and sent Lieutenant Colonel Capers to take charge of the battery and open fire at once.[21] Capers fairly raced his horse to Battery Reed. There he found Lieutenant L. B. Kitching and 15 men from Lamar's Artillery who were assigned to serve the battery of two 24-pounders. Kitching reported that the detachment had just arrived from the country and had no orders, and that neither he nor his men knew anything about the guns or the ammunition. Capers loaded the guns and fired at the target. On the first round, he misjudged the recoil. The gun, elevated about two feet,

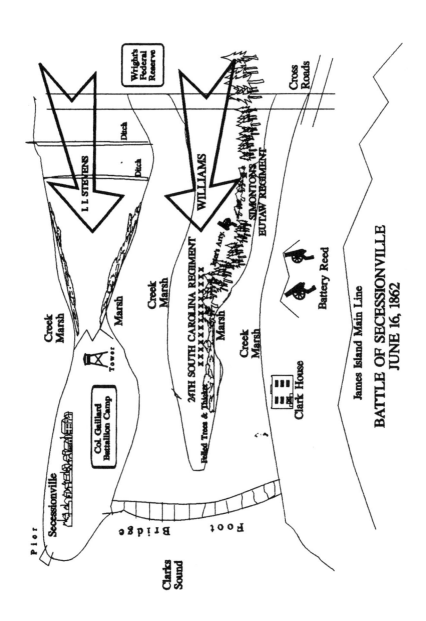

BATTLE OF SECESSIONVILLE
JUNE 16, 1862

37

jumped off its narrow platform, disabled for the remainder of the battle. Warned about the narrow platform, Capers was careful to keep the other gun on its track. Kitching and his men were fast learners and soon the artillery-men were serving the battery well. Capers visited the Clark House and apprised Generals Evans and Smith of the situation. Afterwards, Evans returned Capers to the battery for the remainder of the battle.[22]

Meanwhile, the observers on the gunboats concluded that the scene on the battlefield was "a terrible sight." The sailors observed the brave Federal soldiers breasting the storm of death dealing missiles. Some of the Union soldiers struggled valiantly and finally reached the parapets of Fort Lamar. Just for a moment the Naval observers felt relieved when the Confederate rifle fire subsided. Suddenly, the intensity of the fort's artillery and rifle fire increased again, and the Federals again reeled backward. As Stevens' Division of Union infantry made its final retreat across the cotton fields, the Confederates opened fire with renewed vigor. The Navy suggested that with the expected flank support, the assaulting force might have taken the Tower Battery.[23]

The Federal attack on the flank of Fort Lamar was weak. The 3rd Rhode Island, expecting support from the 3rd New Hampshire, bravely charged the Confederate position. However, the latter regiment came under the Confederate artillery fire and withdrew. The Rhode Islanders noticed the movement and decided that they, too, should retreat.[24] The men from Hagood's Brigade laid down a highly effective small arms fire that no doubt also influenced the Rhode Islander's decision. Union Captain Edwin Metcalf mentioned in his official report "encountering a galling fire from the enemy's sharpshooters."[25]

Colonel Hagood said that the Rhode Islanders "were handsomely repulsed by Colonel C. H. Stevens' skirmishers, except one portion which penetrated to Simonton's line on the left. One of his companies was engaged for a few moments in driving them back...exchanging the first volley at twenty paces...so closely had they approached without being discovered in the dense thicket....[however] the Yankee bolt was shot. They fell back sullenly and without pursuit, leaving dead and wounded upon the field.[26]"

Colonel Stevens considered that his men occupied a reasonably strong defensive position, but such a small force could not mobilize an effective pursuit of the retreating Yankees.

During a momentary lull in the firing, an obviously distressed lieutenant approached Colonel Stevens as he stood immediately behind his men observing the action. The officer had tears in his eyes and informed the colonel that his men were "cut to pieces," and he felt the injured men needed assistance. Stevens immediately elongated his line and protected the lieutenant while he removed his dead and wounded.

The entire skirmish line felt inordinate anxiety because no one knew if friends lived or died. Soon the men began exchanging information about casualties, and the name of each soldier killed made its way down the line. No one showed any emotion or made an outcry. However, a soldier recorded, "One could see by the compressed lips that if the Yankees gave those men another chance...they would pay for their folly."[27]

As the Confederates repulsed the third assault at Fort Lamar, General Benham decided further attacks would be useless and withdrew so the men could "lick their wounds." By 9:00 a.m., the Union forces were in full retreat and the battle of Secessionville was over. A battle that could have been a brilliant victory for the Federals became a bloody repulse, and Benham was the Yankee general who was going to answer for the debacle.[28]

When the Federal troops retreated, the Union gunboats, the *Hale* and the *Ellen*, finally entered the battle. The sailors joyfully grasped the long awaited opportunity and opened fire from the Stono and Folly Rivers with vigor. The boat's large guns hurled shot and shell in the direction of the Confederate defenders. Their blasts also endangered the Federals and killed only one Southerner.

Lieutenant Colonel Capers evaluated the performance of Battery Reed in his official report:

> The effect of our 24-pounder on his [the enemy's] left flank
> was very perceptible at every discharge. I am satisfied that
> the fire of this battery contributed no little to our suc-
> cess...that the general commanding rode to the battery
> during the close of the engagement and warmly thanked us
> for our work.[29]

Afterwards, the Charleston newspapers criticized the Confederate generals because of their reported absence during the battle. However, Generals Smith and Evans were present at the Clark place during the battle. Evans, commander of James Island, accompanied General Pemberton after the battle to inspect the condition of the troops at Fort Lamar. Although Pemberton was the general who actually won the battle, he received no credit. At the Battle of Secessionville, an extremely unusual event occurred: the actual combatants received the honors for the victory, not the generals.[30]

The battle over, the men scoured the battlefield gathering arms, looking after the wounded, and locating the slain. The men experienced for the first time the sad spectacle of witnessing the dead and wounded being removed from the battlefield. One observer noted that the scene was a "heart-rending sight that nerved many an arm to greater strength." Another participant thought that the battlefield offered such horrible scenes that he would forego future ordeals. He recalled that twenty or thirty men, either dying or already dead, filled one small field. One had been in the act of loading his rifle when a charge of grape shot took out the whole of his back, and he lay dead with his hands raised as if he were even then loading his weapon. Another man close by had his leg entirely shot away with only a piece of skin connecting his knee and thigh. One Federal soldier, wounded in his back and throat, lay in the water near the bank and could not move as the continually rising water of the tidal creek reached his shoulders. The Confederates helped the man out of the creek, gave him a drink of water and left him on the field for the litter bearers.

As they retreated, the fleeing Yankees discarded numerous weapons and accouterments. In front of the 24th, the Confederates gathered over 60 weapons, including five Enfield rifles, and large numbers of haversacks, canteens and cartridge boxes.

Some soldiers searched for souvenirs. One found a breast plate, 12 Yankee coat buttons and an enemy cap. He also discovered a supply of cartridges which he vowed to shoot at their former owners. Another man gathered souvenirs for his father and collected a gun strap, four U.S. postage stamps, and a New Hampshire button.[31] The Southerners also found letters that Union soldiers had written and not yet mailed. In one letter, a Federal soldier noted, optimistically, that someone had informed his company "the rebels" would engender only mild resistance, if any at all. Another letter spoke about a company experiencing battle within days after mustering. In addition to letters, the Confederates collected pictures, watches, Yankee money, and gold and silver coins. The souvenirs were dutifully mailed to family members at home.

A few Confederate soldiers gleaned breakfast or lunch from the discarded Federal haversacks, but others could not eat the Yankee food. Later in the war, the soldiers would not be so fastidious and would often welcome food from a Yankee haversack.

While most soldiers quietly returned thanks for safely passing through the battle, one loudly complained because he did not get a shot at an enemy soldier. The same man felt chagrined and embarrassed because his company could not boast of even a single wounded man.[32] With a little more combat experience, the soldiers would feel very thankful for such good fortune.

More Federal casualties occurred during the assault on Fort Lamar than on the flank side of the marsh because of the fort's artillery abetted by Battery Reed. Afterwards, litter bearers spent the remainder of the day carrying the wounded men nearly two miles to the ambulances.[33]

Many Carolinians thought the Yankees fought well and were "a powerful looking set" of men. The prisoners and wounded related that the Federal commanders "swilled the soldiers with liquor" the night before the battle. Several avowed that they never wanted a fight with the Southerners.[34] No doubt, most Confederate soldiers felt the same.

The soldiers' obvious excitement, yet relief, that they had survived a battle experience prevailed throughout the camp. The human carnage moved those who witnessed the battlefield. The men of the 24th did not yet know it, but this was only a taste of the ordeal that lay ahead. However, for the moment, the scene of the Secessionville battlefield was enough.[35]

The search for missing men continued the day after the battle. Private James Tillman, Company I, and several of his comrades searched the battlefield in front of the 24th's position. The searchers sadly found the remains of a missing comrade in some heavy brush.[36]

The next day, Capers voiced his chagrin about the accounts of the battle published in the Charleston newspapers. The news articles identified only the Eutaw Battalion in the account of the skirmish at Secessionville. It mentioned the skill that Lieutenant Colonel Charles H. Simonton, its commander, displayed in handling his men as they charged the enemy. Capers described the events as they actually occurred:

> Simonton had marched his men down the road and Colonels Hagood and Stevens posted him in the woods with our companies...there they lay until the "enemy charging" the wood...fired into him...[and] by the return fire lost men. Neither Stevens nor I will stoop to puff ourselves...Clarence who always does everything carelessly...furnishes...an incorrect...list of our casualties....Hagood & Stevens directed because the Eutaw Battalion has one to write for it they [Hagood & Stevens] are not mentioned.[37]

This is the only account on record that Capers offered criticism of the regiment's adjutant. Lieutenant Palmer added to his brief report, "I don't have time to write anymore," which he probably didn't.

The exhilarating news of the splendid Confederate victory at Secessionville spread rapidly throughout the South. The hearts of the soldiers and citizens alike filled and overflowed, and they gave Joy and Thanksgiving to the Lord for such a stunning and marvelous victory. The Confederates could have won only with His approval. Still, the loss of many Confederate soldiers cast a gloom over the city.

Both sides suffered heavy casualties considering the length of the battle. The hearts of the men of the 24th were sad because of casualties, which included three men killed, seven wounded, and two captured. Lieutenant F. W. Andrews, the regiment's only officer casualty, numbered among the wounded. After the battle, thirteen Yankees lay dead in front of the position defended by the 24th. Colonel Hagood's Brigade reported 20 killed, 52 wounded and 8 missing.[38] The final count indicated a total of 683 Federal casualties and 204 Confederates.

The men of the 24th were extremely cool during the melee, although they realized the danger involved. Many made vows they would serve God and Mother if allowed to survive the ordeal safely. Afterwards, the "would serve" often became "I intend to try." Even so, many preserved the pledge.[39]

Colonel Stevens noted that the men "handled themselves well." He bestowed special recognition to Captain Tompkins of Company K, Lieutenant Beckham of Company G, and the detachment of men who courageously maintained the position in the front of the advancing enemy. The colonel also recognized Major Hammond for bravely remaining at his post in charge of the picket detail on Gill Road and Newtown Cut. Lieutenant Colonel Capers received special mention for bringing Battery Reed into the battle and personally directing the fire of the battery with his usual gallantry and efficiency. General Smith also commended Capers for his service at Battery Reed:

> Colonel: In the absence of General Evans, first in command on the 16th instant, allow me to thank you and the small detachment of South Carolina Artillery under your command for the efficient and distinguished service which was rendered by Battery Reed upon that day. Make known to the detachment my thanks.

Capers responded in writing, "The expression of your approval gives me...and Lieutenant Kitchens...the utmost pleasure...I shall endeavor always to deserve your approbation."[40]

After the hard-fought battle, the new combat veterans coolly resumed the regular picket assignment, almost casually.[41] The entire episode was obviously "all in a day's work."

General Pemberton observed with pleasure the success of his men and published special orders congratulating the troops who engaged the enemy. The general specifically mentioned Capers, Tompkins and Beckham for good conduct.[42]

Capers lamented about the quality of the generals who commanded the men in battle. Even his close and highly respected friend, Brigadier General States Rights Gist, received a critique that offered amelioration. Capers wrote:

> The great deficiency in the military is in generals. Pemberton is no general. General Evans is a coward with a reputation for bravery which he has earned by sending his men and officers where he never dreams of going. He keeps himself out of range and gets away from fire whenever by chance he gets into it. He is reckless, without judgement and terribly pampas and drinks to excess. General Smith is a gentlemen...doesn't use profane language, but he is no he is no coward. General Gist is cool...has a good head and I have great confidence in him...but he is the junior and obeys orders only, without originating them.[43]

Capers made the comments to Lottie with a reminder not to mention his feelings about the generals.[44] However, the qualifications and ability of the Confederate political and military leadership were prime campfire topics affording many hours of enjoyable pastime.

Both armies reorganized after the battle of Secessionville. The Confederates at James Island organized various regiments into brigades, and the 24th became a part of Gist's Brigade. After General Hunter received the report of the battle, he placed General Benham under arrest and shifted command of James Island to General Horatio G. Wright.

The new Union commander anxiously contemplated the adverse living conditions at James Island. The health of the men became his transcending concern. Hunter, too, worried about the unhealthful conditions and warned his superiors that the "sickly months were approaching" and thought, "The climate of Beaufort would be much more ideal for the men". He was concerned about "the...number of men prostrated on James Island...and the increasing sick list...had our presence there been continued."[45]

A Union soldier gave another version of the conditions on James Island:

> The Island was low and marshy, nearly covered with vines, brush, and timber. It was with difficulty we could find enough dry ground to sleep on...countless long-nosed mosquitoes bled us day and night.[46]

Mosquitoes, sandflies, and fleas needed blood to drink regardless of the nationality or race of the provider. Southerners apparently were more impervious to the devilment of the insects than the Northerners. However, the Confederates suffered, too. Colonel T. G. Lamar, of Secessionville, fame and Major Kingman, the 24th Regiment's quartermaster, both died as a result of fever contracted at the island. Private Tillman offered yet another description of the problem: "mosquitoes very annoying."[47]

The 24th benefitted from another regiment's departure. The Soldiers' Relief Association of Charleston received two dozen mosquito nets consigned to the 18th Regiment, which earlier had been transferred to Virginia, so the nets were forwarded to the 24th. Though they were small and protected only one's head from the mosquitos, the men responded eloquently:

> We are very grateful to our fair friends for so useful a present...promise to do our picket duty now in con- tempt...of the mosquitoes and sandfleas, as of the Yankees.

Another participant observed that the complaints of the soldiers "painfully suggests the terrible sufferings of the poor men from heat and mosquitoes."[48]

The appearance of numerous Federal ships and gunboats in the Stono River and performing picket duty in close proximity of the enemy created much anxiety in the soldiers of the 24th. They thought "something was going" on when they spotted the ships. The soldiers speculated about the intentions of the Yankees, and some concluded that the Yankees were "keeping very still" and thought they had "enough fight" for one time. Others surmised that the enemy soldiers were "lying low and making preparations." Debate among the men about the enemy strategy was indeed entertaining, although the Confederates saw the invaders only while both were on picket duty. There the pickets were near enough to speak with each other, though both sides were under precise orders not to speak or converse. Thus both ignored the other's presence. Even with the enemy pickets nearby, the men considered themselves relatively safe since neither would fire unless fired upon. The men of the 24th realized the necessity of picket duty as well as its importance, yet they did not especially relish the duty "under the enemy's very nose."

The Confederates noticed that the Federal picket line had been withdrawn from Grimballs Plantation and reestablished nearer the Legare House. That move intensified speculation among the Confederates that the Yankees were preparing for departure. Others thought that the move was merely a ploy to entice the defenders from behind their strong defensive line and into a trap. The latest rumor that the blue army was actually withdrawing was wonderful news, and the soldiers were ever optimistic that it was true.

Finally, by July 10, 1862, the Federals evacuated James Island. During the embarkation, the Confederate pickets could not determine whether enemy troops were arriving or departing. The Yankee bands played and created much noise and effectively concealed the movement. The exhilarating news confirming the Yankee departure elated the citizens of Charleston as well as the soldiers of the 24th. First and foremost, the city was safe...at least for the moment.[49]

With the Federal army gone, the Confederates immediately entered the vacated Northern camps. The souvenir seeking Confederate soldiers collected many cannon balls of different types and sizes, configurations and shapes. The ammunition was discarded either from enemy gunboats or the batteries located along the shore. The Yankees shaped one like an egg and another was similar to "a butter churn or a wagon hub." A soldier predicted, tongue-in-cheek, that, next, the Yankees would shoot a wagon wheel with each spoke charged with an explosive. After looking over the Federal arsenal, another Confederate soldier observed that the Yankees were "a more enterprising people than we are."[50]

After the excitement of the Secessionville battle and the Federal evacuation of James Island, soldier duties became mundane and tedious. Frequently, the soldiers performed picket duty which became ever more distasteful. However, the duties were more agreeable to those who witnessed the havoc unleashed by battling armies at Secessionville.

The troops constantly wrote the home folk the news from camp. Private John Lewis "Buddy" McGee, Company F, from Anderson, informed his parents that after the Secessionville affair, the regiment relocated their bivouac from Royal's Place one mile west "to a much better place." Buddy enjoyed his assignment with the regimental quartermaster and was "slightly promoted" to second assistant quartermaster. One day a friend gave him four large tomatoes as a lunch supplement that "filled a wash pan," and he thriftily saved the seeds for his Dad's garden. Many soldiers, Buddy included, were deeply religious. Colonel Stevens' brother preached a sermon the preceding evening and John Lewis boasted, "We had the pleasure of hearing a good sermon preached."[51] The men were in fine spirits!

Many men in the regiment were sick. While none were dangerously ill, the large sick list caused an increase in the frequency of picket duty. No doubt, frequent picket duty contributed to an increase in the number of ill soldiers which resulted in a self-fulfilling prophecy.[52]

Typical days were full for the men. The soldiers performed picket duty, stood inspections, cleaned the grounds, participated in dress parades (even on Sunday), attended preaching, and guarded the prisoners. As the men performed the dull garrison duties, they maintained good spirits. Lieutenant Tillman recorded a rumor in camp that reported "two of our pickets were captured & the Yankees were advancing." He added, that the "rumor caused considerable excitement, but it was entirely false."[53]

The troops constantly were concerned about the health and welfare of family members and loved ones at home. When a soldier received a furlough, he usually delivered personal letters and packages to families of his comrades and related news about his friends as well as the war and camp life. Soldiers usually returned from furlough with letters, boxes of food-stuffs, news from families, and the latest community gossip. Sometimes soldiers would learn from a returning comrade that loved ones were ill or in other tragic circumstances. The men frequently complained they did not receive letters from loved ones often enough.[54]

On July 8, 1862, the regiment transferred to Secessionville and Colonel Stevens became post commander. Stevens' new command consisted of the 24th, 51st Georgia and the 46th Georgia Regiments. Capers commanded the 24th. One month later, Gist named Stevens commander of James Island, a much larger and more responsible position. Capers commanded the Secessionville post and Major Hammond the regiment.[55] The regiment would remain there until December 1862.

During the summer of 1862, the Confederate army finally established a program to examine the qualifications of officers. Gist convened a board to examine the officers stationed at James Island, Fort Moultrie, and Charleston.[56] He appointed three lieutenant colonels: Capers; William Butler, 1st Regiment; J. G. Pressley, 25th Regiment; to administer the examination. The officers selected a meeting site at Fort Johnson, but they soon relocated to Military Hall in Charleston.[57] Capers continued the special assignment until October 8, when Lieutenant Colonel Simonton, 25th Regiment, succeeded him. Special assignments such as this one provided the former Citadel professor an opportunity to demonstrate his extensive administrative skills.

Often soldiers would transfer from other units to serve in the same unit with family members. Buddy McGee transferred from the Orr's Regiment to serve with his father's unit, Company F, from Anderson. Soon after Buddy's arrival, Lieutenant G. L. McGee suffered ill health, and the surgeon granted his discharge. After his father's departure, Buddy wished that he was back with his old regiment, which had already seen extensive action in Virginia. A disappointed Buddy, who yearned "to get into the fight," informed his father about his feelings:

> I left my friends to come to this Regt. at your kind request
> and now you left me in most an awful condition. I have
> seen very little pleasure since I came to this Regt.

He, no doubt, missed his father and mentioned the existence of "confusion in the company."

Often friends or relatives indicated a desire to enlist in the army. Buddy's brother, Silvester "Vessie" McGee, became interested. However, Buddy was extremely protective of his "little brother" and strongly advised his parents against the idea:

> I want you to keep Vessie at home as long as possible. He
> knows nothing about hardships, and more than that he is
> entirely too young to stand camp life.

Buddy also wrote to his younger brother suggesting that he should remain at home and described some of the hardships that Vessie would endure if he became a soldier:

> You will not be here one week until you will want to go
> home and (you) will not be allowed to go outside of the
> camp let alone going home and you will get nothing to eat
> but old beef and cow leather bread. If you knew as much
> about it as I do, you would stay where you are.[58]

After Buddy's strong persuasion, Vessie postponed his enlistment, although he lost none of the desire to enlist.

Regiments stationed on the coast frequently received the call and departed for the battle zone, usually Virginia. The camp was rife with rumors that the 24th would leave soon for Virginia. The men did not know why the high command selected a particular regiment for transfer to the battle zone. The 51st Georgia Regiment, in the same brigade as the 24th, departed for Virginia on July 18, 1862. An observer reported, "They were quite happy, such yelling as they did, I never saw before. They all seemed in very fine spirits."[59] On August 9, 1862, an observer recorded the departure of yet another regiment: "Colonel Hagood's Regt. (1st Regt) left this evening for Virginia. We bid them adieu."[60]

Capers commanded the 24th that day and mustered the regiment to wish the departing regiment Godspeed and to present the commander with a present. Lieutenant Colonel Glover, acting commander of the 1st Regiment, "returned it in handsome manner" and the two lieutenant colonels exchanged pleasantries and farewells.[61] Glover departed for the combat zone without having seen his newborn son, who resided in Anderson. Some of the officers speculated that since the 1st Regiment went to Virginia, the 24th would remain at James Island. Although the men were ready and impatient for a combat assignment, one did not materialize.[62]

The routine duties of camp life were boring. At times, the James Island Command tasked the regiment with a variety of details and extra duties. One detail required the command to operate the two marsh batteries that commanded Folly Creek and Light House Inlet.[63] Others worked on the Confederate gunboats under construction. Soldiers griped about the frequent tours of picket duty.

The regiment spent the late summer and fall in a more contented, peaceful, and comfortable garrison life at Secessionville.[64] The heat was oppressive in August, and the men impatiently awaited cooler weather, which would also provide a measure of relief from the dreaded mosquitoes. The troops achieved perfection in performing routine soldier duties. With the arrival of cooler weather, the health of the regiment became "tolerable good." Colonel Stevens invented an ingenious new style oven for baking bread that considerably improved the quality, and the men no longer described the bread as "cow leather bread." Stevens also used his enormous talent keeping the soldiers occupied and yet instilling a sense of accomplishment.

Although the food was relatively good, the troops still prevailed upon the homefolk to provide a box of provisions. Buddy McGee pleaded for clothing, a box of fruit, and anything "pleasing to the eye of a (Regular)." He asked his mother to send him "a lightweight suit" because his suit was too heavy for the summer weather. He also needed two cotton shirts and one pair of cotton drawers. The casualty lists from Buddy's old regiment pained him deeply, especially when the names of several of his old messmates were listed.[65]

The men had not been paid, and they were practically destitute. Colonel Stevens urged Richmond to allocate funds since the men were last paid February 28, 1862, and reminded that the new enlistees had not received the promised bounty:

> The delay in payment...the men are suffering...and their
> families. If anything can be done to facilitate the payment
> it would be of...great advantage.[66]

Known by his men as "The Old Fellow," he never hesitated to act, giving

100 per cent of himself and accepting no less.[67]

Toothache was a fairly common malady among the men, and regimental surgeons usually pulled the tooth that caused the discomfort. Although it was painful, after suffering a day or two with severe pain, the event somehow seemed less intense. Buddy recorded his experience: "It created me...pain but now I think I will rest in peace for awhile."[68]

The soldiers spent many idle hours longing for a furlough, especially when the fruit and watermelons ripened on the farm. McGee gained one of the coveted furloughs during August and September 1862. That was, no doubt, a happy time for the youthful soldier and his family.[69] Buddy, as most members of the 24th, was a proud soldier who willingly served his country, but he still loved his family and home life.

The troops concerned themselves about the local and national political situation. The soldiers enjoyed news articles, especially those published by *The Charleston Mercury*, although the editor often used the newspaper to denigrate favored political leaders. They thought some of the opinions expressed came from "mendacious mouths."[70] The articles were favorite topics at the 24th's bivouac.

Family tragedies often struck members of the regiment. The soldiers grieved for relatives and friends killed, wounded, and maimed as a result of the war. They also grieved for personal tragedies among the homefolk. Lieutenant Colonel Capers' brother, Oddy, a member of Company K, Palmetto Sharpshooters, died on Saturday August 20, 1862, in Virginia. Capers eulogized his brother: "A nobler soul never lived & purer, truer man, never died. Hallowed be his memory."[71]

The war stimulated a religious fervor in many soldiers, and members of the 24th were no different. While under fire at Secessionville, some made serious vows that in the future they would serve God, and, afterwards, many tried to keep those vows.[72] Capers, a product of a religious family, was already deeply religious before the war, and vowed that if he survived the war he would dedicate his life to the Lord's work. He attended church services frequently and started a choir, happily reporting, "Some sing by note." While Lottie was at Cherry Grove Plantation, she and Ellison established a "Mercy Seat" and prayed with each other three times a day on a prearranged schedule, after which the couple felt better. Lieutenant Tillman mentioned that he had attended Sunday church services at "the Colonel's tent."[73]

The "Articles of War" were read to the troops on Sunday, August 3, 1862, at 6 a.m. The army mandated an explanation of the articles on the first Sunday of every month, a routinely dull, boring, and uninspiring session. Usually, the misery of the session ended by 8:30 a.m., and the colonel dismissed the regiment without further formations that day.[74]

During the summer and fall of 1862, several officers resigned. On July

21, 1862, Captain Tompkins, commander of Company K, resigned for health reasons.[75] Captain Thomas, commander of Company H, requested a furlough so he could manage his personal business. However, Colonel Stevens disapproved the request. Incensed, Thomas submitted his resignation, stating that he had lost an arm in the war with Mexico and the law did not require him to serve. Moreover, he said he didn't think one should give his all for his country unless absolutely necessary and at that time such a necessity did not exist. Stevens recommended acceptance because the officer who filled the position should be willing to make the sacrifices that Thomas considered too great, and the War Department accepted the resignation on October 28, 1862.[76]

Private McGee, furlough over, rejoined the regiment at Secessionville early in October. Buddy was happy because Major Kingman retained him with the quartermaster department. While visiting Charleston, the young soldier noticed the nearly completed gunboat, the *Palmetto State*.

Speculation that the Federals would attack Charleston again kept the regiment motivated to construct new entrenchments and strengthen old ones.[77] As the fall season approached, the intense summer heat abated, and many thought the cooler weather would provide a better climate for another Yankee attack.

The month of October was busy for the regiment. General Beauregard, accompanied by Governor Pickens, reviewed the James Island troops, including the 24th. Several men from the regiment volunteered for Naval Service aboard the *Palmetto State*, now ready for active service. Other soldiers with mechanical experience volunteered to assist the boat building project.

South of Charleston, the Yankees occupied the small hamlet of Bluffton, South Carolina. The men theorized that the enemy planned something for the Confederates more intense than a landing there.[78] Finally, the Federals launched an attack toward Pocotaligo. On October 13 the regiment was alerted to prepare and hold themselves ready for a move with one hour's notice.[79] Stevens instructions were explicit: "Keep five days ration of bacon and bread on hand. When ordered to move, if time allowed...cook the bacon. Move without tents or cooking utensils." The same order canceled furloughs. Officers, however, could take leave for a few hours, though they could not remain outside the camp overnight.

Finally, the Federals struck with 5,000 troops, intending to break the railroad at Coosawhatchie.[80] Beauregard sped assistance to Colonel W. S. Walker at Pocotaligo. He mobilized General Gist with three regiments (one of which was the 24th) and a light artillery battery. Beauregard also alerted Colonel Hagood and another 1,000 troops to follow Gist as soon "as transportation was available." On Wednesday, October 22, the regiment boarded the train at the Charleston and Savannah Railroad line not far from

Camp Gist, en route for Pocotaligo.[81] Many of the men assigned to Companies E, D, and F, hailed from the nearby area. In fact, several soldiers were from Coosawhatchie, the target of the Federal attack.

Planning a one-day incursion, the enemy, who heavily outnumbered the Confederates, came up the Broad and Coosawhatchie Rivers in thirteen boats, which included both transports and gunboats.[82] The Federals reached the railroad and had destroyed only four rails of track, which were quickly repaired.[83] The incursion cost both sides. The Federals reported 340 casualties and the Confederates 163.[84]

The 24th arrived at Pocataligo the next morning, October 23, eagerly expecting action. However, by the time the regiment arrived at Pocotaligo, the battle was over, and the Yankees were already aboard the gunboats returning to Hilton Head. Buddy McGee recorded the scene, "The scoundrels fled in confusion to their 'Gun Boats' leaving dead men all along the road." The 24th returned to Secessionville that same night.[85]

While many enlisted men went AWOL, few officers engaged in the practice. One such incident resulted in court-martial and the loss of a highly dedicated Confederate soldier. Captain Pearson, Commander of Company G, requested a few hours leave so he could visit Charleston on Tuesday before the regiment departed for Pocotaligo. Stevens ordered Pearson to return by dress parade that same day, October 21. However, the captain failed to return until the next day and raced to catch up with the regiment already aboard the train en route to Pocotaligo. In addition, he did not contact Stevens upon his return. When the regiment arrived from Pocotaligo on Friday morning, the men unloaded the railroad cars at St. Andrews and hiked to Secessionville. The lame men, including Pearson, gained permission to follow the regiment at a slower pace. The others arrived in camp soon after the main body. However, Pearson detoured to Charleston and finally arrived at Secessionville late that night.[86]

Stevens initiated a court-martial and charged Pearson with absence without leave and disobedience of orders.[87] A rumor prevailed in camp that he would receive a court-martial for violating an order "he could not have well complied with."[88] On November 12, a trial by general court-martial found the captain guilty of three charges and three specifications. The court suspended Pearson from rank without pay or emoluments for three months, and directed that the commander reprimand Captain Pearson in the presence of the regiment.[89]

A successful lawyer by profession, Pearson served as the Master in Equity from Richland District until he raised a company and volunteered for Confederate service. After the court-martial, he immediately submitted an application requesting reassignment to a judge advocate or judicial position. Legal assignments were extremely scarce as there were more applicants than positions. Therefore, the Richmond authorities placed his name on a list of applicants pending a suitable vacancy.[90]

Finally, on February 23, 1863, well into his court-martial sentence, Captain Pearson resigned for health reasons. Stevens described the situation as he saw it:

> Captain Pearson has been frequently absent sick and in my opinion the interest of the service would be very greatly promoted by the acceptance of his resignation.[91]

The Confederate army possessed many strong-willed personalities who worked hard to gain freedom for the new country. Those personalities frequently clashed, usually in the finest sense of honor, although at times the clashes proved detrimental. One such incident occurred at Charleston and deeply affected the life of Colonel Stevens.

Serious personal conflict developed between Colonel Ransom Calhoun, commander of Fort Sumter, and Major Alfred Rhett, a member of Calhoun's command. The feud culminated eighteen months later when Calhoun challenged his subordinate to a duel, which Rhett eagerly accepted. A recent prohibition against dueling had little effect on the two adversaries. In the early morning hours of September 5, 1862, the two officers met at the Washington Race Course (Hampton Park) in Charleston, and Major Rhett's well-aimed shot killed Calhoun on the spot. Afterwards, Major Rhett received a promotion to colonel and replaced Calhoun as commander of Fort Sumter.

General Beauregard convened a court of inquiry consisting of Colonel Peyton H. Colquitt, of the 46th Georgia, Colonel Lamar of Secessionville fame, and Stevens, who became president. After numerous delays, the board finally assembled on October 20, 1862. The court completed the inquiry three weeks later, on November 10, and recommended that General Beauregard institute further proceedings in the case.[92]

Overruling the board, the general decided that Rhett had acted honorably and should not be the first victim of the new law. Beauregard affirmed that in the future he would rigidly enforce the prohibition against dueling and exhorted officers to "forego their personal animosities for country's sake."[93]

Beauregard's action infuriated members of the command, who considered such a finding most odious. In Capers' opinion, the general feared a personal challenge for his own position that would result in his replacement. At times, the young colonel could be tough on senior officers, especially generals. He also had long-term differences of opinion with the radical editor of the *Charleston Mercury*, who was the father of Major Rhett.

In the meantime, on October 30, 1862, Colonel Stevens, inextricably enmeshed in the court, received an urgent message from Pendleton that his wife was stricken. The message advised that he hasten to her side because she was dangerously ill and might not recover. However, the proceedings of the board totally consumed Stevens, and he delayed his departure because his absence would cancel the board and the work already completed. The panel finished its work on November 10, 1862, and the colonel rushed to Pendleton. Unfortunately, when he arrived at his home, he learned that his wife, Ann Bee Stevens, had died Saturday, November 8, 1862, and the family had interred her remains in the family plot at St. Paul's Church in Pendleton the next day.[94] He also discovered the same malady that claimed Mrs. Stevens had also claimed his small son, Lionel, aged 4 years and 7 months.[95]

Ellison Capers commiserated with Lottie about the tragedy. The grief he felt over the death of Mrs. Stevens was evident:

> Is not the death of Mrs. Stevens...sad...? She died on Saturday of diphtheria & was buried on Sund. How differently some men are constituted! Now had I been in Colonel Stevens place, I...have been in Pendleton a week ago. He told me then that his wife had been extremely ill, and the night before the letter was written him she was thought to be dying. This was more than a week ago...he would not ask for a furlough because he was on the Board of Inquiry to investigate the Rhett duel...he said his absence would temporarily dissolve the board. Family first & board after say I.[96]

Clem Stevens' attitude was that of the typical soldier, dedicated to the success of the new country and cause. Although heartbroken, Stevens could not consider making any less of a sacrifice.

The call of duty was equally strong in Ellison as in Clement. However, Capers' family ties apparently were much the stronger. Time would prove that Capers, too, was most willing to make extreme sacrifices for his country, but never at the expense of his family.

Less than one month later, tragedy struck the life of Stevens again. This time, Stevens seemed to blame himself for the tragedy:

> I have just arrived. My little Boy is passing. Slowly passing away. He had been all day anxious to see me. I would not have failed to come for 20 years of life. It does seem as if a heavy curse rests upon me and mine. My love and affection is a blight and a mildew where it rests.[97]

The illness of his son, Hamilton (Hammie), aged 9, resulted in his second son's death. Capers added a sad post-script when he wrote Lottie: "P.S. Colonel Stevens has lost his youngest child too, little Lionel! Poor fellow!"[98]

In short order Colonel Steven's wife, Ann, and two sons, Hammie and Lionel, were gone. Clem was tough, but family tragedy emphasizes issues which are most important.

The men yearned for furloughs so they could visit home and family. Some soldiers even became desperate and slipped away on "French leave" or were "absent without leave," and when apprehended they were court-martialed.[99]

The birth of a child always created a happy time in the regiment. The Capers' second daughter, the couple's third child, was born November 11, 1862, in Columbia.

The same deep-rooted family ties that drove Ellison Capers were typical of the average soldier. Private Isaac Carter, a picket captured at Battery Island, sorely missed his eight children. After the Federals invaded his State, he had felt compelled to enter the army and defend his home. As with most soldiers, he hated the family separation, as well as war, and preferred not to participate, but he could do no less. Within one month after he arrived in camp, the Yankees captured Private Carter, and his family did not know his fate until after he was exchanged.[100] Somehow Carter survived Federal prison, regained his health, and returned to the regiment.

The soldiers usually advised relatives and friends not to join the army. Earlier, Vessie McGee did not enlist because of his brother Buddy's exhortations, although he eagerly awaited the moment he could. However, if the government planned to conscript all white males between the ages of 16 and 60, Buddy thought Vessie would be better off as a member of the 24th. There he and two uncles could protect the younger and less experienced McGee. Finally, Buddy accepted the inevitable, and a delighted Vessie soon joined the regiment at James Island as Private Silvester (Vessie) McGee.[101] Vessie enjoyed camp life, even though he had a cold, and he advised his parents that he was adjusting well: "I am doing very well drilling, but I assure you...there are no fun in it."[102]

The regimental officers served a variety of duties. Capers was appointed to a court-martial board and requested relief because of a heavy workload. The general denied his request:

> No. I appointed the court after carefully thinking of it. I could not admit that you, Capers...are incompetent to the discharge of all duties imposed upon you.

Capers was anything but incompetent and organized the board the next day, November 12, 1862.[103]

Several of the officers submitted resignations, primarily for health reasons. However, occasionally other, more personal reasons, precipitated the action. Captains Thomas and Tompkins and Lieutenant McGee had already departed. Captain Gooding and Lieutenant Doziers' resignation were finally approved. Lieutenant J. P. Tucker submitted his resignation and left for home before receiving approval. The soldiers knowingly confided, "I would not like to be in his shoes." The regiment eventually dropped Lieutenant Tucker from the rolls.[104]

Company F held an election for the vacancy created by the resignation of Lieutenant McGee, Buddy and Vessie's father. Sergeants Samuel W. Sherard and John M. Hall offered for the position. Sherard won the election, receiving one half again as many votes as did Hall. Both sergeants were popular, and the men thought that the election would have been closer.[105]

The camp was rife with rumors that the 24th would transfer to North Carolina because of a Federal threat there. General Gist dined with Capers on the unseasonably warm day of December 9 and claimed he knew "nothing of certainty."[106] However, the men somehow sensed when an action was pending, and a consensus existed that "something was happening."

CHAPTER 3

Defending the Coast

Wilmington & Pocotaligo

After the battle of Pocotaligo, the Confederates spent several hectic weeks wondering where the Federals would strike next. Finally, General Beauregard notified Richmond that the Union general at Hilton Head had loaded the Union army aboard the naval fleet located there, and was en route toward Cape Lookout, North Carolina. They, no doubt, would participate in the Union army's incursion into North Carolina and eventually attack Wilmington. By return wire, Confederate Secretary of War James A. Seddon asked that Beauregard assist Major General William Henry Chase Whiting[1] with the defense of Wilmington. The preservation of the endangered North Carolina area, and one of the few Confederate ports still open, was critical.[2]

As the Federals threatened, Beauregard telegraphed Whiting asking what support he needed and seemed miffed when 18 hours elapsed before receiving a response.[3] Whiting finally responded, and Beauregard sent Brigadier General States Rights Gist with a division of 5,000 men, "all excellent troops." Three light artillery batteries supported the division.[4] Two brigades comprised Gist's Division, the First led by Colonel Stevens, and the Second by Colonel Colquitt, Commander of the 46th Georgia. The 1st Brigade mustered the 24th, the 25th South Carolina, and the 46th Georgia Regiments, and support by Captain William C. Preston's Light Battery.[5] Capers commanded the 24th.

At Secessionville, the camp of the 24th was a mass of excitement. Elated over the call, the troops feverishly prepared for the move, "in light marching order." The troops could take only cooking utensils, two tents per company and two tents for the Field and Staff (F&S) of each battalion. The men hurriedly cooked four days rations, drew 40 rounds of ammunition in cartridge boxes, and packed another 60 rounds for reserve.[6]

After an extremely busy weekend preparing, the regiment departed Secessionville late Sunday afternoon, and arrived, terribly fatigued, at the Charleston train station on Monday, December 14, 1862, at 3:30 a.m. Nearly twelve hours later, the men crammed aboard the uncomfortable railroad cars and departed the city as the train clanked, hissed and slowly scraped its way to Wilmington. Twenty-four hours later, weary after a tiresome journey, but still excited, the regiment reached its destination. The soldiers unloaded the train, traversed the Cape Fear River into Wilmington and bivouacked that night on the banks of the river.[7]

The next day, still excited, the men investigated the town. It stood in a commanding position on a high bluff that rose straight up from the banks of the river. The soldiers discovered two main streets, Front Street along the banks of the river, and Market Street, which ran perpendicular to Front Street. One soldier elicited levity when he expressed an observation that the streets had two directions, uphill and downhill. Streets were quite wide and attractive, displaying many fine buildings that were still whole, as the war had not yet reached into Wilmington. An excessive amount of sand clogged the city's streets, supposedly deposited there by flooding from the river. The soldiers found the city largely unpopulated because citizens had long since deserted the place for safer refuge, either from the threat of the enemy or disease.[8]

The 24th Regiment deployed along the banks of the Northeast River at a railroad bridge or trestle about nine miles northeast of Wilmington. The regiment arrived there on December 17, the same day the Federals attacked the Confederates in front of Goldsboro. Capers found a pleasant area for a bivouac amid a dense grove of pine trees, where the tops came together and formed natural pine top shanties. Captain Sigwald's company, the Marion Rifles, received an outpost assignment across the river from the main bivouac. Capers stationed one section of Preston's Battery (two guns) at the railroad bridge, and placed Company I and the other section of the artillery battery nearby for support.[9] The men immediately fortified the position as well as the approaching roads.[10]

Although the Federal army slowly moved southward, cutting the Weldon Railroad on the Wilmington side of Goldsboro, the enemy objectives were not clear. The South Carolinians momentarily expected a Union cavalry raid on the bridge.[11]

If an army camp was ever rife with rumors, this was it. One rumor purported that the regiment had to move to the support of General G. W. Smith's army at Goldsboro. Another alleged that the regiment was departing Wilmington for Virginia, and still others reported that Whiting had released the 24th back to Charleston. The next day, December 18, even more rumors circulated, equally ridiculous. The rumors were so numerous that Capers could not distinguish "between truth and falsehood" and anxiously contemplated whether he should prepare for a move. A realist, Capers refused to draw in his outposts and prepare for a movement based on the presence of a mere rumor. Perturbed, the young commander sent the adjutant to Wilmington so he could decide whether the regiment should prepare. That afternoon at two o'clock, Palmer returned with the news that the Federals had retreated and, as expected, were concentrating at New Bern. Since the enemy relaxed the immediate pressure on Wilmington, the regiment held its position.[12]

The next day, Quartermaster Sergeant Addison, who made regular messenger and supply trips to Wilmington, returned with word about General Lee's victory at Fredericksburg, Virginia, and the Federal repulse at Goldsboro.[13] Good news always enlivened the regiment's campfire discussions.

The principal subject of conversation at the 24th's campfires was how long the regiment would remain in North Carolina. At first, the prognosticators guessed that the situation would require the regiment's services at Wilmington for only 10 days. The prediction resulted from the news about Lee's victory at Fredericksburg, which meant reduced support for Federal troops in North Carolina. Surely, the men supposed, the Yankees must retreat beyond New Bern, and afterwards Wilmington would be safe.[14]

The weather suddenly turned stinging cold with sharp icy winds blowing out of the north. It didn't usually turn this cold at Charleston so early in the season. The troops huddled over the campfires bundled in their warmest clothing. The men urged the homefolk to knit woolen gloves, socks, and scarfs.[15]

For unknown reasons, General Gist offered Capers an opportunity for relief from duty at Wilmington and a return to Charleston. Capers declined the offer, expressing satisfaction with his position in the 24th:

> I am ready to take any post to which the orders of my
> superiors in the service assign me. It is a principal with me
> not to influence my own position. My life, under God's
> providence, is in his keeping & subject to the orders of my
> country.[16]

Colonel Stevens, his severe family tragedy behind him, finally rejoined the regiment on December 18, 1862. En route, he stopped at Wilmington and briefly visited General Gist.[17] Capers had missed Stevens' strong guiding hand and lamented, "Thank God, Col. Stevens returns to us."[18]

Capers expressed to Lottie his feelings of sympathy for the colonel because of the death of Mrs. Stevens and the two Stevens children:

> Col. Stevens, almost crushed, poor fellow, under his
> tremendous afflictions is with me again, & a nobler, better
> man never lived. - We are warm, confidential friends, & we
> sleep together.[19]

The bivouac at Wilmington was very pleasant. An abundance of straw and blankets provided for the comfort of everyone. The Field and Staff of the regiment bunked in two tents. Stevens, Capers, Ogier, and Palmer shared one of the tents. The remaining members of the Field and Staff shared the other. Captain Steinmeyer described the outpost assignment as his company's most pleasant experience, attesting that it was "little short of a picnic." The local citizens' warm hospitality enhanced the quality of the

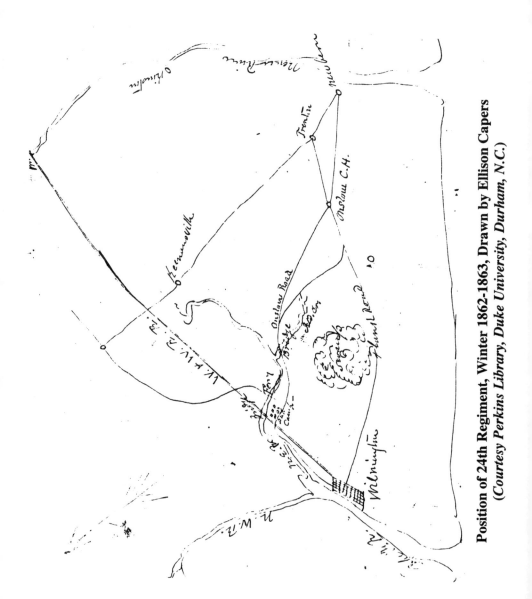

Position of 24th Regiment, Winter 1862-1863, Drawn by Ellison Capers
(Courtesy Perkins Library, Duke University, Durham, N.C.)

58

soldier's sojourn. The assignment was adversely effected only by family separations and the inordinate number of rumors.[20]

The brigade and regimental commanders, Stevens and Capers, reconnoitered the countryside surrounding the bivouac. On December 23 the two men, on horseback, crossed the ferry near the camp and traveled as far as Lane's Ferry, nine or ten miles distant. They observed that the plantations along the river had beautiful and well-tilled fields, and produced corn and ground nuts which would provide sustenance for the army and help feed the civilian population.

The Christmas celebration of 1862 was rather subdued. Two days before Christmas, the regimental officers celebrated the arrival of the holiday season with eggnog.[21] The next day, Christmas Eve, was cloudy and quite cold. On Christmas day, Capers rode into Wilmington and attended church services. On his return he was accompanied by his friend, Lieutenant Colonel Presley of the 25th Regiment.[22] Later that day, the two lieutenant colonels dined together. Other than the family separation, the men, for the most part, enjoyed the Christmas of 1862.

Still, some were disappointed with the holiday season. Many yearned for a furlough so they could visit their loved ones and spend the holidays at home. Vessie McGee expressed mixed feelings when he wrote his parents about his first Christmas away from home: "Pa, this is the dulist Christmas I ever saw." Vessie was homesick and desperately wanted some of his mother's "fresh, homemade crackling bread."[23] Already, he realized that his brother's earlier counsel had been sound.

Major Hammond suffered dreadfully from rheumatism and could not walk without the aid of crutches. The doctor believed the major could not possibly perform military duty until the warm weather arrived and perhaps not even then. Hammond grieved that he could not perform his duties adequately and reluctantly resigned on December 16, 1862. Stevens regretted the ill-health suffered by his friend and wished for the major a speedy recovery. His comment on Hammond's resignation reflected his distress:

> Because of the condition of physical incapacity under
> which Major Hammond suffers, I believe that acceptance
> would be for the good of the service.[24]

Stevens named the regiment's senior captain, Captain Sigwald, commander of Company A, to the position of major of infantry. Afterwards he named Second Lieutenant J. H. Steinmeyer to become commander of Company A. Steinmeyer retained that position until the war ended for him on October 16, 1864, when he was captured at Shipp's Gap, Georgia.[25]

A political action by the South Carolina legislature aroused the ire of both Stevens and Capers. The legislature thought the men should elect regimental officers, and the governing body enacted a military bill into law that revoked the commissions tendered by the governor to the 24th's three field grade officers. Thus, after a year of exemplary performance of duty, the regiment's three principal officers had to stand for election. The law did not affect Major Hammond because of his resignation.[26]

Stevens considered that the bill reflected upon his integrity and honor and immediately submitted his resignation, stating, "I cannot consistent with self respect continue to hold a position to which I have been improperly appointed."[27]

The next day, Capers, equally upset, also submitted his resignation.[28] He followed his letter of resignation with another letter asking General Gist's support for the application:

> You cannot wish me to be so humiliated as to be forced to retain "a position" which is personally unpleasant, & to which I am pronounced as being improperly & unjustly appointed.[29]

Capers also penned a letter to his uncle, South Carolina State Senator Richard Yeadon, expressing outrage over the legislature's decision. Two weeks later, on January 12, 1863, Yeadon responded to his nephew's letter and disclaimed knowledge that the new military bill affected either his nephew or Stevens. The legislature, in fact, was highly appreciative of the character of service that both officers rendered and considered Capers and Stevens "two of the best of our officers." Yeadon also disliked the system of electing officers in the military service and alleged that the system worked only evil. He appealed to the lieutenant colonel's patriotic zeal stating, "Your Country, your wronged, oppressed and tortured Country should be paramount to all other considerations."

The senator encouraged the two officers to file a grievance, but "do your duty...as a part of your duty to God." Yeadon ended his exhortation with an appeal that the two officers recall the resignations:

> As brave men and high souled patriots for my country's sake, for Charleston's sake, for the sake of the women and the children, the brave honorable women and their tender offspring, for God's sake I implore you."[30]

Finally, after several months of confusion, the War Department decided that state laws did not apply to Confederate army regiments. The army considered the law as a recommendation from the state, which it ignored. No evidence exists that Stevens and Capers would not have been reelected had they accepted the legislature's edict.

The men were heavily engaged in strengthening their defensive position that winter. They constructed a new redan on Grady's Hill, and on nearby Blake's Hill the troops erected a simple field work (a redan) supported by a curtain and flanks (trenches). The men cut a road through the swamp connecting the batteries on the two hills and cleared the swamp in front of the works on Blake's Hill that commanded the bridge spanning Island Creek. The two hills were about five miles from the regiment's pine top shanty bivouac. By New Year's Day, the new works were ready for use. Stevens assigned Captain Jones' Company E to build the redan on Blake's Hill, and when it was about half completed, Appleby's Company relieved them.[31] After completing the works, the regiment garrisoned an extremely strong position.

Occasionally Capers, as well as some soldiers, reflected melancholy feelings. Possibly, the moodiness occurred because of absence from home at Christmas, or because they did not attend church services frequently enough. Perhaps the messenger delayed the mail from the homefolk for no good reason. Capers seemed to direct his feelings toward his fellow officers as he wrote:

> I had met but a poor return for the personal, or even public
> attentions & kindnesses I have shown to others. I have been
> recently very much impressed with the conduct of a
> particular officer."[32]

Capers always considered Colonel Stevens his true and noble friend and openly admired his enormous talent. However, occasionally he held some unkind thoughts about his mentor:

> Even as noble, upright and honest a man as Col. Stevens,
> will always use the first person singular. He will allude to
> the toil & labor he has expended on the regiment and
> lesson of discipline he has inculcated & that he knows there
> are many who appreciate his efforts, etc. & never once
> alludes to me.

Finally, Capers calculated the number of days that the 24th was commanded by each of its leaders:

> Stevens: 79 days.
> Capers: 98 days.
> Hammond, Sigwald & Jones: 76 days.
> Add to Capers the months of
> Jan, Feb & Mar: 98 + 98 = 188 days.[33]

Capers hastily added that he did not make the comparison as an adverse reflection on his noble friend, but rather because the discussions concerning the proficiency of the regiment appeared unappreciative of his work. For instance, the 24th constructed some breastworks and redans necessary for defense, which Ellison supervised and completed rapidly and efficiently. However, Capers grumbled that when the new works would be spoken about, "It will be about what Stevens did!" Ellison realized that he would be "rewarded elsewhere."[34] The young officer had few "bad days," but certainly, this was one.

New Year's Day, 1863, dawned clear and cold, full of promise and welcome news. That day, the 24th completed the second redan at Island Creek. Stevens alerted the men that the regiment would return to Charleston on Friday, an announcement that provoked extensive excitement in camp. The men expected to arrive in Charleston on Saturday afternoon and began counting the minutes.[35] Still, the soldiers contemplated the news carefully so if the circumstances changed, they would not suffer disappointment.

Accidents occasionally occurred, many serious, while others were relatively minor. On Friday, January 2, 1863, Capers was the victim of a minor accident that easily could have been fatal. Under Capers' supervision, the soldiers neared the completion of the works located in the swamp at Island Creek. He stood on the trunk of an already fallen tree that leaned about six feet over the water of the creek. Capers was admiring a soldier's handiwork as he cut down another tree. Ellison thought he had plenty of time to move out of its path before the tree would finally fall. However, he did not notice that the axeman had already cut the other side. Another soldier diverted Capers' attention for a fleeting moment as the tree fell. Colonel Stevens had arrived and was still sitting on his horse roared, "LOOK OUT, CAPERS!"

Startled, Ellison saw the tree falling directly upon his head and could not move out of the way, so he stood still, and coolly sidestepped just before the tree struck. The tree brushed past and not a leaf or a twig struck him. However, the tree fell very hard on the tree trunk upon which Capers was standing, and the blow threw him about six feet across another tree trunk. The fall severely bruised his leg just above his knee, and for several days after the incident he could barely walk. Doctor Ogier advised, "Remain quiet for a few days, and it will be alright." His leg healed rapidly, and three days later most of the swelling and soreness had disappeared.[36]

The young colonel made friends with the McNutt family, local residents of quality. After the accident, the McNutts extended Ellison the hospitality of their home and provided him with a comfortable set of quarters. The ladies in the family were lovely, very kind and on Sunday offered their guest a ride in the family buggy to attend church. Capers informed Lottie about the McNutts' gracious invitation and that he attended services at the Episcopal Church in the company of the "delightful society of those charming ladies."[37] Lottie maintained her feelings privately about her husband's activities.

Colonel Stevens reported the completion of the works at Island Creek. Capers didn't see the report, but he was confident that the colonel would assure the full justice for the regiment.[38] Obviously, Ellison had recovered from his recent bout of moodiness.

Finally, on Saturday, January 3, 1863, the men removed tents and loaded the equipment aboard the wagons. Afterwards, the men broke camp at 9:00 a.m., and eagerly started the nine-mile march to the railroad depot.

About one half the distance to Wilmington, a courier arrived with a message from General Gist returning the 24th to camp. General Beauregard was in receipt of late intelligence which indicated he should temporarily halt the return of the troops. The Quartermaster brought word that 1700 enemy troops had transferred from Petersburg to Goldsboro. The men contemplated, "Perhaps, the beaten foe is again after the Weldon & Wilmington Railroad."[39]

The men retraced their tracks and reached the camp late that afternoon, unpacked the equipment and reestablished the camp. The troops, especially those who had families at Charleston, were eager to complete the mission at Wilmington, and were naturally disappointed. Finally, most of the troops from South Carolina and Georgia departed the area, although General Whiting retained Gist's Division.[40]

Members of the 24th were apprehensive concerning the next Federal attack, although a consensus existed that the next target would be the Wilmington and Weldon Railroad. Others thought that the Savannah and Charleston Railroad still offered an inviting target. General Beauregard patiently watched the situation develop, and when the Union forces threatened the Weldon and Wilmington Railroad, he reinforced General Whiting again. By mid-February, the Confederate leaders considered the Weldon and Wilmington railroad secure, and Beauregard called for the return of the troops and heavy guns.[41]

In the meantime, the men continued throwing up earthworks across Grady's field in advance of the batteries constructed two weeks earlier. The left of the works rested on a heavy swamp, and the right ended on an abatis of fallen timber. In general, the area where the 24th expected it would make a strong stand was an impractical swampy country.[42] The soldiers thought it would be too bad for an enemy who might attack the position. Although they didn't show up, the camp was rife with rumors that the Federals would attack there, inspiring the men to work even harder.

Word came from Charleston that Major Kingman, the regimental quartermaster, had died as a result of typhoid fever.[43] Buddy McGee grieved about Kingman's death:

> It was sad news to me, indeed, if I had any friends in camp
> I am certain he was one. He would do anything to accom-
> modate me. I never asked him for a favor but what I got
> it.[44]

On January 19, 1863, General Gist made an official call and stayed for dinner as the honored guest. He spoke about enemy movements and intentions, and discussed the reasons why the troops remained in North Carolina. The general related that a large column of enemy infantry had moved 20 miles from New Bern toward Wilmington. Gist thought the enemy was planning a movement against the Weldon & Wilmington

Railroad, while a stronger column marched on either Wilmington or Weldon.[45] The general speculated that the Federals would have to establish a new supply base if they moved toward Wilmington. The discussion did nothing to still the latest rumors prevalent in the regiment.

Some rumors even reached Charleston. The most serious false report claimed that a battle had been fought at Wilmington, and the Yankees had decimated the Marion Rifles. Shortly after the rumor surfaced, the wife of Private James B. Martin, a member of the Marions, fretted about her husband and anxiously sought information about his fate. Terribly upset, she hurriedly boarded the next train and arrived at Wilmington the following day. Mrs. Martin was happy and relieved when she found her husband safe. The situation embarrassed the young, shy, and loving couple. However, the colonel granted Private Martin a pass and allowed the young soldier and his wife to lodge at a neighbor's house that night.[46] In all probability, embarrassment or not, the Martins were quite happy with the outcome of the escapade.

Another week passed, and concern about the enemy's proximity kept the men diligently working improving the fortifications. Finally, a column of Federal cavalry moved in the direction of Wilmington. Some distance from the city, the Federals met a larger force of Confederate cavalry who dismounted, formed a line of battle, and opened fire. Without hesitation, the Yankee cavalry turned and proceeded in the other direction. A refugee from Morehead City brought news that the enemy only awaited fair weather to advance.[47]

The Confederates captured a Federal steamer, the *Columbia*, on the North Carolina Coast near Masonboro Sound. The steamer had wrecked ashore, and the Confederates at Fort Fisher captured twelve officers and 35 men.[48] This was good news, an inspiring morale builder, for the Confederate troops.

By January 23, 1863, the enemy's advance toward Wilmington by land and sea appeared frustrated. A storm sank the *Monitor* and the *Passaic*, and the *Mantauck* floundered off the North Carolina coast. The heavy seas also severely damaged and partially disabled several other ships in the Union fleet. The latest rumors indicated that those incidents canceled the enemy's designs along the North Carolina coast. The Yankee cavalry advanced again threatening Jacksonville and the country towns of Trenton and Onslow, reaching a point only 40 miles from Wilmington. However, the Federals exerted little effort and only briefly maintained their advanced position.[49] Thus, the immediate danger of a combined Federal land and sea attack on the area guarded by the 24th passed.

In North Carolina, the soldiers engaged in a variety of activities that whiled away the hours other than building fortifications. They hunted deer, repeated rumors, and passed the time usually very pleasantly. One soldier who enjoyed deer hunting confided to his wife that a deer had already run by his stand and was out of range before he noticed it. Stevens scheduled inspections on Sundays, which interfered with some of the soldiers' church attendance.[50] A normal day in camp involved the men in the usual mundane duties. In the mornings, the soldiers drilled, performed camp details, pulled picket, and did similar duties. At 2:30 p.m. they participated in battalion drills and dress parades. As full as the days were, the men still found time for fun and relaxation. The Marion Rifles developed a glee club and practiced singing songs which provided entertainment for the other soldiers. On special occasions, the singers blackened their faces and gave many fine renditions of favorite songs.[51]

The troops remained alert for suspicious characters loitering around camp. One day, a stranger casually meandered about the bivouac. Finally, one alert member of the 24th spotted the character, arrested the man and promptly delivered him to the provost marshal.

News from Charleston, particularly good news, was always the high point of the day. At dinnertime on Saturday, January 31, 1863, news arrived about the capture of an enemy gunboat on the Stono River. When the enemy gunboat sailed up the Stono, Colonel Yates' artillery opened fire from both sides of the river. The battle lasted for about one hour, and the boat "hauled down her flag and surrendered." A total of 180 crewmen were taken prisoner. The Confederates also captured 11 large guns, including several eleven-inch artillery pieces which were larger than any of the Confederate guns at Charleston. Afterwards, the captors proudly anchored the prize at Fort Pemberton.[52] The news of a Confederate success, especially those at Charleston, always added to the excitement level in the camp of the 24th.

That night "the grand news" arrived that the *Chicora* and *Palmetto State*, the recently constructed Confederate ironclad gunboats, had attacked the blockading squadron. The new gunboats sank two enemy ships and put the remainder to flight. Everyone at Charleston believed the blockade lifted, "if it will stay so." When the news reached North Carolina, the men shouted loudly, and the regimental band played its most spirited tunes.[53] News like that was exciting!

Due to illness and other temporary physical disability, several soldiers could not perform regular duties. To alleviate the situation, Colonel Stevens reassigned all "able bodied men" who were assigned duties to administrative positions and replaced the men on special details with "unabled men." Buddy McGee was one of those reassigned and rejoined his company at Wilmington. Although Buddy was disappointed to leave his assignment with the regimental quartermaster, he was happy that he would finally spend time with his brother, Vessie.[54]

The homefolk provided the soldiers with much of their uniforms and clothing. Buddy received warm clothes that fitted "very well" and thanked his mother profusely. For instance, everyone did not receive a coat when the quartermaster issued new uniforms, and only the warm clothes received from home alleviated suffering during cold weather.[55]

The health of the regiment was very good. The regimental surgeon, Dr. M. W. Abney, returned after a month's absence, and he immediately noticed that Capers appeared hale and hearty, saying, "Why Colonel, you are actually stout! I have never seen a man improve so."

Indeed, Capers confided to his wife that he did feel well and that he was getting fat, his coat was tight, his cheeks rotund, and he looked as if he had never been sick, "Thank God for it."[56] The easy camp life at Wilmington without the mosquitos and feverish swamps of James Island proved very healthful. Still, the surgeons counted a few cases of pneumonia, which caused the death of at least one member of the regiment in the Wilmington hospital.[57]

During the next 10 days, a Federal advance toward Wilmington appeared less and less likely, as another situation developed further south along the coast. Northern newspapers reported that the Federals had gathered a large fleet at Beaufort, South Carolina. The size of the armada increased daily and contained fifty-three transports, thirteen gunboats, and four steam frigates. Several were ironclad. On February 3, 1863, General Beauregard alerted the generals at Pocotaligo and Savannah that the Federals would attack either Savannah or Charleston. He also warned Brigadier General W. S. Walker at Pocotaligo "to be prepared."[58] Indeed, the enemy was preparing for an operation.

Daily, General Beauregard's concern escalated. He called for the return of the Georgia and South Carolina troops from North Carolina. The Georgia troops embarked for Savannah first. As soon as the Georgians cleared the transportation, Gist's Division followed.[59]

The 24th, buoyed by the news, broke camp again and started the long and tiring journey to Charleston. The men marched nine miles and boarded the train at Wilmington. Vessie McGee described the experience:

> We had a very fertiging march from our old camp to
> Willmington the road was very bad and muddy they was
> several of the boys gave out bee for they got thar I for one.
> thies long marches is not what they crack up to bee.[60]

Many parents and loved ones were deeply concerned about the comportment of the soldiers. Vessie's mother contacted her brother, Private D. L. Bozeman, and asked that he "take care of Vessie." Bozeman reassured his sister, "You need not be any ways unhappy about him. He is a good a soldier as we have. He is right at his post at every call."[61]

The troops departed North Carolina rapidly. Finally, on the evening of February 12, 1862, the Georgia troops cleared the transportation, and the South Carolinians eagerly boarded the train bound for Charleston. The regiment reached Charleston at midnight on February 13 and established a bivouac on the Citadel Green, now Francis Marion Square.[62] There the men basked in the limelight, surrounded by the doting citizens of the city.

En route from North Carolina, General Gist granted several men brief furloughs so they could visit their families. Capers received permission and left the train as it passed through St. Stephens. He rented a horse, hurried to Cherry Grove Plantation and the loving arms of Lottie and the children.[63] On Sunday at 3:00 a.m., his mind and body refreshed, Capers departed for Charleston and rejoined the regiment bivouacked at the Citadel Green.

Many of the soldiers were homesick and yearned for a furlough. After the sojourn in North Carolina, the troops were happy because they had returned to Charleston and especially enjoyed the pleasant interlude at the Citadel Green. Although the health of the men was "pretty good," a few became slightly ill because of "the change of water." Charleston water was never known for its tastiness. The soldiers whose homes were in other parts of the state were the most homesick. They were anxious for the "day to come" when they could get a furlough. After an extended absence, they "would know how to appreciate their own homes."[64] The men never ceased yearning for the goodness of some home-raised food to caress their palates and constantly urged the homefolk for "a box of provisions."[65]

While camped at the Citadel Green, the Marion Rifles presented a splendid horse to the new regimental major of infantry, Major Sigwald. In his usual straightforward and eloquent manner, Colonel Stevens made the presentation on behalf of the company. The gift, an indication of the esteem the men of his company held for him, delighted the new major who, pleasantly embarrassed, made a warm and feeling reply. Sigwald stated that he would cherish the moment among his happiest reminiscences and named the horse "Marion" as a tribute to his old company.[66]

The Confederates continued to monitor the Union fleet docked at Hilton Head. The fleet finally began moving in the direction of Pocotaligo and the Savannah and Charleston Railroad, which the Confederates considered critical and must be maintained at all costs. Beauregard sent three infantry regiments to defend the railroad at Pocotaligo, one of which was the 24th.[67] The brief, but pleasant, respite on the Citadel Green under the doting eyes of the citizens of Charleston was over.

The move was fast, furious, and, as usual, hectic. Notice arrived on the morning of February 18, 1863, and on the same day at 3:30 p.m., the regiment departed the Citadel Green in light marching order. That night at 8:00 the men crammed into the cars again and arrived early the next morning at 1:00 at the Pocotaligo Railroad Station. For the remainder of the night, the regiment bivouacked on the main stage road between Salkehatchie and Coosawhatchie, about one mile from the station. The next day, the regiment entered a nearby camp recently vacated by a South Carolina reserve regiment which the state had allowed to go home after their enlistment period expired.[68]

The Confederates could only "wait and see" to determine the objectives of the enemy's latest strategy. Possibly, the movements of the fleet were to promote uneasiness among the Confederates. As usual when Federal intentions were unknown to the men, the regiment was rife with rumors. Most reports alleged that over 20,000 enemy troops were preparing for an attack on the Savannah and Charleston Railroad. A prevalent rumor reported the existence of much dissatisfaction in the North because of the war effort. The men gave that news some credence because the Northern press published the report. Some Confederates asked God's divine help to influence the enemy's minds so the Federals would agree to an honorable peace and end the war.[69] Like soldiers in other Confederate regiments, the members of the 24th tired of war and army service rapidly, although the men persevered and loyally supported the Confederate cause.

Several issues were the subject of extensive campfire conversation and discussion in the regiment. For instance, General Beauregard promoted Colonel W. S. Walker to brigadier general for gallant and meritorious conduct at the Battle of Pocotaligo on October 21, 1862. A headline subject was whether the battle was won by General Walker or the troops under his command. The news about the victory at Sabine Pass, Texas, on September 8, 1862, particularly excited the troops. There, a small group of bold Confederate defenders resoundingly defeated a much larger Union force. The men also discussed the news concerning General Magruder's wonderful victories at Galveston, Texas.[70] At daybreak on New Year's day, 1863, the Confederates had stormed that occupied city, drove the Yankees away, and raised the siege.

For unknown reasons, the colonel ordered the men to prepare and keep on hand three days' cooked rations, indicating that the men would soon move again. The soldiers willingly suffered many hardships, although every soldier did not like the moves. One member of the 24th complained to his parents about moving so frequently:

It looks lack that our regiment hast to move more than any

of the rest. we are all worn out movein so much.[71]

Rumors constantly circulated that the Governor called the reserves for three additional months' duty. The McGee brothers thought that was good news because their father, a former officer in the 24th, was a member of the South Carolina reserves. Both men were hopeful that his reserve regiment would report to Pocotaligo.[72] If the governor again mobilized the reserve regiments, they did not report to Pocotaligo while the 24th was there.

The next day, February 26, 1863, was a beautiful warm spring day. The birds were singing and building nests, and the bees were busy gathering nectar. The lilac trees, looking lovely, were blooming early, and the yellow jasmines were in full bloom and looked even more beautiful. Indeed, the men enjoyed a pleasant spring day in the South Carolina Low-Country.[73]

Occasionally, letters were exchanged through the opposing lines under a flag of truce. In the spring of 1863, General Beauregard agreed to such an exchange of with the Federals. Stevens and Capers drew the detail and arranged a meeting so they could make the exchange. The two officers were met by the Federal sentinels and escorted via a leaky rowboat to Port Royal, the Federal headquarters. When the two Confederate officers stepped ashore, Colonel Gilman E. Sleeper, commander of the 4th New Hampshire Volunteers, accompanied by his adjutant, greeted the visitors. Sleeper removed his gauntlet and offered his hand. However, Stevens and Capers considered Sleeper an enemy, a man in the state only for the destruction of many South Carolina institutions, families, homes, and businesses. With those thoughts in mind, the Confederate officer did not take the proffered hand. Capers reported the brief meeting and conversation:

> Sleeper said, "Ah, you won't take the hand, eh?" Capers'
> reply was a polite but firm, "No. Sir." Sleeper replied,
> "Very well then."

The two adversaries delivered their communications and exchanged receipts.

> Sleeper asked, "Do you have any news?" Capers again
> replied politely but firmly, "No sir, nothing of special
> interest."

The errand completed, the two Confederate officers started for their own lines. They did not impart any information, but neither did the Federals.[74]

The Yankee sentinels, all privates, paddled the boat, and after the meeting the same detail returned the Confederate party to the mainland. The privates were very respectful and quite communicative. Capers related, "The men cursed the war and their officers, and said they were heartily sick of it."[75] This is possibly the only time on record that the religiously oriented Capers condoned profanity.

The letters the soldiers received from home usually were very upbeat, yet contained extensive yearning for the presence of absent loved ones. To fathers, the letters brought news of children and intimate details of home life. Even this early in the war, most of the soldiers' families were already smoothing over the hardships they were enduring. Many family members were already depending upon charitable programs for sustenance.

At least a dozen families drove their wagons and camped near the 24th's bivouac.[76] No accommodations were available, and most of the families camped in the wagons. Although uncomfortable, some of the wives moved into tents with their husbands which, at times, raised Lieutenant Colonel Capers' ire:

> In one instance, two sisters, one of them married, spent a
> night in a tent with the husband & three brothers! Of

69

course, they are the very poorest class of people.[77]
Such conduct was shocking indeed.

A favorite pastime was a discussion of the Confederate leadership, and Capers candidly offered his evaluation, usually in confidence, to Lottie. At Pocotaligo, he decided that he liked the new General W. S. Walker very much:

> He is a perfect gentleman in his bearing & it is said that he is a Christian. He does not spend his time at Hd. Quarters, drinking, smoking, and profaning the name of his God, but rides about the country, visits his troops & when the time of trial arrives is with them, to share their dangers and to inspire their actions.[78]

Capers had first observed General Walker after the October 1862 battle of Pocotaligo, and even then he looked like "a military leader in the true sense of that term." Walker was present at the drill of the 24th that same afternoon.[79]

General Walker was the only general who escaped a strong critique by Colonel Capers. He even found traits in Walker that exceeded those of his longtime favorite, General Gist. Capers alleged that Walker had "more brains than Gist" though he doubted that Walker had more "heart" than did General Gist.[80]

Other generals did not fare as well, and some received a stern rebuke:

> Gen. Ripley is simply a less fellow with great energy, fine attainments as an artillery officer & totally wasting in a high sense of honor and was without personal sentiment.
> Gen. Beauregard, though a genius, is too ambitious and too vain to be a fine general. He swerved from the path of duty for political men, as when Rhett induced him to disapprove the findings of the court in the case of his son Alfred.[81]

Most soldiers in the Confederate army considered General Lee the outstanding general, and the members of the 24th agreed with the popular consensus. Capers mentioned the generals whom he favored most, "Johnston and Bragg are my men. Lee is the noblest & best of all." However, Capers confided that he would rather be with his wife, "than to be Lee, Bragg or Johnston." The generals were "no contest" when compared to Lottie, who was his "real general."[82]

Food was somewhat scarce. The typical bill of fare at meals was cornbread and, when it was available, "old tough beef." Some days the men had only "a little piece of bread." The men impressed the shortage of food on their parents and in almost every letter asked for "a box of anything to eat."[83]

Sassafras tea, made from the roots of bushes that grew wild in South Carolina, rapidly became the most acceptable substitute for coffee. The soldiers dug, cleaned, and boiled the roots in fresh water, producing a tasty and wholesome drink or tea that offered limited enjoyment, but it never replaced coffee. Most thought that sassafras tea was more healthful than many of the other coffee substitutes.[84]

The men of the 24th did not especially like Pocotaligo. The dampness of the climate and the heavy night air made the area a health risk to the families camped near the bivouac area. The coughing of the children especially concerned the soldiers, who were glad they resisted bringing their own families to the camp.[85] Private Padgett, Co. I, voiced his opinion about the countryside:

> We fared very well while we were in North Carolina, but
> have reached a place now that I don't like at all. The water
> is very bad, the country is a pond surrounded by mud
> holes.[86]

Padgett's sentiments were, no doubt, echoed by the remaining members of the 24th, except possibly those who hailed from the area.

Two important events transpired on Saturday, the last day of February, 1862. First, the general called for a formal review that consumed the entire morning. The men marched two miles through slimy, oozing mud to reach the parade grounds, which was a virtual quagmire. General Walker expressed his satisfaction with the results of the review, and the occasion passed very well except for the men's extreme dislike of the slimy, stinking mud. That afternoon the colonel mustered the regiment for pay, a pleasant detail, especially since the men had not been paid for several months.[87]

The men were building earth works and rifle pits about four miles from the camp on William Middleton's place. The farms were beautiful and denoted an opulent lifestyle for the occupants. The houses were large, fine ones, with tastefully laid out, well-tended yards and gardens. Yellow jasmine and cloth of gold roses ran up the columns of the piazzas in perfect spirals. In times of peace, the farmers planted rice and earned splendid incomes. As a result of the war, most of the local families sought refuge further inland or in the northern part of the state, and many "fine homes" stood empty.[88] The area, even with its shortcomings to the soldiers, possessed many attractive features. Perhaps the 24th situated its camp in one of the least desirable spots.

Much to the men's dislike, the soldiers constantly constructed batteries, even on Sunday. Some officers thought it unnecessary to work on the Lord's Day, but still they worked. As soon as the soldiers finished one battery, they started another, a bridge, or a causeway and, at times, repaired roads. One day, as the soldiers marched to the work site, troops from another regiment inquired the name of the regiment. The reply, uttered by an unknown soldier, surely reflected the frustration of the entire regiment: "No regiment in particular, we are traveling over the country building batteries."

Since the battle of Secessionville, the men counted over "100 batteries" they had constructed, including those in North Carolina. The troops fervently hoped that the breastworks would prove useful and provide someone protection. Moreover, the soldiers did most of the work on half rations. At Pocotaligo, additional food stuffs were not available on the local market, so the men, in the words of one of the soldiers, "We take what we get and glad to get that."[89]

General Walker assigned three companies of the regiment as support for the batteries on the Combahee and Ashepoo Rivers and the works between the two rivers. Capers commanded the detachment, consisting of Companies F, H, and I. The men were happy they were leaving Pocotaligo and the "pond surrounded by mud holes." The men departed on March 6, 1863, at 9:00 a.m., and reached the new bivouac that afternoon at 3:30. They located the new camp about two-and-one-half miles from the Combahee River Ferry among some pine trees beside the road between the Combahee and the Ashepoo River Ferry.[90] The new bivouac was at an old settlement called Ballouville, about 14 miles from Pocataligo. The members thought it an excellent bivouac that could accommodate the entire regiment, and felt that the troops would fare much better. However, the other companies remained at Pocotaligo. Still, Vessie McGee did not like long marches for any reason, even for a more desirable camp site and wrote, "We had a very tiresome march of it bee for we got to this place."

The men appeared much more satisfied at Ballouville than they had been at Pocotaligo. At the new camp, the "small rashens" immediately improved because of an abundance of wild game to supply the mess:

> We had a old posam for diner. Some other mess had some
> squirrels for dinner. This is the gratis cuntry foe gaim that
> we have ever struck.

As usual, even with the improvement in "the rashens," soldiers pressed parents for "a box of provisions." In the finest spirit of military service and devotion to duty, Vessie began signing his letters, "Your loveing son until death."[91]

From Ballouville, the men of the detachment marched two-and-one-half miles to the Combahee River and constructed the new works. The soldiers thought some of the nearby plantation owners could provide slaves to assist in the task. However, the farmers were concerned with raising crops to supply the army and could not. Although the soldiers considered the wealthy planters selfish, they grudgingly constructed the fortifications by themselves.[92]

Other incidents annoyed the men who were sacrificing so much for the defense of the country. At a bend in the Ashepoo River below one of the firing batteries, a thickly wooded point of land protruded into the river and obstructed the artillery "field of fire." The battery commander cut down the trees to clear the area. Barnwell Rhett, radical Editor of the *Charleston Mercury,* Lieutenant Colonel Capers' old nemesis, owned the land, and petitioned Beauregard, who stopped the cutting of the trees. Ellison thought little of the action and muttered, "And this is the high Priest of Independence of the North."[93] Capers never learned that money is the motivator guiding the behavior of many people, although he recognized his own need for money.

Capers considered his new assignment highly responsible. He commanded all troops stationed between the Combahee and Ashepoo Rivers, which constituted the left flank of General Walker's entire army. The tireless colonel developed a comprehensive plan for the new causeway across the Ashepoo, which the general quickly approved.[94]

The troops thought the area safe from attack, but Beauregard announced that the Federals would next attack along the coast, probably toward the Savannah and Charleston Railroad. The soldiers, aware of the strongly fortified positions in the area, apparently thought differently and allowed that after Beauregard spoke, "It was no need for privates to open their mouths."[95]

A consensus existed among the men that the area was safe from Union attack because the Confederates had already repulsed the Federals twice at the same place.[96] Still, no one knew what the next Federal move might be. Therefore, everyone diligently constructed or strengthened fortifications.

Reports about the activity of the war constantly reached the camp. The Yankees bombarded Fort McAlister, near Savannah, and afterwards the Confederates repulsed a determined Union attack. Another report alleged that the two principal Yankee generals at Hilton Head, Hunter and J. G. Foster, quarreled, and Major General H. W. Halleck settled the dispute by reassigning General Foster. Another report claimed that the Northern Congress had gone out of power, leaving President Abraham Lincoln with unusual authority. He could suspend habeas corpus at will, making him in the opinion of the Southern soldiers, a military dictator.[98] Major General D. H. Hill advanced and offered the enemy battle at New Bern, North Carolina. Latest intelligence reports indicated that the enemy in front of Pocotaligo was moving in the direction of Edisto Island. However, the enemy landed two regiments on Seabrook Island, and the Federals seemed to threaten another foray at Charleston. Such war news was thoroughly discussed at the 24th's campfires.

Essential items such as food, paper and clothing became extremely scarce. The McGee brothers always honored their parents and regardless of the scarcity of paper, they managed to faithfully correspond. They thriftily saved paper and postage by corresponding in the same letter and often shared the paper with their uncles. Vessie wrote that the bivouac at Ballouville was a much better place and the food had improved since the troops arrived there. The colonel purchased fresh shad fish every day from a nearby fishery. Overall, Vessie reported that they were "living as well as we could expect." Even with the improvement in rations, nothing replaced food from the homefolk, and the soldiers constantly asked for "a box" and items of clothing.

Buddy often fulfilled special assignments, or, as Vessie described it, "detached sarvace," representing Colonel Stevens in Charleston on "special business." Vessie sent his parents $30.00 of his pay "because he knew that they needed it worse than he did," and worried until he received a letter verifying the money's arrival.

The men struggled to build the causeways and firing batteries, and the results of the toil slowly began taking shape. Vessie didn't like the constant work assignments and wrote, "We have mor batterys to build than iney other Regt in servace." The boys constantly urged relatives and homefolk to visit the camp. Vessie thought the camp at Ballouville would impress his father.[99]

The health of the detachment at Ballouville was quite good. A few soldiers complained of sore throats, colds or an occasional fever usually developed from sleeping on the ground when pulling picket duty. The colonel excused the ill men from duty for several days.[100]

President Jefferson Davis set aside March 27, 1863, as a day of fasting, humiliation, and prayer. The 24th canceled all drills and work.[101] All the men were not as religious as the lieutenant colonel. However, they enjoyed having the day off from building batteries. Those who could find food did not observe the fast.

Early in April, the Federals slowly concentrated their forces on the Stono and North Edisto Rivers, ostensibly preparing for another attack on Charleston. This time the enemy apparently planned for a land attack on Morris Island, via Folly Island. The enemy strategy called for a simultaneous naval attack upon Fort Sumter, Fort Moultrie, and the batteries defending the outer harbor.[102] As a result, General Beauregard sent a tersely worded message summoning the 24th Regiment:

> Send forward (to Charleston) Stevens' Regiment and
> Preston's Battery at once...[with] three days' provisions
> and light marching order.[103]

The regiment responded rapidly. On April 5, Colonel Stevens and seven companies boarded the railroad cars and departed Pocotaligo the next morning.[104] Capers' detachment departed the bivouac at Ballouville on April 4 at 2:45 a.m. and waited at Green Pond for transportation until 4:00 p. m. the next day. Both contingents of the regiment arrived at James Island too late to reach Secessionville that night and bivouacked along the road.

Finally, after an absence of almost four months, the regiment reached the old bivouac on April 6, 1863. Stevens became commander of East James Island and Capers commanded the military post at Secessionville.[105] The

74

soldiers were glad they were on James Island again, except, of course, the men whose families were visiting at Pocotaligo.

The men anxiously contemplated an attack on Charleston. Buddy McGee excitedly told his parents that one day he was in the top of the tall house at Secessionville and witnessed a Federal attack on Fort Sumter. "It was the proudest thing I ever saw," he wrote, and then reported that the Confederates damaged several ships and sank the Federal ironclad *Keokuk* off Morris Island. As usual, Buddy needed clothing - two cotton shirts, one pair of drawers, two pairs of socks and a hat.[106]

The Confederates closely monitored enemy activity at Charleston. Four Federal regiments landed at Coles Island, and a minimum of 3,300 troops landed on Seabrook Island. General Hagood spotted an enemy assembly of 44 vessels in the North Edisto River.[107] Colonel G. W. C. Lee visited Charleston and inspected the situation. On April 11, Lee counted eight or ten thousand Yankees on the islands near the mouth of the Stono and 5,000 more on Seabrook Island. Colonel Lee urged President Davis to reinforce Charleston with an infantry brigade from Wilmington.[108] However, the enemy did not immediately develop or reveal their strategy.

The men of the 24th enjoyed visiting other fortifications in the area. On April 12, Capers and Acting Adjutant Holmes visited several of the Confederate defenses near Secessionville. First, they visited Morris Island, climbed the "magnificent sand hills," and spotted six turrets and the *Iron Sides* cross the bar. Colonel Robert F. Graham loaned the visitors a splendid marine glass recovered from the *Keokuk*.[109] The glass contained the marking, "U.S.N. No. 72." With the aid of the glass, Capers could plainly see the crew on the deck of the *Iron Sides*, which was accompanied by the sloop of war, *Powhatan*, with many of the other blockaders alongside. The Union Navy obviously was planning for an attack on Charleston.[110] The sailors surely were not discussing the sunken *Keokuk* and her stranded scow, which were in plain view. The two men enjoyed a "grand sight witnessing the fleet of the boastful enemy appear baffled." On the same day, they visited the *Devil*, a Confederate antitorpedo raft and afterwards visited Battery Wagner. The strength of the Confederate fortifications on the islands fascinated the two soldiers.[111]

Occasionally, the two sides exchanged fire. Colonel Stevens reported the results of one such artillery engagement on April 17, 1863:

> After exchanging four shots found that the balls in the ammunition chests were too large for the Parrot guns, and one ball being jammed, I withdrew the guns. The enemy kept up a warm fire for some time but hurt nobody.

Stevens noticed that some of the Federals were leaving Folly Island.[112]

The regiment frequently participated in parades or reviews. On Monday, April 20, 1863, General Beauregard reviewed two brigades, commanded by

The remnants of the colors of the 24th Regiment. The stars
were removed by the men after the surrender in North Carolina.
(*Courtesy Mr. John Bigham, Confederate Relic Room and Museum,
Columbia, S.C.*)

Gist, on James Island. General T. L. Clingman commanded one of the brigades, and Colonel Stevens the other. Capers commanded the 24th. Afterwards, Beauregard presented each of the regiments with a battle flag. The flag was the Starry Cross or the St. Andrew's Cross, also known as "The Beauregard Flag." The 24th Regiment would carry those colors until the end of the war.[113]

The actions of the state legislature still haunted the 24th. The same action that nearly spawned the resignation of the regiment's two senior officers also created turmoil in one of the companies and resulted in the court martial of several soldiers. Under the belief that soldiers were authorized by the state legislature to elect field officers, First Sergeant Melvin L. Kinard thought the men should also elect the new captain who would command Company G. Kinard prepared a petition that specifically asked that the officers decline to rise in grade by appointment and "stand for election." The first sergeant passed the petition among the men for signature.[114]

Private G. C. Jones, when confronted with the petition, passed it to Lieutenant Hamiter, the acting company commander. Hamiter informed Colonel Stevens about the petition. As a military matter, Stevens decided the decision rested with him to "take care of the matter." On the morning of March 8, Lieutenant Hamiter formed the company in front of the colonel's tent, and Stevens called the officers from the other companies as witnesses. The colonel carefully explained that the men were guilty of a "great military impropriety." He explained that he understood the soldiers were acting in ignorance of the consequences. Such an action was improper and "necessarily subversive to all discipline." He informed the signers that discipline could not exist if subordinates could call upon superior officers to resign because "something went awry according to their own ideas." Stevens reassured the men that he did not "blame them as much as he might otherwise have done because of the earlier action by the state legislature as regarded the election of field officers." However, the colonel advised, "The state legislature has no jurisdiction over a Confederate army unit. They simply expressed what amounted to an opinion calculated to do much evil."

Based on the exhaustive explanation, Colonel Stevens gave the men an opportunity to withdraw, and those that did would "no longer share the responsibility of signing the petition." Stevens announced he would consider the latter group "as avowing their determination to abide by the consequences." After a few moments of reflection, most of the men departed the ranks until only a few remained.

Stevens allowed ample time for reflection and decision, and when the time expired, he arrested the remaining men pending trial by court martial. Finally, Sergeants Kinard, J. F. Speck and Charles E. Flynn as well as Privates W. G. Jones and W. D. Morris were charged with "conduct to the

General States Rights Gist
(*From author's collection*)

prejudice of good order and military discipline." In addition, the court martial charges listed four vague military style specifications describing each man's involvement. First Sergeant Kinard was the ring leader of the scheme, perhaps motivated by a desire to become the company commander.

The men did not think they had violated regulations and pleaded "Not Guilty." However, as with any fair-minded and impartial military court, the men were found guilty. The court martial sentence reduced the noncommissioned officers "to the ranks" and confined each man for 14 days in the guard tent. The court did not sentence the privates because of the inordinate amount of time confined pending the court martial. In spite of the court-martial and his reduction in grade, Kinard became an officer by the end of the war.[115] After this incident, the men did not sign additional petitions calling for the resignation or election of officers.

In the meantime, the war was going badly in the west for the Confederates. New Orleans had fallen to the United States Navy, and Union Major General Benjamin Butler had taken over the city. Southern guns bristling on the high bluffs at Vicksburg controlled river traffic. A powerful Union campaign under Major General Ulysses S. Grant was being forced against the Confederacy's stronghold at Vicksburg. If Vicksburg fell, the Confederate States would be severed at the Mississippi River, and the Union would have full access to the waterway.

The Confederate manpower situation was critical. On May 2, 1863, President Davis urgently telegraphed General Beauregard that if the Confederacy were to survive, every available unit must be furnished to other battlefields from the department of South Carolina. Confronted by a strong Federal force, Beauregard hesitantly agreed to provide Lieutenant General Pemberton, now commanding the Confederate army at Vicksburg, with two brigades of "good troops." If attacked, Beauregard was reassured that he would receive reinforcements from other locations.[116]

Beauregard notified Pemberton on May 5, 1863, that he was sending two brigades of troops, one from the Georgia coastal area and one from Charleston:

> I send Gist and [General William Henry Talbot] Walker's Brigades...and two batteries. Keep them together, if practicable, under Gist.[117]

General Beauregard permanently formed Brigadier General States Rights Gist's Brigade, of which the 24th became a member and would remain so for the duration of the War. The brigade consisted of three regiments, one battalion and one artillery battery, which were stationed at Charleston:

Forty Sixth Regiment, Georgia Volunteers, Infantry,
Twenty Fourth Regiment, South Carolina Volunteers, Infantry,
Eighth Battalion, Georgia Volunteers, Infantry,

Sixteenth Regiment, South Carolina Volunteers, Infantry, and Ferguson's Light Battery.

After considerable prodding by President Davis, General Beauregard also sent the brigade of Brigadier General Nathan Evans to Mississippi. Reinforcements now totaled three brigades, supported by two light artillery batteries.[118]

Following more than a year of riding the rails north and south, the 24th was once again on the move. This time it would travel west to Mississippi, boarding railroad cars at Charleston, bound for Augusta. The trip would take the regiment to its destination at Jackson, Mississippi.

CHAPTER 4

THE 24TH BEHAVED FINELY

Johnston's Army of Mississippi

"In Mississippi," Lieutenant Colonel Capers surmised in his diary, "the gallant men of the 24th will be no further from God than at Secessionville." Although apprehensive, the soldiers eagerly and cheerfully accepted the call and found solace in the thought, "The path of duty is the path of safety."[1]

Gist's Brigade departed Charleston on May 6, 1863, and the 24th Regiment arrived at Jackson, Mississippi, on May 13, a journey of eight days and seven nights. The troops changed from train to train to boat and back again six times.[2]

As the rickety railroad train wormed its way past George's Station, and Branchville, South Carolina, headed for Augusta, Georgia, the railroad passed the home areas of four of the regiment's companies. Many men, desperate enough to risk a dreaded court martial, seized the opportunity to leave the train and visit loved ones whom they had not seen in over a year. Between George's Station and Branchville alone, 43 men from one company and 34 from another slipped off the train, and by the time the regiment reached Augusta, over 100 men were missing. Capers left an officer at Augusta to round up the stragglers and head the miscreants to Mississippi, post haste.[3]

Colonel Stevens delayed his departure an extra day so he could assist the quartermaster with the stores and arrived in Mississippi one day after the regiment.[4] Much to his chagrin, he missed the battle of May 14.

By the next afternoon, May 7, 1863, the train was 57 miles beyond Augusta slowly and steadily squirming, chugging, and puffing its way forward. The men found the cars extremely cramped and uncomfortable, but the food was good. For supper, the soldiers ate bread, ham and hard-boiled eggs.[5]

The train finally arrived at Atlanta before daylight the next morning. The 8th Georgia Battalion led the way and the 24th followed with the 46th Georgia third, and then the 16th Regiment.[6] General Gist traveled with the last regiment. At Atlanta, the troops ate a hearty breakfast of boiled ham, eggs, rice, fried bacon and fresh baker's bread still warm from the oven.[7] Capers' brother resided near Atlanta and Ellison expected a visit as the regiment passed through the city. However, as a result of the confusion and the brief hesitation by the trains, the brothers missed each other. Steam was raised, and the train departed Atlanta at 7:30 a. m.

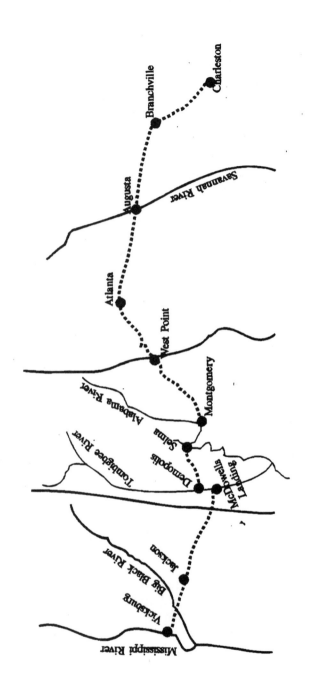

Railroad Route from Charleston, S.C. to Jackson, Miss., May 6-13, 1863.
Drawn by the author from a sketch located at The Citadel Archives, Charleston, S.C.

That afternoon at four o'clock, the rickety train arrived, on schedule, at West Point, Georgia, a small town located on the Georgia and Alabama border. There, a lack of transportation delayed departure until the next day.[8]

The long and tiring journey offered its light moments. Word spread rapidly that Gist's Brigade was aboard the train bound for Mississippi. Crowds of people, mostly old and young ladies, old men and children, both white and black, gathered along the way at every house, station, village or town, to greet and wave the soldiers onward. As the smoking and creaky old train groaned and grunted its way, the crowds cheered and waved, and often displayed Confederate flags. At one train station, twenty women waved handkerchiefs, and at another, a group of women waved an extremely large Confederate flag. Other greeters passed out roses. One pretty lady sent Capers a very large and especially beautiful rose that he remembered to tell Lottie about. While passing a train station, a soldier especially noticed a handsome little boy who held a small Confederate flag and waved it with all his might. Those enthusiastic groups of well wishers helped relieve the rigors of the tedious travel.[9]

The men genuinely appreciated the greetings and responded vigorously. Clarence Palmer, Alfred Holmes, and other members of the regimental staff, full of life and fun loving, constantly shouted "halloo and goodbye" from the train platform to the greeters. An embarrassed Capers noted, "The noble women seemed so sincere...and Palmer and Holmes and the others yelled halloo and goodbye so frequently that those on the train thought that it almost seemed like a farce." Several became hoarse. The Marion Rifles Glee Club responded to the greetings by singing highly spirited songs at every stop.[10]

The regiment arrived at Montgomery, Alabama, at 10:30 p.m. on May 10 and labored all night transferring the baggage from the train onto a boat. Finally, the boat departed Montgomery the next morning at 3:00 a.m. and arrived at Selma the same morning at 10:30. The travelers waited all day for transportation and departed Selma as the sun was setting. They arrived at Demopolis that evening at 10:30.

At Demopolis, the men met a particularly challenging obstacle. There, they boarded a flat-bottom boat that local citizens called "a *Merengo*." One could hardly classify the boat as a passenger boat. However, it was safe enough and finally, after struggling all night, the regiment arrived at McDowell's Landing, five miles away. There, the men left the *Merengo* and boarded another old and rickety train for the final leg of the journey. The train slowly crossed the Alabama and Mississippi line and finally reached Jackson on the afternoon of May 13. Thankfully, the 24th completed the journey without recording a serious accident or mishap.[11]

En route, the 24th passed the 8th Georgia Battalion and was the first unit of its brigade to reach Jackson. The Georgians arrived late the following morning, May 14.

Many of the difficulties experienced during the journey seemed unnecessary. At Selma, the railroad superintendent provided the soldiers a railroad car normally used to transport horses, and horse manure covered the floor. A horrible stench permeated every square inch, and the men revolted and would not board the car. Capers' men swept the car out, and afterwards, with the manure gone and the smell somewhat improved, the men boarded the car. At the same place, the railroad superintendent was particularly uncooperative, and that night assigned 50 members of the 24th for passage on an open flat car. Capers decided that the men were sleepy, and if they fell asleep, they could fall from the car and suffer an injury or even death. Therefore, he informed the railroad official in polite but firm language that he would not allow his men aboard an open car at night. Instead, he would pitch tents and remain at Selma overnight and await safer transportation.[12] The superintendent immediately provided an enclosed car and the regiment proceeded.

The travelers encountered other delays. The lack of coordination among quartermasters delayed progress and created confusion. The quartermaster at Montgomery didn't notify the next station that the brigade was en route, which created another delay at Selma. At Demopolis, the change from the railroad cars to the *Merengo* slowed the movement. The same delay occurred at McDowell's Landing when the situation reversed. To prevent the delay, one suggested building a trestle and laying railroad tracks to connect the railroads.[13]

During the journey, the train rolled through much of the South's prime farmland. The soldiers gratefully noticed that the western farmers planted large crops of grain, such as corn, wheat and oats, which would provide sustenance for the population as well as the army. Of course, many of the legendary cotton fields were still evident.[14]

The Confederate situation at Jackson and Vicksburg was extremely critical. Pemberton had withdrawn into Vicksburg and President Davis sent in General Joseph Eggleston Johnston, the theater/department commander, to raise an army in relief. At that very moment, General U. S. Grant's army of three corps with an estimated strength of 45,000 effectives was preparing for an assault on Jackson.[15] As soon as Gist's Brigade arrived at Jackson, Secretary Seddon reassigned the brigade to Johnston's army.

General Johnston recognized his outnumbered situation, and realized that he must evacuate Jackson. The only reason for making a stand there was to delay the Federal advance long enough to remove the quartermaster stores and public property.[16]

The first night at Jackson, the regiment bivouacked near the train depot and prepared for action at dawn the next morning.[17] Ready for battle, the men slept on their arms that night, anxiously awaiting the arrival of daylight.

General Joseph E. Johnston
*(Courtesy South Caroliniana Library, University of South Carolina,
Columbia, S.C.)*

By the next morning, only a small portion of Gist's Brigade had reached Jackson. Units there included the 24th, five companies of the 46th Georgia, and Captain J. A. Hoskins' Battery of four artillery pieces. General Johnston bolstered the brigade's strength with the assignment of the 14th Mississippi Battalion. The brigade mustered barely 900 troops and was commanded by Colonel P. H. Colquitt, the senior officer present.

A heavy rainfall during the night, coupled with the anxiety about the impending battle, made the night's rest extraordinarily tenuous. However, the regiment came alive before day broke, the men eagerly anticipating the chore that lay ahead. At daylight, the little brigade quietly departed the train depot, and marched toward a defensive position on Clinton Road, ready for whatever the day might bring. The sky was overcast, and rain constantly drizzled and showered upon the men as they trudged toward the assigned position. The inclement weather turned the streets and roads into virtual quagmires that grappled with the soldier's feet as if making every effort to hinder their forward progress.

Confederate Brigadier General John Gregg, in charge of the delaying action at Jackson, was familiar with the area and selected the brigade's position.[18] He ignored the poorly positioned breastworks near the city, and selected a stronger defensive position farther out. Finally, the brigade reached a ridge nearly three miles from Jackson, directly astraddle Clinton Road at the O. P. Wright Farm.[19] Colquitt stationed the 24th on the left side of Clinton Road around the Wright Farm House. The 24th's advanced skirmishers scurried forward a short distance to a garden fence that made a reasonably good breastwork. One gun from Hoskin's Battery prepared for battle supporting the regiment. Colquitt placed the five companies of the 46th Georgia Regiment, the Mississippi Battalion, and the remainder of Hoskin's Battery on the right side of Clinton Road. Colquitt gave Capers full authority over the conduct of the battle on the left side of the road.[20] A Confederate picket line was already on duty in front of the ridge.

Gregg expected the Yankees to advance via Clinton Road. Thus, he placed General William Henry Talbert Walker's Brigade across the Raymond and Mississippi Springs Road two miles from town so he could assist Colquitt, when required. Walker's Brigade mustered the 30th Georgia Regiment, 1st Georgia Sharpshooter Battalion, 3d Kentucky Mounted Infantry, and Martin's Georgia Artillery Battery. Walker's Brigade followed Colquitt's force through Jackson over the "streets of mud." Gregg also alerted his own brigade to stand ready to assist Gist's Brigade. Several units of Mississippi state troops manned the breastworks nearer the city.[21]

The Federals were also up early this day. At 5:00 a.m. Grant put Generals William T. Sherman and James B. McPherson's Corps in motion toward Jackson. Sherman's Corps advanced on the Raymond and Mississippi Springs Road toward General Walker. Simultaneously, McPherson Corps, consisting of six brigades in two divisions, advanced toward the position held by Gist's Brigade.[22] General M. M. Crocker's Seventh Division led the advance of the corps with Colonel T. H. Holmes' Second Brigade across Clinton Road. The other infantry brigades followed, trailed by Dillon's Sixth Wisconsin Battery.[23]

The Federals began to drive in the Confederates pickets at 9:00 a.m. and soon came in contact with the main skirmish line at the Wright Farm House. General McPherson declared that he found "the enemy in strong forces":

> Some of the troops consisted of South Carolina and Georgia regiments, which only arrived the evening before, and had been immediately marched out and placed in position.[24]

Maj. F. Diemling, commander of the Union 10th Missouri Regiment, advanced two miles on Clinton Road and discovered the Confederate location about 9:00 a.m. Diemling reported the defenders supported by four pieces of artillery strongly positioned on "a commanding ridge on the farm of O. P. Wright." The Union 17th Iowa Regiment formed on the Federal left, that regiment's right resting on the Clinton Road and aligned the 80th Ohio on the right of the road. The 10th Missouri Regiment aligned on the right of the 80th Ohio.[25]

As the Federal troops came forward, the 80th Ohio Regiment moved slightly to the left and straddled Clinton Road, largely on the side defended by Colquitt. The 10th Missouri Regiment, as it advanced on the right of the 80th Ohio, moved directly toward the position held by the 24th.

Colquitt's Brigade had been anxiously waiting for about two hours before the enemy appeared. Many of the men thought about the sight and sounds of the battlefield at Secessionville and were conscious of the terror that lay ahead. As the Federals approached, Hoskins' Battery opened fire with one gun and then another. The guns were located so that when fired, the artillery shells passed over the Confederate skirmish line. Soon the enemy artillery responded, and the men of the 24th found themselves under fire from both directions.

One of the first casualties suffered by the 24th was "the sad killing of Orderly Sgt. F. P. Feehan of Co. A." A cannon ball from Hoskins' Battery struck him in the back of his neck and head and he died instantly, a result of friendly fire. Only recently, Steinmeyer had promoted Feehan to First Sergeant. He was an excellent non commissioned officer, a veteran, and highly respected member of the Marion Rifles.[26] After the ball struck Feehan, the men cleared a field of fire for the artillery.

The drizzling rain of that morning increased until it rained heavily and became a severe rainstorm that fell in such torrents that the ammunition was in danger of spoiling. As a result, McPherson delayed his advance for one-and-a-half hours until his men could open their cartridge boxes without risk of wetting the powder.[27] Even during the rainstorm, the Confederate artillery kept up a steady barrage, firing shell and solid shot.[28]

While delayed, the Federals placed three artillery pieces of the 1st Missouri Artillery in position about Mr. Mann's house and waited for the rainstorm to subside. At 11:00 a.m., the rain abated and the battle started with intensity as the Union soldiers reached for the Confederate skirmishers.[29]

As the Federal infantry advanced, the artillery heavily bombarded the Confederate position. The blue regiments advanced about 400 yards across two ridges and hesitated for fifteen minutes, reforming under the crest of a third ridge. Colonel Holmes, the Federal brigade commander, commenced a charge with bayonets fixed and the Northern troops eagerly advanced at the double-quick, cheering wildly. The Federals handily drove in the Confederate skirmishers. They maintained their momentum for another 500 yards and reached the Wright Farm House grounds. The regiment's skirmishers hid themselves and found such protection as was available among the hedges and behind the fences and trees around the house. From that vantage point, such as it was, the 24th, aided by Ferguson's Battery, poured an intense fire of shell, canister, and musketry into the Federals.[30]

87

CROCKLE'S CHARGE AT JACKSON.

**Crocker's charge on Capers' 24th South Carolina
at Wright's Farm**
(*Courtesy Parker Hills, Jackson, Mississippi*)

The 10th Missouri Regiment reeled from the heat of the conflict. Major Diemling recorded, "Here ensued almost hand-to-hand conflict with the 24th Regiment South Carolina Volunteers." The Federals claimed that the 10th Missouri was "suffering severely from the streams of fire" that came from "behind every object which could furnish protection to the enemy." Diemling boasted, "We succeeded in finally dislodging and driving them some 200 yards."[31]

The skirmish line behind the garden fence was highly exposed. Early in the battle, Steinmeyer withdrew the skirmishers to a new "lying low position." He placed the men parallel with the crest of the ridge over which the enemy had to advance. Thus, the skirmishers fired at the enemy from a distance of less than 100 yards as they discerned the heads of the attackers. This was probably the Confederate movement that the Federals interpreted as "gradually driving the Confederates on their main line." When he spotted the movement, Capers advised Steinmeyer to hold his position. However, after learning the reason for the movement, the colonel agreed and the skirmish line remained at the new position.[32]

The men were not fearful despite being heavily outnumbered. They understood the challenge and were highly confident experts in handling the short-range, smooth-bore muskets. One could understand by the determined look on the men's faces and the steel line of their jaws that they were ready. In short order, the skirmishers administered what Steinmeyer described as "a fearful execution."

Some soldiers, however were apprehensive. During the heat of the battle, Major Appleby yelled out, "They are really pouring it to us." Capers could hardly believe his ears. Irate, he immediately sought out Appleby and demanded the meaning of his words. Appleby explained that he did not intend those words to reflect pusillanimity as he was merely commenting. Afterwards, he complained about the younger lieutenant colonel "jacking him up" in a combat situation, and, as a result, an acrimonious relationship developed between the two. Soon after the battle, the homefolk elected the major of infantry to the South Carolina State Senate, and Appleby resigned his commission to serve on another front.[33]

In the meantime, the 75 Confederate skirmishers repulsed three successive enemy charges before retreating.[34] Inevitably, however, the Federals overcome the heavily outnumbered Confederates, even though the defenders made Jackson a difficult and expensive prey. During the melee, Capers received credit for singlehandedly capturing a Union soldier.[35]

Suddenly, Capers realized that the 14th Mississippi and 46th Georgia no longer supported the 24th from the other side of Clinton Road. He sent Adjutant Palmer to find Colonel Colquitt and recommend that the brigade retire. However, Clarence could not find Colquitt, who had already withdrawn the troops on the right of the road. Apparently, the message directing this retirement did not reach the troops on the left side of the road.[36]

Colquitt confirmed that "near 2 o'clock...he received notice that the trains were already on their way," and the quartermaster stores were safe. As a result, the colonel "immediately ordered the entire force to withdraw" and noted that the troops stood steadfast "until given the order." He reported:

> Not a man haved receded an inch...and resisted successfully
> the column of the enemy. All behaved well, officers and
> men...and won my admiration by their coolness and
> bravery.[37]

Until the moment that the brigade retired, the regiment lost few men. Suddenly a Federal ball struck Capers' horse, Hardtimes, in the right shoulder and passed along under the horse's skin for six inches. The ball exited the horse's thick skin and then entered its rider's right leg by piercing the skin on the left of the large bone (fibular) about six inches from his knee. The bullet touched the bone, bending the point of the ball, and stopped under the skin, after barely missing the large artery on the under side of his leg.[38] The shock from the impact of the ball and the subsequent loss of blood weakened Capers, and he passed command of the 24th to Major Appleby to conduct the withdrawal. A participant who witnessed the wounding of the

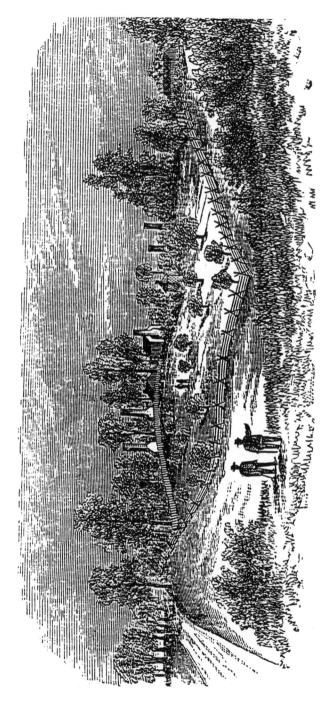

Battleground near Jackson, as sketched by Benson Lossing in April 1866. This view was taken from the open field over which Crocker's troops advanced to the charge. In the middle ground, traversed by a fence, is seen the ravine out of which the Confederates were driven, and on the crest of the hill, where they broke and fled, are seen the chimneys of the ruined mansion of O. P. Wright, on whose farm the battle was fought. The brow of the hill, where the road passes over, is the place where the Confederate cannon were planted.

(Lossing, *The Civil War in America*)

colonel was not sure if the ball which struck Capers came from the front or from the right.

Afterwards, the wounded man rode his "noble little horse, Hardtimes," to a waiting ambulance about one-fourth of a mile in the rear. En route, Sergeant Major Triest gave the colonel "a most welcomed drink of whiskey."[39]

Captain Steinmeyer, proud of the behavior of the skirmishers, boasted that the men had reluctantly retired in good order, as "skirmishers in retreat." The men continued loading and firing as the skirmishers retired before the main battle line of the enemy until the fighting became hand-to-hand and further resistance became futile. This episode ended when it did because of the early retreat of the troops on the right of the road and the hasty withdrawal of the 24th. Steinmeyer thought those movements were premature, allowing the enemy into the rear and preventing the possibility of escape.[40]

The "hasty movement" directed by Appleby was the only options available. Once the other units of the brigade retired, a slower withdrawal would have resulted in additional casualties or even more men captured. The Federals captured about one-half of the 24th's skirmishers, including Steinmeyer and Lieutenant Hawkins. The youthful Steinmeyer, a brave warrior, never fancied the idea of retreat.[41]

During the battle, Lieutenant A. F. Cunningham of Company F, was killed instantly when struck by a Federal ball. He crumpled and fell into one of the flower beds at the Wright House.[42]

The Federals advanced rapidly. In fact, they arrived so swiftly that all four of Hoskins' guns fell into the hands of the enemy, unspiked. The Confederates reported that six horses from the artillery teams had been killed. This, no doubt, accounts for the loss of the invaluable artillery pieces.[43]

The regiment again slogged through the muddy streets, this time toward Jackson. At a point about halfway between the original line of battle and the city, the Confederates turned and momentarily held the Federals at bay. Afterwards, the brigade reached Jackson, traversed the Pearl River, and linked with the balance of Johnston's small army as it retreated toward Canton. The Yankees pursued a short distance, but soon returned to Jackson. The Union army assumed a position behind the breastworks around the city and turned its attention toward a more important objective, Vicksburg.[44]

After the evacuation, Johnston's army marched about five miles and bivouacked along the Canton road for the night. The Battle of May 14, 1863, was over.[45]

During the battle that day, Gist's Brigade lost a total of 198 men killed wounded, and captured. The 24th suffered the most, counting a total of eleven men killed, including the only Confederate officer killed. The

**Photo of historical marker honoring Ellison Capers
at Jackson, Mississippi**
(Courtesy Carl McIntire, Jackson, Mississippi)

regiment suffered badly with 38 wounded and 56 missing or captured for a total of 105 casualties. After the battle, nine of the wounded men died from injuries.[46] The missing men were, for the most part, prisoners whom the Federals paroled soon after the battle.

The Federal Seventh Division reported 265 killed, wounded and captured. Of those, the brigade that led the attack on Gist's Brigade reported 215 casualties. The 10th Missouri and 80th Ohio reported 14 killed and 112 wounded for a total of 126 casualties.[47]

The men of the 24th distinguished themselves during the battle. General Johnston sent Capers his compliments and stated that his aide had reported to him that "the 24th behaved finely."[48] Three days later a proud Capers boasted to his wife, "My men behaved nobly."[49]

The ambulance that transported the wounded Capers away from the battlefield followed behind the troops for a short distance. The road was a deeper quagmire that afternoon than it had been during the morning. The soldiers trudged along, wading through mud that was often knee deep. Finally, the driver managed to find a place where he could guide the ambulance around the 8th Georgia Battalion, which arrived that morning too late to join the brigade at the Wright Farm. The Georgians learned the identity of the wounded officer aboard the ambulance, and as the vehicle

92

passed, gave out a shout that made Capers feel, "There was more to admire in them than to pity in me."[50]

Generals Johnston and Walker, as well as several staff members, visited the ambulance and expressed regrets at the wounded man's misfortune. They also wished him better luck the next time. The visitors congratulated Capers for the regiment's success and offered "to do what they could" to improve his comfort. Someone produced "a gourd of water," and Johnston's medical director offered to dress the wound. However, Capers thought his friend, Dr. Ogier, was on the way, and he would "save him the trouble." Ogier soon arrived but without his medical bag. In the confusion, the men had loaded the medical supplies on other wagons that were far behind. Ogier immediately sent for the bag, but it did not arrive until after nightfall. Since no houses existed along the road, the doctor decided he would remove the ball at Canton. After a painful ambulance ride, they arrived at midnight, and at 2:00 a.m., Ogier skillfully removed the ball and dressed the wound. Capers described the experience, "Such a ride! oh'e!"[51]

Capers recuperated at the home of Mrs. Suber. A Methodist minister, Dr. Thomas, formerly from Abbeville, South Carolina, resided with his daughter, Mrs. Suber, sixteen miles from Canton. The day after the battle, Dr. Thomas and his daughter rode into town and offered Capers the hospitality of their home. The wounded man gratefully accepted and rode to the Subers' home tolerably comfortably. Mrs. Suber, "a whole souled South Carolina lady," called the wounded officer, "Ellison," and nursed him most kindly.

The wounded man rested comfortably at the Suber's residence. After a couple of days, Capers began to feel much better, though still very weak. He recorded that "my wound, though painful, is not dangerous, and I am most kindly provided for by the good family to whose house I was on yesterday brought."[52] The next day, he reassured his wife about the injury, "My wound is doing as well as it possibly could...I am in no pain unless I move."[53]

The news that Capers was recuperating at the Suber home spread rapidly in the local area. Kindly neighbors sent "two vases of flowers," and several made personal visits. By that afternoon, the wounded man could sit up. The injury was still extremely painful. The local attention seemed to make the patient feel better, and he became eager to start for South Carolina and the loving arms of Lottie and the children. Dr. Ogier advised Capers that he should recuperate for two months before resuming military duties.

The Federal occupation of Jackson interrupted the telegraph lines. This caused the wounded soldiers considerable worry because they could not reassure the homefolk. After several days the men discovered they could post letters via the tri-weekly mail from Columbus, Georgia. Capers immediately dispatched a letter and two telegrams advising Lottie that he would soon start the trip home and asked her not to worry:

If I could only lay my head on your dear breast...feel your soft cheek on mine...my own Lottie, I would be happy. Give yourself, my angel, no alarm about my wound. It is not serious and I will start...by the last of this week to your dear bosom.[54]

In the meantime, the soldiers captured at the Wright place on May 14 were held on a field nearby until late that afternoon. A Federal officer informed Steinmeyer that "a Confederate officer" lay dead in the Wright House flower garden. Deeply concerned, Steinmeyer hastened to the spot and discovered Lieutenant Cunningham. He retrieved the dead officer's gold watch and chain, which he mailed to Cunningham's father. The ball that struck down the young officer had cut the long, gold watch chain at its neck.[55]

Steinmeyer requested permission to bury the Confederate dead. The request was obstinately refused by "a very rude old abolitionist major." As a result, the Union soldiers' sympathy was with the prisoners. This indicated that they, too, disliked the major's attitude.[56] No records exist to show who buried the Confederate dead.

The Federals converted the Mississippi State capitol into a temporary prison. About midnight, the Federals marched the prisoners to Jackson and imprisoned the Confederates in the State Capitol. The Federals also used "the jail" for incarcerating several Union soldiers who were awaiting court-martial.[57]

The prisoners were treated very well. The captors made many complimentary references about the bravery and courage displayed by the soldiers of the 24th. Steinmeyer received special recognition when his captors learned that he commanded the Confederate skirmish line on the left of Clinton Road. One Federal officer characterized the 24th's line as that of a brigade, and declared the Confederates "killed off Union soldiers by the hundreds."[58]

One elderly gentleman was captured by the Federals because he inadvertently rode his horse onto the battlefield. The old gentleman stated that the Confederates had killed about 300 Federals that day and testified that most had received head wounds. This news elated the prisoners, especially Captain Steinmeyer, but the report was slightly inflated as the number of Federals killed that day was much less.[59]

Another local citizen, Major George Work, advised Steinmeyer's father of the whereabouts of his son. Work also called upon Colonel Stevens and congratulated the gallantry displayed by the 24th Regiment. Work invited the entire regiment to visit his nearby plantation.[60]

That night, Federal Colonel John N. Cromwell visited the Confederate prisoners at the State House prison. Cromwell shared with Steinmeyer a drink of brandy and some hardtack from his haversack. The prisoners remained the balance of the night downstairs in the State capital. The next morning they were incarcerated upstairs in the Senate chambers.[61]

The morning after the battle, a waiter brought the captured officers a platter of bread and pies with a note from the soldiers of the 80th Ohio Regiment, "Compliments of the 80th Ohio Regiment, to the South Carolina boys who fought on the Clinton Road."[62]

The prisoners had an excellent view of the city. From their vantage point located in the upper story of the State House, they observed the horrible destruction the Federals wrought upon Jackson. The Yankees burned buildings, smashed those that remained as well as their contents, and in general wreaked havoc throughout the city. Steinmeyer felt that the sight gave the observers "ample opportunity to contemplate the horrors of war."[63]

The Federals provided good care for the Confederate wounded. The next day, Steinmeyer visited the wounded and found them in a comfortable and well-tended temporary hospital. He also visited Sergeant Samuel G. Burdit, Sr., of Company F, whose leg the surgeons amputated just above the knee. Burdit suffered dreadfully. He became very despondent from shock and other complications and died soon after the operation.

Two days later, the imprisoned officers received a proposal from the Yankees for parole. General Sherman met with the Confederate prisoners and asked the parolees "to guard the inhabitants (of Jackson) from criminals and other mischievous persons till the civil authorities could restore order and good government." Without hesitation, the two senior officers, Lieutenant Colonel Beverly Kennon, Ordnance Chief, and Captain B. Stevens, Jackson Heavy Artillery, agreed. The prisoners asked for arms. The Federals pointed out that sufficient guns and ammunition were lying around the streets to satisfy the defensive requirements of the parolees. Sherman also suggested that the Confederates use the weapons on Federal stragglers "if they were found depredating." Sherman hurried the withdrawal from the city after he learned that Confederate cavalry was "between Jackson and the Big Black River." As the Union forces departed, Sherman advised the Confederate parolees to remain indoors until "his command was in ranks and under control."[64]

As soon as Sherman's troops vacated Jackson, Colonel Kennon assembled the paroled prisoners and explained the terms of the agreement. Captain Stevens took charge of the general street police or patrol force and asked other paroled members of his company for assistance.[65] A local citizen advised Steinmeyer that the enemy had converted the city hall into a hospital. There, the Federals left three-hundred sick and wounded Union soldiers as well as attending surgeons and nurses. Steinmeyer took charge of the place and formally posted a sentinel as protection for both doctors and patients. The surgeons welcomed the security force and invited the officers to dine with the hospital staff.[66] Afterwards, the captain returned to the State House, now designated as the parolee headquarters.

En route, he witnessed Federal Colonel Cromwell fall from his horse, mortally wounded. A squadron of Confederate scouts who had returned to Jackson immediately after Sherman's departure fired the ball that struck Cromwell. Many thought the shooting of the Yankee colonel was unfortunate and some feared that Sherman might return, shell the city, and punish those in charge. Without hesitation, many local citizens as well as parolees, including the colonel in charge, stampeded away from the city. However, the panic soon subsided and calm reasoning returned. Since the slain officer was a Mason, the local Masonic lodge assured a proper funeral. Steinmeyer deeply regretted Colonel Cromwell's death because of the kindnesses the Northerner had extended the Confederate officers the preceding evening.[67]

After Kennon's departure, the remaining parolees continued to comply with the terms of the parole. Captain Stevens, the senior officer, became post commander, and Steinmeyer took charge of the police detail in addition to the hospital. Soon the city mayor resumed his duties, and Stevens and his company of Mississippi troops departed. The mayor prevailed upon the police and guard detail to remain in Jackson for several additional days. Steinmeyer agreed to remain until the mayor expressed confidence that he could maintain order. When the mayor was satisfied and the agreement with General Sherman was fulfilled, the parolees departed for the Paroled Prisoners Camp at Demopolis, Alabama, and arrived there on May 24, 1863.[68]

The parolee camp detained paroled prisoners until they were exchanged to rejoin the regiment. Major Henry C. Davis commanded the camp and delegated much of the responsibility to Lieutenant T. J. Adkins. The paroled officers dined with the lieutenant. After a few days, Steinmeyer's faithful servant, Sampson, arrived at the camp. Captain A. B. Addison, now resigned as commander of Company D, also visited the men while on his way home. Soon, the men received furloughs, and on June 10, 1863, Steinmeyer departed the parolee camp en route for Spartanburg, South Carolina, via Charleston.[69]

The Paroled Prisoners Camp was a very disagreeable experience for the occupants. In fact, Steinmeyer was extremely unhappy over his treatment and complained bitterly to his congressman, the Honorable W. Porcher Miles. He asked Miles for the plan of organization for "parole camps" and the "jurisdiction given by the government to the officers in command." The grievances were felt by many of the other paroles, especially the officers:[70]

> In becoming a prisoner to the enemy only when escape was impossible and death the alternative...I cannot believe...I forfeited all position in my own army and am to be held as a prisoner...under guard, and subject to...a junior...an inexperienced officer...and kept in durance under a lieutenant who alone controlled us.[71]

Congressman Miles sought information about the camps from Secretary Seddon. The secretary sent the letter to Major Davis for information; Davis denied that conditions were bad and claimed he had little support from the Confederate army:

> Capt. Steinmeyer (especially) called upon me for furlough...which I could not grant. Gen. Johnston gave ...permission to do so. Capt Steinmeyer was the first to avail himself....I had many officers (field & otherwise) who...submitted to the rules...who...testify that they have never been too onerous....no guard...was placed over the camp of Paroled & Ex. Prisoners, nor has any officer exercised jurisdiction...unless by special order from myself.[72]

In the meantime, the Confederate Secretary of War declared field paroles without force and returned the parolees to duty. The action followed a similar action by the Federals that had voided the parole of prisoners granted by General Lee during the Maryland campaign. En route back to the 24th, Steinmeyer visited the Parole Camp as a matter of courtesy. Major Davis leaped at the opportunity and thoroughly scolded Steinmeyer for writing complaints about the camp. The two officers argued, each matching the other's complaint. The confrontation cleared the air and the two warriors parted on friendlier terms. In fact, Davis entrusted Steinmeyer with some important papers for General Leonidas Polk.[73] When he arrived in Mississippi, Steinmeyer delivered his package and happily rejoined his company. He wrote:

> It was no small satisfaction to rejoin my command not the least part was the glad reception extended me by the regimental officers and men.[74]

The Mississippi summer of 1863 was extremely hot and dry. The heat at times became almost unbearable, which was compounded by a chronic shortage of good drinking water. In addition, the men suffered terribly from fatigue, exhaustion, a lack of shoes, clothing and other essential equipment. The poor quality drinking water exacerbated the many cases of dreaded typhoid fever and chronic diarrhea. Although not as fatal as typhoid fever, the latter disease was extremely debilitating.[75]

During the next six weeks, the regiment, in the opinion of the men, aimlessly marched and counter marched all about Mississippi. The men were not certain whether the marches were by design or by circumstance. However, General Johnston was organizing "an army of relief" that was supposed to combine with Pemberton's Army of the Mississippi and so relieve Vicksburg. Johnston divided his army into two wings, one stationed at Jackson and the other at Canton. General W. H. T. Walker headed the second wing which consisted of six brigades, including Gist's Brigade and the 24th. Each move that the regiment made was a result of Johnston's strategy, which bought time until he could amass sufficient manpower and equipment to successfully relieve Vicksburg.

Meanwhile, the night of May 14, 1863, had been uneasy for the troops as they bivouacked in line of battle, expecting a Federal attack at any moment. The small Confederate force awoke early the next morning and continued the march to Calhoun Station. The little army camped at that place for two days and departed on May 17, marching six miles beyond Livingston. The next day the men covered nine miles, and that afternoon they formed a line of battle near Cross Lanes. On July 19, they continued on the Canton Road for 10 miles. The following day the regiment marched still farther along the same road and bivouacked seven miles from the city. On May 21, 1863, the 24th reached a camp one mile from Cordts Pond, where it remained until May 30.[76]

The day after the battle of May 14, a train transporting General Gist and the 16th Regiment approached Jackson. A messenger intercepted the train and advised Gist that Johnston and the army were retiring toward Canton. The troops immediately debarked the train and started toward the new location. Six days later General Gist finally caught up with the brigade.[77]

The news from General Pemberton's army was bad. The poorly planned battles at Champion Hill and the Big Black had been extremely disastrous. Grant's army, soon counting 77,000 men, surrounded Vicksburg, practically holding Pemberton's army prisoner.[78]

On May 25, 1863, General Gist wrote General Beauregard regarding the situation in Mississippi. He regretted that only a small part of the brigade had arrived in time to participate in the hard-fought battle on May 14, but happily recounted the success enjoyed by the 24th:

> The Twenty-fourth Regiment, South Carolina Volunteers, Lieutenant-Colonel (E) Capers commanding, particularly distinguished themselves. Three companies deployed as skirmishers drove three regiments of Federals without giving ground.[79]

Gist, ever optimistic, asserted that "Gen. Johnston is anxiously awaiting reinforcements" to attack Grant's forces at Vicksburg, where he expected success. However, Grant's army mustered between 60,000 and 80,000 well-equipped, heavily entrenched troops that completely invested the city. Gist alleged, "Gen. Pemberton is censured by everyone. He lost nearly all his artillery." On the other hand, Gist related, "The officers, men and citizens have unbounded confidence in Johnston."[80] Gist was obviously confident that the war would soon turn for the better in Mississippi.

Johnston's army grew slowly in manpower but still lacked essential equipment. By early June, the army mustered 24,000 infantry and artillery, plus 2,800 cavalry under Brigadier General W. H. Jackson. Johnston's army was practically without transportation, however, and did not even possess sufficient ammunition.[81] The Big Black River was insurmountable because the army could cross only on a bridge, and it had no pontoons. Grant's army, heavily fortified, guarded each of the existing bridges. The situation was critical, and many thought Johnston would be unable to relieve Pemberton.

The 24th marched again on May 30 and arrived at Yazoo City the next night. A Georgian was disappointed in the appearance of Yazoo City. He opined, "I always thought that Yazoo City was a right smart city, but it is not much of a place." Although no Yankees were there, signs indicated they had visited the place. The men liked the camp at Yazoo City. The soldiers received plenty of good drinking water and purchased extra food from the local market to supplement their diet. At the bivouac near Vernon, foodstuffs were not available on the local market. Water was extremely scarce and often not fit to drink. The Confederates remained two nights and then marched four miles down the Vicksburg Road.[82]

While at Yazoo City, James B. Dotterer, from Charleston, reported for duty. He had resigned from the Citadel and enlisted in Company A of the 24th Regiment. Shortly after joining, Colonel Stevens appointed Dotterer to the position of regimental sergeant major.[83]

In Mississippi, the men became experts at finding potable water. The soldiers drank water from creeks and dry-land ponds. Although "a thick scum" covered the pond water, the men liked it better than the creek water because it tasted better. One soldier observed that the Mississippi pond water was "destitute of tadpoles & wiggletales" that frequently populated South Carolina ponds. Several large cisterns located near the camp did not produce enough water for the entire army. Therefore, the general reserved the clear water for the officers and posted a guard to enforce the rule. The men became experts at securing a drink of the much preferred clear cistern water. Often, the troops paid servants "four bits"[84] for a canteen full, or the men passed themselves as officers and received a refreshing drink. One day Buddy McGee, on duty with the regimental staff, passed himself off as an officer and helped himself. While so engaged, Colonel Stevens and the remainder of the regimental staff officers arrived. The colonel acted quite glad to see Buddy, but the next morning Stevens returned the young soldier to his company. Justice struck in many different ways, and Buddy accepted the reassignment philosophically. Obviously, the enlisted men had to drink whatever water that was available.[85]

Because of the rigors of the marches in the hot and almost waterless countryside, the men found little to like in Mississippi. One observer commented, "The dirtiest roads that I ever saw we have them now -- the roads is just like a dry ash bank. It is just like walking on a bank of flour and hardly any water on the road." The soldiers noticed an abundance of good land that produced cotton and corn but little water. Another homesick soldier rated Mississippi rather harshly, "I have seen none of Mississippi yet that I am willing to live in."[86] Often the troops became exhausted and straggled during the marches. However, they recuperated rapidly and usually caught up with the regiment during the night.

The Richmond authorities desperately prodded General Johnston to launch an attack on Grant's forces, suggesting that a failed attack would be better than no attack. Johnston, a cautious general, considered his options and decided that an attack upon the Federal force was impractical. Every soldier in Mississippi was well aware of the hazardous conditions that confronted Pemberton's army and that time was running out.[87]

Finally, Johnston advised Pemberton on June 4, "All we can attempt to do is save you and your garrison." He urged a simultaneous attack at the same point, or to engineer an escape route that would extricate the besieged army. Pemberton felt that he could not muster sufficient strength to break the siege. In turn Johnston felt that he could not mount a successful initiative alone. However, he argued that a simultaneous effort by both armies might save Pemberton's army.[88] Johnston reconnoitered for a place that would accommodate the coordinated attack, preferring the area north of the railroad, because he thought it offered the greatest chance of success.

In the meantime, General Grant felt secure in his strong entrenchments. Unquestionably, the large force of Union troops stationed around Vicksburg, as well as the many artillery pieces aimed toward that city were overpowering. Grant also considered that his fortifications were well placed along the Big Black and were more than strong enough to resist an advance from that direction. However, the Federals remained on the alert, expecting an imminent attack by Johnston's army.

The 24th, as a part of Johnston's army, continued to march from bivouac to bivouac and camp to camp in the hot, dry state of Mississippi. The army bivouacked four miles from Yazoo City until June 13 and then marched 23 miles to the Big Black River and entered camp at McNamara's Ferry. The next day, the regiment moved four miles, and remained near Vernon until June 30.[89]

Colonel Stevens' personnel problems among his officers continued. He dealt with the divergent personalities in his energetic, forthright manner, adhering to a strong code of discipline. Although Major Appleby had an excellent record, he resigned because he was elected from his home district to the South Carolina State Senate.[90] Later that fall, Stevens met Appleby in Columbia, South Carolina, and wrote Capers about the meeting:

> At Columbia, I met Old Appleby...invited him to my room
> and we had a long talk. He is the same "old two and six
> pence." He was perfectly respectful to me and did not lose
> his temper, but looks upon many of his old grievances with

considerable bitterness. He dwelt at great length on his differences with Ogier... says he most assuredly would have called him to account, ...(unfortunately he died.) He was in Columbia as a member....I think my talk has considerably cooled the old fellow and we parted on friendly terms.[91]

Captain A. B. Addison, Company D, resigned for "physical incapacity and general bad health disqualifying me to discharge the duties of an officer" and departed June 11, 1863.[92] On the same day, Captain Jones, the regiment's senior company commander, was promoted to major of infantry. Stevens also promoted Lieutenant Risher to captain as Commander of Company E. Risher was a devoted South Carolina warrior who was instrumental in forming the company. At the same time, Stevens also promoted Lieutenant John Warren, Second Lieutenant of Company E, to captain.[93]

John McGee received a furlough and visited South Carolina shortly after the battle of Jackson. On his return, Buddy thought that Jackson looked rather desolate. While there, he visited his friends in the hospital and found the patients in good spirits. The wounded men were eager for furloughs so they could convalescence in South Carolina. Afterwards, Buddy walked thirty miles and rejoined the regiment.[94]

Vessie was happy when his brother returned with the latest news from home. He often became discouraged when he didn't receive regular letters. The soldiers seemed disgusted that some of the homefolks were in Jackson "buying up negroes to speculate on" and thought the speculators better "look sharp" or they would be "prest into servace." Vessie McGee "blundered into" Cousin Pinch McGee, a lieutenant in General W. H. Jackson's Cavalry, who was on detached service, recruiting volunteers. Vessie thriftily shared his paper with his brother and also his uncle, Dan Bozeman. Both wrote a few lines. For a happy change the men were getting plenty of beef and cornbread to eat as a result of the good crops produced by the local farmers. The principal campfire subject was the upcoming battle to raise the Vicksburg siege. The soldiers in Johnston's army expected that would be the turning point of the war.[95] They obviously expected success.

The men spent most of the time either on the march or preparing for the march. If other time were available, the men drilled, stood dress parades, and kept the bivouac area neat and tidy. Although idle time was scarce, the soldiers found plenty of time for the favorite pastime of repeating and spreading rumors and starting new ones.

Buddy McGee's writing ability earned him considerable detail time or special assignments with the regimental staff. He secured a position with the division commissary. However, a large number of men from the regiment were already on detached service, and Colonel Stevens canceled the

101

assignment. Perhaps the colonel still remembered the incident at the water cistern. Afterwards, Buddy commiserated with Colonel James McCollough, commander of the 16th Regiment, about the assignment. McCollough counseled that if Buddy had submitted the proper application, Stevens could not stop the assignment. However, Buddy did not pursue the matter, but he still hoped that The Old Fellow would relent. Buddy realized that an assignment providing supplies to 20,000 men would be a challenging task, although he declared, "I would have a better time than I am having now." Buddy soon received "a better assignment," as a clerk on General Gist's staff.[96]

Finally the regiments were fully supplied with ammunition and sufficient transportation and enough pontoon bridges to span the Big Black River. The men speculated, "Gen. Johnston's latest moves are designed to attack Grant's force across the Big Black River." Again, they anticipated an attack at any time. The soldiers were ready. The company commander of Company I, The Edgefield Light Infantry, proudly evaluated his company: "My company is very well drilled, moderately efficient & capable of giving good service."[97] The evaluation was very modest. However, it applied equally well to every company.

By the first of July, Johnston's army mustered nearly 30,000 soldiers. On the 1st, 2nd, and 3rd of July, Johnston reconnoitered the area north of the railroad. He decided that Grant's position was too strong and commenced looking elsewhere. Before he could reconnoiter the area south of the railroad, the Vicksburg garrison capitulated on July 4, 1863.[98]

As General Johnston made his reconnaissances, the regiment moved ever nearer the Big Black River. On July 1, 1863, the 24th moved from its camp near Vernon, Mississippi, to Muddy Creek. The next day the regiment moved from Muddy Creek to Deep Creek and remained there four days. On July 6 the regiment departed Deep Creek, marched to Clinton, and bivouacked there one night. After Vicksburg surrendered, the 24th with Johnston's entire army took a position on the fortified line in front of Jackson and awaited the Federal army.[99]

During those hot, dry days and long marches in Mississippi, General Johnston completed the organization of the army. Gist's Brigade, including the 24th, became a part of General Walker's Division. Walker was a West Point graduate, combat veteran of the Mexican War, and a capable commander well qualified for higher command. Early in the war, President Davis had promoted a political general over General Walker while he was on duty in Virginia. Walker, a proud and chivalrous Southerner, resigned rather than accept what he considered a personal rebuke, and then reentered the Confederate service from his home state of Georgia. As a brigade commander at Savannah, he commanded the brigade of Georgia troops that accompanied Gist's Brigade to Jackson. Johnston promoted Walker to

102

General W. H. T. Walker
(Courtesy Perkins Library, Duke University)

Major General. The two brigades (Gist's and Walker's) remained a part of the division until the death of General Walker during the Battle of Atlanta on July 22, 1864.[100] After Walker's promotion, the brigade became General C. C. Wilson's Brigade until Wilson's death in November 1863.

On July 7, 1863, Johnston positioned his army in front of Jackson. Walker's Division was on the Confederate right center, General Samuel C. French's Division on the left of Walker, and General William W. Loring's Division was on the right. Under General Johnston's latest organization, Walker's Division consisted of four brigades, which were posted on the Jackson defensive line, from left to right: M. D. Ector's, Gregg's, and Wilson's with Gist's in close reserve.[101] Although Gist's brigade was behind the main line, the men were within range of the enemy's rifles and artillery. Walker placed Gist's Brigade in the Old City Cemetery or Burial Grounds, a large graveyard immediately behind the center of the Confederate defensive line. There the men of the 24th Regiment endured a strong artillery barrage for eight days. The men expected to take a position on the main line at a moment's notice.[102]

At first, the men maintained a position on open ground. Soon, they entrenched and every man removed his coat and started digging until the "pitts were deep enough to be able to stand" unseen.[103]

Although in reserve and entrenched, the men still received injuries from

103

the enemy rifle and artillery fire. On the first day, an enemy artillery shell killed a brigade soldier assigned to another regiment who was standing within six paces of members of the 24th. A second artillery shell exploded beneath a stand of stacked arms and destroyed several rifles, and still another shell killed a mule a short distance away.[104] A spent ball struck Vessie McGee on the arm. Although the ball did not break the skin, the blow was very painful and raised a large blue welt.[105] While the McGee brothers were in the trenches, the young soldiers were "fearful that a terrable battle" would soon erupt.[106] Fortunately, the regiment suffered only 20 or 30 men wounded during the entire ordeal. Although one man received a dangerous wound, the 24th did not suffer a single soldier killed or captured.[107] The enemy killed four men assigned to other regiments in Gist's Brigade.

During the siege, the men could not light fires. For six or seven days, the men ate only raw bacon and hard bread. For many, eating raw bacon was a first experience, and many digestive tracts rebelled against the thought of eating the raw meat. However, without fires or means for cooking, the men soon concluded, "It would not do to be too nice about what we got to eat."[108]

Vessie reassured his parents in his letters and displayed his concern for his own safety, although he never doubted that he and Buddy would survive the war. That the brothers were prepared for any eventuality was evident when they wrote home:

> Pa, I don want you or Ma to render yourselves one oz.
> about me and Buddy if we get into battle. I hope we will
> come throu safe and sound. If either of us should git killed
> in Battle, I hope to miat in a better world than this....I
> bought one of the...little testaments the first morning the
> battle commenced and I have bin very attentive to it evir
> since I got it. Ma, I have bin Prayin to my hevenly farther
> to Pardin and forgive my sins. Ma, I want you and Pa to
> Pray for me in absence from you all. Tell Graney to pray
> for me too. I hop the time will soon com when we will all
> get back to Charleston if we eve get back. I hope we will
> all get to go home onst mor.

Vessie added a reassurance to his mother that she should not worry about him being "a good boy."[109] After several days of weathering an artillery barrage, a soldier could look Death in the face and turn easily to the aid of the Supreme Being.

The City of Jackson had received extensive attention during the battle of May 14, and reflected additional signs from the bombardment of the latest siege. General Sherman boasted that on the 12th and 13th of July, the Federals bombed the city dreadfully:

> [I] threw into Jackson about 3,000 rounds mostly from 10
> and 20 pounder Parrots and 12-pounder Napoleons, all of

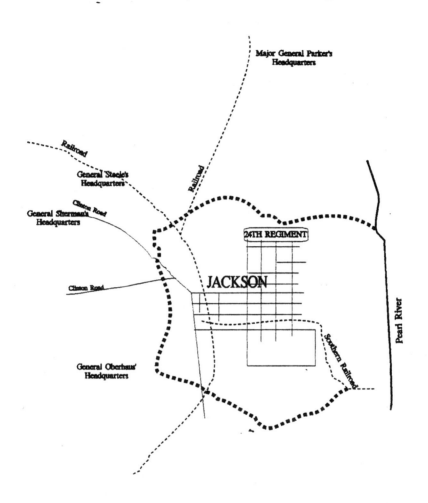

Major General Parker's
Headquarters

Railroad

General Steele's
Headquarters

Railroad

Clinton Road

General Sherman's
Headquarters

24TH REGIMENT

Clinton Road

JACKSON

Southern Railroad

Pearl River

General Oberhaus'
Headquarters

CONFEDERATE DEFENSE LINE AT
JACKSON, MISS. AUGUST 16, 1863

Courtesy Parker Mills.

which did great execution...I...awaited the arrival of the ammunition train to open a furious cannonade on the town from all of our line.[110]

Fortunately for Jackson, the Confederate cavalry intercepted the Federal ammunition train, and it did not arrive. The city already stood in total shambles.

Finally, on the night of July 16, 1863, General Johnston realized the ruin and desolation of Jackson. To preclude additional bombardment, he withdrew the army that night and retired across the Pearl River. The general removed the quartermaster stores and public property, the artillery and wagon train, and safely extricated the entire force.[111] Johnston withdrew the army so quietly and smoothly that the enemy did not know when the defenders departed. One soldier joyously informed his parents that "the fool Yankees" kept up a rapid fire on the vacated positions for several hours after the Confederates were already gone. Another reported that "them scoundrels" made three separate charges before carrying the empty trenches.

That night, the 24th Regiment marched nearly 20 miles and finally arrived footsore and exhausted near Morton, Mississippi, on July 18. The siege of Jackson, July 9-16, 1863, was over.[112]

On the retreat, Vessie McGee came down with an attack of stomach cramps and colic, no doubt caused by a week-long diet of bread, raw bacon, and bad water. His brother and Lieutenant Gray lingered at Vessie's side until the doctor and the colonel arrived. Afterwards, Vessie related the humiliating experience to his parents, "How do you reckon I was treated? The doctor never even got off his horse to examine me and the col. ordered me up lack he was takin to a dog."

After the colonel and the doctor departed, Lieutenant Palmer carried Vessie's rifle and Captain Hill offered his horse. It concerned the soldier that he had not performed duty since the regiment was in the trenches and his letters, no doubt, reflected the feelings of the majority of the soldiers:

> I hop I will soon bee stout again. I recon that I would way 90th lb now. If I could get iney thing that I could eat I would improve rit away but we don't get anything but old tuff beef and corn bred. I do hop in trust that the time is not long whin this terable affare will come to a close when we can get to go home where we can injoy the plesurs of home life.[113]

Companies F and H were assigned two-and-one-half miles away from the regiment as guards for the Morton Depot commissary. This detail relieved the men from the rigors of the march for a few days, and the men finally received enough fairly decent food. Although he was still sick from diarrhea, Vessie kept up on the long marches.[114]

Soon, the Federals, with the entire Jackson area in ruins, returned to the Vicksburg side of the Big Black. As a result, General Johnston started granting furloughs, one per every 25 men. The men were happy about the opportunity and more eager than ever to visit loved ones.

The McGee brothers' mess attendant arranged for a home cooked dinner as the guest of the Whitehead family, who lived near Morton. That evening every member of the mess marched to the Whitehead residence, stacked rifles in the front yard, shyly entered the house, and took a seat at the large dining room table. The men were conscious that they looked extremely ragged, dressed in terribly dirty and frayed breeches. Some of the men thought that the fierce appearance might frighten the Whitehead family; however, no one noticed or mentioned the soldiers' attire. The men sat with bowed heads for the blessing and could hardly wait to attack the scrumptious meal arrayed on the table. The ravenous men ate a full dinner that evening and left for the bivouac with an unusual feeling - a stomach fully satiated with good food.[115]

Since the 24th had arrived in Mississippi, the affairs of the Confederacy were in a changed condition. The Federals had defeated General Lee in Pennsylvania, and both Vicksburg and Port Hudson had surrendered. The Northerners drove General Johnston away from Jackson again, and in South Carolina the enemy practically besieged Charleston by land and sea. The patriotic minded Capers recorded his feelings about the state of affairs: "July 1863 is indeed an eventful month in the history of our struggle."[116]

At 2:40 a.m. July 28, 1863, Capers, now recovered from his wounds, finally boarded the train at Ridgeville, South Carolina, en route to rejoin the regiment. He paused during the journey to visit his brother and sister at Atlanta.[117] Aboard the train, Capers met General Stephen D. Lee, late of the Vicksburg garrison, who eagerly spoke about the siege of Vicksburg and the terrible conditions in the city that had finally caused its surrender. Lee understood that General Johnston would not have been able to raise the siege.

On August 2, 1863, three members of the 24th, also wounded during the May 14 battle of Jackson, joined Capers between Selma and Meridan. The men traveled the remainder of the journey together, and Captain Steinmeyer joined the group farther along the route. The group finally arrived at the regiment at 2:30 p.m., August 3, 1863.[118] That same day, General Gist departed the brigade, furlough in hand, en route for Columbia, South Carolina, and a visit with his new wife.

At Morton, Capers sought out his horse, Hardtimes, also recovered from his wound, and after an absence of seventy days rejoined the regiment two miles from Morton, Mississippi.[119] After visiting Generals Johnston, Walker and Gist, Capers advised Colonel Stevens that he was ready for duty.

As with all the soldiers of the 24th, the health of his loved ones at home deeply concerned the family oriented Capers. He prayed often and asked, "May God protect my best beloved." Letters that arrived on August 10 and 12 indicated that Lottie was recovering rapidly from illness and felt much better. The news temporarily alleviated Capers' concern. Two more letters from Lottie on August 13 and 14 told Ellison about daughter Sue's extreme illness. At 4:35 p.m. on August 22, 1863, Capers received a dispatch from Charleston with terrible news - his daughter, Sue McGill Capers, had died on Monday, August 17, 1863.[120] Heartbroken, the youthful father was thankful that he still had his small son, Frank, whom he adored.

In August, the weather was rather pleasant for Mississippi, and other than the constant marching, duties were relatively boring. When not on the march, the men kept the bivouac clean and drilled frequently, and as always, the soldiers were very unhappy about the latest reduction in rations. The only excitement in camp occurred when Generals Johnston and Walker visited Gist's Brigade on August 14, 1863.[121]

The regiment received little news about the enemy. The Federal army after capturing Vicksburg, its primary objective, apparently gave up trying to bring on a battle with Johnston's army. The Confederate cavalry captured a few Union pickets along the Big Black River; otherwise, the situation was extremely quiet.

During the lull in its marches, the 24th paraded for the two top ranked general officers. Early in August, the 24th exercised the drill and dress parade for General Johnston, and the men thought that the general was impressed with the exhibition. Again on August 17, the regiment exercised another parade. This time the 24th, accompanied by the 46th Georgia, drilled in the presence of Lieutenant General William J. Hardee.[122] The 46th excelled in the manual of arms, but the 24th performed the battalion evolutions even better, and Hardee expressed himself as "much gratified." Apparently all regiments in Johnston's army were not as efficient as those of Gist's Brigade.

Secretary Seddon, who had been unsuccessful in stimulating Johnston to attack Vicksburg, started prodding General Braxton Bragg to launch an attack in Tennessee. To support the effort, Johnston agreed to provide Bragg "a little below 20,000 troops."[123] However, Bragg still declined because of the need to cross the mountains, and President Davis refused to override Bragg's decision.[124] Meanwhile, Union Generals William S. Rosecrans and Ambrose E. Burnside were advancing on Bragg's position. Finally, Seddon transferred Walker's Division, including the 24th, to reinforce the Army of Tennessee at Chattanooga.[125] Once again, the regiment was moving toward a situation that was becoming critical.

Even as the regiment departed Mississippi, typhoid fever and illness began causing considerable distress. Captain James Gist, younger brother of the general, on whose staff he served, died on August 24, 1863. Company

A performed the funeral service, accompanying the 30-year-old Gist's remains to their final resting place, and fired a military salute over his grave.[126]

Upon returning from Captain Gist's funeral, the members of Company A found the regiment ready to board a waiting train, destination Chattanooga. Stevens informed Steinmeyer that new orders arrived after Company A departed for the funeral. The other companies had packed and loaded Company A's supplies and the men marched to the train station ready for an immediate departure.

As the regiment began its move for Chattanooga, Capers received word that his friend, Doctor Ogier, was also a victim of typhoid fever. Ogier, a native of Charleston and formerly the 24th's regimental surgeon, had been promoted to major and appointed surgeon of Walker's Division. Stevens asked his second in command to remain at Morton for an extra day, arrange a proper funeral for Ogier, and afterwards follow the regiment to Tennessee. The next day, Capers accomplished his sad task and departed that night to rejoin the regiment.

When the 24th loaded onto the railroad cars at Morton at 9:30 p.m. on August 25, 1863, the days of trudging around the hot and almost waterless Mississippi were over. Those hardships fully probed the spirit and discipline of the soldiers who passed every test. Many soldiers thought that half the population of Mississippi was pro-Union and that an aggressive conscript officer could find many potential transcripts.[127]

The soldiers rather enjoyed the excitement of the train rides. Although the trip to Tennessee was long and tiresome, the troops confessed to a "nice time on the road." The ladies along the route again greeted the soldiers and offered "baskets of provisions and fruit." Sadly, one man from Company C died when he accidentally fell from the railroad cars. Many lost their hats, but somehow the soldiers found replacements. The lead companies arrived at Tyner's Station near Chattanooga on August 31, 1863.[128] After debarking the train, the men marched six miles along the Tennessee River toward Knoxville.

Finally, the regiment bivouacked beside the river beneath the canopy of a beautiful growth of trees. At the new camp, the men found plenty of good drinking water.[129] Unsure of the situation in Tennessee, the men remained alert and ready for action.

The men from Anderson and Edgefield promptly informed the homefolk that the regiment was near home and pleaded with parents and loved ones to visit. Young Vessie McGee, constantly ill with chronic diarrhea, expressed his feelings about a visit with his parents:

> Pa, I would rather see you and Ma as inybody living. Ma,
> if I was just at home to get chicking sup to drink, I would
> soon get well of the diarrhea.

His brother, in addition to urging a visit, reminded his parents to have a cobbler repair his boots or "have them fixed" because he was "about barefooted."[130]

Capers followed the same route traveled by the 24th the preceding day, travelling through Meridian and Mobile. He rode the steamer *Mary Wilson* across Mobile Bay and boarded another dingy and crowded railroad car that groaned and slowly scraped its way to Montgomery, arriving the next morning at 5:30. Pausing briefly, the train departed for West Point at 7:30 a.m. on August 29. Troops from other regiments and brigades en route for the Army of Tennessee were aboard.[131]

During the momentary pause at Montgomery, Ellison met Mrs. Ogier, the wife of the regiment's late surgeon. The death of her husband afflicted the poor lady terribly, and Capers' sympathy went out to the heartbroken lady. He consoled and reassured her that Dr. Ogier received a proper funeral and gave Mrs. Ogier directions to her husband's grave.[132]

After 22 hours, Capers arrived at Atlanta at 5:30 a.m. and caught up with several companies of the 24th. He departed for Chattanooga in charge of Companies B, G, F and K, traveling aboard a mail train. This group arrived safely near Chattanooga at sunset and bivouacked that night near the train station. After a short, dusty, and dirty march along the East Tennessee & Virginia Railroad, the companies joined the remainder of the regiment the next morning. At the new bivouac, a local lady, Miss Elvira Crews, baked biscuits, fried bacon, and cooked cornbread for the regimental staff.[133] For the hungry men, the thought of homemade flour biscuits and the sounds and odors of the bacon frying crisply, combined with the sweet smell of cornbread, was almost too much to stand.

During the next few days the men explored the new area, and the officers accomplished several administrative details. That afternoon Capers mustered the 46th Georgia for pay, always a pleasant duty. Afterwards, he and Adjutant Palmer rode up Signal Mountain and enjoyed the magnificent view of the west as the sun slowly settled behind the skyline. Two senior officers of the 24th spent the evening at General Gist's headquarters.[134]

As with other camps, the regiment was rife with rumors regarding the movements and intentions of the Federals. The 24th received news that the enemy was moving around the Cumberland Mountains toward the left rear of Bragg's army from a southwesterly direction. The generals expected that the enemy would strike State Road, the main road that ran between Atlanta and Rome and continued into Alabama. The Federals still maintained a large army in the northeast area that mustered 20,000 men. Campfire debates raged about Bragg's strategy to counter the threat. Some thought the general would leave a garrison at Chattanooga and meet the enemy at Rome, and others thought he would select yet another site to offer the Yankees battle. To counter the threat from the direction of Rome, Bragg assigned Walker's entire division as the reserve corps of the army, and Walker detached Gist's Brigade to Rome.[135]

The regiment left Tyner's Station on September 4 and arrived at Rome the next day. The men traveled light, leaving their baggage at Chattanooga in charge of the ill men who could not make the march. The regiment bivouacked near a little creek south of the road between Rome and the Alabama line, about two miles west of town. The remainder of the brigade stopped at Kingston. If a large force of the enemy appeared in the front of the regiment, the brigade's other regiments would come up rapidly.[136]

Reports were circulating that enemy cavalry was crossing the mountain passes at will, especially into Alabama. One report indicated that a large force of cavalry had crossed Sand Mountain and entered Wills Valley, moving toward Gadsden and the Coosa River. General Joseph Wheeler informed Gist that a large force had passed through Neils Gap, located in Lookout Mountain immediately in Wheeler's front! It perturbed the Staff of the 24th that Wheeler did not contest the Federal passages through the mountains. Still other reports claimed that General Rosecrans was making a move in the direction of Rome. If true, Bragg would change his front and meet Rosecrans at Rome.[137] Most of the reports were mere speculation that kept the men entertained and the regiment rife with rumors.

The bivouac at Rome was quite pleasant. The men even bathed in the creek and washed their shirts and breeches. For a change, they even wore reasonably clean clothes. Although still ragged, the clean clothes considerably improved the men's overall appearance. The regimental lieutenant colonel, accompanied by General Gist, attended church services on Sunday.[138]

By September 12, General Bragg evacuated Chattanooga and retired into Georgia.[139] Someone conjectured that if Rosecrans avoided giving Bragg battle, the Confederates had little chance of redeeming Tennessee. That report was not good for the morale of the men.

Preparing for a Federal raid, Colonel Stevens relocated the 24th to the Summerville Road, one mile from Rome toward Alabama on the western side of the road. The transfer alarmed the local people and many abandoned their homes for the protection of the eastern side of the river. The men grieved that the armies of the "wicked & powerful foe" destroyed the peace and security of so many families. However, General Gist received a fairly reliable report that the enemy was not east of Lookout Mountain.[140]

Buddy McGee was practically without shoes and reminded his parents to have his badly needed boots mended. He purchased an old pair of used shoes which he could wear until his boots arrived. One of Buddy's former girl friends, Mollie Harness, had recently married, and Buddy seemed unusually frustrated because his parents did not notify him about the wedding until afterwards:

I have come to the conclusion that you all have been
having such a good time eating pound cake...is why I have
not received any letters from you or mother.

Buddy McGee and M. H. Hall were very happy when they received a
"basket of provisions" from the homefolk, delivered by Cousin Mel Towns
when he returned from furlough. In his next letter, Buddy profusely thanked
his parents for the basket.[141]

The soldiers advised loved ones that the 24th would soon meet the
enemy. The soldiers eagerly expected the fight, because afterwards, the
Confederate army would be able to badger and follow the Union army as it
retreated.[142] Finally, General Bragg sent an urgent message calling for
Walker's Division to join the Army of Tennessee along the banks of
Chickamauga Creek. At 12:00 midnight, on September 16, 1863, the men
cooked three days rations and waited through the next day for
transportation.[143] However, the railroads were operating at capacity
transporting General James Longstreet's Corps to the battlefield.

On September 18, two days after receiving the call, Gist crammed 12
box cars with a portion of the brigade: the 24th, five companies of the 46th
Georgia, and the 8th Georgia Battalion, and started the journey. At 10:00 the
same morning, the train arrived at Kingston and there the soldiers waited
again as trains filled with Longstreets' Corps jammed the railroad. The
hapless soldiers of the 24th could only sit on a railroad siding and watch as
car after car filled with soldiers arriving from Virginia passed.[144] The
regiment waited at Kingston until 8:30 that night before the railroad was
finally clear. Only through pluck and determination did the officers arrange
transportation on the evening of September 18.

As darkness came that day, the stress of the situation increased. They
checked the locomotive and discovered that the fire was dead under the
boiler, and the engineer was no where to be found. Someone thought he had
gone to town intent on finding a place to sleep.

Colquitt, Stevens and Capers made a door-to-door search of the town,
finally locating the residence that housed the locomotive engineer. The man
was sound asleep, exhausted from continuously operating the trains
transporting troops to the battle zone. The engineer, roughly roused from his
slumber, at first claimed the engine was out of order, but the officers knew
better. Stevens put a pistol to the engineer's head and said he would blow
his brains out if the engineer did not return to his place of duty with the
train. Even that seemed not to motivate the engineer, who now pleaded
exhaustion and refused to take the responsibility for the lives of so many
soldiers in his spent condition.[145]

Learning that there was a railroad man in Company A who could
operate the train, Stevens detailed several soldiers to fire the boiler under
that man's guidance. They still needed the regular engineer there to give

directions and practically dragged the exhausted man back to the train cab. Finally, the steam was up, and to the echoes of the rebel yell, the men in the cab gave the whistle a long pull as the creaky train slowly pulled out of Kingston bound for Catoosa Woodshed.[146]

The train did not have enough room to transport Gist's entire brigade. The cars, packed tightly, carried the 24th Regiment, three companies of the 46th Georgia Regiment and the 8th Georgia Battalion. Those men had no idea of the fierceness of the battle or the high number of casualties that awaited the arrival of Gist's Brigade on Sunday at Chickamauga.[147]

Finally, the crowded railroad cars safely completed the all night long unpleasant journey as the train arrived at the Catoosa Woodshed at 10:00 the next morning, on September 19, 1863. The weather turned cold, the first cold snap of the season. The sky was overcast and the wind filled the railroad cars with flying dust that entered every pore and left the men gasping for air.[148]

General Gist, always cool, determined, and unperturbed, arrived at the Catoosa Woodshed with the lead regiment, the 24th. He retrieved his horse and raced forward to General Bragg's headquarters, seeking his brigade's assignment.

CHAPTER 5

CHICKAMAUGA AND CHATTANOOGA

Bragg's Army of Tennessee

The Federals eased into Chattanooga in the summer of 1863, practically without firing a shot. Major General Rosecrans' successful stratagem to occupy the city handily maneuvered Bragg's Army of Tennessee out of the city. Thus, for all practical purposes, the Confederate presence in the entire state of Tennessee ended. However, Rosecrans misread Bragg's withdrawal and decided the Confederate army could be conquered. The Union general divided his force into three wings and pursued the "defeated army."

Suddenly, Bragg realized that the Union army was scattered and presented the opportunity that he had been awaiting! On September 16, 1863, Bragg advised his troops that he would "force the issue" and published an order for battle preparing the army for "an immediate move against the enemy." The Army of Tennessee responded slowly to the call of its commander. By the time the Confederates moved into line of battle, Rosecrans had mustered his scattered troops and offered opposition along the banks of Chickamauga Creek. Determined, Bragg prepared for the battle.[1]

Reinforcements for Bragg's army poured into North Georgia from all directions. General Lee sent Longstreet's Corps from Virginia. General Johnston dispatched two full divisions of troops from Mississippi and planned to send more.[2] Bragg called for Gist's Brigade from Rome, where it had been luxuriating since it arrived from Mississippi, guarding the rear or extreme left of the Army of Tennessee.

As soon as the lead parts of Walker's Division arrived at Chickamauga, Bragg merged Walker and Loring's Division into an army reserve corps and named General Walker corps commander.[3] Part of Walker's Division arrived on the field in time for the battle of September 19. However, some regiments, including the 24th, did not arrive that day.

The men of Gist's Brigade eagerly expected to participate in the battle. However, the journey to the battlefield was long and difficult and fraught with delay. Colquitt, Stevens, and Capers finally accomplished the arrival of the regiment only through highly delicate negotiations, especially at Kingston.

The long and onerous train ride from Kingston ended at Catoosa Woodshed, a small place where the railroad tracks ended. As Gist's Brigade arrived, General Joseph B. Kershaw's South Carolinians, of Longstreet's

Corps, departed for the battlefield.[4]

Impatient for a battle assignment, General Gist advised General Bragg that his brigade was available and ready. Bragg used the brigade to "convey to the army a large ordnance train." As the quartermaster loaded the ordnance train, Gist's Brigade suffered through a long, dusty, windy, and cold day. Finally, at 10:00 that night, the loading was completed, and the men started an all night forced march to Alexander's bridge, 30 miles away. The brigade reached that place as the sun rose on September 20. While the general delivered the brigade's cargo, the physically exhausted men collapsed on the ground and grabbed 20 minutes sleep.[5]

When the ordnance train was taken care of, Gist found General Walker and advised him that the brigade was ready for the fray. As soon as the brigade arrived on the battlefield, Walker placed Gist in charge of Walker's Division, and Colonel Peyton Colquitt, the senior colonel, commanded the brigade.[6]

About 5:00 p.m. on September 19, Leonidas Polk, affectionately known as Bishop Polk, a senior lieutenant general, arrived on the battlefield. Bragg divided the army in two wings and placed Polk in command of the right wing and Longstreet the left. At first Polk assigned Walker's Division as support for General Patrick R. Cleburne, a rising star among the Confederate generals. Later Saturday night, Polk held Walker ready to support General Benjamin F. Cheatham's Division, if needed. In the meantime, Bragg wanted an attack to begin at daylight on September 20. The next morning Walker's Reserve Corps was ready, but no orders initiated the operation.[7]

Finally, the Confederate attack began between 9:00 and 10:00 Sunday morning. A vigorous assault by Generals John C. Breckenridge and Cleburne began on the extreme left of Rosecrans' line near Kelly's farmhouse. Soon, the battle started along the entire line. The Confederate attack met with only limited success, however, and the attack on the Federal left was in jeopardy. Both Breckinridge and Cleburne were withdrawing.[8]

As the Sunday attack began, Walker supported General D. H. Hill, a new corps commander, who had just arrived on the battlefield. About the time Gist arrived, Hill said that he wanted a brigade. Walker informed Hill that a brigade was available immediately behind him, but the general said that he "wanted Gist's Brigade" because he had "heard of that brigade." Walker responded that Gist's Brigade "had just come up," and that Gist commanded Walker's Division, and Colquitt headed the brigade.[9] Hill insisted on Gist's Brigade and gave his instructions for the operation directly to Colquitt.

Apparently Hill realized that the enemy was dealing severely with the Kentuckians and sent Gist's Brigade in support of Helm's Brigade.[10] Colquitt mustered only 980 men.[11] The 16th South Carolina Regiment and seven companies of Colquitt's own regiment, the 46th Georgia, had not yet arrived. In addition, the men were worn out after their night long march with only 20 minutes' rest. Undaunted, the men eagerly anticipated the battle.

Hill informed Colquitt that Breckenridge's troops were engaging the enemy and needed reinforcements. Since other troops were already in place, Colquitt did not reconnoiter the ground over which he was advancing, an error that would be nearly fatal for the entire brigade. The lull in the firing after the repulse of Breckenridge and Cleburne made the enemy's location uncertain. Colquitt advanced due west to support Tennessee Brigadier General Benjamin H. Helm's Brigade.

On the way into the forest, Colquitt met Helm's Brigade retiring in disorder after assaulting the bloody angle.[12] In that action, General Helm had fallen, mortally wounded, at the head of his troops. The remnants of Helm's Brigade cheered loudly as the fresh troops entered the forest. The little brigade was alone and unsupported as it moved forward to assault the strongly entrenched enemy.

The men were eager as they formed in line of battle and fairly leaped into the forest, advancing bravely yet fearfully. The 24th Regiment was on the left, the 8th Georgia Battalion in the center, and the three companies of the 46th Georgia Regiment advanced on the right. Dress was on the 8th Georgia Battalion, at the center of the brigade line. About 11:00 a.m., the advance started. In front of the 24th Stevens, Capers, Jones, and Palmer led the way. Capers' horse, Hardtimes, sniffed the battle and his rider had all he could do to restrain the little animal from bolting. Hardtimes probably remembered the wound that he and his rider received by the same ball at Jackson. Stevens and Palmer rode horses, but Jones was in front of the regiment afoot.[13] Perhaps Jones knew that riding horseback during battle offered a prime target and was, indeed, a dangerous practice.

The Federal main defensive line east of the main Chattanooga road ran a parallel course along the road opposite Kelly's house. North of Kelly's house, the left of the Union line turned sharply north at an angle with the main line and nearly reached the road.[14]

The Federal First Division, commanded by Major General Absalom Baird, occupied the position covering the angle in the Federal line. Baird placed the brigades of Colonel Benjamin F. Scribner and Brigadier General John H. King on the Union left of the angle and Brigadier General John C. Starkweather's Brigade on the right of the angle. King's Brigade guarded the extreme left of Baird's Division as well as the extreme left of the entire Federal line.[15] Baird formed his division in two lines behind a strong barrier of logs, fence rails and felled trees. King's Brigade consisted of United States Army regular troops, including the 15th, 16th, 18th and 19th Regiments. Baird's Division normally claimed three batteries of artillery, but on September 19 the Confederates disabled all but four artillery pieces. The Federals primed the remaining artillery pieces with double-shotted canister

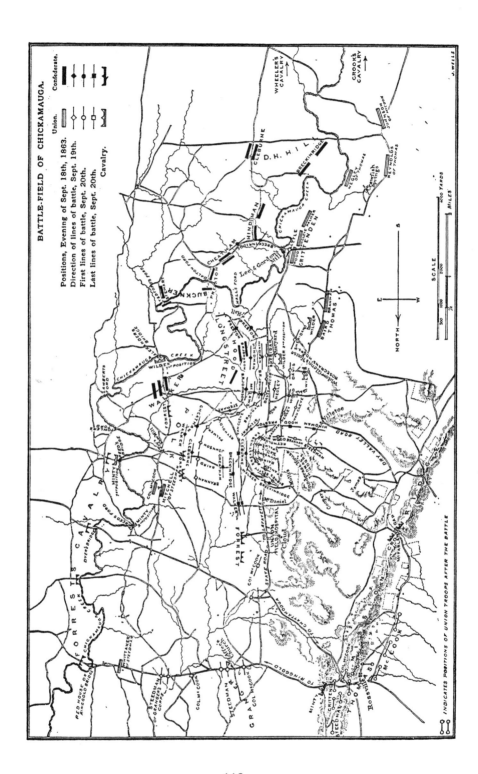

BATTLE-FIELD OF CHICKAMAUGA.

Positions, Evening of Sept. 18th, 1863.
Direction of lines of battle, Sept. 19th.
First lines of battle, Sept. 20th.
Last lines of battle, Sept. 20th.

INDICATES POSITIONS OF UNION TROOPS AFTER THE BATTLE

118

and were ready for action on the 20th.[16] Baird's Division was a formidable foe.

The Federals located their position on top of a slight hill or ridge, hidden deep in the woods. The ground sloped gradually downward toward the Confederate line. Throughout the night of the 19th Baird's men worked feverishly, strengthening the breastworks and increasing the natural camouflage of the position. The next morning, the Yankees awaited the Confederate assault behind a well-built, concealed barrier.

Earlier that morning, at 9:00 a.m., the left of Breckenridge's and the right of Cleburne's Divisions had struck the enemy as the two units moved due west through the woods. Helm's Brigade fell on King's Union brigade and General Lucius E. Polk's Brigade hit the angle guarded by Scribner's Brigade. The assault by the two Southern brigades was fast, furious, and bloody. Helm's Brigade made three separate assaults, and each time the enemy raked the flank as well as the front of the Tennesseans with a terrible fire. The brigade held their ground until General Helm fell, mortally wounded. Exhausted, the remnants of the brigade retired, and about the same time, Scribner repulsed Polk.[17]

Brigadier General David W. Adams' and Brigadier General Marcellus A. Stovall's Brigades of Breckenridge's Division advanced without resistance, moving past Baird's flank onto the Chattanooga road. The two brigades swung around the Union line and attacked Baird from the rear. In turn five brigades from the enemy reserve force pounced upon Adams and Stovall, and repulsed the two attacking brigades.[18] The situation that existed when Hill sent Gist's Brigade to support Breckenridge was extremely hazardous.

At the critical moment of contact with the enemy, Colonel Stevens rode his horse in front, on the regiment's right. Palmer and Capers rode on the left center and Jones walked in front of the left. Suddenly, without warning, the left of the 24th struck the unseen Federal line near the angle. So well was the enemy camouflaged that the 24th on the left of the brigade passed the angle without spotting the enemy until King's Brigade opened fire. The enemy's enfilade fire raked the brigade with musketry and all four pieces of artillery double-shotted with canister. The enemy canister and minié balls came from the left, the front, and even the rear, directly into the ranks of the 24th. When struck, the regiment recoiled and bounced off the Union line. Capers noted, "About 11 or 12 we began to catch it."[19] That was the understatement of the day.

Colonel Stevens, always resourceful, quickly galloped his horse, a blooded stallion, and positioned himself on the left of the regiment. He bellowed, "Change front forward on 10th company, by companies, left half wheel." Stevens' clarion voice rang out the command as if the regiment were on a parade field. The command started the movement that changed the front of the 24th so the men could face the well-camouflaged enemy.

Lieutenant J. Clarence Palmer, the adjutant, a graduate of The Citadel, youthful and full of life, rode beside Capers as the regiment executed the movement. Federal rifle balls were flying in every direction, and the Union artillery was steadily exploding lead death among the men. Noticing the amount of enemy fire that the regiment was sustaining, Palmer observed, "Gee Whiz, Colonel, ain't this hot?" Those words were barely out of his mouth when a minié ball struck him just below the left eye and exited through the back of his head.[20] Palmer died instantly. Some say that he was near enough that bits of his brain splattered Capers' uniform. Others reported that as he fell from his horse, Capers caught him in his arms. No one could do anything more for the lieutenant, and he was carefully and gently laid on the forest floor. The next day Captain Steinmeyer retrieved the body of his friend for burial.[21] There were not many more around like the gallant Palmer.

About the same time that the Union minié ball felled Palmer, Major Jones received a serious wound. An enemy ball passed through his right shoulder.[22]

Capers completed the movement on the left side of the line and told the men to lie down and utilize available cover, if any, on the forest floor. In the new position, the left of the regiment opened a "splendid fire," and Capers turned his attention to assist Stevens in bringing up the right. As those companies moved into position, the enemy rifle fire struck Stevens' horse, the second horse killed under him that day. A soldier handed the colonel the reins of Lieutenant Palmer's mare. As he mounted, a Federal ball struck Stevens and he sustained a serious wound to his back. With the colonel out of action, Capers and the other officers completed the parade-ground maneuver and finally placed the regiment's right on the new line. The men were in a prone position on the forest floor firing as rapidly as possible.[23]

Capers rode toward the right to determine why the brigade units on that side had not come up. He discovered that Colonel Colquitt had received a mortal wound as he brought up the 8th Georgia Battalion and 46th Georgia Regiment.[24] Colquitt fell from his horse in view of both Georgia units, and this stopped the movement in its tracks.

As Capers rode toward the right of the regiment, an enemy ball struck Hardtimes in the windpipe. The wound to the little animal was severe, but he would survive. About the same time, an enemy ball knocked Capers' sword out of his hand. A soldier from Company I retrieved it, and as Capers sheathed the sword, exploding canister struck midway on the scabbard. Within moments, an enemy ball struck Capers' left thigh and inflicted a severe wound. He handed command of the regiment to Captain Hill and almost immediately lost consciousness from the loss of blood. The wounded man next awoke in the "kind hands of a Kentucky surgeon," who saved his life.[25]

By that point in the battle, the enemy fire tore into the ranks of the South Carolinians and Georgians, stopping the brigade in its tracks. The men who were still alive and able continued firing at the enemy, albeit, irregularly.

The entire leadership of the brigade and the 24th Regiment was out of action. The surviving company commanders and other officers focused the men's attention on the enemy. Soon, reinforcements arrived and extricated the remnants of the brigade from the battle. The men retired and reformed the broken ranks in the rear of the other troops and prepared for the afternoon assault.[26] The heavy and unrelenting fire that Sunday morning lasted only about forty murderous minutes. When the brigade withdrew, the Confederate morning assault on the left of the enemy was over.

Captain D. F. Hill, commander of Company F and senior officer present, now commanded the 24th. The senior officer in the brigade, Lieutenant Colonel Leroy Napier, commander of the 8th Georgia Battalion, directed the brigade.[27]

General Gist, commanding Walker's Division during the battle that day, cited the brigade for its display of undauntable courage:

> The enemy now poured forth a most destructive and
> well-aimed fire upon the entire line...though it wavered and
> recoiled under the shock, yet, by the exertions of the gallant
> Colquitt, nobly seconded by Colonels Stevens, Capers,

Jones...other brave and true officers, order was promptly restored. For some twenty-five minutes, the gallant little band withstood the terrific fire and returned it with marked effect. It was here that the Colquitt fell mortally wounded while cheering on his command. In quick succession the iron-nerved Stevens and the intrepid Capers were seriously wounded...many others who deserve to live in their country's memory yielded up their life's blood. One-third of the gallant command was either killed or wounded...I would recommend to the favorable notice of the general commanding the distinguished gallantry of Col. C. H. Stevens, Twenty-fourth South Carolina Volunteers, who, besides being severely wounded, had two horses killed under him.[28]

There were many astute observations made about the battle that morning. Capers thought that early in the battle all the men who sustained wounds received them on the left side of the body, although Jones was wounded in the right shoulder. Afterwards, as Stevens, Capers, Jones, and Johnson rested in the division hospital, the wounded officers worried about the condition of the regiment:

Never was a regiment subjected to a more severe trial of its discipline than was our gallant regiment when it changed its front under that never-to-be-forgotten flank fire. Here we are, Col, Lieut Col, & Major, unable to do anything for the comfort of our noble command. Stevens has just said, "Well Capers, the men have been taught obedience...the captains that are left are equal to their duties & responsibilities. I have no fears for the regiment."[29]

General Hill earned some justifiable criticism for the handling of the attack on Sunday morning. While directing the attack, Hill, normally a fine military tactician, did not maximize the utilization of his forces. Possibly because of the denseness of the forest, he did not realize the magnitude of the threat that existed in front of his position. The general could not have known the strength of the enemy force when he sent Colquitt, with only about 980 men, into the woods in support of the Tennesseans. When Helm's Brigade came stumbling back with Helm dead, Hill should have realized the disastrous consequences that awaited a small or piecemeal commitment. There, readily at hand, stood the balance of General Gist's Division and the brigades of Ector and Wilson. Meanwhile, the "one brigade at a time attack" failed, as did all piecemeal and uncoordinated operations. When he directed the assault, the experienced Walker and Gist idly stood nearby with additional troops available. Yet, Hill for some unknown reasons gave his direction for the assault directly to Colquitt, the acting brigade commander.

The unsuccessful attack by Breckenridge and Cleburne on the rear of Baird's Division, no doubt, would have been successful with support. However, in Hill's defense, no one knew the location of the enemy reserve brigades on the Union left.[30] Hill was normally a brilliant field commander. However, at Chickamauga, he must have left his genius for military action in Virginia. He would pay for his mistakes, and, sadly, the Confederacy would lose the services of a highly capable, although "hard to get along with," combat leader.

The Confederate morning attacks did not carry the left of the enemy. However, the intensity of the morning actions caused the Federals to reinforce the position. The shift of several key divisions from the center and the right of the Federal line obviously weakened the rest of their line. The morning strikes aided Longstreet as he drove the fatal wedge into the Union line later that day.[31]

At 5:00 on Sunday afternoon, General Polk ordered an advance by the entire right wing which was closely coordinated with the left wing. The tightly coordinated advance aided the wedge that Longstreet drove into the heart of the Union line, earning the Confederates the bloody victory. Polk's Brigade of Cleburne's Division pushed through the woods and by hand-to-hand combat swept the angle defended by Baird's Federal Division that had given the 24th so much grief that morning.[32]

Before the afternoon attack, the seven missing companies of the 46th Georgia arrived after the long and dusty forced march from Catoosa Woodshed. With the added men, Gist's Brigade mustered about 1,400 men.

That afternoon, the 24th moved forward with Gist's Brigade and Walker's Division, closely coordinated with Polk's entire wing. Their route passed on the right of the position where the regiment had suffered so badly that morning. This time the 24th raced through the woods and reached the Chattanooga Road, capturing prisoners along the way. That night the troops bivouacked on the west side of the road. The men displayed an enthusiasm rekindled only after a glorious victory as rebel yell after rebel yell echoed from all sides of the battlefield.[33] Victory was wonderful!

That night, the troops felt a fair amount of apprehension as they bivouacked "with the dead and dying." After midnight, the 8th Georgia's picket commander received a false alarm that an enemy column was advancing for a night attack and called out the picket support, the 24th's Company A. Company A responded promptly and brought in several prisoners, but, most importantly, they quieted the apprehensions of the Georgians and prevented the edgy guards from firing into their own men.

Gist's Brigade suffered mightily that fateful day, losing a total of 336 soldiers. The gallant 24th suffered the most damage. They started the battle that morning with 410 men present for duty, and lost 169 officers and men either killed or wounded.

The men of the 24th were especially uneasy that night, principally because of the loss of the regiment's three senior officers. At first, many thought Colonel Stevens' wound was mortal, and the soldiers were thankful when they learned that the wound, although serious, was not mortal. The wounds of Capers, Jones, and Johnson were also serious but not dangerous.

Captain Hill noticed several others with minor wounds or injuries, not counted, among the troops that day. For instance, Hill himself sustained a slight wound to his chest and Steinmeyer suffered a slight injury or wound. Sergeant Major Dotterer received a slight facial wound. Few of the 24th's soldiers failed to receive an injury that day or show the results of a shell fragment or ball.[34] Captain Risher found seven bullet holes in his clothing and equipment and yet escaped without a scratch.

General Walker lauded the leadership of Colonel Stevens. Many leaders of the Army of Tennessee expected he would soon become a brigadier-general and command his own brigade. Walker wrote:

> And that the gallant Stevens of Gist's Brigade, who was
> severely wounded, from what I know of his capacity as an
> officer, from his gallantry on the field and for his devotion
> to the cause, would grace any position that might be
> conferred.[35]

The next morning Captain Steinmeyer directed a detail to search the battlefield for the bodies of missing comrades. Steinmeyer's first concern was for his friend, Lieutenant Palmer. The detail recovered and carefully transferred Palmer's remains to the rear for a proper funeral. The men also buried Color Sergeant J. J. Caminade and Sergeant William P. Ryan of Company A on the battlefield with appropriate honors.[36]

The Sunday morning battle was tough on the soldiers in the 24th, especially color bearers. Besides killing Color Sergeant Caminade of Company A, the Federals severely wounded Color Corporal Hollis. Lieutenant Joseph Evan Morgan of Company K saw the colors of a Georgia Regiment fall to the dust. He ran from his place of safety, picked up the fallen colors and held them high in the air. An observer recalled that "before the breeze could unfurl the colors over his head he was shot dead through the neck."[37]

The record does not reveal the regiment whose colors Morgan raised over his head. However, at that moment, only two Georgia units were positioned near the 24th, the 8th Georgia Battalion and the 46th Georgia Regiment. Most likely the colors belonged to one of those units.

Sergeant Morris Harris of Company A bore the colors of the 24th during the battle on the afternoon of September 20. Captain Hill noticed that Harris carried the colors proudly, with fortitude and acumen, and offered the sergeant the permanent position of regimental color bearer. However, Harris declined, preferring duty with his company.[38]

Captain Steinmeyer had loaned Sergeant Major Dotterer a silver-plated sword with an ivory handle that Dotterer proudly wore during the battle. Afterwards, Dotterer noticed that the hilt was gone, although the blade was still in its scabbard. An enemy ball or shell fragment had struck the sword and separated the hilt from the blade. The sergeant major had used a rifle during the battle that day. He did not miss the hilt until after the battle and could not recall when the enemy missile struck. The next day a member of the command found the hilt of the sword and displayed it as an enemy trophy at the regiment's headquarters. Dotterer saw the hilt, which he rejoined with its blade before returning the sword to its rightful owner.[39]

The warriors of the 24th Regiment were, for the most part, armed with short range, antiquated muskets. Only a few men were armed with the better Enfield rifles. During the retreat, the Union soldiers left an abundant supply of Enfields on the battlefield. The general gave the men of the 24th permission to gather sufficient rifles and arm themselves with the new and better rifles.[40] The Enfield rifles graciously supplied by the enemy elated the troops.

Gist's performance attracted the attention of many that day. Captain Steinmeyer paid a personal tribute:

> I want to pay humble tribute...to the cool, determined courage of Gen. Gist, whose bearing particularly struck us. He followed close up with our line, and stood, in contrast with many others in high rank, with self-possessed coolness and efficiency, from the first to the last.[41]

Word around the campfire was that Gist would soon command his own division. At Chickamauga his performance as commander of Walker's Division reflected his usually cool, competent, and capable demeanor.

The survivors of the battle had received little rest and almost no rations since departing Rome. The next day, Monday, September 21, 1863, the hungry and exhausted men received an issue of rations, of sorts. Late that afternoon the regiment marched in the direction of Chattanooga, but the march ended after nightfall in a "mysterious manner." The soldiers were passing through a neighborhood when they simply stopped and found a place to sleep until the next morning.[42]

The men bedded down while Captains Steinmeyer and Hill remained awake and on watch. They lighted a fire and crouched over the burning embers, soaking up the heat because the night was extremely cold. Suddenly, the cries of a woman in distress startled the two officers. Captain Hill, acting commander, proposed that he investigate the ladies' plight and Steinmeyer remain by the fire on watch. Hill soon returned with a tin plate of corn dodgers in one hand and a pitcher of buttermilk in the other. Captain Hill commented, "This is what a fellow gets for helping a lone woman." The lady became upset because the boys were burning her fence rails. Hill stopped the practice, and the lady generously rewarded him with the corn dodgers and buttermilk. The repast was the first meal of sufficiency that either had eaten since the regiment departed Rome.[43] They devoured the food with relish and cleaned the platter.

Vessie McGee missed the big battle. The surgeon finally realized the soldier was truly sick and assigned him to a convalescent camp at Atlanta. There he was "recuperating finely." His brother hoped Vessie would remain at the camp until he regained his full strength.

Supporting the needs of the soldiers was becoming increasingly difficult for the homefolk, although they continued to provide those items that were available. Mrs. McGee sent a greatly welcomed bundle of cakes to the boys that quickly disappeared. Buddy again reminded his mother that he still needed his boots, and beseeched her for a blanket and "a shirt or two."[44]

Before the battle, Capers presented Private William Rowlinski, Company A, with a small "Bible or Testament." On the front leaf Capers inscribed a personal note:

> To Private Wm. Rowlinski, with the wish of his Colonel
> that he may make as cheerful a soldier of the Cross as he
> does of his regiment.
> Ellison Capers Comd 24th S.C.V.[45]

The morning after the battle Stevens, Capers, Jones, and Johnson reposed in Walker's division hospital established in a tent near the battlefield. On September 23, the surgeons loaded Capers, Jones, and Johnson onto a railroad car with nearly 150 other wounded soldiers and started the uncomfortable journey to the College Hospital in Atlanta. The train arrived at Catoosa Woodshed at sunset and, after a brief pause, continued to Tunnel Hill and stopped there for the night.

The next day, September 24, Jones and Johnson were admitted to College Hospital in Atlanta. Capers met his brother there, and space being limited, the lieutenant colonel received permission to join his family. At 7:00 that same night, Capers, who was able to painfully move about on crutches, departed College Hospital en route for Oxford, Georgia, his brother's home. A few days later, Lottie and Little Frank joined their husband and father at Oxford, "Thank God!"[46]

Stevens, a strongly dedicated over-achiever, delayed his departure from the battlefield for an additional day so he could visit the regiment before beginning the tedious journey.[47] A determined individual, the "Old Fellow" nonchalantly arrived at the regiment riding a little clay bank horse. Officers and men alike cheered the colonel from all sides and extended a genuienly cordial and enthusiastic greeting. Even the soldiers from the brigade's other regiments joined the tumultuous welcome. Stevens, his arm in a sling and his body heavily bandaged, stoically rode down the line of the bivouac and spoke with the men. Stevens' visit was brief because his condition worsened and he was evacuated to the hospital. However, the colonel visited Captain Morgan, who had replaced Captain Hill as acting commander and talked with him about the affairs of the regiment.[48] The Old Fellow was tough.

Capers recuperated rapidly at Oxford. He visited College Hospital on November 9 and found Jones and Johnson still there, healing rapidly.[49] After the visit, he departed for South Carolina to complete his convalescence.

Three days after the battle of Chickamauga, the 16th Regiment finally obtained transportation from Kingston and rejoined the brigade, which was en route to Missionary Ridge.[50] When the 16th arrived, Colonel James McCollough, known to his men as "Old Beeswax," assumed command of the brigade. Gist still headed Walker's Division.[51] The brigade reached Missionary Ridge on September 23, 1863.

Captain Morgan became ill and reported to the hospital, and Captain Steinmeyer, an acting captain, assumed command of the regiment. There were only seven regimental officers, all lieutenants, present for duty. Steinmeyer felt extremely fortunate because he secured the services of Lieutenant Andrews of Company K as adjutant. Andrews was a highly intelligent and reliable officer who maintained the regimental paperwork and proved himself to be an excellent administrator.[52]

Shortly after the battle of Chickamauga, Bragg abolished the army reserve corps and assigned Walker's Division to Longstreet's Corps. The division remained with Longstreet until he departed for Knoxville in November. At that time, Bragg retained Walker's Division with the Army of Tennessee and assigned the division to Hardee's Corps.[53] Even after the departure of Longstreet, Bragg believed he could maintain a siege on the Federal force in Chattanooga until they evacuated the city. Time would prove that General Bragg was making a fatal blunder.

After settling into the bivouac at Missionary Ridge, the soldiers turned their attention to more ordinary activities. Buddy McGee visited many of his old friends who were with the Virginia troops. He thought that the uniforms of Longstreet's troops were in better condition and the eastern soldiers looked better than "we western fellows." Buddy asked his mother to tailor a pair of leggings if she had any "stout cloth" and broadly hinted, "If I had a pair of gloves, I could make good use of them." Vessie returned from the convalescent camp looking "fat and hardy!" In fact, Buddy noted that he looked as fleshy and healthy as he did when he initially entered the service. The illness and death of "Uncle Tillman," Sergeant David Tillman Bozeman, saddened the McGee brothers. In addition to losing a close relative, the boys depended on their uncle "like a father."[54]

For the first few days after the battle of Chickamauga, the regiment bivouacked on the slope of Missionary Ridge, but soon relocated to the valley floor. It rained almost every day and night during the first month after the battle. The rain was cold, and the conditions miserable for exposed men.

The siege of Chattanooga, with Lookout Mountain on the left
(*Battles and Leaders*)

The constant rainfall raised the level of the water in the valley until it covered the entire valley floor, and the men actually stood in water. For relief, the soldiers threw logs together to create crude platforms that would keep their feet out of the dampness.[55]

The excessive rainfall created severe living conditions for the troops, and many men became ill. The small creeks, known as branches, overflowed the banks and flooded the countryside. The swollen creeks prevented the ambulances from reaching the bivouac areas, and many could not receive badly needed medical attention. For the same reason, the commissary department could not provide critically needed food and supplies, and the men subsisted on meager rations. After the war Captain Steinmeyer, the acting regimental commander, recalled, "It is hard to conceive of more deplorable condition, of suffering and of destitution."[56]

The men had scored a magnificent victory at Chickamauga, and suddenly, at Missionary Ridge, they were living little better than "a dog's life." One soldier suggested that the men must "take it like cattle." Blankets were the only shelter the troops had from the rain and chill. At night, the men rested sitting up on the log platforms to keep out of the deep mud holes. The rain continued with little indication of abating. Rations became even shorter. In letters home, the men, with increased, intensity pleaded for boxes of provisions asking for "flour, bacon, dried fruit, and butter." The soldiers especially yearned for molasses "to satisfy a sweet tooth." Buddy McGee declared he would "tote a 25-pound sack of flour on a long march if someone would send him some."[57]

The men worried about the efficiency of the regiment. They thought it was "going down fast," because only two captains commanded companies, and the remainder were in the hands of the lieutenants and sergeants. The soldiers fretted because Colonel Stevens was still absent healing his wound. The tone of the letters to families asking for provisions continued to increase in intensity, which, no doubt, reflected the adverse conditions at Missionary Ridge. Instead of a "box of provisions" or specific items, the men pleaded for "something to eat."[58]

After so many dreary days of rain, cold, and misery that the men lost count, the sunshine finally appeared. The men greeted the "sweet smile of heaven" with rebel yell after rebel yell. The yell was more like a continuous shout that started on the right of the noble army at the top of the ridge and passed all along the Confederate lines. It traveled all the way across Lookout Mountain and entered the Federal lines. There, the rebel yell changed to a distinct huzzah as the exclamations of delight resounded along the entire Federal line. The shouting repeated its course and wavered through the Confederate line again and again.[59] Indeed, the break in the weather provided a time for rejoicing and happiness. The sunshine produced the first recorded "wave."

After a solid month of terrible weather conditions, the arrival of good weather relieved and reinvigorated the men. Finally, the 24th moved out of the water to a position on higher ground nearer Lookout Mountain. In the meantime, Captain Morgan, a senior captain, returned from the hospital and replaced Captain Steinmeyer as regimental commander.[60] Also, some of the other sick and wounded men, now recuperated, began returning from the hospital in Mississippi.[61]

One day in October, 1863, a pretty, petite, Georgia girl, dressed up in neatly fitting male clothing, applied for enrollment. She contacted a lieutenant assigned to General Gist's command who was collecting volunteers at Rome, Georgia. The lieutenant complied with her request, and she was ready for assignment. However, one of the men became highly suspicious of the individual's sex and gently suggested that the volunteer should wear "little ruffled petticoats" and engage in a more feminine occupation. He didn't believe that the "manual of the piece" was appropriate. As a result, General Gist interviewed the lady, and she confessed her sex. The lady said her home was at Gainesville, Georgia, and that her brother had been killed while he served in Virginia, and she considered it her duty to avenge his death. With the approval of her parents, the young lady disguised herself in male attire and applied for entrance into the army. General Gist openly admired her pluck and determination, but he could not allow one of her gender into the brigade and detailed a soldier to escort the lady to Atlanta. En route, she eluded the escort and Gist's Brigade never heard from the highly spirited lady again.[62]

One month after the big battle, the regiment detailed a burial team to visit the Chickamauga battlefield and inter unburied soldiers. It was a gruesome task, but the men were happy when they found no one from the 24th Regiment.[63]

General Bragg announced a policy that increased the recruiting incentive for soldiers - any man who recruited a new soldier would receive a 40-day furlough. The enticement provided an unusually exciting opportunity. The men wrote home soliciting their parents' assistance in finding anyone who was liable for the conscript law, interested in receiving a $50.00 bounty, and who might be induced to join the regiment. The homefolk eagerly searched for someone who would enlist on the behalf of a family member in service.[64] The mere thought of receiving a furlough instantly raised the men's hope.

At the campfires, the subject of recruiting a soldier for the army never ceased as a topic of discussion. Vessie McGee's words probably reflected the feelings of all the soldiers:

> It was intarely up to the folks at home. Ma, if you can get a recruit iney whares this winter for me, I want you to do it. I thik if you and Pa could emagen how glad I would bee to see you all you would get me a recruit if they could be raised, but it looks lack I will never get to go home. Soon crismus will be hear. I saw no plesure last Cristmas and it will be the cace agin I feeare. Pa rot that he was depending on Robert Ruse for my recruit but could not get him as he was engaged to the leegin. I recived a letter from Lewis the other day and he spoke of joining a co. at Columbia. If he could get in it and if not, he would come to our co. I think if I was in his plase, I would coume to our co., if I had to go atall. Ma, if you get this letter before Lewis leeves home I want you to try to get him to com to our co. When he had to go so he can bee wit us. Uncle Davy will treet him just lack a farther would.[65]

The men also constantly pressured the folks at home for a "box of provisions." Finally, the McGee family sent the boys a box with plenty to share with all ten men in the mess. Even with the food from home, Vessie McGee still could not stave off the ravages of dysentery and diarrhea. Although he was hale and hearty after his return from the convalescent hospital, Vessie soon became sickly again.

The soldiers' cravings for boxes from home never ceased. Besides a furlough, the subject of "a box of provisions" from home remained as the principal topic of campfire conversation, or written about in letters to the home folk. The men were elated when they learned that Corporal Bob Black, on furlough in Anderson, might return with a "number of boxes." When Bob finally arrived with the news that he had mailed the boxes from Columbia, the troops were sorely disappointed. "It killed their joy." The boxes would certainly arrive in "a few days," so the men still did not "give up hope or despair." One soldier wrote home and asked that a relative "bring the boxes in person." Desperate as the soldiers were for a furlough, someone would most likely enroll the visitor on the spot and enjoy a long furlough.

The price of food became exorbitant in camp. A messmate bought a handful of little potatoes for $1.00, and another bought a piece of pie the size of his hand for $1.00. Prices were outrageous indeed, considering most men earned only $11.00 per month.

Foragers were sent out every day seeking food, often traveling ten miles to "steal a hog." If successful, the foragers returned with a porker, "butchered it," and sold enough fresh meat to satisfy a mess (10 men) for a more reasonable price, one or two dollars. Vessie McGee sometimes foraged for supplies and always returned with good foodstuffs.[66]

In spite of the occasional receipt of a box from home, the soldiers constantly yearned for more. One man returned from furlough with a bottle of molasses that nearly drove his messmates crazy. None would ask for a share because that soldier would soon exhaust his small supply, too. One soldier asked his parents to send him a "jug of molasses" and that he would pay double the value of molasses sold at home. The homesick men yearned for the moment when they could sit down at the dinner table at home and eat a dish of cold turnips, hogs head, and corn bread. If they had such a meal, they would "not swap places with Gen. Gist."[67]

News of affairs at home often attracted the attention of the troops. One soldier became concerned because he heard "the negroes" had run away. The news was shocking. "They didn't have to work too hard anyway." Afterwards, he wished he was at home so he could "straighten them out."[68] The homefolk still did not divulge the true desolate conditions at home.

The men did not lose their sense of humor. There were jokes about such issues as "swapping places with General Gist" and other camp related nonsensical trivia. Often the conversation turned to food and what the home folks might eat for supper. Those conversations usually worked against them because it made the men even hungrier. One man allowed that he could eat "a Camp Meeting if I had it." The men could not forage, and only meager rations were available from the quartermaster. Unabashed, the soldiers reminded their parents that they depended on "something from the hand of my good parents."[69] The soldiers either asked about or mentioned the subject in practically every letter.[70] Perhaps, the idea "a box from home" was on the way may have, somehow, kept those brave soldiers going.

Chattanooga from the side of Lookout Mountain
(*Battles and Leaders*)

Captain Steinmeyer became the brigade picket officer and performed duty in front of Chattanooga. The picket detail was on the extreme left of the Confederate line, near the base of Lookout Mountain. The line extended along Lookout Creek and fronted a tannery and orchard, then extended into a more wooded area. Upon completion of his first tour of picket duty, Steinmeyer informed headquarters that the escape route was virtually impassable because of the overflowing streams prompted by the month-long rains. There were few bridges, and those that did exist were in poor condition. Steinmeyer reiterated that if the enemy advanced, the picket detail would be in danger of capture.[71] Steinmeyer's warnings were not heeded and on the day of the advance, the enemy captured the entire picket detail. When the attack came, Gist's Brigade had moved to another location and was no longer on picket duty.

At Lookout Creek, Gist's Brigade pickets relieved Jenkins' South Carolina Brigade of Longstreet's Corps. The men of the 24th happily greeted many old friends from home. That night Jenkins' Brigade attacked the Federals on Raccoon Mountain, and reports circulated that the enemy roughly handled the South Carolinians.[72] Perhaps one could find substance in the theory that the western Yankee soldiers were a more formidable adversary than the Easterners.

The Federal pickets on the other side of Lookout Creek were within easy speaking distance. Jenkins' pickets and the enemy reached an agreement and suspended firing at each other until required to do so by higher authority. In that event, each would give the other notice. The pickets also agreed to mutual use of the water from the stream that flowed between their respective lines.[73]

The first night the new picket was on duty at the stream, the Union soldiers proposed to renegotiate and continue the agreement. Sergeant J. R. Howell, of Company A, called the picket officer and reported the Federal proposal. Captain Steinmeyer trusted the enemy with no small amount of trepidation. However, he was reassured when he learned that the agreement involved the word of Masons. Sergeant Howell and the Federal officer on the other side of the creek were members of the fraternity to which Steinmeyer belonged. The picket officer also learned that he could exchange a plug of tobacco for a New York newspaper, a scarce object behind the Confederate lines. Both sides maintained the agreement as long as Gist's Brigade remained on picket duty along Lookout Creek.[74]

Neither side realized that the picket officers knew about the scheme and thought the leaders were opposed to communication between the two picket lines. The soldiers from both sides of the creek waited until the officers looked the other way, then, out of sight of military discipline, they "established free trade." The pickets met at the stream and the Confederates threw across tobacco for coffee or canteens and newspapers. Even with this friendlier aspect of picket duty the men considered the duty very heavy.[75]

Camp conditions remained appalling and no one expected improvement. Even with less rain and more sunshine, many soldiers were still sick because of the constant exposure and poor diet.[76] The surgeons were hopeful that better weather would reduce the sick list.

As the fall season approached, cold mountainous weather began to affect the comfort and health of the troops. The men appealed to the folks at home for warm clothing and blankets. Lieutenant Andrews, commander of Company K, made an appeal for blankets through *The Edgefield Advertiser*, the hometown weekly newspaper. The newspaper published the letter soliciting the generosity of the homefolk. Andrews reported that the men had lost their blankets in Mississippi during the preceding summer, and the men urgently needed warm blankets and bedding because the weather in Tennessee was decidedly colder. Andrews advised that the company quartermaster already had submitted numerous requisitions through army channels, and there were no blankets available. The lieutenant promised that General Gist would retrieve the blankets from South Carolina.

Lieutenant Andrews reminded donors to mark the name of the recipient soldier on the blanket or comforter. He also asked for a few blankets for distribution to the troops who did not have the benefit of family or friends.

Soon after the appeal, General Gist directed that the quartermaster sergeant "travel to Aiken, South Carolina, and pick up supplies."[77] No doubt, those supplies were the blankets.

As a result of inadequate clothing and blankets, the men suffered terribly from the weather, which turned cold earlier this year than usual. In addition to food and blankets, the men constantly asked the homefolk for various articles of warm clothing such as socks, gloves, coats, scarfs, and shoes or boots. As the weather improved, the men's health recovered, although the incidence of illness remained higher than usual because of the cold weather. Vessie McGee had a relapse of diarrhea, and once again "he was poorly."

The soldiers worried about fighting a big battle, and one informed his parents that the regiment was on a "minute's notice alert." If thrust into battle, the McGee brothers hoped their "lives would be spared" and trusted in "The Almighty." Vessie was terribly homesick and yearned for a furlough so he could visit his parents. He wrote home, "I never wanted to see iney body as bad as I want to see you."[78]

Some of the officers considered moving their families to nearby locations. Colonel Sprowl, an old friend of the Capers family, extended an invitation to the family to reside at the Sprowl's pretentious home near Cartersville, Georgia.[79] Capers did not accept Sprowl's invitation because of the proximity to the potential battlefield. Instead, he made arrangements for his family to reside with his brother at Oxford, Georgia, a safer distance away.

The soldiers who were recuperating from wounds at home or in the hospital eagerly looked for news about the regiment. On November 15, Steinmeyer wrote Capers, who was still convalescing in South Carolina, and narrated the exciting events taking place in the Army of Tennessee that affected the 24th. Steinmeyer, eternally optimistic, declared, "We are doing tolerable well in camp." A rumor reported the promotion of Capers to "full colonel," and the men anxiously awaited the truth. "Capt. Morgan commanded the regiment," and "Lts. Hamiter, Moore, Beckham, and Siegler were once more present for duty." Captain Hill was still at home recuperating, but Captain Roddey was better and would return soon. Company commanders worried because the regiment was without a "good doctor." Despite the circumstances, the regiment performed its duty well.

Steinmeyer went on to tell Capers that Longstreet's Corps had departed in the direction of Knoxville, and the 24th was reassigned with Walker's Division to Hardee's Corps. A rumor continued to circulate that Walker's Division might leave for Florida to intercept an invasion there. Presently, the Union troops began moving, but no one in the regiment worried about them.

After the rainy weather ceased, conditions in camp improved somewhat. Diarrhea still wreaked havoc, and food was still scarce. The food situation improved as the men used their ingenuity by employing some devious methods to find new sources of provisions. "Someone, no one knew who," of course, stole a hog and supplied the messes with fresh pork. The next morning the men had a good breakfast of fried pork and flour bread. The quartermaster issues improved and each mess received a small amount of flour twice each week. Even so, every mouth watered as the soldiers yearned for "a good old homemade biscuit." As usual, the men cajoled their parents and homefolk for "food or a box." The McGee brothers thought it strange that the men from the Edgefield company received boxes from home regularly, and the men in the Anderson company seldom received one.[80]

Many of the men had never seen the mountains until the regiment joined the Army of Tennessee. At first, the troops eagerly viewed the cloud wreathed mountain crests and thought that the countryside was beautiful. However, the men decided that the mountain climate caused the regiment's bad health, which would not improve as long as the regiment remained in the mountains. Vessie McGee's words must have echoed the feelings of every soldier in the regiment about the assignment at Missionary Ridge: "I never wanted to leave iney place much wurs than I want to leeve this [place, but] it does not look lack we will leeve hear soon."

In addition to picket duty, the men continued to construct fortifications. One day, as the men worked on a redoubt high on the mountainside, two enemy shells struck the works about two feet above the heads of the workers. Luckily the shells injured no one.[81]

On November 20, 1863, General Gist selected Buddy McGee as his new headquarters clerk. The new assignment pleased Buddy, because he would write official letters, something he enjoyed doing. Buddy soon voiced the opinion that General Gist was a very kind person.[82]

General Bragg noticed the arrival of General Sherman's forces at Chattanooga on November 20, 1863. Movement increased, and three days later he reported "unusual activity in the Union camps."[83] The Federals removed tents and two Federal brigades disappeared before the very eyes of the watching Confederates. However, the only increase in contact between the two armies was sporadic skirmishing. A strong Union force moved up river presumably with intentions of launching an attack. Bragg countered the threat by assigning General Hardee responsibility for defense of the Confederate right. He bolstered Hardee's Corps with the divisions of Cleburne and Walker. Since Walker was still on furlough, Gist commanded Walker's Division.[84] Gist surveyed the situation and told his superiors that the purported Yankee attack on the right was a mere feint, and the serious attack would come toward the Confederate left and center. As usual, Gist was correct, and as soon as Gist's Division departed the Confederate left, the enemy assaulted General Carter L. Stevenson's Division. Stevenson reported that the enemy flanked him, forcing him to fall back on Missionary Ridge. He believed he could have held the mountain if Bragg had retained

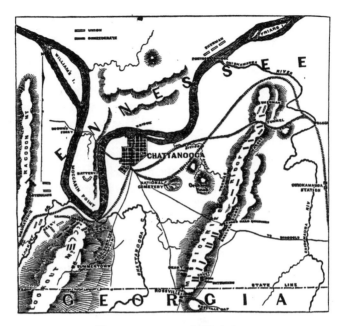

Chattanooga and Vicinity
(Lossing, *The Civil War in America*)

Gist's Division on the left. Since Lookout Mountain was an easy prey, the enemy wasted little time launching a major frontal assault on Missionary Ridge.[85]

On the afternoon before the battle of Missionary Ridge, Gist's Division made a hasty shift and joined Hardee's Corps on the Confederate right. The 24th made another all-night forced march, reaching the new position early the next morning. The regiment immediately formed in line of battle across the tunnel where the East Tennessee and Georgia Railroad passed through Missionary Ridge.

General Cleburne assumed a position across Missionary Ridge on the right of Gist's Division at the extreme right of the Confederate line. Upon reaching the position, Cleburne's Division passed in front of the 24th Regiment. An enemy division was already in line of battle opposite the position, and another was rapidly crossing the Tennessee River. Cleburne greeted the enemy's vigorous advance shortly after he occupied the position.[86]

Cleburne eventually faced a large force of the enemy that included Major General Jefferson C. Davis' Division, three divisions of Major General Sherman's veterans brought from Vicksburg, and Major General O. O. Howard's (Eleventh) Corps.[87] Cleburne held the Federals at bay, directed counter charges and captured eight stands of colors.

136

Gist's Brigade was on the right of the division, and the 24th was on the right of the brigade with Company A in its usual position on the regiment's right. The right of Company A rested on the left of Cleburne's Division. Cleburne himself spoke with Steinmeyer and asked the name of his command. When told, Cleburne remarked, "My command joins yours (Walker's Division)."[88]

The men of Walker's Division were in a perfect location to witness the blue army assault Missionary Ridge. The Federal attack came in columns seven lines deep that charged as many as a dozen times. Captain Steinmeyer was impressed with the scene that developed before his eyes:

> We witnessed the grand spectacle of the attack on Lookout
> and Missionary Ridge...It was a sight...hard to describe or
> forget. The great host, marshalled out in such perfect and
> grand style, was before our eyes, soon...on the tracks of
> Bragg's army.[89]

The Confederate line repulsed every attack. Finally, Brigadier General Arthur Manigault's Brigade gave way, and his men ran like "wild horses" from the center of the line.[90]

Cleburne's Division caught the brunt of the enemy advance on the Confederate right.[91] Late that afternoon, Gist's Division came under enemy fire and the men returned it vigorously, but Gist did not receive the same attention accorded Cleburne. Some companies of the 24th joined in the defense of Cleburne's line to the right, enfilading the Federal attack. As Gist rode forward and reconnoitered the situation, his horse was killed. This was the second mount that the enemy shot from under Gist; he recently had lost another mount at Chickamauga.[92]

Colonel McCollough, Old Beeswax, commanded the brigade. During the battle, McCollough felt extreme trepidation about riding his horse in such an exposed position. General Gist patiently counseled the colonel that he should remain mounted. McCollough, an exceedingly brave Confederate warrior, did not enjoy presenting such an inviting target for the enemy nor the pressure of leading troops into a hot battle. On other battle fields, commanders often advised officers for safety reasons not to remain mounted during the battle.

As darkness fell, the men of Cleburne's and Walker's Divisions were exultant because they thought they had won another victory. However, the exultation didn't last long. The men soon learned that Manigault's Brigade, located in the center of the line, had given away, and the Confederates, including Hardee's Corps, had begun the skedaddle from Missionary Ridge.[93]

As the day ended, the 24th moved by the left flank and halted atop Missionary Ridge. Captain Morgan, the acting regimental commander, threw out Company A as a skirmish line about fifty yards in front of the regiment. Morgan then received confirmation of the terrible news that Bragg's line was broken, and the Federals were advancing rapidly directly in front of the 24th. The order came, "Let no one pass." However, just before the line closed three Confederate horsemen, anxiously seeking their unit, galloped down the road and proceeded along the ridge. The men of the 24th opined, "The three horsemen have gone up the spout." More than a year later Steinmeyer met a prisoner of war at Johnson Island and concluded that the man was one of those who had passed through the regiment's line that fateful night. Without warning, the horsemen had ridden directly into the arms of the enemy.[94]

Bragg signaled the Army of Tennessee to withdraw. He assigned Cleburne's Division as rear guard for Hardee's Corps and Gist's Division as rear guard for Breckenridge.[95] Bragg was in an extremely bad humor and pronounced Breckenridge drunk. He directed that Gist personally take charge of the inebriated corps commander even if he had to load Breckenridge into a wagon and haul him off the field. Bragg continued, "Under no circumstances allow him (Breckenridge) to give an order."[96]

Early the next morning, Brigadier General George Maney's Brigade of Tennessee troops guarded the division's rear as Gist's Division was withdrawn. During the day, an enemy ball seriously wounded Maney, and the stretcher bearers evacuated the general to the hospital. Gist then threw his own brigade out as rear guard in replacement for Maney's Brigade. The men of the 24th successfully disputed every foot of ground until the entire division slowly and surely made its way across Chickamauga Creek near Graysville.

As a part of the rear guard, the 24th brought up the division's rear. After crossing the creek, the men burned the bridge. By the time the division attained the safe side of the creek, night had fallen. The regiment established a skirmish line near the creek and began a night march to safety.[97]

The line of retreat followed the eastern side of Chickamauga Creek. A sharp bend in the creek forced the division to again cross the creek over a railroad trestle and proceed on the western side. A mile-and-a-half farther, the division would recross the creek utilizing yet another railroad trestle. The wagon train had already crossed the final trestle and was well on the way to Ringgold.[98] However, darkness caught the men still on the western side of the creek slowly plodding toward the final trestle.

Suddenly, several artillery blasts and multiple volleys of musketry interrupted the peaceful march. As quickly as it began, it stopped, and the men apprehensively greeted an eerie calm. A column of enemy troops had intercepted the Confederate line and occupied the trestle ahead as well as the one behind. The enemy captured Lieutenant Beauregard, son of the general, and three of the four remaining artillery pieces. In addition to the artillery, the Federals captured three companies of the 16th Regiment.[99]

138

Because the Federals might again intercept the Confederate line, Gist searched for another route across Chickamauga Creek. A local farmer, intimately familiar with the area, informed the general that one mile away there was a spot that the men could wade the river. The 24th brought in the skirmishers and hastily turned toward the ford.[100]

Guided by the farmer, the men rushed toward the ford over a narrow country road that extended along the bank of the East Chickamauga River. It ran up and down the river bank, which at times was so steep that it practically prevented passage. The soldiers did not dawdle. As they raced to the ford, the final artillery piece stalled and blocked the narrow little road. Gist quickly ordered it to be thrown into the river.[101]

For the safety of the division, the general determined that the men should wade the cold and dark water creek as rapidly as possible. The men did not especially favor the wade, but there was no other means of crossing the river to safety. The soldiers did not even consider removing their clothing. There was no time for such ease. Gist and Morgan led the way across the creek, and the men of Gist's Brigade entered the water, so deep that it reached the chests and arm pits of the men. When the waders became top heavy, some of the smaller men stumbled and were assisted by the taller soldiers. The regiment's only losses while fording the river were a few accoutrements.[102]

The men emerged from the creek soaking wet and freezing cold. An observer recorded, "They looked and felt like half-drowned dogs." During the night, the wet clothes froze solid. Private Isaac Carter, Company E, soon entered the hospital suffering from pneumonia, surely a result of that freezing cold wade.[103] He remained a patient in the hospital until his death three months later. The men of the 24th were tough, but not that tough.

General Gist insisted the men ford the creek as quickly and silently as possible and personally supervised the crossing of the entire division. However, when Maney's Brigade arrived, the Tennesseans defiantly took the time to remove and fold their clothing into compact bundles. The men held the bundles out of reach of the water as they waded the river. The Tennesseans arrived on the other side patted themselves dry, and put on their dry clothing, refreshed from "an enforced bath." One of the soldiers of Maney's Brigade suddenly realized that he had left his breeches on the other side of the creek.[104] No one mentioned which was more uncomfortable, "no breeches or frozen breeches."

After fording the creek, Company A threw out skirmishers, who advanced as a forward scouting party, alert for parties of the enemy. As the day was breaking, the division reached the railroad track near Ringgold without further interference. Cleburne's Division turned on the enemy at Ringgold and reeled the advancing enemy backwards.[105]

During the retreat, the regiment's sick men were captured. They had been dispatched toward the rear, shifting for themselves. They had walked six or seven miles and found that it was necessary to lie down beside the road and rest. The ailing men remained there until dark, when the advancing Federals captured the entire group.[106]

It was a tough day for the regiment. The battle had struck that morning before the troops ate, and no food was available until the regiment arrived at Ringgold.

The retreating wagon train also experienced a tough time. One driver, Buddy McGee, started the day with two wagons and ten mules. There were numerous mud holes along the route, and one of the wagons became mired at least 50 times. Since the retreating division was close behind the wagon train, the drover found it necessary to wade into the mud holes and extricate the mired wagons by pressing the wagon wheel with his shoulder. The drover did not like wading into the mud holes so frequently, but, under the circumstances, he did not hesitate. Finally, one wagon was wrecked and later two mules bogged down so deeply in a mud hole that only the animal's heads emerged. The drover reported the condition of two more of the completely spent mules. "I turned them loose to die if they saw proper."[107]

After the war, Captain Steinmeyer recorded that during the retreat Cleburne's and Walker's Divisions were the only "organized part" of the Confederate army. Steinmeyer quickly pointed out that his opportunities for information were narrow, and he could report only those issues that he personally observed and experienced. However, he reassured that the 24th Regiment was not a part of the line that broke, "Rest easy about that!"[108] Actually, the lines of four divisions, Cheatham's, Walker's, Stevenson's and Cleburne's, all constituting Lieutenant General Hardee's Corps did not break that day.

General Gist acquitted himself quite well again. An observer eloquently described the indomitable Gist:

> The whole rear guard was placed under the command of the noble, generous, handsome and brave General Gist, of South Carolina. I loved General Gist, and when I mention his name tears gather in my eyes...he was the handsomest man I ever knew.[109]

Others evaluated General Gist's performance in equally favorable terms:

> Several of the Confederate commanders, however, had either made their reputations or added luster to distinguished careers. States Rights Gist, who... commanded Walker's Division in the battle, raised himself greatly in the esteem of the army.[110]

The battle of Missionary Ridge was over. General Bragg provided General Cooper a most discouraging report on November 30, 1863, deploring the action of his men who had allowed the break in the Confederate line. However, he recognized several of the Generals (Hardee, Cleburne, Gist, William B. Bate, Alfred Cumming, Edward C. Walthall and Lucius Polk) for coolness, gallantry, and successful conduct. Bragg especially mentioned the behavior of Cleburne and Gist during the retreat, and recommended that the Congress recognize Hardee and Cleburne.[111]

The Confederate Congress passed a resolution recognizing Generals Hardee and Cleburne for gallant duty performance. Hardee related to his friends, "I had a handsome fight on the right & for which I have received more credit than I deserve. Such is life."[112] General Hardee was extremely modest.

By now, word of the Confederate disaster spread all over the South, and citizens were heartsick. Colonel Stevens was still on convalescence furlough visiting his mother and sister at Spartanburg, South Carolina, when he learned about the Missionary Ridge skedaddle. Stevens feared the worst for the regiment because of its location on the left center of the Confederate line atop Lookout Mountain. The colonel worried that perhaps the line had broken in the very spot occupied by Gist's Brigade. He did not yet know that Walker's Division had been relocated before the battle started. Stevens expressed his concern for the safety of the army, especially Gist's Brigade and the 24th Regiment on November 28, 1863:

> I am wretchedly uneasy at the news from the army. If Bragg had fallen back voluntarily to Chickamauga, I should not have thought it as a very bad move, since he already had all the advantage of his position on Lookout, but to have been forced back is to my mind very disastrous. Still...he can hold his present position, and cover Long-street's line of communication all may be well...I am very anxious and uneasy about the brigade and regiment...I am miserable until I can hear from them.[113]

General Bragg resigned as Commander of the Army of Tennessee on December 2, 1863, and General Hardee became interim commander, modestly declining permanent command of the Army of Tennessee. He wrote, "I respectfully decline the command if designed to be perma-nent....[I]...will cooperate [with whatever] officer the President may select."[114] General Hardee publicly announced his preference to be General Joseph Eggleston Johnston.

In the meantime, the interim commander published a circular announc-ing the change and reassured the troops, "Let the past take care of itself; we can and must secure the future."

The condition of the Army of Tennessee immediately improved as the interim commander located supplies and provided sustenance for the troops. He replaced lost equipment, artillery, and accouterments and rounded up stragglers, increasing the army's strength by 6,000 troops. Hardee happily turned over an army of 36,017 troops to Johnston, who arrived at Dalton, Georgia, on December 26, 1863.[115]

By December 15, 1863, the remnants of the Army of Tennessee and the 24th Regiment commenced preparing winter quarters at Dalton.[116]

CHAPTER 6

A REGENERATED ARMY

Johnston's Army of Tennessee

The Army of Tennessee crept slowly into winter quarters suffering from the pangs of a severely stunned force. It quickly rebounded with the assignment of a new commander and the institution of judicious and competent leadership.

On December 3, 1863, Walker's Division mustered 3,999 effectives, on December 26, it had 6,978, and, by the end of the year, Walker counted 7,212 effectives.[1] The return of stragglers and men wounded at Chickamauga was primarily responsible for the startling increase in manpower.

The 24th Regiment kept pace with the division. Captain Morgan mustered nearly as many soldiers as Colonel Stevens counted at the battle of Chickamauga. By December 14, 1863, the regiment totaled 403 effectives. Only 342 men had arms. Every man held 35 rounds of ammunition.[2] After Chickamauga and the hardships of Missionary Ridge, the regiment was fortunate to survive. Yet, the 24th was in reasonably good condition and improving daily. In December, 1863, Stevens, Capers, and Jones, the regimental field grade officers, were still absent, convalescing from their wounds, but they would return soon.

General Johnston was named commander of the Army of Tennessee in mid-December, 1863. Unfortunately, Johnston considered the assignment a personal victory over the high command of the Confederate government. He immediately started raising morale and improving the soldier's spirit, an endeavor in which he was completely successful. However, Johnston did nothing that would foster understanding or improve his relations with the Confederate hierarchy, even for the benefit of the army.[3]

By the first of January, the men's morale was much improved since the skedaddle from Missionary Ridge, but the soldiers still lacked the confidence that a victorious army needed. For instance, there was a need for more harmony among the officers, and similar dissatisfaction was expanding among the men. Although the officers and soldiers considered General Johnston entirely acceptable, the men held a pervasive feeling that the President was indulging his "pet army" in Virginia. Minor issues contributed to the anxiety, petty jealously, and rivalry, especially among the officers.[4] The situation changed dramatically as the new commander, General Johnston, adroitly earned the confidence of officers and men alike. By early

January, Johnston visited the command of every general officer. Major Manning, the general's aide, allowed that not one would exchange him, "even for General Lee."[5]

The new commander intuitively understood what actions would rejuvenate the Army of Tennessee. On the first clear day after his arrival, Johnston inaugurated his program of field visits. He rode into General Stevenson's Division unannounced and unheralded, but the identification of the distinguished visitor spread rapidly. The men appeared from the various chores of camp life curious about the new general, and, as they massed together, General Johnston stopped and visited. He took off his hat each time a man saluted. As Johnston kneed his horse and rode away from one of the regiments, a soldier loudly exclaimed his observations: "Look-a-here boys, that's Old Uncle Joe. He ain't proud." Soon the general became known, and when he rode by the soldiers removed their hats, waved and cheered.[6]

On January 23, 1864, the *Charleston Mercury* reported the level of improvement in the Army of Tennessee: "Officers and men from the army encamped near Dalton state the conditions and spirit of our troops was never better than at present...remedied by the appointment of General Johnston..."

On the same day, the *Mercury* offered additional evidence about the improvement in the Army of Tennessee: "The chief feature...is that the troops are reenlisting."

The newspapers specifically reported that Tennessee and Kentucky troops were reenlisting for the war. They never mentioned that the men of the 24th had enlisted for the war two years earlier, while undergoing camp of instruction near Charleston.[7] The 24th was the first regiment of South Carolinians that enlisted for the duration of the war when it mustered, an accomplishment for which the men of the regiment received little credit.

Several weeks later, the Charleston newspapers again lauded the improvement in the Army of Tennessee: "General Johnston...in ninety days he has transformed this army...It is a regenerated army."[8]

The same edition described the dire consequences of the new discipline in the army:

> General Johnston has two modes of stopping desertions.
> One is by liberal furloughs, allowing all to go home by
> turns. The other is by the (code)...death to deserters.[9]

During the entire war, the Confederate army did not execute a single member of the 24th Regiment as a result of sentence by court martial.[10]

By January 27, 1864, General Johnston completed the grand rounds of the Army of Tennessee and identified Gist's Brigade as the "best in the army." He reported, "They look as if they had a man at their head who knew how to do his duty...who took an interest in his men."[11]

Johnston complimented the brigade and asked that others emulate

144

General Gist's example. The general had good reasons for the glowing recommendation. The camp of Gist's Brigade radiated the appearance of a regular village. Their huts were tight and snug, situated on wide streets neatly laid off and beautifully maintained. General Gist clothed and shod his men well, and adeptly drilled the troops in military discipline and tactics. In addition, the brigade received extensive recognition for its admirable conduct covering the retreat from Missionary Ridge.[12] The 24th Regiment contributed its full share toward earning the approbation received by the brigade.

As the men became adjusted to the rigors of winter quarters, the McGee brothers suffered excessive uneasiness. The box that fellow soldier Bill Black had mailed from Columbia in November still had not arrived. Anxiously, Buddy thought that when the box did arrive, the contents surely would be spoiled and inedible. The McGee brothers constantly begged their parents for boxes of provisions and essential items of clothing.[13]

Throughout the army experience, toothache was a malady that affected the well-being of many men. Private Vessie McGee had a toothache, and the pain was excruciating. His top lip swelled double its normal size, and the surgeon and the dentist suggested that he "draw four of my front teeth." Vessie would not consider having the teeth pulled, preferring to have the "teeth plugged."[14] Vessie located a dentist who would do the work for $80.00. The young soldier called on his father for some money, "If he had any to spare." Finally, Vessie learned that he needed "nine plugs" or fillings, which would cost $125.00.

One day Vessie received joyful news from home. His father had discovered a young man confronted with the conscript law who preferred to enlist for an assignment with the 24th Regiment. The news delighted Vessie - all that was needed was for his father to fund the recruit's transportation. Vessie shared his feelings with his parents: "I never want to go home as bad in all my life as I wan to go now. I hope he will come without fale."[15]

If the recruit reported and enlisted, Vessie would receive one of the highly coveted 40-day furloughs. Good news like that could possibly even cure the toothache. Realizing that Vessie was terribly homesick and desperate for a furlough, Mr. & Mrs. McGee had exerted every effort and expense to find someone who would join the army. Finally, the recruit, a man named "Taler," reported, but he could not muster until he presented his papers, which could not be found. Finally, Vessie reluctantly realized that Taler would never muster. The young soldier fretted about the trouble and expense he caused his parents and apologized profusely about the outcome of the affair. Since Taler had no money, Vessie thought his father should collect repayment of the transportation money from Taler's family.[16]

Eventually, General Johnston changed the rules for granting furloughs and authorized one furlough for every ten men present. The companies each selected the men for a furlough by holding "a public name drawing." Neither Vessie nor Buddy gained a furlough during the first drawing. However, the brothers were optimistic they would receive a furlough. Their chances were now as "good as anyone else's."[17]

At Dalton, the winter of 1863/1864 was extremely cold. The cold weather gave the soldiers another outlet for their energies besides starting and repeating rumors, and gossiping. The men, especially the Tennesseans, enjoyed snowball fighting. The contests with snowballs usually began between the men of the same company and regiment. On one occasion, the game elevated and became a contest between the Tennesseans of Cheatham's Division and the Georgians of Walker's Division. The two South Carolina regiments of Gist's Brigade defended their division and entered the contest on the side of the Georgians. The Tennesseans "captured Captain Steinmeyer, Colonel Capers, and Colonel Stevens," who were held as "snowball prisoners."[18] Finally, the snowball battle involved several thousand men. The struggle was as fierce and furious as a battle with the hated Yankees. The air at times was literally white with snowballs. Colonel (later General) George W. Gordon related that more than a hundred snow balls struck him during the melee. After a severe battle, the Tennesseans won. The victors asked for another battle, but the Georgians declined. The Tennesseans, who were more experienced with snow than their former opponents, did not hesitate and started snowball fighting among themselves again.[19]

The rations for the soldiers improved, but food was still somewhat scarce and lacked quality. Many of the men considered that the food was as good as the country could provide. Meals for the troops usually consisted of cornmeal and bacon, and an occasional ration of poor quality beef. The typical bill of fare for breakfast was cornbread and gravy, for dinner or lunch, cornbread and bacon, and for supper or dinner, mush and water. A rumor prevailed that General Johnston issued short rations in camp and fed the men well during the campaign. If true, the soldiers thought it a wise policy.[20]

It always made the soldiers feel better when they received a letter from home. A messmate received a box from home, and "they were living high" when the men ate fried peas for dinner. Almost as good as a letter from home, a new chaplain arrived and was assigned to the 24th. The troops were happy to hear "some good preaching in camp."[21]

As soon as weather conditions permitted, General Johnston reviewed the entire Army of Tennessee. This was the only time the soldiers witnessed the spectacle of 50,000 soldiers collected in one body. Johnston later passed the word that results of the review were very satisfactory.

Training in tactics and discipline of the command included sham battles. General Hardee decided to conduct such an exercise for the training of his corps and invited many citizens and high ranking dignitaries to "observe the show." The general canceled the first one because of inclement weather. General Walker recorded that he had no time for such play:

> The great sham fight did not come off. It was to have taken place yesterday. The cargo of females who came to witness it were disappointed. Sorry on their account, glad on my own for I have no fancy of being shot at for the amusement of anybody.[22]

A few days later, Hardee finally conducted the sham battle for his corps.[23] The 24th Regiment participated.

During winter quarters, General Gist located his brigade, including the 24th Regiment, along Spring Place Road, about two miles east of Dalton, Georgia. In December 1863, the men were busy building crude huts for winter quarters. The huts were made of rough logs and daubed with mud, which sealed out much cold air. After the men completed the huts, the cabins were quite comfortable and served as excellent protection against the elements. The soldiers eagerly anticipated moving into a hut so they could keep dry. Until the men completed the crude huts, they had little shelter from the inclement weather that was already cold and miserable.[24] The men built bunks raised about two feet off the floor around the sides of the cabins. The bedding consisted of one blanket per man. When the weather turned extremely cold, the men tore down the bunks and slept on the bare ground, two men sleeping together. The two soldiers placed one blanket underneath and covered with the other and rose several times during the night to warm themselves by the fire.[25]

Private Elijah Keese, of the Edgefield Light Infantry, Company I, 24th Regiment, was a regular correspondent with his hometown newspaper. He often presented news articles that sparked the home folks' interest and tuned their imagination into the vibrancy of camp life at Dalton. He wrote about many subjects concerning the camp, including the leadership of the generals and conditions that existed in the camp:

> Our cabins are the perfection of comfort, when compared with the way we had been living in the open air like the birds and beasts of the forest. This housing of the men has added much to their health, strength, and efficiency. There is novelty too about our lowly dwellings. After nightfall, when the stars set each upon his ruby lights gleaming from the crowded tenements, looking for all the world like some large and beautiful city. In one street, you hear the cheerful voices saluting the war; over in that regiment yonder, the boys are boisterous, whooping and yelling as if charging a Yankee brigade revives the associations of home...hark! What burst of harmony is that which charms every audi-

tor...makes the sweetest echoes of the evening? It is the Nashville band discoursing eloquent music from the magic notes of the "Anvil." Entranced you listen and forget for a moment that the land is deluged with blood and tears. The gay scenes incident to a state of peace and prosperity float through the imagination...The stern command...right dress... Attention to roll-call! ...recalls you to the painful present and causes you to recollect that a grim visage war has not yet smoothed his wrinkled front. All the men and officers seem to be glad that Gen. Johnston commands the Army of Tennessee....has the most expressive countenance I ever beheld...I saw this lion sit upon his horse for hours while the veterans of our army marched before him in serried ranks to the sound of martial music.[26]

Meanwhile, General Johnston decided the use of privately owned tools to be inefficient and established a centralized system for maintenance, preservation, and issue.[27] The men of the 24th Regiment, who mostly owned their own tools, didn't especially like the change. However, under the new system, every soldier had access to the equipment that was available.[28]

Even with Missionary Ridge in recent memory, the men still regarded the army as having done its duty. The soldiers expected heavy fighting in the spring and the battles would determine if they would become "freemen or vassals of the north."[29]

In February 1864, General Cooper in Richmond asked General Johnston, who badly needed commanders, whether he desired the assignment of Lieutenant General John Bell Hood as a corps commander. Johnston responded, "Lieutenant-General Hood is much wanted here."

General Hood had a reputation as a fearless fighter and a brave and chivalrous Confederate general. He had one leg amputated on the battle field at Chickamauga and one arm hung uselessly in a sling as a result of a combat wound at Gettysburg. Such physical disability would have incapacitated a less indomitable man and even to General Hood, it proved a terrible handicap for field service. Later General Johnston experienced many problems with General Hood, and he lived to regret agreeing to General Hood's assignment. In all probability, General Hood would have been assigned to the Army of Tennessee whether Johnston agreed or not.

A similar situation existed when Major General James Patton Anderson was promoted to Major General and reassigned to Florida in January 1864. Anderson's departure created a major general vacancy in the Army of Tennessee, and Johnston seized the opportunity to recommend Gist for promotion:

Recommend Brigadier States Rights Gist for Major General for assignment to MG Anderson's He is the best qualified for the place. I want really good Major Generals.

In short order, President Davis personally responded: "Before receipt of Gen. Johnston's telegram, Gen. W. B. Bate had been promoted to succeed MG Anderson." General Bate was a brigade commander in the Army of Tennessee.

The absent members of the 24th's Field and Staff began returning in January, 1864. The officers were in reasonably good health, well rested, and again ready for the responsibilities of the regiment. The camp was rife with rumors that Stevens and Capers were receiving promotions. Finally, General Johnston promoted Stevens to brigadier-general on January 20, 1864. Stevens' new brigade was last commanded by Brigadier General Claudius Charles Wilson of Georgia who had died of fever on November 27, 1863, after serving only eleven days. The brigade had been commanded earlier by Major General W. H. T. Walker.[30]

The *Charleston Daily Courier* voiced its pride over the promotion:

> Few promotions in the army have been more judiciously
> made, and none conferred upon a more deserving soldier.[31]

The men of the entire brigade were delighted with General Stevens' promotion and celebrated accordingly. One witness described the scene:

> The word that Gen. Johnston promoted Colonel Stevens to
> general set off a near riot in the gallant regiment. The men
> flowed out of their crude huts to give their beloved com-
> mander their best wishes and the men enthusiastically
> cheered him.

General Stevens succeeded Colonel James C. Nisbet, who had commanded the brigade since Wilson's demise. In Nisbet's eyes, the new general was quite a man:

> A man about 60 years old, of splendid physique, well
> versed by military education and experience in the art of
> war. Although a strict disciplinarian, he soon gained the
> confidence and esteem of his officers and men. He was the
> brother of General W. H. Stevens who built the efficient
> floating battery which defended Charleston.[32]

Some of Colonel Nisbet's facts were incorrect. Colonel Stevens was 42 years of age when he became a brigadier general. Also, the colonel described Stevens' brother as having invented the floating iron battery, when General Stevens himself designed the battery.[33]

On April 15, 1864, General Stevens corresponded with a friend at the War Department indicating disappointment with his new brigade. He described a strong desire for the command of Gist's Brigade and exuded considerable pride in his old regiment, the 24th:

> I think...that my friend Genl. Gist...will be promoted before
> long...I am...anxious to have his brigade. It is...the finest

one in this army...it is one of the best disciplined. I have
long served with it...my old regiment is with it...I have
contributed my share toward its character....My present
brigade is a very inferior one...it is very small...two of the
commands...are of such inferior physical material that they
will melt away before the end of one week's march. These
commands...(have) exempt and discharged soldiers expecting to serve...in Florida....for these reasons, I would desire
to be transferred back...but I cannot make a formal application in advance....I am afraid some other officer maybe sent
and assigned before I can send my application to the War
Department.[34]

General Stevens' letter also noted his pleasure with General Johnston.
He wrote:

Genl. Johnston had a review today of the whole army and
I am led to believe that it was very satisfactory. The men
are better clothed, better shod, better equipped, and armed
than they have ever been and their next fight will, I trust, be
worthy of their great leader.[35]

Those words of approbation toward General Johnston were strong
indeed, considering that General Stevens was the source. Stevens enjoyed
a reputation as a fair officer who practiced stern discipline and steady
behavior. Gist did not gain the expected promotion, and Stevens never
returned to command Gist's Brigade. Even expecting reassignment, General
Stevens set about improving the condition of his new brigade. The reserve
battalion soon was transferred and replaced by the 1st Georgia Regiment.
Stevens instituted an intensive training program in soldier discipline and
tactics at every opportunity that the weather permitted. When inclement
weather prevented outdoors activity, he conducted training sessions indoors.
Stevens, a competent teacher of military tactics and duties, conducted
nightly classes at his headquarters for the officers of the brigade. As a result
of his dedication, his new unit became a splendid brigade that performed
well in battle.[36]

The promotion of Stevens created a ready-made vacancy for Lieutenant
Colonel Capers. With Capers promoted, an opportunity existed for the
promotion of Major Jones. If Jones received a promotion, Captain Hill, the
senior captain in the regiment, could also earn a promotion. Each candidate
for promotion had frequently performed duty at the higher position.[37]

General Walker established an examining board that reviewed Capers'
qualifications. The board consisted of Brigadier Generals Jackson and
Stevens and Colonel Wilkinson, commanding officer of the 8th Mississippi
Regiment. The examining board convened and reviewed Capers' qualifications on February 27, 1864. Capers' competency for command, character,

and sobriety, and knowledge of tactics were completely satisfactory. Based on the review, the board gave a wholehearted recommendation that Capers receive the promotion. The Confederate army promoted Capers with date of rank January 20, 1864.[38]

Another board examined Major Jones thoroughly in tactics and army regulations and found his knowledge satisfactory in both areas. The board was otherwise satisfied with the results of the examination and recommended Jones for promotion. Jones became lieutenant colonel February 20, 1864, with date of rank January 20, 1864, one month earlier.[39]

Captain Hill appeared before the examining board on February 19, 1864. The board found him somewhat deficient in knowledge of tactics and regulations. Nonetheless, Hill's approved conduct in battle and his personal influence in the regiment earned a favorable recommendation. Colonel Capers presented the board with information about Hill's high character as a gentleman and disciplinarian. Based on all the information, the board recommended Hill for promotion. Finally, the army promoted Hill to major on March 2, 1864, which was confirmed on May 18, 1864, with date of rank January 20, 1864.[40]

The new colonel promoted several soldiers filling critical vacancies within the regiment. Capers selected Sergeant Alfred Holmes as the new adjutant, replacing Lieutenant J. Clarence Palmer, who had been killed in battle at Chickamauga. He promoted Lieutenant Steinmeyer to captain and commander of Company A, a position he had long held. In the same company, he selected J. D. Droze for the vacant second lieutenant position. The Confederate Congress passed an act creating the grade of ensign for color sergeants. Capers nominated Color Sergeant Hollis, saying that, "Hollis is a gallant soldier, who has borne the colors of this regiment with distinguished valor on two occasions at Jackson, Miss., and at Chickamauga." The Confederate Adjutant General approved Hollis for promotion to Ensign on April 18, 1864.[41]

Colonel Capers astutely scrutinized the drill and discipline of the regiment and was gratified with its level of efficiency. In early spring, when the weather became warmer and one could move about outdoors more comfortably, the intensity of the training increased, and the men mastered the art of drill and military tactics. Capers boasted about the prime condition of the regiment:

> When the campaign opened in May, Gist's Brigade [which still included the 16th and 24th SCV, the 46th Ga, and the 8th Ga. Bn.] was in fine condition for the work before it, and no part of it in better trim than the Twenty fourth.[42]

General Johnston implemented several other major reorganizations of the army at Dalton. Gist's, Jackson's and Stevens' Brigades now formed Walkers' Division, Hardee's Corps. Mercer's Brigade arrived from

Savannah and added its strength. These four brigades counted fifteen Georgia, two Mississippi and two South Carolina regiments, which gave General Walker a splendid division of 19 regiments. Hardee's Corps claimed twelve batteries of artillery. One of the batteries, Ferguson's, complemented Gist's Brigade.[43]

In early 1864, the Confederate Congress passed an act that required officers to provide sustenance for their servants. The officers had to purchase such supplies in the local neighborhood or utilize supplies brought from home. Each company and regimental commander, including those of the 24th, signed a letter complaining bitterly about the so-called "ration law or servant act." The letter had Gist's approval and stated, "The officers of this brigade would cheerfully make any sacrifice which might be deemed necessary to the maintenance of the army and our cause."

General Stevens became genuinely alarmed about the dilemma and wrote a friend in the War Department a separate letter maligning the new servant ration bill: "The supplies which we bought in advance of the ration law are nearly exhausted, and we must have relief or dispense with servants." Few issues perturbed the officers of the Army of Tennessee as did the so-called "new servant ration law." Possibly, because of the uproar, the government repealed the law forthwith.[44]

The Confederate shortage of manpower was acute. General Cleburne devised a plan that would alleviate the situation by enlisting blacks into the Confederate army. He considered the plan as the only remaining method by which the Southern army could acquire the manpower necessary to achieve its goals.[45] In 1861, 318,000 free blacks resided in the South who owned property valued at 25 million dollars. Some even owned slaves. A small number of white Southerners thought that blacks, too, should defend the country. A number of Southern newspapers were calling for the enlistment of blacks.[46] The population, in general, disagreed.

One night Colonel Nisbet noticed General Stevens ride his horse toward town and thought the journey strange.[47] The next morning, General Stevens confided to Colonel Nisbet that the meeting concerned the issue of enlisting blacks into the Confederate army. Stevens told Nisbet that every general officer except Cleburne was against the plan. Colonel Nisbet responded that he favored enlisting blacks and would gladly lead a black regiment or brigade. Nisbet thought that if President Davis took a bold stand for enlisting blacks, the Congress would have enacted the bill. He considered that President Davis made a serious blunder when he did not support the concept which, with early resoluteness, might have alleviated the manpower weakness of the Confederacy. One year later, the Confederate Congress passed such an act. Nine days before General Lee's surrender, the Confederate army opened a recruiting office in Virginia for the enlistment of blacks.[48]

The proposal upset General Walker even more than it did Stevens. The officers and the soldiers of the 24th did not record how they felt about the proposal, but they, in all probability, agreed with General Stevens.

A religious revival that met the approval of the leaders sprang up in camp during winter quarters. The Chaplains conducted nightly religious services which were attended by soldiers genuinely profound about religious beliefs and the necessity of saving their souls. Constantly, Capers publicly proclaimed that if he survived the war he would serve God for the remainder of his life. The 24th fortunately attracted the services of the capable Rev. F. Auld as chaplain. He presented a truly faithful ministry of the gospel and a "personal friend service" for the soldiers. Many adopted Christian ways during that long, cold winter as a result of Chaplain Auld's efforts.[49]

In the cold month of February 1864, the division called out the 24th on two separate occasions when the enemy threatened the Confederate outposts. On February 11, the regiment marched 20 miles to a community known as Red Clay, camped for the night, and returned by late the next day. The long march caused blisters on the feet of Vessie McGee. The blisters as sure as one foot steps in front of the other, were the result of improper fit or poor quality shoes, if not by marching 20 miles. By the time the regiment arrived at camp, he could scarcely walk. On the evening of February 23, the regiment again moved in the direction of the enemy. This time the men remained in the field until February 28, and then returned to camp and warmer winter quarters without incident.[50]

The first Saturday and Sunday of April were regular seasonal days typical for March. The wind was boisterous and unpleasant, and by midday Sunday, it rained. The colonel and several of the men became ill with violet colds. On Saturday, the ill men spent most of the day in bed, but, they felt better on Sunday.

Dedication of the soldiers in the 24th to the Confederate cause was never questioned. Husbands frequently counseled wives about the hardships of the war and the effects on the soldier's family. Colonel Capers set the example that most of the men followed when he wrote Lottie:

> My dear wife, you must expect difficulties, & meet them with a determined, resolute Christian spirit. - Don't give in to dismay, or discouragement. These are the trials, my Lottie, which war imposes; and the war is a contest for honorable homes & hearts. I pray for you, my dear Angel & with all my heart sympathize with you in every one of your trials & difficulties. I am never tempted to leave the ·support of our cause to come to you, but on the contrary, the very difficulties & anxieties you encounter at Oxford stimulate my heart to more resolution.[51]

From Charleston, an officer brought Capers six bright shiny stars, three for each side of his collar. The new colonel liked the stars because they were metal and of the type that would shine brightly when removed from his jacket and cleaned.[52] The downside was that they were real targets for enemy sharpshooters.

Spring arrived rapidly. Soon, the Army of Tennessee would be called upon to frustrate the advance of Sherman's army. The 24th, in Capers opinion, had achieved its full efficiency and the men exhibited an extraordinary high level of esprit de corps. Ready for the fray, the regiment of South Carolinians would not have to wait long.[53]

CHAPTER 7

THE HUNDRED DAY BATTLE

Johnston's Army of Tennessee

Near the close of April 1864 the sound of the enemy's artillery blasts started drawing nearer, advising all listeners that the Yankee army was on the move. Ever more frequently, the Army of Tennessee called out units to secure defensive positions north of Dalton. Anxiously, the Confederate soldiers awaited the Federal advance, and General Johnston made final preparations for the long awaited battle. The quartermaster stripped the units and transported the spare baggage to the rear. Johnston discreetly gave the members of the command a poignant reminder that families of the soldiers visiting the camp should leave. The Army of Tennessee was ready.

The Federals commenced exerting pressure at all points by May 4, and picket duty for the Southerners became extremely hazardous. The next day, actual fighting started and continued through May 6 along a general line between Ringgold and Tunnel Hill. On the following day, the enemy drove the advanced skirmishers of the Army of Tennessee to a position near Mill Creek Gap. Those actions heralded the actual beginning of the Atlanta Campaign, or the Hundred Day Battle. A member of the 24th, who obviously enjoyed poetry, described his feelings as battle descended upon the two armies, "It was like a meteor streaking across the firmament scintillating small stars before going out in the darkness."[1]

The men were unanimous in thinking that General Johnston had done his work well, and the army was fully prepared for the campaign that lay ahead. No troops of any regiment were more ready or responded with more enthusiasm than did the men of the 24th![2]

Because of his flanking maneuvers, General Sherman earned the sobriquet "The Great Flanker" among the soldiers of the Army of Tennessee. His movements became the Union general's trademark during the next hundred days. He constantly maneuvered the Union army in the direction of the Confederate flanks, first on one side and then the other. His objective was the rear of the Confederate army, something he never accomplished.

General Johnston always implemented a vigorous defensive maneuver that frustrated Sherman's strategy. For each of Sherman's flank movements, Johnston maneuvered the Confederate army in a corresponding move that prevented the Federals from penetrating his army's rear. On numerous

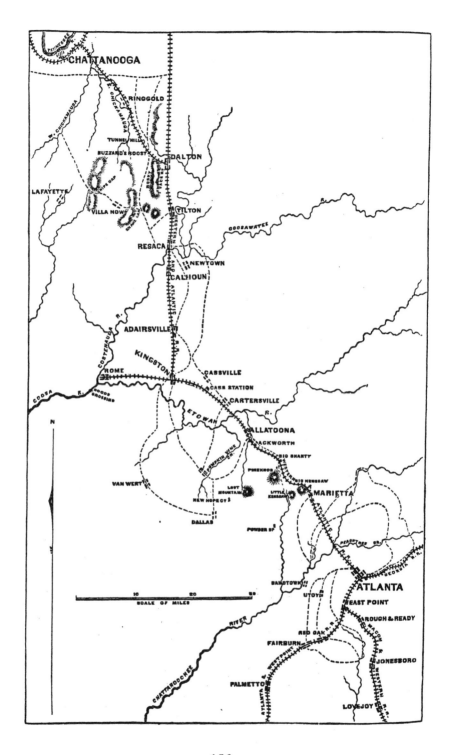

156

occasions, the Yankees considered the Southerners to be trapped. Each time Johnston withdrew, leaving Sherman looking for the Army of Tennessee where it had been. Johnston expected that the Union army would eventually commit a blunder that would give the smaller army an opportunity to counterattack. Such a blunder would, hopefully, allow the Southerners to gain the advantage. Given the disparity in the size of the two forces, Johnston's defensive strategy was the Confederates' only prospect for success.

Johnston did not eagerly assume the tactical offensive and seemed satisfied when the enemy was the aggressor. As a defensive strategist, most military observers considered Johnston's maneuvers as brilliant. An equally brilliant offensive strategy, coupled with the defensive strategy, might have afforded the Confederates a slim chance of success. The battle could not be won with only a defensive strategy.

From Dalton, Old Joe expertly withdrew his entire command in the direction of Resaca. A member of the rear guard who worked all night moving supplies reported, "They were removed, not even losing a cup of meal."[3]

The Federal army bungled a prime opportunity to breach the Confederate rear early in the campaign. The opportunity presented itself on Sherman's first flank movement when General McPherson discovered that Snake Creek Gap was guarded only by the Alabama brigade of Brigadier General James Canty. McPherson lost his nerve and withdrew into the safety of Snake Creek Gap, giving Old Joe time to withdraw the Army of Tennessee from danger. Even Sherman thought McPherson missed a once-in-a-life time opportunity.

Walker's Division, including the 24th Regiment, supported the troops holding Mill Creek Gap and bivouacked in line of battle. The 24th contributed a picket detail. Otherwise, the regiment's involvement was passive.[4]

The leisure time did not last long. On May 9 the Federals pressed the picket line of the 63rd Georgia Regiment of Mercer's Brigade, which was located immediately in front of Gist. Capers sent the Edgefield Light Infantry, Company I, 24th Regiment South Carolina Volunteers, forward in support of the Georgia Regiment. The company commander, Captain Wever, was suffering the agony of a pulled muscle, but he eagerly grasped the opportunity. The Edgefield Light Infantry charged the Federal picket line and regained the lost ground. About 9:00 p.m., the 63rd Regiment's picket line stabilized and Capers withdrew the Edgefield Light Infantry. During the melee, the Federals killed two men and slightly wounded six others. Lieutenant Tillman, the only officer injured, received a slight wound.[5]

Beginning at 10:00 that night the men endured a rapid forced march that lasted all night with the brigade going via Resaca Road to Resaca. The 24th arrived near Resaca about 8:00 the next morning, May 10, 1864. All that day and night, the 24th was in reserve as General Gist held the brigade ready to provide immediate assistance to the embattled force opposing McPherson.[6] Although ready for action, the brigade's services were not needed.

On the next morning of May 11, the Confederates learned that a blue force with an objective of the railroad at Calhoun, was searching for a crossing along the west bank of the Oostanaula River. Gist's Brigade, including the 24th, drew the assignment to intercept the Yankees and immediately departed en route to the Oostanaula. The bridge that spanned the river presented a gruesome scene! The Federals had inflicted a number of casualties on another command that preceded the regiment. The men cautiously and slowly picked their way under artillery fire over the maze of dead soldiers strewn along the bridge. Otherwise, the 24th traversed the river uneventfully and marched along the railroad to a position midway between Resaca and Calhoun. There, the Confederates spotted the Federals and made a charge that recovered a line of entrenchments. The enemy offered little resistance before retiring for safer parts.[7]

The 24th camped until May 14 on the railroad opposite Gideon's Ford about one-half mile from the river. Here they vigilantly watched for an attempt by the enemy to cross. Colonel Capers received a report that the Federals had indeed crossed the river in force about three miles away at McGinnis' Ferry, which was being guarded by the 16th Regiment. The 16th engaged the enemy, but badly needed reinforcement. Again General Gist called on the 24th. The men eagerly raced the three miles to McGinnis' Ferry. There Capers found that the enemy was already across the river, and the 16th Regiment was retiring slowly before a much stronger force. The blue soldiers were advancing into a wooded area and would soon reach a position that would become even more formidable. As the 24th deployed and aligned with the 16th, Capers conferred with Colonel McCullough, and the two colonels decided to counterattack at once. By the time the 24th gained its position, the 16th had already stopped retreating and was firing into the woods. Colonel Capers ordered a charge, and the combined force handily repelled the Federals. The Yankee artillery, posted atop an eminence on the far side of the river afforded the enemy a strong cover fire. As a result of the artillery fire, the Federals recrossed the river in plain sight of the Confederates. After the action, Capers reported that no one in the 24th had received an injury. The 16th Regiment counted several casualties. No one knew the extent of the Federal casualties, although Capers recorded, "I am satisfied that our fire galled him (the enemy) at the river." With the affair over and McGinnis' Ferry secure, the men of the 24th casually returned to Gideon's Ford.[8] All in a day's work.

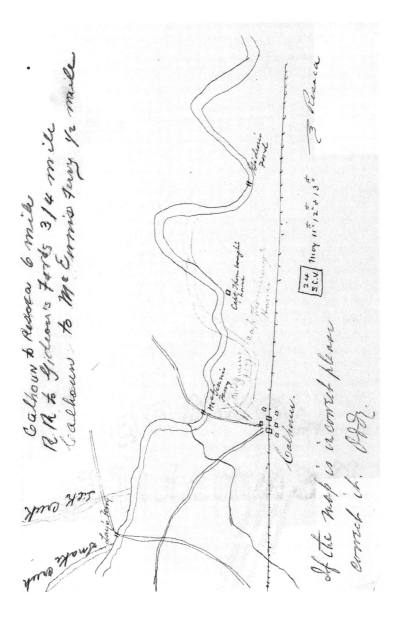

This map shows the location of the 24th Regiment May 11, 12 and 13, 1864. Capers apparently asked someone to review the map and make corrections. The name of the correspondent is unknown.
(Courtesy Duke University, Perkins Library, Capers papers.)

With the addition of General Leonidas Polk's Corps of Mississippi troops and a division of Georgia State Troops, Johnston's army, including cavalry, mustered nearly 70,000 rifles.[9] Sherman's three armies numbered well over 100,000, seriously outnumbering the Army of Tennessee.

General Polk felt extensive personal satisfaction on returning to the Army of Tennessee. The first night that General Polk was present for duty with the Army of Tennessee, he baptized Lieutenant General Hood. A few nights later was General Johnston's turn.[10] Polk was optimistic about the prospects of the army:

> We have as yet not met the enemy in a pitched battle...we
> have...a very fine army...The relations between the general
> officers, Johnston, Hardee, Hood & myself are very
> pleasant...our whole hope and confidence is in God.[11]

The relationships of the senior officers in the Army of Tennessee were destined to change, and not for the better.

In the meantime, the 24th remained on duty opposite Gideon's Ford, constantly alert for an enemy attempt at crossing the river. The men of the regiment were happy with the relaxed duty and the brief respite. On the afternoon of May 15, 1864, Gist's Brigade marched with Walker's Division and reinforced the center of General Johnston's line at Resaca. As the regiment approached the battlefield, the men could hear the increasing roar of the artillery and the constant, shrill rattle of musketry. The chilling sounds urged the men onward with an increased sense of urgency. Colonel Capers observed the situation and proudly described the prevailing attitude as the men awaited the battle, "The men moved with alacrity to the duty assigned them."[12]

The 24th eagerly led Gist's Brigade toward the battle. The brigade was in the lead for Walker's Division. Finally, the troops arrived at the pontoon bridge spanning the Oostanaula. The bridge was under a heavy fire by Federal artillery posted atop an eminence on the far side of the river, well within range. No one hesitated. With a yell, the regiment, Company A in front, unflinchingly crossed the bridge and did not suffer a casualty. The balance of Gist's Brigade followed close behind the 24th and reported seven wounded. Later Capers observed, "The officers and men behaved with steady courage." The 24th moved up with Walker's Division and occupied a reserve position immediately behind Cheatham's Division until 11:00 that night. Although it occupied an exposed position the entire day, the regiment escaped taking casualties.[13]

For two days, Sunday and Monday, Cheatham's Division was bombarded with grape and canister in a Union cannonade of "major proportions." The Union artillery was supported by sharpshooters who poured round after round of minié balls on anything that moved or didn't move, especially anything that appeared Confederate. However, Cheatham's well-entrenched division suffered few casualties. One soldier wrapped his knapsack in a new shawl that he had received from the homefolk and left it lying on the bank at the rear of the trench. It was within easy reach, but the soldier dared not extend his arm to retrieve it. After nightfall the firing ceased, and the soldiers could move safely out of the trenches. The soldier immediately examined his new knapsack and blanket and found both items completely riddled with minié balls. The shawl did not have a piece of material remaining as large as a man's hand.[14]

For three days the enemy hurled furious artillery barrages and repeatedly assaulted the Confederates at Resaca. Each Union assault struck a different point, which the Confederates singularly repulsed. Finally, Sherman, "the Great Flanker," began maneuvering again. Old Joe learned that a large force of Federals had spanned the river the preceding day and if let alone would cut the Confederate communications and supply lines. Johnston implemented his strategy and retired the Army of Tennessee behind the river, and the Federal movement toward the Confederate rear ceased. The Army of Tennessee withdrew that night. Walker's Division recrossed the Oostanaula River, the 24th leading the way once more.[15]

General Walker guided his division to a new destination about two miles southwest of Calhoun, where he halted the march. The 24th stopped near where the Oothkaloga Creek flowed in a westerly direction and entered the Oostanaula River near Tanners' or Lays' Ferry.

Early in the morning of May 16 Hardee's Corps went into bivouac along the Rome road. The right of the corps rested on Oothkaloga Creek, facing in a westerly direction. From that position the men could cover an enemy advance from Tanners and McGinnis' Ferries. The enemy finally moved a large force over the Oostanaula at Tanners' Ferry. The Yankees drove the Confederate pickets until the Federal artillery fire reached Hardee's bivouac.[16]

By that afternoon General Hardee grew tired of the enemy artillery blasts disturbing his bivouac. He asked Walker to reinforce the picket line and repulse the enemy. General Gist drew the assignment, and he selected for the mission the 24th Regiment and Major Arthur Shaaff's 1st Battalion, Georgia Sharpshooters, of Mercer's Brigade.[17]

Gist placed Colonel Capers in charge of the action. Capers planned that Shaff's men would charge the enemy from the right rear, while the 24th assaulted the front. The Georgians reached the assigned position over a trail protected by a stand of woods and shielded by a dense hedge row. They formed a line perpendicular to the South Carolinians. As soon as the Sharpshooters were in position, Capers marched the 24th Regiment into the open. Despite being in full view of the enemy, the regiment prepared for the charge as if on a parade field. The enemy held a position slightly elevated, which created a dangerous situation for the 24th. Colonel Capers rode his steady and twice wounded little horse, Hardtimes, in front of the regiment. Without hesitation, he gave the command that began the charge, and the Georgians wasted no time coming from the other direction "with a yell." Because of the swiftness and vigor of the attack, the enemy fired wildly over the heads of the charging Confederates. The Federals broke into a "precipitous retreat," and as quickly as it began, the battle was over. Colonel P. E. Burke, commander of the enemy force, fell at the head of his troops, mortally wounded. The Confederates captured a few Union prisoners and silenced the artillery fire that had annoyed Hardee's bivouac. They then reestablished the picket line at its former position. Afterwards, an elated Capers boasted, "Both commands behaved in the most admirable order."[18]

After reestablishing the picket line, Capers reported that the 24th had captured 20 prisoners and a large number of accoutrements. He estimated that the enemy suffered twice as many casualties as did the Confederates.[19] The men collected over 50 Yankee knapsacks and a large number of other accoutrements. Captain Steinmeyer exchanged a pair of ragged pants for a brand new pair of U.S. Army regulation blue trousers. As soon as the area was secure and the pickets reestablished, Gist recalled Capers' force. Later that day, General Hardee personally thanked both Capers and Shaaff for their stalwart duty.[20]

The regiment suffered nine killed, thirty wounded, and two men missing during the first days fight. Capers did not bother to report that he himself received a slight wound during the battle. Captain T. C. Morgan, acting major of infantry, and Sergeant Major Dotterer suffered severe wounds during the charge. After the condition of the wounded men stabilized, the surgeons granted the wounded who could travel a convalescence leave, and Dotterer immediately departed for Charleston. However, he was anxious about the regiment and rushed his convalescence so he could rejoin his men. En route to his unit, Dotterer became ill, running a high fever, and the brave regimental Sergeant Major died at Augusta, Georgia. The disease that claimed his life is unknown, possibly typhoid fever. The army returned Dotterer to Charleston and he was buried in a private plot in Magnolia Cemetery.[21]

The newspaper erroneously reported that Captain Steinmeyer, commander of Company A, was killed in battle during the melee. Although Steinmeyer received several wounds and finished the war a prisoner at Johnson Island, he survived. Apparently, the reporter made the erroneous report when someone noticed Steinmeyer chatting with Lieutenant Samuel P. Mims, a member of the 16th Regiment. Later, Mims was killed, and the observer apparently thought the dead soldier was Steinmeyer and so informed a newspaper correspondent.[22] Of course, the report extremely mortified the young captain. Later lists published in the newspaper deleted Steinmeyer's name, but the newspaper never mentioned or highlighted the error.

After the war, Captain Roddey, Company commander of Company H, told his story about the charge at Calhoun, Georgia:

> It impressed me very broadly as much as any occurrence during that campaign for one reason...we charged through a skirt of wood...and stopped at an open place, for about a minute or two...I, and it may be another man or two, went forward 30 yards to an old fence...there was a volley fired by the enemy. At no place during the whole campaign did such a shower of bullets fly so close to me and not one touched me. In a very short time the line came forward and all firing stopped.[23]

General Johnston learned that the Federals had traversed the Oostanaula River, again threatening the Confederate rear. Ole Joe initiated his strategy and abandoned the position. The 24th bivouacked near Adairsville on May 17. The next day, the men resumed the march, passed Kingston, and arrived at another bivouac two miles beyond Cassville.[24]

There, Sherman dispatched his three armies to search for Johnston on three separate roads. Two of the Federal armies converged on Kingston, a move that provided Johnston an unusual opportunity. One corps of General Schofield's Army of the Ohio, the smallest of the three Federal armies, had wandered out by itself. To Old Joe, this was the blunder he awaited, a golden opportunity for the strike! Early in the day of May 19, Hardee's entire corps was formed in two lines of battle, and the commanding general published an order of battle. In conferring with his corps commanders, Johnston listened as Hood and Polk opposed the attack. Although Johnston considered Hardee's position as the weakest, Hardee reassured his commander that he could hold his position. Generals Hood and Polk earnestly beseeched Johnston not to order the attack. Finally, Johnston yielded, a decision he always regretted. Old Joe's detractors contemplated that he lost his nerve.[25] Considerable confusion exists whether Hood or Johnston was right at Cassville. However, little confusion surrounds the actions of the 24th Regiment.

In the meantime, the receipt of orders that the regiment should prepare for an attack elated the soldiers, who prepared for battle with enthusiasm. Johnston positioned Hardee's Corps on the left of the Army of Tennessee. Hardee placed Walker's Division in the center of the corps, and Walker located Gist's Brigade on the left of the division. The 24th and the 46th Georgia were in front of the brigade and immediately behind were the 16th Regiment and the 8th Georgia Battalion. The men faced north on a line that ran due east and west. The 24th stood immediately west of the railroad in an open field. In front, the terrain inclined slightly downward for about one-fourth of a mile and then gradually ascended. The Confederates could see the enemy preparing a position on the crest of the ridge about one mile away. About 2:00 p.m., the Confederate line, including the 24th, moved forward. As it reached the foot of the slope, the line halted with the enemy in full view only three fourths of a mile away.

The Yankees appeared confused and the battle wise veterans of the regiment, eager to attack, could not imagine the cause for the delay. After the regiment held the forward position about thirty minutes, Gist handed Capers his pocket watch and directed, "If the attack was not started by 4:00 p.m., retire the regiment." Capers recorded his exasperation about the movement:

> Precisely at the moment, the entire corps faced by the rear rank and moved in beautiful order to the rear, the enemy not firing a shot at us. We marched back a mile and entrenched our position, expecting an attack every hour.[26]

Earlier, Gist had positioned Steinmeyer's company, the Marion Rifles, at right angles in front of the brigade as skirmishers in advance of Hardee's line of battle. In the distance, Steinmeyer's skirmishers spotted a formation of the enemy concealed from Hardee's line. The left flank of the enemy was toward the Marions, who were posted near "a fine residence just vacated by its owners." Gist visited the position riding his stallion and inspected the disposition of the troops. Before departing the area, he suggested placing sharpshooters at the windows of the residence's upper story. The enemy artillery soon opened a resounding barrage on the Southerners at the farmhouse.

In the midst of the Federal artillery barrage, Major Benjamin Burg Smith, Adjutant General of Gist's Brigade, arrived, bearing instructions to retire. He commented, "Captain, this is a damned hot place." Gist's Brigade would retire first, followed by Stevens' Brigade. As soon as Stevens' Brigade disappeared from view, the skirmishers were to disengage and retire also.

The Company A skirmishers chuckled when the enemy skirmishers "thoughtfully stopped firing" as soon as the Confederate battle lines moved. As Company A started the withdrawal, Smith returned and formed the skirmishers in a line of battle as if he planned a confrontation with the advancing enemy. The Confederate feint provided the men another chuckle when Company A's movement suddenly halted the enemy. After a brief stand, the skirmishers quietly withdrew.[27] No one recorded the casualties sustained, if any, during the melee at the farmhouse.

The men entrenched at the new position and fell sound asleep until the arrival of a messenger alerting the regiment at 1:00 a.m. The messenger directed that the 24th traverse the swift flowing Etowah River, immediately behind the bivouac. After crossing the river, the men marched about two miles and bivouacked for the second time in one night. This time the colonel

164

located the camp along the Allatoona Road. The regiment rested there until May 24.[28]

General Stevens told Captain Steinmeyer that the retreat across the Etowah River was not part of General Johnston's strategy. Stevens alleged that Hood's withdrawal from the Confederate right at Cassville was responsible. Some observers considered that Hood executed a withdrawal based on an informal and unverified report that the enemy was in his rear; some sources indicate that there was at least a squadron of Federal cavalry.[29]

Colonel Capers made a speech challenging the troops at that bivouac on May 22, 1864. He boasted about the accomplishments of the regiment and commented that the embattled country needed even higher sacrifices to achieve the success of the cause.[30]

On May 24 Walker's Division trudged to Dallas and camped. The next day, the division headed down the Allatoona road and entered a bivouac near New Hope Church. There Walker's Division supported General Stewart's Division. Late that afternoon Hooker threw his entire Federal corps upon Stewart's Division, and a severe battle raged until after dark. Capers placed the 24th in close reserve, and although the men did not participate in the action, the regiment still suffered one officer and five soldiers wounded.[31]

Heavy fighting at Pumpkin Vine Creek and Pickett's Mill closely followed the battles at Dallas and New Hope Church. Since Sherman had not made noticeable progress, the Federal general veered left and placed his army across the railroad. Old Joe once more found a position in front of Sherman just northwest of Marietta. The 24th spent much of the time manning the heavy skirmish lines.[32]

Capers spotted a house just beyond a little knoll that the enemy was using as an assembly point on June 1, 1864. Company A drew the detail to charge the place and drive the enemy away. If retention of control of the area was impractical, the men would destroy the house and retire. The little offensive started when the Confederate artillery lobbed several rounds into the area. As soon as the artillery ceased firing, the men dashed across the open area and took possession of the house. Soon, a larger enemy contingent appeared, ready for a counterattack. Without hesitation, the Confederates fired the house and departed the area. Corporal William Kerwick was killed by Union rifle fire while the troops moved across the knoll toward the house. Several of the other boys received slight wounds, but Corporal Kerwick was the only serious injury. The men retrieved Kerwick's remains, and that night his friends buried him on the wild mountain slope. Steinmeyer eulogized the fallen warrior, "He was a heavy, splendid specimen of manhood, and faithful foreign ally and fighter for our cause."[33]

When June 1864 arrived, Walker's Division was on the left of the Confederate line supporting Bate's Division, challenging the Northern forces for the ground near Dallas. Walker's Division lingered in the reserve position until June 4. That night the men made a forced march through a pelting rainstorm, slowly slogging along through ankle-deep mud. The division marched down the Lost Mountain Road and arrived at a new position in the middle of the Confederate defensive line near Gilgal Church. There the men received a much-needed rest and became refreshed both mentally and physically.[34]

At Gilgal Church, Walker's Division again held a reserve position, bivouacking 500 yards behind Stevenson's and Stewart's Divisions. The weather continued unfavorable constantly, raining extremely hard. Capers fashioned a fly with his blue blanket and slept on a stretcher that raised his bed above the wet ground. Even with this meager shelter, he was better off than the men. As usual, many of the men only had nature's cover, the same shelter afforded the birds and beasts of the fields and woods.[35]

The rain practically obliterated the roads. One observer noticed, "The road to Marietta resembles a magnificent canal of mortar. It is filled with wagons and teams...drivers realizing the novelty and importance of his position vie with each other in the accomplishments of splashing, plunging, crashing, and swearing."[36] The only favorable aspect of the excessive rainfall was that it afforded the men an opportunity for a much-needed rest.

The population of Atlanta became extremely worried as the two battling armies drew nearer and nearer to the city, and many were evacuating the town. As Sherman's army approached, those who remained prepared for the worse, yet they hoped it would never happen. Atlanta authorities beseeched the citizens to increase their level of sacrifice:

Let every man, young and old, who can load a musket, or
pull a trigger, prepare for action, and all will yet be well.

However, newspaper editors reassured the public and happily reported the pledges received from the army commander:

Gen. Johnston has assured the authorities here that Atlanta
will be defended to the last extremity, it behooves every
patriot to come to his aid in this critical emergency.[37]

Because of the heavy rainfall, the regiment's normal activity was restricted on Saturday morning, June 4, and the men relaxed in the bivouac. Capers slept late that morning. After rising about 9:30, he leisurely penned a letter to his family. He commented that although Walker's Division had been constantly on the move, lately, for unknown reasons, it had been under fire less than either of Hardy's other divisions. Sherman still hugged the railroad, and no one knew the Great Flanker's intentions; for every move Sherman made Old Joe make a "corresponding move." He added, "I wait with patience and faith for the issue." That morning Ben, Capers' faithful servant, served a breakfast of fried cornbread and ham. The men were now getting an occasional ration of coffee, which was enjoyed even "without milk or sugar!"[38]

The excessive rain caused the suspension of operations for a few days by both armies. Federal deserters declared that the blue army would advance as soon as the roads became passable.[39]

In the meantime, the Confederate army had implicit confidence in its commander, and the troops were in fine spirits. The men were better clad and fed than ever before and occasionally even received a ration of whiskey. On June 11, 1864, Lieutenant General Polk reported strong confidence in the army and that General Johnston was "managing matters very prudently":

> I have never known the army to be...so well organized,
> This is remarkable...the campaign from Dalton...has been
> the hardest I have experienced.[40]

Although many of the men of the Army of Tennessee openly admired and respected General Johnston, everyone did not view his strategy from the same perspective. One of Old Joe's aides foretold the danger that the noble leader of the Army of Tennessee faced when he wrote:

> The enemy at Richmond (whom I regard as the most
> dangerous that this army & its general have) are busy
> criticizing - damning - accusing - undermining - What does
> our general think of all this? He thinks as little of it as of
> the rain and mud through which he has passed, sleepless
> nights and anxious days.[41]

June 9 arrived uneventful, and Hardee's Corps moved in line of battle behind Pine Mountain. Walker's Division supported Bate which held a position on the mountain itself. General Walker was deeply concerned about the weakness of the division line because it extended too far. One brigade occupied a normal three-brigade front and another occupied a two-brigade front. After remonstrating with Hardee, Walker placed his third brigade "in the trenches."[42]

Private James Padgett, Company I, finally received a promotion to lieutenant and was enthusiastic about the latest assignment:

> We are now in position. Our left wing resting on Loss
> [Lost] Mountain a distance of about 9 miles from Marietta
> and our right wing extending across the Chattanooga and
> Atlanta Railroad.

A message from Sherman to Grant that fell into Confederate hands confessed that their repeated flank movements had been unsuccessful. Therefore, Sherman sought permission to launch an assault on the middle of the Confederate line. The information elated the Southerners because they felt they could defend against any army that would make a frontal assault. Part of the reason for such confidence was that the Southern army was usually well entrenched in the Atlanta Campaign. When Hood was given command after Johnston he believed the men would not fight or were

167

cowards because they had been in defensive trenches too long.

Lieutenant Padgett reassured his father of the outcome of the battle if Sherman attacked Johnston from the front, "It is the very thing that the Confederates wanted and Sherman would be the worst whipped man of the war." Padgett was fully confident that the Confederates would "utterly destroy Sherman's whole command." He added his name to the list of Old Joe's admirers when he penned his feelings to his father, "You may rest assured that the army is all right. It has the right man at its head."[43]

The troops were astonished on June 14, 1864, to hear that while at an advanced post atop Pine Mountain, reconnoitering the enemy's position, a 10-pound Parrot solid shot cannon ball struck and instantly killed General Polk!

> The news threw a deep gloom over the whole army, and
> not even Gen. Johnston's death would have been more
> universally regretted.

As General Johnston removed his hat and rendered his last respects, an observer reported, "Tears were seen to trickle down his face." A Louisiana soldier said, "I will gladly lay down and die this moment to bring Genl. Polk back to life." Sam Watkins verbalized how the army felt most eloquently: "His soldiers loved him and honored him and they called him Bishop Polk!"[44]

As the soldiers moved between Pine and Kennesaw Mountains, Hardee's Corps changed its position several times. During that same period, the 24th Regiment brushed the enemy on several occasions. In one of the skirmishes, an enemy minié ball wounded Lieutenant Isaac D. Drose, of Company A, and he received a ten-day convalescence furlough starting June 15.[45]

The men expected an attack on June 17 and hastily threw up temporary breastworks for safety. These were barely complete when the enemy made several charges on the regiment's position. The last charge brought on a sharp fight after nightfall, when the enemy severely handled the pickets in front of the regiment. The regiment reinforced the picket line, and finally held the blue-clad soldiers at bay.[46]

General Gist detailed Steinmeyer as the brigade picket officer and assigned four companies of men from various brigade units as pickets. Company B represented the 24th. When he arrived at the picket area, Steinmeyer found the old picket detail seriously distressed and uncertain about the state of affairs confronting the position. In a steady rain, the new picket officer supplanted the old picket detail with fresh men. The enemy fired constantly during the day, wounding several pickets. One ball passed through the wrapper that Steinmeyer wore between his chest and right arm and severely wounded a courier standing behind him. Yet another ball harmlessly passed through the lower part of Steinmeyer's wrapper.[47]

Brigade picket duty was an unusually hot place. As darkness was falling, the division picket officer informed Captain Steinmeyer that the army was retiring. The 24th provided support for the picket line and covered the division's withdrawal. The picket line maintained its position until the next morning at 1:30. Steinmeyer withdrew the picket line in good order, losing only Private Wiley Bonner, commonly known as "Tipper" among his comrades, who acted as guide for the withdrawing pickets. Tipper fell asleep and remained at his position too long, and the advancing Federals captured the tired picket.

Captain Steinmeyer thought that his tour of duty as the division picket officer was complete the next morning after daylight. Therefore, he released the other three companies to their regiments, and he and Company B rejoined the 24th.[48]

Afterwards, Steinmeyer learned that the picket detail was still needed and recalled the companies, replacing Company B with his own company, Company A. The detail rapidly returned to the outpost and there found Major Whitely of Stevens' Brigade, the division picket officer, under attack. Steinmeyer extended Whitely's line filling an exposed place. Whitely decided that the Federals had flanked the Confederates and they had to retire at once. A retreat conflicted with Steinmeyer's natural resolve to fight when engaged with the enemy, but no other option existed. While traversing a dense swamp, Lieutenant Hawkins discovered a bridge over an otherwise impassable stream. Once the little band crossed the bridge, the pickets deployed and successfully defended the area. Lieutenant Hawkins received a leg wound here.[49] Soon Major Hill, the 24th's popular major of infantry, who had been detailed as the division picket officer, arrived with a fresh picket detail. Steinmeyer recommended that Hill hold the present position because it was more defensible. Nevertheless, the division picket officer thought better and selected the old line as the appropriate position. Steinmeyer assisted the new picket detail into position and afterwards returned to the brigade area. As predicted by the intrepid Steinmeyer, the picket line gave way on the morning of June 18. The Federals drove in the Confederate picket line with much confusion and killed, wounded, and captured many Confederate soldiers. After the picket line gave way, the enemy temporarily penetrated a nearby Confederate skirmish line.[50]

General French's Division was on the right of Walker's Division on the main Confederate line. French discovered that the enemy was only 400 yards away and determined to penetrate his line. As the battle continued throughout the day, French's Division suffered severely while successfully resisting the enemy assault. About the time daylight disappeared that afternoon, French's Division withdrew and established a new line high on the reaches of Kennesaw Mountain.[51]

Finally, on June 19 Walker's Division found themselves in front of Marietta, south and west of Kennesaw Mountain. Here Walker's Division formed the right of Hardee's Corps; it joined General French's Division, which formed the left of Polk's Corps, now commanded by General Loring. Gist's Brigade was on the right of Walker's Division, with the 24th Regiment on the extreme right of Gist's Brigade, touching the left of French's Division. On the left of Walker's Division, in order, were Bate, Cheatham, and Cleburne. The men strongly fortified the line with head logs atop the breastwork and constructed numerous obstructions for an effective abatis in front. If Sherman attacked the center of the Confederate line at that place, it would be, no doubt, to his folly.[52]

The next day, June 20, the enemy again came forward in force and attacked the picket line of Walker's Division, which was manned by the Edgefield Light Infantry, Company I. The enemy positioned their main line of battle about 300 yards in front of Walker's Division. The Yankee small arms and artillery fire constantly rained a leaden hail upon the works occupied by the Confederates. The men, without encouragement, kept their heads down, alert for a new situation or sudden move by the Federals. The weather was extremely hot, and the troops were most uncomfortable while pinned down by the Union fire. General French noticed the heavy enemy artillery barrage on his left, and prepared for an enemy advance. During the action, the Federals killed Major O'Neil of the 16th Regiment as he bolstered the Confederate picket line.[53] As busy as Colonel Capers was on June 20, 1864, he still penned Lottie a letter. That day, he confided the concern he felt for his own safety:

> I bless God for keeping me well & safe. My regt. would be worth but very little, if I was disabled...I feel the impor-tance of my services my sorely pressed country. We must watch & pray, as St. Paul says & fight the valiant fight if we would gain our independence.

He also described the conditions the men endured, although the troops seldom complained about the hardships:

> This army is going through a terrible campaign & thus far stands it well. - Men are more seriously demoralized by personal inconvenience & hardships, such as we have encountered more than by bullets, or shell - but I hope the spell of rain is now over, or soon will be, - but I have not taken as much as a cold from it.

Lottie sent Ellison a new haversack chock full of cakes, breads and potatoes. He thanked her profusely for both the haversack and its contents.[54]

The enemy made another serious attempt at dislodging the pickets of Gist's Brigade with an assault on June 24. General Gist deployed the 24th in front of the brigade as advanced skirmishers. As the incessant firing continued, the men repelled repeated Union assaults and still maintained a viable skirmish line. By day's end, the men were completely worn out and most happy when darkness arrived, and the battle calmed.

During the melee, a member of the 24th captured a Union soldier whose rifle had a strange looking contrivance attached. The soldier had appended a mirror on the stock of his musket that allowed him to sit with his back turned toward the Confederate line and still sight along the barrel of his weapon. Thus, the soldier could fire his weapon from a position of relative safety. The men were not confident the ball would go where the soldier aimed, and if the ball fired in this manner hit anything it would surely be "a stray shot."[55]

The soldiers liked the defensive position at Kennesaw Mountain because it was very strong. Capers handed Company A, The Marion Rifles, the duty of regimental sharpshooters, which meant that the Marions and the enemy remained in constant contact. The Federals made several attempts on the regiment's left flank, but, each time, the Confederates repulsed the intruders. Later, the heavily reinforced Yankees carried a small knoll.

When the Federals reached the hill top, Lieutenant Colonel James Watson of the 40th Ohio returned to the rear. As soon as Watson departed for the rear, the soldiers of the 24th counterattacked and drove the Federals from the knoll. Since he knew the position, Watson returned to secure the hill again. As daylight disappeared and darkness enveloped the area, Watson approached the summit of the hill and there spotted a line of men whom he thought were reinforcements. The Union officer approached the line and asked sharply, "What are you doing here?" The force, which was the 24th Regiment's sharpshooters, answered, "We came after you!" The men leveled about twenty rifles and Watson quickly surrendered. Proudly, the sharpshooters marched the high ranking prisoner into camp.

Steinmeyer had escaped many near misses from enemy rifle fire, but on June 25 his luck finally ran out. While directing the activities of the skirmishers, Captain Steinmeyer received a severe wound, and the stretcher bearers evacuated the injured officer to the hospital. The wound would keep him absent from the army until late September.[56]

Given the circumstances, the soldiers were well-fed. Occasionally, the troops received an issue of sugar and coffee. Lately, those rare luxuries were available often, and, in addition, the men quite frequently received an allowance of whiskey. The soldiers ate quite well, and thus far had to endure no long marches with an empty haversack.

The soldiers of the 24th Regiment trusted General Johnston and knew that he would not commit the men in a useless or unwise battle. When Old Joe was ready for a fight, the soldiers were ready because, "It would be right." The Confederate troops were in fine spirits, and one observer stated simply, "They were fully determined to whip the fight."[57]

Enemy artillery fire commonly swept along the Confederate line, day and night. On June 27 the volume swelled until the entire line came under an abysmal artillery attack. The intensive artillery fire had only one meaning, the Federals would launch a general attack! About 9:30 a.m. the artillery barrage lifted, and the attack began. High on Kennesaw Mountain, General French witnessed the attack from his vantage point and afterwards described the awesome panorama in detail:

> Presently, as if by magic, there sprung from the earth a host of men and in one long waving line of blue. The infantry advanced and the battle of Kennesaw Mountain began. I could see no infantry on my...front. I directed my guns from their elevated position to enfilade Walker's front. In a short time, the flank fire down the line drove them back, and Walker was relieved from the attack.[58]

The Federal advance covered the front of Walker, Bate, Cheatham, and Cleburne's Divisions. The battle of Kennesaw Mountain was intense for each of the divisions.

The enemy handily dispersed the Confederate pickets and assaulted the advanced skirmish line manned by the 24th Regiment. Aided by General French's enfilading artillery fire, the men repulsed every enemy charge with a steady musket fire. Finally, the Federals decided the situation was hopeless, and many of the blue soldiers withdrew to the safety of their breastworks. By dark on June 27, the enemy's main line of battle was within 100 yards of the position held by the South Carolinians. From that position, an observer reported, "The enemy poured in a galling fire of musketry." The nearness of the main skirmish lines of the two antagonists precluded a picket line.[59]

Without pickets in advance of the skirmish line, every man had to remain alert day and night for the possibility of an enemy advance. The Confederates staunchly held the Federals at bay for an entire week until Sherman finally decided the frontal assault could not succeed, and he again reverted to the strategy of flanking movements. General Johnston obligingly made a counter move.

At Kennesaw, the 24th suffered the loss of one officer and nine men killed and four officers and 27 men with serious wounds. In addition, the enemy captured 16 men of the regiment. The total killed, wounded, and captured for the entire 13 days of battling at Kennesaw Mountain was 57. Indeed, the battle had been costly.[60] On the night of July 2, 1864, Capers expressed his frustration with another retreat: "After thirteen days of unceasing exertion, fighting, and watching, we retired from the position."

That night the 24th arrived at a position near Smyrna Church, about five miles south of Marietta, and entrenched there. On July 3, the Federals, close behind, constantly lobbed artillery shells among the entrenching Confederates and killed one man and wounded another. The next day, the Federals continued lobbing artillery shells, but their guns were at a distance of one mile and did little damage. The 24th evacuated the strongly fortified position on July 5 and retired down the Atlanta Road toward the Chattahoochee River. The regiment marched five miles, camped at yet another unfortified position, which they hastily fortified, and remained there until July 9. The only requirement imposed upon the regiment was a picket detail, so most of the men gained a much needed-rest.[61]

The regiment crossed the Chattahoochee River near the railroad bridge on July 9 and entered a bivouac two miles from the river. This time the men arranged the bivouac under some carefully made "bush arbors." The arbors didn't stave off the dampness when it rained, but they did shelter the men from the hot noonday sun. The regiment furnished men for a picket detail along the river, where Union sharpshooters wounded three men with the deadly, long-range Whitworth rifles. The regiment remained at the bush arbor bivouac until July 18.[62]

By July 1864 the regiments and battalions of Brigadier General John King Jackson's Brigade were badly under strength and Jackson's services were needed in Florida. General Walker increased the overall efficiency of his division by reassigning Jackson's individual regiments among his other brigades. As a result, Gist's Brigade temporarily received four new units: the 2d Battalion, Georgia Sharpshooters; the 65th Regiment, Georgia Volunteers; and the 5th and 8th Regiments, Mississippi Volunteers.[63] Although the new units were badly under strength, Gist was happy that the brigade gained the added rifles.

Now that the army was only three miles from the city, the citizens of Atlanta felt miserable and completely stampeded. An observer reported that the women, if anything, were braver about the situation than the men, and the children were even braver than either. General Johnston carefully guarded the ranks of the army from the panic. Some worried that the situation might influence the Confederate Government to withdraw its support of General Johnston.[64]

General Johnston published an address on July 17, 1864, and announced his plan for an attack on Sherman as soon as the Northern army crossed the Chattahoochee. By all indications, Sherman planned a crossing at Roswell, a Chattahoochee River location safely beyond the right flank of the Confederate army. Sherman finally crossed east of Peachtree Creek near the railroad bridge.[65]

Colonel Capers sadly recorded the events that occurred that fateful day as Johnston's enemies struck, quick and hard. The Confederate High Command replaced the beloved leader of the Army of Tennessee with Lieutenant General John Bell Hood. The change in leadership was, without doubt, untimely. General Johnston was the one person who might have

173

thwarted General Sherman's designs for Atlanta.[66] In the meantime, Capers recorded his feeling about reading Johnston's address to the men of the 24th:

> I had the honor to read the commanding general's address to the brigade, and to congratulate the command upon the prospect of a successful battle. The order of battle was received with enthusiasm, and the most confident spirit prevailed. Next day, the 18th, while we were forming to march from our bivouacs to the right a rumor prevailed that General Johnston had been removed from command, and after we had marched some distance on the road to Atlanta a courier handed me a circular order from General Hood, announcing General Johnston's removal and assuming command. Shortly after the farewell address of General Johnston was received and read to the regiment. It is due to truth to say that the reception of these orders produced the most despondent feeling in my command. The loss of the commanding general was felt to be irreparable. Continuing the march and passing by his headquarters Walker's Division passed at the shoulder, the officers saluting, and...the...men taking off their hats. We marched across the railroad and went in bivouac east of the Peachtree road, some three miles from Atlanta. And thus closed the campaign under General Johnston's command.[67]

The men and officers of Stevens' and Gist's Brigades suggested a special salute for General Johnston. At his farewell parade, the men wanted to give him a rousing cheer. However, the general sent word that he preferred "they not do that." General Stevens offered an alternative salute and suggested that, instead of a cheer, the men take off their hats when the regiments marched by Old Joe, which would express the love and respect that the soldiers felt for the former commander. The suggestion was accepted, and every soldier assigned to the 24th removed his hat. Even better, the 24th reported that not a single man deserted the regiment during the campaign led by General Johnston.[68] That accomplishment in itself was a significant salute to the general whom those dedicated, combat-hardened, and battle-wise men loved and respected.

General Stevens expressed the admiration and esteem held for Old Joe by the men in Stevens' Brigade. The men of the 24th Regiment were, in large part, a product molded by the efforts of Stevens, and his words, no doubt, reflected the feelings of those men toward General Johnston:

> That you are no longer...our leader...was received in silence and deep sorrow....the abiding and unlimited confidence...we have felt in the wisdom of your judgement and leadership has sustained us....looked confidently forward to

174

the day of triumph...with you as our leader we should surely march to a glorious victory. This confidence and implicit trust has been in no way impaired and we are ...ready...to obey your orders...to retire before a ...outnumbering foe, or to spend our last drop of blood in the fiercest conflict. Our loss is irreparable, and...this army and our country loses one of its ablest, most zealous, and patriotic defenders...you carry with you the love, respect, esteem, and confidence of the officers and men of this brigade...We would hail with joy your return to command us.[69]

All this was from a man known and respected as a tough disciplinarian and fearless leader. Two days after penning the letter, the Federals mortally wounded General Stevens as he led his brigade into battle at Peachtree Creek.

Sam Watkins described General Johnston's accomplishments from the perspective of the private soldier in the Army of Tennessee. He mentioned the sadness at the loss of Old Joe, and after the war Sam Watkins reflected on the years that passed since he served in the Army of Tennessee:

After twenty years, I can see where General Joseph E. Johnston made many blunders in not attacking Sherman's lines at some point.[70]

In the eyes of the men of the 24th, they had lost the two most beloved leaders of the Army of Tennessee, Generals Johnston and Polk. True, the men wanted to fight, but the same soldiers also wanted leaders interested in their welfare.

The Charleston newspapers continued to support General Johnston and frequently published the opinion that he was "more than a match for Sherman." The newspapers extolled Johnston's strong points:

General Johnston is the bravest and most cool man when under fire that I ever saw. He is almost reckless with his own life, but is exceedingly careful with the lives of his men.[71]

Several years after the war was over, Ellison Capers expressed his feelings about the relief of General Johnston:

Until the 17th of July, I did not once seriously doubt the success of the campaign.[72]

Under General Johnston's command, the 24th served constantly on duty from the beginning of the Atlanta Campaign or The Hundred Day Battle. The soldiers were continuously in the presence of the enemy and performed soldier's tasks, constantly fighting either on picket duty or behind the breastworks. Colonel Capers recorded the hardships and the response of the men of the 24th Regiment:

The month of June was characterized by incessant rain...the

marching and work in the mud were most distressing to the men and officers. Our bivouacs were always in line of battle, often in the trenches and we seldom got a nights rest. At Kennesaw Mountain, particularly, we got but little rest, and for the last five days, none at all...the pluck and spirit of the regiment never failed and I am happy to report that a single man deserted his colors during this trying ordeal.[73]

On the campaign from May 5 - July 18, 1864, the regiment lost 119 officers and men. It entered the campaign on May 5 with 545 men and a full complement of officers.[74]

Thus, the men of the Army of Tennessee completed two-and-one-half months of constant fighting, sacrifice and hardship. Johnston's enemies replaced him when the army and the country, especially Atlanta and the citizens of Georgia, needed him most.[75]

An elated Capers received a letter from his sister Susan bearing the news that he and Lottie were the parents of another daughter. This time Lottie felt less pain and was more comfortable than during her previous confinements. On July 17, 1864, Capers penned Lottie a letter and reassured her that he was safe:

The enemy has crossed the Chattahoochee River just where we would prefer his crossing, near the Roswell Factory. I think...that Johnston will endeavor to strike him in the flank and rear as he moves out toward Atlanta...If not, we will probably line up about Stone Mountain.

Capers was most anxious to hold his new daughter. Two days later he received a slight wound, and, accompanied by his faithful servant Ben, departed the camp en route for Oxford, Georgia, 40 miles from Atlanta. There he visited his wife, son, and new daughter and decided to find safer refuge for his family in South Carolina.[76]

CHAPTER 8

THE HUNDRED DAYS BATTLE

Hood's Army of Tennessee

General John Bell Hood smiled confidently as the word quickly spread that announced his eagerness for battle. He seemed to enjoy being recognized as a fighter. The soldiers knew that General Hood commanding the Army of Tennessee meant that they could expect some hard fighting, and soon.

Many of Hood's peers agreed with the description, and even General Robert E. Lee characterized Hood as "a bold fighter."[1] Sherman was warned by some of the new commander's West Point classmates that Hood would attack without delay. Hood surprised even his nearest confidantes by just how rapidly he did attack.[2]

As the reins of the Army of Tennessee changed hands, General Sherman's converging Union forces threatened Atlanta from three general directions. General George H. Thomas was crossing Peachtree Creek, a few miles north of the city. General Schofield was coming from the northeast, and General McPherson was approaching from the east at Decatur. The most imminent threat came from Thomas' army at Peachtree Creek.

Within 36 hours after his promotion, Hood lashed out, hoping that he would catch Thomas in the act of crossing Peachtree Creek. When Hood's forces arrived on the scene and attacked, Thomas was already across Peachtree Creek and well entrenched. The result was a loss of 8,000 irreplaceable Confederate soldiers, and worse, the Federals were still on the wrong side of Peachtree Creek.[3]

During the battle of Peachtree Creek, the regiment did not accompany Walker's Division or Gist's Brigade. General Hardee reinforced Walthall's Division with the 24th. When the regiment reported to Walthall, the Yankees had repulsed Cantey's Brigade, and Colonel Edward Asbury O'Neal, acting commander of Cantey's Brigade, appealed for reinforcements. The 24th drew the assignment.[4]

Just before the regiment departed for its assignment, Colonel Capers received a slight wound and sought treatment at the hospital.[5] Soon afterwards, the regiment, with Lieutenant Colonel Jones in command, marched down Collier Road and waited at a position near the Olyinska house for orders from O'Neal. There, the sounds of the battle that raged nearby created considerable consternation among the men. While waiting,

General John B. Hood
(*Battles and Leaders*)

the Yankees shot down one of the 24th's soldiers as he performed a work detail. At the same place, the men witnessed Major William Campbell Preston, a South Carolinian and Walthall's chief of artillery, struck down by enemy artillery. As the artillerymen sadly removed Preston's body, the ambulance passed along the 24th's line again.[6] After those two instances, the men hunkered down utilizing all available protection.

The men waited only a short time for orders until O'Neal guided the regiment up a country road toward the sounds of the battle. As the regiment proceeded into position, a stray ball killed another of the 24th's soldiers. Jones formed a line of battle, with one company in front as advanced skirmishers, and moved into the woods, pausing momentarily, readying for the charge. A participant recorded the action:

> Everything was still as death for a few seconds when the
> enemy fired into us at very short range. Our line soon gave
> way and we retreated to the road that we marched up to
> reach the position.[7]

The regiment rallied and quickly advanced a short distance and held that position for the remainder of the battle.

The men grumbled about the assignment. One participant thought O'Neal used the regiment as an extension of his line, because he did not provide a supporting line in front or behind, thereby, leaving the regiment on its own.[8] The situation made for an inordinate amount of apprehension, creating a gloomy outlook among the 24th's battle-wise warriors.

Among the wounded at Peachtree Creek was Private R. J. Rivers, Company D, known as the "one handed man" because he already had a "bad arm." On that day the war ended for him when a Union ball struck his already maimed arm.[9]

That night the news about General Stevens' dangerous wound reached the regiment. The news intensified the gloominess already apparent among the men.

During the melee, Canty's Brigade drove the enemy nearly a mile, captured several works and punished the defenders severely. However, because of a lack of adequate support, O'Neal could not maintain the advanced position, and the enemy compelled the brigade to retire and assume a stronger defensive position. Much to O'Neal's discomfort, the brigade was forced to maintain the latter position until the battle concluded. He complained,

> If the whole of our line had pressed forward with the same
> energy and determination which the troops of this division
> did, we would have carried the day and driven the enemy
> in confusion across the creek.[10]

O'Neal's report seemed to criticize some unit, possibly the 24th, which would have been entirely out of character for the regiment. Possibly, he directed the comment at other regiments or brigades in Walthall's Division which should have supported Cantey's Brigade, or even some of his own regiments. Most likely, the comment was made concerning events before the 24th arrived. However, O'Neal's previous experience as brigade commander in the Army of Northern Virginia had also resulted in disaster.[11]

In 1885, T. A. Stevenson, former private of the 24th, was surprised when he learned that O'Neal was still living and had become governor of his native state, Alabama. Stevenson allowed that O'Neal had been age 50 more than twenty years earlier: "They must be scarce of young governor timber out there or they are like I am - partial to the old soldiers."[12]

While the 24th was detailed for duty with Walthall's Division, the balance of Walker's Division as well as Gist's Brigade heavily engaged the enemy. That afternoon, Lieutenant General Hardee "sallied forth" and struck the Federals at Peachtree Creek with fury. Hardee's men viciously went after the Yankees, and raced through the forest while screaming the rebel yell. At first, the Confederates struck and easily overran Union General John Newton's Division. The charging line soon came up against Ward's, Geary's, Williams', and Palmer's well-entrenched Divisions and were more than the Confederates could handle. As a result, the Federals "rolled the Confederates back, shattered and broken." Hardee reorganized for another charge but decided it was useless.[13]

On July 21, 1864, the day after the battle at Peachtree Creek, Hood decided to feint another attack the next day. The army gave the appearance of falling back into the trenches around Atlanta, and the men labored the entire day entrenching, preparing for the operation on July 22.

During the day, General Gist was wounded by a Yankee sharpshooter. The ball struck Gist in the back near his spine. However, it was "a spent ball" and did little damage. The surgeon bandaged the wound, and Gist was ready for duty again.[14] It would take more than one Northern ball to stop the determined Gist.

That same night Hood placed Hardee in command of another mission against the Federals. Hood sent Hardee around the left flank of McPherson by the way of Decatur to attack from the enemy's flank and rear. At the same time, acting corps commander Cheatham would attack McPherson's army from the front. At precisely 1:00 a.m., July 22, 1864, Hardee moved his corps en route for Decatur feinting a movement through Atlanta. The men exerted extraordinary effort executing the attack, but two divisions of Dodge's Corps formed a new line that blocked Hardee's path and thwarted the strategy. Later, General Hood cited Hardee for not completely turning McPherson's flank. Others thought it was a matter of luck because of the appearance of Dodge's Divisions, which the advancing Federal line had "squeezed out."[15]

During the approach, Gist's Brigade had not come up, and a gap existed between Nisbet (who temporarily commanded Stevens' Brigade), and Cleburne's Division. General Walker rode off searching for Gist's Brigade. In the meantime, Nisbet's Brigade advanced with Bate's Division, although Nisbet remonstrated with General Bate to delay the advance until Gist's Brigade came up. Because too much time had already been lost, General Bate retorted, "It is imperative that the line move forward without further delay."[16]

Walker's advance was delayed by a pond and an extremely impregnable briar patch and other dense undergrowth. General Walker became incensed when Hardee denied permission to skirt the obstruction. Although Hardee apologized, Walker told his aide, "Hardee must answer for this."[17]

General Walker's Division finally overcame the briar patch and charged the enemy's works late that afternoon. It was a piecemeal attack, each brigade charging as it arrived on the field. As with all such piecemeal attacks, the results were disastrous.

During the assault, General Walker noticed that Gist's Brigade was suffering the effects of a heavy fire. Walker personally rushed forward and rallied the men. He discovered the 24th Regiment especially threatened with annihilation:

> Without hesitation, Gen. Walker rode among them, in the middle of the "iron hail" and complimented the gallant regiment for their bravery. Gen. Walker's clarion voice reached out to every soldier, calmed their fears and urged them onward. Gen. Walker waved his hat and extolled the bravery of every man!,
> "Soldiers: Remember Stevens! Remember him!
> One more charge and the day is won! Follow me!"

With a wild cheer those gallant men responded.[18]

Suddenly, the enemy fire hit General Walker's fine grey mare, and she fell heavily. At the same moment that the fearless General Walker stood upright, several enemy minié balls pierced his body, mortally wounding the general. That stopped the renewed vigor of the 24th in its tracks. It could go no farther. Those who saw the brave Walker fall yelled out, "Bring off the general!" Private John Bagley, a member of Company H, 24th Regiment, responded. He gathered General Walker's body in his arms as tenderly as possible under the circumstances and bore him from the field.[19]

While under a strong Confederate fire, Federal Colonel Sheldon, commander of the 18th Missouri, changed the direction of his regimental line. Thus, the Missourians poured a raking fire into the 24th Regiment as it assaulted the Federal position. The regiment trembled and quivered and then reeled backwards by the heavy musket fire of the Missourians. The men searched for cover. Sheldon reported that a general, whom he thought was General Walker, rode into the open field waving his hat and was superbly

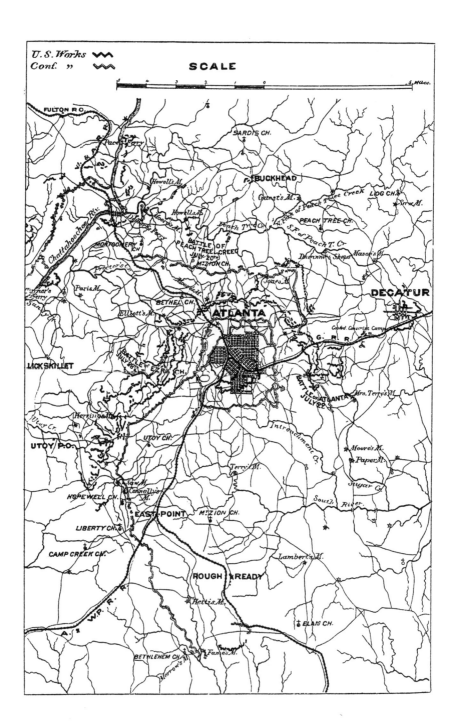

182

The Battle of Atlanta, July 22
from the painting by James E. Taylor
(***Battles and Leaders***)

rallying his troops. Suddenly, the general's horse was riderless. The brave Walker was no more, as already noted.[20]

The troops of the 39th Ohio held a position near the 18th Missouri and the rifle fire of the Ohioans also could have struck General Walker.[21]

About the same time that the enemy shot General Walker, General Gist suffered a severe wound in the hand and wrist. Gist, always determined, resolute, and cool, continued leading the charge. With extraordinary effort, Gist's Brigade reached within 100 yards of the enemy breastworks. For over two hours after the enemy shot General Gist, he performed his duty and sustained the focus of the brigade on its objective. Finally, he fainted from the loss of blood, and the litter bearers sadly bore the brave Gist, unconscious, from the battlefield. Colonel McCullough assumed command of the badly torn and battered brigade as it fell back to some vacated artillery works and reformed. With both Generals Walker and Gist gone, the leadership of Walker's Division suffered considerable confusion. Therefore, for the remainder of the Battle of Atlanta, General Hardee held the division in reserve. Even in the reserve position, the men were still under an intense musket fire. The entire battlefield was a hot place.

Colonel (then Major) Benjamin Burgh Smith, of General Gist's staff, declared that the lack of coordination resulted in the disaster suffered by Walker's Division:

(Gen) Cleburne, after dressing his line made a glorious attack with grand results which; however, only showed what would have been the result if a concerted attack of Hardee's whole corps had been made simultaneously.[22]

Colonel Smith mentioned that Stevens' Brigade, commanded by Nisbet, had also made an unsupported attack with similar disastrous results. Smith blamed the ambivalent effort by Walker's Division on General Bate, whom he alleged, initiated the unsupported attack, saying that it was "imperative that the line move forward." For success in battle that day, Smith concluded that a few more minutes would have made a wise investment.[23] General Bate would bear the responsibility for several other future battles. Bate is the same man that President Davis promoted over the capable and always competent Brigadier General States Rights Gist.

Sergeant John Lewis (Buddy) McGee, of Company K, was killed by the Federals during the battle of Atlanta. His brother, Private Sylvester (Vessie) McGee feeling a great loss, departed the regiment, absent without leave, until September 1864.[24] Information about Buddy's death and grave site are unknown.

After the battle, the *Charleston Mercury* proudly reported the results of the battle:

> The gallant 24th S.C.V. sustained her reputation and was commanded by Lt. Col. Jones. Said one of its officers to me, where all acted their part so well, it would be difficult to particularize. This remark is applicable to the whole brigade (Gist's). Never did men fight better and behave more gallantly. ...[They] exhorted the highest compliments from the veterans of Cheatham.[25]

General Hood complained bitterly that his forces did not accomplish the desired results that day. Even so, he felt that he had halted the Federal movement against the Confederate communications line. He also felt that the troops had fought with spirit and determination, carrying several lines of entrenchments. After the battle, the Yankees entrenched and began the "Siege of Atlanta."[26]

General Gist received treatment at the Confederate hospital at Macon, Georgia. A few days after the battle he was already up and around, not as seriously injured as first presumed.[27] The wound, no doubt, earned the general a much coveted and enjoyed furlough for convalescence which he probably spent with his beautiful young wife in South Carolina.

General Hood's next major movement was down Lick Skillet Road for a bloody battle at Ezra Church on July 28, 1864. However, the 24th Regiment did not participate in the fight at Ezra Church.[28] This battle was as disastrous for the Confederates as the battles of Peachtree Creek and Atlanta (Decatur) had been.

In the meantime, Lottie was resting at Oxford, regaining her strength following the birth of the Capers' new daughter, May, on July 14, 1864. The new baby was the Capers' fourth born and the second surviving child. The Capers' small son, Frank, accompanied his mother at Oxford.

Mrs. Capers clearly understood that Atlanta was in serious danger. Moreover, she knew that the army needed her husband to fight with the other soldiers. Bolstered by her husband's confident letters, she felt the matter would work out and left the situation "in God's hands."

Ellison brought the regimental colors of the 24th and asked his wife to embroider the names of the battles on the flag. She did not complete the task and the flag remains without honors. During her confinement, those colors were hanging from the staff in Lottie's bedroom. The Capers' new daughter, only six days old, also shared the room, lying in her crib.

Oxford was rife with rumors that the notorious Yankee raiders were in the vicinity. However, everyone thought the town safe. Suddenly, one afternoon a lady friend excitedly burst into Lottie's bedroom and fairly blurted the announcement, "Mrs. Capers, the town is full of Yankees." The feared Northern raiders were there.

Lottie's first thought was to hide the colors of the 24th in a safe place. Thinking fast, Lottie quickly removed the colors from the flagstaff and neatly stitched the flag inside a pillow case. She then placed the pillow under her new daughter's head. Mrs. Capers' maid, a free black women, hid the flagstaff under the house. The colors remained safe until she returned them to her husband.

That night, the town was a scene of disorder and confusion. Confined to her bedroom, Lottie could hear the noise of the raiders. However, she did not see any of the Yankee soldiers. Afterwards, she described the scene:

> The uproar of voices in the street and passageways, the
> tramp of horses on the stone pavement of the yard leading
> to the smokehouse, the rude demands of the (Yankee)
> soldiers and the pleading of the ladies to be spared some-
> thing for the family to live.[29]

Suddenly, in the midst of the scene, Frank, the Capers' three-year-old son, burst into Lottie's chamber and announced the most welcome news, almost too good to believe: "Ma! you know Pa is come!"

After his minor wound on July 20, Ellison received a few days leave. He considered Oxford unsafe and resolved that he would remove Lottie and the children to safer sanctuary in South Carolina. En route, Capers found the railroad track destroyed by enemy raiders, stragglers from Major General George Stoneman's command. As a result, he and his faithful servant, Ben, completed the journey on foot, walking 40 miles. Capers asserted, "We have been dodging Yankees all morning." As soon as he arrived at Oxford, Capers rushed to his wife's side. However, the alarm soon went up again,

"YANKEES ARE COMING!" and he fled into the woods to avoid capture. Afterwards, as soon as he could do so undetected, Ben delivered a blanket and some food. For four days and nights Capers moved back and forth between the woods and the house. Daily, he became more anxious about his absence from his place of duty with the regiment. Lottie finally regained her strength sufficiently, and Ellison reminded her that he had to secure her safety and depart for the 24th at once.

A journey of any kind under these conditions was indeed perilous. However, the couple decided that Oxford was in serious danger, and they had to risk the move. Capers located the family carriage and a kindly neighbor loaned a broken-down horse. The family hurriedly departed for the nearest train depot and secured rail passage bound for Uncle Richard Yeadon's home at Kalmia, near Aiken, South Carolina.

Ben drove another wagon with an equally broken-down team of horses by a different route. It was loaded with Lottie's personal effects that he expected to ship from the train station. En route, the Yankee raiders waylaid Ben, stole his money and food, and ransacked Lottie's belongings, searching for anything of value. Since Ben's broken-down horses were better than those of the stragglers, they exchanged horses. Finally, the raiders departed, and Ben finally reached the train station. He then shipped the remnants of his precious cargo to South Carolina.[30]

After a terribly fatiguing trip, especially for a new mother, Capers finally delivered his family safely to Kalmia. The Capers family remained there until early fall, when Lottie rejoined her own family at Cherry Grove Plantation.

The manpower situation in the Army of Tennessee became more critical daily. General Bragg visited the army a second time in July 1864 and summoned General Stephen Dill Lee from Mississippi with 5,000 fresh troops. Hood searched the army for additional replacements and as a result armed "the detail men," (i.e. cooks, wagon drivers, and the extra artillery men), exempting no one except gunsmiths. Hood assigned the newly armed men to duty "in the trenches" and increased the firepower of the army by 4,000 badly needed rifles. The detail men freed the main part of the army from trench duty so they could operate on the flanks of the enemy.[31]

Supplies for man and beast were very meager. Although there still were sufficient rations for the men, forage for the horses became extremely sparse. The men in the trenches ate only crackers after the cooks began using rifles.[32]

Some of the soldiers were still disgruntled over General Johnston's removal and wished for his return. One complained of "prejudice of [President] Davis, to the extent of sacrificing the Army of Tennessee to...his obstinacy [because he] refuses to reconsider."[33] In spite of the discontent over the "loss of their general," the 24th's morale remained high.

186

The siege of Atlanta meant duty in the trenches or "the ditches," a place where the men suffered incredibly from the intense heat as well as the enemy rifle and artillery fire. The men participated in sporadic skirmishing with the enemy and picket duty was extremely precarious. Moreover, the frequent blasts of enemy artillery shells presented danger not only to the men in the trenches but to the citizens of Atlanta.[34]

The soldiers performed picket duty every fourth day and night. On those days, the direct fire of the enemy was even more hazardous than when in the trenches. The "Zit! Zit! Zit!" sound of the Yankee minié balls never stopped. While in the trenches, the troops carefully remained behind the breastworks, and those that became careless suffered the effects of the deadly balls. The soldiers worried about the women and children in the city, even though they endured the bombardment better than the men. The Yankee bombardment of the city inflicted extensive damage to the buildings, but, given the amount of ammunition expended, few lives were lost.[35]

General Sherman's troops were shooting the Confederates with a new missile. It was a zinc washer placed around the minié balls. Some soldiers thought that the Federals deliberately designed the washer to inflict added injuries to the Confederates. Others thought the Yankees dipped the washer in poison to intensify its effects. Actually, the washer was a new invention by the Northerners that aided the chore of cleaning rifle barrels of the black powder crust that formed when the soldiers fired their weapons. The Federals fired the minié ball fitted with the zinc washer every 10th shot. The inventors designed the washers so it would separate from the minié ball. If the washer did not separate from the ball when fired, it did separate upon impact, thereby creating a more serious wound. The soldiers of the 24th didn't like the Yankee zinc washer regardless of the innocence of its purpose.[36]

The men enjoyed few pleasures in the trenches during the siege of Atlanta. However, beginning on August 2, the battlefield action paused briefly until August 5, and General Hood issued the soldiers a ration of whiskey. That day the 24th participated in a severe picket fight with negligible results. The next day, the Federals assaulted the section of defensive line next to the 24th and breached it for a short time. The Tennessee boys who held the line soon rallied, repulsed the attackers and captured 60 Federal soldiers.[37]

Colonel Capers, his family safe and sound at Kalmia and his mind relieved, returned to the battle front. At Augusta, he had some difficulty getting aboard the overloaded trains bound for Atlanta and arranged for a seat only by arriving at the train station early.

Finally, Capers arrived at the trenches occupied by the 24th on Wednesday, August 10, 1864. One soldier approached Capers and exclaimed with much correctness, "Col! I don't want you to leave us any more!" It terribly upset Capers when he found only 247 effectives present for duty with the regiment. The numbers had declined dramatically since Old Joe departed barely three weeks earlier. The men thought the prospects of success for the embattled army depended upon General Wheeler's cavalry, which was operating on the Federal communication line.[38]

Captain L. B. Wever, commander of Company I, suffered the effects of chronic diarrhea that rendered him seriously ill. The medical examining board determined he suffered a general debility and granted Wever a 30-day furlough on August 10. A month later the doctors extended his leave for another 30 days. Captain Wever's health did not improve sufficiently to permit his return to the regiment until March, 1865.[39]

As a result of the close confinement and constant danger of trench warfare, the soldiers yearned for the comfort of their loved ones' arms. The men braved those hot, stinking, uncomfortable, and nasty trenches and confronted a different perilous situation every day, either as a result of battling the enemy or the weather. A cold rain fell on the 8th, 9th, and 10th of August, the type of rain that caused exposed men to catch colds. The colonel and several of the men became ill. During this period, General Gist was absent mending his wounds, and Colonel McCollough commanded the brigade. The men missed both Walker and Gist and were thankful that Gist would return.[40]

Soon after the battle of Atlanta and the death of Walker, General Hardee reorganized his corps and reassigned the brigades of Walker's Division. Gist's Brigade, along with the 24th, drew an assignment to General Cheatham's Division of Tennesseans, and the regiment joined ranks with its former snowball opponents. Since the troops already knew each other, it was an uncomplicated change. The other brigades of Walker's Division were also reassigned. General Steven's old brigade went to Bate's Division and Mercer joined Cleburne.[41] In the meantime, Cheatham temporarily commanded Stewart's Corps, and Brigadier General Maney guided Cheatham's Division.[42]

The Federals burned some of the wagons that contained the records of the Army of Tennessee. The men were happy that the wagons containing personal belongings were not burned.[43]

The officers of the army often performed special details, such as officer of the day, picket officer, etc. On August 15, 1864, the division detailed Colonel Capers as division officer of the day.[44] He completed the assignment in his usually efficient manner.

General Hood issued an edict that soldiers who communicated with the enemy would be shot. Hood thought that this offense occurred because the troops were ignorant of the consequences and advised the men that the Federals used the opportunity to gather intelligence and spy. The picket line of the 24th had communicated and practiced free trade with the enemy at Chattanooga several months earlier. However, after Hood's order the soldiers did not admit to such a practice even if it existed. Confederate soldiers did not wish to aid and abet Federal intelligence gathering.

The delivery of mail was sporadic, and often long periods elapsed between deliveries. The lack of mail intensified the homesickness the soldiers felt for loved ones.[45]

August 17, 1864, was an exciting day for the 24th. The enemy demonstrated seriously along the Confederate main line and struck the area guarded by the regiment's picket line. The demonstration started Wednesday afternoon and finally quieted on Thursday morning. The 24th had four men killed, two on the picket line and two more on the main line.

Several of the officers received wounds even when they were not in the trenches. The enemy wounded one of General Gist's aides by a "stray ball" as he was cleaning his teeth at brigade headquarters. Later the same day, a spent ball struck the acting brigade commander, Colonel McCollough, on the leg, and he departed for treatment. With McCollough in the hospital, Colonel Capers, the next senior colonel, assumed command of the brigade and once again turned command of the regiment to the capable Jones.[46]

The August heat wave worsened the uncomfortable conditions in the trenches. During the intense hot weather, only minor activity emanated from the opposing line, just enough to irritate the defenders. Infrequently, the Federals threw artillery shells into the Confederate lines at night. One shell exploded over the tent occupied by Capers, Hill, and Holmes, and a large fragment sliced through the tent. Fortunately, it did not strike the occupants.

Union raiders destroyed the railroad track, and thereby delayed the mail delivery. The delay of the mail contributed to the homesickness of the soldiers. Ellison was terribly homesick and longed for another furlough. "If I get home," he declared to his wife, "I will spend the time in your arms."[47]

The Confederate army Inspector General arrived to inspect the assigned divisions, brigades, and regiments of Hardee's Corps on August 20, 1864. The inspectors performed a complete inspection so far as the surroundings permitted. The inspectors noticed the "extensive deficiency" of the lack of shoes and clothing. However, there were laudable points: "The appearance of the men indicates (excellent) health, vigor & morale and...evident that if better supplied, no more efficient body of troops bear arms in the Confederate army."[48]

This inspection reinforced the belief that the soldiers of the Army of Tennessee were fine fighting men. One man opined that the western men were the equal of any soldiers fielded by the Confederacy, even those serving in "President Davis' pet Army of Northern Virginia."

The inspector general visited Gist's Brigade and found Capers in command of the brigade and Jones in charge of the 24th. The inspectors determined the regiment counted 26 officers and 276 enlisted men present for duty. The inspector accounted for the absent officers in his report:

Prisoners of war: 3,

Wounded, in the hospital: 7,

Furloughed from the hospital: 3,

Sick, sent in hospital: 1, and

Absent without leave: 2.

The 24th held 577 rifles, either Enfields, Springfields or Macon rifles with globe sights. Sufficient accouterments were available, and every man held 40 rounds of ammunition.

The military bearing of the troops was "soldierly." The inspector determined that the discipline of Gist's Brigade had fallen off since the beginning of the campaign. Even so, its discipline compared favorably with the remainder of the army. Military instruction was good and as complete as practical since the troops were constantly under fire and usually confined to the trenches.

The inspectors rated the sanitary conditions in the trenches very fair and the police of the brigade camp very good. However, personal cleanliness of the troops was not good. That was because the troops had served for an extended period in the trenches. In addition, a serious shortage of soap exacerbated the situation. The men treated the animals well, but forage was sparse.

The division received a good report reflecting a highly trained infantry unit ready for the fray. Actually, the troops were described as dirty, hungry, practically naked, and barefooted. However, their rifles were clean and well maintained, and each soldier had an ample supply of ammunition.[49]

With vigor, General Joseph Wheeler implemented his cavalry operation on Sherman's line of communications. The infantry troops prayed Wheeler would succeed and convince Sherman that he must fight or retreat. However, Wheeler found that the Federals were guarding the railroad strongly with blockhouses at critical points. When he managed to damage the railroad tracks, the Union repair teams laid new tracks rapidly. The strategy was more than General Wheeler could handle, and he soon retreated after suffering exceedingly high losses of men and animals. His efforts brought little Confederate success.[50]

The abominable Union raiders once again broke the railroad line from Macon, and no mail arrived during the weekend of August 20 and 21, 1864. The engineers repaired the railroad tracks and claimed the capture of the entire raider force. The news, true or not, exhilarated the men whose mail the raiders delayed.[51]

The men frequently suffered upset stomachs, and Capers developed the malady on August 22, 1864. That night he actually had a nightmare that revealed his deep concern for his wife when he dreamed she was dead. He woke up, fell asleep again, and had the same dream again.[52] After weeks "in the trenches," the men were entitled to a few nightmares.

When Capers returned from furlough, Ben remained at Kalmia to assist Lottie. Ben fulfilled his responsibility and was returning through Atlanta during the night of August 24. There the city firemen pressed Ben into service to help douse a house fire. On the following day, he finally rejoined the regiment and delivered a letter to Capers from his wife.

More bad news: someone had stolen Capers' beloved little horse "Hardtimes." He cared deeply for the animal, and Capers' heart was broken. The man and the animal had survived many battles and shared many dangerous missions; they had been struck by the same ball at Jackson and had been wounded about the same time at Chickamauga. Ben thought he knew who had stolen Hardtimes and searched "high and low," but it is unclear if he found the treasured animal. Capers grieved over the missing horse as if he were a beloved family member.[53]

Letters, mailed by the soldiers, were not reaching addressees, and this terribly upset the men. The troops often commiserated with loved ones that they were homesick and felt restless and impatient because of the separation.[54]

Delightful news reached the Confederate trenches on Thursday, August 25, 1864. The Federals had vacated their lines and were in full retreat! The Yankees traversed the Chattahoochee River beginning August 27. For the first time in more than a month the men could safely emerge from the ditches during daylight hours. The Confederate soldiers were ready to give pursuit and waited impatiently for the word.[55]

Sherman had no intention of retreating. He decided that Atlanta would not capitulate solely from the effects of an artillery barrage and resurrected his flanking strategy. The Union army quietly slipped out of the works in front of Atlanta and moved toward the Confederate communication line at Jonesboro, the last Confederate rail link.[56] Within one hour after the Yankees departed, the Confederates entered the vacated Federal works.

Five invaluable days passed before Hood finally realized that the enemy intended to strike the railroad at Jonesboro. By the time Hood knew Sherman's destination, the entire Union army had reached Jonesboro, where they traversed the Flint River and fortified a well-selected position across the Macon railroad. After Hood realized Sherman's strategy, he dispatched Hardee with two corps to force the enemy back across the Flint River.[57]

Cheatham's Division, commanded by General George Maney, marched all night from its position near East Point, and reached Jonesboro early on the morning of August 31. The division formed in line of battle with the brigades of Generals George C. Porter, George W. Gordon, John C. Carter, and Gist formed on the west side of the village. Gist's Brigade was on the right of the division, about 200 yards behind Cleburne's Division on the right of the corps' battle line. Bate's Division supported both divisions on the right. The attack was fast, furious, and short lived.

In addition to General Maney, several acting commanders directed the battle that day. Hardee was in command of the entire force and Cleburne commanded Hardee's Corps. Some confusion exists whether McCollough or Capers commanded Gist's Brigade at Jonesboro. General Maney cited McCollough as the leader of the brigade, but others specifically named Capers as brigade commander and Jones as commander of the 24th Regiment. After the war, Capers related that he commanded the brigade from August 10 until General Gist returned on September 5. At Jonesboro, Capers recalled that he commanded the brigade, because McCollough, who had returned from the hospital, preferred to remain with the 16th Regiment.[58]

Cheatham's Division hesitated about 300 yards from the enemy's entrenchments and prepared for the assault. Cleburne, acting corps commander, canceled the initiative, and Maney held his division steady. Next, Cleburne withdrew the divisions to the position held earlier, where the men entrenched. The division reached that position about 10:00 p.m.[59]

After the battle at Jonesboro, Capers' bitterly condemned Hood for procrastinating while Sherman's forces marched toward Jonesboro. The colonel felt that Hood should have forced the issue before the Yankees arrived at Jonesboro:

> Instead of assaulting this force on open ground or on their march to Jonesboro, our troops were led against fortifications which they had been educated to believe could not be carried by a quadruple line of battle...they all knew we had but a single line.[60]

Since early May, the Army of Tennessee had handily resisted Sherman's superior strength. The Confederates constantly erected exactly such fortifications as those they were called upon to assault at Jonesboro. The enemy understood the situation and were elated that the Confederates even considered "storming his fortifications." Capers thought that Sherman won his point:

> He got to Jonesboro and fortified. Now to be attacked in his works was just what he wanted. As our troops (the Confederates) approached to the assault, his men (the enemy's) mounted the breastworks and waved their hats to us to come on. On went many a noble fellow to certain death. So much for the fall of Atlanta.[61]

On August 31, 1864, both Hardee's and Lee's Corps engaged the enemy and battled until dark. Hardee's Corps succeeded in carrying the Federal works, but the enemy repulsed Lee's men. Once again, an outnumbered Confederate force attacked a well-entrenched enemy with little success. This time it was a disaster for the entire South, for Atlanta was lost![62]

Afterwards, Hardee severely criticized Hood because the assault should have occurred as Sherman marched to Jonesboro, and should have been conducted by the entire Army of Tennessee.[63]

On September 5, 1864, Hood provided Richmond with an assessment of the Jonesboro battle of August 31. His report reflected a genuine disappointment with the performance of his army:

> To let you know what a disgraceful effort was made by our men in the engagement of August 31, I give you the wounded in the two corps. Hardee's, 539; Lee's, 946; killed, a very small number.[64]

As Atlanta was vacated, Hood called for Lee's Corps to return and assist the Confederate evacuation. At Jonesboro, Hardee's Corps alone confronted Sherman's entire army.[65]

On the afternoon of September 1, the Federals suddenly realized that only one corps occupied the Confederate works. The Union generals decided that an attack in force could destroy a large portion of the Army of Tennessee. Therefore, without hesitation, the Federals struck. Because the battle on August 31 had decided who would possess Atlanta, the most important Federal objective, the Confederate soldiers never understood why the enemy attacked on September 1. The Southerners were only holding on at Jonesboro until Hood's army could escape Atlanta.[66]

At 1:00 a.m. on the first of September, Hardee shifted Gist's Brigade from the left to the right of his corps. The men marched all night and finally reached the new position. There, the brigade straddled a 10-foot-deep railroad cut on the tip of the Confederate defensive line. Hardee told Capers that Gist's Brigade must hold the right of his line. The position, without fortifications, ran through a thickly wooded undergrowth near the railroad.

Capers placed the 2nd Georgia on the left of the defensive line, with the 24th next. The 24th was actually across the railroad, and the 16th Regiment was on the right side of the 24th. The 46th Georgia Regiment was on the right of the 16th and formed the extreme right of the brigade as well as the corps. Quickly, the men of the 24th increased the strength of the position. First, the soldiers bent over small trees and utilized pocket knives to cut the trunks. They then thickly interlaced the small trees held in place by the stumps, and so formed a "first rate abatis." The men in the rear added some rails and logs, which made a "tolerable breastwork." The men completed these preparations within thirty minutes after reaching the position.[67]

The right of the brigade bent around covering the right of the corps. Such a position would expose the men if an enfilade fire developed from the other side of the railroad. The men built traverses of logs on the left of each company that protected from this possibility. After the battle, Capers reported, "They [the traverses] proved our salvation." Thus prepared, the

193

men awaited the enemy's attack.[68]

With a "superior force," the enemy charged Hardee's Corps about 4:00 p.m. and drove in the brigade skirmishers. The Federals maintained close contact until the Confederate skirmishers reached the main line where they were handily repulsed. However, General Daniel C. Govan's Brigade of Cleburne's Division and General Joseph C. Lewis' Brigade of Bate's Division did not fare as well and gave way. Lewis' Brigade joined Gist's Brigade on the left. When Lewis's Brigade gave way, the 2nd Georgia Battalion on the extreme left of Gist's Brigade also began reeling backwards.

The first Federal assault struck the left of the brigade, and only reached about one half the distance across the front of the 24th. However, When the enemy struck again at 5:30 p.m., the assault reached across the entire front of the regiment.[69] The Federal assault line did not reach the two regiments on the right of the brigade. Afterwards, Union prisoners informed the defenders that Gist's Brigade had faced the entire division of Union General Jefferson C. Davis.[70]

Gist's Brigade fired rapidly and accurately, and the enemy movement toward the Confederate works stopped. In the meantime, as the enemy pressed the 2nd Georgia back, and the pressure extended to the left of the 24th, the enemy occupied the works vacated by the 2nd Georgia. However, the traverses gave the remainder of the brigade good protection. In addition, the enemy fired too high, and little damage was done.

Companies B, G, and K, located on the regimental left, soon began yielding. When Capers spotted the reversal, he directed Lieutenant Beckham to rally his men and retake the area before the enemy occupied it too strongly. Beckham, assisted by Major Smith, Holmes, and Capers, immediately counterattacked. After an extremely hot fight, the men drove the enemy from the works and reoccupied the regiment's traverses. The 2nd Georgia Battalion immediately recaptured the position it had held before the assault, and, as the enemy retired, the men of Companies B, G, and K of the 24th also recovered the places they had held earlier. The brigades of Lewis and Govan also rallied and formed a new position in the rear of the one lost earlier.[71]

During the final assault, Major D. F. Hill, the 24th's highly regarded major, was killed as he rallied the Georgians. Captain Steinmeyer reported that three balls pierced his heart in a space that a man could cover with his hand. Every man in the regiment mourned the loss of their congenial major. Colonel Capers eulogized the exemplary service of the major, saying, "A cool, brave man, and a good soldier, Maj. Hill's loss is deplored by every man and officer of his regiment." Leaders of Hill's quality were rare and becoming scarcer by the day as the hopes of the South waned.

Capers recognized several officers for valiant conduct during the battle.

In addition to Hill, he specifically mentioned Lieutenants Holmes, C. Dudley Easterling, Beckham, and Tandy M. Seigler: "The conduct of officers and soldiers of the Twenty-fourth South Carolina Volunteers in the engagement merited the highest approval."[72] Capers also noted that Jones directed the fire that repulsed every assault made on the center and right side of the regiment.

At midnight on the first day of September, General Hardee visited the 24th to extend his congratulations and tender his personal thanks for their gallant conduct. Hardee personally directed the withdrawal of the brigade to the next position near Lovejoy Station.[73]

In the middle of the next night, Hardee's Corps started the withdrawal. The 24th led the brigade in yet another all night forced march. It arrived at daylight and commenced fortifying. Hood finally completed the evacuation of Atlanta and reunited his army at Lovejoy on September 3.[74]

The Union 2nd Brigade of the 4th Division, 15th Corps entered Jonesboro September 3, 1864, at 3:00 a.m., and captured several of the Confederate wounded. Near Atlanta, the Federals claimed the capture of Gist's servant, horses, and equipment and the near capture of Gist himself. The Federals thought that they missed Gist because he realized his peril at the last moment and leaped aboard a train evacuating the wounded.[75] An independent confirmation of the report has not been located.

Capers agonized that the latest reverses would have an adverse effect on the soldiers from South Carolina. Although Hardee's and Lee's Corps had borne the brunt of the fighting, "Hardee's Corps seemed in good heart." He noted, "The soldiers of the gallant regiment took the fall of Atlanta...(better) than expected, though it is a great blow to the army."[76]

The men of the Army of Tennessee felt that they had suffered one more rebuff for the want of sufficient manpower and the right leader at the right time. Even with this latest blow, the men of the 24th Regiment remained cheerful, ready for the fray, and confident of ultimate victory.[77]

Gist returned to the brigade on September 5, 1864. Hardee immediately placed the recovered general in command of Cheatham's Division, another task he performed flawlessly.[78]

The men worried about Sherman's next move. If the Union general turned toward Macon, the Army of Tennessee would be "in for a long campaign." However, if Atlanta were enough, Sherman would probably provide General Grant some of his troops.[79] At that moment, no Southerner could imagine even in the wildest nightmare the option Sherman would select.

For several days, the two armies did little other than skirmish sporadically on the picket lines and fire minor artillery barrages. Both armies lobbed a few artillery shells at each other around Lovejoy Station with little effect. Stewart and Lee's Corps soon arrived and formed on Hardee's right and rear, and the Army of Tennessee held Sherman's army at bay.[80]

On the morning of September 6, the Confederate skirmishers discovered that the Yankees had quietly withdrawn. Gist's Division reconnoitered the movement, and that afternoon blundered into the enemy's rear guard one and one half miles south of Jonesboro. The adversaries exchanged musket fire, but neither side challenged for battle. Citizens reported that the Federals were en route to Atlanta where Sherman would "rest and recruit his army." Many citizens thought that with Atlanta captured, Sherman would depart for Virginia and assist Grant with the capture of the North's only remaining major military objective, Richmond. In the meantime, Sherman's move back through Jonesboro surprised the Confederates. That night, Gist's Division bivouacked near the town under rainy skies. Lieutenant Tillman was picket officer of the second detail and "captured a few prisoners."[81]

The next day, September 7, was a cloudy and rainy day as Sherman evacuated Jonesboro. Before departing, Sherman visited a Confederate hospital and boasted to the patients that his army would linger at Atlanta, "for rest and then he was going to Andersonville."[82] That night, the brigade posted a picket line north of the town.

Lieutenant Tillman noted that Thursday, September 8, was a cloudy day with an occasional drizzle that did not dampen the spirits of the members of the 24th. One observer allowed that except for the lack of regular mail delivery, "Cheerfulness pervades the corps."[83] As usual, the men of the Army of Tennessee retained an exceptional high level of elan.

On September 9, 1864, Gen. John C. Brown, received an assignment as commander of Cheatham's Division. Brown was promoted over Gist as early as one month previous. Gist was a more senior brigadier general with impeccable credentials who was highly respected and admired by the soldiers of the 24th Regiment. Gist, a man of quality, repeatedly demonstrated extensive ability for higher command and repeatedly rendered flawless performances as a division commander. Perhaps Gist was not promoted because of the Richmond policy that favored the promotion of individuals from Tennessee, or simply because Gist was recovering from his July 22 wound. In future battles, the Army of Tennessee would suffer because the wrong men held the leadership positions. Generals Bate and Brown, who received promotions instead of the talented Gist, would both earn justifiable criticism. Bate already had earned criticism for his actions at the battle of Atlanta, and would soon do likewise at the battles of Franklin and Nashville, and the action at Murfreesboro. Brown's ambivalence may have caused the Confederate fiasco at Spring Hill. At any rate, some extremely unfortunate decisions were being made.

The interruption of the mail service, precipitated by the collapse of Atlanta, adversely affected the morale of the men. The officers of Gist's Brigade, including those of the 24th, signed a petition and asked that

General Hardee support improved mail delivery.[84] The general could do little about the delivery of mail since the Yankee raiders were roaming the countryside with impunity.

From the bivouac at Jonesboro, members of the 24th observed a scene that depicted the true devastation of war. The town was almost completely empty of residents, and those who remained had to draw rations from the army. The enemy left debris, such as unburied dead horses and garbage, strewn about the town. There remained only the bare remnants of homes and farms in the vicinity. A member of the 24th wrote, "It sickens the heart and stomach."[85]

The Confederate army used up the remnants the Federals left at Jonesboro. The generals set up their headquarters in the better houses, and the troops appropriated the last farm animals for their use. The only crop left untouched by the Yankees was the sugar cane, and the Southerners gathered it "by the arms full." Soon there would be nothing left.[86]

The devastation of Jonesboro as well as the irresolute attitude of Confederate leaders concerned Colonel Capers very much. He rode by the hospital and observed some grave diggers cover up four deceased Confederate soldiers in a hole, and then draw the dirt up over the grave like an Indian mound. When asked, the grave diggers did not know the identity of the deceased soldiers. The situation terribly infuriated the religiously oriented Capers and threw him in a bad humor all day. Frustrated over the incident, he was adamant that the surgeons could have identified the soldiers. In contrast, the colonel openly admired the manner the Federals buried deceased Union soldiers: "The slain Yankee soldiers are carefully buried & every grave is marked & fenced in."

On September 1, Capers counted 234 Yankee graves. The burial detail had neatly arranged each grave and clearly marked the name of the occupant at the head of the grave. He lamented about the manner the grave diggers interred Confederate soldiers, "The Confederates are buried in holes (not graves) where they fall."[87]

In the mind of Colonel Capers, discipline and drill were the key ingredients that achieved success on the battlefield. Comparing the "discipline and drill" of the Southerners with that of the Yankees, he thought the Federal army was "much superior" to the Confederates:

> Their generals show a capacity & energy that was far ahead
> of the starved & wretched gentry of the Southerners. This
> was especially true of those who send inadequate orders by
> staff officers & couriers from safe positions, one, two, or
> three miles in the rear. There is nothing so sickening as to
> be commanded by your inferiors...feel but little confidence
> in your leaders.

Most Confederate leaders accompanied the troops during battle.

However, General Hood never once visited the battlefield during any of the battles around Atlanta. A brave and fearless soldier, his severe physical handicaps must have been responsible for his absence.[88]

On September 12, 1864, Hardee named Capers as Post Commander at Jonesboro. The 24th was selected to be provost guard. The regiment established a comfortable bivouac among a splendid grove of trees on the western side of town. From there, the men remained constantly alert for enemy activity.

At Jonesboro, routine military activities returned as the combat situation quieted. General Cheatham resumed command of the division on September 17, and Gist also returned to the brigade.[89] Hardee reviewed his entire corps the same day. The pleasant weather ended, and that night it rained or constantly drizzled until midnight the following night.

Finally, Hardee's Corps departed Jonesboro at 2:00 a.m. on September 19, 1864.[90] In preparation for the march, the men drew three days' rations and afterwards attended "preaching in camp." After the last division cleared Jonesboro, the 24th examined the encampments thoroughly, assuring that no stragglers remained. The regiment departed Jonesboro at sunrise Monday morning. The 24th was the rear guard of the corps as well as the entire army, and Companies A, D, and I were last in line. That day, the men marched 15 miles toward Palmetto.[91]

The 24th stopped at midnight Monday, rested five hours, and resumed the march at daylight. Finally, the regiment caught up with the brigade near Palmetto about 8:00 a.m. The army halted at noon, and the men entrenched. The next day the brigade moved its bivouac about one-half mile and entrenched a new site located at Phillips' farm on the extreme right of the army. The pleasant weather changed somewhat, and the days became warm, cloudy, and rainy. After nearly a week of the tempestuous weather, the men finally greeted the sunshine on September 23. The next day the men completed the entrenchments and fortified the position with a strong abatis. Afterwards, Hardee rode his stallion along the line and admired the soldier's handiwork.[92] Smiling faces reflected the cheerfulness that prevailed in the regiment, although the lack of mail created some unhappiness.

A few days later President Davis visited the camp of the Army of Tennessee. Some men welcomed the visit, while others disparaged it, mainly because he, in the soldiers' view, had unfairly removed their favorite general, Old Joe. When the President showed up on Monday, September 26, 1864, he looked pale and careworn. After considerable hesitation, the men greeted the President with loud shouts of applause. President Davis completed his review of the army, and the 24th returned to its bivouac about 11:00 a.m.[93]

Before the President's speech that morning, Lieutenant Tillman thought there would be a universal call for Johnston's return:

General Johnston is all that is desired. The whole army would hail his return with the wildest shouts of applause, yet our President will not reinstate him. The reception of the president will be icy since he had forfeited all claims our regard and kind consideration. I predict that the President will hear hurrahs for Johnston.

After the President's speech, Tillman's letter seemed less critical of Jefferson Davis:

Gist's Brigade moved out sullenly to be seen by him. We had scarcely taken position before his Excellency appeared and rode slowly along the line, saluting officers and men by raising his hat as he passed by. Though scarcely a man left the bivouac who had not determined to treat him coldly, his calm, pale face and frosty locks created a deep sympathy...the careworn Executive...When General Gist proposed "three cheers for our President" a wild united shout was given. Such as we used to give our great and much loved general...When he was with us and he would ride along the line or encampment.[94]

Although General Hood had been in command for over two months, the men of the 24th still yearned for the return of General Johnston.

The *Charleston Mercury* continued to call for Johnston's return as commander of the Army of Tennessee and correctly predicted that the army would not survive the continuation of Hood. The newspaper recognized the hopelessness of expecting "anything wise, or magnanimous or unselfish from the administration."[95] Even the newspaper could not convince President Davis to replace Hood before he guided the Army of Tennessee to oblivion.

Two days later, the men learned that the President had reassigned General Hardee to Charleston. That night the men of the 24th heard Hardee's farewell address and many of the battle hardened, severely scarred, combat veterans, wept. Another leader whom the men loved, respected, and had long followed was gone. Nevertheless, the men continued the fight, somehow confident of success.[96] Four days after Hardee's departure, Hood recommended Cheatham for promotion.

Hood seemed to blame others for his setbacks. He particularly pointed out "the failures" of Generals Johnston and Hardee, as well as the officers and the men of the army.[97] Hood's problems appeared to be greater than a disabled arm and missing leg.

On September 19, 1864, General Robert E. Lee recommended that President Davis replace Hood with Beauregard. Instead, Davis assigned Beauregard to oversee both Hood's Army of Tennessee and Taylor's Army of Mississippi. In reality, Beauregard would have little authority over either.

One observer noticed that Hood's army no longer resembled the fine army commanded by Johnston. At best, the top commander of the Army of Tennessee was in a perplexing position.[98]

The final aspects of the Atlanta Campaign (also known as the Hundred Day battle) occurred during the period September 12 - 21, 1864. Sherman and Hood agreed upon a 10-day truce to exchange prisoners at Rough and Ready, Georgia. Sherman seized the break in action to give a cold-hearted order that all non combatants in Atlanta evacuate the city. The city's civilians boarded the trains at Lovejoy Station for destinations further south. They were penniless, homeless, and destitute of friends. The worst fears of the citizens of Atlanta had materialized.[99]

For the 24th Regiment South Carolina Volunteers Infantry, the end was just beginning.

CHAPTER 9

HOOD'S TENNESSEE CAMPAIGN

Atlanta abandoned and its residents banished! Not only Georgians, but everyone in the entire South found the unexpected loss of Atlanta difficult to believe. Southerners registered their extreme indignation with a single voice. No one could believe that the population of Atlanta was suffering such a degradation. As the news spread, a deep gloom permeated the country. Although weakened, the Southerners sustained their resolve to continue the battle.

The Army of Tennessee mustered an infantry strength of only 26,000 effectives. With such a small force, even Hood felt that the only opportunity for success was a campaign against Sherman's communications. The general expected that such a campaign might entice the Federal army away from Atlanta and, better yet, out of Georgia. Apparently, Hood discussed his plan with President Davis and received tacit approval on September 25. Within a few days after the President's visit, Hood commenced preparing the Army of Tennessee for its infamous "Tennessee Campaign," a campaign that one might well call *A Journey to Oblivion*.[1]

Hood concentrated the Army of Tennessee near Palmetto, Georgia, a safe distance from Sherman's army. There the men of the 24th quickly rejuvenated themselves. The rigors of hard marching, fighting, and loss of sleep suffered during the Atlanta campaign seemed to fade from memory. An observer ascertained from the relaxed feelings, laughter, and buoyancy that the men exhibited, the regiment was, indeed, again ready for the fray. The soldiers attended Divine services on Sunday, September 11, and prayed for peace. During the following week, the pleasant weather and equally pleasant marching conditions persisted. The slowness of the delivery of mail was the only situation that experienced censure, and that was alleviated somewhat when a limited amount of mail arrived on Wednesday.

After an inordinate three-week delay, the army completed preparations and abandoned Palmetto. The troops began a long march that passed on the western side of Atlanta, and then moved rapidly north.

The men disapproved of the lengthy and apparently needless delay, believing Sherman was gaining time to accumulate sufficient supplies to sustain his army for an entire month. However, members of the 24th considered the move on Sherman's communications to be bold, and they applauded the frankness with which Hood "communicated his general plan to his army." The information "inspirited the troops greatly." Even after the fall of Atlanta, the soldiers were still sanguine of success. Some soldiers were optimistic the regiment would return home by Christmas.

Most of the soldier's clothes were in poor condition, and the home folks were hard-pressed to provide replacement items. Lieutenant Padgett's sister, Mary Ann, sent her brother a new pair of pants, and he responded, "I sewed up and patched the other pair so I am now making out very well."[2] However, many soldiers did not fare as well and wore extremely soiled and ragged clothing and were often barefooted.

The soldiers of the 24th were always proud of their duty performance, but they constantly wished for peace. Lieutenant Padgett's words were, no doubt, apropos for the entire regiment:

> I have never missed any duty that belongs to the service,
> that fell to my share. I have been in every fight and skir-
> mish that my command has been in. We are now resting for
> a while and I hope that the fighting part will never be
> resumed...I am tired of war.[3]

At 7:00 a.m. on September 29, 1864, at 7 a.m., the 24th crossed the Chattahoochee River at Phillips Ferry and started the new campaign. The day was very warm and this made marching conditions disagreeable. The regiment covered 15 miles that day and eight miles the next along the banks of the Chattahoochee. The sun shone brightly and the weather, although still hot, was excellent. At times, the soldiers received a welcome break from the heat when the sky clouded over and threatened rain. At dusk the second day, it rained and afforded the men a measure of relief from the heat. The next morning the marchers departed the bivouac at 6:00 a.m., and covered 10 miles.

As they marched, the soldiers' attention was riveted on the very beautiful countryside that bordered the army's route. The soldiers became especially enthusiastic when the exquisite blue caps of the Kennesaw and Lost Mountains came into view. It rained during the day and again that night, soaking the troops, who stopped for the night wet, soggy, and exhausted at a dreary camp near Souters, Georgia.[4]

The men received a brief respite on Sunday as the soldiers rested until 3:00 p.m. before breaking camp. They marched five miles and encamped again. The day was clear, but the skies clouded over and that night it rained again.

The troops cheerfully endured the long, fatiguing marches and the frequent severe weather conditions as they sought to fight the battle that would win the War. Lieutenant Tillman's words reflected their sense of dedication when he wrote: "I am determined to go through this campaign if God so ordains it & will shield & assist me."[5]

The army correspondent to *The Augusta Constitution* paid a tribute to the South Carolinians:

Gen. Gist is a fine officer - gallant and fearless. He has an excellent command - prominent amongst which is the 24th South Carolina. It is a regiment that will do to tie to. Colonel Capers is a most excellent officer, having everything on the march and elsewhere en militarie. He is a rigid disciplinarian, and commands an enviable fame. The Palmetto State has reason to be proud of all her chivalric sons, and none more than our brigade friends and associates.[6]

The men cheerfully accepted the hardships of the day-after-day journey as the army moved north. On Monday, the men hiked five miles under the skies of yet another hot, humid, rainy day. That night, they camped at Brownsville. The next day, the rain abated somewhat, and the soldiers marched twelve miles along Lost Mountain Road. The regiment camped for the night on Morris' place and constructed a line of fortifications. There Tillman felt ill and reported to sick call suffering, the surgeons thought, the effects of typhoid fever. The army hesitated an extra day on October 5, providing the men a much-needed day of rest. Here the quartermaster issued the men supplies, which were wretchedly inadequate and did not even satisfy minimum essential requirements.[7]

That night, the men suffered the adverse effects of an all-night rainstorm. At 7:00 the next morning, October 6, the soldiers started marching again and trudged eight miles on the Van Wert Road under skies that glowered and dumped rain all day. The roads were heavy and muddy and often the troops struggled through knee-deep mud.[8] The news that Stewart's Corps and the cavalry had destroyed the railroad located between Marietta and the Etowah River heartened and elated the men of the 24th somewhat.

Senior officers continued to recognize the leadership talents of General Gist. From Charleston, Hardee eagerly solicited Gist's services for an assignment at Charleston as soon as the army concluded its latest campaign. The general assured Gist a much-deserved and highly coveted promotion. Capers speculated that if the army promoted Gist, he would, no doubt, receive a promotion and command Gist's Brigade.[9]

Beginning early in the morning of October 7, the regiment marched fourteen miles on the Van Wert Road as the weather improved and the day became clear, warm and quite pleasant. The next day, the troops left the very hilly, rocky, and rather barren countryside and proceeded through the beautiful and productive Enharlee and Cedar Valleys. The pleasant weather continued, and the men marched 18 miles and bivouacked for the night two miles from Cedartown. The next day, the men paused for part of the day. At 3:00 p.m., the regiment broke camp, proceeded eight miles, and finally bivouacked again one mile from Cave Springs, Georgia.[10]

General Beauregard paid the army an official visit at Cave Springs. After consulting briefly with General Hood, he departed for Jacksonville, Alabama, for a meeting with General Taylor.[11] Both meetings apparently were fruitless, since neither of the two field commanders seemed to accept the leadership of Beauregard.

Several senior officers were reassigned or returned to their permanent assignments. General Gist returned to the brigade, after being released from command of Cheatham's Division. General John C. Brown assumed command of Cheatham's old division. The 24th was now part of Brown's Division.[12]

The daily marches continued, long and arduous, without relief. At 6:00 a.m., on Monday, October 10, the men hustled out of the bivouac at Cave Springs, forged ahead 16 miles and traversed the Coosa River at Quinn's Ferry. The regiment went through Coosaville and bivouacked two miles beyond the town. The men exulted as they admired the panorama of the beautiful Armuchee Valley. The call of reveille aroused the men at 4:00 a.m. During the day, the regiment traveled 18 miles, eased through Taylor's Ridge via Daniels' Gap, spanned the Armuchee River, and bivouacked for the night near the river on the Summerville Road. The good weather conditions remained, and the troops marched under skies that were clear, cool and pleasant. The next day, the soldiers maintained a steady gait and marched yet another 20 grueling miles and bivouacked within five miles of Resaca.[13] On October 13, the weather remained clear, cool and pleasant as the regiment traveled 17 miles over good roads through the magnificent Sugar Valley.

During the late afternoon of October 13, the army appeared in full view of an enemy fort at Dalton. General Hood summoned the fort's commander and demanded an immediate surrender. At first, the Union commander refused, because a few days earlier a handful of General Wheeler's cavalry had attempted such a ruse. Brown's Division commenced an assault on the fort. Arrayed in line of battle, the division moved forward with the 24th in the advanced skirmish line. As the troops approached the fort over an open field, the Federals raised several white flags. The Union commander, Colonel L. Johnson, surrendered without firing a shot when he learned the strength of the Confederates.

The Southern soldiers decided it was "their turn to break up the railroads" and accomplished the task with relish. That night, observers saw huge fires for miles along the railroad bed as the men stripped the railroad tracks from the road beds and laid the steel rails across fires. After heating, the soldiers bent and warped the rails into unusable shapes as they delightedly made their own "Sherman's neckties."

The Confederates also appropriated many valuable and much needed military stores and supplies stored at the fort. Colonel Capers secured for himself a good sabre.[14]

On October 14, the regiment awoke at 4:30 a.m. and continued destruction of the railroad until 11:00 a.m. The Army of Tennessee then resumed the journey. The troops passed through Mill Creek Gap and other countryside with which they had become familiar when the army had retreated toward Atlanta. That day they marched 15 miles before camping near Villanow in the Chattooga Valley. The men were worn out and daily became even more exhausted. The next day, the troops trekked eight miles across Taylor's Ridge via Shipp's Gap and bivouacked on the Summerville Road. The regiment had already marched 200 miles since it departed Jonesboro. That night, Captain Roddey returned from the hospital, and, as the senior captain, he assumed the duties of acting major, in the place of Captain Steinmeyer.[15]

As the regiment marched through Shipp's Gap, Union infantrymen were close behind the brigade. The next morning, General Gist assigned the 24th the task of checking the enemy's advance. Gist instructed Capers to detain the enemy as long as practical, but warned him, "Do not lose your regiment!" The regiment deployed at Shipp's Gap about 8:00 a.m. The commander of the 24th established an advanced skirmish line under the direction of the acting major, Captain Roddey. He included the men of three veteran companies in the advanced skirmish line, Company A, under Captain Steinmeyer, Company F, under Captain Sherard, and Company D, under Lieutenant Gray.

The forward skirmishers were placed about one-quarter of a mile down the mountain in front of the regiment's main line. Capers carefully instructed the advanced skirmishers to offer strong resistance and detain the enemy as long as possible. However, when pressed too hard, Roddey's advanced skirmish line should fall back on the right and left of the regiment's main line. Roddey posted a picket about 200 yards in front of the advanced position, one on each flank, and placed a small skirmish line a few yards in front.

A cavalry squadron skirmished with the enemy between the advanced position and the Federal infantry. In short order, the cavalry arrived at a gallop. Roddey asked the cavalry commander to support the Confederate resistance. The cavalry commander retorted, "This is no place for me." With that, the cavalrymen kneed their mounts and galloped away. Before departing, the cavalry commander confirmed that the force in front was Union infantry.[16]

Soon after the cavalry disappeared in the direction of safety, the Federals appeared. Roddey's pickets fired into the approaching enemy and retired, followed closely by enemy skirmishers. As the Yankees appeared in view, Capers visited Roddey's line and found the troops well disposed. He cautioned about an enemy movement on the flanks and lingered with the

Captain John Henry Steinmeyer,
Company Commander, Company A
(Courtesy: War Between the States Museum, Florence, S.C.)

skirmishers as the intensity of the firing increased. By 11:00 a.m., Roddey's small skirmish line became heavily engaged.

The Federals threw a significant force, spearheaded by the 29th Missouri Regiment, against the position. The Union general sent a small demonstrating force of the Missourians in the direction of the Confederate left while a stronger regiment, the 26th Iowa, moved to the right flank of the skirmishers, intent on penetrating the Confederate rear.

After slowing the Federal thrust on the left, Roddey thought he could hold the position and asked Capers for 25 reinforcements. However, Capers observed from his vantage point that the enemy had already trapped the advanced force and counted 17 enemy battle flags in front of Roddey's skirmish line. In short order, Capers heard the enemy shout from each of Roddey's flanks and all firing ceased. Many of the men realized the hopelessness of the situation and ran as hard as they could to escape capture. Those men verified that the enemy penetrated the rear of the skirmishers, preventing an organized retreat. The Federals almost surrounded the entire force of advanced skirmishers.

Capers deployed the main force of the regiment in a manner that provided maximum protection for his flanks. After Roddey's force ceased firing, the enemy charged the 24th's main battle line, which repulsed the Yankee charge with a well-directed fire. Since the enemy could not progress, they entered the woods and attempted another flanking movement. The astute Capers spotted the movement and without hesitation withdrew the regiment with the order, "Pass the defile by the right flank." Each company continued firing until the moment of marching as the regiment withdrew and rejoined the brigade at bivouac two miles away.

The total number of casualties that the regiment suffered as a result of the action was large for a rather small or unimportant skirmish. Reports varied considerably regarding the number of soldiers captured. Sherman claimed that he captured "two companies" of men at Shipp's Gap, an action also known as Taylor's Ridge. Another Union report recorded that a total of 20 men was captured, including three from Company A. Capers indicated a loss of four officers and 40 men. In later writings, he thought that the regiment suffered the loss of 43 officers and men at Shipp's Gap. An accurate count of the number of South Carolinians killed that morning is not known.

Captain Steinmeyer, commander of Company A, who was numbered among the captured men, was interrogated by General Sherman himself. Capers wrote Steinmeyer's father and expressed his regrets at the loss of one of "my best officers and my excellent friend, your son." The colonel also applauded the young officer's gallantry, stating that "(Captain) Steinmeyer was captured after a gallant stand in the front." Steinmeyer, still lame because of his recent wound, could not run rapidly and thereby elude his

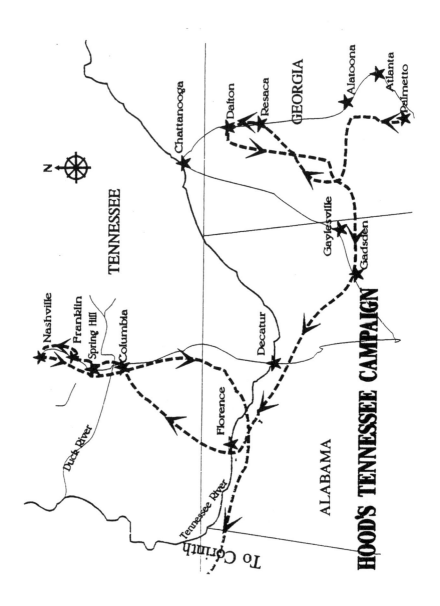

HOOD'S TENNESSEE CAMPAIGN

captors, and recounted that many of the men ran and contrived an escape.[17]

After the war, Steinmeyer intimated that the regiment retreated too soon and practically abandoned the advanced skirmishers. However, the decision to withdraw was based on an overall view of the situation. The main force itself risked capture, and finally retired at the behest of General Gist.[18] Steinmeyer, a brave and resolute Confederate officer, never considered retreat an option and his capture may well have been a result of that innate determination.[19]

Private Sylvester McGee was among the soldiers captured at Shipp's Gap. He did not survive his subsequent imprisonment at Camp Douglas, Illinois, and died in prison from the effects of scorbutis, probably scurvy. For Vessie, the "terrable affare" was over.[20]

The next day, the regiment departed the bivouac at an unusually early hour of 1:00 a.m. The men pressed ahead 22 miles via the Brown Town Valley Road and camped one mile from Alpine. That night, General Hood located his headquarters three miles from the forks of the Alpine and Gaylesville and the Alpine and Summerville roads.[21]

Hood's moves perplexed the Union commander. General Sherman could not decide whether Hood was heading for Tennessee or Alabama or Mississippi. Finally, the game of chase grew tiresome. By the time the Union army reached Gaylesville, Sherman decided Hood would not offer battle and boasted that his army had "ate out this valley good." He then turned his attention elsewhere.[22]

Sherman selected an alternate objective. He would make "the interior of Georgia feel the weight of war."[23] He provided General Halleck with information about his objectives, saying, "The movement is not purely military or strategic, it will illustrate the vulnerability of the South. They don't know what war means."[24]

Surmising that Hood would continue his campaign into Tennessee, Sherman urged Halleck to provide General Thomas at Nashville with "all the troops you can spare." Halleck immediately dspatched General Schofield's army to Nashville.[25] The men of Gist's Brigade, including the 24th Regiment, never looked at Sherman's strategy favorably. When they learned about Sherman's new objectives, the soldiers became deeply concerned for their families, who might be in his path.

Meanwhile, the men were becoming footsore and weary as a result of the long, grueling, daily marches. Fortunately, the cloudy, cool, and pleasant autumn weather held. The next day, October 18, the regiment entered Cherokee County, Alabama, and proceeded along the Turkey Town Valley Road, which circled the base of Lookout Ridge. In favorable weather, the men hiked 10 miles and bivouacked at Davis Cross Roads.[26]

Early the next morning, still weary after a brief night's rest, the regiment continued circling Lookout Mountain via the Blue Pond Road in the direction of Gadsden. As the pleasant weather held, the regiment proceeded 10 miles. The men noticed prime, although rocky and hilly, farm land along the route. As a result of the favorable marching conditions, the soldiers were in unusually high spirits. On October 20, the regiment covered 18 miles and crossed the fast-flowing Coosa River near Gadsden, Alabama. The countryside offered the soldiers beautiful scenery and sincere hospitality from its citizens. The weather remained clear, cool, and pleasant.

Mail arrived as the regiment passed through Cedar Town and was posted again at Gadsden. The delivery of mail always improved the morale of the soldiers who received a letter. The quartermaster issued critically needed supplies to the troops. Shoes arrived at the opportune moment, because 20 men in the regiment were completely barefooted, and the shoes of numerous others were worn out. However, the supplies satisfied only a fraction of the regiment's minimal needs.[27]

Since leaving Jonesboro, the army had marched 257 miles. Although the men still did not know where they were going, the army was one-half the distance to its destination, Nashville, Tennessee.[28]

After a quiet day of rest at Gadsden, the men, unimpressed by the length of the march, started again at 9:00 a.m. on October 22, 1864. They marched 12 miles and bivouacked atop Sand Mountain near the Black Warrior River. An observer considered the mountain a curiosity because it gave the appearance of broad unproductive tableland whose residents were destitute. The mountainous weather made a drastic change and suddenly turned cold. The next morning, the thinly clad troops awoke shivering under a white frost, the first of the year. That day, the regiment forded the Black Warrior River, trudged 20 miles farther, and bivouacked on the Decatur Road near Blountsville. Some of the men straggled but caught up with the regiment at the bivouac that night.[29]

With Sherman's attention directed toward Georgia, the men thought the marches seemed a bit more leisurely, while still long and arduous. On October 24, the route traversed Sand Mountain via the Decatur Road as the troops marched 15 miles over roads that were in excellent condition.

One officer decided everything was "wrapt in mystery" concerning the destination of the army or the purpose of the long marches. The soldiers, however, thought Hood was moving the army in the direction of Tennessee.

The regiment passed through a sparsely settled countryside and noticed considerable wild game. The next day, the canteen detail shot three deer, and the men feasted well that night. A soldier in Company D shot another deer as it leaped over the line of marching men.

The regiment proceeded 15 miles that day, descended Sand Mountain, and entered the Great Tennessee Valley. The men viewed the valley in all its magnificence, a panorama of beautiful scenery provided by the trees dressed in full fall foliage. The view was a spectacle that visibly impressed the men. The regiment bivouacked three miles from Summerville in rain that lasted all night.[30]

On October 26, 1864, the regiment proceeded 18 miles and bivouacked two-and-one-half miles from Decatur, Alabama. That day, the roads were extremely muddy and progress was particularly slow and fatiguing because of the constant rain.

Finally, the soldiers reached Decatur where they rested for the next two days. However, it rained continuously and the respite was most unpleasant. On the second day, the sounds of artillery blasts came from the direction of Decatur, which added apprehension to the men's misery. About nine o'clock the next morning, the regiment marched one mile toward the city and formed in line of battle. Finally, the rain stopped about 4:00 p.m. and the sun broke through the clouds in a most welcome Heavenly smile. The regiment remained in line of battle until about sunset and, without incident, rejoined the division one mile away.

The next day, Friday, Gist's Brigade moved only a short distance and relaxed for the remainder of the day. Since Wednesday night, the Confederate artillery had been firing slowly but steadily. That constant roar, the ground shaking with every blast, made rest at Decatur difficult and kept the men anxious as they expected an attack at every moment. Because they expected imminent battle, the men did not have an opportunity to cook and suffered the uncomfortable pangs of hunger.

Lieutenant Tillman gave in to the constant chills and fever and finally entered the hospital on October 28 at 6:00 p.m., for a three-day stay. The surgeons treated him with a "great deal of quinine & other stuff." He rode in an ambulance on October 29 while the army marched eight miles toward Tuscumbia on the Courtland Road, and again the next day, while the army gained another 16 miles. That day, the men applauded the appearance of Courtland, a beautiful and serene little Alabama village, nestled peacefully in the foothills.

On the last day of October, 1864, the soldiers trekked 15 miles under pleasant skies. The army passed through Tuscumbia and bivouacked one mile west of the almost deserted town. The farther the army proceeded west, the more homesick the South Carolina soldiers became. The men of the regiment had marched a total of 381 long, hard miles since leaving Jonesboro.

Shortages of essential supplies and equipment were becoming even more critical. At Tuscumbia, the quartermaster again issued clothing, shoes, and blankets that still did not meet minimal requirements. The regiment counted 23 men completely barefooted and 113 more that desperately needed shoes. Other supplies were equally inadequate.[31] No one escaped hunger and the men were complaining about the meager rations.

By the time the Army of Tennessee arrived in the splendid valley of the Tennessee, the enemy had already despoiled the countryside. A chimney standing alone was often the only remnant of many of the pretentious homes that once stood there. General Hood published a circular pointing out the desolated area and exhorted every man and officer "to vow the redemption of Tennessee from the grasp of the foe." The soldiers of the 24th, greeted the circular with a "hearty cheer." Many who cheered suffered seriously from the want of food, clothing, and shoes.[32] Lieutenant Tillman returned from the hospital still sick and extremely weak.

The mail seldom arrived and the opportunity to post a letter was equally infrequent. On November 1, Colonel Capers asked a soldier who departed the regiment en route to Virginia to mail a letter. The soldier was traveling via South Carolina. Capers vividly described the journey of the Army of Tennessee:

> Our march from Decatur to (Tuscumbia)...passed through the ample and beautiful valley of the Tenn....the broad noble fields are overgrown with dog fennel and broom grass...the tall isolated chimneys of these once teeming plantations...around the blackened ruins of homes once beautiful...speak to my heart a sad, sad comment on this strange struggle.

The next day, Capers wrote that the army would soon traverse the Tennessee River and boasted, "We will march on Nashville." He concluded that if Sherman followed into Tennessee, the Confederates would give battle, and he confidently expected victory.[33] A delay at Tuscumbia, which gave the Yankees "golden hours" in the race for Nashville, troubled the leaders of the Army of Tennessee. Colonel Capers purchased a new horse that he named Woodfire, after a fine Rockaway horse his father once owned.[34]

Money was becoming extremely scarce. That month, Capers sent his wife $20.00 and had no money left. On a personal note to his wife, Ellison wrote that he felt some mortification because she intimated that he was "a little dashed with crazy."[35] As all soldiers in the 24th, Ellison remained homesick for the tender arms of his loving wife.

During the pause at Tuscumbia, the weather was cold and wet. This made the bivouac very uncomfortable and the regiment's sick list increased. Finally, on November 8, the army broke camp at Tuscumbia and struggled through the rain and mud before bivouacking near the Florence railroad depot. At 1:00 a.m. on November 9, a cold wind sprang up that blew from the south, which gave the men hope that after several days of rain the southern wind would bring sunshine. Lieutenant Holmes, the adjutant, was "all used up" from exposure and fatigue and reported to the hospital.

212

The usually resilient Capers had one of his infrequent bad days. It terribly concerned the regimental commander that he alone was responsible for all the "head work" in the regiment. He thought some officers were willing and ready, but incompetent. Capers grumbled, "The weight of the impact of that word is pregnant with great issues. Incompetence. It is a vampire, everywhere in our army, sucking the very lifeblood of all our efforts." Later, Capers clarified his remarks about incompetence. He did not direct the tirade at the officers of the 24th but at the members of the engineer corps who had trouble spanning the Tennessee River with the pontoon bridge. After receiving his pay, Ellison mailed Lottie $175.00. His bout of moodiness was increased when he learned later the same day that the paymaster at Selma was out of money.[36] The fortunes of the South and its hopes for success were becoming more critical every day.

On November 10, the troops prepared to cross the Tennessee River. However, the pontoon bridge was still out of order and Hood halted the movement until the next day. The men marched one and one half miles away from the river and bivouacked near the railroad.

The weather continued to wreak havoc with the men. The next morning, a white frost covered the ground. Ice formed that evening, and the thinly clad soldiers shivered and suffered badly. Many of the men were loudly voicing complaints about feeling bad, because they were suffering the effects of colds and debility. Several officers were also ill. Lieutenant Tillman thought he had cholera, and Captain Risher regretfully reported to the hospital for treatment because he was suffering the extreme pains of rheumatism.[37]

The regiment lingered at the bivouac near the railroad tracks until November 13. That day, the engineers finally completed the pontoon bridge, and the regiment marched over the river without further delay. As they crossed the river, the bands were playing, raising everyone's spirits. Afterwards, the troops marched four miles and passed through Florence, Alabama. The regiment encamped southwest of the town. The weather was somewhat better that day.

The greetings of the ladies provided one of the lighter moments that somehow alleviated many of the hardships endured on the long forced marches. These ladies were extremely pretty and rendered the army an exceptionally warm greeting. The next day, the regiment "turned out without arms and threw up breastworks." The army lingered at Florence for a full week and constantly labored on improving the fortifications.

The good weather soon disappeared, and the skies steadily dumped rain as conditions deteriorated. Rations became sparse, and the command exasperated the feelings of the men when it declared a fast day. As usual, some of the famished men who found food did not observe the fast. On the following day, a forage party brought in three fat hogs and some turnips, and that night the men satiated their appetites.

The quartermaster issued supplies that still did not satisfy the basic mandatory needs of the soldiers. In the 24th Regiment, 30 soldiers were barefooted and 40 more badly needed shoes. Seventy men had no blankets as the weather turned cold, yet they still cheerfully and dutifully endured the rain and snow.[38]

Sickness, lack of food, and the bad weather all contributed to the soldiers' misery. After Lieutenant Holmes reported sick to the hospital, Colonel Capers detailed Lieutenant William M. Beckham as adjutant. Private George N. Freeman, Company I, became ill and departed for the general hospital. Lieutenant Tillman accompanied the sick soldier part of the way. On November 18, the provost guard arrested Privates Ransom Gregg and John Williams for "illegal foraging." Two days later, the regiment sent out foragers who brought in "three shoats" or young hogs, and the troops again ate well. The weather was cloudy, drizzling rain, windy, and bitter cold.[39] The severe weather held the men in its miserable grip like a hand that clasped a snowball and could not let go.

The regiment received word for a move that the general canceled the next day. The men speculated if he canceled the order because of the rain or other army matters. Some conjectured that Sherman had turned his attention toward Atlanta. Others thought that Hood was awaiting the arrival of cavalry support. One soldier observed the depth of the mud and worried that if the rain continued, the wheels of the wagons and artillery "would be locked fast by the powers of mud." In camp, the shivering men sought shelter in tents and remained reasonably dry.

The lack of comfort and the miserable weather held the attention of the soldiers. Capers expressed his appreciation for the much needed woolen cap and gloves that Lottie sent by Sergeant Major Triest. A friend presented the colonel with two pounds of coffee that he enjoyed. The next day the harsh weather continued cold and damp, with a misting rain. The camp was rife with rumors that Sherman had turned toward Macon.[40]

Colonel Capers made a dire prognostication that almost predicted the future:

> Many of us who survive this contest, will find ourselves poor...dependent...our blood lost...sacrifices made ...suffering endured will neither buy our meat and bread ...nor pay the debts which the necessity...incident to our positions in the war obliged us to contract. Our names may appear in the public prints...to be read as in the disgrace of litigation...we will be, in all respects, subordinated to those who kept one hand on the sword, only, while they gave all else to themselves. They will be as much...more respected after the war...vastly more comfortable.[41]

214

While at the bivouac, Gist's Brigade completed several administrative actions. One was the appointment of an examining board to interview candidates for promotion. The board consisted of Capers and Jones of the 24th and Major Dunlap of the 46th Georgia Regiment. The board interviewed Captain W. G. Foster, commander of the 65th Georgia, for promotion to colonel. On November 15, 1864, the board decided that Foster "exhibited admirable good sense and a fair knowledge of the duties of a regimental commander." The board unanimously recommended the captain for promotion.[42]

The brief respite at Florence, Alabama, offered the men an opportunity for writing letters and attending to personal needs. The colonel had his clothes laundered in town at a cost of $2.00 for five collars, one shirt, three handkerchiefs, one pair of drawers, and a pair of socks. Ben located provisions and that night prepared a dinner of fried chicken, cornbread, boiled Irish (white) potatoes, and turnips. It distressed the soldiers because the quartermaster could not provide adequate forage for the animals.[43]

Their journey started again on November 21, 1864, in a storm of wind, snow and sleet. The day was bitterly cold. The wretched condition of the roads caused the wagon wheels to sink to the hubs in the muck and mire. During the day, the men walked primarily in the woods and across the fields, which provided a better footing than the roads. The quartermaster wagons struck and destroyed Capers' personal buggy. Exerting extraordinary effort, the regiment managed a ten-mile trek. Capers lamented, "My poor fellows whose feet are on the ground." That night was the coldest of the season. The men were without sufficient shelter and blankets; their bivouac was appalling. On November 22, the roads were frozen solid and became slick as the artillery passed. Suffering terribly, the thinly clad troops marched 12 miles, crossed a pontoon bridge over the Tennessee River. The Army of Tennessee once again entered the state of Tennessee.[44]

As the army continued its journey, steadily moving north, the men never ceased suffering because of the lack of adequate rations and clothing. The troops left the bivouac at 8:00 a.m. on November 23 and tramped 16 1/2 miles. The weather was clear but bitter cold, and the ground was frozen solid. The regiment pushed through a barren and poorer section of the country and bivouacked one mile from Waynesboro. The next day the men skirted the town over reasonably good roads and camped 16 miles beyond. Lieutenant Tillman, who was sick, hungry and weak, recorded that rations were scanty. Sergeant Charles Bowers killed a deer, providing a small feast. One deer couldn't last long, though, and the beleaguered quartermaster had to further reduce the men's rations. Finally, rations consisted of only a pitiful amount of scorched corn. Weatherwise, the skies became clear, and although it remained cold, the day was a little more pleasant as the troops plodded along.[45]

The next day, the soldiers progressed 17 miles through Henryville, a dirty little village, where they forded a stream the local people called "Buffalo River." The roads were in good condition, except a little muddy. The men suffered continuously from the inadequate rations. On Saturday, November 26, 1864, the regiment started at 6:00 a.m., and the men hurried through Mt. Pleasant, a pretty village with polite people. The residents of the village extended the soldiers a gracious welcome. The image of the countryside improved and exuded the characteristics of a rich and productive locality. The following day, the regiment trekked 18 miles under more rainy skies and bivouacked two and one half miles from Columbia, Tennessee, which was occupied by a strong enemy garrison.

General Stephen D. Lee's Corps invested the city. That night, the regiment furnished 16 men for picket duty. During the next two days the men relaxed in camp, required only to furnish a daily picket detail of 100 men.[46]

The first night at Columbia, many fine fat hogs, cattle, and chickens were available for the first time in many days. The men finally received an abundance of food and satiated their ravenous appetites.[47] Locally, the Federals left many of the mills intact, but the troops learned that the Yankees had burned the mills farther north.

About 4:00 a.m. on November 28, the regiment was relieved from picket duty and rejoined the brigade located four miles away. At long last, the weather became pleasant.[48] Since leaving Jonesboro, the regiment had traveled 478 1/2 miles.

General Hood confidently envisioned the Army of Tennessee as soon controlling the State of Tennessee. He eagerly added, "Except Nashville, & perhaps even that." This was the news the men of the 24th Regiment enthusiastically awaited.[49] A staff officer proclaimed that the army was "in fine spirits and anxious to meet the enemy." He added, "Tomorrow, we will get our army up...force them (the enemy) to fight or to leave."[50]

By the time dawn broke on the warm and cloudy, late fall day of November 29, 1864, the 24th was already awake. The men energetically prepared for another long, forced march. They started that morning without breakfast, hurried to Davis' Ford, and crossed the Duck River on a pontoon bridge.

A special excitement filled the air. General Hood issued clear directions for Cheatham's and Stewart's Corps to gain the enemy's rear at Spring Hill. Cheatham led the way, followed by Stewart's Corps. Lee's Corps engaged the Yankees practically all day at Columbia, camouflaging the movements of Cheatham and Stewart.

After traversing the Duck River, the regiment continued its rapid march toward the rear of the Federal army. The troops covered 18 miles, following little-used community by-paths and neighborhood roads; part of the time they even marched across open plantations. The rough route made rapid progress difficult, yet the men maintained a rapid gait, steadily moving toward Spring Hill. The men suffered from the want of food and water, but they heartily approved of the speedy forced march and moved "with spirit and excitement." That afternoon, the regiment forded Rutherford Creek and at sunset stopped one mile from Spring Hill.[51]

The Army of Tennessee approached Spring Hill from two directions. Cheatham's and Stewart's Corps advanced from the south, and Forrest's Cavalry came from the east. The cavalry attacked the Union forces. However, their assault made little progress.[52]

About 3:00 p.m., lead elements of Cheatham's Corps arrived at Spring Hill. As the men approached the village, Cleburne's Division attacked with vigor, and the Federals retreated in disorder. Bate's Division, which was following Cleburne, stopped at the Columbia and Franklin Pike. Brown's Division arrived and faced in a northerly direction, and Cleburne aligned with Brown. Soon, Stewart's Corps and Major General Edward Johnson's Division arrived and also aligned with Brown's Division. The Confederates formed 25,000 soldiers in battle array for an attack on 6,000 enemy soldiers that were in full retreat along a line three miles long.[53]

Gist's Brigade formed its line of battle facing Spring Hill, positioned on the extreme left of Brown's Division; the 24th formed on the left of the brigade. The men observed a confused enemy, unprepared for battle, and the soldiers considered it the opportune moment for an assault. They heard the sounds of sporadic fighting as Forrest's cavalry engaged the enemy on the far right of the regiment, and every soldier expected to attack at any moment. Alas! No order came.[54] In later years, the dilemma still puzzled Colonel Ellison Capers: "This state of affairs was, and still is, inexplicable to me."[55]

The head of the enemy column reached the Confederate position about 7:00 p.m., and finally passed about 1:00 a.m., marching unmolested, "rapidly and silently," through Spring Hill. Meanwhile, "The Confederates slept - peacefully out in sight of the whole line."[56]

The night of November 29, 1864, was an anxious one, indeed, for the men of the 24th Regiment. Every one of those battle wise veterans comprehended "the opportunity of the moment." A distressed Ellison Capers could not forthrightly answer the question asked by the men of the 24th, "Why don't we attack the enemy?"

Seldom did Colonel Capers allow himself the frustration that he experienced at Spring Hill as he wrote in his journal:

> Enemy retreating in sight! Time for attack, but no attack!
> Can't imagine why we do not go forward. Gist, Strahl, &
> I ride forward in pistol shot of enemy, at dark. No fires.
> Troops rest on arms in line. Miserable night. Enemy

passing by. Somebody in authority ought to be shot! Marched 18 miles to strike the enemy's rear, reached it, but did not attack a retreating enemy in flank, and in full sight![57]

Colonel Capers rode forward with Brigadier Generals Gist and Otho F. Strahl and observed the enemy's line of retreat and the indefensible position of the Federals. Capers disgustedly drew his pistol from its holster and fired the weapon until empty in the direction of the retreating Union army. He never understood why the Confederates did not attack. In later years, perhaps influenced by General S. D. Lee and Judge J. P. Young, a participant who researched the battle for 30 years, Capers decided that General Brown was at fault. None of the senior generals at Spring Hill accepted responsibility for failure to order the attack. No army from either side during the entire war ever missed a better opportunity for an overwhelming military victory. With that, the Army of Tennessee bungled its last chance. Oblivion was near.

The men's anxiety over missing this opportune moment for victory precluded a full night's rest. Many slept only one hour before reveille sounded the next morning.[58]

The weather smiled favorably on Wednesday, November 30, 1864, and provided a beautiful autumn day. The men arose early and at about 8:00 a.m. Gist's Brigade joined the march on the pike toward Franklin. The soldiers marched eagerly at a rapid pace, Stewart first, followed by Cheatham. The Federals clearly marked the tracks of their retreat by leaving the hulls of 33 burned wagons and numerous dead mules along the pike. They burned the wagons and deliberately killed mules to prevent the animals from falling into the hands of the Confederates.[59]

About 2:00 p.m., Stewart's Corps reached a line of high hills where the enemy had positioned a strong rear guard. This day, the Confederates did not hesitate, and the lead corps sent the enemy's rear guard scurrying for cover. At 3:00 p.m., the two corps hesitated momentarily at the foot of the hills and formed in line of battle. Stewart formed east of the Columbia Pike and Cheatham on the west. Cheatham's Corps placed Cleburne's Division on the right near the Pike, while Brown formed on the left of Cleburne, and Bate rested on the left of Brown. The divisions formed in two lines. Gist's and Gordon's Brigades were first line in Brown's Division. They were supported by the brigades of Strahl behind Gist and Carter behind Gordon. Gist's Brigade was on the left of Brown's Division, and the 24th held the position in the front rank on the left of the brigade. The 16th Regiment was on the right of the 24th as well as the right of the brigade. On the left of the 24th was Bate's Division; the right of Bate's Division next to the 24th was formed by Stevens' old brigade. In this battle order, the Army of Tennessee eased forward with bands playing and battle flags flying. The two corps of

Confederate soldiers scaled the hills that stood between the Confederates and the Yankee entrenchments at Franklin, Tennessee, ready for the assault on the Yankee breastworks.[60]

The enemy held a heavily entrenched position in front of the little city that extended in a semicircle from the Harpeth River on one flank and connected with the Harpeth River on the other. Those works were about one and one-fourth miles from the Army of Tennessee's position across an open field. The Federals had stationed a short line of troops, perhaps one division, about 500 yards in front of the main force. The advanced skirmish line from Lane's Brigade was situated behind an elevated stone fence. The soldiers of Lane's Federal Brigade, including the 97th Ohio, lay there and waited for the Confederates.

As the Confederate army readied for battle, Cheatham remonstrated with Hood about making a frontal assault. He implored, "I don't like the looks of this fight. The Federals have an excellent position and are well fortified." Hood brushed Cheatham's objections aside and responded, "It is better to attack here than at Nashville where they have been entrenching for three years." Without another word, Cheatham turned on his heels and departed for his place of duty.[61]

General Nathan B. Forrest, too, tried his hand at convincing Hood concerning the wisdom of a flanking movement. Forrest suggested that he take his cavalry down the river and attack the flank of the Federal line as Hood attacked from the front. Hood was as impatient with Forrest as he had been with Cheatham, and responded, "There are only a few there and we will have little difficulty with them."[62] That afternoon, Hood determined that the Army of Tennessee would make a frontal assault, without artillery support, on the well-entrenched enemy lines.

The 24th inched slowly forward, formed in line of battle. Colonel Capers rode on horseback in front of the regiment. Lieutenant Colonel Jones stood on the right, silently observing the situation, and the acting major, Captain Bowers, was equally intense on the left of the regiment. Private Adam Carpenter carried the colors, which as always waved silently, furled in the breeze, proudly and defiantly.

As the 24th moved forward, it passed over a small elevation. There, the regiment hesitated momentarily, silently awaiting the general's word for the charge.

General Gist appeared after a few short moments that seemed like an eternity, and rode his horse along the regiment's front. The general approached Capers and gave the order for the brigade to charge simultaneously with Gordon's Brigade. Gist hesitated a fleeting moment and "waved his hat to the gallant Twenty-Fourth." He expressed his confidence in the regiment and "wished victory to the Twenty-Fourth." Then he rode away to perform urgent duties on other parts of the battlefield. Capers

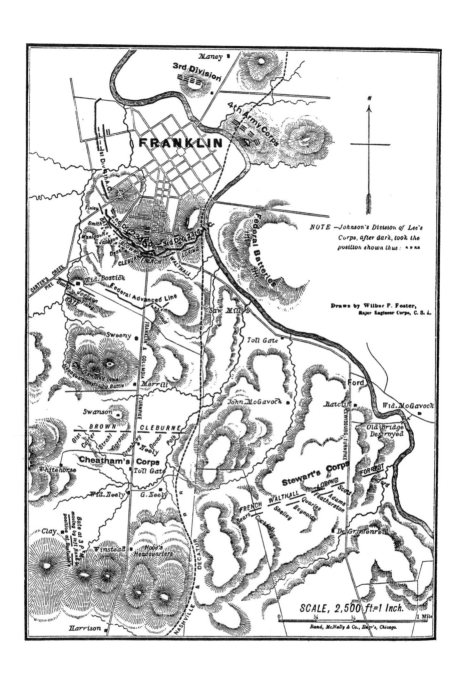

NOTE —*Johnson's Division of Lee's Corps, after dark, took the position shown thus :* ▪ ▪ ▪

Drawn by Wilbur F. Foster,
Major Engineer Corps, C. S. L.

SCALE, 2,500 ft=1 Inch.

Rand, McNally & Co., Bair's, Chicago.

survived the battle and recorded the event:

> I kissed my hand to him and he was soon lost in the smoke
> of battle, never more to be seen in the front of the regiment
> he had assisted in forming, and whose respect & confi-
> dence he had always possessed.

In later years, Capers related other aspects of the event that he experienced that fateful day:

> General Gist rode up to me in the course of the battle and
> called out excitedly...the only time I ever saw him excited
> on a battlefield, ("Colonel, I count on the 24th today.")
> That he could count on the 24th the result showed.[63]

Moments after the General's departure, the enemy's artillery batteries opened at full bore with blasts that rent the air with resounding bursts. The Confederates, prepared and ready for action beheld the battlefield, a magnificent spectacle. The military bands "played their finest and liveliest tunes." Generals were "dashing among the regiments making speeches and barking orders for the attack. Staff officers and couriers were dashing back and forth among the lined up troops receiving and delivering messages. The smoke already generated by the battle from the shell bursts wreathed the air with great circles of smoke."[64] The battlefield provided the troops with a panorama that they would long remember. Capers recorded his personal reaction to the grandeur of the moment, "The sight inspired every man of the Twenty Fourth with the sentiment of duty."[65]

General Hood called the two corps forward at 4:00 p.m.[66] The mighty Army of Tennessee, without hesitation or pusillanimity initiated the assault, one from which it would never recover. The "journey to oblivion" was nearly over.

The blue soldiers who manned the advanced skirmish line that day knew they faced a determined fight. Suddenly, the Confederates advanced "with a bound forward and that familiar yell known all too well." The Federals behind the low stone wall involuntarily recoiled, held steady, and greeted the rapidly advancing Southerners with a hot musket fire. The fight was on![67]

Twenty thousand dedicated Confederate soldiers moved forward as one, their rifles poised and bayonets glinting brightly in the sunlight. The Southerners marched steadily against the foe in "splendid order." The Federal forward force remained only briefly behind the stone wall before starting a hasty retreat toward the main line, firing as they fled. The enemy had constructed a formidable abatis in front of their main line that was hastily opened for the retiring troops. The Confederates quickly spotted the gaps in the abatis and ran as rapidly as possible to gain the openings before the Yankees could close them. The chase was frantic, and, as the troops exited the abatis, the two forces mingled closely. The 44th Missouri

The Battlefield of Franklin, looking north from General Cheatham's Headquarters
(Battles and Leaders of the Civil War)

Volunteers (Unionists) fired a broad side into the fray that injured as many Federal as Confederate soldiers. Some of the blue soldiers did not stop running until they reached safe refuge at the river bank.[68]

Tragedy struck as soon as the regiment came within range of the advanced Federal position. Lieutenant Colonel Jones fearlessly led the right of the regiment directly into the teeth of the enemy's withering rifle fire. One of the very first shots from the advanced troops of Lane's Brigade hit Jones, who fell, dangerously wounded, struck by a minié ball through the jaw and neck. The stretcher bearers at once removed the wounded officer from the battlefield to the division hospital, the A. M. Harrison House, located about one mile behind the lines.[69] There the wounded man received needed medical attention, but the surgeons quickly determined that Jones' wound was mortal.

Shortly after Jones fell, a Federal minié ball disabled Gist's horse. The cool general dismounted and continued cheering his men onward. Shortly, the Federals shot Gist through the thigh. Limping badly, Gist steadfastly remained at his post as he hobbled along the front of his brigade, urging his troops ever forward. Suddenly, Gist was struck by another ball. This time a .58 caliber ball pierced the general's right lung. Capers thought the Yankees shot Gist through the heart and reported that the general died on the battlefield at 5:30 p.m. However, Gist initially survived the wound.

The stretcher bearers removed the unconscious general to the hospital at the Harrison House, where he died that night at 8:30. Captain H. D. Garden and Lieutenant Frank Trenholm, Gist's aides, and Ben Wiley, his loyal servant, attended. Dr. Wright treated the wound. The three men were with Gist until the end and recorded his final words, "Take me to my wife!"[70]

The first line of Brown's Division established itself in the ditch immediately in front of the Federal second line. Once established, Brown's troops never retreated. General Brown himself received a serious wound.

The regiment reached the second line of works "torn and exhausted." Its men maintained their position in the ditch, but they could not cross into the enemy works. Private Adam Carpenter placed the flag of the regiment on the enemy breastworks, and there the colors remained. At one point, a Federal soldier who had designs of seizing the colors of the 24th accosted the color bearer. Carpenter, his ammunition depleted, quickly reacted by picking up a rock and braining his assailant. The proud and defiant colors remained where they were.[71]

Just before the men of the 24th reached the ditch, a Federal minié ball severely wounded Capers in the ankle. One of his soldiers saved the disabled colonel by dragging him into the ditch, where he was safe from further enemy rifle fire. In later years, Capers determined that the soldier was from one of the companies from Edgefield District, but he never learned the

Captain James Tillman, company commander
Company I, 24th Regiment
(Courtesy: George Tillman Bailey, Jr., Wilson, N. C.)

soldier's identity.[72]

The other brigade units arrived at the ditch immediately after the 24th. The 8th Georgia Battalion and the 46th Georgia Regiment also gained a position in the ditch, as equally torn and exhausted as the 24th. On the right of the brigade, the 16th Regiment also reached the second line of the enemy works. Major Smith, the acting commander, scaled the enemy works and captured several prisoners and a sword. During the action, the Yankees severely wounded Smith while he was behind the Union side of the works, but he managed to return to the Confederate side.[73]

Enemy rifle and artillery fire prevented the stretcher bearers from reaching many of the wounded men who fell near the enemy works. Those wounded, including Capers and Smith, suffered without relief until late that night. At approximately the same time that Gist's Brigade became established in front of the enemy's second line of works, Strahl's and Carter's supporting brigades started forward. The two supporting brigades came under a severe artillery fire from as far away as the other side of the Harpeth River. This bombardment literally "tore the lines of the two brigades to pieces." The Federal artillery fire wounded General Strahl and killed his entire staff before the men passed through the abatis. The advancing line trembled and shook but went on with momentum to reach the ditch. But it could go no further.[74]

The Confederates established a line in single rank on the crest of their side of the Federal parapet and maintained pressure on the enemy. The men still in the ditch loaded muskets, passed the weapons to the men on the crest of the works, and thereby increased the rate of fire threefold. The soldiers kept up a steady and effective fire until the enemy ceased firing at 9:00 p.m. That fire, or "show of force," no doubt, held the enemy at bay.[75]

Lieutenant Tillman decided he could scale the second line of works and sought out the badly wounded Capers in order to ask for support of the movement. Tillman suggested that Capers put his hat on his sword and wave it, and the men would go over the ditch.

Capers recognized James Tillman as a man who never needed inspiration for duty and replied, "I am too weak from the loss of blood to do even that."

At that point, Tillman barked out a command mustering Company I for the task. But, the company was very much scattered and mingled with others, and few soldiers heard or comprehended the order. Finally, Tillman succeeded in gathering Privates Carpenter, J. P. Blackwell, Anderson Walls and one unknown soldier from a Georgia Regiment. These brave men eagerly followed Tillman over the top of the second line and into the enemy works.

Tillman and his men found the ditch inside the works full of Yankee soldiers. To prevent capture, the small group of Confederates put on a bold front and "started the bluff game at once." A lieutenant, commander of the Union color company, thought he should "live and fight again" and surrendered first. Later, the small squad from the 24th captured the entire color company as well as the regimental colors of the 97th Ohio. Tillman grabbed the colors held by the enemy color sergeant and told Private Blackwell, "Shoot the color bearer if he does not give up the colors." Blackwell did not have another cartridge, and his gun was empty. However, he responded with "immediate alternate action and clubbed his musket which proved very effective." Tillman handed the flag and the prisoners over to the men on the Confederate side of the works.[76]

Some confusion existed whether the Union color bearer died that day in defense of his colors. The color bearer desperately held onto the colors of the 97th Ohio Regiment and received what everyone thought was a fatal blow. The Confederates left the man for dead on the field, and even the colonel reported that the color sergeant of the 97th Ohio Regiment died in defense of his flag. However, over twenty years later, on November 7, 1885, Capers received a letter from former Federal Private Henry Infield who related that Private Laiken, the 97th Regiment's color bearer that day, had survived the war.[77]

During the melee, Private Blackwell relieved the Federal lieutenant of his sword and pitched it over the works. Lieutenant Padgett of Company E claimed it and Blackwell reported, "He got off with it."[78]

By now the Yankee firing had almost ceased. This indicated to Lieutenant Tillman that he and his small group could capture the enemy's next line. Therefore, the group started over the third line and called for the surrender of the enemy behind the third line. Instead of surrendering, the Federals opened fire and struck three of the five men. Anderson Walls received a wound in his shoulder. The Federals shot down the soldier from the Georgia Regiment and forced Private Blackwell off the third line. The Federal balls pierced 30 holes through Blackwell's blankets and cartridge box. Only Lieutenant Tillman and Private Carpenter emerged unscathed.[79]

Other acts of heroism occurred that were above and beyond the call of duty. Three men from Company H, alone and unsupported, charged over the second line of works and unflinchingly encountered a hot enemy fire. The three Confederates captured two officers and eight men. Private James Whyte Bigham, of Company H, led the group or the crowd as the Southerners called themselves. Privates John Bagley and Hugh T. Bruce ably assisted Bigham in performing the dangerous chore. Bagley was the same brave soldier who had removed General Walker's body from the battlefield during the battle of Atlanta.[80]

Shortly after 9:00 p.m., the Federals ceased firing all along the line. Before midnight, the Union forces slipped quietly away, leaving their dead and wounded. After the enemy retreated, the Confederates occupied the

226

bloody battlefield of Franklin. The battlefield was not worth the costly sacrifice. Six general officers, including Generals Cleburne and Gist, had died, and another was captured as a result of the battle. General Brown was seriously wounded, and a colonel was the ranking officer in the entire division. Few leaders survived to maintain the direction of the army. Although the battle of Franklin ended when General Schofield retired toward Nashville, Hood's army was defeated and would never regain its effectiveness.

After Franklin, the Army of Tennessee became "paralyzed from further effective service."[81] There and then, on the bloody battlefield at Franklin, Tennessee, the mighty Army of Tennessee arrived at oblivion. The real sadness of the situation existed because General Hood either refused to accept or realize the army's condition.

With both Capers and Jones shot down, Captain A. E. Bowers, acting major, commanded the regiment. The ranking officer of Brown's Division was Colonel C. S. Hunt, commander of a Tennessee Regiment. The senior officer of Gist's Brigade was Captain Gillis of the 46th Georgia Regiment, and Captain H. Garden, General Gist's aide, alone represented the brigade staff. In Brown's Division, the major general, four brigadier generals, all the regimental commanders, and most of the staff officers, were either killed or wounded. Even though the division lost its leadership, the survivors stood fast.[82]

The 24th counted few officers available to lead its companies. Those still present were Griffith, Company C; Bowers, Company D; Risher, Company E; Beatty, Company F; Beckham, Company G; McDaniel, Company H; and Tillman, Company I. Capers recognized every officer in the 24th for their leadership and proudly proclaimed that every man in the regiment had performed his duty.[83]

Soon after the battle, Tillman visited Capers at the hospital and delivered the captured colors of the 97th Ohio. Capers considered it an honor when he presented this trophy to the commanding general. Hood received few stands of enemy colors that day, and he expressed his gratification. He returned the colors to the regiment with warmest congratulations. Capers especially recognized Tillman and the other men responsible for seizing the colors.[84]

In later years, Capers and Smith decided that General Bate had precipitated the battle's dreadful outcome by his belated advance on the Federal left. General H. R. Jackson's Brigade advanced on the immediate left of Gist's Brigade, and Tyler's Brigade, commanded by General T. B. Smith, advanced on the left of Jackson. Bate assigned Finley's Brigade, commanded that day by Colonel Robert Bullock, to support both Jackson's and Finley's Brigades. Jackson's Brigade reached the Union second line, and his men swept over it, but Jackson's horse would not vault the ditch.

227

Top photo is gravestone of Lt. Col. Jesse S. Jones
at Cross Swamp Church, Islandton, S. C.
Photo on bottom shows the grave marker adjacent to the
South Carolina monument at the Confederate Cemetery
in Franklin that bears the inscription "JSJ"
(*Photos by author*)

The general rode along his left, seeking a convenient spot where the horse could breach the breastworks. To his dismay, Jackson discovered the left of his brigade broken and retreating in disorder. On the left was a battalion of sharpshooters who often distinguished themselves for standing firm and maintained a well-known reputation for bravery and gallantry. Jackson reassured the men and insisted on a renewed forward movement. However, a brave young officer told him, "We will all be captured! We are again deserted. The entire left of the division has retreated from the field." Jackson's further inspection confirmed that Tyler's Brigade, indeed, had broken a considerable distance from the breastworks and had fallen back on Finley's Brigade. At that time, both brigades retreated behind the protection of a hill. Jackson alleged that not a man from either of those two brigades charged into any part of the enemy's lines that day. Thus, the men of Brown's Division assaulted heavily armed breastworks largely unsupported on the left.[85] The situation spelled disaster.

After the war, Capers and Smith discussed Bate's tardy appearance that day. Bate's Division may have received credit for advancing late that day when actually General Edward Johnson's Division of Lee's Corps should have received the credit. The latter division advanced on the Confederate left late that afternoon.[86]

Meanwhile, the surgeons treated the mortally wounded Jones at the division hospital located at the Harrison house. However, they could not stop the hemorrhage from the terrible jaw and neck wound. His faithful servant, a family slave, remained with Jesse S. Jones as he prepared himself for the inevitable. Jesse wrote two letters and entrusted his servant with his gold watch to deliver only to his brothers. The wounded man suffered terribly for eight days before he finally died. Bishop Quintard visited Jones and the wounded Brigadier General Carter at the Harrison house on the evening of December 7, 1864. The Bishop discovered that Jones' wound, even at that moment, was hemorrhaging badly. As hard as the wounded man fought for life, Jones could survive no longer, and he died during the night, either late on the evening of December 7 or early on the morning of December 8. General Carter died as a result of his wounds soon afterwards. Two more irreplaceable Confederate leaders were gone.

Jones' servant constructed a wooden coffin and buried Jesse in a well-marked grave near the other South Carolina dead. The servant sewed Jones' gold watch into his under clothes and wrapped the two letters in a protective cover before starting the long, sad, trek to the small hamlet of Ashton, South Carolina. There, he broke the news that Jesse was dead and delivered his watch and final letters. After the war, Jesse's brothers returned to Franklin in a horse-drawn wagon and retrieved the deceased soldier's remains. Jesse was reinterred near the graves of his father and mother in the old Jones/Murdaugh cemetery, located at the Cross Swamp Methodist Church near

Islandton, South Carolina. There he rests today, his grave marked with a Confederate headstone. Still located in the Confederate Cemetery at Franklin, adjacent to the South Carolina monument, exists a grave marker with the initials "JSJ."[87]

Colonel Capers expressed his grief at the loss of the regiment's lieutenant colonel:

> Lieut. Col. J. S. Jones died of his wounds at the division
> hospital a few days after the battle. His loss will be much
> felt by the regiment and is greatly deplored by his colonel.[88]

Sergeant P. R. Sine, Company A, 97th Ohio Volunteers Infantry, was in charge of some of the blue soldiers on the Federal advanced line. He left a record of his admiration for the bravery of the Confederate soldiers who assaulted the Union forces that day.

> I hope I may see the day that I can take those brave boys
> who opposed us there by the hand. for I consider them
> brave to a fault. "Hero" does not define their position clear
> enough. I will say there is no precedent for the bravery
> shown there; It was beyond supremacy. No braver men
> ever faced each other on a field of carnage.[89]

Sergeant Sine retreated from Franklin with the 97th Ohio. Almost three weeks later, he pressed through Franklin with the Northern army while pursuing the retreating Confederate army. Nostalgically, Sergeant Sine looked over the battlefield and suddenly caught sight of a plain board marker that stood over a single grave. Sine moved closer so he could read the Confederate marker that indicated the burial place of a group of men, and he recalled the company was from the 24th Regiment: "A captain and twenty-two of his company lie here."[90] Mass burial - a hard ending for twenty-three South Carolinians that is wistfully appropriate for one of the South's last major battles.

Fortunately, Colonel Capers survived and recorded his own impression of deeds of the 24th Regiment at Franklin:

> No command of the army fought with more spirit and
> heroic determination at Franklin than the Twenty Fourth
> South Carolina Volunteers Infantry.[91]

Colonel Capers also reflected on the hardships and suffering borne by the regiment during the two months preceding the battle at Franklin. The men had marched over five hundred miles. The poorly clad soldiers subsisted substantially on short rations and sustenance that often consisted of no more than parched corn and at times little of that:

> Not a single man of the 24th deserted his colors...whenever
> called on to meet the enemy on the picket line, or in battle,
> I always felt the highest pride in the conduct of the Carolin-
> ians...I had the honor to command.[92]

Years later, General Schofield visited Europe and spoke about the battle of Franklin. He told the German Kaiser about the bravery displayed by the soldiers of the Confederate army that day, "The highest exhibition of human courage in the history of the world was the Confederate attack on my breastworks at Franklin."

At Franklin, the 24th Regiment, South Carolina Volunteers, Infantry were in the first line of the assault and did themselves proud!

In 1885, Capers thought that it would be magnanimous if the regiment returned the colors captured at Franklin. After much correspondence between Capers and Colonel John Q. Lane, the commander of the 97th Ohio Regiment, the two leaders coordinated the arrangements. Private J. Preston Blackwell, then a member of the South Carolina House of Representatives, and Private Anderson Walls visited Zanesville, Ohio, and returned the colors on behalf of the members of the 24th Regiment. Other commitments prevented Capers from attending the affair. The 97th OVI Survivors Association named the two ex-Confederate privates and Capers as honorary members on December 3, 1885. Representative Blackwell informed Capers about the esteem voiced by the members of the 97th Regiment:

> [They] loved you better than even their own officers,
> [Capers'] name was mentioned so often and so lov-
> ingly...from the manner in which you were spoken of that
> you were the commander of the 97th Ohio instead of the
> Twenty Fourth S.C.V.[93]

The first day of December, 1864, was a sad day in the history of the Army of Tennessee. The 24th, along with the other regiments, bivouacked near the battlefield and buried the dead. In addition, the survivors visited the wounded in the division hospital at the Harrison house. The men knew they would never see many of the wounded men again. During the day, the few survivors attended the funeral of General States Rights Gist and wished their slain leader a final farewell.[94]

The regiment, devastated by the loss of many troops and senior leaders, reformed its decimated ranks that reflected "sorrow on every face." Captain Griffith, late of Company C, commanded the remnants of the regiment.[95] The actual number of casualties suffered by the 24th at Franklin is unknown. Colonel Capers estimated that one-third of the regiment was either killed or wounded. That would equal about 86 casualties. However, the strength of the regiment during the battle of Franklin is also uncertain, possibly 255 - 260.

The exact number of casualties suffered by the Confederate army that afternoon is unknown. Hood reported shortly after the battle that the army suffered a loss of 4,500 men. However, a more accepted count places the number nearer 7,000 men killed, wounded and captured. The Federal casualty list totaled much less - approximately 2300 killed, wounded and captured.[96]

On the morning of December 2, General Hood marched his army onward, destination Nashville! He could not have fully realized the condition of the mighty Army of Tennessee. Hood's vision did not match the available resources and condition of the army. The Army of Tennessee obediently traveled north, inadequately prepared for the rigors that lay ahead. Somehow the men of the 24th yet expected victory.[97]

A Federal force holding Murfreesboro concerned General Hood, and he dispatched Forrest's cavalry and Bate's Division to challenge the enemy. The Confederates did not capture Murfreesboro, so Hood withdrew Bate. However, he left Forrest at Murfreesboro, confident he could handle the situation. This decision practically eliminated the cavalry as a source of information and intelligence.[98] Afterwards, Hood would desperately need the cavalry at Nashville.

The surgeons loaded the wounded men who could travel aboard available transportation and dispatched them south. On the morning of Saturday, December 3, 1864, Capers and Smith boarded an ambulance bound for Columbia, Tennessee. As they prepared to depart, the two officers visited the more seriously wounded soldiers in the hospital at the Harrison house. There, the remaining patients, for the most part, were in good spirits and well-treated. Capers and Smith departed fully confident that many of the wounded would recover. Even so, they were very saddened with the realization that they would never see some of the men again. On Sunday, the two wounded officers, joined by Captain Waties, another seriously wounded South Carolinian, started the long, painful and tedious journey south. Capers and Smith finally reached South Carolina safely, but Waties' wound hemorrhaged badly and he remained with a Tennessee family until his wound improved.

The troops marched northward again on Saturday before Capers departed Franklin. The regiment traveled 15 miles and bivouacked at Regan's place, less than five miles from Nashville. The next morning, Gist's Brigade, including the 24th, moved forward about one mile and bivouacked in full view of the city. There, the regiment assumed a position in line of battle and entrenched. The enemy commenced a steady artillery barrage on the Confederate line, and the picket lines constantly exchanged rifle fire. The weather was clear and cold, already much too severe for the poorly clad soldiers of the Army of Tennessee.[99]

That night, the men constructed fortifications which were completed by early the next morning. The enemy threw some artillery shells in the direction of the regiment, but the rounds fell short.

The Yankees had ransacked private homes and destroyed or stolen personal property that belonged to the citizens of the area. In the cellar of an empty house, Privates Blackwell and Carpenter found some blackberry wine and shared it with Lieutenant Tillman. The lieutenant donned clean clothes, his first change in three weeks.[100]

The weather remained clear and cold. The next day, Yankee shelling accelerated, and a sharper than usual picket fight erupted. On Monday, December 5, the pickets fought another sharp skirmish on the right, and the 24th made an oblique movement in the event the pickets needed assistance. However, the pickets soon repulsed the Federals, and the regiment resumed its position. The weather continued cloudy and cold, and the Confederates continued to find it extremely difficult to keep warm.[101]

Everything was very quiet on Tuesday, another cloudy, calm, and cold day. The trenches were rife with rumors that Sherman was at Murfreesboro. For the first time since the battle of Franklin, the men were cheerful that day.

Wednesday was cloudy again. The wind suddenly shifted from the south and blew from the northwest, and the weather turned very cold and disagreeable. The enemy advanced a feeble effort toward the right of the regiment that did not succeed in driving in the Confederate skirmishers. For a happy change, the day's rations were good. The next morning, Thursday, December 8, the 24th Regiment and the 2nd Georgia Battalion marched about one mile away and constructed a redoubt. During the day, the men attacked and drove in some Union pickets. They returned to their bivouac at sunset. That day, the men received word that Lieutenant Colonel Jones, released from agony, had died the night before.[102]

The weather turned terribly cold on Friday, December 9, 1864. The wind blew a strong northeast gale and the weather was cloudy, snowing, and sleeting. The troops participated in little activity that day as the snow and sleet swirled around the heads of the soldiers. It required maximum exertion and effort just to keep warm. That night, the men suffered terribly from cold and severe weather as they hovered over the fires, barely keeping warm. Their misery increased the next day. Rations were sparse, and essential supplies such as firewood also became scarce. The ground froze solid, and freezing sleet soon covered the landscape with snow and ice. The barefooted men and those barely shod suffered the most. A rumor passed among the men that the regiment would move, but no one knew where. That night, for the first time in several days, the regiment furnished a picket detail.[103]

Monday morning, Bate's Division finally arrived from Murfreesboro and relieved Brown's Division. The regiment moved two miles farther right with Brown's Division. The severe weather lingered, and the men hunkered over the fires as if held by glue. The enemy offered only token activity that day, lobbing several artillery rounds that fell harmlessly in the direction of the Confederate line. On Tuesday, December 13th, the troops remained in the bivouac one mile from the Murfreesboro Pike. The enemy demonstrated in front of the regiment all day, but they made no move of significance. General Cheatham alerted his old division, and they prepared for a move on

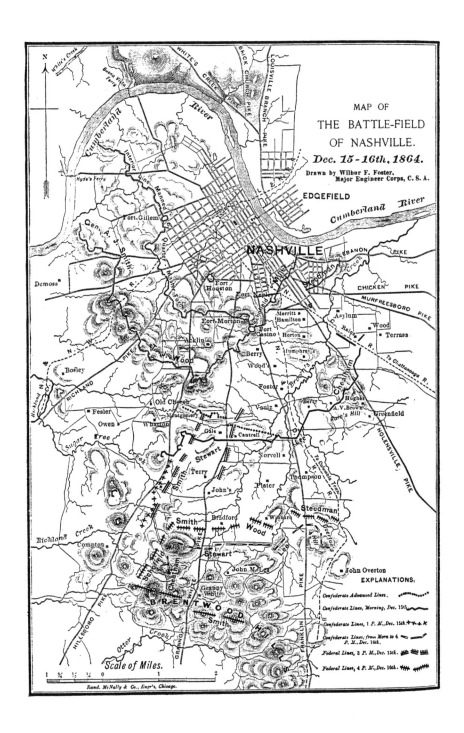

MAP OF
THE BATTLE-FIELD
OF NASHVILLE.
Dec. 15-16th, 1864.

Drawn by Wilbur F. Foster,
Major Engineer Corps, C. S. A.

EXPLANATIONS.

Confederate Advanced Lines.
Confederate Lines, Morning, Dec. 15th.
Confederate Lines, 1 P. M., Dec. 15th.
Confederate Lines, from Morn to 4 P. M., Dec. 16th.
Federal Lines, 3 P. M., Dec. 15th.
Federal Lines, 4 P. M., Dec. 16th.

Scale of Miles.

Rand, McNally & Co., Engr's, Chicago.

short notice. They waited anxiously the entire day, but no orders came. The next morning the sky became overcast at about 10:00. That night, the weather was much warmer and it misted rain. As the snow melted, the conditions became muddy and even more disagreeable. The severe weather remained constant, holding the men in its insufferable grip. Picket fighting intensified that day as the enemy commenced "feeling out" the Confederate right flank. Captain Morgan inspected the regiment's weapons.[104] The army was preparing for something, but no one knew what!

Finally, the fateful day of Thursday, December 15, 1864, arrived. Early that morning, the 24th drew a work detail, and about 9:00 a.m., the brigade recalled the regiment and placed the men under arms. The men formed a line of battle and waited for about five hours. Finally, late that day, the regiment moved six miles to the far left of the Confederate line. All day long, the enemy blasted the area with a heavy artillery barrage. The battle-wise combat veterans knew what that meant: the Federals would make a major attack. However, on the 15th, the Yankees attacked at only one point, capturing several pieces of artillery and three prisoners before the Confederates repulsed the attack. The regiment worked all night fortifying the position.[105]

That night, members of Hood's staff suggested that the general retire the army south of the Duck River. There, he could entrench and make a vigorous stand with at least some assurance of success. Hood would not budge from Nashville. He probably based that decision on an irresistible desire to secure Tennessee for the Confederacy. Also, Hood obviously was unaware of the army's true condition or the strength of General Thomas' forces. General Hood located his headquarters at the Overton House, five miles in the rear of the army and apparently did not visit or inspect the troops at Nashville. During the night of December 15, 1864, Hood sent the wagons back to Franklin. "That move," wrote a staff officer, "prepared the men still more for the stampede the next day." That was a busy night for the soldiers as the Army of Tennessee prepared to receive an all out assault the next day.[106]

Friday, December 16, 1864, dawned cloudy and windy and with sporadic rain. The expected heavy enemy artillery barrage started very early that morning and ceased about 8:00 a.m.[107]

Immediately, General Thomas flung a strong force against General Lee's Corps on the Confederate right. Lee's Corps handily repulsed the attack. On the Confederate left, the Federals attacked even more vigorously. About 3:00 p.m., after numerous assaults along the much too thin line on the Confederate left, the enemy breached the line. The enemy first broke the portion of the thinly manned line defended by Bate's Division. The Yankees penetrated the rear of the Army of Tennessee (something they had never accomplished before) and quickly enveloped Cheatham's entire corps.

235

Some observers alleged that at least part of Bate's Division offered little resistance. However, the Federals killed Colonel William M. Shy, one of Bate's brigade commanders, on an eminence located on the left side of the Granny White Pike; the hill is now known as Shy's Hill in his memory. The Federals also captured General H. R. Jackson, another of Bate's brigade commanders, who commanded Stevens' old brigade. The Yankees also captured General Smith, Bate's remaining brigade commander, but the division commander, General Bate, escaped. This loss of brigade leadership adversely impacted on the ability of the division. About 4:00 p.m., the entire Confederate left collapsed suddenly and without warning.

The Yankees completely overran the entire position guarded by Cheatham's Corps. Almost in the blink of an eye, the army was in full retreat in the wildest disorder. An observer reported, "The proud Army of Tennessee, suddenly and quickly, degenerated into a mob."[108]

Many men threw down their guns and equipment that impeded flight toward Franklin and other points south. An observer described the army as "panic stricken" and said that the woods were "full of running soldiers." One staff officer said, "I shall not attempt to describe, for 'tis impossible to give you any idea of an army frightened and routed."[109]

Numerous officers vainly attempted to rally the troops. The officers would call out, "Halt! Halt!" When one colonel tried, and his troops would not stop or make a stand, he was compelled to join the mass exodus.

A local woman, Mary Bradford, lived along the route of the running men. She ran out of her house under the heavy Union fire. She pleaded with the men, "begging them" to stop and fight "but in vane." As the Army of Tennessee panicked that day, the last vestige of hope for success of the Confederate cause vanished.[110]

Colonel Capers, who missed the battle of Nashville because of his wounds, later contacted Major D. W. Sanders, staff officer of General French's staff. Capers asked Sanders if the 24th behaved well at Nashville. Sanders responded, "Indeed it did."[111]

Few records exist that define the role of the 24th and the early stages of the flight from Nashville. Certainly, the men of the 24th joined in the flight south with the same vigor displayed by the balance of the army.[112] The Federals captured sixty-four men of the 24th Regiment when the position was overrun. The regiment, in the midst of the collapse of Cheatham's Corps, suffered more prisoners that day than any other Confederate regiment. The number of soldiers from the regiment killed at Nashville is unknown. Over 700 unknown Confederate soldiers lie buried at Nashville, and surely some of them were members of the 24th.

Later, Colonel Capers made a sad report concerning the regiment at Nashville: "The 24th S.C.V. lost 1/3 of its numbers, killed, wounded & captured!"[113]

236

Lieutenant Tillman briefly commented about the results of the action at Nashville, "Lost nearly all of our artillery & many (men) were captured."

One report indicated that the army lost 50 pieces of artillery. However, there remained sufficient artillery at Franklin for the defensive needs of the army. By the end of the day on December 16, 1864, the soldiers were no longer a responsible part of an organized army. The men ran all night toward Franklin, a movement by individuals without resemblance of military order and discipline. Even with the severe weather conditions, the rain and mud, the flight of the men covered the ground in record time. Most of the survivors finally reached Franklin by daylight the next morning.[114]

Initially, Lieutenant General Stephen D. Lee earned credit for saving the remnants of the army at Nashville. Until Nashville, his corps was in reasonably good condition, since only one of his divisions had participated in the disastrous battle at Franklin. After Cheatham's line collapsed, Lee withdrew from the Confederate right and gathered enough of his troops to straddle the pike across Overton Hills at Brentwood. Somehow, Lee's Corps held the Federals at bay momentarily. As a result, the speed of the Yankee forward rush slowed just a little. The early winter darkness also aided General Lee's rear guard action. The Yankees, although entirely victorious, could not have realized the magnitude of the victory and did not gain all the fruits they earned. During the rear guard action from Nashville, Lee received a wound in the foot.[115]

The remnants of the Army of Tennessee reorganized at Franklin and prepared for retreat. Hood toyed with the idea of making a stand on the south side of the Duck River. By now, even Hood decided little fight was left in the once mighty Army of Tennessee, and he dismissed the idea. Lieutenant Tillman seized the opportunity of the brief delay and visited the seriously wounded men who were still in the division hospital at the A. M. Harrison house. The surgeons had already sent south the patients who could travel.

On December 17, the army marched 12 miles through rain and mud and bivouacked at Spring Hill in line of battle. That night, the soldiers had no rations and suffered dreadfully. On the 18th of December the army continued the withdrawal.

Meanwhile, at Franklin and Nashville, the enemy rounded up the stragglers as well as the Confederate wounded who remained in the hospital. The Yankees admitted the sick and wounded Confederates who were in critical need of medical attention to Federal military hospitals for treatment. The Federals processed the other captured solders as prisoners of war before sending them to one of the ghastly Northern prisons. If such was possible, those men suffered even more as Yankee prisoners than as Confederate soldiers.[116] As the Federals overran Franklin, they captured twelve more members of the 24th.

237

At Spring Hill, General Cheatham gathered the remnants of his once proud corps and replaced Lee's Corps as rear guard. The 24th as well as the other units of Gist's Brigade participated in Cheatham's rear guard activity. From Spring Hill, the regiment marched eight miles and bivouacked in line of battle in front of Rutherfords Creek. That evening, Colonel John H. Anderson placed Lieutenant Tillman under arrest for shooting a pig in front of the Confederate line.[117] Hunger was rampant.

Before daylight on Monday, December 19, 1864, the pursuing Yankee cavalry caught up with the Army of Tennessee's rear guard at Rutherfords Creek. The few surviving members of the 24th regiment manned the position. The Federals recklessly dashed their mounts among the men of the 24th, who resisted and quickly repulsed the attackers. During the melee, the men of the regiment captured three enemy soldiers and several horses. Tillman reported that the Confederate artillery entered the action, and skirmishing continued until about 2:00 p.m. After the skirmish at Rutherford's Creek, the enemy did not press further that day and the regiment retired four miles closer to Columbia.

There, the men of the regiment assisted in transporting the wagons and remaining artillery pieces across the Duck River. During the crossing, a disagreement erupted between Generals Forrest and Cheatham, two temperamental Tennesseans. Apparently, the disagreement started over who would first utilize the pontoon bridge that spanned the Duck River. As the two old battle scarred warriors turned the air blue with profanity, the wounded General Lee left his ambulance and restored peace. After tempers cooled, the two antagonists apologized, but the record does not reflect whose troops crossed the river first.[118]

After the army safely crossed the Duck River, the men of the regiment helped take up the pontoons that night. The regiment then rejoined Cheatham's Corps and headed south. After spanning the river, Hood handed Forrest's Cavalry rear guard duties and assigned Walthall's Division as infantry support.[119]

The fact that Walthall's Division mustered only 1900 soldiers greatly concerned General Forrest. His concern increased when he learned 400 troops in the division were completely barefooted. Afterwards, the barefooted infantry clearly impressed the general, and he lauded the quality of service they rendered: "They bore their sufferings without murmur and were ever ready to fight the enemy."[120]

Lieutenant Tillman recorded on December 20, 1864, "The weather was unabated in its severity." The weather produced rain, sleet and snow driven by a bitterly cold "cutting northwest wind" accompanied by rain that froze as it fell. The army pushed through the small village of Linville, and then walked 18 miles before stopping at a bivouac along the Pulaski Pike. The men suffered severely from the cold and for the want of clothing and shoes, and complained loudly about the insufficient rations.

The next day the regiment marched 10 miles, pressed through Pulaski, and bivouacked one mile from town. The terrible weather, a combination of snow, wind and bitter cold, continued. The camp was rife with rumors concerning the activities of Sherman's army in Georgia. The men worried about their loved ones, the defenseless old men, women, and children, who resided in Georgia. Many were in the path of the Federal army as it razed the heart of the practically defenseless state.[121]

On Thursday, December 22, 1864, the regiment returned to Pulaski, left the pike, and proceeded down Laurel's Ferry Road, which was in horrible condition, slick and rough. As a result, the Confederates marked their passage with dead horses, mules and broken wagons. A staff officer worried about the need to bridge the Tennessee River, where the pontoons would become critical. He remarked, "The worse loss than all the others is the broken pontoons." He stopped counting after noticing 15 broken pontoons. The same staff officer recorded his impressions of the men's suffering: "Many thousands were barefooted, actually leaving the prints of blood upon the ground, as the enemy pressed us in the rear."[122]

That night, the regiment camped on a beautiful slope eight miles from Pulaski. The terrible weather remained, stormy, clear, cold, icy, and the ground was frozen solid. The wind blew, cold and hard, and magnified the men's discomfort as rations continued scarce. The next day was more of the same, but somehow the men marched 18 miles over the bad roads. Colonel Anderson released Lieutenant Tillman from arrest.[123]

On Christmas Eve, the general detailed the regiment as guards for the supply wagon train. The men marched at sunrise for five miles, then halted and waited for the wagons, which they escorted 10 miles before bivouacking near the Alabama State line.

Christmas Day was gloomy and unhappy for the soldiers of the Army of Tennessee. On that Holy Day, the men marched 18 hard miles through mud and rain and waded Shoal Creek, near the Tennessee River, opposite Bainbridge. On Christmas night, the regiment detailed Lieutenant Tillman and 15 men to picket duty two miles in front of the brigade. The detail returned the following morning at nine o'clock. Two men, Walls and Price, who had recovered from wounds received at Atlanta, returned to duty.[124] The two men could not have known the conditions that prevailed in the regiment, otherwise they might have delayed returning.

When the army reached the Tennessee River, the shortage of pontoons finally became a critical problem. The engineers anxiously counted the pontoons and discussed whether those on hand could bridge the river. General Roddy's Tennessee cavalrymen solved the problem when they raided the enemy camp at Decatur and floated the Yankee pontoons stored there down the river to the waiting Confederates. As a result, a pontoon bridge soon spanned the Tennessee River and the Southerners started across. The men of the 24th threw up earthworks on the river bank to support the artillery defending the pontoon bridge. The men in the fortifications handily repulsed the Union gunboats that soon appeared. On the same day, the quartermaster issued eight biscuits per man for three days rations.[125]

On December 27, 1864, the regiment arose at 2:00 a.m., and safely crossed the mighty Tennessee River over the pontoon bridge. Once across the river, the regiment hesitated until daylight, and then continued the march. The route led the troops through countless untended fields and the army's old camp at Tuscumbia. The men marched 25 miles that day and at 9:00 p.m., bivouacked at Barton Station. The day was cloudy, drizzly, and cold with "mud and water to the excess," and the men straggled badly. When the army crossed the Tennessee River, pursuit by the Federal army ceased.[126]

The members of Gist's Brigade received some hard-earned and well-deserved recognition as they crossed the Tennessee River. General Cheatham recalled the behavior of Gist's Brigade after the ordeal of the retreat:

> Gist's Brigade was the only body of troops in his corps [Hardee's old corps] which crossed the Tennessee...on its retreat from Nashville, marching in order...and under its officers...armed, obedient and organized. Of course the 24th should have its share in the credit due to the good conduct of the brigade.[127]

The march after crossing the Tennessee River became slightly more leisurely without the pressure from the Union troops, and because the severity of the weather abated. The 24th resumed the journey the next morning at 9:00 a.m. It proceeded along the railroad track for 12 miles and camped on the banks of Big Bear Creek. The day was breezy and rather pleasant for marching as the weather became moderate. Some mail caught up with the regiment and Lieutenant Tillman received five letters, "The first news from home in many weeks." The regiment remained in the bivouac until nearly noon the next day before starting the march again. The men walked into Mississippi for eight miles and camped at Iuka. The severe weather returned, and it became cold and unpleasant again.

The regiment was rife with bad rumors about the adverse results of the war effort as well as the atrocities committed by Sherman's army. The rumors created excessive uneasiness among the men, especially those from Georgia, even though none of the rumors was credible.[128]

The 24th tarried at Iuka until Friday, December 30, 1864. The march began again at 8:00 a.m., and the regiment traveled eight miles and bivouacked at Burnsville. That night, for the first time since Christmas Eve, the 24th drew a picket detail. On New Year's Eve, the regiment started again at 8:00 a.m., marched over a dirt road for 12 miles and bivouacked two miles from Corinth. At that bivouac, mail arrived again, and Lieutenant Tillman received two more letters. A bright sunshine finally prevailed all the next day, but the roads were muddy and made marching conditions unpleasant. On New Year's Day, the troops marched through Corinth and bivouacked three or four miles beyond the town on the southeastern side. Some of the men wondered why the army did not bivouac at Corinth because of the strong breastworks there. The weather was clear and created pleasant marching for the first time since the army departed Nashville. Even so, "There was still ice in abundance and the ground was frozen."

The camp was rife with rumors that the Army of Tennessee was going into winter quarters, and still another rumor "factually reported" that Gist's Brigade was en route to South Carolina. James Tillman recorded his thoughts, which must have reflected the feelings of all the soldiers of the Army of Tennessee, "This has certainly been a most gloomy New Year's Day."[129]

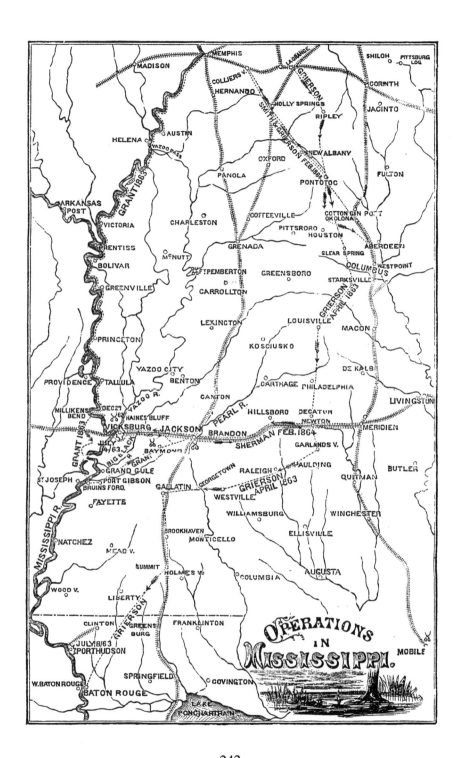

242

CHAPTER 10

MISSISSIPPI TO NORTH CAROLINA

Consolidation and Conclusion

While bivouacked near Corinth, the Army of Tennessee licked its wounds, reorganized, and tried to rebound from the ill-fated campaign. Many thought the task unsurmountable. The indomitable spirit of the men prevailed, although, at that moment, it was seriously flickering.

Each day, the rebuilding process brought a special challenge or difficulty. The leaders astutely realized that a hasty return to normal military activity was imperative, and the application of military discipline provided the cohesion that would renew the army. The leadership of the army immediately inaugurated projects that inculcated the use of military discipline and regulations. Captain D. S. Garden of the brigade staff mustered and inspected the 24th as early as January 3.

James Tillman, curious about his surroundings, obtained a pass and visited Corinth. There, he discovered a small desolate village that had seen too much of war. Tillman mused that the fortifications excelled any that he had ever visited and recorded, "The old works gave notoriety to the place." Within the works, the Confederate army buried many soldiers who died from wounds. In Tillman's view, the deceased warriors were "Gallant Heroes." After his visit, the battle-weary and battle- wise lieutenant concluded, "In fact this place looks like a graveyard." On Friday, January 6, 1865, the regimental commander selected Tillman as adjutant.[1]

Weather and rations improved somewhat while the 24th was at Corinth. Any food at all would have been an improvement over the sustenance that the troops received during December 1864. The weather at times was pleasant, but, for the most part, the days were cloudy, rainy and cold, with an occasional blast of sleet and snow. However, the severity of the weather did not compare with that encountered during the retreat through Tennessee. Rumors claimed that the brigade was going to transfer to South Carolina. The mere thought of such a move raised the spirits of the men. However, as with most rumors, no one could substantiate the report.[2]

Finally, the army started moving again. On January 10, 1865, the 24th broke camp, marched 12 miles and bivouacked at Boonesville, Mississippi. The men arrived cold and fatigued. The troops started again early the next morning, covered 20 miles, and bivouacked at Gun Town. The soldiers received rations from Baldwyn, Mississippi, six miles away. On January 12, the regiment moved out at daylight and marched beside the tracks of the railroad in a southerly direction for 15 miles before stopping three-and-one-half miles from Tupelo. Near the little town of Satillo, the quartermaster issued the men two days' rations. During the first day of the march, the weather was calm and, at times, even pleasant. On the second day, it was clear, cold and windy.[3]

James Tillman's true and loyal servant, Peter, returned that day. No one had seen the man since the debacle at Nashville, and Tillman feared that the Yankees had captured "the poor fellow." Peter somehow had eluded the blue soldiers. Tillman was delighted that Peter, a loyal supporter of the Confederate cause, had made good his escape and found his way back to the regiment.[4]

The 24th arrived at Tupelo on January 13, 1865, and the men rested there until January 24, performing only routine military duties. The rumor persisted that the brigade was en route to South Carolina. No one could verify the report, and all the men could do was patiently await official word from the generals. While camped at Tupelo, the regiment's foraging expeditions became successful, and the sustenance improved significantly. A small amount of mail arrived occasionally, and soldiers who received a letter felt fortunate. Everyday, a member of the brigade staff inspected the regiment. Finally, on January 24, the regiment received an alert for a move, though the destination was unknown. The men cooked three day's rations and marched at daybreak. During the night, the weather, which had been fairly pleasant, turned bitterly cold.[5]

The news of the horrible deeds committed by Sherman's army in Georgia alternately excited and enraged the men. In this regard, the troops, especially those from Georgia, felt no small amount of trepidation for the safety and well-being of their families and loved ones.

Many changes were announced throughout the Army of Tennessee. General Hood resigned his position as commander of the army on January 23, 1865, and departed for Richmond, Virginia. Lieutenant General Richard Taylor assumed temporary command, pending the arrival of General Beauregard. In the meantime, the Confederate Congress named General Robert E. Lee the commander-in-chief of all Confederate Armies. Lee immediately restored General Joseph Eggleston Johnston to his former post as the commander of the Army of Tennessee.[6] This news delighted the men of the 24th, because they would serve once more under the man whom the South Carolinians considered "their general."

The small number of soldiers that the 24th mustered is difficult to estimate. On January 16, 1865, Lieutenant Hawkins counted few men present for duty in Company A, The Marion Rifles, whose members hailed from Charleston. Those still present were Lieutenants Hawkins and Smith, Sergeant Howe, Corporal T. Riggs, Privates Flood, Thomas, Clark, Droze,

Hazzard, Simms and John Scott, a total of eleven effectives. Private Dougherty was sick, though, Lieutenant Hawkins expected him to return soon. Every company was equally small, and the prospects for an increase in manpower were dire.[7]

At sunrise, the men began the march again and reached a new bivouac near Okalona, Mississippi. On January 26, the soldiers covered 19 more miles and bivouacked near Prairie Station. The next day, the regiment stopped at a camp 11 miles beyond West Point. The men observed, "There are splendid crops of corn still in the field, ungathered." On January 28, the worn out men remained in camp all day.

Good news arrived in the form of an order to "Take the train tomorrow morning! Destination: South Carolina!" When they received the order, the men would have broken out in "a wild celebration" if they had not been so exhausted. Although the men did not know the purpose of heading toward South Carolina, a consensus existed that they would defend the state from the invasion of Sherman's army.

The next day, the troops eagerly packed themselves into a railroad car and traveled to Meridian, where they waited all night for transportation. The South Carolinians were eager to get going and impatient with the delay. Because of the news about Sherman's foray through Georgia, the general furloughed the 46th Georgia Regiment until February 13, 1865. On the last day of January, 1865, the remnants of Bate's Division, which followed Brown's Division, arrived at Meridian.[8]

While the soldiers were hurrying toward whatever the future held, Colonel Capers remained in South Carolina nursing his wounded ankle. He was extremely anxious to return to his place of duty with the 24th Regiment. However, early in Hood's Tennessee campaign, Capers recalled that General Gist expected a promotion by the first of the year and thought Capers would also receive a promotion to brigadier general and command the brigade. Capers contacted some of the people Gist mentioned as interested in the advancement of the two South Carolina officers.

Capers started his campaign for a promotion by writing General Johnston and asking for his assistance. Johnston thought the promotion had been earned, but he replied that he probably could not help him because he did not yet have official contact with Richmond.

The colonel contacted General Hardee, who sent a recommendation that directed President Davis' attention to the vacancy created by the death of Gist. Hardee went on to recommend Capers for the vacancy:

> Col. Capers belongs to the same brigade and has served
> with it continuously...I speak...from personal knowl-
> edge...he is one of the most accomplished officers in the
> service...in camp or on the battlefield, he has proved
> himself to be brave, zealous & indefatigable...Among all

245

my acquaintances I don't know an officer...better qualified...or one I would prefer...under my...command in that
grade.[9]

Earlier, several friends sent letters urging that the President approve
Capers' promotion to brigadier general. The list included James L. Orr, W.
D. Simpson, W. Porcher Miles, et al., all well-known politicians and men of
stature and prominence in South Carolina. Each pointed out to President
Davis in glowing terms the reasons that Capers should receive the promotion, noting that he "proved himself a most efficient and competent
officer...by his gallantry and soldierly qualities fairly earned his promotion."

President Davis reviewed the recommendations and was highly
impressed. He handed the package to General Cooper with a note that the
commander of the Army of Tennessee should make a recommendation and
indicate whether Capers was present for duty. On January 28, Johnston,
once again commander of the Army of Tennessee, sent Cooper a message
that fulfilled the requirement established by the President:

Col. Ellison Capers has recovered from his wound. I
recommend his promotion to command Gist's Brigade still
vacant. He is an officer of great merit.[10]

Finally, on March 2, 1865, the Confederate army promoted Capers to
brigadier general. Indeed, General Capers had earned the much coveted
promotion, and he was one of the brightest stars in the Confederate army.

At the time Ellison received his promotion, the 24th had commenced the
long journey toward South Carolina. The men were anxiously trudging the
long, weary route, every day a little nearer their homes. Progress was slow
but steady. At daylight, on February 1, 1865, the regiment boarded the train
at Meridian, Mississippi, and arrived at McDermott's landing on the
Tombigbee River at 11:00 a.m. There, the regiment obtained passage aboard
a boat en route to Demopolis, Alabama, and arrived at 2:00 p.m. At
Demopolis, the men boarded another train, this time bound for Selma,
Alabama, which was reached at 7:00 p.m. Two hours later the troops
boarded yet another boat en route to Montgomery. The men rested the
remainder of the night aboard the dilapidated old boat anchored in the
Alabama River. At daylight the next morning the boat somehow cranked its
poorly maintained engines and started the squeaky journey for Montgomery.
They arrived there safely at noon on February 2, 1865. The regiment
traveled with the remnants of Gist's Brigade, Brown's Division and
Cheatham's Corps.[11]

An independent record of the journey of the regiment between
Montgomery, Alabama, and North Carolina is not available. It is clear that
the regiment traveled with Cheatham's Corps until it reached Montgomery.
Consequently, it is likely that the regiment accompanied the corps for the
remainder of the long trek to North Carolina.

246

On Friday, February 3, Cheatham's Corps, depleted in strength, boarded railroad cars bound for Columbus, Georgia, and arrived the same day. The Confederates departed Columbus at daylight and arrived at Macon at 4:30 p.m., on Saturday. After waiting all day on Sunday, the men again boarded the trains at 8:00 Monday morning and arrived at Midway, Georgia, at 2:00 p.m. At that point, the railroad was interrupted by Sherman's devastation of the countryside, so the troops had to walk until they reached Mayfield. The corps reached Milledgeville and bivouacked for the night. Although it stormed Tuesday morning, the storm proved little deterrence and Cheatham's men pressed onward to Mayfield Station. The men stopped and bivouacked as darkness fell.

The next day, the soldiers arrived at Mayfield Station at noon and boarded railroad cars bound for Augusta. Finally, the soldiers arrived at Augusta at 5:00 p.m., on Thursday, February 9, 1865. The following morning, as the troops from South Carolina cheered, the corps eagerly marched across the Savannah River into South Carolina, prepared to defend the state from the intrusion of Sherman's army. That night, they bivouacked in Edgefield District one mile from the bridge over the Savannah River. The men of Company I and K were home. Word came that a Federal force was approaching Aiken, a distance of only seventeen miles.[12] By Monday the Federals ended the demonstration in front of Aiken and departed in the direction of Columbia, South Carolina.

The possible location where Cheatham would greet Sherman changed daily as the Confederates massed their forces to offer the strongest resistance. On Monday, February 13, Beauregard directed Cheatham's Corps toward Columbia. When all preparations were complete, the corps started in motion again on Wednesday, February 15. It covered 20 miles that day and reached Bauskett's Mills. On Thursday, the corps covered 20 more miles and bivouacked along the road at Norris' Place.

General Cheatham learned that a large force of Federals blocked the route to Columbia, so on Friday morning, February 17, the same day Sherman's troops occupied and burned Columbia, South Carolina, the corps detoured toward McNary's Ferry, where it crossed the Saluda River. The crossing was slow, and several divisions moved up the river three miles and crossed at Holly's Ferry. By 3:00 a.m., Saturday, Cheatham's Corps was safely on the other side of the river and camped 3/4 mile from the ferry. At sunrise, the men departed the bivouac, marched seven miles, and bivouacked two miles beyond the town of Saluda. On Sunday, the corps marched eight miles and reached Newberry at 11:00.[13]

The corps rested for two days at Newberry until Tuesday, February 21, when General Beauregard finally caught up with the army. The general turned the movement toward Charlotte, North Carolina. At daylight, the corps started toward the new destination. After marching 21 miles, General

Beauregard received word to change the destination again, this time to Wilmington, North Carolina. The next day, the men retraced their footsteps to Newberry.

On February 23, General Cheatham loaded the troops aboard railroad cars en route for Pomaria, 17 miles away, and waited there until Sunday, February 26, 1865. The corps traveled 10 miles over rough roads that day, and 17 more miles the next day. During the day, Generals Lowrey and Loring caught up with additional troops. At the Enoree River, the Confederates constructed a ferry to transport the troops across the river. They completed the crossing on March 2, 1865, and bivouacked near Unionville.[14]

The next day, the men crossed the Broad River at Skeift's Ferry and arrived at Chester. On March 4, 1865, their destination changed again, this time to Smithfield, North Carolina. The soldiers departed Chester on March 11. The men traveled by train and arrived at Charlotte that night at 11:00 p.m. They departed Charlotte on Sunday March 12 and reached Salisbury at 4:00 p.m., without incident. At Salisbury, the railroad gauge changed size and the shortage of rolling stock hampered progress. Finally, the troops, including the 24th, arrived at Smithfield, late in the afternoon on Monday, March 20, 1865, the second day of the battle of Bentonville.[15]

Earlier that day the Army of Tennessee's Adjutant General had sent General Johnston a note, "Gist's Brigade is expected today." Johnston advised the adjutant general that he should forward all troops of the Army of Tennessee to the Bentonville battlefield as soon as the units became available. However, Johnston cautioned, "They are not to arrive after dark."[16]

That night, the 24th Regiment bivouacked near the Smithfield railroad depot. Early on March 21, 1865, Cheatham's Corps departed the railroad station and linked with other elements of Johnston's army. The men found the lead units of the army of Tennessee warmly engaged with the Federals. As Gist's Brigade, including the 24th, arrived 10 miles from the Bentonville battlefield, General Johnston withdrew his entire army to a position near Smithfield, behind the Neuse River.[17]

The camp was rife with rumors that the Confederates had retarded and changed the direction of the advance of Sherman's army. The rumors alleged that the Federals were now advancing toward Goldsboro. On March 23, the Army of Tennessee began moving in the direction of Raleigh. The next day, Cheatham's Corps passed through Smithfield and stopped at a point four miles north of the railroad station on the Halifax Road, where it was to remain for the rest of the month.[18]

Since active fighting between the two armies had practically ceased, the army bivouacked near Smithfield on the first of April and remained there until the eighth. The weather, except for the occasional rain, was warm and pleasant. The camp was relatively quiet, and the men of the regiment adapted easily to the relaxed routine of garrison life. The regiment frequently provided a picket detail and held daily dress parades. On April 4, the Army of Tennessee paraded for Generals Johnston and Stewart.

The news about the evacuation and surrender of Richmond reached the Army of Tennessee on April 5. Some men became terribly despondent and despaired about the prospects for a Confederate victory.[19]

Several relatives of the soldiers visited the camp. On one occasion, Captain Tillman was visited by his younger brother, Ben.

On April 9, 1865, the same day General Robert E. Lee surrendered the Army of Northern Virginia, General Johnston reorganized the Army of Tennessee. General John C. Brown, recovered from the wound he had received at Franklin, became the commander of General Cleburne's Division. Johnston returned Cheatham to his old division who was delighted to lead "his boys" once more. "Ol Reliable," Lieutenant General Hardee, headed his old corps.

General Johnston consolidated regiments with less than 400 men present for duty into new regiments, usually with others of the same state. The 24th remained in the same brigade and infantry division, but the regiment consolidated with the 16th Regiment on April 9, 1865. The consolidation of the 24th and the 16th was natural, because both had less than 400 men, both were from South Carolina, and both had served with the same brigade. After the consolidation, the 24th Regiment, South Carolina Volunteers, Infantry, in effect, no longer existed.[20]

The consolidation excited the men. The new regiment became the Consolidated 16th and 24th Regiment, South Carolina Volunteers, Infantry. General Johnston appointed Colonel Benjamin Burg Smith commander of the 16th Regiment to command the new consolidated regiment. Smith, a native South Carolinian and graduate of the Citadel, enjoyed a reputation as a brave and brilliant officer. The men of both regiments knew Smith because he was formerly a member of General Gist's staff and had commanded the 16th Regiment at the battle of Franklin. Captain Morgan, commander of the 24th Regiment, became lieutenant colonel. Captain Gibbes of the 16th Regiment became major and Lieutenant Holmes of the 24th was named adjutant.

The two regiments formed themselves into five companies each. The 24th staffed Companies C, G, H, I and K. The 16th Regiment comprised Companies A, B, D, E, and F.[21]

Colonel Smith promoted several lieutenants to be commanders of the new companies. He promoted James Tillman to command Company G, William M. Beckham, Company H; Adrian C. Appleby, Company I; C. S. Beaty, Company K; and W. Alston Gibbes, of the 16th S.C.V., to command Company C. After the war, Colonel Smith evaluated the performance of the new regiment: "The consolidation behaved well until the unhappy surrender. Very few deserted, the men standing by their guns to the last."[22]

**Colonel B. Burgh Smith, who commanded the Consolidated
16th and 24th Regiment at the conclusion of the war.**
(Courtesy: The Citadel Archives)

General Steven's old brigade had suffered terribly during Hood's Tennessee campaign. The entire brigade formerly commanded so ably by the founder of the 24th could not muster sufficient men needed for a regiment. Instead, Johnston reorganized Stevens' old brigade into a battalion of eight companies and named it, "The First Confederate Georgia Battalion." Major Joseph B. Cummings, Hood's former aide, received a promotion to lieutenant colonel and commanded the new battalion.[23]

With the reorganization in place, the army started in motion again. In the event that negotiations were not successful, General Johnston, a master of defensive strategy, wanted to maneuver and prevent Sherman from pinpointing the location of the Confederate army. In addition, the discipline maintained in the Confederate army would keep the men occupied while the negotiations were taking place.

On April 10, 1865, the soldiers marched in a northwestern direction on the Louisburg road for six miles and camped about 10:00. The new regiment broke camp at sunrise and marched 18 miles before reaching a bivouac within three miles of Raleigh, North Carolina. On the following day, the men passed through Raleigh and marched 10 more miles. Tillman, a bachelor who always enjoyed the greetings of the women, recorded, "A few ladies honored us with their presence upon the sidewalks and balconies."[24]

The appearance of Confederate troops intrigued Southern ladies even at this late date.

On Thursday, April 13, 1865, the regiment clearly heard cannon fire or artillery blasts in the direction of Raleigh. That day, the soldiers marched in the rain 20 miles through Chapel Hill via the Chapel Hill Road. The regiment started at sunrise the next morning and after marching 17 miles bivouacked near Ruffin's Mill. On Saturday, the men waded two rivers, the Haw and the Alamance, and marched a total of 15 miles. It rained most of the day as the men slogged over muddy roads. Completely exhausted, the troops stopped at a bivouac just before dark.[25] No one knew the destination of the regiment.

The men of the 24th made one of their last forced marches on Sunday, April 16, 1865. The march that day covered 15 miles on the Salisbury Road. During the day, the regiment passed a party of scouts escorting 51 Union prisoners and a large herd of captured enemy horses.[26]

In Johnston's Army of Tennessee, the administration of discipline prevailed in spite of the situation. A delegation of officers from a South Carolina regiment petitioned General Johnston for commutation of a court-martial sentence. The court had given a young soldier a death sentence for desertion and scheduled the execution for the next morning. General Johnston's steadfast policy was that he would never set aside the sentence of a proper court-martial verdict. After ascertaining that it actually had been a proper verdict, Johnston stood by his policy and gave the petitioners his customary answer, "No!" Early the next morning, however, he instructed his aide to send an urgent message that General Stewart should "suspend executions till further orders." Thankfully, General Stewart received the message in time and saved not only the young South Carolinian but three other soldiers from the firing squad. The aide later confided that he knew the war was over when the general suspended a sentence imposed by a properly rendered court-martial verdict.[27]

On Monday, April 17, 1865, General Johnston held Cheatham's Division, which included the 24th, at its position near Goldsboro. One of Johnston's staff officers evaluated the dire circumstances of the Confederate army: "As the enemy are all around us, both above, below, and behind, the inevitable inference is that the army is to be surrendered."[28]

The situation was completely hopeless. James Tillman reflected, "The wildest & most humiliating rumors afloat - Lee has surrendered & Johnston makes a proposal to Sherman."[29] Two days later, Tillman recorded the dreadful event in his diary:

Tuesday 18 April 1865

Excitement somewhat subsided. Soldiers cried on yesterday
- Clear in morning cloudy in evening & some rain -
inspection - I greatly fear something terrible is before us -
Oh! God! Save my country & my family from disgrace.

Wednesday 19 April 1865
Rain last night - no mail or news from home besides the
report of our surrender has sorely tried my patience, my
faith, but all things are for the best.

The next day, April 20, 1865, the regiment drilled! The Army of
Tennessee was rife with rumors concerning the surrender and the fate that
awaited the men. On Friday, the troops drilled again, and if Vessie McGee
had been alive he would still "find no fun in it." The weather was mostly
warm and cloudy with occasional hard rains and strong winds. Captain
Wever, although still ill, returned from the hospital. His health was terrible,
and on this day he left for home once more. On Saturday, Captain Tillman
reported, "Rumor yet walks majestically through the army." The weather
was clear and warm, cool and breezy, and especially comfortable at night.[30]

The men departed the bivouac at sunrise the following morning,
marched nine miles on the Greensboro Road, and arrived at a new bivouac
near Centre, North Carolina. No one knew the reason for the move.
However, the weather provided a delightful spring day, clear and breezy and
pleasant for marching. On April 24, 1865, the regiment drilled and held an
inspection and a dress parade. The good weather continued, although many
men were in extremely low spirits over the impending surrender.

General Sherman advised General Johnston that the new United States
President, Andrew Johnson, was refusing the peace treaty the two generals
had agreed upon. Sherman also advised Johnston that he would commence
hostilities again on April 26, 1865, at 11:00 a.m. Johnston alerted his troops
to "hold themselves in readiness" for a move promptly at that time.[31]

In preparation for renewed hostilities, General Johnston inspected the
army to determine its readiness. General Bate inspected the new Consolidated Regiment. Bate congratulated Colonel Smith upon the splendid
condition of their arms, equipment, ammunition, as well as the fighting spirit
that prevailed among the men. Bate reported that the Consolidated Regiment
was ready for the fray. This was a favorable stamp of approval received by
only a small number of regiments assigned to the Army of Tennessee. After
the war, Colonel Smith was still smarting from the behavior of General Bate
and his division at Atlanta, Franklin and Nashville, when he wrote General
Capers, "Would it have been someone else."[32]

At 11:30 a.m., on April 26, the regiment started moving once more. It
marched 10 miles on the High Point Road and reached a point about four
miles from the railroad. The regiment bivouacked along the Salem and
Fayetteville Plank Road. The good weather held.

On April 27, 1865, General Cheatham announced that Generals
Sherman and Johnston had reached another agreement. The new treaty was
approximately the same agreement reached by Lee and Grant in Virginia:

[The men] should sign an obligation not to bear arms against the United States until released from it, and that the troops be marched to their States and there disbanded.[33]

Captain Tillman noted, "The painful suspense is about over," and recorded his feelings about the event in his diary on Friday, April 28, 1865:

By terms of a military convention, this army was surrendered on the 26th inst. & announced today to the troops -
A deep gloom rests upon the army.

Tillman executed the required certificates for drawing specie payment for the troops. He completed the muster rolls and drew a total of $45.00 in silver coin to be paid $1.29 per man to Company G of the new Consolidated Regiment. This was the only payment of specie the troops received during the entire war. In the old 24th, 180 men received the payment, which they affectionately dubbed "The Silver Medal" or "The Legion of Honor."[34]

The next three days were very quiet. On Sunday, the men attended divine services. Afterwards, Tillman completed the required forms and executed the paroles, which were signed by Colonel Smith on Tuesday.[35]

The saddest of all sad days arrived, the war was over! Defeat. The blood, sweat and tears that had been shed was all for naught. The men departed their final bivouac on May 3, 1865, at 10:30 a.m., and marched in a southerly direction, going home. The next day, the regiment covered 20 miles as it passed through Lexington, North Carolina, and camped that night near Salisbury, North Carolina. On the second day of the journey home, Colonel Smith departed toward Greenville, South Carolina, leading a portion of the Consolidated Regiment, the old 16th Regiment.

Lieutenant Colonel Morgan and Companies H, I, K, and F of the 24th Regiment turned toward Chester, Anderson, Abbeville, Edgefield, and Hamburg. The troops from the other companies continued southward toward their homes, still under the command of their respective company commanders.[36]

Captain Joseph K. Risher proudly marched in front of his company, Company E, bound for Colleton District, South Carolina. The men of Company E hailed from rural communities surrounding the small towns of Ashton, Bamberg, Branchville, Lodge, Ruffin, Smoaks, and Captain Risher's own hometown of Williams. Every man arrived home safely with his honor intact, proud of his Confederate army service and the quality of duty that he tendered. So few were left. However, the fierce pride these men displayed was still as strong as when they originally joined with their neighbors to defend their homes more than three years earlier.

Every day the men marched between 10 and 24 miles as they traveled eagerly toward Edgefield. Captain Tillman recorded that he passed out the paroles at Newberry, and finally on Friday, May 12, 1865, the old company, Company I, The Edgefield Light Infantry, arrived at Edgefield. Tillman

The flag of the 24th South Carolina was preserved at the unit's surrender by its commanding officer, but not before several of the men had removed several stars and other sections of the flag as mementoes. The flag measures 44 1/4 inches high, and 48 inches wide. The blue cross is 8 inches wide, with a 3/4 inch edging. The white stars were 3 3/4 inches in diameter. The banner has a 2 3/4 inch side border, and a 2 inch wide blue sleeve for attachment to the pole.

(*South Carolina Relic Room and Museum, Columbia, S. C.*)

distributed the balance of the government property among the soldiers and sadly parted from his old friends and comrades. Afterwards, his duty completed, he made his way home. He arrived home at noon on Friday, May 12, 1865, and was eagerly welcomed by his father, mother, brothers and sisters. He entered his innermost thoughts in his diary, "I feel much happier."[37]

On July 1, 1865, James Tillman recorded that he had given little attention to his diary since his return home from the war:

No note for the time has been taken from the 12th May to 1st July - This came from sickness, feelings of despair, & a desire to let the horrible present sink into oblivion.[38]

Captain James Tillman died later that year. His doctors attributed his death to the result of the injuries and illnesses that he suffered as a soldier in the Confederate army. Here was another uncounted casualty of the war.

At last, the survivors had arrived home. In deference to Private Silvester "Vessie" McGee, the "tarrable affare" was over. Those who survived were sure they would meet those who did not in a better world.

Few regiments in the Confederate army could favorably compare records with that of the 24th. After the war, General Capers repeatedly recognized those who served with the regiment. He often stated that no soldier ever disgraced himself, the regiment, or the Confederate States Army. Instead, the men, as a whole, repeatedly garnished honors for the regiment.

Few men escaped the ravages of the battlefield or illness during the war. An accurate count of those wounded, killed or died of illness is impossible. Many men were wounded several times during different battles or skirmishes. It is safe to estimate that no one who served with the 24th went unscathed. Of those who survived the war, many were crippled for life.

The survivors of the 24th Regiment, South Carolina Volunteers, Infantry, came home from the War with their heads held high. They eagerly expected that the future would hold numerous challenges, and it did. However, each survivor fully realized that he would fight a hated war no more. The War was over.

255

PHOTO GALLERY

Captain W. R. Beckham, company commander, Company G
*(Courtesy of Mr. R. Buff via Confederate Relic Room,
Columbia S. C.)*

**Captain W. R. Beckham, Company G,
with an unidentified drummer boy**
(*Courtesy of John Bigham*)

Private John Wythe Bigham, Company H
(Courtesy of Mr. John Bigham)

Ellison Capers in his cadet uniform at The Citadel
(Courtesy The Citadel Archives, The Citadel, Charleston, S.C.)

Photo of Ellison Capers as Episcopal Bishop of South Carolina
(The Citadel Archives, The Citadel, Charleston, S. C.)

263

Private Adam E. Carpenter, Company I
(Courtesy of Mr. Buck Carpenter, Trenton, S. C.)

Sergeant John E. Holmes, Company K
(Courtesy of Mr. Buck Carpenter, Trenton, S. C.)

265

Second Lieutenant Joseph Marbury Lanham, Company I
(*Courtesy of Rusty Greenland*)

Private Joseph Campbell McClintock, Company H
(Courtesy of Ms. Jean C. Agee, Richburg, S. C.)

Sergeant John L. "Buddy" McGee, Company F
(Courtesy of Mes. Evelyn Leverett)

Private Sylvester "Vessie" Mc Gee, Company F
(*Courtesy of Mrs. Evelyn Leverett*)

Private James Godwin Odom, Company B
(Courtesy of Mr. Henry H. Odom, Dahlgren, Virginia)

Private Sion W. Odom, Company B
(Courtesy of Mr. Henry W. Odom, Dahlgren, Virginia)

Dr. T. L. Ogier, Jr.
(*South Caroliniana Library, University of South Carolina*)

272

Captain James K. Risher, Company commander, Company E
(Courtesy Otto Warren, Orangeburg, S. C.)

Captain John Henry Steinmeyer, Company A
(Courtesy of Clark Cooper, Barnwell, S. C.)

General Clement Hoffman Stevens
(South Caroliniana Library, University of South Carolina)

Headstone of Clement Hoffman Stevens and his wife, Ann B. Stevens,
located in the Episcopal Churchyard, Pendleton, S. C.
(Photograph by Eugene W. Jones, Jr.)

276

Private Thomas J. Strait, Company H
(Courtesy of Mr. Jacob F. Strait, Georgetown, S. C.)

277

Private William A. Syfret, Company C
(Courtesy of William F. Syfret, Walterboro, S.C.)

Captain James Tillman, Company I
(Identification not positive; see page 224)
(*South Caroliniana Library, University of South Carolina*)

Photo taken at Survivor's Reunion at Bamberg, S.C. in 1914.
The bearded veteran, without cane, is identified as Captain Joseph K. Risher
(Courtesy of Otto Warren, Orangeburg, S.C.)

APPENDIX I
BIOGRAPHICAL SKETCHES AND ROSTER
24TH REGIMENT SOUTH CAROLINA VOLUNTEERS INFANTRY

The military service records of the men who served in the 24th Regiment, compiled on microfilm and held by the National Archives, is the starting point for this biographical sketch and roster. In most instances, the service records contained a variety of information about the soldiers. However, the records at the National Archives do not reflect the names of all soldiers who served with the regiment, and the information is quite often incomplete.

The Biographical Sketch and Roster is the product of many sources, other than the military service records. The most important other source is the Memory Rolls held by the South Carolina State Archives, Columbia, South Carolina. For the most part, the Memory Rolls agree with the compiled military service records and often add to the information. Occasionally, the information offered by the Memory Rolls conflicts with the information in the service record, especially in the spelling of names.

Additional information came from rosters prepared by individual soldiers, survivors associations, the United Daughters of the Confederacy, company commanders, battlefield casualty returns, county record books, etc. Other records such as county histories, cemetery records, postwar manuscripts, death records, newspaper reports of battle casualties, obituaries, genealogies, descendant records, Confederate veteran and widow pension records, museum files, and local libraries provided additional information.

If the original entry is from the military service record, additional information from other records was entered without comment. If the original entry is from other than the military service records, the original source is identified. The list contains the names of all soldiers identified by any source, including suspected duplicates, as having served in the regiment. One entry reflects the name from a headstone in Magnolia Cemetery, Charleston, South Carolina. No other record connects that soldier with the regiment.

The compiled service records at the National Archives consist mostly of pay records, and generally reflect the location or status of the soldier at the end of the pay period. An entry, "Absent, in hospital Jan/Feb 1863," means that at the end of February the soldier was in the hospital. He may have been in the hospital only one or more days during the pay period of Jan/Feb 1863. If he was in the hospital at the beginning of January and returned to duty before the end of February, the record most likely would not mention the period of hospitalization. Thus, the sketch would indicate that the soldier was present for duty during the entire period.

Information in some of the records is inconclusive because it does not always reflect the reason for separation. Most records indicate that the soldier was discharged, killed in battle, surrendered, paroled, died in prison, etc. The military service records show that the regiment mustered for pay the final time for the pay period that ended August 31, 1864. The records of many soldiers present that date do not show an outcome of service. After that date, many soldiers met with hazards at the battles at Jonesboro, Lovejoy, Shipps Gap, Franklin, and Nashville, and the march to North Carolina. For instance, no record exists of those killed at Nashville where a large number of unknown Confederate soldiers lie buried, perhaps some of whom were members of the 24th Regiment.

The roster includes all data and facts discovered about a soldier regardless of how unimportant or trivial the information. Scrutiny of the deaths and wounds suffered by those brave warriors may give a small insight into the many hardships they suffered.

Due to the wide range of resources visited in gathering the information in this roster, and discrepancies in spelling, there is, no doubt, some duplication or misinformation. However, it is better to show names who did not serve with the regiment than miss the name of one soldier who did. Therefore, even minimal evidence that a soldier served in the regiment is enough to include that name.

Abbott, Cary, Pvt., Age 21, Co. G, enlisted at Columbia March 19, 1862. At home, furloughed, Jul/Aug 1863. Killed in battle at Chickamauga September 20, 1863. Joseph Abbott, father, filed claim for settlement March 8, 1864.

Abney, M. W., Asst. Surgeon, F&S, appointed at Pocotaligo September 1, 1862. Granted 21 day furlough March 30, 1863. Present for duty through May/Jun 1863. Reassigned August 14, 1863.

Ackerman, J. K., Pvt., Age 20, Co. C, enlisted at George's Station January 7, 1862. Transferred to 11th Regiment June 12, 1862. Killed at Petersburg.

Acock, James A., Pvt., Age 33, Co. A, enlisted at Charleston January 18, 1862. Granted furlough Mar/Apr 1864. Sick, patient in hospital Sep/Oct - Nov/Dec 1863. Sick in hospital Jul/Aug 1864. Signed receipt roll for clothing at Camp Wright November 19 and December 15, 1864. Present for duty with Co. H, 1st Regiment Troops and Defenses, Macon, Ga., Nov/Dec 1864. Paroled at Greensboro.

Acock, Robert, Pvt., Co. B, captured near Jonesboro September 2, 1864. Exchanged at Rough and Ready September 19, 1864.

Adam, P. L., Corp., Age 34, Co. F, from Majors, S. C., enlisted at Anderson January 9, 1862. Patient, Texas General Hosp., Quitman, Miss., April 30 - August 31, 1863. Captured near Jonesboro August 31, 1864.

Exchanged at Rough and Ready September 19, 1864. Captured at Shipp's Gap/Taylor's Ridge October 16, 1864. Surrendered 1865.

Adams, H. C., Pvt., Age 45, Co. E, enlisted at Camp Gist March 15, 1862. Pay stopped for one month due to court martial May/Jun 1862. Sick, patient in hospital Jan/Feb 1863. Killed in battle near Pine Mountain June 15, 1864. Shot in the head during a charge.

Adams, J. C. Buried April 4, 1864, Block A, Row 5, Grave 17, Oakland Cemetery, Atlanta, Georgia. Entry from Oakland Cemetery Records.

Adams, Patrick H., 1Lt., Age 28, Co. I, enlisted at Columbia March 20, 1862. 2Sgt., until elected 3d Lt., May 17, 1862. Commanded Co. I late 1863 and 1864. Wounded, nose, at Chickamauga September 20, 1863. Absent, sick, furloughed September 20 - Nov/Dec 1863. Promoted to Surgeon 1864.

Adams, Preston Lewis, Pvt., Age 36, Co. F, from Anderson District, Majors, S.C., enlisted at Columbia January 13, 1862. Detached service Nov/Dec 1862. Wounded at Jackson May 14, 1863. Captured and paroled May 16, 1863. Absent, wounded, May/Jun 1863. Wounded at Chickamauga. Sick, patient in hospital, October 23, 1863. Captured at Shipp's Gap/Taylor's Ridge October 16, 1864. Sent to Military Prison, Louisville and transferred to Camp Douglas October 29, 1864. Description: complexion, dark; hair, brown; eyes, brown; height, 5 ft. 6 in. Signed oath of allegiance to the United States and released June 17, 1865.

Adams, Thomas J., 1Sgt., Age 28, Co. I and Co. K, enlisted at Columbia March 20, 1862. Patient in hospital at Canton, Miss., May 30 - June 1863. Relieved as 1Sgt., and returned to ranks March 25, 1864. Daily extra duty at brigade Headquarters. Present for duty Jul/Aug 1864. Signed receipt roll for clothing September 10, 1864. Transferred to Co. K during 1864.

Adams, T. J., Pvt., Co. K. Entry from Memory Rolls at State Archives, Columbia, S.C.

Addison, A. B., Capt., Age 40, Co. D, enlisted at Camp Gist January 16, 1862. Company commander. Resigned due to ill health and physical incapacity June 11, 1863.

Addison, Thomas, Capt., F&S, enlisted at Camp Gist January 16, 1862. Absent, granted furlough December 27, 1863. Promoted and transferred to the Quartermasters and Assistant Quartermasters, Army of Tennessee July 20, 1864.

Adger, P. Wounded, leg, May 17, 1864. Entry from *Charleston Mercury* newspaper article.

Agnew, George W., Pvt., Age 20, Co. H, enlisted at Chester April 6, 1863. Sick, patient in hospital at Lauderdale Springs Jul/Aug - Nov/Dec 1863. Issued certificate of disability, dysentery. Description: complexion, fair;

eyes, grey; hair, light; height, 6 ft. 2 in; occupation, farmer; born, Chester District. Died of disease March 14, 1864. G. W. Agnew buried in Oakland Cemetery, Atlanta, Georgia March 14, 1864, Row 4, No. 5, Atlanta Medical College.

Airey, J. D., Asst Surgeon, F&S, appointed July 14, 1862. Present for duty Nov/Dec 1863.

Albers, Henry J., Pvt., Age 38, Co. A, enlisted at Charleston December 31, 1861. Captured near Jackson, Miss., May 14, 1863. Assigned to Paroled Prisoners Camp at Demopolis, June 5, 1863. Killed in battle at Kennesaw Mountain June 23, 1864.

All, G. W., Pvt., Co. E, enlisted at Camp Gist February 28, 1862. Present for duty through May/Jun 1862.

Allison, William S., 1Sgt., Age 21, Co. A, enlisted at Charleston December 31, 1861. Description: complexion, dark; hair, black; eyes, black; height, 5 ft. 6 in. Captured near Jackson, Miss., May 14, 1864. Released Paroled Prisoners Camp June 5, 1863. Captured at Franklin December 17, 1864. Sent to Military Prison, Louisville and transferred to Camp Chase January 2, 1865. Signed oath of allegiance to United States June 12, 1865.

Ammons, Allen, Pvt., Age 31, Co. B, enlisted at Charleston December 12, 1861. Detailed as pioneer by order of Gen. Gist Nov/Dec 1863. Admitted to 1st Mississippi CSA Hospital, Jackson for rheumatism November 8 - 18, 1864. Present for duty through August 31, 1864. Wounded at Franklin.

Ammons, Alpheus, Corp., Co. B, enlisted at Marlboro on March 31, 1862. Sick, patient in hospital Jul/Aug 1863. Promoted to Corp., August 24, 1864. Employed on extra duty at M&C Railroad as bridge builder Nov/Dec 1864. Paroled at Greensboro May 1, 1865.

Ammons, Thomas, Pvt., Co. B, enlisted at Palmetto, Ga., October 12, 1864. Wounded at Franklin November 30, 1864. Admitted to Way Hospital, Meridan, Miss., January 13, 1865. Furloughed. Paroled at Greensboro May 1, 1865.

Anderson, Preston P., Pvt., Age 16, Co. I, enlisted at Columbia March 20, 1862. Died of typhoid fever at Edgefield August 6, 1862.

Andrews, Frederick W., 1Lt., Age 20, Co. K, enlisted at Edgefield April 15, 1862. Promoted to 1Lt., April 23, 1862. Severely wounded at Secessionville June 16, 1862. Wounded at Franklin, simple flesh wound, left forearm and shoulder, November 30, 1864. Captured at Franklin December 18, 1864. Sent to Louisville and transferred to Fort Delaware January 9, 1865. Sent to Camp Chase, March 3, 1865 and transferred to Point Lookout for exchange March 18, 1865. Admitted to the Stuart Hospital, Richmond suffering debilities of an old wound March 27, 1865. Furloughed for 30 days March 29, 1865.

Andrews, George W., Sgt., Co. K, enlisted at Edgefield April 15, 1862. Wounded at Chickamauga September 20, 1863. Furloughed Sep/Oct-Nov/Dec 1863. Wounded near Atlanta July 29, 1864. Surrendered at Greensboro.

Andrews, John, Pvt., Age 62, Co. D, enlisted at Camp Gist January 16, 1862. Discharged because of debility by order of Colonel Stevens February 28, 1862.

Andrews, Milton A., Pvt., Co. C, from Beaufort District, S.C. Captured at Goldsboro, N. C., March 18, 1865. Took oath of allegiance to the United States and released June 6, 1865.

Appleby, A. C., Capt., Co. C, enlisted at Bull Run, Va., May 10, 1861. Elected 2nd Lt March 1, 1864. Originally a member of 2d Regiment. Exchanged with Luke Simpson to serve in his father's company. Granted leave March 31, 1864. Appointed captain and commanded Co. I, Consolidated 16th and 24th Regiment. Paroled at Greensboro May 1, 1865.

Appleby, Albert R., Sgt., Co. C, enlisted at Secessionville June 12, 1862. Transferred from 11th Regiment in place of J. K. Ackerman June 12, 1863. Reduced to ranks July 19, 1864. Killed in battle at Nashville.

Appleby, D. C., 1Sgt., Age 18, Co. C, enlisted at George's Station January 7, 1862. Wounded at Atlanta July 27, 1864. Furloughed. Paroled at Greensboro May 1, 1865.

Appleby, Felix Vivian, Pvt., Age 17, Co. C, from St. George, enlisted at George's Station January 7, 1862 for 12 months. Term of service expired and discharged April 22, 1863. Discharged due to bad health and afterwards joined Troop D, 5th Cavalry. Survived the war. Died October 21, 1911. Widow: Maude Keyon Appleby.

Appleby, Morgan T., Maj., Age 48, Co. C & F&S, enlisted at George's Station December 18, 1861. Raised and commanded company which was known as "Appleby's Company" prior to becoming Co. C, 24th Regiment. Granted leave Nov/Dec 1862. Resigned his commission because he was elected to a four year term as state senator from his home district, St. George's of Dorchester, June 11, 1863. Died 1867.

Appleby, Peter R., Pvt., Age 17, Co. C, enlisted at George's Station January 7, 1862. Absent, sick, at home, surgeon's certificate, October 1862 - October 1863. Wounded at Peachtree Creek. Wounded, granted furlough from Marshall Hospital, Columbus, Ga., July 30, 1864. Signed receipt roll at Marshall Hospital, Columbus, Ga., July 22, 1864. Paroled at Greensboro May 1, 1865.

Arledge, Joseph, Co. G. Entry from original muster roll prepared by Gen. E. Capers.

Arnett, Benjamin O., Pvt., Co. B., enlisted at Marion April 10, 1864. Died of disease at Empire House Hospital, June 3, 1864. Grave located in

Oakland Cemetery, Atlanta, Ga., Row 4, No. 6.

Arnold, G. William, Pvt., Age 17, Co. A, enlisted at Charleston December 31, 1861. Description: complexion, fair; hair, light; eyes, hazel; height, 5 ft. 8 in. Detailed to work on a gunboat at Eason's Foundry, Charleston. Returned to his company because the supervisor could not make him work and he set a bad example for the other detached men. Captured near Marietta July 3, 1864. Sent to Military Prison, Louisville and transferred to Camp Douglas July 18, 1863. Claimed to have been loyal. Forced to enlist in Rebel Army to avoid conscript and deserted to avail himself of amnesty proclamation, etc. Signed oath of allegiance to the United States and released January 13, 1865.

Arthur, M., Pvt., Co. G, enlisted at Pocotaligo March 25, 1863. Substitute for L. M. Caldwell. Absent without leave beginning May 6, 1863. Deserted. Dropped from rolls January 30, 1864.

Artledge, Joseph, Pvt., Co. G. Entry from Memory Rolls at State Archives, Columbia, S.C.

Astle, William B., Pvt., Age 18, Co. A, enlisted at Charleston December 31, 1861. Description: complexion, dark; hair, dark; eyes, blue; height, 5 ft., 4 in. Captured at Franklin December 17, 1864. Sent to Military Prison, Louisville and transferred to Camp Chase January 4, 1865. Signed oath of allegiance to the United States and released June 12, 1865

Augustine, William, Pvt., Co. I, enlisted at North East, N.C., December 15, 1862. Sick in quarters Jul/Oct 1863. Slightly wounded July 22, 1864. Signed receipt roll, by mark, for clothing August 5, 1864. Severely wounded, simple flesh wound to left side of back, at Franklin November 30, 1864. Captured at Franklin December 17, 1864. Admitted as patient due to wounds to No. 1, USA General Hospital, Nashville December 26 1864 - January 3, 1865. Sent to Military Prison, Louisville and transferred to Camp Chase January 11, 1865. Paroled at Camp Chase via New Orleans for exchange May 2, 1865. Married: December 24, 1978. Died October 30, 1915. Widow: Mary Augustine.

Auld, F., Chaplain, F&S. Entry from *Steinmeyer Diary.*

Averett, Douglas, Pvt., Age 40, Co. G, enlisted at Columbia April 12, 1862. Absent, furlough.

Avery, Douglas, Pvt., Co. G. Entry from Memory Rolls at State Archives, Columbia, S.C.

Bagley, John, Pvt., Age 20, Co. H, enlisted at Chester March 19, 1862. Paroled at Greensboro May 1, 1865.

Bagley, Thomas R., Pvt., Co. H, from Well Ridge, enlisted at Chester March 17, 1862. Wounded at Jackson May 14, 1863. Captured and paroled from General Hospital Ross, Mobile, Ala., May 16, 1864. Leg amputated by US Army surgeon. Furloughed for 60 days October 16, 1863. Applied to Confederate Government for artificial limb November

3, 1864.

Bailey, Edward B., Pvt., Age 27, Co. E, from Ruffin, S.C., enlisted at Camp Gist March 19, 1862. Granted furlough Mar/Apr 1863. Sick, patient in hospital at Atlanta, Ga., October 12, 1863. Signed receipt roll for clothing May 19, 1864. Sick in hospital April 10 - Jul/Aug 1864. Survived. Surrendered. Died March 3, 1888.

Bailey, Thomas R., Pvt., Co. G, from Chester District, enlisted at Pocotaligo March 4, 1863. Wounded at Atlanta July 20, 1864. Right arm amputated at Floyd House and Ocmulgee Hospitals, Macon, July 27, 1864. Furloughed.

Bailey, William W., Pvt., Age 24, Co. I, enlisted at Columbia March 20, 1862. Captured at Missionary Ridge November 24, 1863. Sent to Military Prison, Louisville and transferred to Rock Island December 25, 1863. Enlisted in US Navy at Rock Island and transferred to Naval rendezvous at Camp Douglas January 25, 1864.

Balls, James. Pvt., Co. G, from Columbia, enlisted at Columbia March 19, 1862. Captured at Jackson May 14, 1863. Assigned Paroled Prisoners Camp at Demopolis until exchanged. Wounded at Chickamauga September 20, 1863. Shot through both thighs & scrotum. In hospital at Atlanta, Ga., Sep/Oct 1863. Visited home, furlough, Nov/Dec 1863. Captured near Stone Mountain (Covington, Ga.) July 22, 1864. Sent to Military Prison, Louisville and transferred to Camp Chase August 3, 1864. Applied for oath of allegiance November 1864. Died of pneumonia at Camp Chase January 31, 1865. Grave no. 974, located 1/3 mile south of Camp Chase.

Barber, E., Pvt., Co. A, enlisted at Camp Gist March 24, 1862. Present for duty through May/Jun 1862. Transferred to Cavalry.

Barber, W., Pvt., Co. A, enlisted at Camp Gist March 24, 1862. Present for duty through May/Jun 1862. Transferred to Cavalry.

Barden, Garmany H., Pvt., Co. I, from Baxter Stores, enlisted at James Island May 17, 1862. Patient in hospital at Columbia, May/Jun 1862. Wounded, lost finger, patient in hospital at Atlanta, July 22, 1864. Paroled at Greensboro May 1, 1865.

Barnes, Morgan, Pvt., Age 34, Co. H, enlisted at Chester March 19, 1862. Absent without leave Nov/Dec 1862. Mortally wounded in battle at Chickamauga September 20, 1864. Died from wounds received in battle at Chickamauga September 21, 1864. Widow, S. A. Barnes, filed a claim for settlement July 16, 1864.

Barnes, Nickerson, Pvt., Co. H, enlisted at North East, N.C., February 4, 1863. Absent without leave from May 6, 1863 - February 1864. Reported as a deserter. Wounded. Captured at Jonesboro September 2, 1864. Sent to Military Prison, Louisville and transferred to Camp Douglas November 1, 1864. Applied for oath of allegiance in November 1864. Claimed to have been loyal and enlisted to avoid conscription and deserted to avail himself of the amnesty proclamations. Died of brain fever at Camp Douglas November 16, 1864.

Barnes, Owen H., Pvt., Age 20, Co. E, from Branchville, S.C., enlisted March 20, 1862. Pay stopped one month by order of courts martial May/Jun 1863. Admitted to St. Mary's Hospital, La Grange suffering gun shot wound and thumb amputated at first joint June 17, 1864. Signed receipt roll for clothing August 23, 1864. Admitted to St. Mary's Hospital, West Point, Miss., for disease of debilities January 1865. Survived. Surrendered.

Barnes, William G., Pvt., Co. D. from Gillersonville, S.C., enlisted at Camp Gist April 9, 1862. Pay of $6.00 stopped for the loss of bayonet Jan/Feb 1864. Present for duty on all rolls. Paroled at Greensboro May 1, 1865.

Barrentine, Goodwin, Pvt., Co. B, enlisted at Marlboro April 4, 1862. Slightly wounded, hand, at Peachtree Creek July 20, 1864. Captured near Jonesboro August 31, 1864. Exchanged at Rough and Ready September 22, 1864.

Barrow, John L., 1Sgt., Age 25, Co. B, from Bennettsville, enlisted at Marlboro December 4, 1861. Demoted from 1Sgt., to 4Sgt., to 3Sgt., to Pvt., by June 1863. Missing since retreat from Missionary Ridge Jan/Feb-Mar/Sep 1864 Captured at Missionary Ridge or Ringgold, Ga., November 25, 1863. Sent to Nashville and transferred to Rock Island December 6, 1863. Died of chronic diarrhoea June 14, 1864. Buried at Rock Island, Grave number 237.

Barrs, John W., Pvt., Co. C, from George's Station, enlisted at Camp Gist April 12, 1862. Detached service to gunboat from June 1862 to June 1863. Wounded at Chickamauga September 20, 1863. Furloughed Sep/Oct 1863. Absent without leave Nov/Dec 1863. Wounded at Peachtree Creek. Present for duty Jul/Aug 1864.

Barrs, William W., Pvt., Co. C, enlisted at Cole's Island April 24, 1862. Present for duty May/Jun 1862. Died in service.

Bass, Richard, Pvt., Age 25, Co. B, enlisted at Charleston December 4, 1861. Present for duty Jan/Feb 1863. Survived.

Baum, Charles, Pvt., Co. A, enlisted at Camp Gist March 28, 1862. Received payment on descriptive lists January 31, 1864. Commutation. Transferred to another command.

Beaty, C. S., Capt., Age 29, Co. F, from Dry Grove, S.C., Anderson District, enlisted at Columbia January 12, 1862. Appointed 3Corp., December 1, 1862. Promoted 2Corp., January 30, 1863. Promoted 4Sgt., Jun 1, 1863. Promoted to 3Sgt., August 1, 1863. Elected 2Lt., April 11, 1864. Commanded Co. K., Consolidated 16th and 24th Regiment, formed from Co. F and H, 24th Regiment. Paroled at Greensboro May 1, 1865. Died in 1894.

Beckham, George, Pvt., Co. G, from Fairfield, S.C., enlisted at Columbia May 1, 1863. Wounded at Chickamauga September 20, 1863. Furloughed. Patient in hospital at Columbia S.C., Nov/Dec 1863 - August 1864. Signed, by mark, a receipt roll for clothing September 18, 1864. Paroled at Greensboro May 1, 1865.

Beckham, William M., Capt., Age 21, Co. G, enlisted at Columbia April 15, 1862. Detached service as enrolling officer at Columbia July - October 1863. Granted leave March 5, 1864. Commanded Co. H, Consolidated 16th and 24th Regiment, at surrender. Paroled at Greensboro May 1, 1865.

Behling, Henry, Pvt., Co. C, enlisted at Secessionville May 22, 1862. Detached service with Signal Corps at Hardeeville during 1863. Wounded at Chickamauga September 20, 1863. Furloughed. Absent without leave Nov/Dec 1863. Wounded at Nashville. Captured at Nashville December 16, 1864. Sent to Military Prison, Louisville and transferred to Camp Chase January 12, 1865. Transferred to Point Lookout March 26, 1865. Took oath of allegiance to the United States and released June 5, 1865.

Beier, John B., Pvt., Age 31, Co. G, born in Germany, enlisted at Columbia March 19, 1862. Present for duty May/Jun 1862. Description: complexion, florid; hair, light; eyes, blue; height, 5 ft. 8 in. Discharged by surgeon's certificate July 29, 1862.

Beiglin, John, Pvt., Age 29, Co. C, from Reeves Station, enlisted at Camp Gist March 6, 1862. Mortally wounded in battle at Jackson May 14, 1863. Died of wounds July 25, 1863.

Bell, George, Pvt., Co. F, enlisted at Anderson March 10, 1862. Served as a musician, fife(r). Absent, sick, dropped from roll January 1, 1863.

Bell, Joseph B., 3Sgt., Age 23, Co. H, from Lewisville, enlisted at Chester March 19, 1862. Description: complexion, light; eyes, grey; hair, sandy; height, 5 ft, 10 in; occupation, farmer. Mortally wounded in battle at Chickamauga September 20, 1863. Died in hospital at Atlanta of wounds received in battle at Chickamauga October 15, 1863. Eliza J. Bell, Widow, filed for settlement November 30, 1863.

Bennett, Abraham, Pvt., Age 18, Co. E, from Walter Cove, S.C., enlisted at Salkehatchie January 16, 1862. Sick, patient in hospital, Miss., Jul/Aug - Sep/Oct 1863. Absent without leave Nov/Dec 1863. Along route to Atlanta, wounded, right leg, ball passing through. Granted 60 days furlough. Absent without leave from July 27. Surrendered.

Bennett, Charles F., Pvt., Age 20, Co. I, enlisted at James Island November 1, 1862. Transferred from Savannah River Guards, 3rd Regiment October 17, 1862. Sick, patient in hospital in Charleston from April 23 - November 24, 1863. Killed in battle at Potato Hill, 1864. Shot in the lung. Died in Hospital at Dalton May 10, 1864. Reported killed in speech made by Col. Capers, regimental commander, May 22, 1864.

Bennett, C. L., Pvt., Age 21, Co. D, enlisted at Camp Gist January 16, 1862. Present for duty May/Jun 1862.

Bennett, E. C. Buried May 21, 1864 in Oakland Cemetery, Atlanta, Georgia. Entry from Oakland Cemetery Records.

Bennett, G. R., Sgt., Age 22, Co. E, from Stokes, S.C., enlisted at Salkehatchie January 16, 1862. Absent, sick Oct/Nov 1862. Promoted to 5Sgt. Wounded, leg, near Atlanta August 19, 1864. Survived. Married February 1871. Died April 5, 1906.

Bennett, G. W., Corp., Age 25, Co. B, enlisted at Marlboro December 4, 1861. Wounded, arm, at Peachtree Creek July 20, 1864. Furloughed. Survived.

Bennett, John J., Cook, Age 19, Co. B, enlisted at Marlboro December 4, 1861. Deserted about December 15, 1862.

Bennett, John, Pvt., Age 23, Co. E, enlisted at Salkehatchie January 16, 1862. Absent, sick, at home Nov/Dec 1863 - Jan/Feb 1863. Captured near Marietta July 3, 1864. Sent to Military Prison Louisville and transferred to Camp Douglas July 18, 1864. Paroled at Camp Douglas and transferred to Point Lookout for exchange February 20, 1865.

Bennett, William, Pvt., Age 28, Co. E. Wounded along route to Atlanta. Survived. Entry from roster made by Capt. J. K. Risher, Company Commander.

Benton, A. B., Pvt., Age 16, Co. E, enlisted at Dalton, Ga., March 1, 1864. Bounty due for enlistment $50. Paroled at Greensboro May 1, 1865. Born: March 16, 1845.

Benton, Berry W., Pvt., Age 19, Co. E, enlisted at Camp Gist March 20, 1862. Wounded at Chickamauga September 20, 1863. Absent without leave July 9 - August 31, 1864. Patient in Floyd House and Ocmulgee Hospitals, Macon for chronic diarrhoea October 17, 1864. Surrendered.

Benton, E. H., 2Lt., Age 29, Co. E, enlisted at Camp Gist March 2, 1862. Temporarily promoted from Pvt., to 2Sgt., in place of S. C. White who was taken prisoner May 21, 1862. Served as Pvt., for 33 days. Appointed Corp., December 4, 1862. Promoted 5Sgt., June 1863 and 4Sgt., August 1863. Elected 2Lt., January 26, 1864. Killed in battle at Stone Mountain (Battle of Atlanta) July 22, 1864.

Benton, Henry E., Pvt., Age 18, Co. E, enlisted at Camp Gist March 19, 1862, Wounded at Chickamauga September 20, 1863. Slightly wounded, shoulder, July 20/22 1864. Captured near Nashville December 16, 1864. Sent to Military Prison, Louisville and transferred to Camp Chase January 2, 1865. Died at Camp Chase of pneumonia February 20, 1865. Grave # 1415.

Benton, J. D., Pvt., Age 16, Co. E, enlisted at Dalton, Ga., March 20, 1864. Killed in battle at Calhoun or Resaca, Ga. Severely wounded, spine.

Died of wound May 21, 1864. Grave located at Confederate Cemetery, Marietta, Ga.

Benton, J. R., Pvt., Age 24, Co. E, enlisted at Camp Gist March 31, 1862. Wounded, left arm, near Atlanta Jun 21, 1864. Patient in hospital. Arm amputated. Died of wound. Survived. Ed. Note - Military service record reflects individual died. Roster prepared by company commander after the war reflects that individual survived.

Benton, M. C., Sgt., Age 18, Co. E, enlisted at Salkehatchie January 16, 1862. Served as Corp., from March 62 - July 23, 1864. Wounded, eye, at Atlanta August 25, 1864. Blind since.

Benton, Samuel S., Pvt., Co. A, enlisted at Adams Run April 10, 1862. Transferred from Co. B, 3rd Cavalry April 10, 1862. Sick, furloughed Sep/Oct 1863. Absent without leave Nov/Dec 1863. Absent, under arrest, February 3, 1864. Absent without leave August 18, 1864. Signed receipt roll by mark for clothing September 12, 1864. Detached in hospital. Discharged for disability.

Benton, Sam S., Pvt., Age 35, Co. E, from Colleton District, enlisted at Camp Gist March 3, 1863. Signed receipt roll for clothing, by mark, April 5, 1864. Died of disease, chronic diarrhoea, at Marietta, Ga., September 30, 1863. Grave located in Marietta Confederate Cemetery, Grave # 57.

Bethea, A. J., Pvt., Co. B, from Marion, enlisted at Marlboro April 20, 1862. Served as hospital nurse and assistant hospital steward detailed to the medical department Jan/Feb - August 31, 1864. Paroled at Greensboro May 1, 1865.

Bethea, J. E., Pvt., Age 20, Co. B, Born at Marlboro, enlisted at Marlboro December 4, 1861. Description: complexion, fair; eyes, blue; hair, light; height, 6 ft, 3 in. Discharged due to surgeon's certificate for defective eyes January 23, 1862. Discharged again June 23, 1862. Enlisted again April 1, 1863. Died near Yazoo City June 21, 1863.

Bethea, Tristram T., Pvt., Co. B, from Marlboro. Killed in battle at Franklin November 30, 1864. Entry from Memory Rolls at State Archives, Columbia, S.C., and *A History of Marlboro County.*

Beverly, Robert A., Corp., Age 26, Co. B, enlisted at Marlboro December 4, 1861. Promoted to Corp., May/Jun 1863. Sick in hospital at Canton May/Jun 1863. Reported killed at battle at Atlanta July 22, 1864. Also, reported killed in speech to 24th Regiment by regimental commander, Colonel Capers May 22, 1864. Probably killed at the battle of Calhoun May 16, 1864.

Bier, John B., Pvt., Co. G. Entry from Memory Rolls at State Archives, Columbia, S.C.

Biggers or Briggers, W. Buried in Oakland Cemetery, Atlanta, Georgia September 9, 1863 or 1864. Entry from Oakland Cemetery Records.

Bigham, James W., Pvt., Age 27, Co. H, from Cornwell, S.C., Chester District, enlisted at Columbia April 15, 1862. Slightly wounded, hand and ankle, July 20 or July 22, 1864. Description: complexion, dark; hair, dark; eyes, blue; height, 5 ft. 7 1/2 in. Slightly wounded, liver, at Nashville. Captured near Nashville December 16, 1864. Sent to the Military Prison, Louisville and transferred to Camp Chase, January 14, 1865. Signed oath of allegiance to the United States June 12, 1865. Born May 29, 1938.

Bishop, T. J., Pvt., Co. A, enlisted at Wilmington, N.C., February 12, 1863. Served as Drummer Boy. Missing in engagement near Jackson, Miss., May 14, 1863. Deserted at Cordts Pond, Miss., August 30, 1863.

Black, Robert J., Corp., Age 30, Co. F, from Mt. Carmel, Anderson District, enlisted at Camp Gist January 13, 1862. Promoted to 3Corp., August 1, 1863 and to 2Corp., 26 November 1863. Reported as prisoner in the hands of the enemy. Captured at Missionary Ridge November 26, 1863. Sent to Military Prison, Louisville. Transferred to Rock Island December 9, 1863. Tired of CSA. Wished to "take the oath and be loyal." Released at Rock Island May 22, 1865.

Blackwell, J. Preston, Pvt., Co. I, enlisted at James Island May 17, 1862. Slightly wounded, knee, at Chickamauga September 20, 1863. Absent, wounded, Nov/Dec 1863. Wounded at Kennesaw. Wounded at Franklin. Surrendered and paroled at Augusta May 18, 1865.

Bodie, Nicholas, Pvt., Co. I, enlisted at Columbia March 20, 1862. Absent without leave and name canceled on roll April 21, 1862.

Bofil, Paul, Pvt., Age 40, Co. G, enlisted at Columbia March 19, 1862. (Last name may be: Bofile.) Discharged by surgeon's certificate June 11, 1862.

Bolan, M. J., Surgeon, F&S, appointed December 19, 1862. Reassigned July 13, 1864.

Bold, William, Pvt., Co. A., Age 54, enlisted at Charleston December 31, 1861. Detailed to work at Eason's gun boat October 23, 1862. Detailed to work at Eason's until further orders August 11, 1863. Died of disease at Charleston.

Bollinger, W. Jr., Pvt., Co. G. Entry from original muster roll.

Bonner, Wiley, Pvt., Age 28, Co. E, enlisted at Salkehatchie January 16, 1862. Transferred to Co. A. Paroled prisoner with the Vicksburg garrison July 4, 1863. Absent without leave from November 4, 1862 - March 30, 1863. Pay stopped for one short Enfield Rifle and accoutrements, one knapsack, one haversack, one canteen and strap, 25 rounds of ammunition. All returned but the knapsack. Transferred to Co. A, 24 SCVI. Captured near Marietta at Kennesaw Mountain June 19, 1864. Sent to Military Prison, Louisville and transferred to Camp Morton June 27, 1864. Died of inflammation of the lungs at Camp Morton February

13, 1865. Grave number 1404, Green Lawn Cemetery, Indianapolis, In.

Boulware, Green F., Pvt., Age 34, Co. H, from Chester, enlisted at Columbia March 19, 1862. Description: complexion, light; eyes, blue; hair, light; height, 5 ft. 8 in; occupation, farmer; born, Fairfield District. Killed in battle at Chickamauga September 20, 1863. Marg. S. Boulware filed claim for settlement November 10, 1863.

Bowen, G. W., Pvt., Co. G. Entry from Memory Rolls at State Archives, Columbia, S.C., and from original muster roll.

Bowers, Alfred, Pvt., Co. C. Living. Entry from Memory Rolls at State Archives, Columbia, S.C.

Bowers, A. E., Capt., Age 34, Co. D, enlisted at Camp Gist January 16, 1862. Promoted to Capt., June 11, 1863. Furloughed from hospital August 12, 1864. Died of wounds received in battle at Nashville.

Bowers, Charles E. Sgt., Co. D, from Bluffton, enlisted at Hardeeville January 16, 1862. Appointed Sgt., by General Johnston February 1, 1864. Slightly wounded, ear, July 20/22, 1864. Captured near Nashville December 16, 1864. Sent to Military Prison, Louisville and transferred to Camp Chase January 2, 1865. Died of pneumonia January 13, 1865. Grave no. 759, 1/3 mile south of Camp Chase.

Bowers D. U., Sgt., Age 31, Co. D, enlisted at Camp Gist January 16, 1862. Wounded at Secessionville June 16, 1862. Promoted to Sgt., December 5, 1862. Wounded at Chickamauga September 20, 1863. Suffered from chronic diarrhoea and admitted to Floyd House and Ocmulgee Hospitals, Macon September 27, 1863. Furloughed for 30 days September 27, 1863. Furlough extended to Jan/February 1864. Discharged June 30, 1864. Surrendered and paroled at Augusta June 2, 1865.

Bowers, Depena N., Sgt., Co. D. Wounded at Chickamauga. Promoted from ranks. Living. Entry from Memory Rolls at State Archives, Columbia, S.C.

Bowers, H. A., Pvt., Co. D, enlisted at Beaufort District January 15. 1864. Present for duty Jul/Aug 1864. Surrendered and paroled at Augusta May 19, 1865.

Bowers, Mc. R., Pvt., Age 19, Co. D, enlisted at Camp Gist January 16, 1862. Mortally wounded in battle at Jackson May 14, 1863. Died of wound July 2, 1863. Father, Jno. Bowers, filed claim for settlement April 29, 1864.

Bowers, Medicus H., 1Lt., Age 19, Co. D, enlisted at Camp Gist January 16, 1862. Promoted to 1Lt., July 23, 1863. Killed in battle at Chickamauga September 20, 1863. Father, R. C. Bowers, filed claim for settlement April 29, 1864.

Bowers, William R., Pvt., Co. D, from Whippy Swamp, Hampton County, enlisted at Bluffton November 12, 1862. Sick with pneumonia in CSA General Military Hospital, No. 4, Wilmington December 29, 1862 -

January 14, 1863. Furloughed from hospital for 25 days January 14, 1863. Sick in hospital at Atlanta Nov/Dec 1863. Paroled at Greensboro May 1, 1865. Married: September 9, 1868. Died: January 23, 1901. Widow: Delia Clara Bowers.

Bowie, John A., Maj., F&S, Appointed captain, A. C. S. (this was a reappointment) November 12, 1863 to rank from July 3, 1863 and ordered to report to the commissary general. Assigned to Gist's Brigade, Army of Tennessee. Promoted to Major & Chief of Staff at Abbeville January 28, 1865. Ordered to report to Gist's Brigade April 5, 1865.

Bowyer, Thomas M. Pvt., Age 33, Co. B, from Bennettsville, enlisted at Marlboro December 4, 1861. Sick, patient in hospital at Cassville, Ga., Sep/Oct 1863 - Jan/February 1864. Present for duty through August 31, 1864.

Boyd, John L., Pvt., Co. H, enlisted at Chester June 6, 1862. Present for duty through August 31, 1864. Killed in battle at Franklin November 30, 1864. Grave located in Franklin Confederate Cemetery, Section 84, Grave No. 29.

Boyd, S. W., Pvt., Age 19, Co. F, from Anderson, enlisted at Anderson January 13, 1862. Mortally wounded in battle at Chickamauga September 20, 1863. Died of wounds received in battle at Chickamauga October 10, 1863. Died in Fair Grounds Hospital No. 2, Atlanta.

Bozeman, D. L., Sgt., Age 31, Co. F, enlisted at Abbeville May 9, 1862. Promoted to 2Corp., June 1, 1862, detached duty in QM Department. Promoted 1Corp., August 1, 1863. Promoted to 4Sgt., February 1, 1864, in charge of cooking detail. Wounded at Franklin, November 30, 1864. Admitted to Way Hospital, Meridan, Miss., suffering from diarrhoea January 12, 1865. Surrendered 1865. Killed in saw mill accident at Abbeville in October 1868.

Bozeman, D. Tillman, Sgt., Age 44, Co. F, enlisted at Anderson January 13, 1862. Hospital steward. Present for duty through Mar/Apr 1863. Died of disease in fall of 1863.

Brackenridge, Robert W., Pvt., Age 42, Co. I, enlisted at Columbia March 20, 1862. Absent, sick, patient in hospital Sep/Oct 1863. Absent, sick, patient in hospital May 16 - Jul/Aug 1864. Paroled at Greensboro May 1, 1865.

Bradshaw, William H., Pvt., Age 18, Co. F, from Abbeville, enlisted at Anderson April 9, 1862. Wounded and captured at Jackson May 14, 1863. Paroled in hospital May 16, 1863. Name appears on a weekly report of paroled and exchanged prisoners sent to their commands September 21, 1863. Signed, by mark, receipt for clothing December 23, 1863. Absent without leave February 15, 1864. Patient in Ocmulgee Hospital, Macon for diarrhoea Aug/Sep 1864. Served in a detachment guarding Baker Creek Bridge, Muscogee R. R., near Columbus

November 1864. Surrendered 1865.

Brady, Peter, Corp., Age 30, Co. H, from Chester, enlisted at Chester March 19, 1862. Description: hair, black; eyes, black; height, 5 ft. 9 in; occupation, farmer. Died of measles at Columbia June 22, 1862.

Branyan, R. P., Corp., Age 17 1/2, Co. F, from Abbeville, enlisted at Columbia January 13, 1862. Absent, sick, Mar/Apr 1863. Appointed 4Corp., August 1, 1863. In hospital sick October 4, 1863. Promoted to 4Corp., February 1, 1864. Captured near Nashville December 16, 1864. Sent to Military Prison, Louisville and transferred to Camp Chase January 4, 1865. Died of pneumonia at Camp Chase August 17, 1865. Grave # 2061.

Breedlove, John W., Pvt., Age 23, Co. C, enlisted at George's Station January 7, 1862. Absent, sick, patient in hospital Jul/Oct 1862 - Mar/Apr 1863. Brigade teamster Jul/Aug 1864. In hospital at Mobile and Montgomery for debilities November 5 - 22, 1864. Sent to General Hospital November 22, 1864. Paroled at Greensboro May 1, 1865.

Breland, A. B., Pvt., Age 26, Co. E, enlisted at Camp Gist March 2, 1862. Absent, patient in hospital, December 26, 1863. Died of disease in Hospital at Kingston, Ga., December 31, 1863. Widow, A. M. Breland, filed claim for settlement October 26, 1864.

Breland, G. H., Sgt., Age 28, Co. E., enlisted at Camp Gist March 15, 1862. Wounded at Chickamauga September 20, 1863. Absent without leave Jan/Feb 1864. Present for duty Jul/Aug 1864. Signed receipt roll for clothing September 9, 1864. Survived.

Breland, Isaiah, Pvt., Age 47, Co. D, enlisted at Camp Gist January 16, 1862. Sick in hospital Jul/Aug - Sep/Oct 1863. Captured at Shipp's Gap/Taylor's Ridge October 16, 1864. Sent to Military Prison, Louisville and transferred to Camp Douglas. Died of scurvy February 21, 1865. Grave no. 812, Chicago City Cemetery.

Breland, Josiah W., Pvt., Age 41, Co. E, from Colleton County, enlisted at Salkehatchie January 16, 1862. Sick in hospital Jan/Feb 1864. Signed receipt roll for clothing September 9, 1864. Wounded, right leg, Nashville December 16, 1864. Captured at Pulaski, Tenn., December 25, 1864. Admitted to No. 1, USA Gen. Hosp., Nashville, Tenn., February 10 - 14, 1865. Treated for simple flesh wound in right leg. Sent to Military Prison, Louisville and transferred to Camp Chase February 18, 1865. Description: complexion, florid; hair, dark; eyes, grey; height, 5 ft. 11 1/2 in. Signed oath of allegiance to the United States June 13, 1865 and released.

Breland, J. R., Pvt., Age 31, Co. E, born June 20, 1843, from Ruffin, enlisted at Camp Gist March 2, 1862. Died of disease in hospital at Selma, Ala., May 24, 1863.

Breland, S. Lawrence, Pvt., Age 18, Co. E, from Walterboro, S.C., enlisted at Camp Gist March 3, 1865. Wounded at Chickamauga September 20, 1863. Patient at Floyd House and Ocmulgee Hospitals, Macon. Gunshot, right side, through ligaments and escaped through gluten muscles September 16, 1864. Paroled at Greensboro May 1, 1865. Grave located in Breland Family Cemetery, Upper Colleton County, S.C.

Breland, T. A. S., Pvt., Age 23, Co. E, enlisted at Camp Gist March 20, 1862. Absent without leave October 1 - November 1, 1862. Pay stopped one month by court martial in May/Jun 1863. Signed receipt roll for clothing September 9, 1864. Paroled at Greensboro May 1, 1865.

Brigman, L., Pvt., Co. B, conscripted at Marlboro April 1, 1863. Present for duty through August 31, 1864. Survived.

Briscoe, George, Pvt., Co. K, enlisted at Edgefield March 14, 1862. Discharged by medical board May/Jun 1862.

Bristow, Thomas C., Pvt., Age 24, Co. B, enlisted at Marlboro December 4, 1861. Present for duty on all rolls. Deserted April 25, 1865. Paroled at Greensboro May 1, 1865.

Britt, A., Pvt., Co. H, enlisted at Atlanta August 21, 1864. Captured at Jonesboro September 2, 1864. Sent to Military Prison, Louisville and transferred to Camp Douglas November 1, 1864. Mustered into 6th U. S. Vol. Infantry April 3, 1865.

Brower, W., Pvt., Age 19, Co. A, enlisted at Charleston December 31, 1861 for 12 months. Present for duty May/Jun 1862. Transferred to 1st Battalion, South Carolina Sharp Shooters.

Brown, Ambrose, Pvt., Age 40, Co. F, from Greenville, S.C., enlisted at Anderson September 1, 1862. Substitute for Sgt., G. F. Burdit September 11, 1862. Wounded at Chickamauga September 20, 1863. Absent, sick, October 20, 1863 - August 31, 1864. Signed by mark. On duty at Military Prison, Atlanta May/Jun 1864. Captured at Atlanta September 2, 1864. Sent to Military Prison, Louisville and transferred to Camp Douglas November 1, 1864. Claimed to have been loyal, conscripted into the Rebel Army. Deserted to avail himself of the amnesty proclamation. Enlisted in 5th U.S. Vols. April 15, 1865. Living.

Brown, Cornelius J. H., Sgt., Age 28, Co. A, from Charleston, enlisted at Charleston March 17, 1862. Sick at home Sep/Oct - Nov/Dec 1864. Wounded and captured at Jackson May 14, 1863. At Paroled Prisoners in Camp at Demopolis June 5, 1863. Promoted to 1Sgt., March 14, 1864. Signed receipt roll for clothing April 1, 1864. Captured at Shipp's Gap/Taylor's Ridge October 16, 1864. Sent to Military Prison, Louisville and transferred to Camp Douglas October 29, 1864. Description: complexion, fair; hair, brown; eyes, hazel; height, 5 ft. 7 in. Signed oath of allegiance to the United States and discharged June 17, 1865.

Brown, H. H., Pvt., Age 31, Co. F, enlisted at Camp Gist January 13, 1862. Sick at Hospital Jul/Aug 1863. Signed receipt roll for clothing April 1, 1864. Present on all other rolls. Died of disease May 13, 1864.

Brown, Jacob, Pvt., Age 15, Co. D, enlisted at Camp Gist January 16, 1862. Wounded at Chickamauga September 20, 1863. In hospital at Atlanta, Ga., Sep/Oct 1863. Wounded, granted leave Nov/Dec 1863. Signed receipt roll for clothing April 1, 1864. Severely wounded, foot, Jul 20, 1864. Survived.

Brown, J. J., Pvt., Co. D, enlisted at Camp Gist January 16, 1862. Absent with leave, wounded, August 17 - October 17, 1864. Surrendered and paroled at Augusta May 24, 1865.

Brown, John, Sgt., Age 18, Co. D, enlisted at Camp Gist January 16, 1862. Wounded, severely in the thigh, at Legares June 3, 1862. Wounded in 1863. Absent with leave, wounded, May/Jun - Nov/Dec 1863. Killed in battle at Calhoun, Ga., May 16, 1864. (Following information from official service record suspected error). Captured at Fayetteville, N.C., March 10, 1865. Sent to Point Lookout, Md., March 31, 1865. Admitted to USA General Hosp., Point Lookout, Md for chronic diarrhoea July 2 - 6, 1865. Took oath of allegiance to the United States and released June 9, 1865.

Brown, J. K., Pvt., Co. D. Reported killed in battle by speech made by Col. Capers, regimental commander May 22, 1864. Listed as killed in action by *Daily Courier* May 20, 1864.

Brown, Lee, Pvt., Age 17, Co. D, enlisted at Camp Gist January 19, 1862. Wounded at Legares, James Island, June 13, 1862. Killed in battle at Atlanta August 9, 1864.

Brown, Perry W., Corp., Age 21, Co. D, enlisted at Camp Gist January 16, 1862. Promoted to Corp., July 17, 1864. Captured near Nashville December 16, 1864. Sent to Military Prison, Louisville and transferred to Camp Chase January 4, 1865. Description: complexion, florid; hair, light; eyes, blue; height, 5 ft. 10 in. Signed oath of allegiance to the United States June 12, 1865.

Brown, R. Kirk, Pvt., Co. D, enlisted at North East, N.C., February 7, 1863. Absent without leave May/Jun 1863. Sick in hospital and on sick furlough Jul/Aug 1863 - October 7, 1864. Surrendered and paroled at Augusta May 24, 1865.

Brown, R. M. Pursuant to a letter from the AAG, the Provost Marshal in Charleston reported that this soldier presented himself to their office August 11, 1863. He was arrested and lodged in jail.

Brown, Samuel W. E., Pvt., Age 30, Co. F, from Anderson Dist., enlisted at Camp Gist January 13, 1864. Died of typhoid fever at Catoosa Hospital, Griffin, Ga., September 2, 1864.

Brown, T. R., Pvt., Age 18, Co. F, enlisted at Anderson September 19,

1862. Substitute for Corp. S. A. Hutchinson September 19, 1862. Originally mustered as a substitute. Became of age and was entitled and mustered in his own right Jul/Aug 1863. Wounded at Chickamauga September 20, 1863. Absent, wounded, September 20, 1863 - August 31, 1864. Surrendered.

Brown, Ulmer J., Corp., Age 22, Co. D, enlisted at Camp Gist January 16, 1862. Promoted to Corp., June 1, 1863. Absent with leave, wounded, September - December 1863. Wounded at Chickamauga September 20, 1863. Present for duty Jul/Aug 1864. Dead.

Browne, Richard M., Pvt., Age 23, Co. A, enlisted at Charleston December 31, 1861. Detailed to work at arsenal, Charleston April 28 - May/Jun 1863. Sick in hospital Sep/Oct 1863. Reported missing July 3, 1864. He has been heard from and will return to duty in a short time. Paroled at Greensboro May 1, 1865.

Bruce, Hugh T., Pvt., Age 18, Co. H, enlisted at Chester March 19, 1862. Absent, sick, Nov/Dec 1862. Patient for diarrhoea in St. Mary's Hospital, La Grange, Ga. July 17, 1864. Wounded. Paroled at Greensboro May 1, 1865. Applied for Confederate veteran's pension August 10, 1906, as a resident of Arkansas.

Brutus, negro cook. Present for duty Sep/Oct 1862 - Mar/Apr 1863.

Bryan, E. H., Sgt., Age 22, Co. E, enlisted at Salkehatchie January 16, 1862. Promoted to 5Sgt., 4Sgt., 3Sgt., Detailed to provost guard Nov/Dec 1863. Severely wounded, right arm, at Atlanta July 9, 1864. Absent, in hospital, Jul/Aug 1864. Paroled at Greensboro May 1, 1865. Grave located in Bethel United Methodist Church Cemetery, Upper Colleton County, S.C.

Bryan, J. M., Pvt., Age 39, Co. E, enlisted at Salkehatchie January 16, 1862. Discharged by surgeon March 20, 1862. Grave located in Bethel United Methodist Church Cemetery, Upper Colleton County, S.C.

Bryan, J. T., Pvt., Age 26, Co. E, enlisted at James Island November 1, 1862. Absent, sick, in hospital Sep/Oct 1863. Absent without leave Nov/Dec 1863. Died of disease January 13, 1864.

Bryan, Paul W. A., Sgt., Age 22, Co. E, enlisted at Salkehatchie January 16, 1862. Promoted to 3Sgt., 2Sgt., 1Sgt. Slightly wounded, knee, near Calhoun, Ga., May 16, 1864. Signed receipt roll for clothing September 9, 1864. Description: complexion, light; hair, light; eyes, blue; height, 5 ft. 10 in. Captured near Nashville December 16, 1864. Sent to Military Prison, Louisville and transferred to Camp Chase January 2, 1865. Signed oath of allegiance to the United States June 12, 1865.

Bryan, Richard E., Pvt., Age 20, Co. E, enlisted at Salkehatchie January 16, 1862. Absent, sick, in hospital at Atlanta September 2, 1863. Signed receipt roll for clothing May 19, 1864. Absent, sick, in hospital March 25, 1864 - Jul/Aug 1864. Paroled at Greensboro May 1, 1865. Grave located in Bethel United Methodist Church Cemetery, Upper Colleton County, S.C.

Bryan, R. G. W., 1Lt., Age 28, Co. E, enlisted at Salkehatchie January 16, 1862. Promoted to 2Lt., from 1Sgt., May/Jun 1863. Wounded at Chickamauga September 20, 1863. Absent, wounded, granted sick furlough, September 20, 1863 - Jan/Feb 1864. Promoted to 1Lt., August 20, 1864. Slightly wounded, head, at Atlanta July 20, 1864. Sent to hospital. Present for duty Jul/Aug 1864. Surrendered 1865.

Buff, J. Wade, Pvt., Co. I, enlisted at Coles Island March 20 1862. Absent without leave, name canceled on roll.

Bulger, John F., Pvt., Age 21, Co. D, enlisted at Camp Gist April 9, 1862. Missing at Jackson May 16, 1863. Prisoner in paroled prisoners camp at Demopolis May/Jun 1863. Wounded at Chickamauga. In hospital at Atlanta Sep/Oct - Nov/Dec 1863. Description: complexion, light; hair, light; eyes, hazel; height, 5 ft. 9 in. Captured near Nashville December 16, 1864. Sent to Military Prison, Louisville and transferred to Camp Chase January 4, 1865. Signed oath of allegiance to the United States June 12, 1865.

Burdell, Benjamin, Pvt., Age 25, Co. G, enlisted at Columbia March 19, 1862. One month pay stopped by order of court martial May/Jun 1863. Present for duty through August 31, 1864. Signed receipt for clothing September 9, 1864. Employed on extra duty at M. & C. Railroad as a bridge builder Nov/Dec 1864.

Burdett, G. F., Sgt., Age 30, Co. F, from Iva, Anderson County, S.C., enlisted at Camp Gist January 13, 1862. Discharge by substitute A. Brown August 31, 1862. Joined another command. Discharged in N.C. in April 1865. Married August 30, 1883. Died July 16, 1915.

Burdit, Samuel G., Jr., Pvt., Age 19, Co. F, from Moffetsville, enlisted at Anderson January 13, 1862. Worked at salt works Mar/Apr 1863. Sick in Hospital October 23-30, 1863. Sick in hospital January 18 - February 28, 1864. Signed receipt roll for clothing April 1, 1864. Gun shot wound through left hand fracturing the metacarpal bone of little finger July 9, 1864. Furloughed Jul/Aug 1864. Wounded at Franklin November 30, 1864. Treated at Way Hospital, Meridian, Miss for wound January 12, 1865. Paroled at Greensboro May 1, 1865.

Burdit, Samuel G., Sr., Sgt., Age 40, Co. F, enlisted at Anderson January 13, 1862. Promoted to 1Corp., December 1, 1862. Promoted 5Sgt., January 30, 1863. Absent, furlough, Mar/Apr 1863. Promoted to 2Sgt., June 1, 1863. Mortally wounded in battle at Jackson May 14, 1863. Suffered extreme depression after learning his leg had been amputated above the knee. Captured and paroled May 16, 1863. Died from wounds received in battle at Jackson June 30, 1863. Widow, Tempey Burdit, filed claim for settlement February 8, 1864.

Burris, G. B., Pvt., Co. F, disabled from wound received at Atlanta and discharged August 1864. Entry from other roster.

Burris, J. B., Pvt., Age 25, Co. F, from Iva, S.C., enlisted at Anderson June 13, 1862 for 12 months. Absent, sick since reported. Discharged for inability July 29, 1862.

Burris, James N., Pvt., Age 35, Co. F, from Herdmont, Ga., enlisted at Anderson May 24, 1864. Captured at Shipp's Gap/Taylor's Ridge October 16, 1864. Sent to Military Prison, Louisville and transferred to Camp Douglas October 26, 1864. Forwarded to Point Lookout for exchange February 20, 1865. Admitted to Receiving and Wayside Hospital or General Hospital No. 9, Richmond February 28, 1865.

Burton, Benjamin, Pvt., Co. I, enlisted at Columbia March 20, 1862. Absent without leave. Name canceled on roll.

Burton, Charles, Pvt., Co. I, enlisted at Columbia, April 21, 1862. Absent without leave. Name canceled on roll.

Burton, George W., Sgt., Co. K, from Edgefield, enlisted at Edgefield April 15, 1862. Severely wounded at Secessionville June 16, 1862. Granted 60 days leave from the hospital Mar/Aug 1864. Paroled at Greensboro May 1, 1865. Married in September 1864. Died August 30, 1884. Widow: M. J. Burton.

Burton, J. D., Pvt., Age 35, Co. F. From Iva., S.C. Wounded at Jackson, Miss., May 14, 1863. Surrendered. Entry from Memory Rolls at State Archives, Columbia, S.C. and Survivor's Association roster.

Burton, James D., Pvt., Age 32, Co. F, from Iva, S.C., enlisted at Anderson January 13, 1862. Wounded at Jackson May 14, 1863. Captured and paroled in hospital May 16, 1863. One months pay stopped by sentence of court martial for 1 month 6 days absent without leave. Paroled at Greensboro May 1, 1865. Died May 1899.

Burton, James F., Pvt., Co. K, enlisted at Edgefield October 20, 1861. Detailed as hospital nurse in Atlanta April 22, 1864 by order of General Johnston. Captured at West Point, Ga., April 16, 1865. Transferred to Military Prison, Macon, Ga., April 23, 1865.

Burton, Samuel, Pvt., Co. A. Discharged for disability. Entry from Memory Rolls at State Archives, Columbia, S.C.

Busby, Jake N. 1Sgt., Age 23, Co. G, from Alston Depot, enlisted at Columbia April 12, 1862. Appointed 2Sgt., June 1, 1863. Appointed 1Sgt., September 20, 1863. Wounded by gunshot in the back that passed underneath the scapula May 16, 1864. Granted 60 days leave May 30, 1864. Slightly wounded, arm, July 22, 1864. Present for duty August 31, 1864.

Bush, John E., Pvt., Age 18, Co. I, enlisted at James Island May 15, 1862. Slightly wounded, hand, August 31, 1864. Captured near Jonesboro August 31, 1864. Exchanged at Rough and Ready September 19, 1864.

Paroled at Greensboro May 1865.

Bussey, Dempsey C., Pvt., Age 35, Co. I, enlisted at Columbia. April 10 1862. In hospital at Charleston February 15, 1863. Furloughed March 12, 1863. Wounded, ankle and shoulder, at Chickamauga September 20, 1863. Absent, wounded, in hospital Sep/Oct 1863 - Jul/Aug 1864.

Bussy, J. E., Pvt., Co. K, from Orangeburg, enlisted at Edgefield April 15, 1862. Killed in battle at Secessionville June 16, 1862.

Butts, Charles H., Pvt., Co. A, enlisted at Charleston, February 21, 1862. Under arrest for desertion May/Jun 1863. Captured at battle near Jackson May 14, 1863. At Paroled Prisoners Camp at Demopolis June 5, 1863. Absent without leave from paroled prisoners camp from October 1, 1863 to February 1, 1864. Sentenced to deduction of $11.00 per month for four months or a total of $44.00. Died of disease at Marietta.

Butts, J. C., Pvt., Age 22, Co. A, enlisted at Charleston December 31, 1861 for 12 months.

Byrd, A. W. J., Pvt., Age 31, Co. C, enlisted at Camp Gist March 13, 1862. Wounded at Chickamauga September 20, 1863. Furloughed, wounded, Sep/Oct 1863. Absent without leave Nov/Dec 1863. Present for duty Jan/Feb 1864. Absent, sick in hospital, Jul/Aug 1864.

Cadden, R., Sgt., Age 48, Co. C, enlisted at George's Station January 7, 1862. Present for duty through Jan/Feb 1864. One report indicates that he died in service. Another report indicates he survived and died in 1902.

Calder, H., Pvt., Co. B, enlisted at Marlboro, February 4, 1862. Transferred from Co. C, Smith's Battalion June 23, 1862. Killed in battle near Atlanta August 17, 1864.

Calder, Robert, Pvt., Age 21, Co. B, enlisted at Charleston, December 4, 1861. Transferred to 2nd Battalion, S.C. Sharpshooters, 1862.

Caldwell, Luke M., Pvt., Age 35, Co. G, enlisted at Columbia, April 12, 1862. Services requested for detail as a detective because of serious health problem that rendered him unfit for field duty March 28, 1863.

Calhoun, John C., Asst. Surgeon, F&S. Entry from *Edgefield Advertiser* July 20, 1864.

Calhoun, Thomas T., Pvt., Co. I, enlisted at Augusta, Ga., January 4, 1864. Recruit bounty due $50.00. Severely wounded, neck, at Atlanta. Absent, wounded, in hospital August 19, 1864. Paroled at Greensboro May 1, 1865. Died at age 51, December 17, 1896 at Houston, Tex. During battle of Atlanta, he caught a minie ball in neck and carried it until some years after the war when he had it extracted and mounted. He occasionally wore it on his watch chain.

Calk, James, Pvt., Age 27, Co. B, from Marlboro District, enlisted at Charleston December 4, 1861. Discharged by reason of surgeon's certificate at Camp Gist February 1, 1862,. Description: complexion, fair; hair, dark; height, 5 ft. 6 in; occupation: farmer.

Caminade, J. J., Color Sgt., Age 25, Co. A, enlisted at Charleston December 31, 1861. Killed in battle at Chickamauga September 20, 1863. Buried by his friends with military honors on the battlefield at Chickamauga. (See Carinden, S., Co. A.)

Campbell, James N., Pvt., Age 21, Co. F, enlisted at Anderson April 11, 1862. Died of disease at Camp Chattanooga October 9, 1863. Widow, Martha A. Campbell, filed claim for settlement February 8, 1864.

Campbell, John J., Pvt., Age 24, Co. A, enlisted at Camp Gist March 25, 1862. Spent most of war sick in hospital. Complexion, light; hair, light; eyes, blue; height, 5 ft. 10 in. Reported at Northern District, Department of the South, U.S. Provost Marshal, Charleston, as rebel deserter. Took oath to the United States and was discharged April 1, 1865.

Campbell, W. O., Pvt., Age 19, Co. F, from Moffettville, enlisted at Anderson January 13, 1862. Suffered chronic rheumatism. Granted sick furlough from hospital January 26, 1863 for 25 days. Absent, sick, Sep/Oct 1863 - Jul/Aug 1864.

Campbell, O. B., Pvt., Age 19, Co. F. Died in hospital of disease May 21, 1864. Entry from Memory Rolls at State Archives, Columbia, S.C. and Survivor's Association roster.

Cannaday, J. S., Pvt., Age 28, Co. C, enlisted at George's Station January 7, 1862. Died February 20, 1862.

Cannon, Theodore W., Pvt., Co. A, enlisted at Charleston June 18, 1862. Wounded at Jackson. Sick at hospital De Soto, Miss., Jul/Aug - Sep/Oct 1863. Absent, sick, at hospital February 22 - Jul/Aug 1864. Signed receipt for clothing at 3d Gen Hosp, Augusta October 12, 1864.

Capers, Ellison, Brig. Gen., Age 24, Born October 14, 1837 at Charleston, F&S, commissioned at Charleston April 1, 1862. Served in 1st SCM 1860 - 1862. Commandant of a camp of instruction and organization at Camp Gist January - March 1862. Commanded at Cole's Island May 1862. Commanded flank battery of 24 pounders near Clark's House at Battery Reid during Battle of Secessionville. Commanded first attack on enemy at James Island June 3, 1862. Commanded district between the Ashepoo and Combabee Rivers March 1863. Commanded advance in skirmish before Jackson May 1863. Severely wounded, right leg, near Jackson May 14, 1863. Severely wounded, left thigh, at Chickamauga September 20, 1863. Promoted to Colonel January 20, 1864. Wounded, left ankle, at Franklin, November 30, 1864. Appointed Brigadier General as commander of Gist's Brigade March 1, 1865. Paroled at Greensboro May 1, 1865. Married: Charlotte (Lottie) Rebecca Palmer, who died in Columbia August 13, 1908. Capers served as Secretary of State of South Carolina, Priest of the Protestant Episcopal Church,

Bishop of the Diocese of South Carolina, Chancellor of the University of the South. Died August 13, 1908. Buried in the church yard of Trinity Episcopal Church, Columbia.

Carinden, S., Co. A. Grave located in Marietta Confederate Cemetery, Marietta, Ga. Entry from Marietta U.D.C., Kennesaw Chapter # 241, Marietta Public Library, Marietta, Ga. Suspected duplicate of *Caminade, J. J.*

Carpenter, Adam E., Pvt., Age 26, Co. I, from near Johnston, S.C., enlisted at Columbia March 20, 1862. Present for duty on all rolls. Paroled at Greensboro May 1, 1865. Married February 7, 1860. Died July 11, 1907. Widow: Melissa Carpenter.

Carpenter, Isham W., Pvt., Age 33, Co. I, enlisted at Columbia March 20, 1862. Absent, sick, furlough Nov/Dec 1862. Wounded May 16, 1864. Absent, in hospital, Jul/Aug 1864.

Carpenter, J. E. Owen, Sgt., Age 17, Co. I, enlisted at Columbia March 20, 1862. Wounded at Chickamauga September 20, 1863. Wounded June 22, 1864. Promoted from the ranks for meritorious service April 19, 1865. Paroled at Greensboro May 1, 1865.

Carpenter, John, Pvt., Age 21, Co. I, enlisted at Columbia April 19, 1862. Wounded, right thigh, flesh, at Chickamauga September 20, 1863. In hospital at Augusta November 1, 1863 - February 29, 1864. Severely wounded in shoulder at Calhoun May 17, 1864. Absent, sick, furlough to expire November 4, 1864. Signed receipt roll for pay at 2d Ga. Hospital, Augusta, Ga., August 25, 1864. Paroled at Greensboro May 1, 1865.

Carroll, William B.,(Billy), Corp., Age 18, Co. A, enlisted at Charleston February 28, 1862. Captured near Jackson May 14, 1863. Assigned Paroled Prisoners Camp at Demopolis June 5, 1863. Present for duty Jul/Aug 1864. Killed in battle at Shipp's Gap/Taylor's Ridge, Ga., October 16, 1864.

Carston, E. H., Pvt., Co. D, enlisted at Camp Gist May 1, 1862. Discharged May 23, 1862. Entry canceled on rolls.

Carter, Adam, Pvt., Age 30, Co. E, enlisted at Camp Gist March 31, 1862. Captured at Battery Island while on picket duty May 21, 1862. Sent to Hilton Head and thence to Fort Columbus, New York Harbor aboard Steamer *Arago* August 14, 1862. Sent to Fort Delaware, Del., August 23, 1862. Exchanged at Aikens Landing, Va., November 10, 1862. Pay stopped for one month by court martial May/Jun 1863. Severely wounded, left thigh, at Atlanta June 15, 1864. Admitted to St. Mary's Hospital, La Grange, Ga., June 17, 1864. Captured near Nashville December 16, 1864. Sent to Military Prison, Louisville and transferred to Camp Chase January 6, 1865. Died from unknown causes June 2, 1865. Grave no. 2013 located 1/3 mile south of Camp Chase.

Carter, Charles, Pvt., Age 27, Co. E, born in Colleton District, enlisted at Camp Gist March 20, 1862. Wounded at Chickamauga September 20, 1863. Signed receipt roll for clothing October 11, 1864. Absent, sick at home, sick furlough, September 20, 1863 - Jul/Aug 1864. Description: complexion, light; eyes, blue, hair, light; height, 5 ft. 4 in; occupation, farmer. Retired as invalid soldier as consequence of gun shot wound of the neck causing anchylosis of spinal column (cervical vertebrae) October 5, 1864.

Carter, Hanford Duncan, Pvt., Co. E, from Ruffin, S.C. Discharged at Port Royal. Married May 2, 1860. Died November 26, 1914. Wife Mary Louisa Carter. Entry from Civil War Veteran's Widow's pension files at State Archives, Columbia, S.C. Application for pension submitted by widow December 22, 1919.

Carter, Isaac, Pvt., Age 28, Co. E, enlisted at Camp Gist March 20, 1862. Captured at Battery Island while on pickett duty May 21, 1862. Sent to Hilton Head and thence to Fort Columbus, New York Harbor aboard Steamer *Arago* August 14, 1862. Transferred to Fort Delaware August 23, 1862. Exchanged at Aikens Landing, Va., November 10, 1862. Admitted to Moore Hospital or General Hospital No. 24, Richmond with Typhoid fever October 6, 1862. Returned to 24th Regiment Nov/Dec 1862. Sick, entered hospital at Atlanta December 8, 1863. Died of pneumonia February 13, 1864.

Carter, Jacob, Pvt., Age 35, Co. E, enlisted at Pocotaligo March 22, 1863. Discharged on account of physical disability May/Jun 1863.

Carter, Joseph, Pvt., Age 25, Co. E, enlisted at Camp Gist March 20, 1862. Detached to Signal Corps at Hardeeville Feb/Mar - Apr/May 1863. Severely wounded, arm, near Marietta, Ga., June 15, 1864. Furloughed from Hospital for 60 days June 18, 1864. Signed receipt roll for clothing October 11, 1864. Surrendered.

Carter, William M., Pvt., Age 19, Co. E, from Ashton, S.C., enlisted at Salkehatchie January 16, 1862. Pay stopped for one month by court martial May/Jun 1863. Wounded at Chickamauga September 20, 1863. Absent without leave Nov/Dec 1863. Patient at Ocmulgee Hospital, Macon June 1 - July 19, 1864. Present for duty Jul/Aug 1864. Signed receipt roll for clothing July 11, 1864. Discharged about the end of March 1865. Surrendered. Married 1864. Died March 4, 1905.

Cartledge, Jerry S., Pvt., Age 25, Co. I, enlisted at James Island May 17, 1862. Detached service Sep/Oct 1862. Absent without leave December 26-30, 1863. Present for duty Jul/Aug 1864.

Cartledge, Samuel C., Pvt., Age 16, Co. I, from Parkville, Edgefield County, S.C., enlisted at Pocotaligo March 4, 1863. Severely wounded, face, at Dalton 1864. Signed receipt roll for clothing April 1, 1864. Present for duty Jul/Aug 1864. Wounded at Franklin 1864. Survived the

War.

Cartledge, William, Pvt., Co. I, from Edgefield, born April 4, 1844. Wounded through the hip. Entry from Confederate Veteran's Pension records at State Archives, Columbia, S.C.

Caskey, Frank M., Pvt., Co. I, enlisted at Dalton, Ga., March 13, 1864. Bounty due. Died in hospital of disease at Dalton April 19, 1864.

Caskey, Joseph S., Pvt., Age 18, Co. H, enlisted at Chester March 19, 1862. Description: complexion, fair; hair, light; eyes, blue; height, 5 ft. 9 in. Wounded at Franklin, gunshot wound of right thigh and arm (severe), November 30, 1864. Captured at Franklin December 17, 1864. Admitted to No. 1, USA Gen Hosp., Nashville for wounds December 27, 1864 - July 9, 1865. Sent to Nashville military prison. Signed oath of allegiance to the United States and released at Nashville July 9, 1865.

Caskey, Thomas, Co. H. From Chester District. Entry from *Chester County Heritage History*.

Catlett, John, Pvt., Age 35, Co. F, from Anderson, S.C., enlisted at Anderson March 27, 1863. Discharged by substitute M. Simpson April 11, 1863.

Caulk, James C., Pvt., Co. B. Discharged 1862. Died in hospital 1862. Entry from Memory Rolls at State Archives, Columbia, S.C.

Caulk, J. C., Pvt., Co. B. Entry from *History of Marlboro County*.

Chambers, J., Pvt., Co. A, enlisted at Charleston May 1, 1862. Present for duty May/Jun 1862.

Chastrier, C. A., Pvt., Age 40, Co. G, enlisted at Columbia April 12, 1862. Discharged by certificate - never reported for duty.

Chavis, George, Pvt., Age 22, Co. B, enlisted at Charleston December 4, 1861 for 12 months. Died in hospital January 28, 1862.

Chavis, John, Pvt., Age 35, Co. B, enlisted at Charleston December 4, 1861. Wounded, chest, at Legares June 3, 1862. Wounded at Atlanta. Sick furlough Mar/Aug 1864. Paroled at Greensboro May 1, 1865. Died at home 1868.

Chavis, William, Pvt., Age 16, Co. B, enlisted at Charleston December 4, 1861. Complexion: Dark; hair, black; eyes, dark; height, 5 ft, 6 in; occupation, farmer. Discharged by reason of surgeons certificate June 23, 1862.

Cherry, Elijah, Pvt., Co. H, enlisted at Chester July 16, 1862. Absent, sick at home, in hospital at Columbia and granted sick furlough May/Jun 1863 - March 1, 1864. Died at home. Killed by accident at home.

Cherry, John H., Pvt., Co. H, from Chester District, enlisted at Chester February 14, 1863. Died of disease near Chattanooga November 20, 1863. Mother, Deborah Cherry, filed claim for settlement March 12, 1864.

Cherry, W. T., Pvt., Age 20, Co. A, enlisted at Charleston December 31,

1861. Detailed to work on Eason's gunboat October 23, 1862 - August 31, 1863. Absent without leave from September 1, 1863 through August 1864. Transferred to Marine service.

Chesher, Hezekiah, Pvt., Age 45, Co. D, enlisted at Camp Gist January 16, 1862. Description: complexion, dark; hair, dark; eyes, grey; height, 5 ft. 8 in; born, Beaufort District; occupation, farmer. Discharged July 25, 1862. Surrendered and paroled at Augusta May 23, 1865.

Chevees, William, Pvt., Stevens' Regiment. Died February 3, 1862. Entry from Tombstone located at Magnolia Cemetery, Charleston, S.C.

Christian, David W., Sgt., Age 34, Co. K, enlisted at Edgefield April 12, 1862. Detailed as a shoemaker at Columbus, Ga., October 28, 1862. Employed on extra duty as a shoemaker at Columbus January 1865.

Clark, George, Pvt., Age 23, Co. A, enlisted at Charleston December 31, 1861. Severely wounded, leg, at Kennesaw Mountain Jun 20, 1864. Signed receipt for clothing September 21, 1864. Present for duty on all rolls. Paroled at Greensboro May 1, 1865.

Clark, James, Pvt., Age 18, Co. C, enlisted at Georges Station January 7, 1863. Died March 24, 1862 at James Island, S.C.

Clark, John C., Pvt., Co. B, conscripted at Marlboro April 1, 1863. Slightly wounded, shoulder, May 16, 1864. Signed receipt roll for clothing September 9, 1864. Captured near Nashville December 16, 1864. Sent to the Military Prison, Louisville and transferred to Camp Douglas December 24, 1864. Signed by mark. Mustered into 5th U. S. Volunteer Infantry April 6, 1865,.

Clark, Samuel J. M., Pvt., Age 29, Co. I, enlisted at Columbia March 20, 1862. Transferred to 3rd Regiment, South Carolina Cavalry. Died 1889. Grave located in Lawtonville Cemetery, Hampton County, S.C.

Clark, Sandy, Pvt., Co. D, enlisted at Camp Gist January 19, 1862. Teamster. Colored. Discharged March 6, 1863.

Clark, William, Pvt., Co. I, enlisted at Columbia April 21, 1862. Absent without leave. Name canceled from roll.

Clarke, David Z., Pvt., Age 41, Co. I, from Edgefield District, enlisted at Columbia March 20, 1862. In hospital at Rome Ga., Sep/Oct 1863. Fined $10.00 for absent without leave Jul/Aug 1864. Captured near Nashville December 16, 1864. Sent to Military Prison, Louisville December 20, 1864 and transferred to Camp Douglas December 22, 1864. Discharged at Camp Douglas June 18, 1865.

Clayton, John W., Corp., Age 21, Co. A, enlisted at Charleston December 31, 1861. Under arrest for absent without leave May/Jun 1862. Captured July 20, 1864. Killed in battle at Atlanta.

Clinkscales, Jas. L., 4Corp., Age 18, Co. F, born at Anderson, enlisted at Anderson January 13, 1862. Discharged by substitute W. B. F. Cook, June 23, 1862. Enlisted May 6, 1863. Slightly wounded at Chickamauga September 20, 1863. Wounded in hands of enemy July 20, 1864. Appointed 4Corp., April 12, 1864. Description: complexion, fair; hair, red; eyes, blue, height, 5 ft. 10 in; occupation, farmer. Killed in battle at Peachtree Creek July 20, 1864.

Clinkscales, R. P., Pvt., Age 18, Co. F, from Twiggs, S.C., enlisted at Anderson February 20, 1862. Wounded at New Hope Church June 29, 1864. Paroled at Greensboro May 1, 1865.

Cochran, Robert A., 1Lt., Co. K, enlisted at Edgefield July 1, 1862. Sent to South Carolina to round up all stragglers and deserters and receive volunteers for the 24th Regiment August 1863. Promoted to 1Sgt., March 1, 1864. Wounded, groin, at battle of Atlanta July 22, 1864, Promoted to 2Lt., August 17, 1864. Wounded at Jonesboro. Commanded Co. K, Consolidated 16th and 24th Regiment at surrender. Paroled at Greensboro May 1, 1865.

Cohen, A. P., Cook, Age 32, Co. D, enlisted at Camp Gist January 16, 1862. Free negro. Died in hospital at Savannah November 15, 1862.

Coleman, John L., Pvt., Co. I, enlisted at Columbia July 2, 1862. Captured at Covington, Ga., July 22, 1864. Sent to Military Prison, Louisville and transferred to Camp Chase August 4, 1864. Paroled at Camp Chase and transferred for exchange to City Point, Va., March 4, 1865. Paroled prisoner, sick, suffered chronic diarrhoea and admitted to 4th Division, Jackson Hospital, Richmond March 13, 1865.

Coles, J. D., Co. I. Wounded January 11, 1865.

Collier, Edward, Pvt., Co. I, enlisted at Columbia March 20, 1862. Absent by permission, canceled on roll.

Collier, J. Buried at Oakland Cemetery, Atlanta, Ga., April 20, 1864. Entry from Oakland Cemetery records.

Collins, James, Pvt., Co. K, enlisted at Edgefield April 13, 1862. Captured at battle of Secessionville June 16, 1862. Admitted to USA General Hospital, Hilton Head. Sent north. Sent from Hilton Head to Fort Columbus, New York Harbor on Steamer *Arago* August 14, 1862.

Collins, Jonathan, Pvt., Age 34, Co. H, enlisted at Chester March 19, 1862. Sick in Hospital Sep/Oct 1863. Died of typhoid fever in hospital at Atlanta April 18, 1864. Mother, Sarah Collins, filed claim for settlement May 21, 1864.

Collins, Thomas J., Pvt., Age 26, Co. H, enlisted at Chester March 19, 1862. Wounded at Chickamauga September 20, 1863. In hospital at Atlanta. Absent without leave since February 27, 1864 - August 31, 1864. Severely wounded at Chickamauga, shot through the body. Retired.

Collins, Tom, Pvt., Co. K. Died in hospital in 1863. Entry from Memory Rolls at State Archives, Columbia, S.C., and roster prepared by Capt. R. A. Cochran, Company Commander.

Connerly, John W., 1Sgt., Age 23, Co. C, from Branchville, S.C., enlisted at Georges Station January 17, 1862. Promoted from Pvt., to 4Sgt., 3Sgt., 2Sgt., 1Sgt. Severely wounded, arm, July 20, 1864. Absent, wounded, July 20, 1864. Wounded at Peachtree Creek. Furloughed. Survived the war.

Connel, Charles R., Pvt., Age 40, Co. C. Entry from Memory Rolls at State Archives, Columbia, S.C.

Cook, Clinton, Pvt., Co. C. Died since the war. Entry from roster prepared by Capt. W. C. Griffith, Company Commander.

Cook, James C., Pvt., Age 23, Co. A, enlisted at Charleston December 31, 1861 for 12 months. By order of Gen. Beauregard transferred to Navy Dept., October 16, 1862. Absent without leave, deserted en route from Miss., at Atlanta. Court martialed and sentenced to stoppage of 1 months pay, $11.00 Nov/Dec 1863. Captured near Jonesboro September 1, 1864. Exchanged September 22, 1864. Captured at Shipp's Gap/ Taylor's Ridge October 16, 1864. Sent to Military Prison, Louisville and transferred to Camp Douglas October 29, 1864. Description: complexion, light; hair, brown; eyes, brown; height, 5 ft. 7 in. Signed oath of allegiance to the United States and discharged July 17, 1865.

Cook, J. F., Co. H, from Chester District. Entry from *Chester Country Heritage History*.

Cook, J. W., Pvt., Age 17, Co. F, from White Oak, Ark., enlisted at Anderson January 13, 1862 for 12 months. Substitute for W. J. Simpson February 11, 1862. Discharged, under 18 years of age January 29, 1863.

Cook, Redding, Pvt., Age 46, Co, D, enlisted at Camp Gist February 20, 1862. Present on all rolls. Paroled at Greensboro May 1, 1865.

Cook, Samuel, Pvt., Age 25, Co. I, from Tuckers Pond, S.C., enlisted at Columbia March 20, 1862. Admitted to CSA General Military Hospital, No,. 4, Wilmington for pneumonia December 29, 1862. Returned to duty January 7, 1863. Admitted to hospital at Charleston April 23, 1863. Absent, sick, September 6, 1863 - August 31, 1864. Surrendered and paroled at Augusta May 18, 1865.

Cook, William, Pvt., Co. G, enlisted near Dalton, Ga., February 20, 1864. Signed receipt roll for clothing April 1, 1864. Wounded at Atlanta July 22, 1864. Gun shot wound, ball entered his head in front of left ear and lodged. Facial bones fractured July 28, 1864. Sent home on "furlough of indulgence" August 31, 1864.

Cook, W. B. F., Pvt., Age 16, Co. F, from Walton, Ark., enlisted at Anderson June 24, 1862. Substitute for J. L. Clinkscales June 24, 1862. Discharged for underage. Presently 18 years of age April 15, 1863.

Coon, F. A., Corp., Age 17, Co. G, enlisted at Columbia April 15, 1862. Granted ten day furlough April 29, 1863. Appointed Corp., June 1, 1863. Wounded at Chickamauga September 20, 1863. Hospitalized in Columbia October 1863 - Jan/Feb 1864. Signed receipt roll for clothing at Ladies Gen. Hosp. No. 3, Columbia, S.C., March. 17, 1864. Present for duty August 31, 1864.

Cooper, Fred, Pvt., Age 40, Co. G, enlisted at Columbia March 19, 1862. Detached to work on gunboat at Easons at Charleston from Sep/Oct 1862 until further orders.

Cope, E., Drummer, Co. B, enlisted at Marlboro April 1, 1863. Absent without leave May 6, 1863. Declared deserter Nov/Dec 1863. Survived.

Cope, John J., Pvt., Co. B, enlisted at Marlboro March 31, 1862. Sick in hospital in Georgia Sep/Oct 1863. Died in hospital at Atlanta November 16, 1863. Grave located in the Confederate Section, Oak Hill Cemetery, Newman, Ga.

Copeland, A. E., Pvt., Age 33, Co. E, enlisted at Camp Gist March 20, 1862. Absent, sick in hospital and at home, from December 10, 1862 to December 1864. Signed receipt roll for clothing at General Hospital, No. 2 Columbia December 7, 1864. Surrendered.

Copeland, Isaac L. E., Pvt., Age 30, Co. E, enlisted at Camp Gist March 20, 1862. Killed in battle at Chickamauga September 20, 1863.

Copeland, J. J. J., Pvt., Age 22, Co. E, enlisted at Camp Gist May 1, 1862. Substitute for J. C. Padgett April 30, 1862. Sick in hospital at Rome, Ga., September 19, 1863. Wounded and admitted to hospital August 3, 1864. Killed in battle at Atlanta.

Cornelius, Alexander, Pvt., Age 37, Co. G, enlisted at Columbia March 19, 1862. In hospital May/Jun 1862. Sick, admitted to hospital, Mar/Apr 1863. Died in Medical College Hospital, Atlanta, December 29, 1863. Buried December 30, 1864. Grave located in Oakland Cemetery, Confederate Section, Atlanta, Row 7, No. 7.

Council, Charles Robert, Pvt., Age 34, Co. C, from Reevesville, enlisted at Georges Station January 7, 1862. Assigned to commissary department June 1862. Earned extra pay of $20.00 per month as commissary sergeant. Paroled at Greensboro May 1, 1865. Married May 20, 1868. Died December 24, 1888. Buried in Reevesville. Widow Mildred Rebecca Council.

Council, C. J., Ord. Sgt., F&S. Entry from Memory Rolls at State Archives, Columbia, S.C.

Covington, Harris, Pvt., Co. B, enlisted at Marlboro March 26, 1862. Transferred to 26th Regiment November 15, 1862. Died 1876.

Covington, James R., Pvt., Age 27, Co. H, enlisted at Chester March 19, 1862. Detached service to Russel's work shop, Charleston, from Sep/Oct 1862 to August 31, 1864. Living.

Cox, Abraham, Pvt., Co. I, born at Edgefield District, enlisted at Augusta, November 23, 1862. Transferred from Co. A, 63rd Ga., to Co. I, 24th Regiment July 9, 1864. Description: complexion, light; hair, sandy; eyes, gray; Height, 5 ft., 6 in; occupation, student. Wounded, left forearm flesh impairing use of flex of muscle, August 14, 1864. Granted certificate of disability for retiring of invalid soldiers January 27, 1865. Surrendered and paroled at Augusta May 18, 1865.

Cox, Henry C., Pvt., Co. I, Age 19, from Edgefield District, enlisted at Augusta April 10, 1862. Transferred from Co. A, 63rd Ga., to Co. I, 24th Regiment July 9, 1864. Wounded at Atlanta July 18, 1864. Patient at Floyd House and Ocmulgee Hospitals, Macon for gun shot wound through back part of neck flesh July 21, 1864. Furloughed for 60 days July 22, 1864. Paroled at Greensboro May 1, 1865.

Craft, George Anderson, Pvt., Age 18, Co. F, enlisted at Anderson December 22, 1862. Patient at Hospital for wound received at Jackson May 14, 1863. Patient at Loring's Division Hospital, Lauderdale and 1st Mississippi CSA Hospital, Jackson July 12, 1863. Absent, wounded, May 14, 1863 - Jan/Feb 1864. Present for duty August 31, 1864. Wounded at Shipp's Gap/Taylor's Ridge October 16, 1864. Surrendered 1865.

Craft, John M., Sgt., Age 35, Co. F, from Craftsberry, S.C., enlisted at Charleston January 13, 1862 for 12 months. Discharged by furnishing a substitute, L. Howell, February 13, 1862. Joined another command. Died July 22, 1915, grave located at New Bethel Cemetery, Elbert County, Ga.

Craft, Matthew, Pvt., Age 35, Co, G, enlisted at Columbia March 19, 1862. In hospital at Benton, Miss May/Jun 1863. Detached service and in hospital at Columbia October 20 - December 1863. Absent without leave July 23 - August 31, 1864.

Craft, Moses, Pvt., Age 32, Co. G, enlisted at Pocotaligo March 1, 1863. One month pay stopped by order of court martial May/Jun 1863. Signed receipt roll for clothing, by mark, January 13, 1864. Severely wounded, both thighs, at Calhoun, Ga., May 16, 1864. Wounded at Atlanta July 22, 1864. Captured near Nashville December 16, 1864. Sent to Military Prison Louisville and transferred to Camp Chase January 4, 1865. Description: complexion, fair; hair, light; eyes, black; height, 5 ft. 10 in. Signed oath of allegiance to the United States June 12, 1865.

Crafton, Snowdon S., Pvt., Age 26, Co. I, enlisted at Coles Island April 21, 1862. Wounded at Chickamauga September 20, 1863. Absent, wounded, September - December 1863. Missing in battle July 22, 1864. Killed in battle at Decatur July 22, 1864.

Craps, J. J., Pvt., Age 18, Co. D, enlisted at Camp Gist January 19, 1862. Present for duty through May/Jun 1862.

Craps, William J., Pvt., Age 37, Co. D, enlisted at Camp Gist February 16, 1862. Absent with leave, wounded, Sep/Oct - Nov/Dec 1863. Signed receipt roll for clothing June 7, 1864. Mortally wounded in battle at Franklin November 30, 1864. Captured at Franklin December 18, 1864.

Lower third left leg amputated February 17, 1865. Treated by Lorne's stimulants and supporting diet for chronic diarrhoea. Died of exhaustion at USA General Hospital, Nashville March 11, 1865. Grave no. 12462, City Cemetery, Nashville. (Ed. note - name spelled *Craps, Carpps, Crapse, Crape,* and *Cropps*).

Crawford, Gibson G., Pvt., Co. B, enlisted at Marion June 30 1862. Sick in the hospital at Secessionville Sep/Oct 1862. Transferred to the Navy April 30, 1864.

Crawford, H. B., Corp., Co. B, enlisted at Marion April 1, 1862. Wounded, admitted to hospital, August 31, 1864. Deserted April 25, 1865. Paroled at Greensboro May 1, 1865.

Crawford, J. C., Corp., Co. F, enlisted at Camp Hampton December 1, 1864. Paroled at Greensboro May 1, 1865.

Crawford, W. H., Sgt., Co. B, enlisted at Marion March 31, 1862. Sick at home Sep/Oct - Nov/Dec 1862. Promoted to Corp., Jan/Feb 1863. Wounded at Peachtree Creek. Promoted to 5Sgt., August 24, 1864. Signed receipt roll for clothing September 19, 1864. Signed receipt roll for clothing at Hosp. Fort Valley, Ga., November 1, 1864. Captured near Nashville December 16, 1862. Sent to Military Prison, Louisville and transferred to Camp Douglas December 21, 1864. Mustered into the 6th U. S. Vol. Infantry April 2, 1865.

Crews, J. J. W., Pvt., Co. D, enlisted at Beaufort District, January 15, 1864. Sick in hospital Jul/Aug 1864. Listed on a muster roll of Co. C, 1st Regiment Troops and Defenses, stationed at Camp Wright, Macon Nov/Dec 1864. Signed receipt roll for clothing November 15 and December 17, 1864.

Crews, Joseph W., Pvt., Co. D, enlisted at Camp Gist April 9, 1862. Absent without leave Nov/Dec 1863. Patient at St. Mary's Hospital, La Grange, Ga., and Ocmulgee Hospital, Macon, Ga., suffering from debility July 29, 1864. Transferred August 23, 1864. Present for duty August 31, 1864. Signed receipt roll for clothing November 5 and December 17, 1864 at Camp Wright located near Macon.

Crews, Moses, Pvt., Age 28, Co. D, enlisted at Camp Gist January 19, 1862. Captured near Jackson May 17, 1863. Prisoner in paroled Camp May/Jun 1863. Signed receipt roll for clothing April 1, 1864. Captured near Marietta June 19, 1864. Sent to Military Prison, Louisville and transferred to Camp Morton June 26, 1864. Died from inflammation of the lungs December 4, 1864. Grave no. 1182, Green Lawn Cemetery, Indianapolis, Ind.

Crook, Joseph T., Pvt., Age 26, Co. H, enlisted at Chester March 19, 1865. Detailed driving wagons (Teamster) for commissary department Oct/Nov 1863. Paroled at Greensboro May 1, 1865.

Crook, W. Benjamin, Pvt., Age 42, Co. C, enlisted at Georges Station

311

January 7, 1862. Killed in battle at Chickamauga September 20, 1863. Grave located in Confederate Cemetery, Marietta, Ga.

Crook, W. Hemphill, Pvt., Co. H, enlisted at Chester February 17, 1864. Bounty due. Absent, sick, at hospital August 31, 1864. Died of disease in Georgia 1864.

Crosby, Abraham, Co. E, from Smoaks, S.C. Discharged at surrender. Married February 1866. Died July 1866. Entry from Confederate Veteran pension records at State Archives, Columbia, S.C.

Crosby, Elias, Pvt., Age 17, Co. E, enlisted at Camp Gist March 3, 1862. Wounded at Chickamauga September 20, 1863. Absent, at home, sick furlough, September 20, 1863 - Jan/Feb 1864. Treated for acute diarrhoea at 1st Mississippi CSA Hospital, Jackson January 13, 1865. Paroled at Greensboro May 1, 1865.

Crosby, H. E., Pvt., Age 21, Co. E, enlisted at Camp Gist March 2, 1862. Wounded at Atlanta. Signed receipt roll for clothing September 9, 1864. Paroled at Greensboro May 1, 1865.

Crosby, Jacob D., Pvt., Age 30, Co. E, enlisted at Camp Gist March 20, 1862. Twenty days pay stopped for absence without leave Nov/Dec 1862. Pay stopped for one month by court martial May/Jun 1863. Wounded at Chickamauga. Captured near Marietta July 2, 1864. Sent to Military Prison, Louisville and transferred to Camp Morton July 12, 1864. Description: complexion, florid; hair, dark; eyes, hazel; height, 5 ft. 8 3/4 in. Signed oath of allegiance to the United States and released May 18, 1865.

Crosby, J. C., Pvt., Age 32, Co. E. Entry from Memory Rolls at State Archives, Columbia, S.C.

Crosby, John Greene, Pvt., Age 18, Co. E, from Ruffin, S.C., enlisted at Charleston March 20, 1862. Wounded, hand, at Jonesboro. Present for duty on all rolls through Jul/Aug 1864. Survived. Married September 28, 1865. Died November 4, 1911.

Crosby, Malaha Paulers, Co. E, from Round, S.C. Discharged at Moncks Corner in April 1865. Married April 1, 1870. Entry from Confederate Veteran records at State Archives, Columbia, S.C.

Crosby, Samuel, Pvt., Age 18, Co. E, enlisted at Charleston January 16, 1862. Discharged by surgeon's certificate February 28, 1862. Enlisted at Pocotaligo March 3, 1863. Deserted April 16, 1863.

Crosby, William, Pvt., Age 27, Co. E, enlisted at Salkehatchie January 16, 1862. Pay stopped for one month by court martial May/Jun 63. Absent without leave Nov/Dec 1863. Severely wounded, leg, May 16, 1864. Furloughed from hospital for 60 days with an extension of 30 days June 1864. Survived.

Cunningham, A. F., 3Lt., Age 22, Co. F, enlisted at Anderson January 13, 1862. Absent, sick furlough, Jan/Feb 1863. Killed in battle at Jackson

May 14, 1863. Shot and killed in a flower garden in front of the O. P. Wright farm house. Capt. Steinmeyer returned Lt. Cunningham's gold watch, with the chain cut due to the passage of the bullet, to the deceased soldier's father.

Cunningham, J. R. McD., Pvt., Age 30, Co. F, enlisted at Anderson July 16, 1862. Mortally wounded in battle at Chickamauga September 20, 1863. Died from affects of wounds the next day September 21, 1862. Grave located in Confederate Cemetery, Marietta, Ga.

Cunningham, S. A. L., Pvt., Age 21, Co. F, from Buckhammam, Ga., enlisted at Anderson January 13, 1862, for 12 months. Conscripted for the War Jan/Feb 1863. Wounded at Jackson. Wounded at Chickamauga September 20, 1863. Absent, wounded, in hospital at Columbia, furloughed, September 20, 1863 - August 31, 1864. Surrendered 1865.

Curry, Thomas H., 1Lt.., Age 16, Co. I, enlisted at Columbia March 20, 1862. Present for duty on all rolls. Paroled at Greensboro May 1, 1865.

Dansby, Isaac, Pvt., Age 25, Co. G, born Abbeville District, enlisted at Columbia April 12, 1862. At home, furlough, Jul/Aug 1863. Sent off with the wagons and never heard from since February 22, 1864. Died at home. Attorney, R. Hawthorn, filed a claim for settlement September 8, 1864.

Dantzler, Jacob. S., Pvt., Age 25, Co. C, enlisted at Camp Gist April 1, 1862. One months pay stopped by court martial May/Jun 1863. Absent, sick, furloughed July 25, 1864. Signed receipt roll for clothing October 10, 1864. Captured near Franklin December 17, 1864. Sent to Military Prison, Louisville and transferred to Camp Douglas December 20, 1864. Claimed to have been loyal. Enlisted to avoid conscription, was captured & desired to take the oath of allegiance to the United States and become a loyal citizen. Discharged at Camp Douglas May 16, 1865.

Davis, Henry, Pvt., Co. A. Captured at Franklin, December 17, 1874. Sent to Military Prison, Louisville and transferred to Camp Chase January 4, 1865. Died of pneumonia at Camp Chase January 15, 1865. Grave no. 777, Quarters.

Davis, I. A. D., Pvt., Age 22, Co. G, enlisted at Columbia April 12, 1862. Absent without leave.

Davis, Jakes A., Pvt., Co. G. Entry from Memory Rolls at State Archives, Columbia, S.C. (Name on original muster roll.)

Davis, James, Pvt., Age 32, Co. A, enlisted at Charleston December 31, 1861. Wounded at Chickamauga September 20, 1864. Absent, wounded, Sep/Oct 1863 - Nov/Dec 1863. Sentenced by court martial to stoppage of one months pay - $11.00, Jan/Feb 1864. Detailed to drive pontoon wagon Jul/Aug 1864.

Davis, Samuel N., Pvt., Age 17, Co. A, enlisted at Charleston December 31, 1861. Absent without leave from September 20, 1863 - October 20,

1863. Sentenced by court martial to stoppage of one months pay $11.00 Jan/Feb 1864. Captured near Marietta July 2, 1864. Sent to Military Prison, Louisville and transferred to Camp Douglas July 18, 1864. Claimed to have been loyal. Forced into Rebel Army to avoid conscript and deserted to avail himself of amnesty proclamation August 17, 1864. Enlisted in 6th U. S. Vols., April 1, 1865. Editors Note - Official records show Davis' first name as "L." until he was captured and then it is listed as Samuel N. Other rosters only show a Samuel N. Davis.

Davis, Pringle, Pvt., Age 18, Co. A, enlisted at Charleston December 31, 1861. Severely wounded, side, arm and right thigh, June 19, 1864. Absent, wounded, Jul/Aug 1864. Died of disease in Union prison at Camp Chase.

Dawkins, W. L., Pvt., Age 38, Co. G, born at Fairfield, enlisted at Columbia, March 19, 1862. Killed in battle at Secessionville, June 16, 1862.

Dawkins, McL., Pvt., Co. G. Entry from Memory Rolls at State Archives, Columbia, S.C., and original muster roll.

Day, Willian, Pvt., Age 40, Co. B, from Bennettsville, enlisted at Marlboro December 4, 1861. Mortally wounded in battle at Chickamauga September 20, 1863. Died of wounds September 22, 1863.

Deal William M., Pvt., Age 37, Co. I, enlisted at Columbia March 20, 1862. Absent, sick, in hospital October 15, 1863 - Nov/Dec 1863. Died at Fair Ground Hospital No. 2, Atlanta December 31, 1863. Funeral December 31, 1864. Grave located at Oakland Cemetery, Confederate Section, Atlanta. Contractor paid $11.50 to conduct funeral.

Dean, J. Madison, Corp., Co. K, enlisted at Edgefield April 15, 1862. Present on all rolls. Paroled at Greensboro May 1, 1865.

Dean, Starling, Pvt., Age 45, Co. D, enlisted at Camp Gist January 19, 1862. Died in Tennessee October 5, 1863. Mother, Henrietta Dean, submitted claim for settlement April 29, 1864.

Delaughter, John W., Pvt., Co. I, from Franklin, S. C., a farmer, enlisted at James Island July 1, 1862. Present on all rolls. Extra daily duty with infirmary corps Jul/Aug 1864. Paroled at Greensboro May 1, 1865.

DeLoach, Charles, Pvt., Age 32, Co. D, enlisted at Charleston March 1, 1862. In hospital at Charleston Nov/Dec 1862. Sick in tent Jan/Feb 1863. Wounded and admitted to hospital July 20, 1864. Living.

DeLoach, Jesse, Pvt., Co. D. Entry from Memory Rolls at State Archives, Columbia, S.C.

Derrick, Simeon Paul, Pvt., Age 16, Co. I, enlisted at Columbia April 19, 1862. Discharged for chronic rheumatism July 23, 1862. Enlisted at Pocotaligo March 10, 1863. Present for duty from May - December 1863. Severely wounded, arm and leg, May 16, 1864. Died of disease at Catoosa Hosp., Griffin, Ga., June 25, 1864. Grave located at Stonewall Cemetery, Griffin, Ga.

Devore, John, Pvt., Co. K, enlisted at Edgefield March 10, 1862. Discharged by medical board May/Jun 1862. Admitted to CSA General Hospital, No. 11, Charlotte for treatment of pneumonia. Released February 9, 1865.

Devore, Richard, Pvt., Co. G, enlisted at Columbia May 1, 1863. Assigned to company from camp of instruction at Columbia. Absent without leave August 25 - October 1863. Severely wounded at Atlanta July 22, 1864. Killed in battle at Franklin. Grave located in Franklin Confederate Cemetery, Section 83, Grave no. 10.

Dewett, Daniel F., Corp., Age 24, Co. C, enlisted at Georges Station January 7, 1863. Absent, sick, in hospital Jan/Feb 1863. Signed receipt roll for clothing April 1, 1864. Paroled at Greensboro May 1, 1865.

Dickard, William D., Pvt., Age 32, Co. F, nickname "Billy," from Teagle's Store, S.C., enlisted at Anderson January 13, 1862. Present on all rolls. Paroled at Greensboro May 1, 1865.

Dixon, Thomas E., Pvt., Age 21, Co. A, enlisted at Charleston December 31, 1861. Wounded near Jackson May 14, 1863. Captured and paroled in hospital May 16,1863. Signed receipt roll for clothing April 1, 1864. Captured at Jonesboro September 2, 1864. Sent to Military Prison, Louisville and transferred to Camp Douglas October 29, 1864. Claimed to have been loyal, enlisted under false representations, desired to avail himself of the amnesty proclamation. Mustered into 6th U. S. Vols., March 25, 1865.

Dixon, Thomas, Jr., Pvt., Age 23, Co. A, enlisted at Charleston December 31, 1861. Detailed to work at government foundry at Greenville and arsenal at Charleston June 5, 1863 - August 1864. Signed receipt roll for clothing at C.S. Arsenal September 29, 1864. Signed receipt roll for clothing September 29, 1864. Worked as a founder in the manufacture of ordnance stores. Transferred to civil service.

Doltun, J. B., Sgt. Maj., F&S, enlisted at Yazoo City June 2, 1863. Ed. Note - This is suspected duplicate of Dotterer, J. B., Sgt. Maj.

Donnelly, H., Pvt., Age 18, Co. A, enlisted at Charleston March 17, 1862. Signed by mark. One months pay deducted by sentence of court martial Jul/Aug 1863. Signed receipt roll for clothing September 9, 1864. Captured at Franklin December 17, 1864. Sent to Military Prison, Louisville and transferred to Camp Chase January 4, 1865. Description: complexion, light; hair, light; eyes, gray; height, 5 ft. 4 in. Signed oath of allegiance to the United States June 12, 1865.

Donnelly, William, Pvt., Age 20, Co. A, enlisted at Charleston, March 17, 1862. Present for duty May/Jun 1862. Discharged, physically disabled.

Doolittle, Benjamin, Pvt., Age 22, Co. I, enlisted at Columbia April 11, 1862. Discharged by surgeon's certificate, chronic rheumatism, July 6, 1862.

Dorn, George, Pvt., Co. K. Killed in battle at Jonesboro. Entry from Memory Rolls at State Archives, Columbia, S.C.

Dorn, James, Pvt., Co. K, enlisted at Edgefield, March 1, 1863. Present on all rolls. Paroled at Greensboro May 1, 1865.

Dorn, John, Pvt., Co. K, enlisted at Edgefield February 18, 1862. Sent to hospital at Rome September 11, 1863. Furloughed home October 1, 1863. Died of disease in hospital October 7, 1863.

Dorn, John J., Pvt., Co. K, enlisted at Edgefield April 15, 1862. Absent, sick, in hospital at Lauderdale Springs, Miss., July 21, 1863 - Jan/Feb 1864. Paroled at Greensboro May 1, 1865.

Dorn, W., Pvt., Co. G, enlisted Columbia May 1, 1863. Assigned to company from camp of instruction at Columbia May/Jun 1863. Left in hospital at Selma July - September 1863. Supposed to have died at Selma, AL., September 1, 1863. A notation appears on the record, "The information is not official."

Dorn, Wright Peter, Pvt., Co. K, enlisted at Edgefield March 10, 1862. Sent to division hospital, sick, October 24, 1863. Died of disease in Asylum Hospital, Dalton, Ga., November 15, 1863.

Dotterer, James B., Sgt. Maj., Co. A & F&S, enlisted at Yazoo City, Miss., June 3, 1863. Citadel cadet, class of 1863. Appointed Sergeant Major, September 1, 1863. Slightly wounded, head, at Chickamauga September 20, 1863. Severely wounded, chest, at Calhoun, Ga., of May 16, 1864. Recovered from wound, en route returning to regiment, became ill and died of disease at Augusta. Grave located in private lot at Magnolia Cemetery, Charleston. (See Doltun, J. B.)

Dougherty, Thomas, Pvt., Age 23, Co. A, enlisted at Charleston December 31, 1861. Present on all rolls. Paroled at Greensboro May 1, 1865

Dozier, James A., 1Lt., Co,. K, enlisted at Edgefield April 23, 1862. Resigned by reason of surgeons certificate based on ill health October 7, 1862.

Drawdy, A., Pvt., Co. E, enlisted at Dalton, Ga., May 10, 1864. Absent without leave July 25 - August 1864. Prisoner. Survived.

Drawdy, D. C., Pvt., Age 38, Co. E, enlisted at Salkehatchie January 16, 1862. Discharged by substitute February 28, 1862.

Drawdy, P. W., 2Lt., Age 33, Co. E, enlisted at Camp Gist, March 15, 1862. Elected 2Lt., Co. E, examined him and found him incompetent for the promotion. Position in company rendered very painful by the circumstances. Requested transfer to Captain Campbell's Cavalry Company, Colonel Colcock's Regiment.

Drawdy, D. E., Pvt., Age 42, Co. E, enlisted at Salkehatchie January 16, 1862. Discharged by surgeon's certificate March 20, 1862.

Drawdy, John, Pvt., Age 17, Co. E, enlisted at Salkehatchie January 16, 1862. Discharged because of small size March 20, 1862.

Drawdy, William P., Jr., Pvt., Age 18, Co. E, from Colleton District, enlisted at Camp Gist March 8, 1862. Substitute for D. C. Drawdy March 1, 1862. Transferred to the 2nd Battalion, Sharpshooters and retransferred January 15, 1863. Released from hospital June 29, 1863. Surgeon wrote letter to Commanding Officer that soldier was "Absolutely in need" of one pair of pants, one shirt, one pair of trousers and one jacket. Absent, sick, in hospital Mar/Apr - May/Jun 1863. Admitted to Ocmulgee Hospital, Macon, Ga., for Veal. Sclopt. June 23 - 29, 1864. Admitted to 1st Mississippi CSA Hospital, Jackson, Miss., November 4 - 7, 1864. Present for duty Jul/Aug 1864. Died of disease.

Drawdy, William Daniel, Sr., Pvt., Age 38, Co. E, enlisted at Pocotaligo March 20, 1863. Admitted to 1st Mississippi CSA Hospital, Jackson suffering diarrhoea acuta June 6, 1863. Sent to General Hospital July 8, 1863. Wounded, neck, near Atlanta. Survived.

Driggers, Charles O., Pvt., Co. B, from Bennetsville, enlisted at Marlboro October 16, 1862. Wounded at Chickamauga September 20, 1863. In hospital and on sick furlough September 20, 1863 - August 31, 1864

Driggers, Matthew C., Pvt., Age 43, Co. B, enlisted at Marlboro December 4, 1861. Sick in hospital at Charleston Jan/Feb 1863. Died of disease at home September 21, 1863.

Driggers, Robert, Pvt., Age 33, Co. B, enlisted at Marlboro December 4, 1861. Absent without leave May/Jun 1863. Absent, sick, in hospital and furloughed September - February 1864. Died at home February 22, 1864.

Driggers, William, Pvt., Age 35, Co. B, enlisted at Marlboro December 4, 1861. Absent, sick, in hospital at Lauderdale Springs July - October 1863. Admitted to Walker's Division Hospital, Lauderdale and Jackson's Cavalry Division Hospital, Old Marion, Miss., August 10 - October 1863. Present for duty Jul/Aug 1864. Wounded at Atlanta. Died at home.

Droze, Isaac (J.) D., 2Lt., Co. A, enlisted at Camp Gist April 8, 1862. Elected 2Lt., February 11, 1864. Wounded at Kennesaw Mountain. Killed in battle at Atlanta July 22, 1864. Grave located in Stoneman Cemetery, Griffith, Ga. Widow, Eugenia Droze, resided at 555 King St., Charleston, S.C.

Droze, William W., Pvt., Co. A, enlisted at Charleston July 7, 1862. Sick furlough Nov/Dec 1862. Sick at hospital August 29, 1863 - August 1864. Signed receipt roll for clothing November 15, 1864. Present for duty January 16, 1865.

Drumm, Daniel, Pvt., Age 27, Co. H., enlisted at Chester March 19, 1862. Absent, sick, in hospital July 29, 1864. Died of disease, pneumonia, at Catoosa Hospital, Griffin, Ga., August 14, 1864. Grave located at Stonewall Cemetery, Griffin, Sapulding County, Ga. Married December

8, 1856. Widow, Sarah Drumm resided at Edgemoor, S.C.

Druges, Whitfield, Pvt., Co. B. Captured near Nashville December 16, 1864. Sent to Military Prison, Louisville and transferred to Camp Douglas December 24, 1864. Signed oath of allegiance to United States and discharged June 19, 1865.

Duane, T., Pvt., Co. G. Entry from original muster roll.

Dukes, George M., Pvt., Age 26, Co. C, from Colleton District, enlisted at Georges Station January 7, 1862. Captured at Chickamauga September 20, 1863. Sent to Military Prison, Louisville and transferred to Camp Douglas October 2, 1863. Discharged June 20, 1865. Married October 11, 1889. Widow, Mary Catherine Dukes.

Dukes, James P., Pvt., Age 24, Co. C, enlisted at Georges Station January 7, 1862. Mortally wounded in battle at Chickamauga September 20, 1863. Died of wounds received in battle at Chickamauga December 11, 1863.

Dukes, William W., Pvt., Age 30, Co. C, enlisted Georges Station January 7, 1862. Sick in hospital at Atlanta and furloughed Jul/Aug - Sep/Oct 1863. Signed receipt roll for clothing at Camp Wright December 14, 1864. Name listed on muster roll of Co. E, 1st Regiment Troops and Defenses, at Camp Wright near Macon Nov/Dec 1864.

Duncan, John, Pvt., Age 23, Co. I, enlisted at Columbia, March 20, 1862. Wounded at Secessionville June 16, 1862. Reported missing in battle. Captured at Secessionville June 16, 1862. Sent to Fort Columbus, New York Harbor aboard Steamer *Arago*. Transferred to Fort Delaware August 23, 1862. Exchanged at Aikens Landing, Va., November 10, 1862. Returned to Camp January 22, 1863. Absent without leave May 7 - Jul/Aug 1863. Absent, sick, in hospital at Atlanta September 20, 1863 - Nov/Dec 1863. Signed receipt roll for clothing November 13, 1863.

Duncan, William, Pvt., Co. I, enlisted at Columbia, March 20, 1862. Discharged at Coles Island for disability May 10, 1862.

Dunlap, Jacob, Pvt., Age 19, Co. F, enlisted at Anderson March 27, 1862. Died of disease February 2, 1864.

Dunn, Alexander, Pvt., Co. B, from Bennetsville, enlisted at Marlboro April 14, 1862. Died in camp October 18, 1863.

Dunn, Joel, Pvt., Age 40, Co. G, enlisted at Columbia, March 19, 1862. In hospital May/Jun 1862. One months pay stopped by order of court martial May/Jun 1863. Absent without leave November 27 - December 1863. Sick in hospital in Atlanta January 20 - February 1864.

Durean, William, Pvt., Cop. I. Discharged. Entry from *Edgefield Advertiser*.

Durr, W. D. W., Pvt., Age 22, Co. C, enlisted at Georges Station January 7, 1862. Sick in hospital and furloughed May/Jun - Sep/Oct 1863. Absent without leave Nov/Dec 1863. Signed receipt roll for clothing September

9, 1863. Discharged due to physical disability January 15, 1864.

Dutton, John D., Pvt., Age 23, Co. F, from Hartwell, Ga., enlisted at Anderson January 13, 1862. Description: complexion, fair; hair, dark; eyes, blue; height, 5 ft. 7 in; occupation, farmer. Discharged for inability June 27, 1862.

Easterling, C. Dudley, 1Lt., Age 22, Co. B, from Marlboro, enlisted at Marlboro, December 4, 1861. Promoted to 1Lt., January 27, 1863. Granted leave of absence of 30 days January 20, 1865. Description: complexion, light; hair, auburn; eyes, dark; height, 5 ft. 10 in. Captured at Marlboro District March 5, 1865. Sent from New Bern, N. C., to Hart's Island, New York Harbor April 10, 1865. Transferred to Fort Delaware April 16, 1865. Signed oath of allegiance to the United States and released Jun 17, 1865.

Easterling, J. N., Pvt., Age 17, Co. B, enlisted at Marlboro December 4, 1861. Detached as Provost Guard by order of Gen. Gist Nov/Dec 1863. Captured at Jonesboro September 1, 1864. Sent to Military Prison, Louisville, transferred to Camp Douglas October 28, 1864. Claimed to have been loyal, conscripted into the Rebel Army and deserted to avail himself of the amnesty proclamation. Mustered into the 5th United States Volunteer Infantry April 14, 1865.

Easterling, John T., Corp., Age 17, Co. B, enlisted at Marlboro, December 4, 1861. Appointed Color Corporal at Secessionville April 18, 1863. Promoted to Corp., August 24, 1864. Present for duty on all rolls. Killed in battle at Franklin November 30, 1864. Grave located in Franklin Confederate Cemetery, Section 83, Grave No. 5.

Easterling, William B., Sgt., Age 18, Co. B, from Marlboro District, enlisted at Marlboro December 4, 1861. Slightly wounded, thigh, July 20/22, 1864. Promoted 2Sgt., August 24, 1864. Present for duty on all rolls. Seriously wounded at Franklin November 30, 1864. Middle third right arm amputated December 1, 1864. Captured at Franklin December 17, 1864. Admitted to No. 1, USA General Hospital, Nashville December 27, 1864 - January 7, 1865. Sent to Military Prison, Louisville and transferred to Camp Chase January 15, 1865. Description: complexion, dark; hair, dark; eyes, brown; height, 5 ft. 8 in. Signed oath of allegiance to the United States June 13, 1865. Discharged June 14, 1865.

Easterling, W. L., Pvt., Age 37, Co. B, enlisted at Marlboro December 4, 1861. In charge of baggage at Secessionville. Captured at Jackson May 14, 1863. Assigned to Paroled Prisoners Camp at Demopolis June 5, 1863. Slightly wounded, hand, July 20/22, 1864. Treated at Floyd and Ocmulgee Hospitals, Macon for wound, left hand, (flesh wound) but serious July 15, 18, 22, 25, 1864. Signed receipt roll for clothing July 25, 1864. Wounded at Franklin November 30, 1864. Survived.

Eddings, Charles, Teamster, Co. D, enlisted at Camp Gist January 13, 1864.

Colored. Discharged January. 13, 1864. Negro.

Eddings, Kelly, Teamster, Co. D, enlisted at Camp Gist January 13, 1864. Colored. Discharged January 13, 1864. Negro.

Eddings, Nat, Teamster, Co. D, enlisted at Camp Gist January 13, 1864. Colored. Discharged January. 13, 1864. Negro.

Edmonston, Edward, Pvt., Age 28, Co. A, enlisted at Charleston, December 31, 1861. Detailed to work on roads by order of General Gist Nov/Dec 1863. Captured near Marietta July 2, 1864. Sent to Military Prison, Louisville and transferred to Camp Douglas July 18, 1864. Claimed to have been loyal, enlisted in the Rebel Army to avoid conscription and desired to take oath of allegiance to the U.S. and become a loyal citizen. Died from small pox December 13, 1864. Grave located near Camp Douglas. Ed. Note - name also spelled Edmundson.

Edmondson, Charles, Pvt., Co. A. Wounded at Chickamauga. Died in Union prison at Camp Chase. Entry from Memory Rolls at State Archives, Columbia, S.C.

Edwards, Owen, Pvt., Age 40, Co. G, enlisted at Columbia March 19, 1862. Sick in hospital March 19, 1862 - October 1862. Discharged January 20, 1863.

Elam, J. M., Pvt., Co. G, enlisted at Knoxville, Tenn., May 24, 1862. Attached to Company G, May 24, 1863 and returned to his command August 10, 1863.

Elder, Elijah, Pvt., Age 36, Co. H, enlisted at Chester District March 19, 1862. Present for duty on all rolls. Signed receipt roll for clothing September 9, 1864. Paroled at Greensboro May 1, 1865.

Ellen, R. M., Pvt., Co. B, enlisted at Marion March 31, 1862. Absent, sick, in hospital at Atlanta, Ga., Sep/Oct 1863. Signed receipt roll for clothing April 1, 1864. Patient in hospital August 1864. Paroled at Greensboro May 1, 1865. Deserted April 23, 1865.

Ellen, William B., Pvt., Co, B, enlisted at Marion April 28, 1862. Sick in Camp and Bell Hospital at Rome Jul/Aug - Sep/Oct 1863. Overpaid, pay stopped for two months Nov/Dec 1863. Admitted to hospital February 23, 1864. Present for duty August 31, 1864. Signed receipt roll for clothing September 9, 1864. Died at home.

Ellenburg, J. R., Pvt., Co. K, enlisted at Edgefield March 14, 1862. Patient in hospital at Columbia February 23 - Jul/Aug 1864. Surrendered and paroled at Augusta May 18, 1865.

Ellis, Joseph S., Pvt., Age 18, Co. A, enlisted at Charleston December 31, 1861. Transferred to Navy Department by order of General Beauregard October 6, 1862.

Ellis, Oscar A., Sgt., Age 23, Co. D, enlisted at Camp Gist January 16, 1862. Promoted to 5Sgt., May 27, 1863 and promoted to 4Sgt., and 3Sgt. Wounded at Chickamauga September 20, 1863. Reduced to ranks

June 30, 1864. Signed roll for clothing September 9, 1864. Signed receipt roll for clothing September 9, 1864. Captured at Shipp's Gap/Taylor's Ridge October 16, 1864. Sent to Military Prison, Louisville and transferred to Camp Douglas November 29, 1864. Forwarded to Point Lookout for exchange, February 20, 1865. Admitted to Receiving and Wayside Hospital or General Hospital No. 1, Richmond February 28, 1865. Surrendered and paroled at Tallahassee, Fla., May 10, 1865.

Ellison, David, Pvt., Co. F., Consolidated 16th and 24th Regiment, enlisted at Columbia November 5, 1864. Paroled at Greensboro May 1, 1865.

Elrod, D. S., Pvt., Age 35, Co. F, from Holland's Store, S.C., enlisted at Anderson March 28, 1862. Wounded and captured near Jackson May 14, 1863. Paroled in hospital May 16, 1862. Absent, sick, Nov/Dec 1862. Absent, wounded, May 16, 1863 - August 31, 1864. Surrendered.

Enzminger, J. W., Co. G. Entry from original muster roll.

Enoch, Phillip Mathew, Age 20, Co. E, born January 27, 1843. Killed in battle of Chickamauga, September 20, 1863. Grave located in National Cemetery at Chattanooga. Entry from *Cemeteries of Upper Colleton County, South Carolina.*

Esdorn, John F., Pvt., Age 23, Co. A, enlisted at Charleston December 31, 1861. Wounded and captured near Jackson May 14, 1863. Paroled in hospital May 16, 1863. Absent, wounded in hospital at Lauderdale Springs, Miss., May 14, 1863 - Jul/Aug 1864. Wounded so seriously as to disqualify him for further service and active duty for life. Signed receipt roll for clothing November 11, 1864. Retired December 27, 1864. Assigned to Post Commissary February 16, 1865. Died of disease at Charleston.

Etheridge, William Wade, Pvt., Age 30, Co. F, from Antreville, S.C., enlisted at Anderson January 13, 1862. Slightly wounded at Jackson July 16, 1863. Wounded at New Hope Church June 1864. Wounded at Shipp's Gap/Taylor's Ridge October 16, 1864. Captured near Nashville December 16, 1864. Sent to Military Prison, Louisville and transferred to Camp Chase January 4, 1865. Description: complexion, light; hair, light; eyes, hazel; height, 5 ft. 9 in. Signature by mark. Signed oath of allegiance to the United States June 12, 1865.

Eustice, William, Pvt., Co. G. Entry from Memory Rolls at State Archives, Columbia, S.C., and original muster roll.

Evans, Arch B., Pvt., Age 35, Co. F, from Holland's Store, enlisted at Anderson, April 10, 1862. Discharge granted for physical disability by the Examining Board at Columbia, January 12, 1863.

Evans, J. M., Pvt., Age 33, Co. F, from Lowndesville, S.C., enlisted at Anderson March 11, 1863. Slightly wounded by artillery shell during siege of Jackson July 9-16, 1864. Wounded at Chattahooche. Gun shot wound fracturing the bone of the big toe of right foot July 9, 1864. Furloughed 60 days July 13, 1864. Paroled at Greensboro May 1, 1865.

Evans, J. O., Pvt., Age 30, Co. F, from Moffetsville, S.C., enlisted at Anderson April 8, 1862. Absent, sick, Nov/Dec 1862. Detached duty as teamster, Morton, Miss., July - October 1863. Signed receipt roll for clothing April 1, 1864. Ambulance driver Jan/Feb - Mar/Aug 1864. Surrendered.

Evans, Thomas H., Pvt., Age 36, Co. H, enlisted at Chester Dist., March 19, 1862. Wounded at Kennesaw Mountain. Absent without leave July 30, 1864 - August 31, 1864. Paroled at Greensboro May 1, 1865.

Evans, T. W., Co. C, Gist's Brigade, from Chester District. Entry from *Chester County Heritage History.*

Evans, W. A., Pvt., Age 18, Co. F, from Moffetsville, S.C., enlisted at Anderson April 1, 1862. Wounded at Decatur, right hand causing amputation of middle finger, July 22, 1864. Approved for 60 days leave July 29, 1864. Paroled at Greensboro May 1, 1865. Died in 1889.

Farley, Jno., Pvt., Co. G. Detached to work in shops. Entry from letter written by Col. Ellison Capers to his wife September 7, 1863, and original muster roll.

Farmer, B. D., Pvt., Co. C, from Wilson County. Paroled at Provost Marshal's Office, Goldsboro.

Farmer, J. A., 24th Regiment. Entry from tombstone located in Confederate Section, Magnolia Cemetery, Charleston, S.C.

Farmer, Isaac, Pvt., Age 28, Co. C, enlisted at Georges Station January 7, 1862. Present for duty on all rolls. Present for duty through August 1864. Survived and relocated to North Carolina.

Faust, Sumpter, Pvt., Co. G, enlisted at Columbia May 1, 1863. Assigned to company from camp of instruction at Columbia May/Jun 1863. Wounded and captured at Missionary Ridge November 27, 1863. Died of dysentery at US Military Hospital Prison, Nashville, Tenn., December 7, 1863. Grave no. 5737.

Feehan, F. P., Sgt., Age 20, Co. A, enlisted at Charleston, December 31, 1861. Orderly Sergeant. Killed in battle at Jackson May 14, 1863. Struck by a cannon ball from Confederate artillery piece, striking him in the back of his neck and head. A gallant, efficient and faithful soldier. He was among the first and probably the very first casualty from Co. A, during the battle of Jackson May 14, 1864.

Fennell, Robert H., 2Lt., Age 23, Co. H, enlisted at Chester Dist., March 19, 1862. Elected 2Lt., January 15, 1863. Furloughed April 30, 1863. Captured at Chickamauga September 20, 1863. Sent to Military Prison, Louisville and transferred to Johnson's Island October 5, 1863. Transferred to City Point for exchange, February 24, 1865. Admitted to Receiving and Wayside Hospital, or General Hospital No. 9, Richmond

March 3, 1865.

Ferrell, C. D., Pvt., Age 19, Co. E, enlisted at Camp Gist March 20, 1862. Absent, sick, hospitalized in Mississippi, Jul/Aug 1863 - July 18, 1864. Captured at Yazoo City July 19, 1864. Received at Camp Morton August 7, 1863. Enlisted in 7th Ind. Cav., August 1863. Died at Camp Morton September 22, 1863. Ed. Note - Name also listed as C. E. Ferrell, also Ferell, Ferrel, Ferrall. Dates are confusing, may be two soldiers.

Ferrell, C. E., Pvt., Age 21, Co. E. Died of disease at Cordt's Pond, Mississippi. Entry from roster prepared by Capt. Joseph K. Risher, Company Commander.

Fesyemnson, William, Buried June 21, 1864 in Block D, Row 3, Oakland Cemetery, Atlanta, Georgia. Entry from Oakland Cemetery Records. Name may be spelled *Feysterman*.

Fewox, James, Pvt., Co. C. Name listed on roster prepared by Capt. A. C. Appleby, Company Commander.

Fewox, Jerry, Pvt., Co. I, Consolidated 16th and 24th Regiment, enlisted at Georges Station March 14, 1865. Paroled at Greensboro May 1, 1865.

Fewox, John, Pvt., Age 16, Co. C, enlisted at Georges Station January 7, 1862. Absent, sick, furloughed, Sep/Oct 1863. Paroled at Greensboro May 1, 1865.

Fewox, W., Pvt., Co. C, enlisted at Georges Station March 4, 1865. Paroled at Greensboro May 1, 1865.

Fields, Peter, Pvt., Age 20, Co. B, enlisted at Marlboro December 4, 1861. Absent, sick at home, Sep/Oct - Nov/Dec 1862. Absent without leave Jan/Feb 1863. Absent, sick at home, May/Jun 1863. Absent without leave May 5, 1863 - August 31, 1864. Died at home in 1863.

Finley, A., Pvt., Co. D, enlisted at Camp Gist, April 9, 1862. Present for duty May/Jun 1862.

Finley, J. J., Pvt., Age 35, Co. F, enlisted at Anderson January 13, 1862. Discharged for inability/disability February 24, 1862. Died December 1891.

Finley, John, Pvt., Age 32, Co. G, enlisted at Columbia April 12, 1862. Sick, patient in hospital at Columbia, May/Jun - Sep/Oct 1862. Absent, patient in hospital at Columbia, Jan/Feb 1862. Absent, sick in hospital, Nov/Dec 1863. Wounded at Kennesaw Mountain, hospitalized at Columbia August 31, 1864. Discharged April 1865. Married January 15, 1874. Died September 4, 1895. Widow Mary C. Finley.

Fisher, Co. H, from Chester District. Died in Georgia. Entry from *Chester County Heritage History*.

Fitch, R. G., Pvt., Co. G, enlisted at Columbia May 1, 1863. Assigned to company from camp of instruction at Columbia. Patient in hospital at Newman, Ga., Sep/Oct 1863. Killed near Kennesaw Mountain July 4,

1864. He was visiting friends in Co. K when a shell exploded overhead. A fragment struck a pole and ricocheted striking and cutting off the back of his head. Buried by his friends in Co. K.

Fitchue, James, Pvt., Age 32, Co. A, enlisted at Charleston December 31, 1864. Detailed to work at Camerons Foundry, Charleston April 12, 1862 - Jun/Jul 1863. Transferred to civil service. Killed while working on South Carolina Railroad, detached at the time, Jul/Aug 1863.

Fleming, A. M., Pvt., Co. F, from Honea Path, S.C., enlisted at Camp Gist March 28, 1862. Present on all rolls. Present for duty through August 31, 1864. Survivor. Died in 1888.

Fleming, A. M., Pvt., Age 32, Co. F, from Honea Path, S.C. Surrendered. Entry from Memory Rolls at State Archives, Columbia, S.C.

Fleming, George M., Pvt., Age 18, Co. F, from Abbeville, enlisted at Abbeville January 11, 1862. Wounded and captured near Jackson May 14, 1863. Assigned to Paroled and Exchanged Prisoners Camp at Demopolis June 5, 1863. Slightly wounded, hand, at Calhoun, Ga., May 16, 1865. Captured at Shipp's Gap/Taylor's Ridge October 16, 01864. Sent to Military Prison, Louisville and transferred to Camp Douglas October 29, 1864. Description: complexion, fair; hair, dark; eyes, blue; height, 5 ft. 10 in. Signed oath of allegiance to the United States and discharged June 17, 1865. Moved to Texas.

Fleming, Warren S., Pvt., Age 18, born September 1, 1847, Co. F, from Honea Path, S.C., enlisted at Abbeville, February 16, 1864. Bounty due. Present for duty through August 31, 1864. Captured at Shipp's Gap/Taylor's Ridge. Surrendered.

Fletcher, Nicholas, Pvt., Age 36, Co. B., enlisted at Charleston December 4, 1861 for 12 months. Died in camp at Secessionville of typhoid fever November 19, 1862.

Fludd, James, Pvt., Co. A, enlisted at Camp Gist April 8, 1862. Detailed to work on Eason's gunboat, Charleston October 23, 1862 - December 12, 1863. Sick at hospital Jul/Aug 1864. Signed, by mark, receipt roll for clothing November 15, 1864. Paroled at Greensboro May 1, 1865.

Flynn, Charles E., Sgt., Age 18, Co. G, enlisted at Columbia March 19, 1862. Under arrest Mar/Apr 1863. Charged with initiating and passing a petition for the men to be allowed to elect their captain and first lieutenant. Reduced to ranks by court martial May 1, 1863. Captured at Jackson May 14, 1863. Assigned to Paroled Prisoner Camp at Demopolis June 5, 1863. Killed in battle at Chickamauga, September 20, 1863. Father, Patrick Flynn, filed claim for settlement March 5, 1864.

Fogarty, J., Pvt., Co. G, enlisted at Secessionville April 24, 1863. Received as a substitute for Pvt. Jos. Lorich April 24, 1863. Deserted May 4, 1863. Dropped from the roll January 30, 1864.

Folk, Henry N., Pvt., Age 29, Co. D, from Colleton District. Captured near

Nashville December 16, 1864. Sent to Military Prison, Louisville and transferred to Camp Chase January 4, 1865. Description: complexion, dark; hair, dark; eyes, gray; height, 5 ft. 10 in. Signed oath of allegiance to the United States June 12, 1865.

Folk, Jacob L., 1Lt., Co. D, from Whippy Swamp, enlisted at Camp Gist April 9, 1862. Captured near Jackson May 14, 1863. Assigned to Paroled Prisoners Camp at Demopolis June 5, 1863. Description: complexion, florid; hair, dark; eyes, blue; height, 5 ft. 8 in. Elected 2Lt., and promoted to 1Lt., September 20, 1863. Captured at Nashville December 16, 1864. Sent to Military Prison, Louisville and transferred to Johnson's Island December 22, 1864. Signed oath of allegiance to the United States and released June 16, 1865.

Fowler, James L., Pvt., Age 30, Co. F, from Anderson, S.C., enlisted at Anderson January 13, 1862. Transferred to Smith's Battalion Sharp Shooters August 10, 1862 to November 25, 1862. Wounded, ankle, at Charleston. Wounded in engagement in shoulder near Jackson May 14, 1863. Captured and paroled in hospital May 16, 1863. Captured at Missionary Ridge, November 26, 1863. Discharged at Rock Island Prison July 1865. Surrendered.

Frank, Henry, 1Sgt., Age 28, Co. G, enlisted at Columbia March 19, 1862. Absent, sick in hospital at Columbia, Jan/Feb 1862. Appointed 1Sgt., June 1, 1863. Wounded in engagement near Jackson May 14, 1863. Killed in battle at Chickamauga, September 20, 1863.

Freeman, William Dixon, Pvt., Age 21, Co.D, from Beaufort District, enlisted at Camp Gist January 16, 1862. Captured at Jackson May 14, 1863. Assigned to Paroled Prisoners Camp at Demopolis June 5, 1863. Exchanged August 17, 1863. Furloughed 30 days. Gunshot wound, first phalanx of little finger amputated at Floyd House and Ocmulgee Hospitals, Macon June 24, 1863. Captured near Nashville December 16, 1864. Sent to Military Prison, Louisville, transferred to Camp Douglas, December 22, 1864. Discharged June 19, 1865.

Freeman, George M., Pvt, Co. I, enlisted at James Island November 10, 1862. Absent without leave December 20-31, 1863. Wounded, arm and knee, June 15, 1864. Sent from regiment to general hospital November 15, 1864. Surrendered and paroled at Augusta May 18, 1865.

Freeman, J., Pvt., Age 26, Co. D, enlisted at Camp Gist January 16, 1862. Present for duty Sep/Oct 1862.

Freeman, James E., Pvt., Age 24, Co. D, enlisted at Camp Gist March 10, 1862. Mortally wounded in battle at Kennesaw Mountain. Died July 30, 1864. Grave located in Confederate Grave Yard near Milner, Pike County, Georgia.

Freeman, John Nelson, Pvt., Age 22, Co. D, enlisted at Charleston March 10, 1862. Wounded at Chickamauga. Sick in hospital Nov/Dec 1863.

Sick in hospital at Greensborough, Ga., Jul/Aug 1864. Surrendered and paroled at Augusta May 25, 1865.

Freeman, Philip, Pvt., Age 24, Co. D, from Gillersonville, enlisted at Camp Gist January 16, 1865. Present on all rolls. Paroled at Greensboro May 1, 1865.

Gadd, Wm. W., Pvt., Co. B, enlisted at Marlboro March 31, 1862. Present for duty May/Jun 1862. Transferred 1862.

Gaddy, John, Pvt., Co. B, enlisted at Marion March 31, 1862. Present on all rolls. Captured at Nashville December 16, 1864. Sent to Military Prison, Louisville and transferred to Camp Douglas December 24, 1864. Discharged June 19, 1865.

Gailey, Albert, 2Lt., Age 33, Co. F, enlisted at Abbeville June 1, 1862. Exchanged from Aikens Regiment, Partisan Ranger for D. R. McClellan November 17, 1862. Absent, sick, patient in hospital, Jul/Aug - Sep/Oct 1863. Elected 2Lt., January 20, 1864. Granted leave March 28, 1864. Killed in battle, inside the Lock's Fort within the enemy's works, at Franklin, November 30, 1864. "A good citizen, a brave Confederate soldier, and was a most worthy gentleman. Held in highest esteem by all the officers and men of his command." Grave located in the Confederate Cemetery, Section 85, Grave No. 31, at Franklin "near where he gave his life for his home and his country."

Gaines, Jno. Pvt., Co. G. Entry from Memory Rolls at State Archives, Columbia, S.C.

Galphin, Milledge, Pvt., Co. I, enlisted at Coles Island May 7, 1862. Discharged for disability at James Island May 26, 1862.

Garner, Jerry, Pvt., Co. G, from Beaufort District. Description: complexion, dark; hair, dark; eyes, hazel; height 5 ft. 8 in. Captured at Fayetteville March 30, 1865. Sent to Point Lookout, Md. Signed oath of allegiance to the United States and released June 27, 1865.

Garner, Samuel, Pvt., Co. I, from Trenton, S.C., enlisted at Edgefield March 10, 1865. Paroled at Greensboro May 1, 1865. Married 1872. Died December 24, 1914. Widow Susan E. Garner.

Garris, Calvin, Corp., Age 26, Co. E, enlisted at Salkehatchie January 16, 1862. Wounded at Chickamauga September 20, 1863. Absent with leave Sep/Oct 1864. Absent without leave Nov/Dec 1863. Severely wounded, arm and hip, at Calhoun Ga., May 17, 1864. Killed in battle at Franklin November 30, 1864. Grave located in Franklin Confederate Cemetery, Section 84, Grave no. 30.

Garris, John, Pvt., Age 43, Co,. E,. enlisted Camp Gist January 16, 1862. Wounded and sent to hospital. Died at Newsome Hospital, Cassville, Ga., December 15, 1863.

Garris, S. P. J., Pvt., Age 18, born October 6, 1842, Co. E, from Smoaks, S.C., enlisted at Camp Gist January 16, 1862. Present on all rolls.

Present for duty August 31, 1864. Surrendered. Discharged from service at Newberry, S.C., March 1865. Married November 18, 1924. Died December 24, 1931. Widow resided at Denmark, Bamberg County, S.C.

Gauff, J., Pvt., Co. G, enlisted at Columbia May 9, 1864. Never was paid. Absent without leave June - August 1864.

Gentry, Davie O., Pvt., Age 18, Co. F, enlisted at Anderson, March 27, 1863. Wounded near Jackson May 14, 1863. Killed in battle at Chickamauga September 20, 1863.

Gentry, John A., Pvt., Age 24, Co. F, from Eton, Ga., enlisted at Anderson, June 13, 1862. Medical Examining Board, Dalton granted two months leave for chronic diarrhoea, extreme emaciation and debility June 23, 1863. Granted 60 days for same reasons June 23, 1864. Captured at Shipp's Gap/Taylor's Ridge October 16, 1864. Sent to Military Prison, Louisville and transferred to Camp Douglas October 29, 1864. Description: complexion, fair; hair, dark; eyes, hazel; height, 5 ft. 8 in. Signed oath of allegiance to the United States and discharged June 17, 1865.

George, Henry, Pvt., Age 20, Co. E, enlisted at Camp Gist April 1, 1862. Absent with leave Sep/Oct 1863. Absent without leave Nov/Dec 1863. Captured near Nashville December 16, 1864. Sent to Military Prison, Louisville and transferred to Camp Chase January 4, 1865. Description: complexion, light; hair, light; eyes, hazel; height, 5 ft. 6 in. Signed oath of allegiance to the United States June 12, 1865.

George, James, Pvt., Co. C, enlisted at Georges Station, January 7, 1862. Killed in battle at Chickamauga September 20, 1863.

George, Jacob L., Pvt., Age 25, Co. E, enlisted at Camp Gist January 16, 1862. Pay stopped for one month by court martial May/Jun 1863. Captured at Resaca May 16, 1864. Sent to Military Prison, Louisville and transferred to Military Prison, Alton, Ill., May 25, 1864. Transferred to Camp Douglas August 23, 1864. Died of Pneumonia December 24, 1864. Grave no. 323, Block 2, Chicago City Cemetery.

George, Richard, Pvt., Age 26, Co. E, enlisted at Salkehatchie January 16, 1862. Mortally wounded at Chickamauga September 20, 1863. Died of wounds received in battle at Chickamauga, Institute Hospital, Atlanta October 23, 1863. Buried October 23, 1863. Grave located in Oakland Cemetery, row 13, # 3, Confederate Section, Atlanta. Contractor paid $11.50 to conduct funeral.

German, Francis, Pvt., Co. I, enlisted at Columbia April 21, 1862. Absent without leave. Name canceled on roll.

German, Richard P., Pvt., Co. K, enlisted April 15, 1862. Wounded at Secessionville June 16, 1862. Sick in hospital at Texas General Hospital, Quitman, Miss., July 21, 1863. Transferred to Breckinridge's Division Hospital, Marion, Miss., September 13, 1863. Paroled at

Greensboro May 1, 1865.

Gibson, Dexter, Pvt., Age 16, Co. G, enlisted at Columbia, April 12, 1862.

Gibson, James D., Sgt., Co. G, enlisted at Columbia March 19, 1862. Present on all rolls. Captured at Nashville, December 16, 1864. Sent to Military Prison, Louisville and transferred to Camp Chase January 4, 1865. Admitted to USA General Hospital, No. 12, Vicksburg for intermittent fever May 17 - 31, 1865. Paroled at Camp Chase via New Orleans for exchange May 2, 1865. Admitted to USA General Hospital No. 12, Vicksburg for intermittent fever May 17 - May 31, 1865.

Gibson, Osborne, Pvt., Age 38, Co. H, enlisted at Chester District, March 19, 1862. Detailed to pioneer Nov/Dec 1863. Assigned ambulance corps March 1 - August 31, 1864. Paroled at Greensboro May 1, 1865.

Gilchrist, D. J., Pvt., Co. K, enlisted at Edgefield April 15, 1862. Furnished a substitute in the person of W. T. Stillman May/Jun 1862.

Gile, Robert, Pvt., Co. A. Reported captured at Macon by the 1st Brigade, 2d Cav. Div., April 20 and 21, 1865.

Gill, Henry D., Pvt., Co. G, enlisted at Columbia March 19, 1862. Captured in engagement near Jackson, Miss., May 14, 1863. Assigned to Paroled Prisoners Camp at Demopolis June 5, 1863. Sick, patient in hospital at Atlanta Sep/Oct 1863. Sick, patient in hospital at Columbia, S.C. Jan/Feb 1864. Present for duty Nov/Dec 1863.

Gillespie, Thomas J., Pvt., Age 27, Co. H, enlisted at Chester District, March 19, 1865. Died of disease in McPhersonville Hospital at Pocotaligo March 26, 1863.

Gillis, Joseph, Pvt., Age 28, Co. A, enlisted at Charleston, December 31, 1861. Blacksmith. Detailed for government work at Russells Charleston October 4, 1862 - Jul/Aug 1863. Killed in battle at Atlanta August 5, 1864.

Ginn, Amos, Pvt., Age 22, Co. D, enlisted at Camp Gist February 10, 1862. Present on all rolls to capture. Captured near Nashville December 16, 1864. Sent to Military Prison, Louisville and transferred to Camp Chase January 4, 1865. Description: complexion, dark; hair, dark; eyes hazel; Height, 5 ft. 4 in. Signed oath of allegiance to the United States June 13, 1865.

Ginn, Charles, Pvt., Age 45, Co. D, enlisted at Camp Gist January 16, 1862. Sick, patient in hospital at Atlanta, Jul/Aug - Sep/Oct 1863. Paroled at Greensboro May 1, 1865.

Ginn, Martin, Pvt., Co. D. Discharged at Camp Chase. Living. Entry from Memory Rolls at State Archives, Columbia, S.C.

Ginn, Robert, Pvt., Age 17, Co. D, enlisted at Camp Gist January 16, 1862. Missing in engagement near Jackson May 14, 1863. Sick, patient in hospital, Eufaula, Ala., Jul/Aug 1864. Name appears on muster roll of Co. C, 1st Regiment Troops and Defenses, Macon Nov/Dec 1864.

Signed, by mark, receipt for clothing at Camp Wright December 15, 1864.

Ginn, W. M., Pvt., Age 37, Co. D, enlisted at Camp Gist February 10, 1862. Present for duty on all rolls. Signed receipt roll for clothing September 9, 1864. Paroled at Greensboro May 1, 1865.

Glanton, Patrick H., Pvt., Co. I, enlisted at James Island May 17, 1862. Sick, patient in hospital October 10 through October 1863. Died at his home, Edgefield District, December 14, 1863.

Glaze, Richard, Pvt., Co. K, enlisted at Edgefield April 15, 1862. Detailed as Teamster July 1, 1862. Patient in the hospital at Canton, Miss., May/Jun 1863. Died in the Lauderdale Springs Hospital August 4, 1863. Father of Pvt. William Glaze.

Glaze, William, Pvt., Age 15, Co. K, born at Turkey Creek, S.C., January 16, 1847, enlisted at Edgefield February 26, 1862. Shocked by shell at Peachtree Creek, but it did no harm except leave him deaf for awhile. Wounded at Decatur near Atlanta July 22, 1864. Wounded through both legs and crippled for life. Taken by ambulance from Atlanta to hospital at Macon August 31, 1864. Granted several 60 day furloughs until the end of the war.

Glover, George, Pvt., Co. H, enlisted at Chester April 15, 1862. Detached service at Russel's Work Shop, Charleston, September 1862 - August 21, 1863. Killed in battle at Peachtree Creek July 20, 1864.

Glover, Joseph, Pvt., Co. H. Killed in battle at Atlanta. Entry from Memory Rolls at State Archives, Columbia, S.C.

Glover, William J., Pvt., Age 20, Co. I, enlisted at Columbia April 19, 1862. Present on all rolls. Paroled at Greensboro May 1, 1865.

Goff, William G., Pvt., Age 35, Co. G, enlisted at Columbia, April 12, 1862. Absent, sick. Never shown present for duty.

Goff, Wm. Pvt., Co. I. Entry from article in *Edgefield Advertiser*.

Goiris, John, Co. G. Entry from original muster roll.

Gooding, R. B., Pvt., Age 25, Co. D, enlisted at Charleston March 10, 1862. Present for duty May/Jun 1862.

Gooding, William J., Capt., Age 26, Co. D, appointed at Camp Gist January 19, 1862. Company Commander Co. D. Tendered resignation because of ill health and unable to perform duties August 12, 1862. Resignation accepted effective November 11, 1862.

Googe, Brantley W., Corp., Age 28, Co. E, enlisted at Camp Gist January 6, 1862. Promoted to Corp., May 28, 1863. Sick, furloughed, Sep/Oct 1862. Absent, sick in hospital, Jul/Aug 1863. Died in Lee Hospital at Lauderdale, Miss., August 28, 1863. Mother, Miley Googe, filed claim for settlement April 29, 1864.

Gordon, James J., Pvt., Age 40, Co. C, enlisted at Camp Gist March 2, 1862. Substituted in place of W. Weathers August 1, 1862. Sick in hospital and furloughed November 20, 1863 - Jul/Aug 1864. Lost during retreat from Dalton to Atlanta.

Gordon, J. G., Pvt., Age 23, Co. F, from Storeville, S.C., enlisted at Columbia January 13, 1862. Wounded at Lovejoy Station September 13, 1864. Present on all rolls. Paroled at Greensboro May 1, 1865.

Gordon, W. M., Pvt., Age 18, Co. F, from Storeville, S.C., enlisted at Anderson February 13, 1864. Signed receipt roll for clothing July 28, 1840. Discharged for organic heart disease that existed prior to entry into the service September 21, 1864. Description: complexion, fair; hair, dark; eyes, blue; height, 5 ft. 6 in; occupation, farmer.

Gortney, James M., Pvt., Age 18, Co. F, enlisted at Anderson April 1, 1863. Killed in battle at Jackson May 14, 1863. Father, David Gortney, filed claim for settlement August 15, 1863.

Gray, James A., 1Lt., Age 31, Co. F, from Moffetsville/Anderson, S.C., enlisted at Anderson January 13, 1862. Promoted to 1Sgt., November 7, 1862. Elected 2Lt., January 30, 1863. Granted furlough April 30, 1863. Promoted 1Lt., vice Lt. Sherard January 20, 1864. Captured at Shipp's Gap/Taylor's Ridge October 16, 1864. Sent to Military Prison, Louisville and transferred to Johnson's Island October 26, 1864. Description: complexion, dark; hair, dark; eyes, blue; height, 6 ft. 1 and 1/2 in. Signed oath of allegiance to the United States and released June 16, 1865.

Gray, R. A., Pvt., Age 30, Co. F, from Twiggs, S.C., enlisted at Anderson January 13, 1862. One months pay stopped by sentence of court martial for 1 month 19 days absent without leave Jan/Feb 1864. Slightly wounded at Atlanta July 22, 1864. Admitted Ocmulgee Hospital, Macon July 24, 1864. Furloughed July 29, 1864. Surrendered 1865.

Gray, Randolph F., Sgt., Age 24, Co. A, enlisted at Charleston December 31, 1861. Detailed to work on Eason's gun boat, Charleston October 23, 1862. Detailed until further orders August 1, 1863. Transferred to Civil Service. Married Mary E. Gray March 6, 1873. Died January 10, 1892.

Grayson, Arthur B., Corp., Age 20, Co. E, from Colleton Dist, enlisted at Camp Gist March 19, 1862. Absent without leave Mar/Apr 1863. Slightly wounded, shoulder, May 16, 1864. Signed receipt roll for clothing September 9, 1864. Captured near Nashville December 16, 1884. Sent to Military Prison Louisville and transferred to Camp Chase January 4, 1865. Description: complexion, dark; hair, black; eyes, black; height, 5 ft. 10 in. Signed oath of allegiance to the United States June 13, 1865. Name also spelled *Grason and Gracen.*

Grayson, Edward H., Corp., Age 16, Co. D, from Beaufort County, enlisted at Camp Gist January 19, 1862. Patient in McPhersonville hospital Mar/Apr 1862. Wounded at Jackson. Captured near Nashville December 16, 1864. Sent to Military Prison, Louisville and transferred to

Camp Chase January 4, 1865. Description: complexion, dark; hair, black; eyes, black; height 5 ft. 4 in. Signed oath of allegiance to the United States June 12, 1865.

Grayson, James, Pvt., Co. D, enlisted at Camp Gist January 19, 1862. Sick in MacPhersonville Hospital at Savannah, Ga., Mar/Apr 1863 - Jul/Aug 1864. Signed receipt roll for clothing March 24, 1864. Dropped from rolls by order Jul/Aug 1864.

Grayson, William S., Pvt., Age 25, Co. E, from Ruffin, S.C., enlisted at Camp Gist March 19, 1864. Substitute for Hardy Herndon. Pay stopped for one month by order of court martial May/Jun 1863. Signed receipt roll for clothing April 1, 1864. Absent without leave July 24 - August 1864. Severely wounded, thigh and arm, at Calhoun, Ga., furloughed, May 16, 1864. Surrendered. Discharged March 1865. Grave located in Pine Grove No. 1 Baptist Church Cemetery, Upper Colleton County, S.C. Widow applied for pension and signed by mark. Pension application has last name spelled *Gracen* which is probably the same person as Grayson. Married May 13, 1867. Died July 9, 1908. Widow Mary Grayson. Name also spelled *Grason and Gracen*.

Green, George G., Pvt., Co. B, enlisted at Marlboro June 22, 1864. Paroled at Greensboro May 1, 1865. Sent to hospital April 10, 1865. Died of disease in hospital six days before the surrender in 1865.

Green, John B., 2Lt., Age 19, Co. B, occupation, farmer, enlisted at Marlboro December 4, 1861. Promoted 4Sgt., August 24, 1864. Wounded in the fighting at Atlanta. Signed receipt roll for clothing September 9, 1864. Wounded at Franklin. Wounded twice at Nashville. Present on all rolls. Paroled at Greensboro May 1, 1865.

Green, Samuel, Pvt., Age 28, Co. G, from Columbia, enlisted at Columbia April 12, 1862. Absent without permission May/Jun 1862. Sick in quarters Sep/Oct 1862. Detached to work in State service at Columbia Nov/Dec 1862 - Sep/Oct 1863. Detached to work in Railroad Shops, Columbia January 25, 1864. Detailed by Secretary of War, CSA, to work for South Carolina Railroad Company for 60 days March 24, 1864. Description: complexion, dark; hair, dark; eyes, grey; height, 5 ft. 6 in; occupation, mechanic.

Green, William J., 2Lt., Age 23, Co. B, enlisted at Marlboro December 4, 1861. Promoted to 2Lt., from 1Sgt., May 4, 1863. Detached service in South Carolina from Jul/Aug 1863 to Jan/Feb 1864. Absent, leave of absence, February 12 - 28, 1864. Killed in battle at Peachtree Creek July 20, 1864.

Gregg, Ransom, Pvt., Age 24, Co. I, enlisted at Columbia March 20, 1862. Transferred to Sharpshooters August 9, 1862. Wounded at Franklin November 30, 1864. Surrendered and paroled at Augusta May 25, 1865.

Gressett, Tatum, Corp., Age 29, Co. C, enlisted at Georges Station, January

7, 1862. Sick in hospital at Atlanta Jul/Aug 1863. Mortally wounded in battle at Calhoun, Ga., May 16, 1864. Died from effects of wounds in Hospital No. 12, Fair Ground Hospital, Atlanta May 22, 1864. Buried May 23, 1864. Grave located in Oakland Cemetery, Confederate Section, Atlanta, Ga., Row 15, No. 4. Name may be listed as *J. Grissett*.

Griffin, J. D., Pvt., Co. G. Entry from Memory Rolls at State Archives, Columbia, S.C., and original muster roll.

Griffin, John W., Pvt., Age 16, Co. B, enlisted at Marlboro, December 4, 1861. Died in hospital at Brandon, Miss., Jul/Aug 1863.

Griffin, William, 2Lt., Age 42, Co. B, enlisted at Marlboro, December 4, 1861. Elected 2Lt., however, the regimental commander considered the soldier entirely unqualified for the position of an officer. Resigned due to unavoidable circumstances July 4, 1862.

Griffith, James, Pvt., Age 37, Co. E, enlisted at James Island December 1, 1862. Absent, sick in hospital and furloughed, October 15, 1862 - Jan/Feb 1863. Absent without leave Nov/Dec 1863. Absent, sick at home, furloughed, October 30 , 1863 - Jan/Feb 1864. Signed receipt roll for clothing at Gen. Hosp. No. 2, Columbia, S.C. July 30 and August 4, 1864. Captured near Nashville December 16, 1864. Sent to Military Prison, Louisville and transferred to Camp Chase January 4, 1865. Died of pneumonia March 21, 1865. Grave no. 1724 located 1/3 mile south of Camp Chase.

Griffith, W. C., Capt., Age 30, Co. C, enlisted at Georges Station, January 7, 1862. Promoted to Capt., May/Jun 1863. Company commander of Co. C. Commanded 24th Regiment at Nashville.

Grimes, W. A., Pvt., Age 25, Co. F, enlisted at Anderson January 13, 1862. Present for duty on all rolls. Admitted to Way Hospital Meridan, Miss., for wound January 25, 1865. Paroled at Greensboro May 1, 1865.

Grimsley, Irvin, Pvt., Age 35, Co. G, enlisted at Columbia, March 19, 1865. In hospital at Columbia Jan/Feb 1863. In hospital at Canton and Lockheart, Miss., May 21, 1863 - Jan/Feb 1864. Severely wounded, breast, at Atlanta July 22, 1864. At home, furloughed. Married July 1865. Died August 2, 1897. Josephine Grimsley, signed widow's pension application by mark.

Grooms, Absalar, Pvt., Age 26, Co. A, from Summerville, S.C., enlisted at Charleston July 7, 1862. Sick at Bell Hospital, Rome and Bell Hospital, Eufaula, Ala., September 17, 1863 - March 21, 1864. Present for duty August 31, 1864. Description: complexion, dark; hair, dark; eyes, dark; height, 5 ft. 6 in. Rebel deserter and refugee at Northern District, Department of the South, Provost Marshal, Charleston March 31, 1865. Took oath and was discharged March 27, 1865.

Gruver, Jno. T., Pvt., Age 20, Co. A, enlisted at Charleston, December 31, 1861. Present for duty May/Jun 1862. Transferred to Wilmington

Cavalry.

Hagood, J. C., Pvt., Age 37, Co. G, enlisted at Columbia March 19, 1862. Present for duty May/Jun 1862.

Hagood, Jno. D., Pvt., Co. G. Entry from original muster roll.

Hailey, William, Pvt., Age 30, Co. C. Discharged at Charleston in 1862. Entry from Memory Rolls at State Archives, Columbia, S.C.

Haithcock, Robert, Pvt., Co. B, enlisted at Marlboro March 31, 1862. Present through August 31, 1864. Although, shoe less and lame, he still marched. Captured at Shipp's Gap/Taylor's Ridge October 16, 1864. Sent to Military Prison, Louisville and transferred to Camp Douglas October 29, 1864. Enlisted in Co. I, 6th U. S. Volunteers April 2, 1865.

Hall, A. J., Pvt., Age 28, Co. F, from Iva, S.C., enlisted at Anderson March 28, 1862. Wounded at Chickamauga. Patient at hospital October 18, 1863 - Nov/Dec 1863. Absent without leave December 25, 1863 - August 31, 1864. Surrendered.

Hall, A. M., Pvt., Age 31, Co. F, enlisted at Anderson January 13, 1862. Wounded and captured at Jackson May 14, 1863. In Paroled Prisoners Camp at Demopolis June 5, 1863. In hospital and furloughed from hospital Sep/Oct 1863. Died of disease November 1863.

Hall, Bartley Dejarnett, Co. F, Age 28, born 1834 in Anderson County. Farmer. Parents: Father, Ezekial Hall I; Mother, Frances Evelyn Byrd Tucker. Died in 1902 in Anderson County, S.C. Entry from *Sons of Confederate Veterans Ancestor Album.*

Hall, Davis, Pvt., Age 31, Co. F, from Antrevele, S.C., Living. Individual was sick and left with citizen near Yazoo City, Miss. Never heard from again. Entry from Co. F, 24th S.C.V. Survivors Association roster and McGee ltr dtd August 8, 1863. Memory Rolls at State Archives, Columbia, S.C., indicate Hall "Surrendered 1865."

Hall, E., Pvt., Age 26, Co. F, Iva, S.C., enlisted at Anderson January 13, 1862 for 12 months. Conscripted for the war Jan/Feb 1863. Absent, sick, August 1864. Paroled at Greensboro May 1, 1865.

Hall, James, Pvt., Age 23, Co. B, enlisted at Marlboro December 4, 1861. Detailed to Commissary department August 63. Assigned duty with commissary department. Paroled at Greensboro May 1, 1865.

Hall, J. D., Pvt., Age 38, Co. F, enlisted at Abbeville, April 6, 1863. Patient at 1st Mississippi CSA Hospital, Jackson February 16, 1864. Transferred to General Hospital February 27, 1864. Detached service March 1, 1863 - Jan/Feb 1864. Surrendered at Citronelle, Ala., May 10, 1865. Paroled at Meridian, Miss., May 13, 1865.

Hall, John, Pvt., Age 31, Co,. G, enlisted at Columbia March 19, 1862. Discharged October 20, 1862.

Hall, John G., Pvt., Age 37, Co. F, from Iva, Anderson District, S.C., enlisted at Anderson January 13, 1862. Sick at hospital Jul/Aug 1863 -

Sep/Oct 1863. Absent without leave Nov/Dec 1863 - August 31, 1864. Wounded January 29, 1864. Description: complexion, fair; hair, light; eyes, blue; height, 5 ft. 11 in.; occupation, farmer. Discharged because of surgeon's certificate of disability October 10, 1864. Married May 24, 1854. Died August 19, 1893.

Hall, J. H., Pvt., Co. G. Entry from Memory Rolls at State Archives, Columbia, S.C.

Hall, Jno. L., Pvt., Co. G. Entry from original muster roll.

Hall, John M., 1Lt., Age 25, Co. F, enlisted at Anderson January 13, 1862. Promoted to 5Sgt., December 1, 1862. Promoted to 4Sgt., January 30, 1863. Elected 3Lt., May 28, 1863. Promoted to 1Lt., by Brig. Gen. S. Jones. Sick at hospital Jul/Aug 1863. Died of disease in hospital at Macon August 30, 1863.

Hall, J. W., Co. G. Entry from original muster roll.

Hall, L. M., Pvt., Age 46, Co. F, from Storeville, S.C., enlisted at Anderson January 13, 1862. Company commissary. Wounded near Jackson May 14, 1863. Detached to guard baggage at Macon by order of General Johnston. Name listed on muster roll of Co. D, 2d Battalion, Troops and Defenses, Camp Wright, Macon December 31, 1864. Surrendered 1865. Died July 1, 1902. Grave located at Cross Roads Church, Hall Township, Anderson County.

Hall, L. O., Pvt., Age 24, Co. F, from Anderson, enlisted at Anderson January 13, 1862. Discharged for inability due to chronic diarrhoea May 29, 1862. Enlisted April 11, 1863. Patient in hospital at Rome, Ga., Sep/Oct 1863. Absent without leave Nov/Dec 1863 - Mar/Aug 1864. Description: complexion, fair; hair, red; eyes, blue; height, 5 ft. 8 in; occupation, farmer. Absent without leave November 1863 - August 31, 1864. Paroled at Greensboro May 1, 1865.

Hall, M. H., 1Sgt., Age 34, Co. F, enlisted at Anderson June 13, 1862. Promoted to 4Sgt., December 1, 1862. Promoted 3Sgt., January 30, 1863. Promoted to 1Sgt., June 1, 1863. Captured at Missionary Ridge November 26, 1863. Died of disease in prison May 14, 1864.

Hall, Whitner, Pvt., Age 26, Co. F, enlisted at Anderson January 13, 1862. Killed in battle at Jackson May 14, 1863.

Hall, W. C., Pvt., Age 22, Co. F, enlisted at Anderson January 13, 1862. Killed in battle at Jackson, May 14, 1863.

Halverson, Joseph, Pvt., Age 18, Co. A, enlisted at Charleston February 14, 1862. Killed in battle at Jackson May 14, 1863. A promising young corporal and one of the best loved comrades in the company.

Hamilton, Edward G., Sgt., Age 24, Co. H, enlisted at Chester March 19, 1862. Musician. Signed receipt roll for clothing April 1, 1864. Wounded at Atlanta August 10, 1864. Absent with leave August 1864. Living.

Hamilton, Eli C., Corp., Age 22, Co. H, from Chester District, enlisted at

Chester March 19, 1862. Patient in hospital May/Jun 1862. Description: hair, light; eyes, blue; height, 5 ft. 10 in, occupation, farmer. Died of measles at Columbia July 4, 1862. Married December 20 1860. Widow Sallie A. Hamilton.

Hamilton, Edwin W,., Pvt., Age 20, Co. A, enlisted at Charleston, December 31, 1862. Sick in hospital September 17, 1863 - Jan/Feb 1864. Present for duty Jul/Aug 1864. Patient for Orchitis at 1st Mississippi CSA Hospital, Jackson November 8, 1864. Furloughed May 9, 1865.

Hamilton, James H., 2Lt., Age 26, Co. H, from Chester District, enlisted at Chester March 19, 1862. Absent, sick, May/Jun 1862. Description: hair, dark; eyes, blue; height, 5 ft. 11 in; occupation, mechanic. Died of fever at Columbia August 28, 1862. Margaret Ann Hamilton, Widow, filed claim for settlement.

Hamilton, Pleasant, Pvt., Age 37, Co. K, enlisted at Edgefield April 15, 1862. In hospital at Charleston Mar/Apr 1862. Died of disease in Fair Ground Hospital No. 2, Atlanta October 16, 1863. Buried October 17, 1863. Grave located in Oakland Cemetery, Confederate Section, Atlanta.

Hamilton, Theodore, Pvt., Age 25, Co. A, enlisted at Charleston December 31, 1861. Received court martial for overstaying leave and disobedience of orders April 22, 1863. Pled guilty and was sentenced to 17 days hard labor. Captured at Jackson May 14, 1862. Assigned to Paroled Prisoners Camp at Demopolis June 5, 1862. Absent without leave from parole camp Jul/Aug 1863. Arrested for overstaying leave of absence. Pay stopped from August 1 - September 15, 1863. Wounded at Atlanta. Reported missing July 20, 1862. Captured July 20, 1864. Died at Camp Chase.

Hamiter, Hilliard D., Capt., Age 40, Co. G, enlisted at Columbia March 19, 1862. Detailed to recruiting service Sep/Oct 1862. Promoted to Capt., February 23, 1863. Wounded at Chickamauga September 20, 1863. Furloughed February 18, 1963 - Jan/Feb, 1864. Severely wounded, head, in the battle of Atlanta July 22, 1864. Patient in hospital at Columbia, S.C. August 31, 1864. Accounted for by medical authority for absence, wounded, September 22, 1864.

Hammond, A. J., Maj., F&S, from Hamburg, S.C., appointed at Charleston, April 1, 1862. Raised Co. I, The Edgefield Light Infantry. Promoted to Major of Infantry April 1, 1862. Resigned for physical incapacity, rheumatism, unable to walk without crutches, December 16, 1862.

Hanberry, Decanna W., 2Lt., Age 28, Co. D, enlisted at Camp Gist, January 19, 1862. Furloughed Mar/Apr 1862. Absent, sick, furloughed Sep/Oct 1862. Sick in quarters Jan/Feb 1863. Resigned, unwilling to be examined for promotion April 29, 1863.

Hanna, J. T., Sgt., Age 35, Co. F, from Varennes, S.C., enlisted at Anderson

March 28, 1862. Promoted 1Corp., June 1, 1863. Promoted to 5Sgt., August 1, 1863. Absent, sick in hospital, October 15, 1863. Absent without leave July 1864. Reduced to ranks. Paroled at Greensboro May 1, 1865.

Harden, William H., Pvt., Co. I. Surrendered and paroled at Augusta May 28, 1865.

Hardy, E. Wilbur F., Pvt., Co. F, enlisted at Anderson March 21, 1863. Bounty due $50.00. Clerk, assigned to brigade quartermasters department. Killed in siege of Atlanta while on picket duty August 17, 1864.

Harley, William, Pvt., Age 21, Co. C, enlisted at Georges Station January 7, 1862. Discharged for rupture July 11, 1862. Joined cavalry and captured.

Harling, Elbert, Pvt., Co. K, enlisted at Edgefield May 13, 1862. Sent home, sick furlough, October 22 - Nov/Dec 1862. Entered hospital at Charleston Jan/Feb 1863. Patient in Walker's division hospital at Lauderdale, Miss., and Breckinridge's division hospital, Marion, Miss., July 21, 1863 - Nov/Dec 1863. Patient in hospital at Augusta July 24 - August 31, 1864. Patient at Ladies Hospital, Montgomery, November 15, 1864. Surrendered and paroled at Augusta May 19, 1865.

Harper, J. W., Pvt., Age 36, Co. E, enlisted at Salkehatchie January 16, 1862. Absent at home, sick, furloughed, October 20, 1863 - Jan/Feb 1864. Wounded at Dalton. Signed receipt roll for clothing September 9, 1864. Paroled at Greensboro May 1, 1865.

Harrington, James T., Pvt., Age 17, Co. A, enlisted at Charleston December 31, 1861. Absent without leave May 1, 1863 - January 14, 1864. (8 1/2 months). Sentence by court martial to stoppage of one months pay $11.00. Captured at Kingston, Ga., May 18, 1864. Sent to Military Prison, Louisville and transferred to Rock Island Barracks May 27, 1864. Enlisted in U. S. Navy June 10, 1864.

Harris, Morris, Sgt., Age 21, Co. A, enlisted at Charleston December 31, 1861. Sick in camp, furloughed, Nov/Dec 1863 - March 2, 1864. Absent, sick in hospital, Jul/Aug 1864. Captured near Stone Mountain/Oxford, Ga., July 22, 1864. Sent to Military Prison, Louisville and transferred to Camp Chase August 4, 1864. Paroled at Camp Chase and transferred to City Point via Point Lookout, Md., for exchange March 4, 1865.

Harrison, C. A., Pvt., Co. K, enlisted at Edgefield May 13, 1862. Rejected by surgeon. Died 1863.

Harrison, G. A., Pvt., Co. K. Surrendered and paroled at Augusta May 19, 1865.

Harrison, John E., Pvt., Co. K, enlisted at Edgefield April 1, 1862. Discharged by medical Board May/Jun 1862.

Harrison, J. William, Pvt., Co. K, enlisted at Edgefield May 13, 1863.

Musician. Patient in hospital May/Jun 1862. Absent, sick in hospital at Atlanta, August 31, 1863. Died in hospital at Atlanta September 20, 1863. Grave located at Oakland Cemetery, row 20, # 2, Atlanta, Ga.

Harrison, Robert, Pvt., Age 38, Co. E, from Colleton District, enlisted at Camp Gist January 16, 1862. Died at Secessionville August 31, 1862.

Hartin, John, Pvt., Age 35, Co. G, enlisted at Columbia March 19, 1862. Discharged by surgeon certificate June 11, 1862.

Hartson, W. C., Pvt., Age 35, Co. G, enlisted at Columbia March 19, 1862. Absent without leave Mar/Apr 1862. Entry canceled.

Harvey, W. M., Pvt., Age 37, Co. D, enlisted at Camp Gist January 19, 1862. Absent without leave Jan/Feb 1863. Patient in MacPhersonville hospital Mar/Apr 1863. $20.00 pay stopped by order of court martial for absent without leave May/Jun 1863. Absent, sick in hospital, Sep/Oct 1863. Died at home in Beaufort District November 5, 1863.

Hawkins, William G., 1Lt., Age 27, Co. A, enlisted at Charleston December 31, 1861. Promoted to 1Lt February 23, 1863. Captured near Jackson May 14, 1863. Assigned to Paroled Prisoners Camp at Demopolis June 5, 1863. Wounded, thigh, at Kennesaw Mountain and sent to hospital June 19, 1864. Medical authority (wounded) given for absence September 22, 1864. Paroled at Greensboro May 1, 1865.

Hazzard, John, Pvt., Co. A, enlisted at Camp Gist April 8, 1862. Reported missing supposed to be in hands of enemy July 20/22, 1864. Heard from and he will return to duty in a short time. Present on all rolls. Paroled at Greensboro May 1, 1865.

Headden, Joseph (Joe), Pvt., Co. C, enlisted at Pocotaligo February 24, 1863. Absent, sick in hospital, Sep/Oct 1863. Absent, sick in hospital at Summerville, Jul/Aug 1864. Paid from descriptive list July 7, 1864.

Heaton, David W., Pvt., Age 17, Co. C, from Reevesville, S.C., enlisted at Georges Station February 18, 1862. Slightly wounded, arm, at Calhoun Station May 16, 1864. Wounded at Franklin. Present on all rolls. Paroled at Greensboro May 1, 1865.

Heaton, George, Pvt., Age 40, Co. C, enlisted at Secessionville October 15, 1862. Died at Kingston Hospital, Ga., January 14, 1864.

Heaton, William, Pvt., Age 21, Co. C, enlisted at George's Station January 7, 1862. Died of disease at Charleston March 4, 1862.

Heaton, William M., Pvt., Age 22, Co. F, enlisted at Anderson April 8, 1864. Absent, sick, May/Jun 1862. Missing July 20, 1864. Killed in battle at Peachtree Creek July 20, 1864. Mary Ann Heaton, wife, filed claim for settlement January 11, 1865.

Haydon, Joe, Pvt., Co. C. Still living. Entry from roster prepared by company commander.

Hendrix, D. J., Pvt., Age 32, Co. G, enlisted at Columbia March 19, 1862. Absent without leave Mar/Apr 1862. One months pay stopped by order of court martial May/Jun 1863. Detailed to work on roads Nov/Dec 1863. Sick in hospital at Columbia April 18, 1864 - August 31, 1864. Signed receipt roll for clothing October 29, 1864. Patient at Concert Hall Hospital, Montgomery, Ala., November 15, 1864.

Henry, William, Pvt., Age 36, Co. D, enlisted at Camp Gist January 16, 1862. Transferred to Navy September 30, 1862.

Herndon, G. W., Pvt., Age 29, Co. E, enlisted at Camp Gist, March 20, 1862. Pay stopped for one month by order of court martial May/Jun 1863. Absent, sick in Breckinridge's Division Hospital No. 1, Lauderdale Springs, June 28, 1863 - Sep/Oct 1863. Patient in Blackie Hospital, Madison, Ga., Jan/Feb 1864. Died of disease June 20, 1864.

Herndon, Hardy, Pvt., Co. E, enlisted at Charleston January 16, 1862 for 12 months. Present January 16 to February 28, 1862.

Herndon, James E., Pvt., Age 23, Co. E, enlisted at Salkehatchie January 16, 1862. Present on all rolls. Killed in battle at Chickamauga September 20, 1863.

Herndon, Josiah L., Corp., Age 20, Co. E, from Midway Station, Barnwell District, S.C., enlisted at Charleston February 15, 1862. Absent without leave, returned October 1862. Wounded at Chickamauga. Captured at Chickamauga September 20, 1863. Sent to Military Prison, Louisville and transferred to Camp Douglas October 7, 1863. Description: complexion, fair; hair, light; eyes, blue; height, 6 ft. 1 in. Signed oath of allegiance to the United States and discharged June 16, 1865.

Herron, E. E., Pvt., Age 40, Co. F, enlisted at Anderson March 28, 1862. Died of disease, remittent fever, at Fever Bell Hospital, Rome, Ga., September 9, 1863.

Herron, V. W., Pvt., Age 36, Co. F, enlisted at Anderson March 28, 1862. Sick at James Island July 1862. Died of disease in hospital at Noonan, Ga., October 10, 1863. Grave located in Confederate Grave Yard near Milner, Pike County, Ga.

Hill, D. F., Maj., Age 30, Co. F and F&S, enlisted at Anderson January 13, 1862. Furloughed April 30, 1863. Wounded in the breast at Chickamauga. Absent, patient in hospital at Atlanta October 17, 1863. Appeared before major promotion examining board February 19, 1864. The board found him somewhat deficient in knowledge of tactics and regulations but in consideration of his approved conduct in battle, his influence in the regiment, his character as a gentleman and disciplinarian as presented by his commanding officer, the board recommended Capt. Hill for promotion to major. Date of appointment, March 2, 1864. Date of confirmation May 18, 1864. To take rank January 20, 1864. Date of acceptance April 12, 1864. Killed in battle at Jonesboro September 1, 1864. Buried at Lovejoy's Station on M & W Railroad in Clayton County, Georgia.

Hill, Jacob D., Musician, Co. C, enlisted at Pocotaligo March 2, 1863. Present for duty on all rolls through Jul/Aug 1864. Still living after the War.

Hill, Lawrence, Pvt., Age 13, Co. G, enlisted at Columbia March 19, 1862. Drummer boy. Absent, furloughed, May/Jun 1862.

Hinson, Evander A., Pvt., Age 21, Co. B, enlisted at Marlboro December 4, 1861. Entered hospital January 23, 1864. Died of disease June 17, 1864.

Hinson, James P., 1Sgt., Age 26, Co. B., enlisted at Charleston December 4, 1861. Detached service in South Carolina Jul/Aug - Nov/Dec 1863. Promoted 1Sgt., August 24, 1864. Paroled at Greensboro May 1, 1865. Deserted April 23, 1865.

Hinson, P. H., Corp., Co. B, enlisted at Marlboro April 13, 1861. Wounded September 20, 1863. Sick furlough October 15 - Nov/Dec 1863. Sent to hospital February 23, 1864. Severely wounded, arm, July 22, 1864. Signed receipt for clothing at 2d S.C. Hospital, Florence, S.C., December 14, 1864. Survived.

Hipott, Peter, Pvt., Co. C. Died at St. George. Entry from Dorchester County Enrollment book.

Hitt, Tucker L., Pvt., Age 31, Co. I, enlisted at Columbia March 20, 1862. Transferred to Sharpshooters October 16, 1862. Absent, sick at hospital and furloughed, April 5 - 30, 1863. Wounded at Franklin.

Hoagland, Charles, Pvt., Age 35, Co. G, enlisted at Columbia March 19, 1862. Died at Columbia April 19, 1862. Born in New York.

Hobbs, William E., Sgt., Co. K, enlisted at Edgefield April 15, 1862. Absent without leave Jan/Feb 1862. Wounded near Atlanta July 5, 1864. Died of gangrene at Academy Hospital, Forsythe, Ga., August 9, 1864. Buried as unknown soldier.

Hodge, Alvin, Pvt., Co. I, enlisted at Augusta April 1, 1864. Recruit bounty due ($50.00). Wounded July 22, 1864. Sent to hospital.

Hodge, G. W., Pvt., Co. H, enlisted at Chester March 29, 1863. Wounded. Present on all rolls. Paroled at Greensboro May 1, 1865.

Hodge, Moses, Pvt., Age 28, Co. A, enlisted at Charleston February 17, 1862. Absent without leave from September 8, 1862. Arrested and incarcerated in Charleston Jail for desertion December 17, 1862. Released from arrest and returned to duty with his company by command of General Beauregard April 25, 1863. Captured at Jackson May 14, 1863. Assigned to Paroled Prisoners in Camp at Demopolis June 5, 1863. Absent without leave June 1 - October 6, 1863. Absent, sick in hospital, Jul/Aug 1864. Description: complexion, dark; hair, dark; eyes, blue; height, 5 ft. 10 in. Reported to Northern District, Department of the South, US Provost Marshal, Charleston March 31, 1865 as rebel deserter or refugee. Took oath and discharged.

Hodges, Alfred, Pvt., Age 18, Co. I. Entry from Memory Rolls at State

Archives, Columbia, S.C.

Hodges, John H., Pvt., Age 23, Co. B, enlisted at Marlboro March 22, 1862. Signed receipt roll for clothing April 1, 1864. Present on all rolls. Died of disease June 30, 1864. Buried June 30, 1864. Grave located in Oakland Cemetery, Confederate Section, Atlanta.

Hodges, R. C., Pvt., Age 18, Co. B, enlisted at Charleston December 4, 1861. Present on all rolls. Paroled at Greensboro May 1, 1865.

Hogarth, Edmond A., Pvt., Age 18, Co. D, from Beaufort District, enlisted at Camp Gist January 19, 1862. Sick, furloughed, Sep/Oct 1862. Furloughed, approved by General Johnston, Jan/Feb 1864. Wounded in battle at Franklin. Captured near Nashville December 16, 1864. Sent to Military Prison, Louisville and transferred to Camp Chase January 4, 1865. Description: complexion, dark; hair, dark; eyes, brown; height 5 ft. 10 in. Signed oath of allegiance to the United States at Camp Chase June 12, 1865.

Hoke, John C., Pvt., Age 26, Co. H, from York District, enlisted at Chester March 19, 1862. Absent, sick, May/Jun 1864. Absent, at Secessionville as a guard, Nov/Dec 1862. Wounded at Chickamauga September 20, 1863. Absent, patient in hospital at Marietta, Sep/Oct 1863. Wounded at Nashville. Captured near Nashville December 16, 1864. Sent to Military Prison, Louisville and transferred to Camp Douglas December 24, 1864. Discharged June 19, 1865.

Holiday, Thomas, Pvt., Co. K, enlisted at Edgefield March 19, 1863. Confined in guard house Mar/Apr 1863. Sent to hospital May 7, 1862. Died at Hospital No. 2, Atlanta, May 14, 1864. Buried May 16, 1864. Grave located in Oakland Cemetery, Atlanta.

Holaday, William J., Pvt., Age 20, Co. I, enlisted at James Island May 17, 1862. Wounded, patient in hospital, June 21, 1864. Wounded, gunshot left thigh, fracture, upper third, severe, at Franklin November 30, 1864. Captured at Franklin December 18, 1864. Died of wounds in No. 1, USA, General Hospital, Nashville March 17, 1865. Marital status single. Reference, Miss Mary Harder, Perkins Store, S. C. Left no effects. Grave located at the City Cemetery, Nashville. Grave No. 12592.

Holliday, William, Pvt., Age 18, Co. I. Killed in battle at Atlanta. Entry from Memory Rolls at State Archives, Columbia, S.C., and listed in *Edgefield Advertiser.*

Hollingsworth, P., Pvt., Co. K, enlisted at Edgefield March 14, 1862. Discharged by medical board May/Jun 1862.

Hollingsworth, Thomas, Pvt., Co. K, enlisted at Edgefield March 15, 1863. Absent without leave May 7, 1862 - Jul/Aug 1863. Absent without leave January 20, 1864 - August 31, 1864. Surrendered and paroled at Augusta May 18, 1865.

Hollingsworth, William H., Pvt., Co. K. Entry from Memory Rolls at State Archives, Columbia, S.C.

Hollis, John J., Corp., Age 26, born September 6, 1835, Co. H, from Richburg, Chester County, S.C., enlisted at Chester March 19, 1862. Musician. Brother of Peter T. Hollis. Absent, sick, May/Jun 1862. Promoted to 4Corp., June 1, 1864. Signed receipt for clothing September 9, 1864. Paroled at Greensboro May 1, 1865.

Hollis, Peter T., Ensign, Age 18, Co. H, from Carmel Hill near Richburg, Chester County, enlisted at Chester March 19, 1862. Color Sergeant. Appointed special grade of Ensign as color bearer. Brother of John J. Hollis. Absent, sick, May/Jun 1862. Wounded at Chickamauga. Wounded at Kennesaw Mountain. Promoted Ensign April 18, 1864. Wounded in the back August 2, 1864. Admitted to St. Mary's Hospital, La Grange August 3, 1864. Disabled for two months. Rejoined regiment at Nashville. Description: complexion, dark; hair, dark; eyes, dark; height, 6 ft. Captured at Nashville December 16, 1864. Sent to Military Prison, Louisville and transferred to Johnson's Island December 22, 1864. Signed oath of allegiance to the United States and released June 16, 1865. Married Victoria Gaston in 1869. Fathered 8 children. Elected to South Carolina Legislature in 1893.

Hollis, T. J., Co. H. Entry from *Chester County Heritage History*.

Holloway, John B., Pvt., Age 18, born January 12, 1846, Co. I, from McCormick, S.C., enlisted at Abbeville February 20, 1864. Recruit bounty due $50.00. Returned from hospital January 14, 1865. Paroled at Greensboro May 1, 1865.

Holloway, J. S., Pvt., Co. K, enlisted at Edgefield May 13, 1862. Rejected by surgeon.

Holloway, Thomas, Pvt., Age 40, Co. G, enlisted at Columbia, March 19, 1862. Absent without leave Nov/Dec 1862. Captured at Jackson May 14, 1863. Assigned to Paroled Prisoners Camp at Demopolis June 5, 1863. Left sick in camp on retreat from Missionary Ridge. Captured at Missionary Ridge November 25, 1862. Sent to Military Prison, Louisville and transferred to Rock Island December 26, 1863. Died of diarrhoea January 16, 1864. Grave No. 204, south of Prison Barracks, Rock Island.

Holmes, Alfred, 1Lt., F&S, from Hamburg, S.C., enlisted at Camp Gist April 1, 1862. Appointed Ordnance Sergeant May 1, 1862. Appointed Adjutant, 1Lt., to take rank April 4, 1864. Accepted May 7, 1864. Paroled at Greensboro May 1, 1865. Married November 27, 1877. Died October 24, 1905. Widow Ellen C. Holmes.

Holmes, Edward M., Pvt., born 1845, Co. K, enlisted at Edgefield March 26, 1864. Wounded, right shoulder, near Atlanta July 22, 1864. Furloughed from hospital for 30 days July 27, 1864. Wounded at

Franklin. Paroled at Greensboro May 1, 1865.

Holmes, J. A., Pvt., Co. I, enlisted at Corinth June 8, 1864. Transferred by order of General Johnston from Co. B, 14th Miss., to Co. I, 24th S.C., July 14, 1864. Paroled at Greensboro May 1, 1865.

Holmes, J. Ervin, Sgt., Co. K, enlisted at Edgefield April 15, 1862. Promoted to Sgt., August 17, 1864. Slightly wounded at Chickamauga September 20, 1863. Wounded, admitted to Way Hospital, Meridian, Miss., January 20, 1865. Present on all rolls. Paroled at Greensboro May 1, 1865.

Holson, Joseph Madison, Pvt., Age 18, Co. I, enlisted at Columbia, April 15, 1862. Slightly wounded, hand, at Resaca May 17, 1864. Admitted to hospital. Paroled at Greensboro May 1, 1865.

Horn, Christopher, Pvt., Co. K, enlisted at Edgefield June 1, 1862. Present for duty Nov/Dec 1862. Deserter. Sgt. J. E. Morgan and Pvt. J. E. Holmes were sent to Ashville, N.C., to arrest and return Pvt. Horn to the regiment May 7, 1863.

Horn, David M., Sgt., Age 19, Co. C, from Georges Station, enlisted at Georges Station January 7, 1862. Patient at CSA General Military Hospital, No. 41, Wilmington, for pneumonia January 10 - 23, 1863. Absent, sick in hospital, February 24, 1864. Wounded, simple flesh wound of left ankle, at Franklin November 30. 1864. Captured December 17, 1864. Admitted to No. 1, USA General Hospital, Nashville December 26, 1864 - January 17, 1865. Sent to Military Prison, Louisville and transferred to Camp Chase January 18, 1865. Description: complexion, dark; hair, dark; eyes, gray; height 5 ft. 7 in. Signed oath of allegiance to the United States June 13, 1865.

Horn, James, Pvt., Co. K, enlisted at Edgefield April 15, 1862. Severely wounded at Secessionville and sent to the hospital June 16, 1862. Furloughed home, returned to duty Sep/Oct 1863. In hospital February 23, 1864. Patient in hospital May 18, 1864 - August 31, 1864. Signed, by mark, receipt roll for clothing at Ladies General Hospital, No. 3, Columbia July 27, 1864.

Horn, J. S. W., Pvt., Age 27, Co. C, enlisted at Georges Station January 7, 1862. Detached service to Gun Boat November 1862. Detailed until further orders to J. M. Eason Gun boat August 11, 1863. Present at Eason's December 20, 1864.

Horn, Kit., Pvt., Co. K. Deserted at Dalton in 1864. Entry from list prepared by company commander after the war.

Horne, Richard, Pvt., Co. K, enlisted at Dalton, Ga., January 24, 1864. Absent without leave Jan/Feb 1864.

Horton, Henry C., Sgt., Age 33, Co. D, enlisted at Camp Gist January 19, 1862. Sick, furloughed, Sep/Oct 1862. Sick, patient in hospital at Lauderdale Springs July - September 13, 1863. Died September 13,

1864.

Horton, Henry, Pvt., Co. D. Wounded at Atlanta. Living. Entry from Memory Rolls at State Archives, Columbia, S.C.

Houtzinger, Frank, Pvt., Co. G. Entry from Memory Rolls at State Archives, Columbia, S.C.

Howard, Dan H., Pvt., Age 18, born April 18, 1845, Co. F, from Whitehall, S.C., enlisted at Anderson, November 25, 1862. Employed in salt works Mar/Apr 1863. Wounded, patient in hospital and furloughed from hospital Sep/Oct 1863. Absent without leave October 25, 1863 - Jan/Feb 1864. Sick, in hospital at Columbia, March 1 - August 31, 1864. Signed receipt roll for clothing at General Hospital No. 2, Columbia July 12 and August 5, 1864. Surrendered. Discharged at Columbia, S.C., April 9, 1865. Resided at Abbeville, S.C., after the war.

Howard, James W., Pvt., Age 35, Co. I, enlisted at Columbia March 20, 1862. Detailed to the brigade commissary department July - October 1863. Extra or daily duty with brigade commissary department Jul/August 1864. Signed receipt roll for clothing September 9, 1864. Present for duty on all rolls. Paroled at Greensboro May 1865.

Howe, John W., 1Sgt., Age 36, Co. A, enlisted at Charleston, December 31, 1861. Slightly wounded, side, June 19, 1864. Present for duty on all rolls. Paroled at Greensboro May 1, 1865.

Howel, L. M., Pvt., Age 19, Co. F, from Georgia, enlisted at Columbia February 13, 1862. Substitute for J. M. Craft February 13, 1862. Transferred to Smith's Batt. Sharpshooters August 10 - December 20, 1862. Patient in hospital October 14, 1863. Died of disease November 22, 1863.

Howel, M. P. L., Pvt., Co. F, from Georgia, enlisted at Anderson April 4, 1862. Transferred to Smith's Batt. Sharpshooters August 10, 1862. Arrested and confined in Charleston County jail for robbery until brought to trial December 20, 1862. Provost Marshal ordered to return Pvt. Howel to his company if he had not been tried by court martial prior to January 19, 1863. Substitute for L. M. Howell. Died of disease November 22, 1863. Grave located in the Confederate Section, Oak Hill Cemetery, Newman, Ga.

Howel, R. P., Pvt., Age 35, Co. F, enlisted at Anderson March 27, 1863. Present on all rolls. Present for duty August 31, 1864. Assigned as pontoon train teamster by order of General Johnston. Surrendered 1865. Died in the asylum in 1887.

Howell, John Joseph, Pvt., Age 14, born July 28, 1848, Co. C, enlisted at Augusta May 6, 1863. Suffered slight flesh wound. Description: complexion, light; hair, light; eyes, blue; height, 4 ft. 2 in; occupation, student. Discharged, under eighteen years of age, October 16, 1863.

Howell, John R., Sgt., Age 41, Co. A, enlisted at Charleston December 31,

1861. Wounded and captured in engagement near Jackson May 14, 1863. Assigned to Paroled Prisoners Camp at Demopolis June 15, 1863. Detailed to brigade Quartermaster Department Jan/Feb 1864 - May 11, 1865. Paroled at Greensboro May 1, 1865.

Howle, Henry R., Pvt., Age 18, Co. I, enlisted at Montgomery, Ala., June 8, 1863. Sick in division hospital October 10 - 31, 1863. Paroled at Greensboro May 1, 1865.

Hubbard, Martin, Pvt., Co. B, from Cheraw, S.C., enlisted at Marlboro April 1, 1863. Conscript. Wounded at Chickamauga. Slightly wounded at Calhoun May 17, 1864. Gunshot wound through the left fore arm, ball passing between the bones. Granted 60 day furlough by Medical Examining Board May 30, 1864. Signed receipt roll for clothing September 9, 1864. Paroled at Greensboro May 1, 1865. Deserted April 25, 1865.

Hudson, A. B., Pvt., Age 29, Co. E, enlisted at Charleston February 26, 1862. Captured at Battery Island May 21, 1862. Sent to Fort Columbus, New York Harbor aboard Steamer *Arago* from Hilton Head August 14, 1862. Transferred from Fort Columbus to Fort Delaware August 23, 1862. Exchanged at Aikens Landing, Va., October 12, 1862. Granted 30 days leave from General Hospital Camp Winder, Richmond October 30, 1862. Wounded at Chickamauga September 20, 1863. Killed in battle at Atlanta August 10, 1863.

Hudson, B. C., Pvt., Age 28, Co. E, enlisted at Salkehatchie January 16, 1862. Captured at Battery Island May 21, 1862. Sent to Fort Columbus, New York Harbor aboard Steamer *Arago* from Hilton Head August 14, 1862. Sent from Fort Columbus to Fort Delaware August 23, 1862. Died of disease at Fort Delaware September 4, 1862.

Hudson, Joshua, Pvt., Age 31, Co. E. Died in "Northan Prison." Entry from roster prepared by Capt. Joseph K. Risher, Company Commander, Co. E.

Hudson, William J., Pvt., Age 20, Co. E, enlisted at Camp Gist March 20, 1862. Wounded at Chickamauga September 20, 1863. Absent without leave Nov/Dec 1863 - February 13, 1864. Wounded along route to Atlanta. Sick in hospital June 20 - Jul/Aug 1864. Signed, by mark, receipt roll for clothing at General Hospital, No. 1, Columbia, S.C., August 1, 1864. Paroled at Greensboro May 1, 1865.

Hughey, Miles, Pvt., Co. D, enlisted at Camp Gist April 9, 1862. Detached service, driving wagon to Selma, Ala., Mississippi, and other places, by order of General Johnston August 1, 1863 - August 1864.

Hughey, William R., Pvt., Co. D, enlisted at Camp Gist April 9, 1862. Sick, furloughed, Sep/Oct 1863. Absent without leave October 7 - December 1862. Pay stopped by sentence of court martial. Absent without leave August 30 - October 6, 1863. Absent, sick in hospital, Jul/Aug 1864.

Paroled at Greensboro May 1, 1865.

Hunsinger, F., Pvt., Age 33, Co. G, born in Germany, enlisted at Columbia March 19, 1862. Present on all rolls. Killed in battle at Chickamauga September 20, 1863.

Hunt, Briton, Pvt., Age 18, Co. C, enlisted at Camp Dalton February 10, 1864. Bounty due $50.00 bounty. Captured at Cassville, Ga., May 17, 1864. Sent to Military Prison, Louisville and transferred to Rock Island May 25, 1864. Enlisted U. S. Navy June 10, 1864.

Hunt Elijah, Pvt., Co. C. Captured near Kennesaw. Supposed to be dead. Entry from roster prepared by Capt. W. C. Griffith, Company Commander.

Hunt, John, Pvt., Age 26, Co. C, enlisted at Georges Station January 17, 1862. Absent, sick in Hospital at Yazoo City, May/Jun 1863. Furloughed February 22, 1864. Absent, wounded, in hivision hospital Jul/Aug 1864.

Hunt, Joseph, Pvt., Co. G, enlisted at Columbia March 19, 1862. Killed in battle at Secessionville June 16, 1862.

Hunt, Thomas, Pvt., Age 40, Co. G, enlisted at Columbia April 12, 1862. Absent sick.

Hussey, Edward L., Pvt., Age 29, Co. C, enlisted at Charleston March 2, 1862. Detached on gun boat construction from June 1862 to January 17, 1864. Wounded at Franklin. Paroled at Greensboro May 1, 1865. Died at St. George, S.C., 1903.

Hussey, Simeon A., Pvt., Age 23, Co. C, from Branchville, enlisted at Charleston March 13, 1862. Absent sick June 30 - October 31, 1863. Captured at Chickamauga September 20, 1863. Sent to Military Prison, Louisville and transferred to Camp Douglas October 4, 1863. Description: complexion, fair; hair, auburn; eyes, blue; height, 5 ft. 8 in. Signed oath of allegiance to the United States and discharged June 16, 1865. Died in Florida in May 1929.

Hutchinson, J. A., Sgt., Age 27, Co. F, enlisted at Columbia January 13, 1862. Promoted 2Sgt., November 7, 1862. Promoted 1Sgt., January 30, 1863. Killed in battle at Jackson May 14, 1863.

Hutchinson, S. A., Corp., Age 31, Co. F, enlisted at Columbia January 13, 1862. Discharged by substitute, T. R. Brown, September 18, 1862. Description: complexion, fair; hair, dark; eyes, blue; height, 5 ft. 8 in; occupation, farmer.

Hutto, Jacob, Pvt., Age 43, Co. C, enlisted at Camp Gist March 7, 1863. Killed in battle at Chickamauga September 20, 1863.

Hutto, William Pvt., Age 31, Co. C, enlisted at Georges Station January 7, 1862. Absent, sick, furloughed, Sep/Oct 1863. Absent without leave Nov/Dec 1863. Wounded at Kennesaw, Ga. Absent, wounded, furloughed, August 20, 1864.

Hyatt, Alfred, Pvt., Age 28, Co. C, enlisted at Georges Station January 17, 1862. Absent, sick, May/Jun 1863. Detached on gunboat at Charleston Sep/Oct 1863. Wounded at Marietta. Absent, wounded, furloughed, July 12, 1864.

Hyatt, Jeff., Pvt., Co. C. Supposed to be living. Entry from roster held by Citadel Archives.

Hyatt, Joseph K.,., Pvt., Co. C, enlisted at Camp Dalton December 16, 1863. Absent, sick, patient in hospital January 20, 1864. Absent, sick, furloughed, August 18, 1864. Still living.

Hyatt, J. M., Pvt., Age 30, Co. C, enlisted at George's Station January 7, 1862. Absent without leave from May 6 - Sep/Oct 1863. Absent, sick, Nov/Dec 1863. Absent, sick, furloughed, December 12, 1863. Died June 26, 1864. Grave located in Oakland Cemetery, Confederate Section, Atlanta. Last name maybe shown as "Natt".

Hyatt, Mellard, Pvt., Age 30, Co. C, enlisted at George's Station January 7, 1862. Mortally wounded in battle at Kennesaw Mountain. Died from effects of wound July 3, 1864.

Hyatt, Peter, Pvt., Age 17, Co. C, enlisted at George's Station January 7, 1862. Signed by mark. Present on all rolls through August 1864. Signed receipt roll for clothing September 9, 1864.

Hyatt, W. R., Pvt., Age 25, Co. A, enlisted at Charleston December 31, 1861. Discharged for disability June 19, 1862.

Infinger, Daniel W. Pvt., Age 32, Co. C, enlisted at Charleston January 25, 1862. Severely wounded, head, at Kennesaw Mountain. Absent, wounded, furloughed, July 10, 1864. Paroled at Greensboro May 1, 1865.

Irvin, Pvt., Co., A. Captured at Nashville. Entry from article in the *Daily Courier*.

Jackson, James W., Sgt., Age 26, Co. A, enlisted at Charleston December 31, 1861. Signed receipt roll for clothing April 1, 1864. Present on all rolls through Jul/Aug 1864. Wounded at Shipp's Gap/Taylor's Ridge. Fell into the hands of the enemy; although, severely wounded, his leg was broken, made good his escape from the enemy and arrived safely home to Charleston. Admitted to 1 Div 15 AC Hospital October 16, 1864. Left with a citizen at Lafayette, Ga., October 18, 1864. Complexion, dark; hair, dark; eyes, dark; height, 5 ft. 6 in. Reported himself as a deserter to U.S. Provost Marshal, Northern District, Department of the South, Charleston. Took the oath of allegiance to the United States and was discharged March 11, 1865.

Jackson, Oliver S., Pvt., Age 30, Co. C, enlisted at Charleston March 18, 1862. Died May 21, 1862. Grave located at Magnolia Cemetery, Charleston.

Jacobs, Asbury B., Pvt., Co. B, enlisted at Marlboro April 14, 1862. Under arrest, one month wage forfeited by court martial Nov/Dec 1862. Present on all rolls through August 1864. Paroled at Greensboro May 1, 1865. Deserted April 25, 1865.

Jacobs, John P., Cook, Age 21, Co. B, enlisted at Marlboro December 4, 1861. Absent without leave Nov/Dec 1862. Two months pay stopped for absence without leave by order of court martial May/Jun 1863. Absent without leave September 22 - December 1863. Three months pay stoppage for absent without leave by order of court martial Jan/Feb 1864. Present for duty August 31, 1864.

Jennings, Henry T., Pvt., Age 35, Co. I, enlisted at Marlboro December 4, 1861. Rejected by surgeon April 21, 1862. Enlisted at Pocotaligo, March 10, 1863. Captured at Chickamauga September 20, 1863. Sent to Military Prison, Louisville and transferred to Camp Douglas October 1863. Paroled at Camp Douglas exchanged at City Point March 14, 1865. Admitted to Receiving and Wayside Hospital, or General Hospital No. 9, Richmond March 12, 1865 and transferred to Jackson Hospital, Richmond March 22, 1865. Diagnosis scarbutis. Furloughed for 60 days March 27, 1865. Surrendered and paroled at Augusta May 24, 1865.

Johnson, Andrew, Pvt., Age 26, Co. E, enlisted at Salkehatchie January 16, 1862. Wounded at Chickamauga September 20, 1863. Absent without leave Nov/Dec 1863. Slightly wounded, breast, July 20/22, 1864. Captured near Nashville December 16, 1864. Sent to Military Prison, Louisville and transferred to Camp Chase January 6, 1865. Description: complexion, dark; hair, black; eyes, dark; height 5 ft. 9 in. Signed oath of allegiance to the United States June 13, 1865.

Johnson, Isaac, Corp., Age 24, Co. B, enlisted at Charleston, December 4, 1861. Present on all rolls. Killed in battle at Peachtree Creek July 20, 1864.

Johnson, Isaac, Pvt., Age 27, Co. E, enlisted at Salkehatchie January 16, 1862. Present on all rolls. Killed in battle at Chickamauga September 20, 1863.

Johnson, J., Pvt., Co. E, enlisted at Colleton, December 23, 1861. Nurse at hospital. Absent with leave Sep/Oct 1862.

Johnson, John C., Pvt., Co. H, enlisted at Chester March 19, 1862. Assigned as Secessionville Hospital steward, March 1862 - October 1863. Sick, patient in division hospital and hospital at Atlanta, October 1863 - February 1864. Detached service as hospital druggist at Griffin, Ga., March - August 1864. Furloughed for 60 days by Examining Board, Griffin March 16, 1865. Signed receipt roll for clothing at Direction Hospital, Griffin, Ga., June 30, 1864. Died of disease.

Johnson, R., Capt., Age 35, Co. B, enlisted at Charleston, December 4, 1861. Promoted Capt., May/Jun 1863. Absent, granted sick leave (at home) Sep/Oct 1863. Furloughed March 5, 1864. Severely wounded, right arm amputated, at battle of Atlanta July 22, 1864. Furloughed from hospital August 4, 1864. Died 1884.

Johnson, Thomas, Pvt., Age 20, Co. A, enlisted at Charleston December 31, 1861. Sick, patient in hospital at Charleston, Nov/Dec 1862. Absent without leave September 8 - December 16, 1862. Captured near Marietta, July 2, 1864. Sent to Military Prison, Louisville and transferred to Camp Douglas July 18, 1864. Applied for oath of allegiance, claims to have been loyal, forced to enlist in Rebel Army to avoid conscript and deserted to avail himself of amnesty proclamation. Paroled at Camp Douglas and exchanged at Point Lookout February 20, 1865. Admitted to Receiving and Wayside Hospital or General Hospital No. 9, Richmond, February 28, 1865 and sent to Camp Lee March 1, 1865.

Johnson, William, Col. Sgt., Co. H. Died November 4, 1863. Entry from UDC Pamphlet, *Confederate Dead Buried in Charleston*, dated May 3, 1880.

Johnston, B. M., Pvt., Age 28, Co. C, enlisted at Georges Station January 17, 1862. Wounded at Chickamauga September 20, 1863. Absent, wounded and furloughed, Sep/Oct 1863. Slightly wounded, shoulder, at Marietta July 20/22, 1864. Paroled at Greensboro May 1, 1865.

Johnston, Jesse C., Pvt., Age 20, Co. D, enlisted at Hardeeville January 16, 1862. Description: complexion, dark; hair, black; eyes, black; height, 6 ft. 2 in; occupation, farmer. Died in Tennessee October 31, 1863. Mother, Elizabeth Johnston, filed claim for settlement August 30, 1864.

Jones, Gabriel Capers, Pvt., Age 35, Co. G, enlisted at Columbia March 19, 1862. Received court martial for passing a petition to elect company commander and lieutenant. Found guilty but received no sentence, April 22, 1863. Sick, patient in hospital and furloughed September 1, 1863 - August 31, 1864. Died of disease at home September 22, 1864.

Jones, G. R., Pvt., Age 18, Co. G, enlisted at Columbia March 19, 1862. Present for duty through May/Jun 1862.

Jones, Joseph A., Pvt., Age 19, Co. B, enlisted at Marlboro December 4, 1861. Color Corporal. Absent, sick in hospital at Atlanta, Sep/Oct - Nov/Dec 1863. Present for duty August 31, 1864. Killed in battle at Franklin November 30, 1864. Grave located in Section 85, Grave 33, Confederate Cemetery, Franklin.

Jones, Jesse Stancel, Lt. Col., Age 27, Co. E & F&S, a farmer from Ashton, S.C., enlisted at Charleston January 16, 1862. Commanded company known as The Colleton Guards and Captain Jones' Company. Promoted to major June 11, 1863. Severely wounded, shoulder, at Chickamauga September 20, 1863. Absent, wounded, Nov/Dec 1863. Promoted to lieutenant colonel January 20, 1864. Examined thoroughly in tactics and army regulations. The Board, satisfied with the result of the examination, recommended promotion February 20, 1864. Date of appointment, March 28, 1864. Date of confirmation May 18, 1864. To take rank (Date of rank) January 20, 1864. Date of acceptance April 11, 1864. Mortally wounded in battle at Franklin. Received a gun shot wound to jaw and neck. Died at the division hospital, A. M. Harrison House, during the night of December 7, 1864. Grave located at Cross Swamp Church near Islandton, S.C. A marker inscribed "JSJ" exists in the Confederate Cemetery at Franklin.

Jones, Nelson, Pvt., Age 30, Co. G, enlisted at Columbia March 19, 1862. Sick Sep/Oct 1862 - Jan/Feb 1862. Wounded at Chickamauga September 20, 1863. Absent, patient in hospital and furloughed, September 1863 - Jan/Feb 1864. Signed receipt roll, by mark, for clothing at General Hospital No. 1, Columbia, S.C., January 13, 1864. Assigned post duty at Columbia February 29 - August 31, 1864.

Jones, Samuel, Pvt., Age 30, Co. E, enlisted at Salkehatchie January 16, 1862. Discharged by surgeon for disability, hernia, May 21, 1862. Description: complexion, dark; hair, black; eyes, black; height, 5 ft. 8 in; occupation, farmer.

Jones, S. A., Pvt., Co. G. Entry from Memory Rolls at State Archives, Columbia, S.C.

Jones, William P., Pvt., Age 43, Co. I, enlisted at Columbia March 20, 1862. Present on all rolls. Killed in battle at Chickamauga September 20, 1863.

Jones, William S., Pvt., Co. F, from Georgia, enlisted at Anderson April 22, 1863. Captured at Missionary Ridge November 25, 1863. Sent to Military Prison, Louisville and transferred to Rock Island December 10, 1863. Died of erysipelas April 2, 1864. Grave located at Rock Island Confederate cemetery no. 975.

Jones, William T., Pvt., Age 22, Co. F, enlisted at Pocataligo March 21, 1863. Captured at Missionary Ridge, November 25, 1863. Sent to Military Prison, Louisville and transferred to Rock Island December 16, 1863. Signed oath of allegiance to the United States and released March 7, 1865.

Jones, William W., Pvt., Age 22, Co. B, enlisted at Marlboro December 4, 1861. Detached as pioneer by order of Maj. Gen. Walker from Nov/Dec 1863 through August 31, 1864. Wounded at Atlanta. Died of disease at home.

Judy, David, Pvt., Age 36, Co. C, enlisted at Georges Station January 7, 1862. Absent, sick in hospital, Jan/Feb 1863. Absent, sick in Lauderdale Springs Hospital, Jul/Aug - Nov/Dec 1863. Absent sick, furloughed, August 20, 1864.

Judy, George W., Pvt., Age 22, Co. C, from St. George, enlisted at Georges

Station January 7, 1862. One month pay stopped by court martial May/Jun 1862. Absent, sick, at Rome Sep/Oct 1863. Absent without leave Nov/Dec 1863. Absent, sick in hospital, Jul/Aug 1864. Signed receipt for clothing at 3d Gen Hosp., Augusta October 10, 1864. Still living. Discharged April 1865. Died August 28, 1919. Widow Annie L. Judy.

Judy, Jacob, Pvt., Co. C. Entry from Dorchester County Enrollment Book.

Judy, James, Pvt., Age 29, Co. C, enlisted at Georges Station January 7, 1862. One month pay stopped by order of court martial May/Jun 1863. Absent, sick patient in hospital at Rome, Sep/Oct 1863. Wounded at Franklin. Admitted for diarrhoea to Way Hospital, Meridian, Miss January 12, 1865. Transferred to hospital at Marion, Ala.

Judy, John, Pvt., Age 18, Co. C, enlisted at Georges Station January 7, 1862. One month pay stopped by court martial May/Jun 1863. Wounded at Chickamauga September 20, 1863. Furloughed. Killed in battle at Atlanta August 3, 1864. Buried on Mr. Ripley's lot one mile north of passenger depot on right, Peachtree Street Road, Atlanta, Georgia.

Judy, Lewis, Pvt., Age 26, Co. C, enlisted at Georges Station March 18, 1862. Wounded at Chickamauga September 20, 1863. Furloughed. Present on all other rolls. Paroled at Greensboro, N.C., May 1, 1865.

Judy, William, Sr., Pvt., Age 46, Co. C, enlisted at Georges Station January 17, 1862. Absent without leave Jun/Oct 1862. Detached service with pay (guard duty) Nov/Dec 1862. Absent, detailed to hospital at Newman, Ga., Jul/Aug 1864. Supposed to be living.

Judy, William, Jr., Pvt., Age 16, Co., C, enlisted at Pocotaligo February 24, 1863. Wounded at Chickamauga September 20, 1863. Absent, wounded, patient in hospital and furloughed at Columbia Sep/Oct 1863 - Jul/Aug 1864. Signed receipt for clothing at Newsome Hosp., Cassville, Ga., November 9, 1864. Signed receipt roll, by mark, for clothing at Newsome Hospital, Cassville, Ga., November 9, 1865. Admitted to CSA General Hospital, No. 11, Charlotte, with v.s. upper extremities, right, February 6 - 18, 1865.

Junkin, W., Pvt., Co. G, enlisted at Columbia May 1, 1863. Assigned to company from camp of instruction, Columbia. Absent, sick at home, February 18, 1864. Absent, sick, patient in hospital, June - August 31, 1864.

Justi, William, Pvt., Age 25, Co. G, enlisted at Columbia March 19, 1862. Sick, patient in hospital, May/Jun 1862. Sick in quarters Sep/Oct 1862. Absent without leave and pay stopped for 42 days Nov/Dec 1862. One month's pay stopped by order of court martial May/Jun 1863. Patient in hospital at Lauderdale, Miss., Jul/Aug 1863. Left sick in camp during retreat from Missionary Ridge. Captured at Missionary Ridge November 28, 1863. Sent to Military Prison, Louisville and transferred to Rock

Island December 3, 1863. Released May 16, 1865. Description: complexion, light; hair, light; eyes, blue; height, 5 ft. 7 in.

Kease, B. M., Pvt., Age 16, Co. D, enlisted at Camp Gist March 15, 1862. Present for duty May/Jun 1862.

Kee, Hiram, Pvt., Age 46, Co. H., enlisted at Chester March 19, 1862. Absent, sick since reported May/Jun - Sep/Oct 1862. Absent, sick, Jul/Aug 1863. Wounded at Chickamauga. Drove wagon in pontoon train March - August 31, 1864. Signed receipt roll, by mark, for clothing fourth Quarter 1864. Wounded at Franklin. Died soon after the war.

Kee, John H., Pvt., Co. H, enlisted at Chester March 2, 1863. Wounded at Chickamauga September 20, 1863. Furloughed. Wounded, furloughed, February 13 - March 13, 1864. Absent, sick, March - August 31, 1864. Paroled at Greensboro May 1, 1865.

Kee, William M., Pvt., Age 22, Co. H, enlisted at Chester March 19, 1862. Transferred to Co. A. 6th Regiment January 22, 1863.

Keenan, James, Pvt., Age 19, Co. A., from Charleston, enlisted at Charleston January 31, 1862. Captured at Jackson May 14, 1863. Assigned to Paroled Prisoners Camp at Demopolis June 5, 1863. Absent without leave from parole camp from July 12 to December 12, 1863. Captured near Marietta July 3, 1864. Sent to Military Prison, Louisville and transferred to Camp Douglas July 18, 1864. Claimed to have been loyal, forced to enlist in Rebel Army to avoid conscript and deserted to avail himself of amnesty proclamation. Discharged May 16, 1865.

Keese, Elijah, Pvt., Age 37, correspondent for *Edgefield Advertiser*, enlisted at Columbia, March 20, 1863. Absent, patient in hospital at Selma, Ala., May 11, 1863. Detailed to brigade commissary department Jul/Oct 1863. Sick, furloughed, April 1864. Extra daily duty brigade commissary department Jul/Aug 1864. Signed receipt roll for clothing September 9, 1864. Surrendered and paroled at Augusta May 19, 1865.

Kelly, G. W., Pvt., Age 30, Co. F, enlisted at Anderson March 11, 1863. Absent, sick, patient in hospital July 20, 1863 - Jan/Feb 1864. Patient, ill with abscess popliteal at Ross Hospital, Mobile, Ala., November 12, 1863. Sent to General Hospital, Atlanta, December 8, 1863. Absent without leave February - August 31, 1864. Admitted to Way Hospital, Meridian, Miss., March 25, 1865. Transferred. Surrendered 1865. Died 1868.

Kelly, J. Benjamin, Pvt., Age 19, Co. A, enlisted at Charleston February 17, 1862. Discharged by surgeon's certificate because of physical disability September 30, 1862.

Kelly, Rivers S., Pvt., Age 21, Co. A, from Charleston, enlisted at Charleston January 17, 1862. Detailed to work on roads by order General Gist Nov/Dec 1863. Captured at Kennesaw Mountain July 3, 1864. Sent to

Military Prison, Louisville and transferred to Camp Douglas July 18, 1864. Applied for oath of allegiance February 1865. Claimed to have been loyal, enlisted to avoid conscription and deserted to avail himself of the amnesty proclamation. Description: complexion, fair; hair, light; eyes, hazel; height 5 ft. 9 in. Signed oath of allegiance to the United States and released May 19, 1865.

Kemp, Louis H., Sgt., Co. K, enlisted at Edgefield April 13, 1862. Absent, patient in hospital suffering Otitis at Wilmington, Nov/Dec 1862 - Jan/Feb 1863. Slightly wounded at Chickamauga September 20, 1863. Severely wounded, head, at Jonesboro September 1, 1864. Paroled at Greensboro May 1, 1865.

Kennedy, John, Pvt., Sgt., Age 37, Co. A, enlisted at Charleston December 31, 1861. Assistant to Ordnance Sgt., at Secessionville June 1862. Assisted Ordnance Dept., Mar/Apr 1863 - Nov/Dec 1863. Absent, sick, patient in hospital, February 18 - April 20, 1864. Died April 20, 1864.

Kerwick, William, Corp., Age 26, Co. A., enlisted at Charleston December 31, 1861. Although captured and paroled, he was reported killed at Jackson May 14, 1863. Assigned to Paroled Prisoners Camp at Demopolis June 5, 1863. Absent without leave, pay stopped July 15 - October 15, 1863. Under arrest for absent without leave Nov/Dec 1863. Killed in battle at Kennesaw Mountain or New Hope Church June 1, 1864. A heavy, splendid speciman of manhood, faithful foreign ally and fighter for our cause. Buried on the wild mountain slope by members of his company.

Key, Richard S., 2Lt., Age 43, Co. I, enlisted at Columbia, March 20, 1862. Promoted to 2Lt., April 1, 1862. Absent, sick, furloughed, May/Jun - Sep/Oct 1862. Resigned due to ill health November 12, 1862.

Kidd, William, Pvt., Co. K, enlisted at Edgefield April 15 1862. Received as substitute. Patient at CSA General Military Hospital, No. 1, Wilmington for pneumonia December 25, 1862 - January 7, 1863. Confined in guard house Jan/Feb 1863. One month's pay stopped by court martial Mar/April 1863. Absent without leave August 31 - Nov/Dec 1863. Deserted en route to Chickamauga. Dropped from the rolls January 19, 1864.

Killian, Henry V., Pvt., Age 27, Col H, enlisted at Chester, March 19, 1862. Detached service aboard gunboat at Charleston Sep/Oct 1862 - January 1, 1864. Killed in battle at Pine Mountain June 10, 1864.

Kimbrell, James, Pvt., Age 26, Co. I, enlisted at Columbia March 20, 1862. Present on all rolls through Nov/Dec 1863. Killed in battle at Calhoun, Ga., May 16, 1864. Buried in same grave with Pvt. Preston O. Sullivan.

Kinard, Isaac, Pvt., Age 22, Co. E, enlisted at Walterboro, S.C., January 4, 1862. Pay stopped for one month by order of court martial May/Jun 1863. Killed in battle at Chickamauga September 20, 1863. Grave located in Confederate Cemetery, Marietta, Ga.

Kinard, Melvin L., 2Lt., Age 24, Co. G, enlisted at Columbia, March 19, 1862. Promoted to 1Sgt., Mar/Apr 1862. Sick in quarters Nov/Dec 1862. Under arrest Mar/Apr 1862. Found guilty by court martial of serving on a committee that petitioned for the captain and first lieutenant of the company to be elected by the men rather than accept a promotion March 6, 1863. Ordered reduced to ranks and confined to the guard house for 14 days. Granted furlough July 30, 1863. Elected 2Lt., May 4, 1863. Wounded at Chickamauga. Absent, sick, patient in hospital at Columbia, November 25, 1863. Sick, furloughed July 29, 1864. Absent, at home sick, furlough, August 31, 1864. Wounded at Franklin.

King, George W., Pvt., Age 20, Co. I, enlisted at Columbia March 20, 1862. Absent, sick, patient at Fairground Hospital No. 2, Atlanta October 1, 1863. Died of disease at Atlanta October 8, 1863. Grave located in Oakland Cemetery, Confederate Section, Atlanta.

Kingman, R. H., Maj., F&S, appointed at Charleston April 1, 1862. regimental quartermaster. ADC to Colonel Stevens. Died at Columbia, S.C., January 2, 1863. Contracted typhoid pneumonia while performing duty at Secessionville. Funeral January 4, 1863. Grave located at Wentworth Street Church, Charleston.

Kinsey, R., Pvt., Age 30, Co. E, enlisted at Charleston March 19, 1862.

Kinsey, W. B., Pvt., Age 18, Co. E, enlisted at Charleston March 20, 1862. Captured at Chickamauga September 20, 1863. Sent to Military Prison, Louisville and transferred to Camp Morton October 9, 1863. Paroled at Camp Morton and exchanged at City March 4, 1865. Traveled from Camp Morton to City Point via Baltimore, Md. Surrendered.

Kirkpatrick, Henry, Pvt., Co. D, Teamster, enlisted at Camp Gist January 19, 1862. Colored. Discharged January 13, 1864. Negro.

Kizer, David F., Pvt., Age 24, Co. C, from St. George, S.C., enlisted at Secessionville May 22, 1862. Detached service Jun/Oct 1862. Absent without leave for one month, pay stopped for that time Nov/Dec 1862. Worked extra duty as blacksmith March - May 1864. Present for duty Jul/Aug 1864. Still living at the end of the war. Discharged 1865. Married 1848. Died October 1887.

Kizer, John, Pvt., Age 18, born January 11, 1840, Co. C, enlisted at Georges Station January 7, 1862. One month pay stopped by court martial May/Jun 1863. Present for duty Jul/Aug 1864. Admitted for treatment of wound to Way Hospital, Meridian January 9, 1865.

Kizer, Peter, Pvt., Co. C. Entry from Dorchester County Enrollment Book.

Kizer, Preston A., Sgt., Age 22, Co. C, from St. George, Colleton District, enlisted at Georges Station March 5, 1862. Detached by Maj. Gen. Pemberton without pay May/Jun - Nov/Dec 1862. One month pay stopped by court martial May/Jun 1863. Wounded at Chickamauga September 20, 1862. Captured near Nashville December 16, 1864. Sent to Military Prison, Louisville and transferred to Camp Chase January 14, 1865. Description: complexion, light; hair, light; eyes, blue; height 5 ft. 10 in. Signed oath of allegiance to the United States June 12, 1865.

Kizer, Pinckney C., Corp., Age 19, Co. C, from Colleton District, enlisted at Georges Station January 7, 1862. Several periods of detached service by order of Maj. Gen. Pemberton without pay. Signed receipt roll for clothing April 1, 1864. Captured near Nashville December 16, 1864. Sent to Military Prison, Louisville and transferred to Camp Chase January 4, 1865. Description: complexion, dark; hair, dark; eyes, blue; height, 5 ft. 7 in. Signed oath of allegiance to the United States May 12, 1865.

Knight, D. A., Pvt., Age 24, Co. C, enlisted at Camp Gist March 25, 1862. Died April 25, 1862.

Knight, Thomas, Pvt., Age 42, Co. A, enlisted at Charleston January 6, 1862. Transferred to Smith's Battalion.

Koon, Frank A., Corp., Co. G, from Columbia, enlisted in July 1862. Discharged from the service at the surrender April 12, 1865. Married November 25, 1869. Died September 21, 1899. Widow T. Z. Koon. Entry from Confederate Veteran pension records and Memory Rolls at State Archives, Columbia, S.C.

Kruer, Henry, Pvt., Age 19, born March 5, 1843, Co. A, from Charleston, enlisted at Charleston January 25, 1862. Captured July 12, 1863. Claimed to have deserted from the Rebel Army at Charleston July 14, 1864. Signed oath of allegiance to the United States and to remain north of the Ohio River July 16, 1864. Description: complexion, light; hair, brown; eyes, blue; height, 5 ft. 4 in. Sent from the Dept of the Cumberland to be released north of the Ohio River July 16, 1864.

Ladden, Redin, Corp., Age 40, Co. C. Died of disease at home in 1864. Entry from Memory Rolls at State Archives, Columbia, S.C.

Lamdsy, J. W., Co. C. Buried August 30, 1864 in Oakland Cemetery, Atlanta, Georgia. Entry from Oakland Cemetery records.

Landrum, Benjamin F., Pvt., Age 20, Co. I, enlisted at Secessionville October 20, 1862. Detached to Medical Department in South Carolina April 12 - August 31, 1864. Detailed extended January 9, 1865. Discharged April 5, 1865 at Augusta, Ga.

Landrum Byron W., Sgt., Age 18, Co. I, enlisted at Columbia March 20, 1862. Absent, sick at hospital, September 4 - October 31, 1863. Present for duty through August 1864.

Lanham, Byron N., Sgt., Co. I. Died after the war. Entry from Memory Rolls at State Archives, Columbia, S.C.

Lanham, George B. Corp., Age 34, Co. I, from Edgefield District, enlisted at Columbia March 20, 1862. Absent, sick in Hospital at Lauderdale Springs, Miss., August 3 - October 31, 1863. Severely wounded, thigh, July 22, 1864. Admitted to Ocmulgee Hospital, Macon July 25, 1864. Furloughed August 16, 1864. Surrendered and Paroled at Augusta May 18, 1865.

Lanham, James M., 1Lt., Age 35, Co. I, enlisted at Columbia March 20, 1862. Promoted to 1Lt., April 1, 1862. Absent, sick, April 4, 1862 - August 22, 1863. Resigned, disabled suffered diphtheria, August 12, 1863. Paroled at Greensboro May 1, 1865.

Lanham, Joseph Marbury, 2Lt., Age 18, Co. I, enlisted at Columbia March 20, 1862. Furlough Nov/Dec 1863. Promoted from the ranks to 2Lt., for meritorious service April 9, 1865. Present on all rolls. Paroled at Greensboro May 1, 1865.

Lanier, Jabez J., Pvt., Age 35, Co. I, enlisted at Columbia March 20, 1862. Died of typhoid fever at Charleston June 1, 1862.

Larecy, Joel W., Pvt., Age 29, Co. C, enlisted at Georges Station January 7, 1862. Detached at Canton guarding baggage May/Jun 1863. Killed near Atlanta by the railroad cars while en route from Mississippi to Chattanooga August 30, 1863. (See Louissey, Joel, Pvt.)

Larkin, N., Pvt., Co. F. Dead. Entry from Co. F, 24th Regiment Survivors Association Roster.

Latham, J. B., Pvt., Age 40, Co. F, enlisted at Anderson April 1, 1862. Bounty due. Died of disease at the Second Georgia Hospital, Augusta, July 4, 1864.

Lee Henry D., Sgt., Age 26, born October 25, 1834, Co. A., from Charleston, enlisted at Charleston December 31, 1861. Detailed to work on Eason's gunboat October 23 - December 1862. Captured at Jackson May 14, 1863. Assigned to Paroled Prisoners Camp at Demopolis June 5, 1863. Killed in battle at Calhoun, Ga. Mortally wounded in battle, shot in abdomen, at Calhoun Ga., May 16, 1864. Reported killed in speech by Col. Capers, regimental commander, May 22, 1864.

Lee, James N., Pvt., Age 30, Co. G, enlisted at Columbia April 12, 1862. Absent without leave April 1862.

Lee, James W., Co. G. Entry from original muster roll.

Leitner, Jno. W. Pvt., Age 31, Co. G, enlisted at Columbia March 19, 1862. Detailed to work on the gunboats at Charleston October 24, 1862 to January 1, 1864. Mortally wounded in battle at Atlanta July 22, 1864. Died July 25, 1864. Widow, C. C. Leitner, filed claim for settlement February 13, 1865.

Lemon, James M., Pvt., Age 33 Co. H., enlisted at Chester March 19, 1862. Absent, sick, May/Jun 1862. Absent, sick at division hospital, Sep/Oct 1863. Absent without leave since the retreat at Missionary Ridge Nov/Dec 1863. Captured at Missionary Ridge November 25, 1863.

Killed in battle at Lookout Mountain. Reported, "Lost at Lookout Mountain."

Lemon, John M., Pvt., Age 21, Co. H, enlisted at Chester March 19, 1862. Absent, sick, May/Jun 1862. Fined $.50 damage to his musket Nov/Dec 1862. Absent, sick, Mar/Apr - May/Jun 1863. Absent, sick at division hospital Sep/Oct 1863. Absent, sick, furloughed, Nov/Dec 1863. Absent without leave January 6 - February 1864. Reported missing July 20/22, 1864. Returned. Died of disease at Street Hospital, Milledgeville, Ga., March 13, 1865. His effects consisted of two pair of socks, one blanket and $8.50 in currency.

Lenderman, J. H., Pvt., Co. E, Consolidated 16th and 24th Regiment, enlisted at Columbia June 5, 1861. Paroled at Greensboro May 1, 1865.

Lever, James W., Pvt., Age 35, Co. G., enlisted at Columbia March 19, 1862. Detached service to Eason's Shipyard to work on gunboat October 24, 1862 - January 1, 1864. Present for duty August 31, 1864. Signed receipt roll for clothing September 9, 1864.

Lever, James W., Pvt., born October 18, 1849, Co. G, from Columbia, Richland County, S.C. Married June 1, 1882. Died June 2, 1895. Widow Sallie E. Lever. Entry from Confederate Veteran pension records at State Archives, Columbia, S.C.

Lever, Stephen S., Sgt., Age 38, Co. G, enlisted at Columbia March 19, 1862. Absent, sick, furloughed May/Jun 1862. Sick in hospital at Columbia Sep/Oct 1862. Departed this life in hospital at Columbia November 10, 1862. Widow, Susan A. Lever, filed claim for settlement July 30, 1864.

Leverett, C. J. Pvt., Co. F. Died of disease. Entry from Co. F, 24th Regiment Survivors Association roster.

Leverett, John B. Sr., Pvt., Age 18, born December 22, 1844, Co. F, from Henderson, S.C., enlisted at Anderson November 25, 1862. Captured at Shipp's Gap/Taylor's Ridge October 16, 1864. Sent to Military Prison, Louisville and transferred to Camp Douglas October 26, 1864. Description: complexion, fair; hair, light; eyes, grey; height 5 ft. 16 in. Signed oath of allegiance to the United States and discharged June 17, 1865. Last name also spelled Leverette. In late years was partially blind and deaf from the results of disease contracted during the war.

Leverett, Thomas S., Pvt., Age 20, Co. F, from Anderson District, enlisted at Anderson February 1, 1862. Absent, patient in division hospital, Sep/Oct 1863. Died of disease at Academy Hospital, Marietta, Ga., February 1, 1864. Grave located in Confederate Cemetery, Marietta, Ga., Grave no. 160. Left effects of $73.00.

Leverette, C. S., Pvt., Age 22, Co. F. Died of Disease. Entry from Memory Rolls at State Archives, Columbia, S.C.

Leverette, D. C., Pvt., Age 23, Co. F, enlisted at Columbia January 013,

1862. Absent, sick, Nov/Dec 1862. Died of typhoid fever at Citadel Square Hospital, Charleston, January 9, 1863. Buried same day. Grave located at Magnolia Cemetery.

Leverette, William Harvey, Pvt., Age 34 Co. F, enlisted at Anderson January 13, 1862. Absent, sick, Nov/Dec 1862. Absent, sick patient in hospital, Jul/Aug 1863. Absent without leave Sep/Oct 1863. Died of disease in hospital at Cassville, Ga., January 23, 1864. Left effects of $20.00.

Lewis, John L., Sgt., Age 21, Co. A, enlisted at Charleston December 31, 1861. Captured at Jackson May 14, 1863. Assigned to Paroled Prisoners Camp at Demopolis June 15, 1863. Killed in battle near Kennesaw Mountain July 2, 1864.

Lewis, W. S., Sgt., Age 25, Co. B, from Brightsville, S.C., enlisted at Charleston December 4, 1861. Sick in camp Nov/Dec 1862. Absent, sick, patient at hospital, Jul/Aug 1863. Absent, sick at home in S.C., furloughed, Sep/Oct 1863. Promoted to 3Sgt., August 24, 1864. Paroled at Greensboro May 1, 1865. Deserted April 25, 1865. Died 1896.

Liles, S. H., Pvt., Age 16, Co. B, enlisted at Marlboro December 4, 1861. Present on all rolls. Killed in battle at Kennesaw Mountain June 21, 1864.

Lipford, A. T., Asst. Surgeon, F&S, appointed November 28, 1862. Ordered by General Walker to report to 24th Regiment.

Lipford, James Alexander, 1Sgt., Co. H, enlisted at Chester March 19, 1862. Mortally wounded in battle at Jackson May 14, 1863. Died at Canton, Miss., June 27, 1863, from wounds received in battle at Jackson. Widow, Ellen Lipford, filed claim for settlement March 11, 1864.

Lipford, John G., Sgt., Age 18, Co. H, enlisted at Chester March 19, 1862. Description: complexion, fair; hair, light; eyes, grey; height, 5 ft. 11 in; occupation, student. Discharged because of disability June 23, 1862.

Lipford, W. W., Pvt., Co. H, enlisted at Dalton, Ga., April 16, 1864. Wounded. Paroled at Greensboro May 1, 1865.

Litner, J.W., Pvt., Co. G. Mortally wounded in side, July 22/24, 1864. Entry from *Charleston Mercury* article.

Little, James C. Pvt., Co. B, enlisted at Marion April 15, 1862. Sick, at home, furloughed, Mar/Apr 1863. Died at home May 13, 1863.

Locklear, Andrew, Pvt., Age 30, Co. G, from Richland District, enlisted at Columbia March 19, 1862. Wounded at Chickamauga September 20, 1863. Patient in hospital at Columbia October 1863 - Jan/Feb 1864. Slightly wounded, face and hip, July 20/22, 1864. Signed receipt roll for clothing September 9, 1864. Wounded by cannon ball, simple flesh wound of right leg, middle, at Franklin November 30, 1864. Captured at Franklin December 17, 1864. Admitted to No. 1, USA General Hospital, Nashville, Tenn., December 26, 1864 - January 31, 1865.

Description: complexion, dark; hair, dark; eyes, grey; height 5 ft. 10 in. Sent to Military Prison, Louisville and transferred to Camp Chase February 13, 1865. Signed oath of allegiance to the United States June 13, 1865. Last name spelled as Lockler, Lockier, Lockleyer, Lockliar, and Locklear.

Lockier, A., Co. G. Entry from original muster roll.

Lockler, William, Pvt., Age 20, Co. A, enlisted at Charleston, December 31, 1861. Slightly wounded, hip, and sent to hospital July 20/22, 1864. Surrendered at Greensboro.

Long, Jacob M., Corp., Age 16, Co. D, from Beaufort District, enlisted at Camp Gist January 16, 1862. Wounded at Chickamauga. Absent, granted furlough due to wound, Sep/Oct - Nov/Dec 1863. Signed receipt roll for clothing April 1, 1864. Promoted to Corp., June 1, 1864. Reduced to ranks July 17, 1864. Absent, sick, furloughed, August 20 - October 20, 1864. Description: complexion, fair; hair, light; eyes, blue; height 5 ft. 10 in. Captured at Nashville December 16, 1864. Sent to Military Prison, Louisville and transferred to Camp Chase January 4, 1865. Signed oath of allegiance to the United States June 12, 1865.

Long, John Oliver, Pvt., Age 24, Co. F, enlisted at Columbia January 13, 1862 for 12 months. Absent, sick, May/Jun 1862. Absent, sick, Nov/Dec 1862. Conscripted for the war Jan/Feb 1863. Absent without leave Jan/Feb 1863. Mortally wounded in battle at Jackson May 14, 1863. Captured near Jackson May 14, 1863, and paroled in the hospital May 16, 1863. Died in hospital of wounds received in battle at Jackson June 17, 1863.

Long, L. W., Pvt., Age 20, Co. F, enlisted at Anderson January 13, 1862 for 12 months. Died of disease March 10, 1862.

Long, William H., Pvt., Age 24, Co. F, enlisted at Anderson January 13, 1862. Absent, patient in hospital, Jan/Feb 1863. Wounded at Jackson May 14, 1863. Captured May 14, 1863. Paroled in hospital May 16, 1863. Absent, wounded, alternately furloughed and hospitalized at Columbia, June 1863 - August 31, 1864. Surrendered 1865.

Long, W. H., Pvt., Age 23, Co. G, enlisted at Columbia March 19, 1862. Transferred to the Naval Service October 24, 1862.

Loomas, John, Pvt., Age 23, Co. G, enlisted at Columbia April 12, 1862. Expected to be transferred from Capt. Hampton's Company April 15, 1862. Ed. Note - The record is not clear whether he ever joined 24th Regiment.

Lott, G. P., Co. E, from Walterboro. Married 1858. Died November 2, 1892. Widow Kaity Catherine Lott. Entry from Confederate Veteran pension records at State Archives, Columbia, S.C.

Louissey, Joel, Pvt., Age 30, Co. C. Killed by cars at Atlanta. Entry from Memory Rolls at State Archives, Columbia, S.C. Ed. note: Suspected duplicate of Larecy.

Loveless, Benjamin Franklin, Pvt., Co. I, enlisted at Charleston February 15, 1863. Died at Canton, Miss., May 31, 1863. Died of wounds received in battle at Jackson. Left personal effects of $4.35. Name also shown as Lovelace.

Lovick, J. A., Pvt., Co. G, enlisted at Secessionville August 16, 1862. Absent, sick in quarters, Nov/Dec 1862. Present Jan/Feb 1863.

Lowe, Z. H., Pvt., Age 18, Co. C, enlisted at Georges Station January 7, 1862. Present May/Jun 1862.

Lyons, John S., Pvt., Age 35, Co. E, enlisted at Camp Gist March 20, 1862. Absent without leave Nov/Dec 1862. Absent, sick at home, Jan/Feb 1863. Absent without leave Jul/Aug - Sep/Oct 1863. Absent without leave July 20 - August 1864. Furloughed from hospital. Surrendered. In 1865, discharged at Dalton, Ga., at end of war. Died October 12, 1874. Widow Mary Jane Lyons.

Lyons, W. M., Pvt., Age 35, Co. E, enlisted at Camp Gist April 2, 1862. Pay stopped for one month by order of court martial May/Jun 1863. Wounded at Chickamauga September 20, 1863. Absent, sick, furloughed, September 20, 1863 - February 1864. Slightly wounded, hands, July 22, 1864. Absent, sick, furloughed, October 28 to November 21, 1864.

Mallett, John, Pvt., Age 21, Co. I, from Tuckney Pond, S.C., enlisted at Columbia March 20, 1862. Died of typhoid fever in CSA General Hospital, No. 4, Wilmington, N. C., January 3, 1863. Left effects of a few sundries.

Mallett, Preston S. B., Pvt., Age 18, Co. I, enlisted at North East, N.C., January 1, 1863. Killed on the pickett line at Atlanta August 17, 1864.

Mallonee, J. C., Sgt., Age 25, Co. B, enlisted at Marlboro December 4, 1861. Present through June 1862. Transferred to 26th Regiment in 1862.

Malphrus, W. F., Pvt., Age 20, Co. D, enlisted at Camp Gist January 16, 1862. Absent, sick in hospital, Sep/Oct 1863. Absent, sick, furloughed, Nov/Dec 1863. Present for duty Jan/Feb 1864. Absent, wounded and with leave, July 26 - September 26, 1864. Living.

Manker, Robert J., 1Lt., Age 40, Co. D, enlisted at Camp Gist January 19, 1862. Promoted from 1Sgt. to Lt. December 5, 1862. Wounded in engagement near Jackson May 14, 1863. Resigned, refused to appear before examining board, June 1, 1863. Conscripted and assigned to Co. D, as a Pvt., July 26, 1863. Deserted July 29, 1863. Arrested and charged with desertion but he proved that he was over conscript age and the charges were dropped.

Manning, John J., Pvt., from Herdsmont, Ga. Wounded May 14, 1863 at Jackson, Miss., May 14, 1863. Wounded at Resaca, Ga., May 15, 1864.

Surrendered 1865. Entry from Memory Rolls at State Archives, Columbia, S.C., and Survivor's Association roster. [Ed. note - Possible duplicate of Manning, Joseph J.]

Manning, Joseph J., Pvt., Date of Birth: March 28, 1864, Age 24, Co. F, from Herdsmont, Ga., enlisted at Anderson January 13, 1862. Transferred to Smith's Batt. Sharpshooters August 10, 1862 - December 25, 1862. Wounded at Jackson May 14, 1863. Captured and paroled in hospital May 16, 1863. Slightly wounded at Calhoun, Ga., May 15, 1864. Signed receipt roll for clothing April 1 and September 9, 1864. Captured at Shipp's Gap/Taylor's Ridge October 16, 1864. Sent to Military Prison, Louisville and transferred to Camp Douglas October 29, 1864. Description: complexion, fair; hair, light; eyes, grey; height 5 ft. 6 in. Signed oath of allegiance to the United States and discharged June 17, 1865. Died October 9, 1907. Grave located in Bethlehem Cemetery, Herdmont, Ga. (See Manning, John J.)

Manuel, Richmond Milford, Pvt., Co. D, enlisted at Beaufort District, January 15, 1864. Captured near Nashville December 16, 1864. Sent to Military Prison, Louisville and transferred to Camp Douglas December 22, 1864. Discharged June 19, 1865.

Maree, John J., Pvt., Co. A, enlisted at Charleston April 30, 1862. Sick at Charleston Nov/Dec 1862 - May/Jun 1863. Not accounted for May 20, 1863 - August 28, 1863. Absent, sick in hospital, Nov/Dec 1863. Detached to work at Arsenal, Selma, by order of Secretary of War, December 28, 1863. Surrendered and paroled at Augusta May 23, 1865. Name also spelled Meray.

Maree, William. S. Corp., Co. A, Age 22, enlisted at Charleston December 31, 1861. Color Corporal Sep/Oct 1863 - Jan/Feb 1864. Promoted from ranks to Color Sergeant. Absent without leave August 16, 1864. Wounded at Kennesaw Mountain. Paroled at Greensboro May 1, 1865.

Margart, G. M., Musician, Co,. C, enlisted at Pocotaligo April 1, 1863. Wounded, admitted to hospital and furloughed for 10 days, Jul/Aug 1864. Paroled at Greensboro May 1, 1865.

Margart, George, Pvt., Co. A, Drummer Boy. Discharged because of disability. Entry from Memory Rolls at State Archives, Columbia, S.C. May be duplicate of Margart, G. M.

Marsh, William, Pvt., Age 18, Co. E, enlisted at Charleston March 2, 1862. Born March 13, 1844. Died of disease in service of his country at Secessionville December 15, 1862. Grave located at Bethel United Methodist Church, Upper Colleton County, S.C.

Martin, H. A., Pvt., Age 25, Co. E, enlisted at Salkehatchie January 16, 1862. Transferred to Capt. Campbell's Company, 11th Regiment Jan/Feb 1863.

Martin, Jabez, Pvt., Co. K, enlisted at Edgefield August 12, 1862. Furloughed for 30 days by Hospital Newnan, Ga., July 1863. Absent, furloughed, February 9, 1864. Absent without leave August 31, 1864. Paroled at Greensboro May 1, 1865.

Martin, James B., Pvt., Age 26, Co. A, from Charleston, enlisted at Charleston February 21, 1862. Captured near Vicksburg and paroled with the Vicksburg Garrison July 12, 1863. Absent, paroled pending exchange, Jul/Aug - Sep/Oct 1863. Absent without leave Nov/Dec 1863. Slightly wounded, foot, Jul 20/22, 1864. Captured at Shipp's Gap/Taylor's Ridge October 16, 1864. Sent to Military Prison, Louisville and transferred to Camp Douglas October 29, 1864. Description: complexion, fair; hair, brown; eyes, blue; height 5 ft. 10 in. Claimed to have been loyal enlisted to avoid conscription and deserted to avail himself of the amnesty proclamation. Signed oath of allegiance to the United States and discharged May 17, 1865.

Martin, J. Bracknell, Pvt., Co. I, enlisted at Charleston February 18, 1863. Furlough April 1863. Absent, sick in division hospital and furloughed, October 10, 1863 - January 13, 1864. Slightly wounded, foot, near Calhoun, Ga., May 16, 1864. Absent, sick, in hospital August 27, 1864. Surrendered and paroled at Augusta May 30, 1865.

Martin, Joel, Pvt., Co. G, enlisted at Columbia April 7, 1864. Present February 29 - August 31, 1864.

Martin, John Bryant, Pvt., Age 16, Co. I, enlisted at Columbia March 20, 1862. Present on all rolls. Paroled at Greensboro May 1, 1865.

Martin, Lafyette, Pvt., Co. K. Died in hospital of disease December 12, 1863. Entry from Memory Rolls at State Archives, Columbia, S.C.

Martin, Sol, Pvt., Age 21, Co. E, enlisted at Salkehatchie January 16, 1862. Transferred to Capt. Campbells Co., 11th Regiment, SCV Jan/Feb 1863.

Martin, Whitfield, Pvt., Co. K, enlisted at Edgefield August 15, 1862. Present on all rolls. Signed receipt roll for clothing April 1, 1864. Killed in battle at Peachtree Creek July 20, 1864.

Mason, J. F., Pvt., Co. C. Commutation of rations while on sick furlough September 28 - November 26, 1863.

Mathis, Robert W., 2Lt., Age 18, Co. I, enlisted at Columbia April 18, 1862. Wounded at Chickamauga September 20, 1863. Absent, wounded, September 20, 1863 - Nov/Dec 1863. Promoted to 1Sgt., from the ranks March 26, 1864. Signed receipt roll for clothing September 9, 1864. Promoted 2Lt., for meritorious service April 9, 1865. Paroled at Greensboro May 1, 1865. Applied as a resident of Arkansas for pension August 15, 1903. Died November 1908. Widow applied for pension August 11, 1908.

Mathis, William T., Pvt., Co. K, enlisted at Edgefield April 15, 1862. Received permission to visit Charleston October 17, 1862 and not yet returned (October 31, 1862). In guard house, one month's pay stopped

Nov/Dec 1862. Absent without leave July 31 - August 31, 1863. Slightly wounded, leg, at Chickamauga September 20, 1863. Furloughed home October 1, 1863 - Jan/Feb 1864. Absent without leave Mar/Aug 1864. Surrendered at Augusta and paroled May 19, 1865.

Maxey, M., Pvt., Age 21, Co. A, enlisted at Charleston December 31, 1861. Wounded at Chickamauga. Absent, wounded, Sep/Oct - Nov/Dec 1863. Paroled at Greensboro May 1, 1865.

Maxwell, Thomas, Pvt., Age 25, Co. K, enlisted at Edgefield April 15, 1862. Patient in hospital May/Jun 1862. Description: complexion, light; hair, light; eyes, blue; height 6 ft. 3 in. Occupation, farmer. Discharged because of chronic rheumatism August 23, 1862.

Maxwell, P. J., Capt., & Asst. Surgeon, F&S, from Georgetown, assigned early in 1864. Entry from Memory Rolls at State Archives, Columbia, S.C.

Mays, John A., Pvt., Age 37, Co. I, enlisted at Columbia, March 20, 1862. Absent, sick, furloughed, Sep/Oct 1862. Signed receipt roll for clothing January 30, 1864. Captured at Marietta or Pine Mountain June 15, 1864. Sent to Military Prison, Louisville and transferred to Rock Island June 24, 1864. Transferred for exchange February 25, 1865. Patient at 3d Division, General Hospital, Camp Winder, Richmond and transferred to Receiving and Wayside Hospital or General Hospital No. 9, Richmond March 9, 1865. Transferred to Jackson Hospital, Richmond and granted furlough, March 8, 1865.

McAdams, John O., Corp., Co. F, from Storeville, S.C., enlisted at Anderson April 8, 1862. Absent, sick in hospital, Jul/Aug 1863. Paroled at Greensboro May 1, 1865.

McAdams, William T., Pvt., Age 24, Co. F, from Little Creek, Ga., enlisted at Columbia January 13, 1862. Absent, patient in hospital of Camp of Convalescents, Rome, Ga., Sep/Oct 1863. Wounded at Peachtree Creek July 20, 1864. Absent, wounded, August 31, 1864. Surrendered 1865.

McArdle, P., Pvt., Age 48, Co. C. enlisted at Georges Station January 7, 1862. Discharged July 18, 1862.

McBride, Edward L., Pvt., Co. F. Died of disease in 1864. Entry from Memory Rolls at State Archives, Columbia, S.C., and Survivors Association roster.

McBride, Edward L., Pvt., Age 20, Co. G, enlisted at Columbia January 13, 1862. Died in the hospital at Atlanta September 30, 1863. Left effects of $3.00 currency.

McCabe, George W., Sgt., Age 25, Co. A, enlisted at Charleston, December 31, 1861. Present on all rolls. Surrendered at Greensboro.

McCalister, George W., Pvt., Age 34, Co. F, enlisted at Anderson March 27, 1863. Absent sick at hospital Jul/Aug - Sep/Oct 1863. Returned to duty November 11, 1863. Captured at Ringold during retreat from Missionary Ridge, November 27, 1863. Sent to Military Prison, Louisville and transferred to Rock Island December 14, 1863. Died from Variola (smallpox) February 1, 1864. Grave no. 337, South of Prison Barracks.

McCalister, J. A., Pvt., Age 39, Co. F, enlisted at Columbia January 13, 1862. Absent, sick, May/Jun 1862. Signed receipt rolls for clothing May 14 and June 7, 1864. Died of disease at Stout Hospital, Milledgeville, Ga., June 24, 1864. Effects burned at Madison, Ga.

McCalister, O. B., Pvt., Age 36, Co. F, enlisted at Camp Gist March 28, 1862. Absent, sick, May/Jun 1862. Absent, sick, Nov/Dec 1862. Killed in battle at Jackson May 14, 1863.

McCantell, Patrick, Pvt., Co. C. Entry from Dorchester County Enrollment Book.

McCants, James N., Pvt., Age 30, Co. H, enlisted at Chester District, March 19, 1862. Absent, sick, furloughed, Sep/Oct 1863. Absent without leave Nov/Dec 1863. Signed receipt roll for clothing at General Hospital No. 1, Columbia, S.C., February 24, 1864. Absent, sick in hospital at Columbia, January - August 1864. Died after the war.

McCaughran, James, Pvt., Co. H, enlisted at Chester District March 19, 1862. Absent, sick, Jan/Feb 1863 - Jan/Feb 1864. Signed receipt roll for clothing at Ladies General Hospital, No. 23, Columbia, S.C., November 1863. Detached service by order of the Secretary of War Mar/Aug 1864. Paroled at Chester May 5, 1865.

McCauly, Mack, Pvt., Age 30, Co. C, enlisted at Charleston March 20, 1862. Transferred to 2 Batt. S.C. Sharpshooters October 1862.

McClelland, David R., Pvt., Co. F, from Newell, S.C., enlisted at Columbia January 13, 1862. Patient in hospital October 13, 1862. Requested by Aiken's Partisan Rangers and transferred to Co. G, Aiken's Partisan Rangers November 4, 1862. Exchanged for A. Gaily from Cavalry. Name also spelled McClellan.

McClintock, James, Pvt., Co. G. Captured at Nashville. Died disease. Entry from roster prepared by company commander.

McClintock, John H., Corp., Age 19, Co. H, enlisted at Chester March 19, 1862. Absent, sick, May/Jun 1862. Wounded at Chickamauga September 20, 1863. Furloughed September 30 - Nov/Dec 1863. Wounded at Franklin November 30, 1864. Captured at Franklin December 18, 1864. Admitted to No. 1, USA General Hospital, Nashville, with gunshot fracture of left arm January 16, 1865. Anterior posterior flap amputation middle third left arm, two ligatures applied January 20, 1865. Returned to Provost Marshal March 1, 1865. Admitted to Eruptive USA General Hospital, Louisville March 5, 1865. Died in small pox hospital of small pox March 7, 1865. Grave no. 31, Range No. 62, Cave Hill Cemetery. Father, John McClintock, Chester Courthouse, Chester District, S.C.

McClintock, Joseph, Pvt., Co. H, enlisted at Chester May 16, 1862. Absent sick May/Jun 1863 - Jan/Feb 1864. Signed receipt roll for clothing at Gen. Hospital, No. 2, Columbia, S.C. Absent, sick, July 20, 1864 - August 31, 1864. Captured at Nashville December 16, 1864. Sent to Military Prison, Louisville and transferred to Camp Douglas December 24, 1864. Discharged June 19, 1865.

McClintock, Joseph Campbell, Corp., Age 33, Co. H, from Rock Hill Cross Roads, S.C., enlisted at Chester June 6, 1862. Appointed Corp., January 1, 1864. Present on all rolls. Patient for diarrhoea at Ocmulgee Hospital, Macon May 16 - 21, 1864. Slightly wounded, shoulder, July 20/22, 1864. Captured near Nashville December 16, 1864. Sent to Military Prison, Louisville and transferred to Camp Chase January 6, 1865. Description: complexion, fair; hair, black; eyes, blue; height, 6 ft. 1 in. Signed oath of allegiance to the United States June 12, 1865.

McClintock, Robert Y., Corp., Age 21, Co. H, enlisted at Chester March 19, 1863. Present on all rolls. Killed in battle at Chickamauga September 20, 1863.

McCollum, Hugh, Pvt., Co. B., enlisted at Marlboro April 19, 1862. Absent, sick at home, Sep/Oct 1862. Captured at Jackson May 14, 1863. Assigned to Paroled Prisoners Camp at Demopolis June 15, 1863. Promoted from ranks 1863. Paroled at Greensboro May 1, 1865.

McCormack, John E., Pvt., Date of Birth: December 12, 1839, Age 22, Co. E, from Colleton District, enlisted at Salkehatchie January 16, 1862. Furloughed Mar/Apr 1863. Pay stopped for one month by court martial May/Jun 1863. Wounded at Chickamauga September 20, 1863. Absent due to wound Sep/Oct 1863. Captured near Nashville December 16, 1864. Sent to Military Prison, Louisville and transferred to Camp Chase January 4, 1865. Description: complexion, dark; hair, lite; eyes, hazel; height, 5 ft. 10 in. Signed oath of allegiance to the United States June 12, 1865. Died November 18, 1925. Grave located in Westview Cemetery, Augusta, Ga.

McCormack, Joseph W., Corp., Age 26, Co. E, enlisted at Camp Gist January 16, 1862. Transferred to 2nd Battalion Sharpshooters and retransferred January 15, 1863. Wounded at Franklin November 30, 1864. Gunshot fracture both bones right forearm immediately above wrist joint, middle third forearm amputated December 6, 1864. Captured at Franklin December 17, 1864. Admitted to No. 1, USA General Hospital, Nashville December 23, 1864 - January 3, 1865. Anterior posteriad flap amputation through middle third forearm performed before admission to U.S.A. General Hospital. Sent to Military Prison, Louisville and transferred to Camp Chase January 11, 1865. Description: complexion, dark; hair, dark; eyes, blue; height, 5 ft. 8 1/2 in. Signed oath of allegiance to the United States June 13, 1865.

McCullum, J. E., Pvt., Co. A, enlisted at Charleston May 5, 1862. Absent sick at hospital Sep/Oct 1863 - Jan/Feb 1864. Present for duty Jul/Aug 1864. Transferred to Marine service, Navy April 11, 1864.

MacDaniel, H. C., Pvt., Age 21, Co. B, enlisted at Marlboro December 4, 1861. Description: complexion, fair; hair, sandy; eyes, blue; height 5 ft. 0 in; occupation, farmer. Discharged by reason of physical debility June 23, 1863.

McDaniel, J. Martin, 1Lt., Age 30, Co. H, from Richburg, enlisted at Chester March 19, 1862. Promoted from 2Lt., to 1Lt., January 13, 1863. Leave approved for July 30, 1863. Leave approved for January 31, 1864. Present on all rolls. Paroled at Greensboro May 1, 1865.

McDaniel, William, Sgt., Age 20, Co. I, enlisted at James Island May 17, 1862. Promoted to 4Sgt., from the ranks March 8, 1864. Severely wounded, side, at Decatur, Ga., July 22, 1864. In hospital.

McDonald, Charles B., Pvt., Co. A. enlisted at Camp Gist March 28, 1862. Transferred to Navy Department by order of Commanding General October 6, 1862.

McDonald, Richard, Pvt., Co. A, enlisted at Camp Gist April 8, 1862. Discharged, physically disabled.

McDowell, Benjamin F., Pvt., Co. K, enlisted at Edgefield February 18, 1862. Absent, sick patient in hospital, July 20, 1863. Transferred to hospital at Launderdale Springs July 21, 1863. Missing during the retreat from Missionary Ridge. Captured at Graysville, Ga., November 27, 1863. Sent to Military Prison, Louisville and transferred to Rock Island December 14, 1864. Died from infirmity February 16, 1865. Grave No. 567 located south of prison barracks.

McDowell, William W., 2Lt., Co. K, enlisted at Edgefield April 15, 1862. Slightly wounded, arm, at Chickamauga September 20, 1863. Furloughed home October 1, 1863. Promoted to Corp., August 19, 1864. Wounded, neck, at Franklin November 30, 1864. Treated for wound at Way Hospital, Meridian, Miss., January 11, 1865. Furloughed. Paroled at Greensboro May 1, 1865.

McGarity, Andrew, Corp., Age 23, Co. H, from Rock Hill Cross Roads, S.C., enlisted at Chester March 19, 1862. Appointed 4Corp., June 30, 1863. Absent, sick, furloughed, Sep/Oct 1863. Patient at Ocmulgee Hospital, Macon May 16 - 23, 1864. Absent without leave and reduced to ranks May 30, 1864. Sick four months. Approved for 60 days furlough by Medical Examining Board, Dalton, sick with chronic diarrhoea with extreme emaciation and debility June 22, 1864. Paroled at Greensboro May 1, 1865. Absent, admitted to hospital by medical officer, April 25, 1865. Paroled at Methodist Church Hospital May 2, 1865. Record reflects two paroles, one from hospital and the other from Company H.

McGarity, Henderson, Sgt., Age 37, Co. H, enlisted at Chester March 19,

1862. Appointed 4Corp., Sep/Oct 1862. Wounded at Jackson, Miss. Appointed 5Sgt., June 30, 1863. Captured near Nashville December 16, 1864. Sent to Military Prison, Louisville and transferred to Camp Chase January 6, 1865. Died of pneumonia March 11, 1865. Grave no. 532, located 1/3 mile south of Camp Chase.

McGarity, James, Pvt., Age 17, Col. H, enlisted at Chester March 19, 1862. Reported missing July 20/22, 1864. Returned. Furloughed from hospital August 31 - October 10, 1864. Captured at Nashville December 16, 1864. Sent to Military Prison, Louisville and transferred to Camp Douglas December 24, 1864. Discharged June 19, 1865.

McGee, A. J., Pvt., Age 22, Co. F. Surrendered 1865. Entry from Memory Rolls at State Archives, Columbia, S.C. May be duplicate of McKee, A. J.

McGee, Aaron W., Pvt., Co. F. Surrendered 1865. Entry from Memory Rolls at State Archives, Columbia, S.C. May be duplicate of McKee, Aaron W.

McGee, G. L., 1Lt., Age 43, Co. F, from Walhalla, S.C., enlisted at Anderson January 13, 1862. Absent, sick leave, May/June 1862. Father of brothers John Lewis and Silvester McGee. Resigned due to ill health July 15, 1862.

McGee, J. Anderson, Pvt., Co. G, from Iva, S.C., enlisted at Columbia, May 1, 1863. Absent, patient in hospital at Rome, Ga., Sep/Oct 1863. Detailed to hospital as nurse at Griffin, Ga., Nov/Dec 1863. Wounded at Atlanta July 22, 1864. Admitted to hospital for flesh wound of right thigh, general health, good.

McGee, John Lewis, Nickname - Buddy, 1Sgt., Age 20, Co. F, enlisted at Anderson April 9, 1862. Transferred from Orr's Regiment in exchange for I. B. Newton April 9, 1862. Transferred to serve in Father's [G. L. McGee] company. Detached service as assistant in Quartermaster Department. Assigned as private secretary to colonel. Clerk at General Gists quarters Jan/Feb 1864. Appointed 3Sgt., April 12, 1864. Missing supposed to be in the hands of the enemy July 22, 1864. Killed in battle at Decatur July 22, 1864. [Ed. note - His letters are used in the narrative. Brother of Silvester McGee.]

McGee, John O., Pvt., Age 19, born March 20, 1843, Co. F, from Iva, S.C., Anderson District, enlisted at Anderson January 13, 1862. Absent, sick at hospital, Jul/Aug 1863. Furloughed from hospital Sep/Oct 1863. Absent without leave Nov/Dec 1863. Captured at Taylor's Ridge October 16, 1864. Sent to Military prison, Louisville and transferred to Camp Douglas October 29, 1864. Description: complexion, fair; hair, light; eyes, blue; height, 5 ft. 6 in. Signed oath of allegiance to the United States and discharged June 17, 1865.

McGee, J. R. O., Pvt., Age 30, Co. F. Surrendered 1865. Entry from

Memory Rolls at State Archives, Columbia, S.C.

McGee, Silvester, (Nickname - Vessie), Pvt., Co. F, enlisted at Anderson November 25, 1862. Slightly wounded at Jackson July 9-16 1863. Struck on arm by a spent ball that raised a large blue welt. Absent, sick in convalescent camp, September 1863. Absent without leave August 15 - 31, 1864. Captured at Shipp's Gap/Taylor's Ridge October 16, 1864. Sent to Military Prison, Louisville and transferred to Camp Douglas October 29, 1864. Died of scorbutis (scurvy) January 30, 1865. Grave near Camp Douglas. Name also shown as *Sylvester* and *S. W.* [Ed. Note - His letters are used in narrative.]

McGee, William A., Nickname - Billie, Pvt., Age 18, Co. F, from Anderson, S.C., enlisted at Columbia January 13, 1862. Detached service as wagoner Oct/Sep - Nov/Dec 1862. Extra daily duty as teamster Nov/Dec 1863. Detached to ordnance team Jan/Feb 1864. Assigned to ordnance department Mar/Aug 1864. Paroled at Greensboro May 1, 1865. Died at Deans, S.C., in 1902.

McGill, William, Pvt., Co. F, from Moffatsville, S.C., enlisted at Anderson August 15, 1864. Absent without leave Mar/Aug 1864. Patient at Watts Hospital, Montgomery, Ala., November 15, 1864. Survivor. Surrendered 1865.

McIndoo, (no first name given), Pvt. Co. A, enlisted at Charleston May 1. Present for duty May/Jun. (no year given).

McKee, A. J., Pvt., Co. F, enlisted at Anderson January 13, 1862 for 12 months. Absent, sick, Nov/Dec 1862. Conscripted for the War Jan/Feb 1863. Absent without leave Jan/Feb 1863 - August 31, 1864. Survivor. Died of disease July 7, 1888.

McKee, Aaron W., Pvt., Age 25, born August 21, 1836, Co. F, from Iva, S.C., enlisted at Anderson May 9, 1862. Sick, patient in hospital, Jul/Aug 1863. Captured at Missionary Ridge November 25, 1863. Sent to Military Prison, Louisville and transferred to Rock Island December 13, 1863. Transferred to Fort Columbus and exchanged at Boulwares Wharf, Va., March 6, 1865. Admitted to Jackson Hospital, Richmond, and furloughed for 30 days, March 8, 1865. Surrendered.

McKee, John O., Pvt., Age 19, Co. F, From Anderson District, enlisted January 13, 1862. Absent sick Jul/Aug - Sept/Oct 1863. AWOL Nov/Dec 1863. Captured at Shipp's Gap/Taylor's Ridge October 16, 1864. Sent to Military Prison, Louisville and transferred to Camp Douglas October 29, 1864. Description: complexion, fair; hair, light; eyes, blue; height, 5 ft. 6 in. Discharged at Camp Douglas on June 17, 1865.

McKee, J. R. O., Pvt., Age 28, Co. F, from Iva, S.C., enlisted at Anderson January 13, 1862. Wounded at Jackson May 14, 1863. Absent, wounded September 1863 - February 1864. Detached, enrolling officer over Anderson District by order of the Secretary of War Mar/Aug 1864. Surrendered.

McMahan, A. H., Pvt., Age 28, Co., F, enlisted at Anderson December 22, 1862. Captured at Ringold/Missionary Ridge November 26 1863. Sent to Military Prison, Louisville and transferred to Rock Island December 10, 1863. Died of diarrhoea January 27, 1865. Grave no. 288, located south of prison barracks.

MacPhail, John, Pvt., Age 40, Co. F, enlisted at Camp Gist March 28, 1862. Absent, sick, May/Jun 1862. Absent, sick, Nov/Dec 1862 - Mar/Apr 1863. Absent without leave May/Jun 1863. Absent sick since May 1862. Absent, sick, furloughed, Sep/Oct 1863 - Nov/Dec 1863. Absent, sick, Nov/Dec 1863. Died of disease January 1864. Name also spelled *McPhail.*

McPhail, Junius W., Pvt., Age 34, Co. F, from Storeville, S.C., enlisted at Columbia January 13, 1864. Six balls passed through his clothing at Jackson. Absent, sick, furloughed from hospital, Jul/Aug - Sep/Oct 1863. Absent, sick, April 1864. Paroled at Greensboro May 1, 1865. Died July 24, 1895.

McQuaig, Henry Thomas, Corp., Age 20, born March 10, 1841, Co. B, enlisted at Marlboro December 4, 1861. Absent, sick, furloughed, Sep/Oct 1862. Company commissary 1863. Company courier. Promotion to Corporal announced during a speech made by Colonel Capers, regimental commander, May 22, 1864. Paroled at Greensboro May 1, 1865. Deserted April 25, 1865.

McRae, W. J., Pvt., Co. B, enlisted in Florida October 30, 1862. Captured at Jackson May 14, 1863. Assigned to Paroled Prisoners Camp at Demopolis June 15, 1863. Absent without leave Sep/Oct 1863. Captured at Chattanooga as deserter from Rebel Army October 9, 1863. Signed oath of allegiance to the United States October 1863. Description: complexion, fair; hair, brown; eyes, grey; height, 6 ft. 0 in. Conscript deserter. Released after taking oath to go north of Ohio River October 20, 1864. Died at home.

McWaters, James D., Pvt., Age 17, Co. H, enlisted at Chester District March 19, 1862. Died of disease at Charleston July 28, 1862. Father, John McWaters, filed claim for settlement October 13, 1862. Grave located at Magnolia Cemetery, Charleston.

McWeaver, G., 1Sgt., Co. K. Wounded at Peachtree Creek. Entry from Memory Rolls at State Archives, Columbia, S.C.

Medlin, J., Pvt., Age 32, Co. B, enlisted at Charleston December 4, 1861. Present for duty through May/Jun 1862. Discharged 1862.

Medlin, J. T., Pvt., Age 15, born April 22, 1845, Co. B, from Brownsville, Marion County, S.C., enlisted at Charleston December 4, 1861. Description: complexion, fair; hair, light; eyes, blue; height, 5 ft 0 in;

occupation, student. Discharged by reason of surgeon's certificate February 1, 1862. Married March 1, 1893. Died October 10, 1920. Widow - Ann Eliza Medlin.

Medlin, J. W., Pvt., Age 17, Co. B, enlisted at Charleston December 4, 1861. Description: complexion, fair; hair, black; eyes, dark; height, 5 ft. 0 in; occupation, student. Discharged by reason of surgeons certificate February 1, 1862.

Medlock, Martin, Pvt., Age 35, Co. I, enlisted at Columbia March 20, 1862. Absent, sick, May/Jun 1863. Absent, patient in hospital, August 30, 1863. Died of disease. Widow, Tabitha E. Medlock, filed a claim for settlement May 23, 1864.

Meekins, O. F., Pvt., Co. B, enlisted at Marion April 19, 1862. Present for duty through August 31, 1864. Present on all rolls. Mortally wounded in battle at Jonesboro September 1, 1864. Died at Blind School Hospital. Grave located in Rose Hill Cemetery, Macon, Bibb County, Ga. Father, E. J. Meekins, filed claim for settlement October 17, 1864.

Meekins, P. B., Pvt., Co. B, enlisted at Marlboro April 18, 1862. Sick in hospital in Rome and Columbia September 1863 - August 31, 1864. Paroled at Greensboro May 1, 1865. Deserted April 25, 1865.

Meekins, William E., Corp., Co. B, enlisted at Marion March 31, 1862. Absent, sick at home Sep/Oct 1862. Killed in battle at the Battle of Atlanta July 22, 1864. Father, E. J. Meekins, filed claim for settlement October 17, 1864.

Melton, Jesse, Pvt., Age 40, Co. H, enlisted at Chester March 19, 1862. Absent sick May/Jun 1862. Paid 50 cents for damage to musket Nov/Dec 1862. Died of disease at Fair Ground Hospital No. 2, Atlanta September 24, 1863. Buried in Oakland Cemetery, Atlanta, Ga., September 25, 1863. (Name may be spelled Milton on cemetery records.) Effects include $118.25. Father, Joseph Melton, filed claim for settlement of November 2, 1863.

Melton, Mike, Pvt., Age 30, Co. H, enlisted at Chester District, March 19, 1862. Patient in hospital May/Jun 1862. Wounded at Chickamauga September 20, 1862. Absent, patient in hospital at Columbia, Sep/Oct 1863 - Jan/Feb 1864. Signed receipt roll, by mark, for clothing at General Hospital No. 1, Columbia January 18, July 28 and August 24, 1864. Paroled at Greensboro May 1, 1865. Married - September 22, 1892. Died - August 7, 1908. Widow - Georgiana Melton.

Meray, John J., Pvt., Co. A., Discharged, physically disabled. Entry from Memory Rolls at State Archives, Columbia, S.C. May be duplicate of Marer, John J.

Metts, Jacob, Pvt., Age 18, Co. C, enlisted at Camp Gist March 5, 1862. Wounded at Lovejoy Station. Paroled at Greensboro May 1, 1865.

Metts, William, Pvt., Co. C, enlisted at Camp Gist March 18, 1862. Absent without leave May/Jun 1862. Absent, sick, patient in hospital at Columbia, Mar/Apr 1863. Died May 1, 1863.

Michael H., Pvt., Co. E, enlisted at Charleston January 16, 1862. Discharged on account of color February 28, 1862.

Miles, Alexander, Pvt., Age 34, Co. G, enlisted at Columbia March 19, 1862. Detached service to Easons Foundry to work on gunboat Nov/Dec 1862 - Nov/Dec 1863. Captured near Nashville December 16, 1864. Sent to Military Prison, Louisville and transferred to Camp Chase January 4, 1865. Paroled at Camp Chase and exchanged at New Orleans May 2, 1865.

Miles, Charles R., Pvt., Age 23, Co. G, enlisted at Columbia March 19, 1862. Absent, sick, patient in hospital at Columbia, Sep/Oct 1862. Absent without leave May 16, 1863 - August 31, 1864.

Miles, Francis, Pvt., Age 35, Co. G, enlisted at Columbia March 19 1862. Detached service to Easons Foundry to work on gunboat at Charleston October 24, 1862 - December 31, 1863. Present to August 31, 1864. Patient at Stonewall Hospital, Montgomery, Ala., October 15 - November 15, 1864.

Miles, Francis A., Pvt., Age 18, Co. I, enlisted at Pocotaligo March 1, 1863. Discharged because of underage by command of the Secretary of War November 23, 1863. Enlisted at Smyra Church, Ga., June 1, 1864. Recruit bounty paid. Captured at Franklin December 18, 1864. Admitted as a convalescent to No. 1, USA General Hospital, Nashville December 25, 1864 - January 7, 1865. Sent to Military Prison at Louisville and transferred to Camp Chase January 15, 1865. Died of pneumonia at Camp Chase Hospital February 9, 1865. Grave no. 1145 located 1/3 mile south of Camp Chase.

Miles, James E., Pvt., Age 33, Co. G, enlisted at Columbia March 19, 1862. Absent without leave May/Jun 1862. Patient in hospital at Montgomery Jul/Aug - Sep/Oct 1863. Absent, sick, patient in Ladies Hospital at Montgomery, Feb/Aug 1864 - November 15, 1864.

Miles, Jesse, Pvt., Age 25, Co. G, enlisted at Columbia March 19, 1862. Sick, patient in hospital at Columbia, Mar/Apr 1862. Killed in battle at Atlanta July 22, 1864.

Miles, John L., Pvt., Age 20, Co. I, enlisted at Columbia March 20, 1863. Absent, sick, furloughed, May/Jun 1862. Absent, sick, patient in hospital at Canton, Mississippi, and furloughed, June 26, 1863 - October 8, 1864. Paroled at Greensboro May 1, 1865.

Miles, Milton L., Pvt., Age 24, Co. I, enlisted at Columbia March 20, 1862. Absent on sick furlough May/Jun 1862. Absent, sick, furloughed, November 20, 1862 - December 1862. Absent, sick, patient in Lauderdale Springs Hospital August 5, 1863 - October 1863. Wounded, simple flesh wound, left leg, at Franklin November 30, 1864. Captured at

Franklin December 17, 1864. Admitted to No. 1,. USA, General Hospital, Nashville December 27, 1864 - February 8, 1865. Sent to Military Prison, Louisville and transferred to Rock Island February 18, 1865. Transferred to Point Lookout and exchanged March 23, 1865. Admitted to Jackson Hospital, Richmond March 24, 1865. Furloughed for 60 days March 28, 1865.

Miley, G. W., Pvt., Age 27, Co. E, enlisted at James Island May 14, 1862. Color Guard. Died of dysentery in an Alabama hospital June 24, 1863.

Miley, J. C., Sgt., Age 17, Co. E, enlisted at Salkehatchie January 16, 1862. Color Guard. Wounded at Stone Mountain July 22, 1864. Patient in Floyd House and Ocmulgee Hospital for wound. Amputation of right foot and ankle July 23, 1864. Assigned to invalid ccrps, P. A. C. S., Augusta February 6, 1865. Admitted for v.s. lower extremities, right, to CSA General Hospital, No. 11, Charlotte February 6 - 10 1865. Furloughed February 10, 1865. Surrendered.

Miley, J. K., Pvt., Age 24, Co. E, enlisted at James Island May 16, 1862. Detached service to work on gunboat in Charleston Oct/Nov 1862 - December 31, 1863. Present Jul/Aug 1864. Signed receipt roll for clothing April 1, 1864. Killed in battle at Jonesboro.

Miley, J. W., Pvt, Age 18, Co. E, from Lodge, S.C., enlisted at Dalton, Ga., March 20, 1864. Slightly wounded, thigh, at Calhoun, Ga., May 16, 1864. Absent, sick, patient in hospital August 25, 1864. Surrendered and discharged at end of war in 1865. Married - January 8, 1867. Died September 28, 1915. Widow - A. P. Miley.

Milford, L. C., Pvt., Co. F, from Abbeville, S.C., enlisted at Abbeville February 16, 1864. Severely wounded, leg, July 22, 1864. Mortally wounded in battle at Decatur July 22, 1864. Died from wounds at Forsythe, Ga., August 18, 1864. Buried as unknown soldier. Father, T. B. Milford, filed claim of settlement January 11, 1865.

Millen, Eli Harper, Sgt., Age 21, Co. H, enlisted at Chester April 11, 1862. Wounded at Chickamauga September 20, 1863. Appointed Sgt., January 1, 1864. Wounded at Franklin. Captured at Franklin December 17, 1864. Admitted as convalescent to No. 1, USA General Hospital, Nashville, December 28, 1864 - January 7, 1865. Sent to Military Prison, Louisville and transferred to Camp Chase January 15, 1865. Signed oath of allegiance to the United States to remain in the Loyal states during the war, released March 16, 1865.

Millen, John A., 2Lt., Age 31, Co. H., enlisted at Chester July 20, 1862. Elected 2Lt., December 15, 1862. Detailed to return deserters from South Carolina to their commands Jul/Aug - Nov/Dec 1863. Wife Maria L. Millen. Mortally wounded in battle at Franklin November 30, 1864. Captured at Franklin December 18, 1864. Admitted to No. 1, USA General Hospital, Nashville December 28, 1864. Died of exhaustion caused by gunshot fracture of Tarsus, right foot December 28, 1864. Buried in Grave No. 10795, Nashville City Cemetery December 30, 1864.

Miller, Henry C., Pvt., Age 17, Co. B, enlisted at Marlboro December 4, 1861. Transferred to Co. G, 8th Regiment April 28, 1863. Lost leg.

Miller, J. B., Pvt., Co. G. Entry from Memory Rolls at State Archives, Columbia, S.C.

Miller, Lawrence J., 2Lt., Co. I, enlisted at James Island May 17, 1862. Absent without leave December 15 - 31, 1863. Absent, sick, furloughed August - October 19, 1864. Promoted from the ranks of Co. I, 24th Regiment to 2Lt., for meritorious service April 9, 1865. Paroled at Greensboro May 1, 1865.

Miller, Robert M., Pvt., Age 27, Co. H, enlisted at Columbia March 19, 1862. Mortally wounded in battle at Chickamauga September 20, 1863. Died of wounds in hospital at Atlanta October 8, 1863. Buried October 6, 1863. Grave located in Block A, Row 14, Grave 32, Oakland Cemetery, Confederate Section, Atlanta.

Miller, Robert, Co. G. Entry from original muster roll.

Miller, William, Pvt., Age 25, Co. A, enlisted at Charleston March 17, 1862. Present May/Jun 1862. Discharged physically disabled.

Millis, A. B., Pvt., Co. H. Retired from wounds received at Chickamauga. Living. Entry from roster prepared by company commander.

Mills Robert, Pvt., Co H, enlisted at Chester October 1, 1862. Wounded at Chickamauga September 20, 1863. Furloughed Nov/Dec 1863. Absent without leave Jan/Feb 1864. Absent with leave and retired because of wounds August 31, 1864.

Mims, William P., Pvt., Age 16, Co. I, enlisted at Edgefield March 1, 1865. Paroled at Greensboro May 1, 1865.

Minnis, William A., Musician, Age 17, Co. E, enlisted at James Island March 24, 1863. Drummer. Present on all rolls. Signed receipt roll for clothing August 26, 1864. Paroled at Greensboro May 1, 1865.

Minter, W. C., Pvt., Co. G, enlisted at Wedowie, Ala., May 24, 1863. Assigned to Co. G, by order of General Johnston May/Jun 1863. Returned to his command August 10, 1863.

Mitchell, E. Marshal, Pvt., Age 30, Co. F, enlisted at Anderson January 13, 1862. Died of disease at Ballouville, S.C., April 4, 1863.

Mitchum, A. C., Pvt., Co. G, enlisted at Pocotaligo March 19, 1863. Absent without leave left Camp March 23, 1863. Deserted and dropped from the roll January 30, 1864.

Mock, J. David, Pvt., Co. D, enlisted at Pocotaligo February 20, 1863. Absent, sick, patient in hospital Sep/Oct - Nov/Dec 1863. Absent, sick, furloughed August 17 - October 17, 1864. Paroled at Greensboro May 1, 1865.

Mock, W. Thomas, Pvt., Age 21, Co. D, enlisted at Camp Gist January 19, 1862. Wounded at Secessionville. Absent, sick, furloughed Sep/Oct 1862. Twenty days pay stopped by order of court martial Nov/Dec 1862. Pay stoppage for the loss of bayonet, $6.00 Jan/Feb 1864. Captured at Franklin November 30, 1864. Sent to Military Prison, Louisville and transferred to Camp Douglas December 6, 1864. Discharged June 18, 1865.

Moody, Jno. A., Sgt., Age 40, Co. G., enlisted at Columbia March 19, 1862. Absent without leave May/Jun 1863. Absent, patient in hospital at Rome Sep/Oct 1863. Present to August 31, 1864.

Moore, Benjamin, Corp., Age 30, Co. A, enlisted at Charleston December 31, 1861. Present Mar/Apr 1862. Accidentally killed at Folly Island May 1862. Member of group of soldiers from Cole's Island foraging for beef rations.

Moore, H. F., Pvt., Age 35, Co. F, enlisted at Anderson March 27, 1863. Mortally wounded in battle at Jackson May 14, 1863. Captured and paroled in hospital May 16, 1863. Died of wounds in hospital at Jackson. Widow, Susanna Moore, filed claim for settlement July 28, 1863.

Moore, J. Ezra, Pvt., Age 22, Co. I, enlisted at Columbia March 20, 1862. Missing since battle July 20, 1864. Suppose in hands of enemy. Killed in battle at Peachtree Creek 1864.

Moore, Thomas B., 2Lt., Age 26, Co. B, enlisted at Marlboro December 4, 1861. Appointed 2Lt., August 14, 1862. Absent, sick at home Sep/Oct 1862. Absent, sick at home April 27, 1863. Absent, sick, Jul/Aug 1863. Absent without leave since retreat from Missionary Ridge November 25, 1863. Dropped November 14, 1864. Died 1873.

Morgan, David, Pvt., Co. K, enlisted at Edgefield April 15, 1862. Died in camp at Dalton January 9, 1864. Widow, Frances Morgan, filed claim for settlement January 23, 1865.

Morgan, G. E., Co. K. Grave located in Marietta Confederate Cemetery, Marietta, Ga. Entry from *List in Marietta Confederate Cemetery*, taken from U.D.C. Records, Kennesaw Chapter # 241 as published in *Georgia Genealogical Society Quarterly*, Vol. 14, No. 2, Summer 1978, located in the Marietta Public Library, Marietta, Ga. Suspected duplicate entry of Joseph Evan Morgan.

Morgan, Joseph Evan, 2Lt., Co. K, enlisted at Edgefield April 15, 1862. Killed in battle at Chickamauga September 20, 1863. Killed while attempting to rally a Georgia Regiment. Morgan was the third man killed under the flag of the Georgia Regiment. He saw the colors fall and ran to pick it up, and although he was warned of the peril, he could not see the Confederate colors dragged in the dust. He bravely unfurled the colors, looking up at the same time, and before the flag caught the breeze, he was immediately shot through the neck and died on the field. He was buried in a trench on the battle field and a friend reported that his body was "never recovered." (See G. E. Morgan.)

Morgan, Thomas C., Lt. Col., Co. K, & F&S, enlisted at Edgefield April 15, 1862. Promoted Capt., April 23, 1862. Wounded, left side of the throat, at Chickamauga. Wounded at Calhoun. Wounded near Atlanta and sent to hospital July 22, 1864. Promoted Maj., September 1864. Promoted to Lt. Col., Consolidated 16th & 24th Regiment April 9, 1865. Paroled at Greensboro May 1, 1865.

Morgan, Tyler Whitfield, Corp., Co. K, enlisted at Edgefield July 1, 1862. Sent to hospital at Rome September 17, 1863. Absent, sick, furloughed Nov/Dec 1863. Signed receipt roll for clothing September 9, 1864. Wounded at Franklin. Admitted to Lay Hospital, Meridian, Miss, for wound January 11, 1865. Surrendered and paroled at Augusta May 18, 1865. After the War, he moved to Texas and died at Kansas City May 2, 1893. Earlier he was described as, "Broken down in health and only 30."

Morgan, Wm. T., Pvt., Co. G, enlisted at Anderson April 29, 1862. Absent, sick, May/Jun 1862. Killed in battle at Jackson May 14, 1863.

Morrell, John, Pvt., Age 37, Co. G, enlisted at Columbia March 19, 1862. Killed in battle at Secessionville June 16, 1862. Widow, Elizabeth Morrell, filed claim for settlement January 9, 1863.

Morris, Joseph, Pvt., Co. K, enlisted at Edgefield February 12, 1864. Sent to hospital July 1864. Due $50.00 bounty. Admitted to Way Hospital, Meridian, Miss January 28, 1865.

Morris, W. D., Pvt., Age 35, Co. G, enlisted at Columbia March 19, 1862. Absent without leave and sick in hospital Nov/Dec 1862. Under arrest Mar/Apr 1863. One month's pay stopped by order of court martial May/Jun 1863. Received court martial for passing a petition seeking to elect the captain and first lieutenant of the company. Found guilty but sentence commuted to time already spent in guard house awaiting trial April 23, 1864. Absent without leave April - August 31, 1864.

Morris, William, Pvt., Age 41, Co. A, enlisted at Charleston December 31, 1861 for 12 months. Detailed to work on Eason's gunboat by order of the Commanding General. Died of typhoid fever in Citadel Square Hospital, Charleston, while detached service to work on gunboat at Easons Foundry November 16, 1862. Grave located in Magnolia Cemetery, Charleston.

Mosiley, J. L., Pvt., Co. G. Entry from Memory Rolls at State Archives, Columbia, S.C.

Moyers, Alex., Pvt., Age 20, Co. C, enlisted at Secessionville September 1, 1862. Absent, sick, patient in hospital at Columbia Mar/Apr 1863. Absent, sick, May/Jun 1863. Absent, sick, patient in hospital at Atlanta

Jul/Aug 1863. Absent without leave Sep/Oct 1863. Paroled at Greensboro May 1, 1865.

Moyers, N., Pvt., Age 30, Co. C, from Reeves, enlisted at Secessionville September 1, 1862. Paid $50.00 bounty. Absent, sick, Jan/Feb 1863. Killed in battle at Chickamauga September 20, 1863.

Mulligan, B. A., Pvt., Age 20, Co. D, enlisted at Camp Gist January 16, 1862. Transferred to Co. F, 11th Regiment, November 8, 1862.

Mulligan, Frank, Pvt., Age 51, Co. D, enlisted at Camp Gist February 21, 1862. Description: complexion, light; hair, gray; eyes, blue; height, 5 ft. 8 in; occupation, teacher. Discharged by reason of lumbago and debility due to age October 16, 1862.

Mulligan, Wash, Pvt., Age 43, Co. D, enlisted at Camp Gist January 19, 1862. Present Sep/Oct 1862.

Munds, William, Cook, Age 20, Co. D, enlisted at Camp Gist January 16, 1862. Absent, sick, patient in hospital at Atlanta Nov/Dec 1862. Colored. Reported missing in engagement near Jackson May 14, 1863. Present Jul/Aug 1864.

Murphy, W. M., Corp., Co. G. Entry from Memory Rolls at State Archives, Columbia, S.C.

Murphy, William P., Pvt., Age 24, Co. G, enlisted at Columbia March 19, 1862. Absent without leave May/Jun 1863. Absent, patient in hospital at Rome. Sep/Oct 1863. Detailed to hospital duty at Griffin Nov/Dec 1863. Absent, sick, patient in hospital at Lumpkin, Ga. Jan/Feb 1864. Present for duty Mar/Aug 1864. Signed receipt roll for clothing September 29, 1864.

Murray, T. J., Lt., Age 33, Co. C, enlisted at Georges Station January 17, 1862. Died of disease 1862.

Muse, Julius E., Pvt., Age 35, Co. I, enlisted at Columbia March 20, 1862. Absent, sick, Sep/Oct 1862. Present for duty Jul/Aug 1864. Extra daily duty division hospital Jul/Aug 1864.

Nardin, Walter H., Asst. Surg., F&S, Appointed at High Point, NC, April 4, 1863. Paroled at Greensboro May 1, 1865.

Natt, J. M. H., Co. C. Buried June 26, 1864 in Oakland Cemetery, Atlanta, Georgia. Entry from Oakland Cemetery records. (See Hyatt, J. M., Pvt., as possible duplicate.)

Neely, J. B., Pvt., Age 25, Co. G, enlisted at Columbia March 19, 1862. Discharged September 1, 1862.

Nelson, Horatio, Pvt., Age 26, Co. G, enlisted at Columbia March 19, 1862. Patient in hospital May/Jun 1862.

Nelson, John, Pvt., Co. G, enlisted at Columbia November 1, 1862. Killed in battle at Chickamauga September 20, 1863.

Nelson, Joseph H., Pvt., Age 23, Co. G, enlisted at Columbia March 19, 1862. Present on all rolls. Captured near Nashville December 16, 1864.

Sent to Military Prison, Louisville and transferred to Camp Chase January 14, 1865. Description: complexion, dark; hair, dark; eyes, black; height, 5 ft. 11 in. Signed oath of allegiance to the United States June 12, 1865.

Neuffer, C. Jr., Co. G. Entry from original muster roll.

New, Benjamin, Pvt., Co. K, enlisted at Edgefield April 15, 1862. Patient in hospital Sep/Oct 1862. Absent without leave January 1 - August 31, 1864. Deserted.

New, Ben., Pvt., Co. H. Deserted 1863. Entry from Memory Rolls at State Archives, Columbia, S.C. Ed. Note - Possible duplication of New, Benjamin.

New, Edward, Pvt., Age 28, Co. K, enlisted at Edgefield April 15, 1862. Discharged by surgeons certificate, heart disease, June 15, 1862. Description: complexion, light; hair, brown; eyes, blue; height, 6 ft. 0 in. Died 1862.

New, Pickens, Pvt., Age 25, Co. K, enlisted at Edgefield April 15, 1862. Wounded during the battle of Secessionville June 16, 1862. Patient in hospital June - October 1862. Confined to guard house Jan/Feb 1863. One months pay stopped by court martial Mar/Apr 1863. Admitted to hospital at Atlanta September 6 - Nov/Dec 1863. Captured near Nashville December 16, 1864. Sent to Military Prison, Louisville and transferred to Camp Chase January 4, 1865. Description: complexion, fair; hair, light; eyes, blue; height, 5 ft. 1 3/4 in. Signed oath of allegiance to the United States June 12, 1865.

Newel, Isaiah J., Pvt., Co. F, enlisted at Columbia January 13, 1862 for 12 months. Conscripted for the war Jan/Feb 1863. Absent, sick, March/Apr 1863. Absent, patient in hospital Rome Sep/Oct 1863. Captured at Shipp's Gap/Taylor's Ridge October 16, 1864. Sent to Military Prison, Louisville and transferred to Camp Douglas October 29, 1864. Description: complexion, fair; hair, red; eyes, grey; height 5 ft. 5 in. Signed oath of allegiance to the United States and discharged June 17, 1865. Died of disease at home after the war.

Newel, Thomas A., Pvt., Co. F, enlisted at Columbia January 13, 1862 for 12 months. Died of disease April 6, 1862.

Newton, Isaac B., Pvt., Co. F, enlisted at Anderson January 13, 1862 for 12 months. Exchanged to Orrs Regiment for J. L. McGee April 11, 1862.

Newton, Joseph N., Pvt., Co. F. Exchanged for J. D. McGee to Orr's Regiment. Entry from Memory Rolls at State Archives, Columbia, S.C., and Survivor's Association roster.

Nichols, Sam, Cook, Age 43, Co. A, enlisted at Charleston December 31, 1861. Absent, sick, Sep/Oct - Nov/Dec 1862. Discharged January 1, 1863.

Nicholson, J. A., Pvt., Age 22, Co. K, enlisted at Edgefield April 15, 1862.

Discharged by surgeons certificate, consumption, June 6, 1862. Description: complexion, fair; hair, light; eyes, blue; height, 6 ft. 0 in; occupation, farmer.

Nix, Larken, Pvt., Age 39, Co. F, enlisted at Columbia January 13, 1862. Transferred to Smith's Battalion, Sharpshooters, August 10 - December 25, 1862. Absent, sick, Mar/Apr - Jul/Aug 1863. Detailed as nurse to hospital at Columbia Sep/Oct 1863 - August 31, 1864. Signed by mark. Signed receipt roll for clothing, General Hospital, No. 2, Columbia August 8, 1864. Surrendered 1865.

Nobles, Elliot, Pvt., Age 21, Co. E, enlisted at Walterboro January 4, 1862. Absent, furloughed from hospital for 60 days, August 9, 1864. Surrendered.

Nobles, John, Pvt., Age 23, Co. E, enlisted at Salkehatchie January 16, 1862. Absent, with leave furlough from hospital for 30 days, October 17, 1863. Absent without leave Nov/Dec 1863. Absent, sick, patient in hospital February 1864. Died of disease in hospital at Dalton February 23, 1864.

Nobles, Joshua, Pvt., Age 28, Co. E. Died of disease at Dalton, Ga. Entry from Memory Rolls at State Archives, Columbia, S.C.

Norton, Elias, Pvt., Age 23, Co. B, enlisted at Marlboro December 4, 1861. Absent without leave August 1863. Detailed as regimental teamster January - August 1864. Admitted to St. Mary's Hospital, West Point, Miss., January 13, 1865. Admitted to Way Hospital, Meridian suffering with debility, January 15, 1865.

Norton, J. P., Pvt., Age 22, Co. B, enlisted at Marlboro December 14, 1861. Present May/Jun 1862. Died of disease at hospital 1862.

Norton, Samuel S., Pvt., Co. B, enlisted at Marlboro April 1, 1863. Absent sick at home Sep/Oct 1863. Absent without leave Nov/Dec 1863. Detailed as teamster for supply trains February 18 - August 1864. Absent, sick, patient in Polk Hospital, Atlanta and Ocmulgee Hospital, Macon for rubeola Jun/Jul 1864. Killed in battle at Nashville 1864.

O'Briant, Asbury C., Pvt., Co. F, enlisted at Anderson April 10, 1862. Absent, sick, patient in hospital June - August 1863. Died of disease 1863.

Odom, Daniel A., Pvt., Age 30, Co. B, enlisted at Marlboro December 4, 1861. Present for duty May/Jun 1862. Transferred to 2nd Battalion, South Carolina Sharpshooters, 1862.

Odom, Henry E., Pvt., Age 20, Co. B, enlisted at Marlboro December 4, 1861. Killed in battle at Jackson May 14, 1863.

Odom, James Godwin, Pvt., Co. B, enlisted at Marlboro May 28, 1862. Absent, sick at home, Sep/Oct 1863. Absent without leave Nov/Dec 1863. Wounded at Peachtree Creek. Died in hospital 1864. Prior to enlisting in 24th Regiment, Odom served one year in Co. G, 8th

Regiment stationed in Virginia.

Odom, J. Leonard, Pvt., Age 18, Co. B, enlisted at Marlboro December 4, 1861. Absent, sick at home, Nov/Dec - Jan/Feb 1864. Captured at Nashville December 16, 1864. Sent to Military Prison, Louisville and transferred to Camp Douglas December 24, 1864. Mustered into the 6th U. S. Vol. Infantry April 2, 1865.

Odom, Leander, Pvt., Co. D. Captured near Jonesboro September 1, 1864. Exchanged at Rough and Ready September 19, 1864.

Odom, Phillip E., Pvt., Co. B, enlisted at Marlboro April 1, 1863. Conscript. Signed receipt roll for clothing at 3d Gen Hosp., Augusta October 19, 1864. Signed receipt roll for clothing at 3d General Hospital, Augusta, October 19, 1864. Paroled at Greensboro May 1, 1865. Deserted April 25, 1865.

Odom, S. Durnat, Co. B, enlisted January 6, 1862. Married October 20, 1879. Died October 25, 1914. Widow - Sarah A. Odom. Entry from Confederate Veteran pension records at State Archives, Columbia, S.C.

Odom, Sion W., Pvt., Co. B, enlisted at Marlboro May 29, 1862. Alumnus of Brewton Fork High School. Detailed to signal corps at Pocotaligo Mar/Apr - May/Jun 1863. Killed in battle at Chickamauga September 20, 1863. Prior to enlisting in the 24th Regiment, Odom served one year in Co. G, 8th Regiment stationed in Virginia.

Ogier, T. L., Jr. Surgeon, F&S, Appointed at Pocotaligo September 1, 1862. Acting brigade Surgeon May/Jun 1863. Promoted to Major and division surgeon July 1863. Died from disease, typhoid fever, at Morton, Mississippi August 9, 1863.

O'Kief, Owen, Co. G. Entry from original muster roll.

Ollis, O. A., Pvt. Surrendered at Tallahassee, Fla May 10, 1865. Paroled May 18, 1865.

Orchard, John, Pvt., Age 32, Co. A, enlisted at Charleston February 27, 1862. Detailed to Easons Foundry to work on gunboat at Charleston by order of the Commanding General. Transferred to Navy Department by order of the Commanding General August 14, 1862.

O'Rourke, James W., Pvt., Age 18, Co. A, enlisted at Charleston December 31, 1861. Absent without leave December 15, 1862 - February 20, 1863. Under arrest, confined in guard house for desertion Mar/Apr 1863. Absent, sick, patient in hospital at Montgomery Jul/Aug 1863 - Jul/Aug 1864.

Ouzts, Ab, Pvt., Co. K. Died in hospital 1862. Entry from Memory Rolls at State Archives, Columbia, S.C.

Ouzts, A. S., Pvt., Co. K, enlisted at Edgefield April 15, 1862. Present May/Jun 1862. Surrendered at Tallahassee May 10, 1865. Paroled at Albany May 23, 1865. (Ed. note - The name Ouzts is sometimes spelled Outzs and both ways on most records).

Ouzts, Franklin, Pvt., Co. K, enlisted at Edgefield March 7, 1862. Patient in hospital at Columbia Mar/Apr 1862. Killed in battle at Chickamauga September 20, 1863.

Ouzts, Isaac, Pvt., Co. K, enlisted at Edgefield March 1, 1863. Present on all rolls. Paroled at Greensboro May 1, 1865.

Ouzts, James T., Pvt., Co. K, enlisted at Edgefield April 15, 1862. Musician. Present on all rolls. Paroled at Greensboro May 1, 1865.

Ouzts, J. K., Pvt., Co. K, enlisted at Edgefield January 25, 1864. Absent without leave May - August 1864.

Ouzts, Marion, Pvt., Co. K. Discharged by medical board April 1863.

Ouzts, Peter, Pvt., Co. K, enlisted at Edgefield April 15, 1862. Present for duty on all rolls. Paroled at Greensboro May 1, 1865.

Ouzts, Shemuel W., Pvt., Co. K, enlisted at Edgefield April 15, 1862. Musician. Patient in hospital at Yazoo City, Mississippi May/Jun 1863. Mortally wounded in battle at Calhoun, Ga., May 16, 1864. Died from wounds May 30, 1864.

Outzs, T., Pvt., Co. K, enlisted at Edgefield March 10, 1862. Present for duty Mar/Apr 1862.

Ouzts, Thomas J., Pvt., Co. K, enlisted at Edgefield March 15, 1862. Sent to hospital May 21, 1864. Surrendered in Hospital at Citronelle, Ala., May 4, 1865. Paroled at Meridian, Miss., May 12, 1865.

Overstreet, Labon, Pvt., Co. D, enlisted at Camp Gist March 31, 1862. Transferred to Sharpshooters and returned Jan/Feb 1863. Detached service driving pontoon train by order of General Johnson June 1864. Captured near Nashville December 16, 1864. Sent to Military Prison, Louisville and transferred to Camp Chase January 4, 1865. Died of pneumonia March 5, 1865. Grave no. 563, located 1/3 mile south of Camp Chase.

Owens, Robt. T., Pvt., Age 25, Co. G, enlisted at Columbia March 19, 1862. Drummer/musician. Wounded at Atlanta August 1864. Paroled at Greensboro May 1, 1865.

Padgett, Andrew R., 2Lt., Age 25, Co, E, enlisted at Salkehatchie January 16, 1862. Promoted to 4Corp., May/Jun 1862. Reduced to ranks by court martial May 30, 1863. Detailed to drive ambulance Nov/Dec 1863. Promoted to 4Sgt., February 20, 1864. Promoted to 2Lt., July 15, 1864. Wounded. Granted leave of absence 30 days January 20, 1865. Surrendered.

Padgett, Daniel, 2Lt., Age 27, Co. E, enlisted at Camp Gist January 16, 1862. Resigned June 13, 1862.

Padgett, David, Pvt., Age 30, Co. E, enlisted at Pocotaligo March 31, 1863. Pay stopped for one month by court martial May/Jun 1863. Absent, sick at home, furloughed October 20, 1863 - Jan/Feb 1864. Died of disease.

Padgett, Emanuel, Pvt., Age 29, Co. E, enlisted at Salkehatchie January 16, 1862. Wounded at Calhoun, Ga. Absent, patient in hospital, wounded, left hip and side, July 20, 1864. Patient at Ocmulgee Hospital, Macon, for V.S. compound fracture, left tibia, November 17, 1864 - January 15, 1865. Surrendered.

Padgett, Henry, Pvt., Age 19, Co. E, from Branchville, enlisted at Charleston March 17, 1862. Pay stopped for one month by order of court martial May/Jun 1863. Wounded at Chickamauga September 20, 1862. Gunshot wound through left thigh at Calhoun, Ga., May 16, 1864. Furloughed from hospital for 60 days with extension of 30 days May 30, 1864. Died.

Padgett, Isham, Jr., Pvt., Age 24, Co. E, enlisted at Salkehatchie January 16, 1862. Absent, sick, patient in hospital at Columbia Mar/Apr - May/Jun 1863. Absent, sick, patient in Georgia hospital September 2, 1863. Died of disease at Cassville, Ga., February 19, 1864.

Padgett, Isham, Sr., Pvt., Age 41, Co. E, enlisted at Salkehatchie January 16, 1862. Absent sick at home Nov/Dec 1862 - Jan/Feb 1862. Absent without leave Mar/Apr - May/Jun 1863. Mortally wounded in battle at Chickamauga September 20, 1863. Wounded, patient in hospital September 20, 1863 - April 13, 1864. Died of wounds April 13, 1864.

Padgett, James, Pvt., Age 22, Co. E, enlisted at Salkehatchie January 16, 1862. Absent, sick, patient in hospital Nov/Dec 1862. Sick with pneumonia, furloughed 15 days January 10, 1863. Pay stopped for one month by court martial May/Jun 1863. Mortally wounded in battle at Chickamauga September 20, 1863. Died of wounds at Fairgrounds Hospital, Atlanta, December 7, 1863. Left effect of $1.55. Contractor paid $11.50 to conduct funeral. Buried December 7, 1863 in Oakland Cemetery, Atlanta, Ga., Row 6, #5.

Padgett, James, Co. C. Died at Atlanta Medical College Hospital April 13, 1864. Grave located in Oakland Cemetery, Atlanta, Ga., Row 5, No. 12. Entry from Oakland Cemetery records. (Ed. Note - Two soldiers named "James Padgett" are buried there.}

Padgett, James D., 2Lt., Age 30, Co. I, enlisted at Columbia March 20, 1862. Absent, sick, patient in hospital, furloughed April 17 - May/Jun 1863. Promoted to 2Lt., March 27, 1864. Killed in battle at Franklin November 30, 1864. Grave located in Franklin Confederate Cemetery, Section 83, Grave No. 6.

Padgett, J. C., Pvt., Age 28, Co. E, enlisted at Charleston March 20, 1862. Discharged by enlistment of substitute, J. C. Copeland, April 30, 1862.

Padgett, Job, Pvt., Age 25, Co. E, enlisted at Salkehatchie January 16, 1862. Pay stopped for one month by court martial May/Jun 1863. Surrendered.

Padgett, Joel, Jr., Pvt., Age 18, Co. E, from Branchville, enlisted at Camp Gist March 15, 1862. Pay stopped for one month by court martial May/Jun 1863. Wounded, received gun shot wound through left ankle, at Chickamauga September 20, 1863. Wounded at Atlanta. Surrendered.

Padgett, Joel, Sr., Pvt., Age 24, Co. E, from Branchville, enlisted at Salkehatchie January 16, 1862. Under arrest October 1863. Absent, sick, patient in hospital Nov/Dec 1862. Detached as hospital guard Mar/Apr 1863. Absent without leave May/Jun 1863. Absent without leave Nov/Dec 1863. Absent, sick at home, furloughed December 15, 1863 - July 31, 1864. Absent without leave August 1, 1864. Surrendered.

Padgett, Hugo Sheridan, Pvt., Age 30, Co. E, enlisted at Salkehatchie January 16, 1862. Transferred to 2nd Battalion, Sharpshooters, and retransferred January 15, 1863. Pay stopped for one month by court martial May/Jun 1863. Detailed to drive a wagon October 15 - December 1863. Absent, sick, patient in hospital July 22 - August 1864. Surrendered. Grave located in The Hagan Family Cemetery, Upper Colleton County, S.C.

Padgett, Thomas, Pvt., Age 22, Co. E, enlisted at Salkehatchie January 16, 1862. Pay stopped for one month by court martial May/Jun 1863. Captured at Chickamauga September 20, 1863. Sent to Military Prison at Louisville and transferred to Camp Douglas October 4, 1863. Died of smallpox November 1, 1864. Grave located near Camp Douglas.

Palmer, Joseph Clarence, 1Lt., and Adjutant, F&S, enlisted at Charleston April 4, 1862. Former member of Boykin's S. C. Rangers. Lt. Col. Capers made a special request to the Secretary of War, CSA, Mr. Benjamin Judah, to obtain the services of Lt. Palmer as Adjutant, 24th Regiment. Killed in battle at Chickamauga September 20, 1863. The fatal ball passed through his head entering below the left eye. Citadel graduate, Class of 1861. Grave located in Confederate Cemetery, Marietta, Ga.

Pardue, David, Pvt., Co. K, enlisted at Edgefield April 15, 1862. Discharged by surgeons certificate June 3, 1862. Died in hospital.

Pardue, John, Pvt., Co. K, enlisted at Adams Run February 12, 1862. Present Jan/Feb - Mar/Aug 1864. Deserted at Dalton, Ga., 1864.

Pardue, John F., Co. K. Died September 9, 1872. Widow Mary S. Pardue. Entry from Confederate Veteran pension records at State Archives, Columbia, S.C.

Pardue, L., Co. H, 24th Regiment. Discharged. Entry from *Chester County Heritage History* and roster prepared by company commander.

Parham, Andrew, Pvt., Age 20, Co. B, enlisted at Marlboro December 4, 1861. Absent, sick, patient in hospital at Secessionville Sep/Oct 1862. Sick in quarters Jan/Feb 1862. Wounded at Atlanta. Signed receipt roll for clothing at General Hospital, No. 1, Columbia July 28, 1864. Paroled at Greensboro May 1, 1865. Deserted April 25, 1865.

Parham, Samuel, Pvt., Co. B, enlisted at Marlboro May 29, 1862. Absent without leave May/Jun 1863. Wounded at Chickamauga September 20, 1863. Patient in hospital at Marietta Sep/Oct 1863. Killed in battle at Peachtree Creek July 20, 1864.

Parker, Matthew, Pvt., Co. F, from Holland's Store, S.C., enlisted at Anderson November 7, 1862. Wounded at Jackson May 14, 1863. Captured and paroled in hospital May 16, 1863. Admitted Ocmulgee Hospital, Macon, with diarrhoea chronic and with great emaciation July 19, 1864. Furloughed for 60 days July 22, 1864. Paroled at Greensboro May 1, 1865.

Parker, William W., Pvt., Age 23, Co. B, from Bennettsville, enlisted at Marlboro December 4, 1861. Died of typhoid fever in hospital at Griffin, Ga., October 2, 1863. Effects consisted of sundries and $19.00. Buried at Griffin, Spaulding Co., Ga.

Parker, Wm., Pvt., Co. B. Killed in battle at Peachtree Creek, July 20, 1863. Entry from *A History of Marlboro County*.

Parkman, John P., Pvt., Age 30, Co. I, enlisted at James Island May 17, 1862. Absent, sick, Sep/Oct 1862. Died at Edgefield October 29, 1862.

Parkman, Lewis, Pvt., Co. K, enlisted at Edgefield March 1, 1862. Present for duty on all rolls. Paroled at Greensboro May 1, 1865.

Patat, Lewis P., Pvt., Age 23, Co. A, enlisted at Charleston December 31, 1861. Captured near Marietta, Ga., July 2, 1864. Sent to Military Prison, Louisville and transferred to Camp Douglas July 18, 1864. Description: complexion, dark; hair, dark; eyes, hazel; height, 5 ft. 7 in. Signed oath of allegiance to the United States and discharged June 6, 1865. Married September 19, 1867. Died February 28, 1899. Widow, Mary E. Patat, resided at 207 King St., Charleston, S.C.

Patrick, Benjamin B., Pvt., Age 36, Co. C, enlisted at Charleston March 4, 1862. Absent, sick, May/Jun 1863. Absent without leave July 16, 1863 - August 31, 1864.

Patrick, George W., Pvt., Age 20, Co. C, enlisted at Georges Station, January 7, 1862. Present through May/Jun 1862. Discharged at Charleston 1862.

Patrick, John, Pvt., Age 24, Co. C, enlisted at Georges Station January 7, 1862. Transferred to the 2nd Batt. Sharpshooters and deserted to return to his original company. Tried by court martial. Sentenced to six months hard labor with ball & chain February 12, 1863. Court lenient, in consideration of extenuating circumstances. Lost leg at Fort Sumter.

Patrick, William, Pvt., Age 35, Co. C, enlisted at Georges Station January 7, 1862. Wounded at Kennesaw. Admitted to CSA General Hospital No. 1, Charlotte March 16, 1865. Transferred to another hospital April

21, 1865.

Patterson, Wm. B., Sgt., Age 27, Co. F, enlisted at Anderson January 13, 1862. Appointed 4Corp., December 1, 1862. Promoted to 3Corp., January 30, 1863. Promoted to 5Sgt., June 1, 1863. Promoted to 4Sgt., August 1, 1863. In hospital sick October 4, 1863 - December 31, 1863. Died of disease January 1, 1864.

Patterson, W. H., 1Lt., Age 25, Co. C, enlisted at Georges Station January 7, 1862. Absent, sick, patient in hospital, Jul/Aug 1863. Absent without leave Nov/Dec 1863 - August 31, 1864. Dropped November 14, 1864.

Peak, Samuel. L., Pvt., Co. G, enlisted at Columbia April 7, 1864. Captured near Nashville December 16, 1864. Sent to Military Prison, Louisville and transferred to Camp Chase January 4, 1865. Died of variola (abcess behind the leg) February 13, 1865. Grave located 1/3 mile south of Camp Chase.

Pearson, A. W., Pvt., Co. G, Consolidated 16th and 24th Regiment, enlisted at Tupelo, Miss., January 20, 1865. Paroled at Greensboro May 1, 1865. Deserted April 19, 1865.

Pearson, John H., Capt., Age 43, Co. G, enlisted at Columbia April 19, 1862. Lawyer and Master In Equity for Richland County before the war. Commander Co. G which was known as Captain Pearson's company. Court martialed for overstaying leave, not reporting to his commander upon return to duty after an absence, and absent without permission. Sentenced to be reprimanded in front of regiment, and forfeiture of rank and pay for three months. Resigned due to ill health February 23, 1863.

Pearson, P. P., Pvt., Age 14, Co. G, enlisted at Columbia April 12, 1862.

Pearson, R. R., Pvt., Age 18, Co. G, enlisted at Columbia April 12, 1862. Absent sick.

Peel, Freeman, Pvt., Co. B, enlisted at Marlboro April 1, 1862. Absent without leave Sep/Oct 1863. Severely wounded, shoulder, July 20, 1864. Captured near Nashville December 16, 1864. Sent to Military Prison, Louisville and transferred to Camp Douglas December 24, 1864. Discharged June 19, 1865. Died 1881.

Pendarvis, J. A., Pvt., Age 23, Co. C, enlisted at Georges Station January 7, 1862. Died August 26, 1862. Grave located in Magnolia Cemetery, Charleston.

Pendarvis, J. D. C., Corp., Age 18, Co. C, from St. George, S.C., enlisted at Georges Station January 7, 1862. Color Corporal. Wounded at Chickamauga September 20, 1862. Absent, wounded, Sep/Oct - Jan/Feb 1864. Wounded at Nashville. Paroled at Greensboro May 1, 1865.

Pendarvis, John, Pvt., Age 25, Co. C, enlisted at Georges Station January 7, 1862. Detached service to Easons to work on gunboat at Charleston Jul/Aug 1862 - January 7, 1864. Absent, sick, furloughed, August 8, 1864.

Pendarvis, J. T., Pvt., Age 31, born September 21, 1838, Co. C, from Summerville, S.C., enlisted at Georges Station January 7, 1862. Detached service to Easons to work on gunboat at Charleston June 1862 - January 7, 1864. Severely wounded, through the left shoulder, at Calhoun, Ga., May 16, 1864. Wounded, leg, at Franklin November 30, 1864. Captured at Franklin December 17, 1864. Admitted for gunshot fracture of right tibia, middle 3 inches, to No. 1, USA General Hospital, Nashville December 26, 1864 - January 17, 1865. Sent to Military Prison, Louisville and transferred to Camp Chase January 20, 1865. Description: complexion, dark; hair, dark; eyes, dark; height, 5 ft. 8 1/2 in. Signed oath of allegiance to United States June 13, 1865.

Pendarvis, J. T., Pvt., Age 25, Co. C, enlisted at Charleston February 21, 1862. Died in 1862.

Perdue, Leander, Pvt., Age 24, Co. H, enlisted at Chester March 19, 1862. Discharged.

Perry, Calvin, Musician, Age 25, Co. A, enlisted at Charleston December 31, 1861. Discharged January 24, 1863.

Phillips, Preston, Corp., Age 19, born January 3, 1845, Co. D, from Garnett, S.C., enlisted at Camp Gist January 16, 1862. Slightly wounded at Jackson 9-16, 1862. Wounded at Chickamauga. Absent without leave for six days and pay stopped for that time Nov/Dec 1863. Promoted to Corp., July 21, 1864. Wounded, shoulder, at Jonesboro. Paroled at Greensboro May 1, 1865.

Phillips, William, Pvt., Age 26. Co. D, enlisted at Camp Gist January 19, 1862. Pay stopped ($26.00) by order of court martial for absent without leave May/Jun 1863. Absent without leave August 30 - October 6, 1863. Wounded at Kennesaw Mountain. Absent, wounded, June 16 - September 16, 1864.

Poag, James, Co. H. Entry from *Chester County Heritage History*.

Polk, John, Pvt., Age 25, Co. I. Transferred to Sharpshooters. Entry from Memory Rolls at State Archives, Columbia, S.C.

Polk, Joseph, Pvt., Co. I, enlisted at James Island June 4, 1862. Received as substitute for Thomas J. Thurmond June 4, 1862. Transferred to Sharpshooters August 9, 1862.

Pope, W. J. D., Pvt., Co. D. Entry from Memory Rolls at State Archives, Columbia, S.C.

Poznanski, Gustavus. Killed at Secessionville June 16, 1862. Entry from UDC Pamphlet, *Confederate Dead Buried in Charleston*, May 3, 1880.

Preacher, J. Minney, Pvt., Age 25, Co. E, enlisted at Salkehatchie January 16, 1862. Pay stopped for one month by court martial May/Jun 1863. Absent, sick, patient in hospital June 29 - August 31, 1864. Died of disease.

Preacher, W. E., Corp., Age 19, Co. E, enlisted at Camp Gist March 3,

1862. Slightly wounded, breast, July 20/22, 1864. Promoted to Corp., July 24, 1864. Captured near Nashville December 16, 1864. Sent to Military Prison, Louisville and transferred to Camp Chase January 4, 1865. Died of pneumonia February 17, 1865. Grave no. 314, 1/3 mile south of Camp Chase.

Prescott, Memphis W., Sgt., Age 18, Co. I, enlisted at Columbia April 5, 1862., Promoted 2Sgt., May 18, 1862. Wounded, right arm, at Chickamauga September 20, 1863. Absent Sick September 20 - Nov/Dec 1863. Killed in battle at Peachtree Creek July 20, 1864.

Prevaux, C., Pvt., Co. E, enlisted at Charleston January 16, 1862. Discharged on account of color February 28, 1862.

Prevaux, S., Pvt., Co. E, enlisted at Charleston January 16, 1862. Discharged on account of color February 28, 1862.

Prewette, Phillip H., Pvt., Age 17, Co. F, enlisted at Columbia January 13, 1863. Signed receipt roll for clothing April 1, 1864. Present on all rolls. Killed in battle at Franklin November 30, 1864. Killed inside enemy's works. Grave located at Franklin Confederate Cemetery, Section 84, Grave No. 28.

Price, Abram, Pvt., Co. K, enlisted at Edgefield September 15, 1863. Absent, sick, February 23, 1864. Admitted for chronic diarrhoea to Way Hospital, Meridian March 25, 1865. Furloughed. Surrendered at Greensboro.

Price, John L., Pvt., Age 18, Co. I, enlisted at Augusta April 20, 1864. Recruit bounty due $50.00. Absent, sick, Jul/Aug - October 8, 1864. Wounded at Franklin. Paroled at Greensboro, May 1, 1865.

Price, John W., Pvt., Age 17, Co. I, enlisted at Columbia, April 20, 1862. Present on all rolls. Paroled at Greensboro May 1, 1865.

Price, Joseph, Pvt., Age 30, Co. I, enlisted at Augusta April 10, 1862. Absent, sick, patient in hospital July 20 - August 1864. Paroled at Greensboro May 1, 1865.

Price, Robert, Pvt., Age 20, Co. I, enlisted at Pocotaligo March 10, 1863. Absent without leave November 24 - December 1863. Signed receipt roll for clothing at Camp Wright December 16, 1864. Provost Guard with Co. D, 2d Battalion, Troops and Defenses, Camp Wright, Macon December 31, 1864. Captured at Macon April 20, 1865.

Priester, Andrew H., Pvt., Co. D, enlisted at Secessionville November 29, 1862. Absent, sick, furloughed, July 20 - September 2, 1864. Captured at Franklin December 17, 1864. Sent to Military Prison, Louisville and transferred to Camp Chase January 4, 1865. Paroled at Camp Chase via New Orleans for exchange May 2, 1865. Admitted to USA General Hospital No,. 2, Vicksburg for acute diarrhoea May 29 - 31, 1865.

Priester, Jacob R., Pvt., Age 26, born July 14, 1838, Co. D, from Brunson, enlisted at Camp Gist January 16, 1862. Absent, sick, patient in hospital and furloughed Jul/Aug - Sep/Oct 1863. Absent without leave Nov/Dec 1863. Wounded, hip, at Atlanta. Absent with leave, wounded, August 15 - September 15, 1864. Surrendered and paroled at Augusta May 25, 1865.

Priester, J. R., Pvt., Co. E, enlisted at Dalton, Ga., April 29, 1864. Killed in battle near Resaca, Calhoun, Ga. Died of wounds May 18, 1864.

Priester, J. W., Co. C, from Varnville, S.C. Married June 6, 1907. Died March 22, 1917. Widow Ella Catherine Priester. Entry from Confederate Veteran pension records at State Archives, Columbia, S.C.

Priester, William S., Pvt., Co. D, enlisted at Camp Gist November 19, 1862. Pay stoppage for loss of bayonet, $6.00, Jan/Feb 1864. Present for duty on all rolls. Discharged at Camp Chase.

Priester, W. W., Pvt., Age 19, Co. D, enlisted at Camp Gist January 16, 1862. Present for duty on all rolls. Surrendered and paroled at Augusta May 25, 1865.

Priester, William W., Pvt., Co. D. Killed at Dalton, Ga. Entry from Memory Rolls at State Archives, Columbia, S.C.

Prince, Edward C., Pvt., Age 39, Co. F, enlisted at Columbia, January 13, 1862. Wounded and captured at Jackson May 14, 1863. Listed at Paroled Prisoners in Camp at Demopolis June 5, 1863. Present on all rolls. Patient at Floyd House and Ocmulgee Hospital, Macon with chronic diarrhoea September 21, 1864. Died from the effects of disease in 1864.

Prince, Jesse, Pvt., Age 30, Co. I, enlisted at Columbia April 15, 1862. Absent, sick, patient in Lauderdale Springs hospital July 18 - October 31, 1863. Absent slightly wounded, leg, sent to hospital July 22, 1864. Wounded at Franklin.

Prince, Joseph, Pvt., Age 33, Co. I, enlisted at Columbia February 29, 1864. Bounty due ($50.00). Absent, sick with dropsy, patient in Ocmulgee Hospital, Macon September 24, 1864. Transferred to Augusta September 25, 1864. Discharged at Augusta, Ga., 1865. Married December 23, 1873. Died October 30, 1899. Widow, Angie B. Prince.

Prince, Samuel, Pvt., Age 17, born November 25, 1847, Co. I, from Edgefield, enlisted at Augusta April 20, 1864. Recruit bounty due ($50.00). Slightly wounded, hand, and sent to hospital, finger amputated, July 22, 1864. Wounded at Franklin November 30, 1864. Captured December 17, 1864. Sent to USA, General Hospital, Nashville for treatment December 27, 1864 - May 30, 1865. Wounded by conical in front left femur, lower third of thigh. Lateral flap amputation lower third left thigh December 1, 1864. Admitted with small pox to No. 11 (Small Pox), USA, General Hospital, Nashville May 30 - June 17, 1865. Released and furnished transportation to Charleston, S.C., June 25, 1865.

Proctor, Balam, Pvt., Age 25, Co. C, enlisted at Georges Station January 7, 1862. Died of disease at James Island December 14, 1862.

Proctor, Jesse, Pvt., Co. C. Entry from roster made by Capt. W. C. Griffith, Company Commander.

Proctor, Joseph, Pvt., Age 22, Co. C, enlisted at Georges Station January 7, 1862. Wounded at Jackson. Absent, sick, Nov/Dec 1862. Absent, sick, patient in hospital at Atlanta Sep/Oct 1863. Admitted to Ocmulgee Hospital, Macon with pneumonia July 9, 1864. Transferred to 3d Ga Hospital, Augusta July 23, 1864. Died of pneumonia August 4, 1864.

Proctor, Micajah, Pvt., Age 18, Co. C, enlisted at Camp Gist March 16, 1862. Mortally wounded in battle at Jackson May 14, 1863. Absent, patient in hospital and furloughed due to wounds June 1863 - August 1864. Died of wounds June 15, 1863.

Proctor, Morgan, Pvt., Co. C. Entry from Dorchester County Enrollment Book.

Proctor, Mike C., Pvt., Age 36, Co. H, enlisted at Chester April 15, 1862. Absent, sick, patient in Macon Hospital, Miss., Sep/Oct - December 6, 1863. Died of disease in hospital at Macon, Miss., December 6, 1863. Effects consisted of $10.00. Widow, Mary Proctor, filed claim for settlement.

Proctor, Morgan, Pvt., Age 18, Co. C. Wounded at Chickamauga September 20, 1863. Still living. Entry from Memory Rolls at State Archives, Columbia, S.C.

Proctor, William M., Pvt., Age 38, Co. H, enlisted at Chester March 19, 1862. Died of disease in hospital at Columbia June 20, 1862. Widow, Martha M. Proctor filed claim for settlement July 16, 1862.

Pruitt, P. H., Pvt., Co. F,. Killed in battle inside the enemy's works at Franklin, Tenn., November 30, 1864. Entry from Survivor's Association roster.

Prusner, William, Pvt., Age 18, Co. G, enlisted at Columbia March 19, 1862. Transferred to the Naval Service October 24, 1862.

Pulaski, F. W., Pvt., Age 26, Co. C, enlisted at Georges Station January 7, 1862. Absent, sick, patient in field hospital Sep/Oct 1863. Wounded, patient in hospital Jul/Aug 1864. Killed in battle at Atlanta. Grave located in Stonewall Cemetery, Griffin, Ga.

Quarles, Oscar J., Corp., Age 17, Co. I, enlisted at Columbia March 20, 1862. Absent, sick, patient in hospital at Lauderdale Springs, Miss., July 18 - October 31, 1863. Promoted to Corp., from the ranks April 1, 1864. Slightly wounded, knee, at Dalton. Wounded at Franklin. Admitted for wound to Way Hospital, Meridian January 12, 1865.

Quick, Alexander, Pvt., age 22, born August 7, 1839, Co. B, from Marlboro, S.C., enlisted at Marlboro April 3, 1862. Present on all rolls. Signed receipt roll for clothing September 9, 1864. Paroled at Greensboro May

1, 1865.

Quick, James, Pvt., Age 34, Co. B, enlisted at Charleston December 4, 1861. Sick at home Sep/Oct 1862. Sick in hospital at Atlanta Sep/Oct - Nov/Dec 1863. Absent without leave Mar/Aug 1864. Died of disease at home.

Quick, Murdock, Pvt., Age 37, Co. B, enlisted at Charleston December 4, 1861. Sick at home Sep/Oct 1863. Absent without leave Nov/Dec 1863. Furloughed, sick, August 31, 1864. Paroled at Greensboro May 1, 1865. Deserted April 26, 1865.

Rabon, John, Pvt., Age 40, Co. G, enlisted at Columbia, March 19, 1862. Absent, sick, patient in the hospital at Summerville May/Jun - Sep/Oct 1862. Six days pay stopped for absent without leave Nov/Dec 1862. Sick, patient in hospital at Columbia Jan/Feb - Jul/Aug 1863. Captured near Nashville December 16, 1864. Sent to Military Prison, Louisville and transferred to Camp Chase January 4, 1865. Died of pneumonia January 24, 1865. Grave no. 861, located 1/3 mile south of Camp Chase.

Radcliffe, T. W., Co. G. Entry from original muster roll.

Ralph, James L., Pvt., Age 30, Co. H, enlisted at Chester March 19, 1862. Sick with hernia in 1st Mississippi, CSA Hospital, Jackson June 1863. Absent, sick, patient in hospital at LaGrange, Ga., Sep/Oct 1863. Absent, sick, patient in hospital at Columbia February 8 - August 31, 1864. Paroled at Greensboro May 1, 1865.

Ramsey, David, Pvt., Age 23, Co. E, enlisted at Charleston March 20, 1862. Pay stopped for one month by court martial May/Jun 1863. Present for duty on all rolls. Surrendered. Discharged in Virginia. Married November 1, 1869. Died May 6, 1906. Widow Abigail Ramsey.

Rascoe, Harris, Pvt., Age 24, Co. B, enlisted at Charleston December 4, 1861. Died at Charleston June 5, 1862. Attorney, John McQueen, on behalf of Martha Rascoe, filed a claim for settlement. Grave located at Magnolia Cemetery, Charleston.

Rateree, Thomas, Pvt., Age 37, Co. H, enlisted at Chester March 19, 1862. Absent, sick, Jan/Feb 1863. Wounded at Jackson, Miss., and Chickamauga. Furloughed from hospital Mar/Aug - October 16, 1864. Paroled at Greensboro May 1, 1865. Name also spelled Ratteree.

Raul, John, Pvt., Age 16, Co. G, enlisted at Columbia April 12, 1862.

Rawlings, Rev., Pvt., Co. G. Entry from Memory Rolls at State Archives, Columbia, S.C.

Ravenel, St. Julian, Surgeon, F&S. Assigned to regiment in April 4, 1862. Transferred to hospital duty May 1863.

Real, Albert, Pvt., Co. K, enlisted at Edgefield March 15, 1862. Patient in hospital at Lauderdale Springs 21 July - December 1863. Medical Examining Board, Dalton granted 60 days furlough for chronic diarrhoea with extreme emaciation and debility June 8, 1864. Surrendered and paroled at Augusta May 18, 1865. Name also spelled Reel.

Redish, Isham, Corp., Age 25, Co. E, enlisted at Salkehatchie January 16, 1862. Reduced to ranks March 12, 1862. Absent, sick, patient in hospital Jan/Feb 1863. Died in hospital of disease June 30, 1863.

Reddish, Peter, Pvt., Age 28, Co. E, enlisted at Salkehatchie March 20, 1862. Absent without leave October 1862. Pay stopped for one month by court martial May/Jun 1863. Detailed as teamster to Mississippi July 22, 1863. Died in hospital of disease September 30, 1863. Married 1859. Widow Mary Redish.

Reed, Hardy, Pvt., Age 19, Co. D, enlisted at Camp Gist January 19, 1862. Transferred to Sharpshooters and returned Jan/Feb 1863. Deserted July 21, 1863.

Reese, J. D., 1Sgt., Age 30, Co. B, enlisted at Marlboro December 4, 1861 for 12 months. Died of disease February 22, 1862.

Reeves, George, Pvt., Age 22, Co. C, enlisted at Camp Gist March 5, 1862. Absent, sick, patient in hospital in Columbia Jan/Feb - May/Jun 1863. Wounded at Chickamauga. Present for duty through August 1864. Extra daily duty as cook Jul/Aug 1864.

Reynolds, Alexandrew, Pvt., Co. K, enlisted at Edgefield April 15, 1862. At home, sick, furloughed Nov/Dec 1862. Absent, admitted to hospital in Charleston Jan/Feb 1863. Patient in hospital Jan/Feb 1864. Furloughed for seventeen days March 13, 1864. Absent without leave April 1 - August 31, 1864. Surrendered and paroled at Augusta May 20, 1865.

Reynolds, E. H., Pvt., Co. K, enlisted at Edgefield April 15, 1862. Furnished substitute, J. A. Reynolds, May/Jun 1862. Surrendered and paroled at Augusta May 18, 1865.

Reynolds, John Simmons, Sgt., Age 17, Born April 18, 1841, Co. I, from Abbeville, enlisted at Columbia March 20, 1862. Present on all rolls. Slightly wounded, arm, near Marietta June 15, 1864. Slightly wounded, hip, August 31, 1864. Admitted to Way Hospital, Meridian for diarrhoea January 12, 1865. Wounded at Greensboro. Promoted to 2Sgt., for meritorious service April 9, 1865. Paroled at Greensboro May 1, 1865. Parents: Father, Larkin Reynolds; Mother, Mary D. Simmons. After the War, he was a farmer and solicitor and died February 17, 1919 in a Confederate home at Columbia.

Reynolds, Joseph A., 1Sgt., Co. K, enlisted at Edgefield April 15, 1862. Substitute for E. H. Reynolds. Patient in hospital May/Jun 1862. Promoted to 1Sgt., August 17, 1864. Paroled at Greensboro May 1, 1865.

Rice, W. R., nickname "Billie," Pvt., Co. F, enlisted at Anderson September 18, 1862. Wounded at Jackson May 14, 1863. Captured and exchanged at Jackson May 14, 1863. Assigned to Paroled Prisoners Camp at

Demopolis June 5, 1863. Present on all rolls. Captured at Shipp's Gap/Taylor's Ridge October 16, 1864. Sent to Military Prison, Louisville and transferred to Camp Douglas October 29, 1864. Died of small pox December 10, 1864. Grave located near Camp Douglas.

Rigby, E. L., Pvt., Age 17, Co. C, from Reevesville, S.C., enlisted at Georges Station January 17, 1862. Detached in commissary department May/Jun 1863. Captured at Chickamauga September 20, 1863. Sent to Military Prison, Louisville and transferred to Camp Douglas October 4, 1863. Description: complexion, light; hair, light; eyes, blue; height, 5 ft. 6 in. Signed oath of allegiance to the United States and discharged June 16, 1865.

Riggs, Langdon C., Pvt., Age 18, Co. A, enlisted at Charleston, December 31, 1861. Sick at home Sep/Oct 1862. Sick in Charleston and Columbia Nov/Dec 1862 - May/Jun 1863. Sick, patient in hospital Sep/Oct 1863. Wounded, right hand, at Shipp's Gap/Taylor's Ridge, October 16, 1864. Signed receipt roll for clothing November 16, 23, and December 22, 1864. Paroled at Greensboro May 1, 1865.

Riggs, Thomas L., Corp., Co. A, enlisted at Camp Gist April 12, 1862. Promotion to corporal announced during speech by regimental commander May 22, 1864. Present for duty on all rolls. Signed receipt roll for clothing September 9, 1864. Admitted to CSA General Hospital, No. 11, Charlotte for acute diarrhoea March 11 - 25, 1865. Sent to hospital April 25, 1865. Paroled at Greensboro May 1, 1865.

Risher, Joseph K., Capt., Age 27, Co. E, enlisted at Camp Gist January 16, 1862. Promoted to Capt., Co. E, June 11, 1863. Company Commander. Absent, sick, patient in Fairground Hospital, Atlanta October 12, 1863. Present for duty through August 1864. Twice slightly wounded. Patient at Ocmulgee Hospital, Macon for chronic rheumatism October 23 - 26 1864. Patient in Ocmulgee Hospital, Macon for rheumatism November 4 - 16, 1864. Survived. Paroled at Greensobor, May 1, 1865.

Ritter, Henry R., Corp., Age 20, Co. E, from Branchville, enlisted at Salkehatchie January 16, 1862. Pay stopped for one month by court martial May/Jun 1863. Captured at Chickamauga September 20, 1863. Sent to Military Prison, Louisville and transferred to Camp Douglas October 10, 1863. Description: complexion, dark; hair, light; eyes, blue; height, 5 ft. 11 in. Signed oath of allegiance to the United States and discharged June 16, 1865.

Ritter, Reddin, Pvt., Age 18, Co. E, enlisted at Charleston March 20, 1862. Pay stopped for one month by court martial May/Jun 1863. Severely wounded, foot, at Chickamauga. Admitted to the hospital. Absent, sick, patient in hospital February 1864. Wounded, admitted to hospital, July 20, 1864. Surrendered.

Rivers, Colin, Pvt., Co. D. Died of disease at home. Entry from Memory

Rolls at State Archives, Columbia, S.C.

Rivers, Ruben Jordan, Pvt., Co. D, from Crockettville, enlisted at Camp Gist April 9, 1862. Sick, furloughed Sep/Oct 1862. Wounded, hand, at Peachtree Creek about 4 miles from Atlanta. Wounded in crippled arm. Absent with leave August 17 - October 17, 1864. Disabled from further service. Living. Married February 27, 1866. Died August 27, 1898. Widow Mahala H. Rivers.

Rivers, W. W., Pvt., Co. D, enlisted at Camp Gist March 26, 1862. Present for duty on all rolls. Signed receipt roll for clothing July 12, 1864. Living.

Roberts, W. A., Pvt., Age 35, Co. D, enlisted at Camp Gist March 10, 1862. Discharged May 16, 1862.

Robertson, T. Patrick, Pvt., Date of Birth: July 26, 1840, Age 22, Co. I, enlisted at James Island May 17, 1862. Absent in hospital August 30, 1863. Signed receipt roll for clothing April 1, 1864. Wounded and captured near Calhoun, Ga., May 16, 1864. Sent to Military Prison, Louisville and transferred to Rock Island May 27, 1864. Wounded while in prison. Enlisted at Rock Island Barracks in US Army for frontier service October 15, 1864. Exchanged at Boulwares Wharf, Va., March 5, 1865. Suffered debilities and admitted to Jackson Hospital, Richmond. Granted 30 days furlough March 8, 1865. Survived. Died October 3, 1913. Grave located in Mt. Gilead United Methodist Church Cemetery, Raymond, Ga.

Robertson, William L., Pvt., Co. I, enlisted at James Island May 17, 1862. Captured at Chickamauga September 20, 1863. Sent to Military prison, Louisville and transferred to Camp Douglas October 14, 1863. Paroled at Camp Douglas and exchanged at City Point, Va., March 14, 1865. Admitted to Jackson Hospital, Richmond with rheumatism March 22, 1865. Granted 60 days furlough March 27, 1865.

Robertson, William T., Pvt., Co. K, enlisted at Morgan, Ga., August 16, 1861. Transferred from 25th Georgia Regiment September 24, 1862. Absent in hospital October 24 - Nov/Dec 1863. Medical Examining Board, Dalton, approved 40 days disability leave for emaciation and debility consequent of typhoid fever June 30, 1864. Wounded near Atlanta and admitted to hospital August 12, 1864. Paroled at Greensboro May 1, 1865.

Robinson, Benjamin E., 2Lt., Age 30, Co. A, enlisted at Charleston December 31, 1861. Captured at Jackson May 14, 1865. Assigned to Paroled Prisoners Camp at Demopolis June 5, 1863. Thirty dollars deducted from pay for apprehension, absence without leave Jul/Aug 1863. Wounded at Chickamauga. Promoted to 2Lt., Jul/Aug 1864. Captured at Nashville December 16, 1864. Sent to Military Prison, Louisville and transferred to Johnson Island December 22, 1864.

Description: complexion, dark; hair, dark; eyes, blue; height, 5 ft. 9 in. Signed oath of allegiance to the United States and released June 17, 1865. Married September 20, 1860. Died July 8, 1911. Widow, Agnes B. Robinson, resided at 252 Coming Street, Charleston, S.C.

Robinson, Stephen, Drummer, Co. A, enlisted at Pocotaligo April 1, 1863. Reported missing at Jackson May 14, 1863. Absent without leave May/Jun 1863. Deserted at Pocotaligo or Jackson May/Jun 1863. Discharged because of disability.

Robinson, William, Pvt., Age 18, Co. A, enlisted at Charleston December 31, 1861. Present for duty on all rolls. Surrendered at Greensboro. Reported by Charleston Courier November 3, 1864, that Pvt. Robinson was prisoner of war at Camp Douglas. Ed Note. Unable to verify.

Rochelle, J. Archielaus, Pvt., Age 17. Co. I, enlisted at Dalton, Ga., February 15, 1864. Bounty of $50.00 due. Slightly wounded, shoulder, at Atlanta. Killed in battle at Franklin. Grave located in Section 83, Grave No. 7, Confederate Cemetery, Franklin, Tenn.

Rochelle, William J., Pvt., Age 18. Co. I, born December 7, 1843, eighteen miles east of Edgefield Courthouse, enlisted at James Island May 17, 1862. Musician in regimental band. Admitted to hospital at Chickamauga. Rejoined regiment at Missionary Ridge. Present for duty on all rolls. Paroled at Greensboro May 1. 1865.

Roddey, W. Lyle, Capt., Age 28, Co. H, from Chester enlisted at Chester March 19, 1862. Promoted to Capt., December 1, 1862. Inspected and mustered 2d Artillery Regiment, Mar/Apr 1863. Wounded, shoulder, at Chickamauga. Wounded at Dalton and sent to the hospital May 28, 1864. Absent, wounded, furloughed May 28 - August 31, 1864. Wounded, forehead, near Jonesboro. Captured at Shipp's Gap/Taylor's Ridge October 16, 1864. Sent to Military Prison, Louisville and transferred to Johnson Island October 28, 1864. Description: complexion, fair; hair, dark; eyes, blue; height, 5 ft. 6 in. Signed oath of allegiance to the United States and released June 16, 1865.

Rodgers, Paul, Pvt., Co. D, enlisted at Camp Gist January 19, 1862. Colored. Teamster. Discharged March 6, 1863.

Rodgers, William Edward, Sgt., Age 33, Co. I, enlisted at Columbia March 20, 1862. Absent, detached to recruiting service in South Carolina, July 1 - October 31, 1863. Assigned as company Ordnance Sergeant for faithful service April 9, 1865. Paroled at Greensboro May 1, 1865.

Rodman, Alexander K., Pvt., Age 37, Co. H, enlisted at Chester April 15, 1862. Captured at Jackson May 14, 1863. Absent wounded Jul/Aug 1863. Listed at Paroled Prisoners Camp at Demopolis June 5, 1863. Wounded at Chickamauga. Captured at battle of Missionary Ridge at Graysville, Ga., November 25, 1863. Sent to Prison Hospital, Nashville for chronic diarrhoea. Died January 1, 1864. Buried January 2, 1864.

Grave no. 547.

Rolfe, Q. W., Pvt., Co. K. Surrendered at Greensboro. Entry from Memory Rolls at State Archives, Columbia, S.C.

Rollings, L. P., Pvt., Co. G, enlisted at Columbia March 19, 1862. Substitute for J. C. Hargood. Detached December 3 - 31, 1862. Detached service to shipyard to work on gunboat at Charleston April 19 - Jul/Aug 1863. Absent without leave Sep/Oct 1863. Captured during retreat from Missionary Ridge November 25, 1863. Sent to Military Prison, Louisville and transferred to Rock Island December 13, 1864. Died December 24, 1863. Grave no. 53, south of prison barracks.

Rouse, W. R., Corp., Co. D, enlisted at Camp Gist January 16, 1864. Transferred to Smith's 2nd Batt. S.C. Sharp Shooters October 16, 1862.

Row, John E., Pvt., Age 30, Co. G, enlisted at Columbia March 19, 1862. Captured at Jackson May 14, 1863. Assigned to Paroled Prisoners in Camp at Demopolis June 5, 1863. Patient in hospital at Demopolis Jul/Aug 1863. Patient in hospital at Selma, Ala., Sep/Oct 1863. Discharged from service because of total blindness November 17, 1863.

Rowe, J. H,., Pvt., Co. B, enlisted at Marlboro April 5, 1862. Present for duty on all rolls through August 31, 1864. Signed receipt roll for clothing at Marshall Hospital, Columbus, Ga., June 1, 1864.

Rowe, William D., Pvt., Age 25, Co. B, enlisted at Charleston December 4, 1861. Sick, patient in hospital at Gainesville, Ala., Jul/Aug 1863. Absent, sick at home Jan/Feb 1864. Absent without leave August 31, 1864. Signed receipt roll for clothing November 14 and December 17, 1864. Died 1896.

Rowell, C. Perry, Pvt., Age 16, Co. D, enlisted at Camp Gist January 19, 1862. Guard duty Jan/Feb 1863. Detached service to Summerville, South Carolina, Mar/Apr 1863. Present for duty Jul/Aug 1864. Discharged at Camp Chase, prisoner of war camp.

Rowell, William J., Pvt., Age 20, Co. D, from Beaufort District, enlisted at Camp Gist, March 25, 1862. Present for duty on all rolls through August 31, 1864. Captured near Nashville December 16, 1864. Sent to Military Prison, Louisville and transferred to Camp Chase January 4, 1865. Description: complexion, light; hair, light; eyes, blue; height 5 ft. 8 in. Signed oath of allegiance to the United States June 12, 1865.

Rowlinski, William, Pvt., Co. A, enlisted at Camp Gist April 16, 1862. Captured near Jackson May 14, 1863. Assigned to Paroled Prisoners Camp at Demopolis June 5, 1863. Wounded at Atlanta. Captured at Peachtree Creek July 20, 1864. Sent to Military prison, Louisville and transferred to Camp Douglas August 1, 1864. Applied for oath of allegiance December 1864. Claimed to have been loyal, enlisted through false representations. Captured and desires to take the oath of allegiance to United States and become a loyal citizen. Description: complexion, dark; hair, red; eyes, grey; height, 5 ft. 8 in. Signed oath of amnesty and discharged May 15, 1865. After the war, he moved to Volusia County, Fla.

Ruff, Benjamin Franklin, Pvt., Age 20, Co. G, enlisted at Columbia April 12, 1862. Killed in battle at Jackson May 14, 1863.

Rush, H. J., Pvt., Co. K, enlisted at Edgefield, March 14, 1863. Severely wounded, shoulder, at Chickamauga September 20, 1863. Furloughed from hospital November 1, 1863 - August 1864. Surrendered and paroled at Augusta May 20, 1865.

Rush, W. H., Pvt., Co. K. Entry from Memory Rolls at State Archives, Columbia, S.C.

Rushing, T. O., Pvt., Age 18, Co. D, enlisted at Camp Gist January 19, 1862. Absent, wounded, granted furlough Sep/Oct - Nov/Dec 1863. Paroled at Greensboro May 1, 1865.

Russell, James, Cook, Age 25, Co. C, enlisted at Charleston January 7, 1862. Free negro. Cook for company. Captured November 25, 1863. Later reported killed at Missionary Ridge.

Russell, Levy, Cook, Age 21, Co. C, enlisted at Georges Station January 7, 1862. Free negro. Cook for the company. Signed, by mark, receipt roll for clothing September 9, 1864.

Ryan, Henry J., Pvt., Age 37, Co. A, enlisted at Charleston December 31, 1861. Acting commissary at Secessionville Nov/Dec 1862. Killed in battle at Jackson May 14, 1863. "A most estimable man, exempt from military service for three reasons: physical disability, age bordering the exemption period, and by profession a printer. He was respected by all. Declined offer to move to the rear and took a position where he could use his rifle. He fell like the patriotic soldier he was, facing the enemy."

Ryan, William P., Pvt., Age 19, Co. A, enlisted at Charleston December 31, 1861. Detached to work at Camerons & Co., by order of Commanding General April 12, 1862 - Jul/Aug 1863. Killed in battle at Chickamauga September 20, 1863. Buried with military honors on the battlefield at Chickamauga. Grave located in Confederate Cemetery, Marietta, Ga.

Sadler, J. K., Sgt., Age 33, Co. F, enlisted at Columbia January 13, 1862. Promoted to 3Sgt., November 17, 1862. Promoted to 2Sgt., January 30, 1863. Killed in battle at Jackson May 14, 1863. Middle initial also shown as "H."

Sandeford, J. M., Sgt., Co. D, enlisted at Camp Gist January 16, 1862. Transferred to the Dixie Rangers March 20, 1862.

Sanders, Isaac, Pvt., Age 34, Co. B, enlisted at Marlboro December 4, 1861. One month's wages stopped by court martial for absent without leave Nov/Dec 1862. Present for duty through Nov/Dec 1863. Wounded at Dalton 1864. Dropped dead of apoplexy (stroke) at Dalton, Ga., January 15, 1864.

Sanders, John Leard, Pvt., Age 27, Co. H, from Chester, enlisted at Chester March 19, 1862. Wounded at Chickamauga September 20, 1863. Assigned ambulance corps August 31, 1864. Present on all rolls. Paroled at Greensboro May 1, 1865. Wife, Jane Sanders, resided at Route 3, Chester S.C.

Sauls, Abram, Pvt., Age 25, Co. D, enlisted at Charleston January 16, 1862. Captured at the battle of Jackson May 14, 1863. Prisoner in paroled camp May/Jun 1863. Present for duty on all rolls through August 31, 1864.

Sauls, James, Pvt., Age 21, Co. D, enlisted at Camp Gist January 18, 1862. Absent, wounded, granted leave Sep/Oct 1863 - Jan/Feb 1864. Sick, patient in hospital at Augusta Jul/Aug 1864. Paroled at Greensboro May 1, 1865.

Sauls, J. M., Pvt., Age 19, Co. D, enlisted at Camp Gist January 16, 1864. Absent without leave September 20 - October 30, 1863. Present for duty August 31, 1864.

Sauls, John, Pvt., Age 45, Co. D, enlisted at Camp Gist January 19, 1862. Deserted May 7, 1863. Ordered dropped from the rolls Jan/Feb 1864.

Sauls, Josiah, Pvt., Age 21, Co. D, enlisted at Charleston March 10, 1862. Captured near Jonesboro August 31, 1864. Exchanged at Rough and Ready September 19, 1864. Captured near Nashville December 16, 1864. Sent to Military Prison, Louisville and transferred to Camp Chase January 4, 1865. Description: complexion, florid; hair, dark; eyes, blue; height, 5 ft. 9 in. Signed oath of allegiance to the United States June 12, 1865.

Scott, James, Pvt., Age 23, Co. A, enlisted at Charleston December 31, 1861. Absent, sick, patient in hospital at Charleston Nov/Dec 1862. Absent without leave Jan/Feb 1863. Captured and paroled while patient in hospital May 16, 1863. Captured at Nashville December 16, 1864. Enlisted in United States service and transferred from Camp Chase to Chicago March 20, 1865.

Scott, John E., Pvt., Age 23, Co. A, enlisted at Charleston December 31, 1861. Wounded at the battle of Jackson May 14, 1863. Absent, wounded, patient in hospital, Macon Jul/Aug 1863. Captured at Nashville December 16, 1864. Sent to Military Prison, Louisville and transferred to Camp Chase January 6, 1865.

Scott, John, Pvt., Age 17, Co. A, enlisted at Charleston January 16, 1862. Absent, sick, patient in hospital at Charleston Nov/Dec 1862 - Jan/Feb 1863. Absent, wounded, Sep/Oct 1863. Absent, sick, patient in hospital Nov/Dec 1863. Signed receipt roll for clothing July 23, 1864. Present for duty August 31, 1864.

Scott, J. M., Co. B, 24th S.C.V. Died in hospital near Fortress Monroe and buried south side of the creek August 1, 1864. Entry from article in

Daily Courier.

Scott, L., Pvt., Co. A, enlisted at Camp Gist, March 28, 1862. Present for duty May/Jun 1862. Died of disease at Charleston early in the War. Died June 23, 1862.

Scott, R. E., Pvt., Co. A, enlisted at Charleston December 31, 1861. Wounded at Jackson May 14, 1862. Absent wounded May/Jun 1863 - Jul/Aug 1864.

Scott, W. P., Co. D, enlisted at the end of 1864. Discharged May 1865. Married 1879. Died August 11, 1910. Widow Leaninio Scott. Entry from Confederate Veteran pension records at State Archives, Columbia, S.C.

Sease, George, Pvt., Co. D, enlisted at Beaufort District August 15, 1864. Bounty due fifty dollars. Paroled at Greensboro May 1, 1864.

Seigler, Gibson H., Corp., Co. K., enlisted at Edgefield April 15, 1862. Severely wounded, head, at Chickamauga September 20, 1863. Absent wounded Sep/Oct 1863 - August 31, 1864. Retired and assigned to invalid corps November 9, 1864.

Seigler, H. G., Corp., Co. K, enlisted at Edgefield March 15, 1863. Sent to hospital at Rome September 17, 1863. Absent, sick, furloughed Nov/Dec 1863. Promoted to Corp., August 17, 1864. Present for duty August 31, 1864. Killed in battle at Jonesboro September 1, 1864.

Seigler, Irvin, Pvt., Age 37, Co. C, enlisted at Georges Station January 7, 1862. Absent, sick, patient in hospital at Canton, Miss., May/Jun - Jul/Aug 1863. Absent, sick, patient in hospital Jul/Aug 1864. Paroled at Greensboro May 1, 1865. Married October 26, 1861. Died December 1907. Widow, Catherine Seigler, resided at Grover, S.C.

Seigler, Jacob, Pvt., Age 42, Co. C, enlisted at Georges Station January 7, 1862. Discharged because of physical disability June 29, 1862. Description: complexion, dark; hair, dark; eyes, dark; height, 5 ft., 6 in.

Seigler, Tandy M., 1Lt., Co. K, enlisted at Edgefield April 15, 1862. Elected 2Lt., May 5, 1863. Absent, patient in hospital at Rome and furloughed home October 1863. Paroled at Greensboro May 1, 1865.

Seigler, Thomas, Pvt., Age 25, Co. G, enlisted at Columbia March 19, 1862. Absent, sick, patient in hospital at Columbia May/Jun 1862. Discharged September 1, 1862.

Seigler, W., Co. C, enlisted March 7, 1862. Discharged March 17, 1862.

Sexton, Cornelius, Pvt., Age 36, Co. H, enlisted at Chester March 19, 1862. Absent, sick, May/Jun 1862. Description: complexion, fair; hair, light; eyes, blue; height, 5 ft. 11 in. Discharged by reason of disability August 20, 1862.

Sexton, Daniel, Pvt., Age 39, Co. H, enlisted at Chester March 19, 1862. Absent, sick, May/Jun 1862 - Jan/Feb 1863. Present, sick, Mar/Apr 1863. Died after War.

Shafer, John, Pvt., Co. K, enlisted at Edgefield April 15, 1862. Absent, sick, patient in hospital July 24, 1863. Died at Funderdale Springs Hospital August 21, 1863.

Shark, J. M., Pvt., Age 32, Co. G, enlisted at Columbia March 19, 1862. Discharged October 18, 1862. Name appears as Sharp on some rosters.

Sharpton, Alexander, Pvt., Age 35, Co. I, enlisted at Columbia March 20, 1862. Patient in hospital at Charleston February 13, 1863. Absent, sick, furloughed and patient in hospital at Augusta May 1, 1863 - August 31, 1864. Transferred from 2d Georgia Hospital, Augusta, November 26, 1863. Suffered with lumbago.

Sharpton, E. Moody, Pvt., Age 16, Co. G, enlisted at Columbia April 5, 1862. Died of typhoid fever in hospital at Charleston August 7, 1862.

Shaw, William C., Pvt., Age 18, born November 6, 1843, Co. F, from Abbeville, enlisted at Anderson April 6, 1862. Absent, sick, chronic diarrhoea with debility and extreme emaciation, granted 40 days furlough by Medical Examining Board, Dalton December 9, 1863. Signed receipt roll for clothing April 1, 1864. Wounded at battle of Atlanta, July 22, 1864. Paroled at Greensboro May 1, 1865.

Sheider, J. W. C., Pvt., Co. C. Entry from Dorchester County Enrollment Book.

Shelton, John, Pvt., Co. I, enlisted at Charleston February 18, 1863. Present on all rolls. Paroled at Greensboro May 1, 1865.

Sherard, J. W., Sgt., Age 34, Co. F, from Moffatsville, S.C., enlisted at Columbia January 13, 1864. Appointed 2Corp., December 1, 1862. Promoted 1Corp., January 30, 1863. Promoted to 3Sgt., June 1, 1863. Wounded at Jackson May 14, 1863. Captured and paroled, patient in hospital May 16, 1865. Promoted 2Sgt., August 1, 1863. Absent wounded May - December 1863. Admitted to hospital by medical officer April 25, 1865. Admitted to CSA General Hospital, No. 11, Charlotte, N.C. for debility April 28, 1865. Paroled at Greensboro May 1, 1865. Married December 18, 1849. Died November 26, 1909. Widow Asenath Sherard.

Sherard, Samuel W., Capt., Age 29, Co. F, from Jefferson, Ga., enlisted at Charleston January 13, 1862. Elected to 1Lt November 7, 1862. Wounded at Jackson May 14, 1863. Absent, sick, patient in hospital at Atlanta October 17, 1863. Promoted Capt., January 20, 1864. Slightly wounded, breast, July 20, 1864. Captured at Shipp's Gap/Taylor's Ridge October 16, 1864. Sent to Military Prison, Louisville and transferred to Johnson's Island October 28, 1864. Description: complexion, fair; hair, light; eyes, hazel; height, 5 ft. 9 in. Signed oath of allegiance to the United States and released June 16, 1865. Grave located in Jefferson City Cemetery, Jefferson, Ga.

Sherard, Thomas A., Pvt., Co. F, from Moffatsville, S.C. Discharged

January 1862. Died January 18, 1895. Entry from Memory Rolls at State Archives, Columbia, S.C., and Survivors Association roster.

Shider, T. D., Pvt., Age 16, Co. C, enlisted at Georges Station January 17, 1862. Wounded at Jackson May 14, 1863. Absent, patient in hospital, furloughed May - October 1863. Absent wounded in hospital Jul/Aug 1864. Signed receipt roll for clothing September 9, 1864. Paroled at Greensboro May 1, 1865.

Shirley, Cal. W., Pvt., Age 35, Co. G, enlisted at Columbia March 19, 1862. One months pay stopped by order of court martial May/Jun 1863. Present for duty on all rolls.

Shirley, Hampton, Pvt., Co. G, enlisted Webster, Miss., April 15, 1862. Captured near Nashville December 16, 1864. Sent to Military Prison, Louisville and transferred to Camp Chase January 4, 1865. Died February 12, 1865. Grave no. 719, located 1/3 mile south of Camp Chase.

Shirley, William, Sgt., Age 33, Co. G, enlisted at Columbia March 19, 1862. Absent, sick, patient in hospital May/Jun 1862. Appointed Corp., June 1, 1863. One month's pay stopped by order of court martial May/Jun 1863. Present for duty on all rolls. Killed at Franklin. Grave located in Confederate Cemetery, Franklin, Section 83, Grave No. 12.

Shotz, A., Pvt., Co. G. Entry from Memory Rolls at State Archives, Columbia, S.C.

Sigwald, Christian B., Maj., Age 34, Co. A. enlisted at Charleston December 31, 1862. Commanded company. Promoted to regimental major of infantry January 2, 1863. Resigned because of physical disability due to chronic inflammation of the bladder and prostate gland March 23, 1863.

Simmons, William, Pvt., Co. D, enlisted at Camp Gist April 9, 1862. Absent without leave Jan/Feb 1863. Absent without leave from August 30 - October 16, 1863. Absent, sick, patient in hospital Jan/Feb 1864. Captured at Shipp's Gap/Taylor's Ridge October 15, 1864. Sent to Military Prison, Louisville and transferred to Camp Douglas October 29, 1864. Died of small pox December 1, 1864. Grave located near Camp Douglas.

Simmons, William M., Teamster, Co. D, enlisted at Camp Gist January 19, 1862. Colored. Teamster. Discharged March 10, 1862.

Simms, William, Pvt., Co. A, enlisted at Camp Gist March 25, 1862. Expert hospital clerk. Absent, sick, at home Sep/Oct 1862. Assigned as assistant in hospital Nov/Dec 1862. Assigned as assistant in hospital department Mar/Apr 1863. Assigned as assistant in hospital May/Jun - Jul/Aug 1864. Signed receipt roll for clothing April 1, 1864. Worked as nurse with brigade surgeon. Druggist for regiment. Paroled at Greensboro May 1, 1865.

Simpson, C. M., Pvt., Age 27, Co. C, enlisted at Georges Station January 7, 1862. Died of disease August 10, 1863.

Simpson, Green S., Sgt., Age 22, Co. H, enlisted at Chester March 19, 1862. Wounded at Chickamauga September 20, 1863. Severely wounded, side and arm, July 20/22, 1864. Furloughed from hospital Mar/Aug 1864, returned to duty October 16, 1864. Admitted to CSA General Hospital No. 11, Charlotte, NC, for fracture of left wrist January 15, 1865. Returned to duty February 14, 1865. Paroled at Greensboro May 1, 1865.

Simpson, James A., Pvt., Co. F, enlisted at Anderson October 17, 1862. Substituted for R. Sadler. Present for duty on all rolls. Wounded and thought in hands of enemy July 20, 1864. Killed in battle at Peachtree Creek.

Simpson, Jesse M., Pvt., Co. F, enlisted at Anderson January 13, 1862. Died of disease March 10, 1862.

Simpson, Luke, Pvt., Age 17, Co. C, enlisted at Georges Station January 17, 1862. Transferred to 2nd South Carolina December 29, 1862.

Simpson, Matthew, Pvt., Co. F, enlisted at Anderson April 12, 1863. Substituted for John Catlet. Absent, sick, January 1864. Died of disease in hospital at Marietta March 1, 1864. Grave located in Confederate Cemetery, Marietta, Ga.

Simpson, Thomas, Sgt., Age 40, Co. H, enlisted at Chester March 19, 1862. Furloughed Mar/Apr 1863. Severely wounded at Chickamauga and disabled September 20, 1863. Patient in Augusta and Atlanta hospitals Sep/Oct 1863 - Jan/Feb 1864. Absent without leave August 1864. Admitted to CSA General Hospital, No. 11, Charlotte with V.S.L., leg, September 29, 1864. Furloughed October 11, 1864. Retired as a result of wounds received at Chickamauga. Living after the war.

Simpson, William P., Pvt., Age 18, born December 23, 1844, Co. H, from Edgemoor, Chester County, S.C., enlisted at Chester March 19, 1862. Wounded at Chickamauga. Present on all rolls. Paroled at Greensboro May 1, 1865.

Simpson, Wm. J., Pvt., Co. F, enlisted at Anderson January 13, 1862. Discharged by substitute, J. W. Cook, February 18, 1862. Joined another Command.

Sistrunk, S. O., Pvt., Age 17, Co. C, enlisted at Georges Station January 7, 1862. Discharged February 5, 1862.

Smith, A., Pvt., Co. E. Absent without leave May/Jun 1863.

Smith, Albert Rhett, Corp., Age 20, Co. E, enlisted at Salkehatchie January 16, 1862. Reduced to Pvt., March 15, 1862. Detached service to work on gunboat at Charleston Oct/Nov 1862 - August 31, 1864. Detailed until further orders December 20, 1864. Surrendered.

Smith, Andrew Washington, Sgt., Age 23, Co. E, enlisted at Salkehatchie

January 16, 1862. Wounded, hips, at Pine Mountain June 15, 1864. Absent, patient in hospital August 31, 1864. Surrendered. Died July 21, 1887.

Smith, Benjamin Burgh, Col., F&S. Appointed regimental commander, Consolidated 16th and 24th Regiment at High Point North Carolina April 9, 1865. Wounded at Franklin. Commanded the 16th Regiment at Franklin. Prior to that time, served as staff officer, Gist's Brigade. Paroled at Greensboro May 1, 1865. Brought home the battle flags of both regiments. Delivered the colors of the 24th Regiment to General Capers after the war. Col. Smith was never assigned to the 24th Regiment until the consolidation.

Smith, B. Franklin, Corp., Co. K, enlisted at Edgefield April 15, 1862. Sent to hospital June 29, 1862 - Nov/Dec 1862. Absent without leave Jan/Feb 1863 - Jan/Feb 1864. Dropped from the roll February 19, 1864.

Smith, Calvin, Pvt., Age 20, Co. H, enlisted at Chester March 19, 1862. Absent, left sick in Mississippi July 4, 1863. Absent, sick, Jul/Aug 1863. Died of disease near Brownsville, Miss., July 11, 1863.

Smith, Edward, Pvt., Co. G. Entry from Memory Rolls at State Archives, Columbia, S.C.

Smith, E. C., Pvt., Age 30, Co. G, enlisted at Columbia March 19, 1862. Transferred to the Naval Service October 24, 1862.

Smith, F. F., Pvt., Co. G. Entry from Memory Rolls at State Archives, Columbia, S.C.

Smith, George H., Pvt., Age 22, Co. D, enlisted at Camp Gist January 18, 1862. Captured at Jackson May 14, 1862. Assigned Paroled Prisoners Camp at Demopolis June 5, 1863. Exchanged August 24, 1863. Present for duty on all rolls through August 31, 1864.

Smith, Henry, Pvt., Age 23, born March 9, 1839, Co. E, from Walterboro, enlisted at Camp Gist April 2, 1862. Absent, sick, patient in the hospital Jan/Feb 1863 - Mar/Apr 1863. Absent, sick, patient in Bell Hospital, Rome September 9, 1863. Absent without leave Nov/Dec 1863. Slightly wounded, thigh, at Peachtree Creek July 20, 1864. Absent, patient in hospital Jul/Aug 1864. Captured near Nashville December 16, 1864. Sent to Military Prison Louisville and transferred to Camp Douglas December 22, 1864. Discharged at Camp Douglas June 20, 1865.

Smith, James M., 2Lt., Age 31, Co. A, enlisted at Charleston December 31, 1862. Declined promotion to 2d Lieut of Co. A, 24th Regiment March 16, 1862. Promoted from 1Sgt., to 2Lt., May 4, 1863. Slightly wounded, thigh, at Kennesaw and sent to hospital July 2, 1864. Wounded during Hood's Tennessee Campaign, admitted to Way Hospital, Meridian, January 25, 1865. Granted leave of 30 days January 20, 1865. Surrendered at Greensboro.

Smith, Joe, Pvt., Co. F, from Graniteville, S.C. Discharged. Living. Entry from Survivor's Association roster.

Smith, John, Pvt., Co. C, enlisted at Camp Gist March 13, 1862. Transferred to Maj. Smith's Batt. Sharp Shooters October 16, 1862.

Smith, John, Pvt., Age 32, Co. F, enlisted at Columbia January 13, 1862. Discharged for inability July 6, 1862.

Smith, John O., Pvt., Age 21, Co. D, enlisted at Camp Gist January 19, 1862. Absent, wounded, Sep/Oct 1863. Absent without leave Nov/Dec 1863. Wounded, hand, near Atlanta July 26, 1864. Signed receipt roll for clothing April 1, 1864. Absent with leave wounded July 26 - September 26, 1864. Captured at Nashville December 16, 1864. Sent to Military Prison, Louisville and transferred to Camp Chase January 4, 1865. Died of Variola February 16, 1865. Grave No. 1285, located 1/3 mile south of Camp Chase.

Smith, J. Washington, Pvt., Age 30, Co. E. Surrendered. Entry from Memory Rolls at State Archives, Columbia, S.C.

Smith, J. T., Pvt., Age 20, Co. E, enlisted at Salkehatchie January 16, 1862. Died of disease February 18, 1863.

Smith, J. W., Pvt., Age 27, Co. E, enlisted at Salkehatchie January 16, 1862. Absent, sick, patient in hospital at Noonon, Ga., September 2, 1863. Detailed to work on road Nov/Dec 1863. Sick, patient in hospital August 20, 1864. Signed receipt roll for clothing at Blackie Hospital, Augusta October 27, 1864. Admitted to CSA Hospital No. 11, Charlotte, for gastritis, January 15, 1865. Returned to duty January 21, 1865. Surrendered. Grave located in J. W. Smith Cemetery, Upper Colleton County, S.C.

Smith, Joseph, Pvt., Age 28, Co. E. Died of disease at Charleston. Entry from Memory Rolls at State Archives, Columbia, S.C., and roster prepared by Captain Joseph K. Risher, company commander.

Smith, Joseph, Pvt., Co. F. Discharged July 6, 1862. Entry from Memory Rolls at State Archives, Columbia, S.C., and McGee letter of July 6, 1862.

Smith, Joseph B., Pvt., Age 29, Co. K, enlisted at Edgefield April 15, 1862. Description: complexion, light; hair, light; eyes, blue; height, 5 ft. 10 in; occupation, overseer. Discharged for physical disability, incapacity to use left arm due to old injury to scapula June 7, 1862. Name also shown as Josiah.

Smith, Kimmie S., 2Lt., Age 40, Co. D, enlisted at Camp Gist January 16, 1862. Promoted to Sgt., December 5, 1862. Assigned picket duty Jan/Feb 1863. Promoted to 3Lt., May 28, 1863. Wounded at Chickamauga September 20, 1863. Absent wounded Sep/Oct 1863. Promoted to 2Lt., Jul/Aug 1863. Resigned April 1, 1864.

Smith, Lovett K., Pvt., Co. G, enlisted at Secessionville July 20, 1862. One months pay stopped by order of court martial May/Jun 1863. Mortally wounded in battle at Chickamauga September 20, 1863. Died from wounds in hospital at Atlanta October 31, 1863. Effects valued at $6.50. Mother, Catherine L. Smith, filed claim for settlement April 2, 1864.

Smith, M., Co. G. Entry from original muster roll.

Smith, Paul, Pvt., Age 17, Co. E, enlisted at Dalton, Ga., February 20, 1864. Bounty for enlisting $50.00. Admitted for chronic diarrhoea to Ocmulgee Hospital, Macon May 21, 1864. Absent without leave August 6, 1864. Furloughed from hospital. Surrendered.

Smith, Riley, 1Sgt., Co. H, enlisted at Chester June 30, 1862. Appointed 1Sgt., June 30, 1863. Wounded. Present on all rolls. Paroled at Greensboro May 1, 1865.

Smith, W., Pvt., Co. F, enlisted at Anderson Sep/Oct 1863. Absent without leave Sep/Oct 1863 - Jan/Feb 1864. Dropped from roll Jan/Feb 1864.

Smith, W. G., Corp., Age 38, Co. G, enlisted at Columbia March 19, 1864. In hospital May/Jun 1862. Captured at Jackson May 14, 1863. Assigned Paroled Prisoners Camp at Demopolis June 5, 1863. Absent, sick, in hospital at Columbia Jul/Aug 1863. Wounded at Chickamauga September 20, 1863. Patient in hospital at Columbia Nov/Dec 1863 - Jan/Feb 1864. Signed receipt roll for clothing at Ladies General Hospital, No. 3, Columbia, S.C. March 17, 1864. Admitted for Feb. Renuit. to Ocmulgee Hospital, Macon May 22, 1864. Died May 28, 1864. Left effects of one vest, one pair pants, one pair socks, one pair shoes, 2 pairs drawers, one shirt, one hat, one blanket, one haversack, one pocket book, currency of 25 cents. Grave located in Rose Hill Cemetery, Macon, Ga.

Smoke, William P., Pvt., Age 17, Co. E, enlisted at Salkehatchie January 16, 1862. Absent, sick, patient in hospital at Montgomery August 28 - Jan/Feb 1863. Absent, sick, patient in hospital Jul/Aug - Sep/Oct 1863. Died of disease in Alabama Jan/Feb 1864. Left effects of $12.20. Name maybe spelled *Smoak*.

Snider, George E., Pvt., Age 30, Co. D, enlisted at Camp Gist April 9, 1862. Sick, furloughed, Sep/Oct 1862. Wounded at Chickamauga. Absent with leave wounded Sep/Oct 1863. Absent without leave Nov/Dec 1863. Sick in hospital at Dalton Jan/Feb 1864. Signed receipt roll for clothing March 28 and April 1, 1864. Wounded in hospital July 20, 1864. Captured at Nashville December 16, 1864. Sent to Military Prison, Louisville and transferred to Camp Chase January 4, 1865. Description: complexion, dark; hair, black; eyes, black; height, 5 ft. 6 in. Signed oath of allegiance to the United States June 12, 1865.

Souter, H. G., Sgt., Age 25, Co. G, enlisted at Columbia March 19, 1862. Promoted to Corp., Jan/Feb 1863. Promoted to 3Sgt., Sep/Oct 1863. Wounded and taken prisoner at Jackson May 14, 1863. Paroled in hospital May 16, 1865. Wounded at Chickamauga September 20, 1863.

Home, furloughed, Sep/Oct - Nov/Dec 1863. Wounded, patient in hospital at Atlanta and Griffin, Ga., Jan/Feb - Mar/Apr 1864. Assigned Provost duty with Co. D, 1st Regiment Troops and Defenses, Camp Wright, Macon Nov/Dec 1864.

Southerlin, William, Pvt., Age 27, Co. E, enlisted at Salkehatchie January 16, 1862. Present on all rolls. Died of disease in Georgia December 7, 1863.

Spearman, William M., Pvt., Co. F, enlisted at Anderson April 14, 1862. Discharged by surgeons certificate April 14, 1862. Enlisted at Anderson March 27, 1863. Absent, sick, patient in hospital Jul/Aug 1863. Died of disease in hospital at Lauderdale Springs, Clark County, Miss., September 23, 1863. Left effects of $18.75. Susan A. Spearman, Widow, filed claim for settlement Feb 8, 1864.

Spears, James Edwin, Capt., Age 25, Co. B, from Bennettsville, enlisted at Marlboro December 4, 1861. Absent without leave Jan/Feb 1863. Citadel graduate Class of 1859. Resigned January 27, 1863. Died at home 1865.

Speck, Frank D., Co. G. Entry from original muster roll.

Speck, J. F., Sgt., Age 25, Co. G, enlisted at Columbia March 19, 1862. Absent, sick, furloughed May/Jun 1862. Sick, in quarters Sep/Oct 1862. Absent without leave Nov/Dec 1862. Under arrest Mar/Apr 1863. Court martialed for passing a petition asking that the company officers, captain and first lieutenant, not to accept promotion but to stand for election by the men. Sentenced to 14 days in guard house and reduced to ranks May/Jun 1863. Absent in hospital at Canton May/Jun 1863. Detailed to brigade and regiment hospital Sep/Oct 1863 - August 31, 1864. The *Charleston Courier*, November 3, 1864, reported that Speck was prisoner of war at Camp Douglas.

Spell, D. Yancey, Sgt., Age 18, Co. E, enlisted at Salkehatchie January 16, 1862. Absent, sick, October 1862. Pay stopped one month by court martial May/Jun 1863. Promoted to 3Corp., June 1, 1863. Killed in battle at Calhoun, Ga., May 16, 1864.

Spell, H. T., Pvt., Age 21, Co. A, enlisted at Charleston January 17, 1862. Absent without leave, one month and two days, during which time pay was stopped Nov/Dec 1862. Transferred to Co. B, 3rd Cavalry Regiment Mar/Apr 1863.

Spell, James E. F., Pvt., Age 32, Co. A, enlisted at Charleston January 6, 1862. Captured at Jackson May 14, 1862. Assigned Paroled Prisoners Camp at Demopolis June 15, 1863. Absent without leave, pay stopped from May 28 - September 2, 1863. Under arrest Nov/Dec 1863. Captured near Marietta, Ga., July 3, 1864. Sent to Military Prison, Louisville and transferred to Camp Douglas July 18, 1864. Claimed to have been loyal, forced to enlist in Rebel Army to avoid conscript and deserted to avail himself of amnesty proclamation. Died of small pox October 7, 1864. Grave located near Camp Douglas.

Spell, John D., Corp., Age 33, Co. A, enlisted at Charleston December 31, 1861. Absent without leave August 21 - 31, 1864. Signed receipt roll for clothing June 30, 1864. Signed receipt roll for pay September 12, 1864. Last paid to January 1, 1864. Surrendered at Greensboro.

Spell, W. Allen, Pvt., Age 18, Co. A, enlisted at Charleston January 17, 1862. Mortally wounded in battle at Chickamauga September 20, 1863. Died in hospital at Atlanta October 31, 1863. Grave located in Oakland Cemetery, Confederate Section, Atlanta, Row 15.

Stacks, F. J., Sgt., Co. F, enlisted at Anderson April 10, 1862. Appointed 3Corp., June 1, 1863. Promoted 3Corp., August 1, 1863. Promoted to 1Corp., February 1, 1864. Promoted to 5Sgt., April 12, 1864. Slightly wounded, shoulder, at Peachtree Creek July 20, 1864. Present on all rolls. Paroled at Greensboro May 1, 1865. Died December 4, 1886.

Stanton, E. G., Pvt., Age 18, born July 17, 1843, Co. B, from Smithville, Marlboro County, S.C., enlisted at Marlboro April 8, 1862. Absent, sick, at home May/Jun 1863. Absent, patient in hospital at Atlanta Nov/Dec 1863. Absent, sick, at home Jan/Feb 1864. Severely wounded resulting in the resection of the left shoulder joint July 22, 1864. Patient in hospital at Macon August 1864. Killed in battle at Franklin November 30, 1864.

Stanton, Milton B., Pvt., Age 18, Co. B, enlisted at Marlboro May 10, 1864. Signed receipt roll for clothing September 9, 1864. Captured at Franklin December 18, 1864. Admitted to No. 1, USA General Hospital, Nashville for treatment of acute diarrhoea December 26, 1864. Transferred to Provost Marshal January 17, 1865. Sent to Military Prison, Louisville and transferred to Camp Chase January 20, 1865. Died of diarrhoea June 15, 1865. Grave no. 2041 located 1/3 mile south of Camp Chase.

Stanton, Noah, Pvt., Co. B, from Bennettsville, enlisted at Marlboro April 8, 1862. Absent, sick, patient in Bell Hospital, Rome Sep/Oct 1863. Signed receipt roll for clothing April 1, 1864. Captured near Jonesboro September 1, 1864. Exchanged at Rough and Ready September 19, 1864. Killed in battle at Franklin November 30, 1864.

Stedwell, D. S., Co. E. Died at Gate city Hospital. Buried in Oakland Cemetery, Atlanta, Ga., July 29, 1864, Row 5, No. 37. Entry from Oakland Cemetery records. Name may be listed as *Steadwell*.

Steinmeyer, John H., Jr., Capt., Age 26, Co. A, from Spartanburg, enlisted at Charleston December 31, 1861. Acting regimental Quartermaster at North East Bridge Nov/Dec 1862. Captured near Jackson May 14, 1863. Assigned Paroled Prisoners Camp at Demopolis June 5, 1863. Promoted Capt., and commanded Co. A, February 23, 1863. Slightly wounded, left leg, at Chickamauga September 20, 1863. The *Charleston Mercury* newspaper edition of May 20, 1864, erroneously reported that Capt. Steinmeyer had been killed in battle May 17, 1864. Severely wounded, shoulder, at Kennesaw June 25, 1864. Granted leave January 21, 1864. Captured at Shipp's Gap/Taylor's Ridge October 16, 1864. Sent to Military Prison, Louisville and transferred to Johnson's Island October 28, 1864. Description: complexion, dark; hair, dark; eyes, blue; height, 5 ft. 6 in. Signed oath of allegiance to the United States and released June 16, 1865. As City of Charleston alderman served on committee to visit New Orleans and retrieve sword which General Beauregard willed to the city in 1893.

Stevens, Benjamin, Teamster, Co. D, enlisted at North East, NC, January 1, 1863. Negro. Discharged August 18, 1863.

Stevens, Clement Hoffman, Col., F&S, Commanded regiment April 1, 1862 - January 19, 1864. Raised regiment. Signed certificate as inspector and mustering officer January 20 - February 18, 1862. In command of East James Island, Mar/Apr 1863. Severely wounded, breast and arm, at Chickamauga September 20, 1862. Promoted to Brig. Gen., and assigned to brigade command January 20, 1864. Mortally wounded in battle at Peachtree Creek July 20, 1864. Shot by minie ball behind the right ear. Died in the hospital July 25, 1864. Initially buried at Magnolia Cemetery, Charleston July 27, 1863. The Sons of the Confederate veterans and the United Daughters of the Confederacy placed a marker at his grave in Magnolia Cemetery, Memorial Day, May 10, 1989. Evidence exists that he was reinterred in St. Paul's Churchyard at Pendleton, S.C., next to his wife and two sons, Hamilton and Reginald. The same plot other family members, including his mother, Ann Bee Stevens; his brother-in-law Gen. Bernard E. Bee, killed in battle at the First Manassas; and his brother, Navy Lt. T. K. Stevens, killed in battle at Red River, Louisiana.

Stevens, Frank, Teamster, Co. D, enlisted at Camp Gist February 1, 1862. Colored. Present on rolls through Mar/Apr 1863.

Stevens, Thomas, Teamster, Co. D, enlisted at Camp Gist June 19, 1862. Colored. Present on rolls through Mar/Apr 1863.

Stevenson, Amaziah F., Pvt., Age 37, Co. F, from Georgia, enlisted at Anderson March 6, 1862. Killed in battle at Jackson May 14, 1863. Widow, Mary A Stevenson, filed claim for settlement November 16, 1863.

Stevenson, A. T., Pvt., Co. F, enlisted at Anderson January 13, 1862 for 12 months. Conscripted for the war Jan/Feb 1863. Captured at Jackson May 14, 1863. Assigned Paroled Prisoners Camp at Demopolis June 5, 1863. Absent, patient in division hospital Sep/Oct 1863. Captured at Ringgold, Ga., during retreat from Missionary Ridge November 26,

1863. Sent to Military Prison, Louisville and transferred to Rock Island December 14, 1864. Died January 7, 1864. Grave No. 159, located south of prison barracks.

Stevenson, John A., Pvt., Age 33, Co. F, from Centerville, S.C., enlisted at Anderson March 16, 1862. Absent, sick, Nov/Dec 1862 - Jan/Feb 1863. Under arrest Sep/Oct 1863. One month's pay stopped by sentence of court martial for 42 days absent without leave Jan/Feb 1864. Signed receipt roll for clothing September 9, 1864. Captured near Nashville December 16, 1864. Sent to Military Prison Louisville and transferred to Camp Chase January 4, 1865. Description: complexion, dark; hair, black; eyes, blue; height 5 ft. 5 in. Signed oath of allegiance to the United States June 12, 1865.

Stevenson, Thomas A., Pvt., Age 20, Co. F, from Iva, Anderson County, S.C., enlisted at Anderson May 3, 1864. Absent sick August 1864. Captured near Nashville December 16, 1864. Sent to Military Prison, Louisville and transferred to Camp Chase January 4, 1865. Description: complexion, dark; hair, black; eyes, blue; height 6 ft. 0 in. Signed oath of allegiance to the United States June 12, 1865.

Stevenson, Thomas Dean, Pvt., Age 20, Co. F, from Holland's Store, S.C., enlisted at Anderson January 13, 1862. Present for duty on all rolls. Captured at Shipp's Gap/Taylor's Ridge October 16, 1864. Sent to Military Prison, Louisville and transferred to Camp Douglas October 29, 1864. Description: complexion, fair; hair, light; eyes, blue; height, 5 ft. 8 in. Signed oath of allegiance to the United States and discharged June 17, 1865. Married December 27, 1883. Died June 27, 1914.

Stevenson, W. Foster, Pvt., Age 28, Co. F, enlisted at Anderson January 13, 1862. Reported missing near Jackson May 14, 1863. Absent, sick, June 1864. Died of disease June 1864.

Stewart, Jackson, J., Pvt., Age 32, Co. H, enlisted at Chester March 19, 1862. Description: hair, light; eyes, grey; height, 6 ft. 1 in; occupation, farmer. Died of measles at Charleston June 9, 1862. Grave located in Magnolia Cemetery, Charleston.

Stewart, James L., Pvt., Age 20, Co. F, enlisted at Anderson January 13, 1862. Description: complexion, fair; hair, dark; eyes, blue; height, 5 ft. 4 in; occupation, farmer. Discharged for inability June 20, 1862.

Stewart, James W., Pvt., Co. F, enlisted January 13, 1862. Died of disease 1864. Entry from Memory Rolls at State Archives, Columbia, S.C., and Survivors Association roster.

Stewart, James W. Sr., Pvt., Age 37, Co. F, enlisted at Anderson January 13, 1862. Absent, patient in hospital at Rome Sep/Oct 1863. Absent, sick, February 13, 1864. Absent without leave May 1864. Paroled at Greensboro May 1, 1865.

Stewart, John, Pvt., Co. F, from Twiggs, S.C., enlisted at Anderson March

27, 1863. Absent, sick, Mar/Apr 1863. Discharged for inability at Calhoun, Ga. May 15, 1863.

Stewart, John W., Pvt., Age 18, Co. F, from Moffatsville, S.C., enlisted at Anderson January 13, 1862. Company commissary Mar/Apr 1863. Wounded at Chickamauga September 20, 1863. Absent, wounded, patient in hospital Columbia Sep/Oct 1863 - Mar/Aug 1864. Signed receipt roll for clothing September 9, 1864. Paroled at Greensboro May 1, 1865. Died 1899.

Stewart, L. B., Pvt., Age 17, Co. E, enlisted at Dalton, Ga., February 20, 1864. Bounty due for enlisting $50.00. Slightly wounded, leg, at Peachtree Creek July 20, 1864. Patient in hospital Jul/Aug 1864. Surrendered.

Stewart, Littleton G., Pvt., Co. F, enlisted at Anderson March 28, 1862. Fifteen days pay stopped Nov/Dec 1862. Absent sick Nov/Dec 1862 - Jan/Feb 1863. Mortally wounded in battle at Jackson May 14, 1863. Captured and paroled in hospital May 16, 1865. Died in hospital at Jackson of wounds May 14, 1863.

Stewart, William Alexander, Pvt., Age 25, born 1843, Co. F, from Donalds-ville, S.C., enlisted at Anderson January 13, 1862. Absent, sick, Nov/Dec 1862. Absent, sick, Mar/Apr 1863. Sick, patient at General Hospital, Point Clear, Baldwin Co., Ala., July 17 - August 31, 1863. Slightly wounded, hand, near Atlanta July 20/22 1864. Signed receipt roll for clothing April 1, 1864. Seven times slightly wounded, skin cut each time. Paroled at Greensboro May 1, 1865. Married April 2, 1886. Died August 14, 1913. Resided at Abbeville, S.C.

Stewart, William F., Pvt., Age 39, Co. F, enlisted at Anderson June 13, 1862. Captured at Jackson May 14, 1864. Assigned Paroled Prisoners Camp at Demopolis June 5, 1863. Extra or daily duty working on road Nov/Dec 1863. Present for duty on all rolls. Paroled at Greensboro May 1, 1865.

Stillman, William T., Pvt., Co. K, enlisted at Edgefield April 15, 1862. Absent without leave Jul/Aug - Nov/Dec 1863. Mortally wounded, leg broken, in battle at Calhoun, Ga., May 16, 1864. Died from wounds in hospital at Atlanta May 20, 1864. Left $28.00. Wife, J. H. Stillman, filed claim for settlement November 14, 1864. Grave located in Oakland Cemetery, Confederate Section, Atlanta. Name may be shown as Sullivan.

Stoddard, W., Cook, Age 48, Co. F, enlisted at Anderson March 10, 1862. Company cook. Discharged for inability October 20, 1862.

Stoddard, William, Cook, Co. F. Cooked faithfully to the end. Entry from Survivors Association roster.

Stogner, John, Pvt., Age 25, Co. B, enlisted at Marlboro, December 4, 1861 for 12 months. Present for duty December 4, 1861 - February 28, 1862.

Stone, Oliver, Pvt., Age 16, Co. D, enlisted at Camp Gist March 1, 1862. Patient, in hospital wounded at Marietta, Ga., Sep/Oct 1863. Absent, wounded, furloughed Nov/Dec 1863 - Jan/Feb 1864. Killed in battle at Kennesaw Mountain June 1864.

Stone, Wm. T., Pvt., Co. D, from Coosawhatchie, enlisted at Camp Gist April 9, 1862. Present on all rolls. Captured at Shipp's Gap/Taylor's Ridge October 16, 1864. Sent to Military Prison, Louisville and transferred to Camp Douglas October 29, 1864. Description: complexion, fair; hair, brown; eyes, gray; height, 5 ft. 7 in. Signed oath of allegiance to the United States and discharged June 17, 1865.

Strait, Thomas J., Sgt., Age 15, Born at Chester District December 25, 1846, Co. H. Enlisted at Louisa Courthouse, Va., in Co. A, 6th Regiment March 12, 1862. Exchanged with Albert Thomas and joined 24th Regiment November 1, 1863. Absent, sick, patient in hospital at Atlanta Jan/Feb 1864. Present for duty Mar/Aug 1864. Wounded in the breast at Lovejoy Station. Reenlisted for the War. Bounty due. Received seven bullet holes in his clothing and wounded at Franklin November 30, 1864. Although disabled, he walked home barefooted. Rejoined the 24th in North Carolina in March 1865. Medical board disqualified him for further active service. Married twice: first to Kate A. Lathrop of Abbeville, and second to Ella Ruff of Lexington County, S. C. Graduated S. C. Medical College and practiced medicine in Chester, S.C. Moved to Lancaster County in 1885. Elected to State Senate 1890. Elected to United States Congress in 1892. Died April 28, 1924 and buried at Westside Cemetery, Lancaster, S.C.

Strickland, John C., Sgt., Age 18, Co. E, enlisted at Salkehatchie January 16, 1862. Sgt., to March 13, 1862. Pvt., Mar/Apr 1862. Acted Corporal in place of C. P. Wilson taken prisoner 21 May 1862, May/Jun - Oct/Nov 1862. Pvt., December 31, 1863 - July 15, 1864. Promoted to Sgt., July 16, 1864. Wounded, head, at Atlanta September 1864. Paroled at Greensboro May 1, 1865.

Strickling, John, Pvt., Age 47, Co. D, enlisted at Camp Gist January 16, 1865. Present on all rolls. Killed in battle at Peachtree Creek July 20, 1864.

Stroble, Charles, Pvt., Age 32, Co. A, enlisted at Charleston December 31, 1861. Absent, sick, patient in hospital, Demopolis, Ala., Jul/Aug - Sep/Oct 1863. Transferred to Confederate States Navy August 11, 1864.

Strom, G. W., Corp., Co. K, enlisted at Edgefield February 2, 1864. Bounty due $50.00. Present for duty Mar/Aug 1864. Wounded, leg, at Franklin November 30, 1864. Paroled at Greensboro May 1, 1865.

Strom, Harrison, Corp., Co. K, enlisted at Edgefield April 5, 1862. In hospital May/Jun 1862. Reported missing in engagement near Jackson May 14, 1863. Killed in battle at Jonesboro.

Strom, J. E., Pvt., Co. H, Consolidated 16th and 24th Regiment, enlisted at Edgefield March 20, 1865. Paroled at Greensboro May 1, 1865.

Strom, Hag., Pvt., Co. K. Entry from Memory Rolls at State Archives, Columbia, S.C.

Strom, James H., Pvt., Age 23, Co. K, enlisted at Edgefield April 15, 1862. Description: complexion, light; hair, light; eyes, blue; height 5 ft. 10 in; occupation, farmer. Discharged for consumption May 9, 1862.

Strom, J. P., Pvt., Co. K, enlisted at Edgefield May 26, 1864. Present for duty Mar/Aug 1864. Wounded at Franklin November 30, 1864. Paroled at Greensboro May 1, 1865.

Strom, Patrick H., Sgt., Co. K, enlisted at Edgefield April 15, 1862. Slightly wounded at Chickamauga September 20, 1863. Absent, admitted to division hospital October 24, 1863 - Nov/Dec 1863. Patient in hospital at Columbia April 20 - August 31, 1864. Signed receipt roll for clothing at General Hospital No. 2, Columbia, August 4 and 18, 1864. Paroled at Greensboro May 1, 1865.

Strom, S. B., Pvt., Co. K, enlisted at Edgefield August 17, 1863. Bounty due $50.00. Sick in division hospital August 24 - 31, 1864. Paroled at Greensboro May 1, 1865.

Strom, T., Pvt., Co. K. Entry from Memory Rolls at State Archives, Columbia, S.C.

Strom, W. H., Pvt., Co. K, enlisted at Edgefield October 8, 1863. Due $50.00 bounty. Captured near Nashville December 16, 1864. Sent to Military Prison, Louisville and transferred to Camp Chase January 4, 1865. Enlisted U. S. Army April 22, 1865.

Strom, William H., Pvt., Co. I, enlisted at Bells Valley, Tenn., November 12, 1863. Present Nov/Dec 1863.

Strom, W. Silas, Pvt., Co. K, enlisted at Edgefield July 20, 1864. Due $50.00 bounty. Killed in battle at Franklin November 30, 1864.

Strother, J. C., Pvt., Co. G. Entry from Memory Rolls at State Archives, Columbia, S.C.

Stubbs, Daniel F., Pvt., Age 19, Co. B, enlisted at Marlboro December 4, 1861. Wounded at Chickamauga September 20, 1863. Patient in Hospital and at home furloughed Sep/Oct 1863 - August 31, 1864. Disabled wounded and discharged 1864.

Stubbs, Jackson A., Pvt., age 18, born November 18, 1843, Co. B, from Brightsville, Marlboro County, S.C., enlisted at Marlboro April 16, 1862. Sick, patient in hospital at Gainesville, Ala., Jul/Aug 1863. Patient in hospital at Griffin, Ga., Nov/Dec 1863. Absent, sick, at home Jan/Feb - September 15, 1864. Signed receipt roll for clothing at General Hospital No. 1, Columbia, S.C., March 25 and 31, 1864. Paroled at Greensboro May 1, 1865.

Stubbs, J. L., Sgt., Age 22, Co. B, enlisted at Marlboro December 4, 1861.

Received court martial for over staying leave and sentenced to be placed under arrest for three days April 22, 1863. Absent, sick, at home in S.C. Sep/Oct - Nov/Dec 1863. Sick, patient in hospital at Columbia January - August 1864. Signed receipt roll for clothing at General Hospital,. No. 1, Columbia, January 16, March 28, and August 1, 1864. Survived.

Stubbs, Thomas, Pvt., Age 18, Co. B, enlisted at Marlboro December 4, 1861. Sick, patient in hospital in Atlanta Sep/Oct - Nov/Dec 1863. Signed receipt roll for clothing at Oliver Hospital LaGrange, Ga., April 1, 1864. Sick furlough to expire September 15, 1864. Signed receipt roll for clothing at 2d S.C. Hospital, Florence, S.C., December 10, 1864.

Sturznegger, Samuel C., Pvt., Age 40, Co. I, enlisted at Columbia March 20. 1862. Discharged because of physical disability at James Island May 29, 1862.

Sullivan, Preston O., Pvt., Co. I, enlisted at James Island July 1, 1862. Wounded at Chickamauga September 20, 1863. Absent, wounded, Nov/Dec 1863. Killed in battle at Calhoun, Ga., May 16, 1864. Death reported to regiment in speech by Colonel Capers May 22, 1864. Buried in same grave with Pvt. James Kimbrell.

Sullivan, Sampson W., Pvt., Age 29, Co. I, enlisted at Columbia March 20, 1862. Present on all rolls. Killed in battle at Chickamauga September 20, 1863. Grave located in Confederate Cemetery, Marietta, Ga.

Sulman, W. T., Co. K. Died at Atlanta Medical College Hospital. Buried on May 20, 1864 in Oakland Cemetery, Atlanta, Ga., Row 10, No. 5. Entry from Oakland Cemetery records. Name maybe also shown as Sullivan.

Swearingen, Abner, Age 30, Pvt., Co I, enlisted at Columbia February 25, 1864. Recruit bounty due ($50.00). Present for duty Jul/Aug 1864. Signed receipt roll for clothing September 9, 1864. Captured at Nashville and never heard of again.

Sweat, Harris, Pvt., Co. B, enlisted at Marlboro April 8, 1862. Transferred 2nd Batt. S.C. Sharpshooters October 30, 1862. Discharged 1863.

Sweat James, Pvt., Co. B, enlisted at Marlboro April 1, 1862. Wounded at Chickamauga September 20, 1863. Sick, furloughed Sep/Oct - Nov/Dec 1863. Sick, patient in hospital Mar/Aug 1864. Died at home in 1869.

Sweat, John W., Pvt., Age 26, Co. B, enlisted at Marlboro December 4, 1861. Absent, sick, patient in hospital at Lauderdale Miss Jul/Aug - Nov/Dec 1863. Present for duty August 31, 1864. Survived. Died at home.

Sweat, Lumfor, Pvt., Co. B, Colored. Wounded, arm, at Calhoun May 17, 1864. Entry from *Charleston Mercury* article.

Sweat, Sam, Pvt., Co. B, from Marlboro County. Slightly wounded, arm, at Calhoun, Ga., May 16, 1864. Wounded at Peachtree Creek. Died of wounds in 1864.

Sweat, Simeon, Pvt., Age 26, Co. B, enlisted at Marlboro December 4,

1861. Wounded August 15, 1864. Patient in hospital August 31, 1864. Killed in battle at Nashville 1864.

Syfret, William, Pvt., Age 23, Co. C, from Orangeburg District, enlisted at Camp Gist March 5, 1862. Wounded at Chickamauga. Sick, patient in hospital at Rome Sep/Oct 1863. Wounded through middle 1/3 of left leg July 24, 1864. Slightly wounded, thigh, July 20/22, 1864. Patient in Ocmulgee Hospital at Macon October 11, 1864. Transferred to Augusta October 12, 1864. Furloughed.

Swygert, S. D., Co. G. Entry from original muster roll.

Talbert, George W., 2Lt., Co. K, enlisted at Edgefield April 15, 1862. Elected 2Lt., December 5, 1862. Resigned April 18, 1863.

Tatum, F. P., 3Lt., Age 26, Co. B, enlisted at Marlboro, December 4, 1861. Wounded at Peachtree Creek July 20, 1863. Elected 3Lt., August 24, 1864. Present for duty on all rolls. Wounded at Franklin November 30, 1864. Admitted for wound to St. Mary's Hospital West Point, Miss., January 8, 1865. Leave of absence granted by surgeon's certificate January 3, 1865. Paroled June 9, 1865.

Taylor, James, Pvt., Age 30, Co. G, enlisted at Columbia March 19, 1862. Present for duty on all rolls through August 31, 1864. Killed in battle at Franklin November 30, 1864. Grave located in Franklin Confederate Cemetery, Section 83, Grave No. 11.

Taylor, John, Pvt., Co. K, enlisted at Edgefield February 25, 1863. Present for duty on all rolls. Slightly wounded, leg, near Jonesboro September 2, 1864. Signed, by mark, receipt roll for clothing at Hill Hospital, Cuthbert, Ga., October 31, 1864. Paroled at Greensboro May 1, 1865.

Taylor, Samuel H., Pvt., Co. F, enlisted at Anderson March 28, 1862. Absent, sick, Mar/Jun 1863. Captured at Missionary Ridge November 26, 1863. Admitted to No. 2, USA General Hospital, Nashville December 8, 1863. Sent to Military Prison, Louisville and transferred to Rock Island January 4, 1864. Transferred to US Navy, May 23, 1864. Captured and joined the enemy. Supposed to be dead, was in Vermont when last heard from.

Taylor, T. L., Pvt., Co. F, enlisted at Anderson April 1, 1864. Bounty due. Present for duty Mar/Aug 1864. Killed in battle at Franklin November 30, 1864. Grave located at Franklin Confederate Cemetery, Section 84, Grave No. 27.

Taylor, Tolliver L., Pvt., Co. F. Killed in battle at Jackson, Miss., May 14, 1863. Entry from Memory Rolls at State Archives, Columbia, S.C.

Taylor, W. B. F. P., Pvt., Age 21, Co. F, from Equality, S.C., enlisted at Anderson January 13, 1862. Absent, sick, Mar/Apr - May/Jun 1863. Captured at Ringgold, Ga., November 27, 1863. Sent to Military Prison, Louisville and transferred to Rock Island December 14, 1863. Transferred for exchange March 2, 1865. Died February 15, 1902.

Taylor, William, Pvt., Co. F., from Starr, S.C., enlisted at Anderson March 28, 1862. Present for duty Jan/Feb 1864. Absent, sick, Mar/Aug 1864. Surrendered 1865.

Taylor, Wesley J., Pvt., 24, Co. F, from Anderson, enlisted at Anderson January 13, 1862. Wounded near Jackson May 14, 1863. Absent, sick, patient in hospital, furloughed, Mar/June - Jul/Aug 1863. Absent, sick, February 23, 1864. Assigned as nurse at division hospital Mar/Aug 1864. Wounded at Franklin November 30, 1864. Wounded admitted to Way Hospital, Meridian, Miss., January 13, 1865. Furloughed. Surrendered 1865.

Terry, C. M., Sgt., Age 33, Co. D, enlisted at Camp Gist January 16, 1862. Present for duty May/Jun 1862. Last paid September 15, 1862. Discharged September 15, 1862.

Terry, William P., Pvt., Co. D. Captured at Nashville, December 16, 1864. Sent to Military Prison, Louisville and transferred to Camp Chase January 4, 1865. Died of pneumonia February 1865. Grave no. 730 located 1/3 mile south of Camp Chase.

Thomas, Albert, Pvt., Age 30, Co. H, enlisted at Chester March 19, 1865. Absent, sick, Sep/Oct - Nov/Dec 1862. Exchanged for T. J. Strait, Co. A, 5th Regiment, November 1, 1863.

Thomas, Charles M., Pvt., Age 30, Co. I, enlisted at Columbia March 20, 1862. Absent, wounded, and supposed in hands of enemy May 9, 1864. Dangerously wounded, thigh broken, in battle May 1864. Killed in battle at Dalton.

Thomas, G. W., Pvt.,. Co. K. Wounded at Franklin. Entry from Memory Rolls at State Archives, Columbia. Entry added to Co. K roster by General Ellison Capers.

Thomas, James Alexander, Capt., Age 34, Co. H, enlisted at Chester March 19, 1862. Commanded company known as Capt. Thomas' company. Resigned to take care of personal business October 29, 1862. Lost left arm during Mexican War in 1848. Raised company from Richburg community of Chester county. Elected company commander of Capt. Thomas' company, which became Co. H, 24th Regiment.

Thomas, Lewis, Pvt., Age 22, Co. A, enlisted at Charleston December 31, 1861. Assigned to ambulance corps February 20, 1864. Present on all rolls. Paroled at Greensboro May 1, 1865. Wife's name Sarah E. Thomas.

Thomas, Philip, Sgt., Age 32, Co. D, enlisted at Camp Gist January 16, 1862. Captured near Jackson May 14, 1863. Assigned Paroled Prisoners Camp at Demopolis June 5, 1863. Exchanged August 9, 1863. Promoted to 5Sgt., Mar/Apr 1862; to 4Sgt., Sep/Oct 1862; to 3Sgt., Mar/Apr 1862; to 2Sgt., Jul/Aug 1863. Although slightly wounded, finger, July 20/22 1864, he remained on duty. Present on all rolls through Jul/Aug 1864. Signed receipt roll for clothing September 9, 1864. Captured at Nashville December 16, 1864. Sent to Military Prison, Louisville and transferred to Camp Chase January 4, 1865. Description: complexion, florid; hair, dark; eyes, blue; height, 5 ft. 10 in. Signed oath of allegiance to the US June 12, 1865.

Thomas, Stephen, Pvt., Co. K, enlisted at Edgefield March 6, 1862. Reported missing after engagement near Jackson May 14, 1863. Severely wounded, thigh, near New Hope Church and sent to hospital June 4, 1865. Surrendered and paroled at Augusta May 20, 1865.

Thomas, William, Corp., Co. D, enlisted at Beaufort District July 15, 1861. Promoted to Corp., February 2, 1864. Present on all rolls. Killed in battle at Peachtree Creek July 20, 1864.

Thomasson, M. N., Pvt., Co. A, enlisted at Charleston May 1, 1862. Sick, patient in hospital at Summerville Sep/Oct 1862. At regimental camp confined to guard house, under arrest Nov/Dec 1862. Sick, patient in Citadel Square Hospital, Charleston Jan/Feb 1863. Discharged for disability March 27, 1863.

Thompson, Elijah, Pvt., Age 22, Co. E, enlisted at Salkehatchie January 16, 1862. Transferred to 2nd Battalion, Sharpshooters, and retransferred January 15, 1862. Sick, patient in hospital at Yazoo City May/Jun - Jul/Aug 1863. Pay stopped for one month by court martial May/Jun 1863. Sick, patient in Hospital July 22 - August 3, 1864. Signed, by mark, receipt roll for clothing September 10, 1864. Surrendered.

Thompson, J. J., Pvt., Age 40, Co. B, enlisted at Charleston December 4, 1861. Description: complexion, fair; hair, dark; eyes, blue; height 5 ft. 6 in; occupation, farmer. Discharged by reason of surgeon certificate at Camp Gist February 1, 1862.

Thompson, John O., Pvt., Co. C, enlisted at Georges Station January 7, 1862. Absent, sick, patient in hospital in Summerville Jan/Feb - Mar/Apr 1863. Absent without leave December 15, 1863 - August 31, 1864. Supposed to be dead.

Thompson, J. S., Pvt., Co. H. Wounded. Living after the war. Entry from roster prepared by company commander.

Thompson, Solomon J., Pvt., Age 33, Co. H, enlisted at Chester March 19, 1862. Absent, sick, Sep/Oct 1862. Discharged from the army in hospital at Columbia November 15, 1862.

Thurmond, George W., Pvt., Age 31, Co. K, enlisted at Edgefield July 1, 1862. Patient in hospital February 23, 1864. Painfully wounded, hand, two fingers amputated, near Atlanta and sent to hospital July 22, 1864. Wounded at Franklin November 30, 1864. Captured at Columbia, Tenn., December 22, 1864. Admitted to No. 1, USA General Hospital Nashville for wound, character unknown. Lower third left arm amputated January 1865. Lost two fingers of his right hand at battle of

Atlanta. Lost his left arm at Franklin. Sent to Military Prison, Louisville and transferred to Camp Chase February 3, 1865. Transferred to Point Lookout for exchange March 26, 1865. Admitted to USA Small Pox Hospital, Point Lookout April 8, 1865. Released at Point Lookout after taking the oath of allegiance to the United States June 4, 1865.

Thurmond, Phillip M., Pvt., Co. I, enlisted at Pocotaligo March 10, 1863. Wounded in battle at Jackson July 12, 1863. Absent, patient in hospital July 14 - October 1863. Absent, sick, patient in hospital August 1864. Killed in battle at Franklin November 30, 1865. Grave located in Franklin Confederate Cemetery, Section 83, Grave No. 9.

Thurmond, Thomas J., Pvt., Age 31, Co. I, enlisted at Columbia April 18, 1864. Replaced by substitute Joseph Polk June 4, 1862. Surrendered and paroled at Augusta May 20, 1865.

Tidwell, S. P., Pvt., Age 30, Co. G, enlisted at Columbia March 19, 1862. Sick, patient in hospital May/Jun 1862. Detached to work on gunboat at Charleston Nov/Dec 1862 - Nov/Dec 1863. Mortally wounded in battle at Atlanta July 22, 1864. Two fingers of right hand amputated in hospital. Died September 17, 1864. Left no effects. Grave located in Stonewall Confederate Cemetery, Griffin, Ga.

Till, Henry, Pvt., Age 20, Co. E, enlisted at Salkehatchie January 16, 1864. Pay stopped for one month by court martial May/Jun 1863. Sick, patient in Walker's Division Hospital at Lauderdale August 1, 1863 - January 14, 1864. Died of disease January 14, 1864.

Tillman, James A., Capt., Age 19, Co. I, born June 4, 1842, enlisted at Columbia March 20, 1862. Wounded, left arm broken, at Chickamauga September 20, 1863. Promoted 1Lt., January 24, 1864. Seriously wounded, both legs, at Calhoun, Ga., May 16, 1864. Absent sick furloughed from hospital July 8, 1864. Wounded at Franklin. At the battle of Franklin, assisted by four other soldiers, crossed unsurmountable second line and captured the colors of 97th Regiment OVI. The regimental commander sent the trophy to General Hood who returned the colors to Captain Tillman with his thanks. Granted 30-day leave of absence January 23, 1865. Paroled at Greensboro May 1, 1865. Died at home of injuries/wounds sustained during the war June 4, 1866. His diary is referred to in the narrative. Older brother of South Carolina Governor Pitchfork Ben Tillman.

Timmerman, Benjamin, Pvt., Co. K, enlisted at Edgefield February 18, 1863. Died in hospital at Marietta September 15, 1863.

Timmerman, David, Pvt., Co. K, enlisted at Edgefield April 15, 1862. Admitted to hospital at Rome September 15, 1863. Absent, sick, furloughed Nov/Dec - Jan/Feb 1864. Admitted to hospital July 16, 1864.

Timmerman, Frank A., Pvt., Co. K, enlisted at Edgefield April 15, 1862.

Captured at Chickamauga September 20, 1863. Sent to Military Prison, Louisville and transferred to Camp Douglas October 1863. Died of typhoid fever January 30, 1864. Grave no. 991, Chicago City Cemetery. Fort Douglas death roster reflects name as T. A. Timmerman.

Timmerman, F. H., Pvt., Co. K. Died in hospital January 20, 1864. Entry from Memory Rolls at State Archives, Columbia, S.C.

Timmerman, George H., Pvt., Co. K, enlisted at Edgefield April 15, 1862. Patient in hospital May/Jun 1862. Admitted to General hospital September 25, 1863. Died November 18, 1863.

Timmerman, George H., Pvt., Co. K, enlisted at Edgefield January 25, 1864. Due $50.00 bounty. Present for duty through August 31, 1864. Killed in battle at Jonesboro.

Timmerman, Henry, Pvt., Co. K. Killed in battle at Chickamauga. Entry from Memory Rolls at State Archives, Columbia, S.C.

Timmerman, Simeon, Pvt., Co. K, enlisted at Edgefield March 10, 1862. Discharged by medical board May/Jun 1862.

Timmerman, William, Pvt., Co. K, enlisted at Adams Run February 15, 1863. Signed receipt roll for clothing April 1, 1864. Paroled at Greensboro May 1, 1865.

Tindol, James H., Pvt., Age 16, Co. D, enlisted at Camp Gist January 16, 1862. Absent, sick, in hospital Jul/Aug 1863. Died in hospital August 30, 1863.

Tompkins, Samuel S., Capt., Co. K, from Edgefield, enlisted at Edgefield April 15, 1862. Served as a Major and voluntary ADC to General Bonham at the battle of Bull Run July 21, 1861. Afterwards, he raised a company and was elected captain. One of eight brothers in Confederate service. Resigned due to serious health problems August 14, 1862. Father of Daniel H. Tompkins future Secretary of State of South Carolina.

Torlay, Alonzo G., Pvt., Age 18, Co. A, enlisted at Charleston March 9, 1862. Detached to work as a mechanic at arsenal Charleston Sep/Oct 1862 - May/Jun 1863. Present for duty August 31, 1864. Died of disease at Selma, Ala.

Torry, W. F., Pvt., Co. G, enlisted at Columbia April 7, 1864. Wounded at Calhoun May 16, 1864. Patient in hospital through August 31, 1864.

Townsend, W. S., Corp., Age 17, Co. B, enlisted at Marlboro December 4, 1861. Transferred to Smith's Batt. S.C. Sharpshooters June 23, 1862. Transferred to 26th Regiment as 4th Sgt.

Trawick, Peter, Pvt., Age 26, Co. B, enlisted at Marlboro December 4, 1861. Detached to work on gun boat in Charleston Nov/Dec 1862 - Nov/Dec 1863. Absent without leave August 31, 1864. Killed in battle at Franklin November 30, 1864.

Traxler, James J., Pvt., Age 18, Co. C, enlisted at Camp Gist March 3, 1862.

Died in Lauderdale Springs Hospital of disease July 25, 1863. Mother, Susan Pendarvis, filed claim for settlement December 12, 1864.

Trevett, J. W., Pvt., Age 28, Co. G, from Richland County, S.C., enlisted at Columbia March 19, 1862. Detached for the regimental band. Drummer. Musician. Signed receipt roll for clothing September 30, 1863. Present on all rolls. Captured at Franklin December 17, 1864. Admitted as convalescent to No. 1, USA General Hospital, Nashville December 27, 1863 - January 13, 1865. Sent to Military Prison, Louisville and transferred to Camp Chase January 11, 1865. Description: complexion, florid; hair, light; eyes, blue; height, 5 ft. 11 1/2 in. Signed oath of allegiance to the United States June 13, 1865.

Triest, M., Sgt. Maj., F&S, enlisted at Camp Gist January 20, 1862. Present on all rolls. Quartermaster Sergeant. Paroled at Greensboro May 1, 1865.

Tucker, A. C., Pvt., Age 18, Co. I, enlisted at Augusta April 20, 1864. Recruit bounty due ($50.00) Absent, wounded, at Atlanta August 9, 1864. Patient in hospital Jul/Aug 1864. Returned to duty from hospital January 14, 1865. Admitted to CSA General Hospital, No. 11, Charlotte, for chronic diarrhoea March 11, 1865. Returned to duty March 14, 1865.

Tucker, Hampton B., Pvt., Co. I, enlisted at James Island May 17, 1862. Severely wounded near Dalton May 9, 1864. Patient in hospital Jul/Aug 1864.

Tucker, J. P., 2Lt., Age 33, Co. F, from Storeville, S.C., enlisted at Anderson December 10, 1861. Absent without leave Nov/Dec 1862. Resigned October 1862. Dropped from the rolls January 22, 1863. Died at Iva, S.C., in 1902.

Tucker, Pickens L., 2Lt., Age 17, Co. I., from Dark Corner, S.C., enlisted at Columbia March 20, 1862. Present for duty Nov/Dec 1863. Promoted to 2Lt., March 17, 1864. Granted leave April 1, 1864. Killed in battle at Kennesaw 1864. Father, Atticus Tucker.

Turner, Daniel, Pvt., Age 15, Co. B, enlisted at Marlboro December 4, 1861. Appointed Drummer April 1, 1863. Present for duty on all rolls through August 31, 1864. Captured near Jonesboro September 1, 1864. Exchanged at Rough and Ready September 19, 1864. Paroled at Greensboro, May 1, 1865. Deserted April 26, 1865.

Turner, Jack, Pvt., Co. B. Died 1895. Entry from Thomas, A. W., *History of Marlboro County.*

Turner, James, Pvt., Age 21, Co. B, enlisted at Marlboro December 4, 1861. Pay stoppage for accoutrements and bayonet Nov/Dec 1863. Present for duty on all rolls. Signed, by mark, receipt roll for clothing September 9, 1864.

Turner, John, Cook, Age 51, Co. A, enlisted at Charleston December 31,

1861. Discharged January 15, 1863.

Turner, John, Pvt., Age 44, Co.B, enlisted at Marlboro December 4, 1861. Admitted to hospital February 23, 1863. Absent without leave August 31, 1864.

Turner, Levy, Pvt., Age 25, Co. B., enlisted at Marlboro December 4, 1861. Absent without leave May/Jun 1863. Captured at Nashville December 16, 1864. Sent to Military Prison, Louisville and transferred to Camp Douglas December 24, 1864. Discharged June 6, 1865. Died at home.

Turner, William, Pvt., Co. B, enlisted at Marlboro April 1, 1862. Absent without leave, one months pay retained by court martial Nov/Dec 1862. Died in Wayside Hospital at Charleston May 6, 1863. Widow, Caroline Turner, filed claim for settlement November 19, 1863. Grave located in Magnolia Cemetery, Charleston.

Tuten, J. A., Pvt., Age 33, Co. D, enlisted at Camp Gist March 1, 1862. Sick, furloughed, Sep/Oct 1862. Assigned guard duty Jan/Feb 1863. Absent without leave May/Jun. Absent with leave Jul/Aug - Sep/Oct 1863. Absent, sick, furloughed Nov/Dec 1863 - September 2, 1864.

Tuten, Joseph J., Sgt., Age 27, Co. D, enlisted at Camp Gist January 16, 1862. Absent, sick, furloughed Sep/Oct 1862. Promoted to Corp., December 6, 1862. Wounded, absent with leave to September 2, 1864. Mustered with Co. C, 1st Regiment Troops and Defenses, Camp Wright, Macon Nov/Dec 1864. Captured by US 1st Brigade, 2d Cav. Div. Macon, Ga., April 30, 1865.

Tuten, J. W., Pvt., Age 20, Co. A, enlisted at Charleston December 31, 1861. Present for duty May/Jun 1862.

Ulmer, L. G., 2Lt., Age 18, Co. E, enlisted at Camp Gist March 3, 1862. Absent without leave October 1862. Absent without leave Nov/Dec 1863. Present for duty on all rosters through Jul/Aug 1864. Surrendered.

Usher, Charles, Pvt., Age 35, Co. B, enlisted at Marlboro, December 4, 1861. Absent, sick, patient in hospital and sick, at home, July/Aug - Sep/Oct 1863. Absent without leave Nov/Dec 1863. Admitted to hospital at Atlanta by Lt. Smith February 26, 1863. Signed receipt roll for clothing October 6, 1863. Died of ascites in hospital at Fosythe, Ga., March 21, 1864. Buried as unknown soldier. Personal effects consisted of sundries and $21.25.

Utsey, D. M., Corp., Age 39, Co. C, enlisted at Georges Station, January 7, 1862. Sick, patient in hospital at Atlanta Jul/Aug 1863. Died at Georges Station September 24, 1863.

Utsey, Isoc Simmons, Pvt., Co. C, from St. George, S.C. Served in 11th and 24th Regiments. Married June 5, 1860. Died April 17, 1881. Widow Mary E. Utsey. Entry from Confederate Veteran pension records at State Archives, Columbia, S.C.

Utsey, John S., Pvt., Age 18, Co. C, enlisted at Georges Station January 7,

1862. Exchanged in place of G. W. Patrick August 29, 1862. Wounded at Chickamauga September 20, 1863. Absent wounded Sep/Oct - Jan/Feb 1864. Killed in battle at Kennesaw. Killed while on pickett duty at Smyrna Church Line June 1864.

Utsey, Isaac V., Pvt., Age 30, Co. C. Discharged at Charleston 1862. Entry from Memory Rolls at State Archives, Columbia, S.C.

Varn, P. M. E., Pvt., Age 19, Co. E, enlisted at Camp Gist March 13, 1862. Killed in battle at Chickamauga September 20, 1863.

Varnadore, Henry, Pvt., Co. E, from Walterboro, S.C., enlisted at Dalton, Ga., April 1, 1864. Bounty due for enlistment $50.00. Discharged at the end of the war. Surrendered. Married October 12, 1872. Died May 6, 1885.

Vaugh, Alfred, Pvt., Age 18, Co. E, enlisted at Salkehatchie January 16, 1862. Forty days pay stopped for absence without leave Nov/Dec 1862. Detailed as a teamster January 10, 1864. Paroled at Greensboro May 1, 1865. Deserted April 17, 1865. Last name also shown in record as Vaughn and Vaughan.

Vaughan Samuel D., Pvt., Age 18, Co. E, enlisted at Camp Gist April 20, 1862. Admitted to Ocmulgee Hospital, Macon, with acute dysentery May 22 - 29, 1864. Present on all rolls. Paroled at Greensboro May 1, 1865.

Vaughan, Stephen, Pvt., Age 22, Co. E, enlisted at Salkehatchie January 16, 1862. Absent, sick, patient in hospital at Augusta September 30 - October 1863. Sick, patient in hospital February 20 - July 22 1864. Furloughed from hospital for 60 days July 22, 1864. Admitted to CSA General Hospital, No. 11, Charlotte, with V.S. lower extremities, left, January 19 - February 10, 1865. Furloughed February 10, 1865.

Wagstaff, J. G., Pvt., Age 51, Co. H, enlisted at Chester March 19, 1862. Absent without leave Sep/Oct 1862. Detached in Quartermaster Department Jan/Feb - Sep/Oct 1863. Ambulance driver Jan/Feb 1864. Signed receipt roll for clothing April 1, 1864. Sick, patient at hospital at Columbia May 30 - August 31, 1864. Transferred to service in the Quartermasters Department under Capt. J. H. Stout August 18, 1864. Determined unfit for field service, detailed to other service by General Hood September 24, 1864. Paroled at Chester May 5, 1865.

Walden, Washington A., Pvt., Age 27, Co. A, enlisted at Charleston December 31, 1861. Absent, sick, patient in hospital at Charleston Sep/Oct 1862. Detailed to pioneer corps by order General Walker Nov/Dec 1863 - Jul/Aug 1864. Present for duty August 31, 1864. Surrendered at Greensboro. Name also shown as Walling.

Walker, Daniel, Pvt., Age 36, Co. I, enlisted at Columbia April 7, 1862. Wounded, leg, at Chickamauga September 20, 1863. Absent, wounded, patient in hospital September 20, 1863 - August 1864. Signed receipt roll for clothing at General Hospital, No. 2, Columbia, S.C. July 28 and August 5, 1864. Killed in battle at Franklin. Grave located at Franklin Confederate Cemetery, Section 83, Grave No. 8.

Walker, James D., Pvt., Age 26, Co. E, enlisted at Salkehatchie January 16, 1862. Captured at Chickamauga September 20, 1863. Sent to Military Prison, Louisville and transferred to Camp Douglas October 4, 1863. Died of debility from small pox December 11, 1864. Grave no. 247, located Block 2, Chicago City Cemetery.

Walker, L. B., Pvt., Age 27, Co. E, enlisted at Pocotaligo March 31, 1863. Killed in battle at Chickamauga September 20, 1863.

Wall, J. E., Pvt., Co. D, enlisted at Camp Gist April 9, 1862. Absent, patient in hospital at Columbia Mar/Apr 1863. Died of disease at Columbia April 29, 1863.

Wall, John G., Pvt., Co. F, enlisted January 13, 1862. Captured at Nashville December 1864. Entry from roster of Co. F.

Wall, M. H., Pvt., Co. D, enlisted at Camp Gist April 9, 1862. In hospital at Charleston Nov/Dec 1862. Patient in hospital at Columbia Mar/Apr 1863. Absent without leave, $21.00 stopped from pay by order of court martial May/Jun 1863. Sick in hospital Sep/Oct - Jul/Aug 1864. Dropped from rolls Jul/Aug 1864.

Wallace, Hugh K., Co. H, enlisted at Dalton, Ga., March 13, 1864. Bounty due. Absent, sick, August 31, 1864. Captured near Nashville December 16, 1864. Sent to Military Prison, Louisville and transferred to Camp Douglas December 24, 1865. Died of pleuritis January 22, 1865. Grave no. 558, Block 2, Chicago City Cemetery. Name shown as Wallace, *M*., on Camp Douglas death list.

Wallace, J. B., Pvt., Age 15, Co. B, enlisted at Marlboro December 4, 1861. Wounded July 12, 1864. Patient in hospital August 31, 1865. Paroled at Greensboro May 1, 1865. Deserted April 26, 1865. Moved to Texas.

Wallan, John W., Pvt., Age 21, Co. A, enlisted at Charleston December 31, 1861. Detailed to work on Eason's gunboat October 13, 1862. Detailed to work at Arsenal, Charleston April 27, 1863 - May/Jun 1863. Wounded and sent to hospital Jul/Aug 1864. Signed receipt roll for clothing November 11, 1864. Surrendered at Greensboro. Name also shown as Wallin, Wallen, and Waller.

Wallin, Henry C., Pvt., Co. A. Surrendered at Greensboro. Entry from Memory Rolls at State Archives, Columbia, S.C.

Walls, Anderson, Pvt., Co. I, enlisted at Pocotaligo March 10, 1863. Absent at hospital August 30, 1863 - January 3, 1864. Absent, sick, patient in hospital July 17, 1864 - August 1864. Wounded at Franklin.

Walls, V. O., Pvt., Co. D, enlisted at Camp Gist April 9, 1862. Present for duty May/Jun 1862.

Walters, Hamp, Pvt., Age 29, Co. C, enlisted at Georges Station January 7,

1862. Detached without pay by order of Maj. Gen. Pemberton May 30, 1862. Detached service without pay November 21 - December 21, 1862. Absent, sick, home in S.C. May/Jun -Jul/Aug 1863. Present for duty Jul/Aug 1864. Survived.

Walters, John Amanuel, Pvt., Age 19, born May 6, 1843, Co. C, from Reevesville, enlisted at Camp Gist March 18, 1862. One months pay stopped by court martial May/Jun 1863. Captured at Chickamauga September 20, 1863. Sent to Military Prison, Louisville and transferred to Camp Douglas October 4, 1863. Description: complexion, fair; hair, light; eyes, blue; height 5 ft. 9 in. Signed oath of allegiance to the United States and discharged June 16, 1865.

Walters, Middleton, Pvt., Age 17, Co. C, enlisted at Georges Station January 17, 1862. Killed by train. Died April 11, 1862.

Walters, Richard, Pvt., Age 36, Co. C, enlisted at Georges Station January 7, 1862. Detached by order of Maj. Gen. Pemberton without pay May 30, 1862. One month's pay stopped by court martial May/Jun 1863. Wounded at Chickamauga. Present for duty Jul/Aug 1864.

Walters, R. M., Corp., Age 28, Co. C, enlisted at Camp Gist March 6, 1862. Absent, sick, patient in hospital and furloughed Mar/Apr - May/Jun 1862. Wounded at Chickamauga September 20, 1863. Furloughed Sep/Oct 1863. Paroled at Greensboro May 1, 1865.

Walters, S. D., Pvt., Age 17, Co. C, enlisted at Georges Station January 7, 1862. One month pay stopped by court martial May/Jun 1863. Absent, sick, patient in hospital Jul/Aug 1864. Paroled at Greensboro May 1, 1865.

Warner, D., Pvt., Co. C, enlisted at Camp Gist March 13, 1862. Present for duty May/Jun 1862. Discharged at Charleston 1862.

Warren, Darby M., Pvt., Age 20, Co. E, enlisted at Camp Gist March 19, 1862. Died at Secessionville Hospital October 9, 1862.

Warren, E., Pvt., Age 18, born 1846, Co. E, from Smoaks, enlisted at Dalton, Ga., May 1, 1864. Bounty due for enlistment $50.00. Present for duty Jul/Aug 1864. Wounded at Jonesboro. Signed receipt for clothing November 28, 1864. Surrendered. Discharged at Goldsboro April 1865. Grave located Baptist Church Cemetery, Smoaks.

Warren, John, Capt., Age 24, Co. E, from Williams, enlisted at Camp Gist January 16, 1862. Granted leave February 2, 1863. Promoted Capt., June 11, 1863. Dangerously wounded, left knee, in battle near Atlanta. Leg amputated. Died as a result of wounds in hospital at Atlanta July 6, 1864. Brother-in-law of Company Commander, Joseph K. Risher.

Warren, Thomas, Pvt., Age 68, Co. D, enlisted at Camp Gist January 16, 1862. Present for duty Mar/Apr 1862.

Warren, W., Pvt., Co. G, enlisted at Columbia March 13, 1863. Seriously wounded at Chickamauga. Absent, patient in hospital at Marietta and

Montgomery Sep/Oct 1863 - August 1, 1864.

Waters, David P., Pvt., Age 38, Co. H, occupation mechanic, enlisted at Chester March 19, 1862. Present for duty March 19 to April 30, 1862. Transferred to 17th Regiment. Grave located in Union Cemetery, Richburg, S.C.

Waters, John A., Pvt., Age 20, Co. F, from Texas, enlisted at Anderson January 13, 1862. Present on all rolls through August 31, 1864. Supposed to be in Mississippi when last heard from. Surrendered 1865.

Waters, John, Pvt., Co. B, enlisted at Marlboro April 14, 1862. Absent sick at home Sep/Oct 1863. Absent without leave in S.C. Nov/Dec 1863 - Jan/Feb 1864. Signed receipt roll for clothing 2d N.C. Hospital., Columbia, S.C. July 12, 1864. Absent, patient in hospital at Columbia August 31, 1864. Paroled at Greensboro May 1, 1865.

Watt, Andrew J., Pvt., Co. F, from Deans, S.C., enlisted at Anderson March 27, 1863. Wounded and captured at Jackson May 14, 1863. Paroled in hospital May 16, 1863. Absent, wounded, furloughed or in the hospital at Columbia May 1863 - August 31, 1864. Surrendered. Died June 10, 1891.

Watt, John G., Pvt., Age 33, Co. F, from Moffatsville, S.C., enlisted at Anderson January 13, 1862. Captured May 14, 1863. Paroled prisoner June 1863. Absent without leave August 1863. Absent, wounded, July 22, 1864. Wounded at Nashville. Captured near Nashville December 16, 1864. Sent to Military Prison, Louisville and transferred to Camp Chase January 14, 1865. Description: complexion, light; hair, light; eyes blue; height, 5 ft. 6 in. Signed oath of allegiance to the United States June 12, 1865.

Watt, John T., Pvt., Co. F. Surrendered 1865. Entry from Memory Rolls at State Archives, Columbia, S.C.

Watt, John W., Pvt., Co. F, from Moffattsville, S.C., enlisted at Anderson April 1, 1864. Bounty due. Absent, sick with chronic diarrhoea and general debility, patient in Floyd House Hospital, Macon August 5, 1864. Present for duty August 31, 1864. Surrendered 1865. Died in 1887.

Watts, Henry, Pvt., Co. G, enlisted at Columbia March 19, 1865. Sick, furloughed and in hospital at Columbia Sep/Oct - Nov/Dec 1862. Sick, furloughed, and patient in hospital at Columbia Nov/Dec 1863 - Jan/Feb 1864. Died at General Hospital No. 1, Columbia April 25, 1864. Signed, by mark, receipt roll for clothing at General Hospital No. 1, Columbia, S.C., January 13 and 18, 1864. Mother, Ady Watts, filed claim for settlement May 21, 1864.

Way, John, Pvt., Co. C, enlisted at Secessionville July 3, 1862. Present for duty on all rolls through Jul/Aug 1864. Signed, by mark, receipt roll for clothing at Marshall Hospital, Columbus, Ga., June 21, 1864. Still living.

Way, William E., Pvt., Age 26, born January 18, 1845, Co. C, enlisted at Georges Station January 7, 1862. Wounded at Chickamauga September 20, 1863. Furloughed Sep/Oct 1863. Absent without leave Nov/Dec 1862. Wounded at Kennesaw Mountain. Present for duty Jul/Aug 1864. Discharged April 1865. Married October 14, 1870. Died 1897. Widow Mary E. Way.

Wayne, Daniel G., 1Lt., Age 44, Co. A., enlisted at Charleston December 31, 1864. In charge of camp at Secessionville Nov/Dec 1862. Resigned due to physical limitations February 23, 1863.

Weathers, Jacob, 2Lt., Age 40, Co. C, enlisted at Georges Station January 7, 1862. Promoted 2Lt., October 27, 1862. Wounded at Chickamauga September 20, 1863. Died of wounds received in battle at Chickamauga November 20, 1863.

Weathers, John L. E., Sgt., Age 21, Co. C, enlisted at Georges Station January 17, 1862. Killed in battle at Chickamauga September 20, 1863.

Weathers, J. W., Pvt., Age 29, Co. C, enlisted at Camp Gist March 2, 1862. Present for duty May/Jun 1862.

Weathers, Peter Daniel, Pvt., Age 17, Co. C, from Harleyville, S.C., enlisted at Georges Station February 19, 1864. Absent, sick, patient in hospital Mar/Apr 1863. Sick in S.C. Jul/Aug 1863. Absent without leave Sep/Oct 1863. Paroled at Greensboro May 1, 1865. Died June 24, 1911. Widow Mrs. M. F. Weathers.

Webb, James Marion, Pvt., Age 18, Co. F, enlisted at Anderson January 13, 1862. Sick, patient in hospital at Lauderdale Springs, Miss Jul/Aug - Sep/Oct 1863. Absent, sick, February 10, 1864. Died of typhoid fever at Manassas, Ga., March 4, 1864.

Weeks, John J., Pvt., Age 16, Co. C, enlisted at Georges Station January 7, 1862. Patient at CSA Military Hospital, No. 4, Wilmington, N. C., for pneumonia January 4 - 23, 1863. Admitted to CSA General Military Hospital, No. 4, Wilmington with debilities January 30 1863. Furloughed for 25 days January 31, 1863. Wounded at Chickamauga September 20, 1863. Absent, sick, furloughed September 20, 1863 - Jan/Feb 1864. Present for duty Jul/Aug 1864. Admitted to Way Hospital, Meridan, Miss., suffering chronic diarrhoea with extreme emaciation and debility February 18, 1865. Granted 60 days furlough by Medical Examining Board, Lauderdale, Miss February 21, 1865. Died of wounds at Augusta in 1865.

Weeks, J. M., Sr., Pvt., Co. C. Entry from Dorchester County Enrollment Book.

Weeks, R. S., 2Lt., Age 21, Co. C, enlisted at Georges Station January 7, 1862. Elected 2Lt., May 4, 1863. Granted leave January 29, 1864. Slightly wounded at Resaca May 16, 1864. Present for duty on all rolls.

Wounded at Franklin. Granted 30 day leave of absence January 25, 1865. Paroled at Greensboro May 1, 1865.

Weeks, Zachariah P., Sgt., Age 20, Co. C, enlisted at Georges Station March 20, 1862. Appointed Sgt., December 1, 1862. Killed in battle at Chickamauga September 20, 1863. Mother, Martha Weeks, filed claim for settlement October 26, 1864.

Welch, Edgar H., Pvt., Age 19, Co. A, enlisted at Charleston December 31, 1861. Absent without leave Sep/Oct 1862. Absent without leave September 20 - December 20, 1863. Sentenced to one months pay stopped ($11.00) Jan/Feb 1864. Deserted May 26, 1864. Reported missing - heard from and would return to duty in short time. Surrendered at Greensboro.

Welch, James, Pvt., Age 34, Co. I, enlisted at Columbia April 15, 1862. Absent, patient in hospital July 21 - 31, 1863. Signed receipt roll for clothing April 1, 1864. Present for duty Jul/Aug 1864. Died of hydrothorax in hospital of Army of Tennessee February 24, 1865. Grave located in Rose Hill Cemetery, Macon, Ga.

Wells, B. W., Pvt., Co. D, enlisted at Camp Gist April 19, 1862. Detached service at Wilmington Nov/Dec 1862. Absent without leave August 30 - October 6, 1863. Captured near Marietta June 17, 1864. Sent to Military Prison, Louisville and transferred to Camp Morton June 28, 1864. Paroled at Camp Morton and forwarded via Baltimore to Point Lookout for exchange February 19, 1865.

Wells, Eldred, Pvt., Age 24, Co. D, enlisted at Camp Gist April 9, 1862. Slightly wounded, shoulder, July 20, 1864. Absent without leave Jan/Feb 1863. Absent without leave August 30 - October 16, 1863. Captured near Marietta June 17, 1864. Sent to Military Prison, Louisville and transferred to Camp Morton June 27, 1864. Signed by mark. Paroled at Camp Morton and exchanged at City Point, Virginia, March 4, 1865.

Wells, Gansey H., Pvt., Co. D, enlisted at Beaufort District, March 15, 1864. Bounty due fifty dollars. Sick, patient in hospital, Macon Jul/Aug 1864. Captured near Nashville December 16, 1864. Died of pneumonia at Military Prison Hospital No. 2, Louisville January 18, 1865. Grave No. 11, located Range 62, Cave Hill Cemetery, Louisville.

Wells, Jasper W., 2Lt., Age 35, Co. I, enlisted at James Island May 17, 1862. Elected 2Lt., November 27, 1862. Killed in battle at Chickamauga September 20, 1863. Effects were sundries. Administratrix, Margaret E. Wells, filed claim for settlement March 1, 1864.

Westbury, Daniel, Pvt., Co. C. Survived. Entry from Dorchester County Enrollment Book.

Westbury, David H., Pvt., Age 30, Co. C, enlisted at Georges Station January 7, 1862 for 12 months. Absent, sick, October 1862. Discharged, term of service expired Jan/Feb 1863. Killed by accident.

Westbury, Thomas, Pvt., Co. C. Survived. Entry from Dorchester County Enrollment Book.

Wever, George Mc., 1Sgt., Co. K, enlisted at Edgefield April 15, 1862. Patient in hospital May/Jun 1862. Absent, sick, patient in hospital at Augusta and at home furloughed Nov/Dec 1862 - Sep/Oct 1863. Absent without leave Nov/Dec 1863 - Jan/Feb 1864. Severely wounded, ankle, at Peachtree Creek July 20, 1864. Patient in hospital at Griffin, Ga., August 31, 1864. Lost a leg at Peachtree Creek. Disabled for further service.

Wever, Lafayette B., Maj., Age 36, Co. I, enlisted at Columbia March 20, 1862. Promoted to captain vice Capt. A. J. Hammond who was promoted to Maj., April 1, 1862. Granted furlough April 30, 1863. Absent, sick, August 30 - Nov/Dec 1863. Absent, sick, patient in hospital May 19 - Jul/Aug 1864. Surrendered and paroled at Augusta May 18, 1865.

Whetsell, Jacob J., Pvt., Co. C, from Orangeburg and Reevesville S.C., enlisted at Camp Gist April 6, 1862. Wounded at Marietta. Patient in Floyd House Hospital, Macon with gun shot wound, flesh, to the abdomen. Granted 30 days furlough July 4, 1864. Paroled at Greensboro May 1, 1865.

Whitaker, Gabriel, Teamster, Co. D, enlisted at Charleston May 16, 1862. Discharged January 13, 1864. Negro.

Whitcofski, John F., Pvt., Co. A. Transferred to Smith's Battalion. Entry from Memory Rolls at State Archives, Columbia, S.C.

White, J. N., Sgt., Age 18, Co. E, enlisted at Salkehatchie January 16, 1864. Absent without leave Sep/Oct 1863. Sick, patient in hospital February, 1864. Died of disease in Georgia hospital April 1, 1864.

White, John, Teamster, Co. D, enlisted at Camp Gist February 1, 1862. Colored.

White, John T., Corp., Co. F, from Anderson, S.C., enlisted at Anderson May 14, 1862. Absent, sick, Nov/Dec 1862. Appointed 4Corp., February 1, 1864. Appointed 3Corp., Mar/Aug 1864. Absent sick August 1864. Survived. Surrendered. Died 1899.

White, Joseph W., Pvt., Age 19, Co. H, enlisted at Chester March 19, 1862. Detached driving wagon Jul/Aug - Sep/Oct 1863. Wounded at Franklin. Paroled at Greensboro May 1, 1865.

White, S. C., 2Lt., Age 22, Co. E, enlisted at Salkehatchie January 16, 1862. Promoted to 2Sgt., April 15, 1862. Captured at Battery Island May 21, 1862. Transported from Hilton Head to Fort Columbus, New York Harbor via Steamer *Arago* August 14, 1862. Transferred to Fort Delaware August 23, 1862. Exchanged at Aikens Landing, Va., October 12, 1862. Promoted to 2Lt., September 1863. Killed in battle at

Chickamauga September 20, 1863. Grave located at Marietta Confederate Cemetery, Marietta, Ga.

White, William, Pvt., Age 35, Co. A, enlisted at Charleston, December 31, 1861. Present for duty Mar/Apr 1862. Discharged, physically disabled.

White, William, Pvt., Co. K, enlisted at Edgefield April 15, 1862. Detailed as a guard at Secessionville Nov/Dec 1862. Absent, sick, furloughed Jan/Feb 1863. Granted furlough of 30 days February 4, 1863. Killed in battle at Chickamauga September 20, 1863. Widow, Sarah White, filed claim for settlement January 23, 1865.

Whitman, Elijah P., Pvt., Co. F, enlisted at Anderson January 13, 1862 for 12 months. Patient in hospital May/Jun 1862. Died of disease August 4, 1862. Widow, P. L. Whitman filed claim for settlement April 6, 1863.

Whitman, William J., Pvt., Co. F, enlisted at Anderson April 12, 1862. Killed in battle near Jackson May 14, 1863. Widow, Elizabeth Whitman, filed claim for settlement February 8, 1864.

Wilbur, Hardy, Pvt., Co. F, from Georgia. Killed in battle at Atlanta. Entry from Memory Rolls at State Archives, Columbia, S.C.

Wilburn, W. F., Co. H. Died of wounds in Georgia. Entry from *Chester County Heritage History.*

Wilder, E., Pvt., Co. G, enlisted at Columbia May 1, 1862. Assigned to regiment from Camp of Instruction, Columbia. Patient in hospital at Rome, Ga Sep/Oct 1863. Absent without leave December 15, 1863. Paroled at Greensboro May 1, 1865.

Wilhite, T. T., Pvt., Co. K, enlisted at Edgefield April 15, 1863. Severely wounded, mouth, at Chickamauga September 20, 1863. Absent wounded Sep/Oct 1863 - Jan/Feb 1864. Severely wounded, spine, near Atlanta July 22, 1864. Sent to hospital. Never returned to duty.

Williams, Augustus, Pvt., Co. D, enlisted at Camp Gist April 2, 1862. Transferred to Sharpshooters and retransferred to the regiment. Wounded, fingers shot off, and patient in hospital Jul/Aug 1864. Wounded, admitted to Way Hospital, Meridian, Miss January 11, 1865. Furloughed.

Williams, F. B., Corp., Co. D, enlisted at Camp Gist January 16, 1862. In hospital at Charleston Jan/Feb 1863. Wounded near Jackson May 14, 1863.

Williams, James H., Pvt., age 20, Co.D, enlisted at Camp Gist January 16, 1862. Reported missing near Jackson May 14, 1863. Sick, patient in hospital at Daresville, Ga., Jan/Feb 1864. Sick, furloughed, June 11 - September 11, 1864. Admitted to Ocmulgee Hospital Macon for insanity September 26 - October 8, 1864. Captured at Nashville, Tenn., December 16, 1864. Sent to Military Prison, Louisville and transferred to Camp Chase January 4, 1865. Description: complexion, fair; hair, light; eyes, blue; height, 5 ft. 8 in. Signed oath of allegiance to the

United States June 12, 1865.

Williams, John Henry, Corp., Age 25, Co. D, enlisted at Camp Gist February 20, 1862. Promoted to Corp., September 26, 1863. Reduced to ranks May 30, 1864. Sick, patient in hospital Jul/Aug 1864. Wounded at Franklin November 30, 1864. Admitted to St. Mary's Hospital January 7, 1865. Hospitalized in Georgia, Alabama and Mississippi.

Williams, John S., Pvt., Co. K, enlisted at Edgefield March 1, 1863. Slightly wounded, leg, at Chickamauga September 20, 1863. Absent, furloughed because of wound Sep/Oct 1863 - Jan/Feb 1864. Slightly wounded, leg, July 20, 1864. Returned to company. Wounded near Atlanta August 17, 1864. Died September 9, 1864. Killed in battle at Atlanta. Grave located in Confederate Graveyard near Milner, Pike County, Ga.

Williams, Joseph, Pvt., Age 15, Co. B, enlisted at Marlboro December 4, 1861. Died of pneumonia at Fair Ground Hospital, Macon June 20, 1864.

Williams, J., Co. C. Buried June 4, 1864 in Oakland Cemetery, Atlanta, Ga. Entry from Oakland Cemetery records.

Williams, Lary, Pvt., Age 20, Co. B, enlisted at Marlboro January 24, 1862. Wounded, admitted to the hospital August 15, 1864. Signed receipt for clothing October 1, 1864.

Williams, Pressly M., Sgt., Co. K, enlisted at Edgefield April 15, 1862. Absent sick May/Jun 1863. Transferred to Co. B., 6th S.C. Cavalry, December 3, 1863.

Williams, Robert H., Pvt., Age 20, Co. I, enlisted at Coles Island May 12, 1862. Absent sick at hospital in Charleston May/Jun - Nov/Dec 1862. Wounded, leg, at Chickamauga September 20, 1863. Detached hospital duty Montgomery April 1, 1864. Wounded at Franklin November 30, 1864.

Williams, Thomas B., Sgt., Age 32, Co. D, enlisted at Camp Gist January 16, 1862. Detached service in the country Mar/Apr 1863. Signed parole until exchanged at Canton, Miss., July 18, 1863. Patient in hospital at Canton May/Jun 1863. Absent, wounded, Jul/Aug - Sep/Oct 1863. Promoted to Sgt., May 30, 1864. Paroled at Greensboro May 1, 1865.

Williams, Thomas, Pvt., Age 45, Co. B, enlisted at Marlboro December 4, 1862. Sick, at home, Sep/Oct 1863. Absent without leave Nov/Dec 1863. Detailed as teamster August 31, 1864. Survived.

Williams, Thos., Pvt., Co. B. Died 1864. Entry from *A History of Marlboro County*.

Williams, W. Harvey, Pvt., Co. A, enlisted at Charleston, April 15, 1862. Sick, patient in hospital at Montgomery Jul/Aug 1863 - Jan/Feb 1864. Detailed to Breckinridge's Division Hospital No. 2, Lauderdale Springs, Miss., as a nurse by order of General Johnson September 23, 1863. Present for duty Jul/Aug 1864. Discharged, physically disabled.

Williamson, Carnot B., 1Lt., Age 31, Co. G, enlisted at Columbia March 19, 1862. Detached to recruiting service for 14 days April 1863. Furloughed April 30, 1863. Promoted to 1Lt., February 23, 1863. Patient in hospital at Rome Sep/Oct 1863. Sick, patient in hospital at Columbia October 1, 1863. Absent without leave June 1 - August 31, 1864.

Willoughby, Rich, Pvt., Age 27, Co. B, enlisted at Marlboro March 26, 1862. Sick, patient in the hospital at Columbia Sep/Oct 1862. Discharged by Surgeons certificate November 17, 1862.

Wilson, Bird, Pvt., Age 26, Co. H, from Langsford, enlisted at Chester March 19, 1862. Absent, sick, May/Jun - Sep/Oct 1862. Severely wounded, leg at Calhoun, Ga., May 16, 1864. Signed, by mark, receipt roll for clothing at Cannon Hospital, LaGrange, Ga., June 18, 1864. Captured at Jonesboro September 2, 1864. Sent to Military Prison, Louisville and transferred to Camp Douglas November 1, 1864. Description: complexion, light; hair, red; eyes, blue; height, 5 ft. 5 in. Signed oath of allegiance to the United States and discharged June 12, 1865.

Wilson, Calvin P., Corp., Age 38, Co. E, enlisted at Camp Gist March 15, 1862. Promoted to Corp., Mar/Apr 1862. Captured at Battery Island May 21, 1862. Sent from Hilton Head to Fort Columbus, New York Harbor aboard Steamer *Arago* August 14, 1862. Sent from Fort Columbus to Fort Delaware August 23, 1862. Exchanged at Aikens Landing, Va., October 2, 1862. Died December 4, 1862. Died of disease at home.

Wilson, Frank, Pvt., Co. K, enlisted at Secessionville April 25, 1862. Deserted April 15, 1863.

Wilson, George, Pvt., Co. H, enlisted at Chester May 21, 1863. Captured at Chickamauga September 20, 1863. Mortally wounded at Chickamauga. Lost at Chickamauga. Supposed wounded and died.

Wilson, Henry W., Pvt., Age 41, Co. H, enlisted at Chester April 14, 1862. Present for duty Mar/Apr 1863. Wounded at Calhoun, Ga. Dead.

Wilson, J. C., Pvt., Co. C, enlisted at Coles Island April 13, 1862. Wounded at Chickamauga September 20, 1863. Severely wounded, thigh, at Calhoun Station, Ga., May 16, 1864. Captured at Nashville December 16, 1864. Sent to Military Prison, Louisville and transferred to Camp Chase January 4, 1865. Died of pneumonia January 28, 1865. Grave no. 920, 1/3 mile south of Camp Chase.

Wilson, James J., Sgt., Age 45, Co. C, enlisted at Georges Station January 7, 1862. Absent, sick, patient in hospital at Point Clair, Ala., Jul/Aug 1863. Died in Fair Ground Hospital No. 2, Atlanta October 14, 1863. Grave located in Oakland Cemetery, Atlanta. Widow, Susan B. Wilson, filed claim for settlement February 15, 1864.

Wilson, James., Pvt., Age 18, Co. C. Killed in battle at Chickamauga. Entry from Memory Rolls at State Archives, Columbia, S.C.

Wilson, L. M., Pvt., Age 17, Co. E, enlisted at Dalton May 1, 1864. Furloughed from hospital and absent without leave August 3, 1864. Wounded at Calhoun and Jonesboro. Survived.

Wilson, W. H., Pvt., Co. H, enlisted at Chester April 14, 1862. Present for duty on all rolls through August 31, 1864. Admitted to 1st Mississippi CSA Hospital, Jackson, for gunshot wound November 10 - December 5, 1864. Captured at Egypt Station, Miss., December 28, 1864. Sent to Military Prison, Alton, Ill., and exchanged at Point Lookout February 21, 1865. Admitted to Receiving and Wayside Hospital or General Hospital No. 9, Richmond March 6, 1865.

Wimberly, Augustus, Pvt., Age 23, Co. C, enlisted at Georges Station January 7, 1862. Assigned to Quartermasters Department Jun/Oct 1862 - Jan/Feb 1863 and May/Jun 1863. Died in Gate City Hospital, Atlanta September 12, 1863. Left $33.00. Contractor paid $11.50 to perform funeral.

Wimberly, J. S., Pvt., Co. C. Survived. Entry from Dorchester County Enrollment Book.

Wimberly, Lewis, Pvt., Age 19, Co. C, enlisted at Georges Station January 7, 1862. Absent, sick, Nov/Dec 1863. Signed receipt roll for clothing November 23, 1863. Absent, sick at hospital, February 24, 1864. Patient at Floyd House and Ocmulgee Hospitals, Macon for chronic diarrhoea, granted 60 days furlough March 10, 1864. Absent, sick, furloughed August 15, 1864.

Wimberly, Nathaniel L., Sgt., Age 24, Co. C, from St. George, enlisted at Georges Station January 7, 1862. Present on all rolls. Paroled at Greensboro May 1, 1865. Married July 5, 1898. Died October 4, 1917. Widow Dora Wimberley.

Wimberly, R., Pvt., Co. C. Entry from roster prepared by company commander.

Wimberly, W., Co., C. Buried October 7, 1863 in Confederate Section, Oakland City Cemetery, Atlanta, Ga. Entry from Oakland Cemetery Record.

Winn, Augustus, Pvt., Co. K, enlisted at Edgefield April 15, 1862. In hospital May/Jun 1862. Present for duty Jan/Feb 1863. Died of disease.

Winn, E. C., Pvt., Age 17, born August 1, 1846, Co. K, from Plum Branch, S.C., enlisted at Edgefield July 20, 1864. Due $50.00 bounty. Severely wounded, leg, near Atlanta July 22, 1864. Furloughed from hospital for 60 days July 27, 1864. Young recruit shot in the thigh. Had not been with the regiment for one hour. Discharged at Hamburg in May 1865. Suffered from thigh wound the rest of his life.

Winn, Robert M., 2Lt., Co. K, enlisted at Edgefield July 1, 1862. Elected to 2Lt., January 26, 1864. Killed in battle at Peachtree Creek July 20,

1864. Mother, F. L. Winn, filed claim for settlement November 4, 1864.

Winn, W. A., Pvt., Co. K, enlisted at Edgefield April 15, 1862. Admitted to hospital at Rome and furloughed home October 1 - Nov/Dec 1863. Died at Hospital No. 2, Atlanta May 11, 1864.

Winningham, Thomas, Pvt., Age 27, Co. C, enlisted at Georges Station January 17, 1862. Present for duty on all rolls through Jul/Aug 1864. Extra daily duty with infirmary corps.

Wisher, J. W., Pvt., Co. H, enlisted at York, S.C., November 8, 1862. Absent, sick, Mar/Apr - Jul/Aug 1863. Absent without leave July 1, 1863 - Nov/Dec 1863. Absent, sick, in hospital Jan/Feb 1864. Died in Hospital at Cassville, Ga., February 14, 1864. Effects none.

Witcofsky, J. F., Pvt., Age 26, Co. A, enlisted at Charleston December 31, 1861. Present for duty May/Jun 1862. Transferred to Smith's Battalion.

Wolf, William, Corp., Age 30, Co. G, enlisted at Columbia March 19, 1862. Severely wounded, ear, at Atlanta July 22, 1864. Patient at hospital at Columbia August 31, 1864.

Wolton, H. C., Pvt., Age 40, Co. A, enlisted at Charleston December 31, 1861. Present for duty on all rolls through Jul/Aug 1864.

Woodle, Edward, Pvt., Co. B, enlisted at Marlboro April 1, 1862. Present for duty on all rosters through Jan/Feb 1864. Wounded, thigh broken, July 20, 1864. Captured at Peachtree Creek July 20, 1864. Admitted to No. 1, USA General Hospital, Nashville for simple flesh wound of left thigh, severe, July 29, 1864. Treated with Gator dressings. Transferred to Provost Marshal November 23, 1864. Sent to Military Prison, Louisville and transferred to Camp Douglas December 1, 1864. Paroled at Camp Douglas and exchanged at City Point March 14, 1865. Admitted to Jackson Hospital, Richmond with V.S. right thigh March 22, 1865. Furloughed for 60 days March 28, 1865.

Woodle, Hinson, Pvt., Co. B, enlisted at Marlboro December 4, 1861. Mortally sounded in battle at Chickamauga September 20, 1863. Died of wounds September 22, 1863.

Woodley, John, Pvt., Co. B, enlisted at Marlboro March 26, 1862. Absent, sick, at home Sep/Oct 1862 - Jul/Aug 1863. Absent without leave Sep/Oct 1863. Paroled at Greensboro May 1, 1865.

Wright, David G., Pvt., Co. B, enlisted at Marlboro Apr 1, 1863. Sick, at home, in S.C., Sep/Oct 1863. Present for duty Jan/Feb 1864. Died of disease September 15, 1864. Grave located in Confederate Cemetery, Marietta, Ga.

Wright, Daniel, Pvt., Co. B. Died 1862. Entry from *A History of Marlboro County.*

Wright, George W., Pvt., Age 50, Co. G, born in England, enlisted at Columbia March 19, 1862. Captured near Jackson May 14, 1863. Assigned Paroled Prisoners in Camp at Demopolis June 5, 1863.

Description: complexion, light; hair, light; eyes, grey; height 5 ft. 6 in; occupation, blacksmith. Discharged for physical disability, double hernia of immense size, June 10, 1863.

Wylie, Brown W., Pvt., Co. H, enlisted at Chester March 19, 1864. Wounded at Chickamauga. Paroled at Greensboro May 1, 1865.

Wylie, Newton I., Sgt., Age 39, Co. H, enlisted at Chester March 19, 1862. Absent sick Nov/Dec 1862. Wounded and captured near Jackson May 14, 1863. Absent, sick, furloughed Sep/Oct 1863. Absent, sick, patient in hospital August 31, 1864. Paroled at Greensboro May 1, 1865.

Wylie, Philip C., Pvt., Age 33, Co. H, enlisted at Chester March 19, 1862. Absent, sick, patient in hospital, Atlanta Jan/Feb 1864. Wounded August 5, 1864. Killed in battle at Atlanta.

Yeargan, Rufus, Pvt., Age 34, Co. F, from Moffatsville, S.C., enlisted at Anderson January 13, 1862. Sick, patient in hospital October 1862. Signed receipt roll for clothing at General Hospital No. 2, Columbia, S.C., February 12, 1864. Absent, sick, February 15, 1864. Slightly wounded, leg, at Calhoun, Ga., May 16, 1864. Cook for company. Captured at Shipp's Gap/Taylor's Ridge October 16, 1864. Sent to Military Prison, Louisville and transferred to Camp Douglas October 29, 1864. Description: complexion, fair; hair, auburn; eyes, blue; height, 5 ft. 8 in. Signed oath of allegiance to the United States and was discharged June 17, 1865. Died at Anderson, S.C., in 1902.

Yelldell, William Alonzo, Corp., Age 16, Co. I, enlisted at Columbia March 20, 1862. Slightly wounded, side, July 22/24, 1864. Killed in the trenches at Atlanta July 27, 1864.

Yonce, Gabriel, Pvt., Age 18, Co. I, enlisted at Columbia April 10, 1862. Present for duty May/Jun 1863. Mortally wounded in battle at Chickamauga. Died from effects of wound at 2d Georgia Hospital, Augusta, Ga., October 22, 1863.

Yonce, Henry Wesley, Pvt., Age 18, Co. I, enlisted at Columbia April 10, 1862. Mortally wounded in battle at Chickamauga September 20, 1863. Died of wounds in hospital at Augusta October 22, 1863. Effects consisted of sundries and $13.50.

Young, Robert H., Pvt., Co. F., enlisted at Anderson January 1, 1863. Shot through at Jackson. Wounded near Jackson May 14, 1862. Captured and paroled in hospital May 16, 1863. Absent sick Nov/Dec 1863. Died of disease in hospital at Kingston, Ga., January 2, 1864.

Young, Samuel O., Pvt., Age 35, Co. G, enlisted at Columbia March 19, 1862. Wounded near Jackson May 14, 1865. Died of continued fever at Bell Hospital, Rome September 23, 1863. Effects consisted of sundries and $11.00. Grave located in Confederate Section, Myrtle Hill Cemetery, Rome, Ga.

Young, William H., Pvt., Age 20, Co. F, enlisted at Anderson January 13,

1864. Died of disease November 19, 1864. Effects consisted of $5.00. Grave located in Confederate Cemetery, Marietta, Ga.

Young, William W., Pvt., Age 18, Co. G, enlisted at Columbia March 19, 1862. Captured near Jackson May 14, 1863. Killed in battle at Atlanta July 22, 1864.

Zimmerman, Dave, Pvt., Co. K. Entry from Memory Rolls at State Archives, Columbia, S.C.

Zimmerman, F. H., Pvt., Co. K. Died in hospital January 20, 1864. Entry from Memory Rolls at State Archives, Columbia, S.C.

Zimmerman, George, Pvt., Co. K. Killed in battle at Jonesboro. Entry from Memory Rolls at State Archives, Columbia, S.C.

Zimmerman, G. H., Pvt., Co. K. Died in hospital November 8, 1863. Entry from Memory Rolls at State Archives, Columbia, S.C.

Zimmerman, Henry, Pvt., Co. K. Killed in battle at Chickamauga. Entry from Memory Rolls at State Archives, Columbia, S.C.

Zimmerman, W. H., Pvt., Co. K, enlisted at Pocotaligo April 1, 1863. Severely wounded, side and arm, at Chickamauga September 20, 1863. Absent sick from wound Sep/Oct 1863 - Jan/Feb 1864.

Zimmerman, Wm., Pvt., Co. K. Surrendered at Greensboro. Entry from Memory Rolls at State Archives, Columbia, S.C.

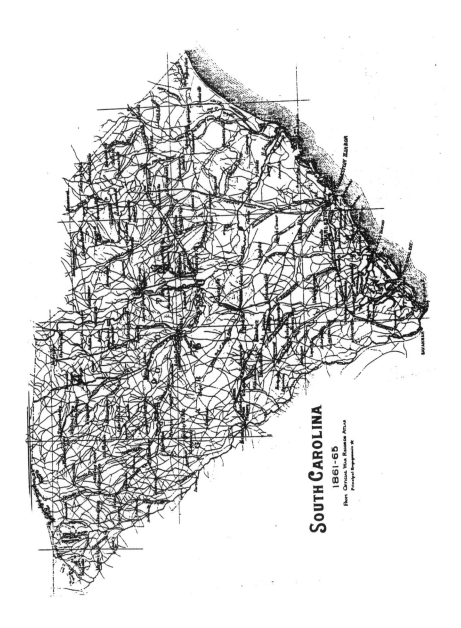

SOUTH CAROLINA
1861-65
FROM OFFICIAL WAR RECORDS ATLAS
Principal Engagements X

APPENDIX II
ROSTER
OF
THE CONSOLIDATED 16TH AND 24TH REGIMENT
SOUTH CAROLINA VOLUNTEERS INFANTRY,
ORGANIZED AT GREENSBORO, NORTH CAROLINA,
APRIL 9, 1865.

NAME	RANK	NEW CO	OLD CO	16TH	24TH
Adkins, Samuel	Pvt	E		x	
Alexander, R. H.	Capt	E	A	x	
Ammons, A.	Corp	C	B		x
Ammons, T.	Pvt	C	B		x
Appleby, A. C.	Capt	I	C		x
Appleby D. C.	1Sgt	I	C		x
Appleby P. R.	Pvt	I	C		x
Armstrong, J. D.	Pvt	D	I	x	
Ashmore, A. M.	Corp	E	B	x	
Austin, J. H.	Pvt	E	A	x	
Bagley, J.	Pvt	C	H		x
Bagwell, B. R.	Corp	F		x	
Bagwell, J. S.	Pvt	F	E	x	
Banon, W. A.	Pvt	E		x	
Barbery, T.	Pvt	A	F	x	
Barden, G.	Pvt	G	I		x
Barns, W. G.	Pvt	I	E		x
Barton, J. G.	Pvt	A		x	
Bates, William P.	Pvt	D	G	x	
Batson, D. F.	2Lt	D	G	x	
Beaty, C. S.	Capt	K	F		x
Beckham, G. N.	Pvt	G	G		x
Beckham, W. M.	Capt	H	G		x
Benson, John	Pvt	F	C	x	
Benton, A. B.	Pvt	B	D		x
Bethea, A. J.	Hosp Stew	F&S	B		x
Bolin, T. G.	Pvt	A		x	
Boling, S. Calvin	Pvt	D	G	x	
Bowers, W.	Pvt	I	D		x
Brackenridge, R. W.	Pvt	G	I		x
Bradley, J. W.	Pvt	E	A	x	
Bradley, S. R.	Pvt	E	A	x	

Bramlett,. R. E.	Pvt	E	A	x	
Breedlove, J.	Pvt	I	C		x
Breland, S. L.	Pvt	B	D		x
Breland, F. A. S.	Pvt	B	D		x
Bridges, L. W.	Pvt	E		x	
Brissey, Charles	Pvt	E		x	
Briston, F.	Pvt	H		x	
Brock, W. C.	Pvt	I	F	x	
Brown, E.	Pvt	A	F	x	
Brown, J. C.	Pvt	B	H	x	
Brown, J. W.	Pvt	B	H	x	
Browne, Thomas	Pvt	E	B	x	
Brown, R. M.	Pvt	E	A		x
Bruce, H. T.	Pvt	K	H		x
Bryan, E. H.	Sgt	B	E		x
Bryan, R. E.	Pvt	B	E		x
Bryson, J. M.	Pvt	F		x	
Burditt, S. G.	Pvt	K	F		x
Burditt, B. William	Pvt	D	I	x	
Burditt, S. G.	Pvt	G			x
Burn, R. L.	2Lt	F	A	x	
Burns, B. F. M.	Pvt	E	A	x	
Burns, William	Pvt	D	G	x	
Burrell, J.	Corp	B	H	x	
Burton, G. W.	Sgt	H	K		x
Burton, J. D.	Pvt	K	F		x
Bush, John E.	Pvt	G	G		x
Calhoun, T. T.	Pvt	F	I		x
Campbell, Boling	Pvt	F	C	x	
Canada, J. L.	Corp	A	F	x	
Cantrell, H.	Pvt	A	H	x	
Carpenter, A. E.	Pvt	G	I		x
Carpenter, J. E. O.	Sgt	G	I		x
Carsister, John	Pvt	G	I		x
Carter, Thomas	Musician	F&S	E	x	
Cathran, J. L.	Pvt	F	E	x	
Chapman, J. C.	Pvt	F	E	x	
Chavis, J.	Pvt	H	B		x
Clark, G.	Pvt	H	A		x
Clark, T. M.	Pvt	F		x	
Clinkscales, R. P.	Pvt	K	F		x
Cochran, R. A.	1Lt	H	K		x
Cook, R.	Pvt	I	E		x

434

Cook, W. G. C.	Pvt	E	A	x	
Cooper, T. A.	Pvt	D	G	x	
Cooper, William H.	Surgeon	F&S	F&S	x	
Council, C. R.	Pvt	I	C		x
Cox, H. C.	Pvt	G	G		x
Cox, J. E.	Pvt	E		x	
Cox, J. P.	Pvt	E		x	
Cranford, H. R.	Pvt	H	B		x
Crawford, J. C.	Corp	F	E	x	
Croft, T. G.	Major	F&S	F&S	x	
Crook, J. T.	Pvt	C	H		x
Crosby, E.	Pvt	B	D		x
Crosby, H. E.	Pvt	B	D		x
Curry, Thomas H.	1Lt	G	I		x
Dale, W. B.	Asst. Surg.	F&S		x	
Daugherty, T.	Pvt	C	A		x
Davenport, C. A.	Pvt	E	B	x	
Davenport, O.	Pvt	F	E	x	
Davis, Abner	Pvt	F	E	x	
Davis, G. W.	Pvt	C	B	x	
Davis, M. L.	Pvt	F	E	x	
Dean, J. M.	Corp	H	K		x
Delaughter, John W.	Pvt	G			x
Dewitt, D.	Corp	I	C		x
Dickard, W.	Pvt	K	F		x
Dillard, G. M.	Pvt	A	F	x	
Dorn, James	Pvt	H	K		x
Dorn, J. J.	Pvt	H	K		x
Edwards, L. Berry	Pvt	D	I	x	
Elder, E. J.	Pvt	C	H	X	
Ellege, S.	Pvt	B		x	
Ellen, R. M.	Pvt	H	B	x	
Ellison, David	Pvt	F	E	x	
Ellison, Joel	Musician	F&S	E	x	
Elrod, J. N.	Sgt	E	B	x	
Evans, J. M.	Pvt	K	B	x	
Evans, T. H.	Pvt	K	F		x
Evans, W. A.	Pvt	K	F		x
Farmer, W. P.	Pvt	B	D	x	
Farr, Jerry	Pvt	F	C	x	
Fewox, J.	Pvt	I	C		x
Fewox, W.	Pvt	I	C		x
Fieldin, George	Pvt	D	I	x	

Finch, T. N.	Pvt	E	B	x	
Fludd, James	Pvt	C	A		x
Flynn, J. F.	Pvt	A	F	x	
Forister, J. B.	Corp	D	I	x	
Foster, J. A.	Pvt	A	F	x	
Fowler, B. M.	Pvt	E	F	x	
Fowler, J. G.	Pvt	B	H	x	
Freeman, P.	Pvt	I	E		x
Furman, C. M.	Capt	B	H	x	
Garden, G. J.	Pvt	K	F		x
Garner, Samuel	Pvt	G	K		x
Garrett, Benjamin B.	Pvt	D	I	x	
Garrett, G. Y.	Pvt	E	B	x	
Garrett, John	Pvt	E	B	x	
Garrison, W. D.	2Lt	E		x	
Gault, J. W. P.	Pvt	D	I	x	
German, R. P.	Pvt	H	K		x
Gibbes, W. Allston	Capt	C	D	x	
Gibson, O.	Pvt	K	H		x
Ginn, C.	Pvt	I	E		x
Ginn, W.	Pvt	I	E		x
Glenn, B. B.	Corp	C	A	x	
Glenn, T. W.	Pvt	E	A	x	
Glenn, W. F.	Pvt	E	A	x	
Glover, W. J.	Pvt	G			x
Goldsmith, Thomas	Pvt	D	I	x	
Goodlett, J. H.	Ord. Sgt.	F&S		x	
Goodlett., W. M.	1Lt	B	D	x	
Gorden, J. G.	Pvt	K	F		x
Granger, E.	Pvt	E	B	x	
Granger, S.	Pvt	E	B	x	
Granger, William	Corp	E	B	x	
Green, G. G.	Pvt	C	B	x	
Green, J. B.	2Lt	C	B	x	
Greer, C. B.	Pvt	A	F	x	
Gridley, I. A.	1Lt	E	A	x	
Griffith, J. W.	Pvt	E	B	x	
Griffith, W. B.	Pvt	E	B	x	
Grimes, W. A.	Corp	K	F		x
Groce,. W. H.	Corp	F	C	x	
Guest, S. M.	Pvt	B		x	
Gunnells, R. T.	Pvt	F	E	x	
Halcom, J. J.	Pvt	B		x	

436

Halcom, John	Pvt	B		x	
Hall, E.	Pvt	K	F		x
Hall, James	Pvt	C	B		x
Hall, L. O.	Pvt	K	F		x
Hamly, G. Smith	Pvt	D	I	x	
Hamley, J. T.	Pvt	D	I	x	
Hammett, Z.	Pvt	A	F	x	
Hammond, R. G.	Pvt	E	A	x	
Hanna, J. T.	Pvt	K	F		x
Harbin, A. V.	Pvt	A	F	x	
Hardin, G. I.	Pvt	A	F	x	
Harper, J. W.	Pvt	B	D		x
Harrison, John R.	Sgt	D	I	x	
Hawkins, E.	Pvt	A	F	x	
Hawkins, John	Pvt	E	A	x	
Hawkins, J. R.	Pvt	A	F	x	
Hawkins, W. C.	Pvt	B	D	x	
Hawkins, W. G.	1Lt	C	A		x
Hazzard, John	Pvt	C	A		x
Heaton, D.	Pvt	I	C	x	
Hellums, James M.	Pvt	D	G	x	
Hellums, Virgil A.	Pvt	D	G	x	
Hinson, J. P.	1Sgt	H	B		x
Hodge, G. W.	Pvt	K	H		x
Hodges, R. C.	Pvt	C	B		x
Hodges, W. L.	1Lt	D	I	x	
Hollis, J. J.	Pvt	I	H		x
Holloway, John	Pvt	G	I		x
Holmes, A.	Adjutant	F&S	F&S		x
Holmes, E. M.	Pvt	H	K		x
Holmes, J. A.	Pvt	G	I		x
Holmes, J. E.	Corp	H	K		x
Holson, Joseph M.	Pvt	G	I		x
Holtzclaw, G. W.	Capt	A	F	x	
Howard, A.	Pvt	B	H	x	
Howard, James	Pvt	G	I		x
Howe, J. W.	Pvt	C	A		x
Howell, J. R.	Sgt	C	A		x
Howle, R. H.	Pvt	G	I		x
Hubbard, M.	Pvt	H	B		x
Hudson, W. M.	Pvt	B	D		x
Hughes, J. F.	Pvt	E	A	x	
Hughey, W.	Pvt	I	E		x

Name	Rank				
Hurt, Riley W.	Pvt	D	I	x	
Hussey, E. L.	Corp	G	C		x
Infinger, D.	Pvt	I	C		x
Jacobs, A. B.	Pvt	C	B		x
Jamison, W. D.	2Lt				
Jordan, G. W.	Pvt	F	E	x	
Jordan, Isaac	Pvt	F	E	x	
Jordan, W. T.	Pvt	F	E	x	
Johnson, Tyre W.	Pvt	I	G	x	
Johnston, B. M.	Pvt	I	C		x
Jones, J. M. H.	Corp	D	I	x	
Jones, W. T.	Pvt	E	A	x	
Judy, L.	Pvt	I	C		x
Kee, J. H.	Pvt	K	H		x
Kemp, L. H.	Pvt	H	K		x
Killett, John A.	Pvt	D	I	x	
Land, Stephen	Pvt	F	C	x	
Langford, Joab	Pvt	D	G	x	
Langford, W. H.	Pvt	D	G	x	
Lanham, James M.	2Lt	A	I		x
Lanham, J. M.	2Lt	G	I		x
Lenderman, F. M.	Pvt	E	B	x	
Lenderman, J. H.	Pvt	E	B	x	
Lewis, W. S.	Sgt	H	B		x
Ligon, W. B.	Sgt	A	K	x	
Linder, Willis I.	Pvt	D	I	x	
Lipford, W. W.	Pvt	K	H		x
Locke,. William B.	Pvt	D	I	x	
Long, A. P.	lSgt	A	K	x	
Long, W. G.	Musician	F&S	F&S	x	
Mahaffey, Hoy J.	Pvt	D	I	x	
Margart, G. M.	Pvt	C	C		x
Martin, Jabe	Pvt	H	K		x
Martin, J. Bry	Pvt	G	K		x
Mathis, Robert W.	2Lt	G	I		x
Mallox, T. R.	Musician	F&S		x	
Maxey, M.	Pvt	C	A		x
McAdams, J. O.	Corp	K	F		x
McCallum, H.	Pvt	C	B		x
McCleery, Robert	Sgt	F	E	x	
McCrary, William K.	Pvt	D	I	x	
McCullough, J. L.	Capt	F	E	x	
McDaniel, J. M.	1Lt	K	F		x

McDonell, W. W.	Corp	H	K		x
McGarrity, A.	Pvt	K	H		x
McGee, W. A.	Pvt	K	F		x
McKenzie, W. G.	Surgeon	F&S		x	
McNeely, James	Sgt	F	K		x
McPeden, J.	Corp	D		x	
McPhail, J. N.	Pvt	K	F		x
McQuaig, W.	Pvt	C	B		x
Meekins, P. B.	Pvt	H	B		x
Melton, M.	Pvt	K	H		x
Merce, W. S.	Pvt	C	A		x
Metts, J.	Pvt	I	C		x
Middleton, B. E.	Pvt	D	G	x	
Miles, John L.	Pvt	G	I	x	
Miller, E.	Pvt	A	F	x	
Miller, J.	Pvt	A	F	x	
Miller, L. J.	2Lt	G	I		x
Mims, William P.	Pvt	G	I		x
Minniss, W. A.	Pvt	B	E		x
Mock, J. D.	Pvt	I	E		x
Moon, B. F.	Pvt	F	C	x	
Moon, J. W.	Pvt	B		x	
Morgan, J. H.	Pvt	B	H	x	
Morgan, L. J.	Pvt	B	H	x	
Morgan, T. C.	Lt Col	F&S	K		x
Myers, A.	Pvt	I	C		x
Nardin, Waller H.	Asst. Surg.	F&S	F&S		x
Neal, Samuel F.	Pvt	D	G	x	
Nix, Elijah	Pvt	D	G	x	
Nunnelly, F. F.	Sgt	D	I	x	
Odom, P. E.	Pvt	H	B		x
Ouzts, Isaac	Pvt	H	K		x
Ouzts, J. T.	Pvt	H	K		x
Ouzts, P.	Pvt	H	K		x
Owens, D. C.	Pvt	F	E	x	
Owens, Robert T.	Pvt	K	F		x
Parham, A.	Pvt	H	B		x
Parker, M.	Pvt	K	F		x
Parkman, L.	Pvt	H	K		x
Parrish, J. W.	Pvt	B	D	x	
Payne, Aaron	Pvt	E	B	x	
Peace, L.	Corp	A	F	x	
Pearson, A. W.	Pvt	G	G		x

Phillips, P.	Corp	I	E		x
Phillips, W. S.	Pvt	F	E	x	
Pike, L. M.	Pvt	A	F	x	
Pendarvis, J. D.	Pvt	I	C		x
Prewitt, J.	Pvt	B	H	x	
Price, John	Pvt	G	C		x
Price, John L.	Pvt	G	I		x
Price, Jospeh	Pvt	G	I		x
Pusley, M. C.	Sgt	D	G	x	
Quick, A.	Pvt	C	B		x
Quick, M.	Pvt	C	B		x
Rains, E. P.	Pvt	A	F	x	
Rains, J. T.	Pvt	A	F	x	
Ralph, J. L.	Pvt	K	H		x
Rataree, T.	Pvt	K	H		x
Reynolds, J. A.	2Lt	H	I		x
Reynolds, John S.	Sgt	G	K		x
Rhods, William	Pvt	B	D	x	
Richardson, T. J.	Pvt	E	A	x	
Riggs, L. C.	Pvt	C	A		x
Riggs, T. L.	Corp	C	A		x
Risher, J. K.	Capt	I	E		x
Robbertson, M. K.	Sgt	B	H	x	
Roberts, E. G.	Capt	D	I	x	
Robertson, W. T.	Pvt	H	K		x
Rochelle, W. J.	Musician	G	I		x
Rochelle, W. G.	Pvt				x
Roddy, J. J.	Pvt	A	F	x	
Roddy, W. P.	Pvt	A	F	x	
Rodgers, W. E.	Sgt	G	I		x
Ross, W. M.	Pvt	A	F	x	
Rushing, T. O.	Corp	I	E		x
Sanders, J.	Pvt	K	H		x
Sauls, J.	Pvt	I	E		x
Scott, James	Pvt	F	E	x	
Scott, W.	Musician	F&S	E	x	
Scruggs, William	Pvt	D	I	x	
Sease, George	Pvt	I	D		x
Seigler, I.	Pvt	I	C		x
Seigler, T. M.	1Lt	I	K		x
Sexon, Thomas	Pvt	E		x	
Shaw, W. C.	Pvt	K	F		x
Shelton, John	Pvt	G	I		x

Sherad, J. W.	Sgt	K	F		x
Shider, T. D.	Pvt	I	C		x
Shockley, Spartan	Pvt	D	G	x	
Simmons, John H.	Pvt	D	I	x	
Simms, W.	Pvt	C	A		x
Simpson, G. S.	Corp	K	H		x
Simpson, W. P.	Pvt	K	H		x
Sims, Y. O.	Pvt	F	E	x	
Sitton, W. L.	Pvt	D	G	x	
Smith, B. B.	Col	F&S	F&S	x	
Smith, Fielding	Pvt	F	E	x	
Smith, G. L.	Corp	A	F	x	
Smith, J. A.	Pvt	E	B	x	
Smith, J. O.	Pvt	E	A	x	
Smith, R. E.	Pvt	E		x	
Smith, Riley	1Sgt	K	H		x
Smith, W. J.	Pvt	E	A	x	
Southern, G. J.	Pvt	B		x	
Sprouse, John	Pvt	F	C	x	
Stacks, F. J.	Sgt	K	F		x
Steward, J. W.	Pvt	K	F		x
Stewart, A. A.	2Lt	B	H	x	
Stewart, J. W.	Pvt	G	F		x
Stewart, W.	Pvt	K	F		x
Stewart, W. A.	Pvt	K	F		x
Stewart, W. H.	Pvt	D	I	x	
Stiles, L.	Pvt	B	D	x	
Strange, C.	Pvt	F		x	
Strickland, J. C.	Corp	B	D		x
Strom, G. W.	Corp	H	K		x
Strom, J. E.	Pvt	H	K		x
Strom, J. P.	Pvt	H	K		x
Strom, P. H.	Sgt	H	K		x
Strom, S. B.	Pvt	H	K		x
Stubbs, J. A.	Pvt	C	B		x
Sudduth, E. P.	Sgt	A	F	x	
Sudduth, W. L.	Pvt	A	F	x	
Sullivan, J. R.	Pvt	F	E	x	
Tate, S. G.	Pvt	F	C	x	
Taylor, J.	Pvt	H	K		x
Taylor, W. N.	Pvt	A	F	x	
Thackston, G. W.	2Lt	E			x
Thomas, L.	Pvt	C	A		x

441

Thompson, F.	Pvt	B	H	x	
Thompson, G. T.	Pvt	F		x	
Thompson, J. T.	Pvt	F	E	x	
Thompson, Harris	Pvt	F	E	x	
Thompson, S. P.	Pvt	B	E	x	
Thompson, T. G.	Pvt	F	E	x	
Tillman, James A.	Capt	G	K		x
Timmerman, W.	Pvt	H	K		x
Trammell, C. P.	Corp	B	H	x	
Traznham, J. J.	Pvt	F	E	x	
Triest, M.	QM Sgt	F&S	F&S		x
Tritty, W. W.	Sgt	E	A	x	
Turner, D.	Pvt	C	B		x
Vance, S. G.	Pvt	F	E	x	
Vaughan, C. C. P.	Pvt	E	B	x	
Vaughan, J. H.	Corp	A	F	x	
Vaughan, J. M.	Pvt	A	F	x	
Vaughan, J. P.	Pvt	A	F	x	
Vaughan, A.	Pvt	A	E		x
Vaughan, J. D.	Pvt	B	E		x
Virden, P. J.	Sgt	D	I	x	
Wade, William H.	Pvt	D	G	x	
Walker, J. L.	1Lt	A	F	x	
Wallace, J. B.	Pvt	C	B		x
Walters, R. M.	Sgt	I	C		x
Walters, S. D.	Pvt	I	C		x
Walton, D. S.	Musician	F&S	A	x	
Ward, J. F.	Pvt	A	F	x	
Ward, J. W.	Pvt	F	C	x	
Waters, J.	Pvt	C	B		x
Weeks, R. S.	2Lt	K	F		x
Wethers, P.	Pvt	I	C	x	
Wherle, B.	Musician	F&S	A	x	
Whetsel, J. I.	Pvt	I	C		x
White, John J.	Pvt	D	I	x	
White, J. W.	Pvt	K	H		x
Wickliffe, Robert	Pvt	E	A	x	
Wigginton, W. J.	Pvt	D	G	x	
Wilder, E.	Pvt	G	I		x
Williams, T. B.	Sgt	I	E		x
Wilson, B. F.	Pvt	A	F	x	
Wilson, R. A.	Pvt	A	F	x	
Wilson, C.	Pvt	A	F	x	

Wimberly, N. L.	Sgt	I	C		x
Woodley, J.	Pvt	C	B		x
Wordlaw, D. L.	Pvt	F		x	
Wordlaw, J. C.	Pvt	F		x	
Wylie, I. N.	Pvt	K	H		x
Wylie, W. B.	Pvt	K	H		x
Yeargin, W. C.	Pvt	E		x	

SEAL OF SOUTH CAROLINA.

Abbreviations used in the Notes

NA   National Archives
OR   *Official Records of the War of the Rebellion* (all references are to Series I)
SCA   South Carolina Archives
SCHS   South Carolina Historical Society
SCL   Caroliniana Library, University of South Carolina
TSLA   Tennessee State Library and Archives

Chapter 1
1.   *Battles and Leaders*, Vol. IV, p. 314; Nesbit, p. 209; *Savannah Republican*, July 25, 1864. A second account of the battle in which Stevens was wounded said he was pinned beneath his horse when it fell. When he was removed by aides he stood up and was immediately struck behind the right ear by a minié ball.
2.   Nesbit, p. 209; *The Charleston Mercury*, July 28, 1864. There is considerable debate whether Stevens' remains were later removed to St. Paul's Church-yard, Pendleton, S.C. Magnolia Cemetery records indicates he is still there. Evidence that his remains were removed is more circumstantial. His family erected a headstone at Pendleton, and it seems unlikely they would have placed the stone at any place other than at his actual grave. Paul Stevens, a family descendent, wrote that Stevens' remains were removed to Pendleton, although he gave no details. In 1880, the United Daughters of the Confederacy (UDC) published a list of Confederate dead buried at Charleston. The list did not include Stevens' name, although his name is mentioned elsewhere in the pamphlet. On Confederate Memorial Day, in 1989, the UDC and Sons of the Confederate Veterans(SCV) placed a monument at the site of Stevens' original interment with the belief that his remains were still at Magnolia Cemetery.
3.   Warner, p. 291; Stevens letter, October 5, 1861, SCHS.
4.   Warner, p. 291; Stevens papers, SCL. Colonel Stevens and Dr. St. Julian Ravenel, a famous Charleston businessman, were business associates in the phosphate fertilizer business.
5.   Evans, p. 16.
6.   Stevens papers, SCL.
7.   Steinmeyer, p. 6, SCL.
8.   Steinmeyer Diary, pp. 1-4, SCL.
9.   RG 109, SC Records, Microcopy M267, NA. Camp Magnolia was located near Charleston in the area known as the Charleston neck area.
10. Capers letter, December 21, 1861, Citadel.
11. Capers letter, November 25, 1861, Citadel.
12. Cross, p. 1; Capers letters, November 25-26, 1860, Citadel.
13. Law, pp. 20-21; Capers letter, December 21, 1861, Citadel.
14. Capers papers, recruiting handbill, Citadel; *The Charleston Mercury* dated

December 28, 1861. There were two advertisements in the newspaper, "Who will go with us?" and "A regiment for immediate service."

15. RG 109, SC Records, Microcopy M267, NA; Capers sketch, Citadel.
16. Capers letter, January 25, 1862, Citadel.
17. *Ibid.*
18. Capers letter, January 21, 1862, Citadel. Capers' wife resided at Cherry Grove Plantation in Berkeley District. Later she joined her husband in Charleston.
19. *Ibid.*
20. Capers sketch, Citadel.
21. Capers sketch, Citadel. There is no record as to what became of the set of colors sewn by Mrs. Stevens. Capers duly recorded the history of the colors that survived the War. That flag is deposited with the Confederate Relic Room, Columbia, S.C.
22. Steinmeyer, p. 6, SCL.
23. *Ibid.*
24. Capers letter, December 19, 1861, Citadel; RG 109, SC Records, Microcopy M267, NA; Edgefield Survivors Association Records, SCL.
25. Prior to the Civil War, the State of South Carolina was organized into "districts." The first county in the state was established in 1868 and the final one over 30 years later.

Company	District	County
A	Charleston	Charleston
B	Marlboro	Marlboro
C	Colleton	Dorchester
D	Beaufort	Hampton/Jasper
E	Colleton	Colleton
F	Anderson	Anderson/Abbeville
G	Richland	Richland/Lexington
H	Chester	Chester
I	Edgefield	Edgefield
K	Edgefield	Aiken

26. RG 109, SC Records, Microcopy M267, NA. Normally, a group of local citizens joined together to form a company from a local community. Most companies proudly bore a variety of names. For many, the name they selected, other than that of their company commander, has been lost. Companies, when accepted for service, were either signed to a camp of instruction or directly to a regiment by the State of South Carolina Adjutant and Inspector General.
27. RG 109, SC Records, Microcopy M267, NA; Steinmeyer diary, SCL. This company derived from a Fire Company, known as the Marion Fire House, stationed on Columbus Street in Charleston.
28. Thomas, p. 215; RG 109, SC Records, Microcopy M267, NA.
29. Appleby, p. 3; RG 109, SC Records, Microcopy M267, NA.
30. RG 109, SC Records, Microcopy M267, NA; Capers papers, Citadel.

31. *The Charleston Courier*, January 4, 1862; Risher papers, Warren; RG 109, SC Records, Microcopy M267, NA; US Census 1850.
32. RG 109, SC Records, Microcopy M267, NA.
33. AAG letter, not dated, SC Archives; RG 109, SC Records, Microcopy M267, NA.
34. Stevens, Book 2, p. 68; RG 109, SC Records, Microcopy M267, NA.
35. AAG letter, not dated, SC Archives; RG 109, SC Records, Microcopy M267, NA.
36. Chapman, p. 422; RG 109, SC Records, Microcopy M267, NA.
37. Stevens letter, April 14, 1862; RG 109, SC Records, Microcopy M267, NA; A&IF file, NA.
38. Capers sketch, Citadel.
39. Capers letter, April 13, 1862, Citadel. Mr. Rhett was the editor of the radical newspaper, *The Charleston Mercury*.
40. Capers letter, January 1, 1862, Duke.
41. Tillman diary, Clemson.
42. Steinmeyer diary, p 6, SCL. Coles Island was a fairly prominent islet located at the mouth of the Stono River, next to Folly Island. It is now under water.
43. *Ibid.*
44. *Ibid.*
45. Steinmeyer diary, p. 6, SCL.
46. *OR*, Vol. XIV, pp. 492, 493.
47. Capers letter, May 7, 1862, Citadel.
48. *OR*, Vol. XIV, p. 490.
49. Capers letter, May 19, 1862, Citadel.
50. Sterling, p. 74. Fort Ripley was located inside the Charleston Harbor between White Point Gardens and Fort Johnson. Fort Ripley was also known as the Middle Ground Battery.
51. Wilcox, p. 31.
52. Capers letter, May 17, 1862, Citadel.
53. Stevens letter, May 16, 1862; A&IF File, NA.
54. Steinmeyer, p. 7, SCL.
55. *Ibid.*; RG 109, SC Records, Microcopy M267, NA.
56. Padgett letter, May 3, 1862, AWC.
57. Capers letter, May 21, 1862, Citadel.
58. Padgett letter, May 3, 1862, AWC.
59. *Ibid.*
60. RG 109, SC Records, Microcopy M267, NA.
61. Padgett letter, May 3, 1862, AWC.
62. Steinmeyer, pp. 7-8, SCL.
63. Stevens letter, May 15, 1862, NA.
64. Stevens letter, May 13, 1862, NA.
65. Steinmeyer, p. 8, SCL.
66. Gist letter, May 10, 1862, NA.
67. *Ibid.*

68. Stevens letter, May 15, 1862, NA.
69. Capers letter, May 17, 1862, Citadel.
70. *Ibid.*
71. Steinmeyer diary, p. 7, SCL.
72. Capers letter, May 17, 1862, Citadel.
73. *Ibid.*
74. Steinmeyer diary, p. 7, SCL.
75. *Ibid.*
76. *Ibid.*
77. *Ibid.*
78. *Ibid.*
79. Steinmeyer diary, p. 8, SCL.
80. *Ibid.*
81. Capers letter, May 21, 1862, SCL.
82. *OR*, Vol. XIV, p. 18.
83. *Ibid.* The names of the men who were captured that are listed in the *Official Records, War of the Rebellion* do not agree with the names listed in RG 109, SC Records, Microcopy M267.
84. *Ibid.*
85. RG 109, SC Records, Microcopy M267, NA.
86. *OR*, Vol. XIV, p. 507.
87. Wilcox, pp. 53-54.
88. *OR*, Vol. VI, p. 248.
89. Warner, p. 30.
90. Warner, p. 476. Colonel Clement Hoffman Stevens and Union General I. I. Stevens were not related.
91. Burton, p. 93.
92. Capers letter, June 5, 1862, Citadel.
93. Evans, p. 13.
94. *OR*, Vol. XIV, p. 523.
95. Burton, p. 93; Johnson, p. 39.
96. Johnson, p. 25.
97. Hagood, Tracy Diary, May 31, 1862.
98. *Ibid.*
99. *Ibid.*
100. Hagood, Tracy Diary, June 2, 1862.
101. *OR*, Vol. XIV, pp. 29-30.
102. Gavin, p. 83.
103. *OR*, Vol. XIV, pp. 29-30.
104. *Ibid.*
105. *Ibid.*
106. Capers letter, June 5, 1862, Citadel.
107. Gavin, pp. 77-91. Several accounts of the skirmish from the Union point of view survive.
108. Steinmeyer diary, p. 9, SCL. This item is based on an entry in Captain

Steinmeyer's diary and offers the only evidence that Colonel Stevens was present during the melee at LeGares Place. If not at the battle, then Captain Steinmeyer described the action of that morning when Lieutenant Colonel Capers placed the Marions Rifles in some woods as advanced skirmishers. Possibly, Steinmeyer was confused as to who placed the Marions in the woods that day. Capers' account was written two days after the battle, and Steinmeyer's account was written twenty or twenty-five years after the war.

109. Gavin, p. 90.
110. *OR*, Vol. XIV, p. 30.
111. Hagood, Tracy diary, June 3, 1862.
112. Capers letter, June 5, 1862, Capers.
113. Hagood, Tracy diary, June 7, 1862.
114. Capers letter, June 9, 1862, Citadel.
115. *The Hartford Daily Courant*, December 9, 1904, Duke.
116. *Ibid.*, December 9, 1904. In his book about his father, Walter Capers, author of *Ellison Capers Bishop-Soldier Bishop*, relates a very interesting anecdote about Ellison capturing a Union soldier at the Battle of Jackson, Mississippi, on May 14, 1863. However, there is no other evidence that Lieutenant Colonel Capers captured a prisoner at Jackson, and the capture of Private Woodford at James Island in 1862 is not included in Walter Capers' book. Therefore, it seems that Walter Capers related a capture that actually took place at James Island on June 7, 1862. Walter Capers possibly quoted a family or oral history event that went slightly awry or used a source not located by this writer.
117. *The Hartford Courant*, December 9, 1904.
118. Hagood, Tracy Diary, June 10, 1862.
119. *OR*, Vol. XIV, p. 567.

Chapter 2
1. Wilcox, pp. 33-34.
2. Capers letter, June 17, 1862, Duke; Waties letter, June 17, 1862, SCL; Evans, p. 94; Burton, pp. 104-105. Battery Reed was named for Captain Reed of Lamar's artillery.
3. Hagood, p. 89.
4. *OR*, Vol. XIV, pp. 42-51.
5. *Ibid.*, p. 52.
6. *Ibid.*
7. *The Daily Courier*, Dec 10, 1862.
8. *Ibid.*; *OR*, Vol. XIV, pp. 59, 91, 94, 99, et al. Official reports each give a different time that the Federals arrived at Fort Lamar. General I. I. Stevens reported his division in motion at 4:00 a.m., which lends credence that the first gun was fired in the defense of Fort Lamar between 4:30 and 5:00 a.m. Colonel C. H. Stevens reported a messenger notified him at daylight and he was a distance away from the fort. Stevens notified Colonel Hagood and that officer recorded he had been notified at 4:30 a.m. General Evans thought

Colonel Hagood notified him at 2:00 a.m. Probably, through a lack of timepieces, the time of the day was largely estimated.

9.   *The Daily Courier*, December 10, 1862.
10. Hagood, p. 93.
11. Evans, p. 88.
12. *Ibid.*
13. Hagood, p. 95.
14. *Ibid.*
15. Hagood, p. 93.
16. Smythe Letter, June 17, 1862, SCHS.
17. *OR*, Vol. XIV, p. 91; Burton, p. 107.
18. Smythe letter, June 17, 1862, SCHS; Waties letter, June 17, 1862, SCL.
19. Waties letter, June 17, 1862, SCL.
20. Smythe letter, June 17, 1862, SCHS; Waties letter, June 17, 1862, SCL.
21. *OR*, Vol. XIV, p. 1014.
22. *OR*, Vol. XIV, p. 1014; Capers letter, June 17, 1862, Citadel.
23. *The Charleston Courier*, December 10, 1862.
24. *OR*, Vol. XIV, p. 84.
25. *Ibid.*
26. Hagood, p. 96.
27. Smythe letter, June 17, 1862, SCHS; Hagood, p. 95.
28. *OR*, Vol. XIV, p. 51; Wilcox, p. 35.
29. *OR*, Vol. XIV, p. 1014.
30. Burton, p. 112; Capers letter, June 16, 1862, Citadel.
31. Waties letter, June 17, 1862, SCL; Smythe letter, June 17, 1862, SCHS.
32. Waties letter, June 17, 1862, SCL.
33. Smythe letter, June 17, 1862, SCHS.
34. *Ibid.*
35. *Ibid.*
36. Tillman diary, June 7, 1862, Clemson. Private James Tillman, who later became a captain and commander of Company I, 24th Regiment, was the older brother of future South Carolina Governor Ben Tillman.
37. Capers letter, June 17, 1862, Citadel.
38. *OR*, Vol. XIV, p. 90. *The Charleston Mercury*. June 25, 1862.
39. Waties letter, June 17, 1862, SCL.
40. *OR*, Vol. XIV, pp. 1014-1015; Capers letter, June 22, 1862, Citadel. There is a small monument located on James Island near the location of Battery Reed that bears the name "Ellison Capers." The history of the marker is lost. However, someone apparently placed the monument there in honor of Capers' fine service of June 16, 1862.
41. *OR*, Vol. XIV, p. 102.
42. Evans, p. 91.
43. Capers letter, June 17, 1862, Citadel.
44. *Ibid.*
45. *OR*, Vol. XIV, p. 107.

46. Gavin, p. 80.
47. Tillman diary, July 21, 1862, Clemson.
48. Smithe, p. 145. The article was originally published by *The Daily Courier*, July 26, 1862.
49. Hagood, Tracy diary, July 8, 1862. There is no apparent reason that the Confederates did not launch, at least, an artillery barrage against the Federals while they were loading their boats.
50. McGee letter, July 6, 1862, SCL.
51. McGee letters, June 25-28, and July 6, 1862, SCL. The preacher was probably Colonel Peter Faysoux Stevens who was married to Ellison Capers' sister. He was also the brother of Clement Hoffman Stevens.
52. McGee letters, June 25, and June 28, 1862, SCL.
53. Tillman diary, July 21, and August 9, 1862, Clemson.
54. McGee letter, July 6, 1863, SCL.
55. First Military District, Special Order No. 12, July 8, 1862, NA.
56. Department of SC, Ga & Fla., General Order No. 49, July 23, 1862, SA; RG 109, SC Records, Microcopy M267, NA.
57. *Ibid.*
58. McGee letter, July 18, 1862, SCL.
59. McGee letter July 18, 1862, SCL; Hagood, Tillman diary, August 9, 1862. At that time, there were only two South Carolina infantry regiments permanently assigned to duty with the Army of Tennessee.
60. Hagood, Tillman diary, August 9, 1862.
61. Capers letter, August 9, 1862, Citadel. "Presents" indicate the exchange of mementos that reflected the esteem that existed between the regiments. There is no record of what the exchanged gifts or mementos were.
62. The men of the 24th were unaware of the criteria for selection for an assignment to the battle zone. If Colonel Capers knew, his copious letters failed to reveal that fact. The 24th was a well trained and disciplined regiment with two outstanding officers providing the leadership. Perhaps the regiment was retained in South Carolina due to the political connections of its leadership, or the top generals wanted to retain the "best regiment" in Charleston. However, neither of these theories is verified.
63. Capers letter, August 9, 1862, Citadel; McGee letters, July 21, 31, 1862, SCL.
64. Steinmeyer diary, p. 10, SCL.
65. Steinmeyer diary, p. 10, SCL; McGee letter, July 18, 1862, SCL.
66. Stevens letter, June 24, 1862; RG 109, SC Records, Microcopy M267, NA.
67. Nisbet, p. 171; McGee letters, SCL; Warner, p. 291; Moseley letter, Editor's file. Warner indicates that Stevens' men called him "Rock." After the war, Captain Steinmeyer wrote a sketch about General Stevens that indicates the men called him "Rock" or "Old Rock." Both Colonel Nisbet and the McGee brothers referred to Stevens as the "Old Fellow." It is not clear whether "Rock," "Old Rock," or "The Old Fellow," were commonly accepted sobriquet(s) for Colonel Stevens. Stevens could have easily earned such

sobriquets for his bravery and steadfastness.

68. McGee letter, July 22, 1862, SCL.
69. McGee letters, July 21 and 22, 1862, SCL.
70. Capers letter, August 9, 1862, Citadel.
71. Capers diary, September 16, 1862, Citadel.
72. Waties letter, SCL.
73. Capers letter, August 18, 1862, Citadel. Tillman diary, Clemson.
74. Capers letter, August 3, 1862, Citadel.
75. RG 109, SC Records, Microcopy M267, NA.
76. *Ibid.*
77. McGee letter, October 3, 1862, SCL.
78. *Ibid.*
79. RG 109, SC Records, Microcopy M267, NA.
80. *OR*, Vol. XIV, p. 149.
81. *OR*, Vol. XIV, pp, 649, 651.
82. *OR*, VOL. XIV, p. 179.
83. *OR*, Vol. XIV, p. 186.
84. *OR*, Vol. XIV, pp 148-149, 180. McGee letter, October 25, 1862, SCL.
85. McGee letter, October 25, 1862, SCL.
86. RG 109, SC Records, Microcopy M267, NA.
87. *Ibid.*
88. McGee letter, November 10, 1862, SCL.
89. RG 109, SC Records, Microcopy M267, NA; A full copy of the court-martial charges and specifications, as well as the findings of the court is found in Captain Pearson's Confederate service record.
90. *Ibid.*
91. RG 109, SC Records, Microcopy M267, NA.
92. Capers letter, February 26, 1863, Duke.
93. Rhett papers, SCHS.
94. Capers letter, November 11, 1862, Duke; Stevens essay, not dated, SCL; Hennessey, p. 52. Mrs. Stevens' mother, a descendant of the famous French Huguenot "Faysoux" family of Charleston, was sister to the mother of Colonel Stevens. Her brother was General Bernard E. Bee, who became renowned for applying the sobriquet "Stonewall" to General Thomas Jonathan Jackson. Mrs. Stevens is interred in the family plot near her brother and beside her husband in the Church Yard, at St. Paul's Church, Pendleton, S.C.
95. *Ibid.* Moseley family record of burial at St. Paul's Cemetery, Pendleton, S.C.
96. *Ibid.*
97. Capers papers, Stevens' note, not dated, NA. Even under these conditions, Stevens' mind was on his duty when he asked Capers to take his place on a court-martial board. There can be no doubt as to the sacrifice that this brave man was willing to contribute to his country.
98. Capers letter, December 9, 1862, Duke.
99. Capers letter, December 9, 1862, Citadel; RG 109, SC Records, Microcopy

M267, NA.
100. RG 109, SC Records, Microcopy M267, NA.
101. McGee letter, November 10, 1862, SCL.
102. McGee letter, December 4, 1862, SCL. Although Vessie was not as articulate as his brother, John Lewis, he, too, wrote super expressive letters.
103. Capers letter, November 11, 1862, Citadel.
104. RG 109, SC Records, Microcopy M267, NA. McGee letter, November 10, 1862, SCL.
105. *Ibid.*
106. Capers papers, NA.

Chapter 3
1. Warner, pp. 334-335. Whiting was a West Point graduate who attained the highest grades ever achieved until that time. Prior to his assignment to Wilmington, he was chief engineer for General Joseph E. Johnston, and served as a division commander at during the Seven Days Battles. Whiting constructed Fort Fisher, guarding the sea approach to Wilmington. He was seriously wounded and captured in January 1865 and died from his wounds as a prisoner of war on March 10, 1865.
2. *OR*, Vol. XIV, p. 711.
3. *OR*, Vol. XIV, pp. 711, 713-714.
4. *Ibid.*
5. Capers letter, December 28, 1862, Duke.
6. *OR*, Vol. XIV, p. 711.
7. Capers letter, December 16, 1862, Duke.
8. Capers letter, December 18, 1862, Duke.
9. *Ibid.*
10. Evans, p. 110.
11. Evans, pp. 364-365.
12. Capers letter, December 18, 1862, Duke.
13. Capers Diary, December 18, 1862, Citadel.
14. Capers letter, December 18, 1862, Duke.
15. *Ibid.*
16. Capers diary, December 22, 1862, Citadel.
17. Capers letter, December 19, 1862, Duke.
18. *Ibid.*
19. Capers diary, December 22, 1862, Citadel; Capers letter, December 23, 1862, Duke. The "affliction" mentioned refers to the death of Colonel Stevens' wife and two small sons.
20. Steinmeyer diary, p. 11, SCL.
21. Capers diary, December 23, 1862, Citadel.
22. Capers diary, December 22, 24-25, 1862, Citadel.
23. McGee letter, December 25, 1862, SCL.
24. RG 109, SC Records, Microcopy M267, NA.
25. *Ibid.*

26. Capers diary, December 27, 1862, Citadel.
27. Stevens letter, December 27, 1862, NA.
28. Capers letter, December 23, 1862, NA.
29. *Ibid.*
30. Yeadon letter, January 12, 1863, Capers papers, NA. Mr. Richard Yeadon was Ellison Capers' uncle. He was also a member of the South Carolina legislature (Senate) and resided at Kalmia, near Aiken. This letter is mentioned here at length to demonstrate the feelings of many of the homefolk toward the war effort, especially the political leadership.
31. Capers diary, December 27, 1862 - January 1, 1863, Citadel.
32. Capers letter, December 29, 1862, Citadel. Capers never identified the officer, but, it was most probably either Major Hammond or Quartermaster Sergeant Addison. Hammond was the only F&S officer who frequently visited Wilmington. Addison was a noncommissioned officer who made daily trips to Wilmington with the mail and other official communications. Since Capers referred to the person as an "officer," Hammond appears to be the most likely person.
33. *Ibid.*
34. Capers letter, December 29, 1862, Citadel.
35. Capers letter, January 1, 1863, Duke.
36. Capers letter, January 14, 1863, SCL.
37. *Ibid.*
38. *Ibid.*
39. Capers letter, January 4, 1863, Citadel.
40. *OR*, Vol. XIV, p. 742.
41. *OR*, Vol. XIV, p. 744.
42. Capers diary, January 13, 1863, Citadel.
43. *Ibid.*
44. McGee letter, January 5, 1863, SCL.
45. Capers letter, January 19, 1863, Duke.
46. *Ibid.*
47. Capers diary, January 21 - 25, 1863, Citadel.
48. Capers diary, January 21, 1863, Citadel.
49. Capers letter, January 22, 1863, Duke.
50. Capers letter, not dated, Citadel.
51. Capers letter, January 30, 1863, Duke.
52. Capers letter, January 31, 1863, Duke; McGee letter, February 1, 1863, SCL.
53. *Ibid.*
54. McGee letter, February 1, 1863, SCL.
55. *Ibid.*
56. RG 109, SC Records, Microcopy M267, NA.
57. *Ibid.*
58. *OR*, Vol. XIV, pp. 760-761, 768.
59. *OR*, Vol. XIV, p. 764.
60. McGee letter, February 16, 1863, SCL.

61. Bozeman letter, February 17, 1863, SCL.
62. Steinmeyer diary, p. 11, SCL. The Citadel relocated to another area in Charleston. The Citadel Green mentioned here was renamed Francis Marion Square.
63. Capers diary, March 30, 1863, Citadel.
64. McGee letter, February 16, 1863, SCL.
65. Bozeman letter, February 17, 1864, SCL.
66. Steinmeyer diary, p. 11, SCL. *The Charleston Courier*, March 24, 1863.
67. *OR*, Vol. XIV, p. 768.
68. *Ibid.*
69. *Ibid.*
70. *Ibid.*
71. McGee letter, February 20, 1863, SCL.
72. McGee letter, February 20, 1863, SCL.
73. Capers letter, February 26, 1863, Duke.
74. Capers letter, February 26, 1863, Duke; McGee letter, March 2, 1863, SCL.
75. Capers letters, February 23 and March 1, 1863, Duke.
76. Capers letter, March 1, 1863, Duke.
77. Capers letter, February 28, 1863, Duke.
78. *Ibid.*
79. *Ibid.*
80. Capers letter, April 26, 1863, Duke.
81. *Ibid.*
82. Capers letter, February 26, 1863, Duke. There is no indication whether Capers wrote about General Albert Sidney Johnston or General Joseph Eggleston Johnston. Since A. S. Johnston had been killed in battle ten months earlier, the reference is more likely made to J. E. Johnston.
83. McGee letter, March 2, 1863, SCL.
84. Capers letter, March 7, 1863, Duke.
85. Capers letter, March 1, 1863, Duke.
86. Padgett letter, April 21, 1863, AWC.
87. RG 109, SC Records, Microcopy M267, NA; Capers letter, February 28, 1863, Duke; McGee letter, March 2, 1863, SCL.
88. Capers letter, March 3 1863, Citadel.
89. McGee letter, March 2, 1863, SCL.
90. Capers letter, March 7, 1863, Citadel. Many years earlier, a settler named Ballou had chosen the same ridge as a "healthy place" and built his home there. As a result, the place became known as Ballouville. The settlement no longer exists and maps of the area made in 1820 and 1860 do not reflect the location of the settlement.
91. McGee letter, March 7, 1863, SCL.
92. Steinmeyer diary, p. 11, SCL; Capers letter, March 7, 1863, Citadel; McGee letter, March 7, 1863, SCL.
93. *Ibid.*; McGee letter, March 7, 1863, SCL.
94. Capers papers, NA.

95. McGee letters, March 7, 15-16, 22, 1863, SCL.
96. Capers letter, March 15, 1863, Citadel.
97. Steinmeyer diary, p. 11, SCL.
98. *OR*, Vol. XIV, p. 878.
99. McGee letters, March 7, 15, 16, 22, 1863, SCL.
100. McGee letter, March 16, 1863, SCL.
101. Capers papers, NA.
102. Evans, p. 194.
103. *OR*, Vol. XIV, p. 878.
104. *OR*, Vol. XIV, p. 879.
105. Capers diary, April 9, 1863, Citadel.
106. McGee letter, April 12, 1863, SCL.
107. *OR*, Vol. XIV, p. 33.
108. *OR*, Vol. XIV, p. 34.
109. Evans, p. 195. Graham was the commander of the 21st Regiment, South Carolina Volunteers, Infantry. At the time of Capers' visit, Graham commanded the defenses of Morris Island.
110. *OR*, Vol. XIV, p. 942.
111. Capers, letter, April 13, 1863, Citadel; *OR*, Vol. XIV, p. 926.
112. RG 109, SC Records, Microcopy M267, NA.
113. Capers diary, April 9, 1863, Citadel; Capers letter, June 11, 1889. This is the same flag on display at The War Memorial Museum, 920 Sumter St., Columbia, S.C.
114. RG 109, SC Records, Microcopy M267, NA.
115. RG 109, SC Records, Microcopy M267, NA.
116. *OR*, Vol. XIV, pp. 924, 942.
117. *OR*, Vol. XIV, p. 926. Walker's brigade was stationed on the coast of Georgia, below Savannah. This message asking that the two brigades be placed under Gist equates to General Beauregard recommending that Gist be promoted to Major General. The two brigades were in Mississippi only a short time when Brigadier General W. H. T. Walker, the commander of the other brigade, was promoted. Walker was a West Pointer and well qualified for the promotion and many thought he could have excelled at even a higher level of command. Although, Gist was not a West Pointer, he was, indeed, well qualified for promotion to major general, too.
118. *OR*, Vol. XIV, p. 956.

Chapter 4
1. Capers letter, May 6, 1863, Citadel.
2. Capers letter, May 12, 1863, Citadel. George's Station is now St. George, South Carolina.
3. Capers letter, May 7, 1863, Citadel. George's Station is now St. George, South Carolina.
4. Evans, p. 204; Capers letter, May 7, 1863, Citadel. At the time, Capers informed his wife that Stevens "left the train at Branchville" and gave no

reason. Capers' diary mentions only that Stevens delayed 24 hours.

5. *Ibid.*
6. Capers letter, May 9, 1863, Citadel.
7. Capers letter, May 8, 1863, Citadel.
8. *Ibid.*
9. Capers letter, May 7, 1863, Citadel; Steinmeyer diary, p. 7, SCL.
10. *Ibid.*
11. Capers letter, May 12, 1863, Citadel.
12. *Ibid.*
13. *Ibid.*
14. *Ibid.*
15. Evans, p. 204.
16. *Clarion Ledger*, July 14, 1957.
17. Evans, p. 204; Capers letter, May 17, 1863, SCL.
18. Evans, p. 205; *OR*, VOL. XLII, Part 1, p. 594. Brigadier General John Gregg, a native of Alabama was killed in action in Virginia on October 7, 1864, at the head of his men.
19. *The Clarion Ledger*, Jackson, Mississippi, Sunday March 14, 1982. Mr. O. P. Wright was born at Lawrence, S. C., in 1810, the oldest of 10 children of General Thomas Wright. His mother was the aunt of William Simpson, Governor of South Carolina, 1878-1880 and South Carolina chief justice 1880-1890. Wright did not serve in the military but lost his wealth during the War. He recouped some of his losses after the War, and at his death in 1876 he owned 400 acres of land.
20. Evans, p. 204-205; *The Clarion Ledger*, Jackson, Mississippi, July 14, 1957.
21. *Ibid.*
22. *OR*, Vol. XXIV, Part 1, p. 638.
23. *OR*, Vol. XXIV, Part 1, p. 723; Evans, p. 209.
24. *OR*, Vol. XXIV, Part 1, p. 638.
25. *OR*, Vol. XXIV, Part 1, p. 782.
26. RG 109, SC Records, Microcopy M267; Steinmeyer diary, p. 12.
27. *OR*, Vol. XXIV, Part 1, p. 638.
28. *OR*, Vol. XXIV, Part 1, p. 782.
29. *Ibid.*
30. *Ibid.*
31. Steinmeyer diary, p. 12, SCL; *OR*, Vol. XXIV, Part 1, pp. 782-783.
32. Steinmeyer diary, p. 12, SCL.
33. Stevens letter, November 27, 1863, Duke.
34. Capers letter, May 26, 1863, Citadel.
35. Capers, pp. 64-65. This story is quoted from a book written by Lt. Col. Capers' son, Walter Capers. This researcher has been unable to independently verify the story. It is interesting that Ellison did not mention this incident to Lottie when he wrote her about his experiences of May 14. Moreover, Capers had no quarters that day and did not find a house in which to stop to get his wound treated until 2 a.m. the next morning. Based on the foregoing, it

appears that this story is possibly a family story gone somewhat awry. It may relate the details about Lieutenant Colonel Capers personally capturing a Union soldier on June 3, 1862, at James Island. This writer cannot state that the incident is erroneous, only that he has been unable to independently verify the anecdote.

36. *OR*, Vol. XXIV, Part 1, p. 786.
37. *Ibid.*
38. Capers letter, May 17, 1863, SCL.
39. Capers letter, May 17, 1863, SCL. This is the only time on record that the highly religious Capers "took a drink of whiskey."
40. Steinmeyer diary, p. 13, SCL.
41. *Ibid.*
42. Steinmeyer diary, p. 13, SCL; *OR*, Vol. XXIV, Part 1, p. 783.
43. *OR*, Vol. XXIV, Part 1, p. 786.
44. *Ibid.*
45. RG 109, SC records, Microcopy M267, NA.
46. Confederate Deaths, Jackson, Mississippi, Courtesy Mr. Parker Hills, Jackson, MS.; *OR*, Vol. XXIV, Part 1, p. 787.
47. *OR*, Vol. XXIV, Part 1, p. 751.
48. Capers letter, May 17, 1863, SCL.
49. *Ibid.*
50. *Ibid.*
51. *Ibid.*
52. *Ibid.*
53. *Ibid.*
54. *Ibid.*
55. *Ibid.*
56. *Ibid.*
57. Steinmeyer diary, p. 15, SCL.
58. Steinmeyer diary, p. 14, SCL.
59. Steinmeyer diary, pp. 14-15, SCL.
60. Steinmeyer diary, p. 15, SCL.
61. *Ibid.*
62. *Ibid.*
63. *Ibid.*
64. RG 109, SC Records, Microcopy M267, NA; Steinmeyer diary, pp. 15-16, SCL.
65. Steinmeyer diary, p. 16, SCL.
66. *Ibid.*
67. *Ibid.*
68. RG 109, SC Records, Microcopy M267, NA; Steinmeyer diary, pp. 16-17, SCL.
69. RG 109, SC Records, Microcopy M267, NA; Steinmeyer diary, p. 17, SCL.
70. RG 109, SC Records, Microcopy M267, SCL. There is a similarity between letters written to one's congressman and the answers received during the War

For Southern Independence and the present time, i.e. there is little change in the bureaucratic tone of responses.

71. Steinmeyer letter to Congressman Miles, July 1, 1863; RG 109, SC Records, Microcopy M267, NA.
72. Maj. Davis' letter to Sec. Seddon, August 6, 1863, RG 109, SC Records, Microcopy M267, NA.
73. Steinmeyer diary, p. 17, SCL.
74. *Ibid.*
75. RG 109, SC Records, Microcopy M267, NA.
76. *Ibid.*
77. *OR*, Vol. XXIV, Part 3, pp. 524-525, 920.
78. *OR*, Vol. XXIV, Part 2, pp. 148, 159.
79. *OR*, Vol. XXIV, Part 3, p. 920.
80. *Ibid.*
81. Evans, p. 209.
82. RG 109, SC Records, Microcopy M267, NA; Purvis letter, June 1, 1863, Georgia Archives.
83. RG 109, SC Records, Microcopy M267, NA; Steinmeyer diary, p. 17, SCL.
84. A U.S. quarter cut in half equaled two bits in the wartime Southern economy. The Confederate government did not mint metal coins in quantity.
85. McGee letter, June 21, 1863, SCL.
86. Purvis letter, June 1, 1863, Georgia Archives.
87. Evans, p. 209.
88. *Ibid.*
89. RG 109, SC Records, Microcopy M267, NA.
90. *Ibid.*
91. Stevens letter, November 28, 1863, Duke; McGee letter, September 25, 1863, SCL; Nisbet, p. 171. Stevens referred to Appleby as "The Old Fellow," a sobriquet by which some men also called Colonel Stevens.
92. RG 109, SC Records, Microcopy M267, NA.
93. *Ibid.*
94. McGee letter, June 15, 1863, SCL.
95. McGee letter, June 20, 1863, SCL.
96. McGee letter, June 21, 1863, SCL.
97. Evans, p. 210; RG 109, SC Records, Microfilm M267, NA.
98. Capers sketch, Citadel.
99. *Ibid.*
100. Warner, pp. 323-324; RG 109, SC Records, Microcopy M267, NA; *OR*, Vol. XXIV, Part 3, p. 1041.
101. *OR*, Vol. XXIV, Part 1, p. 245.
102. McGee letter, July 16, 1863, SCL; Howell letter, July 24, 1990, author's file. In 1895, the city renamed the graveyard "The Greenwood Cemetery."
103. McGee letter, August 2, 1863, SCL.
104. *Ibid.*
105. McGee letter, Jul 24, 1863, SCL.

106. McGee letter, July 16, 1863, SCL.
107. McGee letter, July 24, 1863, SCL.
108. McGee letter, August 2, 1863, SCL.
109. *Ibid.*
110. *OR*, Vol. XXIV, Part 2, p. 535.
111. *OR*, Vol. XXIV, Part 1, p. 208.
112. RG 109, SC Records, Microcopy 267, NA.
113. McGee letter, July 31, 1863, SCL.
114. McGee letter, August 2, 1863, SCL.
115. McGee letter, August 2, 1863, SCL.
116. Capers journal, Citadel.
117. Capers diary, July 28-29, 1863, Citadel.
118. Capers journal, Citadel; McGee letter, August 2, 1863, SCL.
119. Capers diary, August 25, 1863, Citadel.
120. Capers letter, August 23, 1863, Citadel.
121. Capers diary, August 10-15, 1863, Citadel.
122. Lieutenant General Hardee, who had been assigned to the Army of Tennessee, was reassigned to assist General Johnston and arrived at Morton, Mississippi, on July 19, 1863. He remained with Johnston until assigned command of the Vicksburg parolees in August. During his assignment with Johnston, his status was unclear except for two weeks when he commanded the army in Johnston's absence.
123. *OR*, Vol. XXIV, Part 3, p. 1037.
124. *OR*, Vol. XXX, Part 4, pp. 529-530.
125. Capers diary, August 25, 1863, Citadel.
126. Steinmeyer diary, p. 18, SCL.
127. McGee letter, September 1, 1863, SCL.
128. RG 109, SC Records, Microcopy M267, NA.
129. *Ibid.*
130. *Ibid.*
131. Capers diary, August 28, 1863, Citadel.
132. *Ibid.*
133. Capers diary, August 30-31, 1863, Citadel.
134. Capers diary, September 2, 1863, Citadel.
135. Capers letter, September 2, 1863, Duke.
136. Capers letter, September 6, 1863, Duke; McGee letter, September 6, 1863, SCL.
137. Capers letter, September 3, 1863, Duke.
138. Capers diary, September 6-13, 1863, Citadel.
139. Capers diary, September 12, 1863, Citadel.
140. Capers letter, September 16, 1863, Duke.
141. McGee letter, September 14, 1863, SCL.
142. *Ibid.*
143. McGee letter, September 17, 1863, SCL.
144. McGee letter, September 18, 1863, SCL.

145. *South Carolina at Chickamauga*, Confederate Veteran.
146. *Ibid.*
147. *Ibid.*
148. Capers diary, September 19, 1863, Citadel.

Chapter 5
1. *OR*, Vol. XXX, Part 2, p. 37. General Bragg issued Army of Tennessee General Order 180 on September 16, 1863, advising his troops that he planned a battle.
2. *OR*, Vol. XXX, Part 4, p. 541.
3. *OR*, Vol. XXX, Part 2, p. 14.
4. Evans, p. 284.
5. Evans, p. 244.
6. Evans, p. 240.
7. Evans, p. 241.
8. *Ibid.*
9. Evans, p. 284.
10. Evans, p. 285.
11. *OR*, Vol. XXX, Part 2, p. 245.
12. Capers sketch, Citadel.
13. Evans, p. 286; Capers memo, June 19, 1891, NPS.
14. Capers sketch, Citadel.
15. *Ibid.*
16. *Ibid.*
17. Capers sketch, Citadel.
18. *Ibid.*
19. Steinmeyer diary, SCL; Capers memo, January 19, 1891, NPS.
20. Steinmeyer diary, p. 20, SCL.
21. Steinmeyer diary, p. 19, SCL.
22. Capers memo, June 9, 1891, NPS.
23. Evans, p. 286; Capers memo, June 19, 1891, NPS.
24. *Ibid.*
25. *Ibid.*
26. *Ibid.*
27. Capers sketch, Citadel.
28. *OR*, Vol. XXX, Part 2, p. 247.
29. Capers memo, June 19, 1891, NPS.
30. Capers sketch, Citadel.
31. Evans, p. 287.
32. Capers sketch, Citadel.
33. Steinmeyer, p. 19, SCL.
34. Steinmeyer diary, p. 20, SCL; McGee letter, September 25, 1863, SCL.
35. *OR*, Vol. XXX, Part 2, p. 242.
36. Steinmeyer diary, p. 19, SCL.
37. Confederate Veteran, Vol. 10, p. 340.

38. Steinmeyer diary, p. 210, SCL.
39. Steinmeyer diary, p. 20, SCL. The sword, less the hilt, is presently in the hands of Captain Steinmeyer's descendants.
40. Steinmeyer diary, p. 20, SCL.
41. *Ibid.*
42. *Ibid.*
43. Steinmeyer diary, p. 21, SCL.
44. McGee letter, September 25, 1863, SCL.
45. Rowlinski letter, not dated, attached to Steinmeyer letter, Nov 5, 1891, SCL. The front leafs that contained Capers' note were subsequently stolen. Private Rowlinski, who survived the war, wanted to leave the Bible to his children to remember him by after he was "dead and gone." He thought it would be more meaningful if Colonel Capers would write the message in the Testament again. Rowlinski followed proper military protocol. He sent the little Bible to his old company commander with the request that Captain Steinmeyer send it on to Capers. Steinmeyer promptly sent the Bible to the now Bishop Capers who was happy to oblige.
46. Capers diary, October 6, 1863, Citadel.
47. Capers diary, September 21, 1863, Citadel.
48. Steinmeyer diary, p. 21, SCL; McGee letter, September 25, 1863, SCL.
49. Capers diary, November 10, 1863, Citadel.
50. Steinmeyer letter, Nov 1863, SCL.
51. Steinmeyer diary, p. 22, SCL.
52. Steinmeyer diary, p. 21, SCL.
53. *OR*, Vol. XXXI, Part 3, p. 804.
54. McGee letter, October 7, and October 11, 1863.
55. Steinmeyer diary, p. 21, SCL.
56. *Ibid.*
57. McGee letter, October 18, 1863, SCL.
58. *Ibid.*
59. Steinmeyer diary, p. 21, SCL.
60. Steinmeyer diary, p. 22, SCL.
61. McGee letter, October 18, 1863, SCL.
62. *The Edgefield Advertiser*, October 1863.
63. McGee letter, October 26, 1863, SCL.
64. *Ibid.*
65. *Ibid.*
66. McGee letters, November 11, 16, 1863, SCL.
67. McGee letter, October 26, 1863, SCL.
68. *Ibid.*
69. *Ibid.*
70. *Ibid.*
71. Steinmeyer diary, p. 22, SCL.
72. *Ibid.*
73. *Ibid.*

74. *Ibid.*
75. McGee letter, November 11, 1863, SCL.
76. McGee letter, October 26, 1863, SCL.
77. RG 109, SC Records, Microcopy M267, NA; *The Edgefield Advertiser*, October 17, 1863. Aiken, South Carolina, was located in Edgefield district.
78. McGee letter, November 1, 1863, SCL.
79. Steinmeyer letter, November 15, 1863, Duke.
80. McGee letter, November 11, 1863, SCL.
81. McGee letter, November 16, 1863, SCL.
82. McGee letter, November 20, 1863, SCL.
83. *OR*, Vol. XXXI, Part 2, p. 667.
84. *OR*, Vol. XXXI, Part 2, pp. 671, 678.
85. Steinmeyer diary, p. 23, SCL; McGee letter, November 30, 1863, SCL.
86. *OR*, Vol. XXXI, Part 2, pp. 745-753.
87. *Ibid.*
88. Steinmeyer diary, p. 22, SCL.
89. *Ibid.*
90. Steinmeyer diary, p. 22, SCL; McGee letter, November 30, 1863, SCL.
91. *OR*, Vol. XXXI, Part 1, p. 749.
92. *Ibid.*
93. *Ibid.*; McGee letter, December 4, 1863, SCL.
94. Steinmeyer diary, p. 23, SCL. Captain Steinmeyer did not record the name of the officer he met at Johnson Island.
95. *OR*, Vol. XXXI, Part 2, p. 679.
96. Gale/Polk records, Sewanee. Letter from General Braxton Bragg to Major E. T. Sykes, Feb 8, 1873. The original of the letter is in the Archives of the Southern Historical Society at Richmond, Va. Bragg wrote, "I sent for the commander of the rear guard Brig Genl. Guist (misspelled in Bragg's letter) of S. C. and told him not to leave Genl. B - and if necessary, to put him in a wagon and haul him off. But under no circumstances to allow him to give an order."
97. Steinmeyer diary, p. 23, SCL.
98. McGee letter, November 30, 1863, SCL; Hall diary, Vol. 1, p. 92, UNC.
99. Steinmeyer diary, p. 23, SCL; Hall diary, Vol. 1 p. 92, UNC.
100. Steinmeyer p. 23, SCL; McGee letter, November 30, 1864, SCL; Hall diary, Vol. 1, p. 93, UNC.
101. Steinmeyer diary, p. 23, SCL.
102. Steinmeyer diary, p. 23, SCL; Hall diary, p. 93, UNC.
103. Hall diary, p. 93, UNC; RG 109, SC records, Microcopy M267.
104. Hall diary, p. 93, UNC.
105. Steinmeyer diary, p. 23, SCL.
106. McGee letter, November 30, 1863, SCL.
107. *Ibid.*
108. Steinmeyer letter, November 9, 1877, Duke.
109. Watkins, p. 127. Watkins wrote the statement after the war. Apparently, the

"tears gather in my eyes" statement was mentioned because Gist was killed at Franklin.

110. Hughes, p. 177; *OR*, Vol. XXXI, Part 2, p. 666.
111. *OR*, Vol. XXXI, Part 2, p. 666.
112. Beckwith papers, UNC.
113. Stevens letter, November 28, 1863, Duke.
114. Manning letter, January 4, 1864, SCL; *OR*, Vol. XXXI, Part 3, pp. 764-765; Hughes, Chapter 11. The latter reference discusses in detail the reasons General Hardee declined the position.
115. *OR*, Vol. XXXI, Part 3, p. 685; Hughes, p. 188.
116. Steinmeyer diary, p. 24, SCL.

Chapter 6
1. *OR*, Vol. XXXI, Part 3, pp. 783, 880, 883.
2. *OR*, Vol. XXXI, Part 3, p. 885.
3. Manning letter, January 4, 1864, SCL.
4. *Ibid.*
5. *Ibid.*
6. *Ibid.*
7. RG 109, SC Records, Microcopy M267, NA; *The Charleston Mercury*, January 23, 1864.
8. *The Charleston Mercury*, April 5, 1864
9. *Ibid.*
10. RG 109, SC Records, Microcopy M267, NA.
11. Manning letter, January 28, 1864, SCL. Manning wrote, "He (Johnston) published a general order complimenting Gist's (brigade) & asking the other genl. officers to emulate his example."
12. Manning letter, January 28, 1864, SCL.
13. McGee letter, January 4, 1864, SCL.
14. McGee letter, December 21, 1863, SCL.
15. *Ibid.*
16. McGee letter, February 14, 1864, SCL.
17. McGee letter, January 23, 1864, SCL.
18. Steinmeyer letter, May 29, 1899, Duke; Burt diary, GHS.
19. Steinmeyer letter, May 29, 1899, Duke.
20. Hall diary, Vol. 1, p. 100, UNC.
21. McGee letter, February 23, 1864, SCL. At this point in time, the letters written by the McGee brothers cease. They wrote wonderfully vivid sketches of the life of the Confederate soldier fortunate enough to have been assigned to the gallant 24th. They suffered terribly. Yet, they never lost their pride in themselves, their uniforms, or their will to serve. Still it was their fervent hope that the "terrable affare" would soon end and they could go home for good. Buddy McGee was killed during the Battle of Atlanta on July 22, 1864. The Federals captured Vessie at Shipps Gap on October 16, 1864. He died in prison from "scorbutis," probably exacerbated by the poor prison conditions.

The record is not clear if the boys received a leave while they were at Dalton, although they probably did. After Buddy's death, the record indicates that Vessie went AWOL, possibly as a reaction to losing his brother, whom he idolized. Vessie returned to duty in time to start Hood's Tennessee Campaign. The McGee brothers' experiences were a common story of the men who served in the regiment. Those letters most assuredly brought life to this manuscript.

22. Walker letter, April 2, 1864, Duke.
23. Hall diary, Vol. 2, p. 19, UNC.
24. McGee letter, December 21, 1863, SCL.
25. Hall diary, Vol. 1, p. 99, UNC.
26. Kease was a regular correspondent to the newspaper, the *Edgefield Advertiser*, published weekly in his hometown of Edgefield, South Carolina.
27. Hall diary, Vol. 1, p. 101, UNC.
28. *Ibid.*
29. *OR*, Vol. XXXII, Part 2, p. 762. Apparently President Davis had already decided to assign General Hood to the Army of Tennessee whether Johnston agreed or not. The purpose of his inquiry to General Johnston is unknown.
30. General Wilson died of disease at Ringgold, Georgia, November 27, 1863. His promotion had been announced 11 days before his death. The Confederate Senate confirmed the promotion posthumously.
31. *Daily Courier*, February 19, 1864.
32. Nisbet, p. 170.
33. Dictionary of American Biography, Vol. 17, pp. 607-608; *Daily Courier*, February 19, 1864; Steinmeyer letter, November 15, 1863, Duke; Nesbit, p. 170.
34. Stevens letter, April 15, 1864, SCL.
35. *Ibid.*
36. Stevens letter, April 15 1864, SCL; Julian letter, January 30, 1961, SCL.
37. RG 109, SC Records, Microcopy M267, NA.
38. *Ibid.*
39. *Ibid.*
40. *Ibid.*
41. Steinmeyer diary, p. 24, SCL; RG 109, SC Records, Microcopy M267, NA.
42. Capers sketch, Citadel.
43. *Ibid.*
44. Capers letter, April 19, 1864, NA; Stevens letter, April 19, 1864, Duke. The name of General Stevens' friend is unknown.
45. Buck, pp. 41-53, 360-362; Nesbit, p. 172; *OR*, Vol. LII, Part 2, pp. 595, 608.
46. Nesbit, p. 171.
47. Nesbit, p. 171. Colonel Nesbit refers to Colonel Stevens as the "Old Fellow."
48. Nesbit, p. 175.
49. Steinmeyer diary, p. 24. SCL. The "personal friend service" equates to personal counseling.
50. RG 109, SC Records, Microcopy M267, NA; McGee letter, February 21,

1864, SCL.
51. Capers letter, April 24, 1864, Duke.
52. *Ibid.*
53. Steinmeyer diary, p. 24, SCL.

Chapter 7
1. *The Edgefield Advertiser*, May 1864, SCL. Written by Private E. Keese who was a member of the 24th and a correspondent to his hometown newspaper.
2. *OR*, Vol. XXXVIII, Part 3, p. 713; Hall diary, Vol. 2, p. 19, UNC; Hughes, p. 198; *The State*, May 11, 1893.
3. Steinmeyer diary, p. 25, SCL; Hall diary, Vol. 2, p. 20, UNC; Symonds, p. 97.
4. *The State*, May 11, 1893; *OR*, Vol. XXXVIII, Part 3, p. 713.
5. *OR*, Vol. XXXVIII, Part 3, p. 713; RG 109, SC Records, Microcopy M267, NA.
6. *OR*, Vol. XXXVIII, Part 3, p. 713.
7. Steinmeyer diary, p. 25, SCL; *OR*, Vol. XXXVIII, Part 3, p. 713.
8. *The State*, May 11, 1893; *OR*, Vol. XXXVIII, Part 3, p. 714.
9. Gale/Polk papers, Sewanee.
10. *Ibid.* Mrs. Johnston asked General Polk to baptize her husband. It is not known if this request was made as a result of the Bishop baptizing General Hood or not.
11. *Ibid.* Some historians allege that the senior officer relationships were never very good. However, General Polk obviously thought differently.
12. *OR*, Vol. XXXVIII, Part 3, p. 714.
13. *Ibid.* Steinmeyer diary, p. 25, SCL.
14. Hall diary, Vol. 2, p. 23, UNC.
15. *OR*, Vol. XXXVIII, Part 3, p. 714; Mackall letter, May 16, 1864, UNC.
16. *OR*, Vol. XXXVIII, Part 3, p. 714.
17. *Ibid.*
18. *OR*, Vol. XXXVIII, Part 3, pp. 379, 714.
19. *OR*, Vol. XXXVIII, Part 3, p. 714.
20. *OR*, Vol. XXXVIII, Part 3, pp. 379, 714; Steinmeyer diary, p. 25, SCL.
21. *OR*, Vol. XXXVIII, Part 3, pp. 714-715; Steinmeyer diary, p. 25, SCL; Magnolia Cemetery records; *Charleston Mercury*, May 21, 1864.
22. Steinmeyer diary, p. 26, SCL; *The Charleston Mercury*, May 20, 1864.
23. Roddey letter, July 16, 1885, Duke.
24. *OR*, Vol. XXXVIII, Part 3, p. 715.
25. Symond, p. 97; *OR*, Vol. XXXVIII, Part 3, p. 616.
26. *OR*, Vol. XXXVIII, Part 3, pp. 715-716. The fact that General Gist gave Colonel Capers his watch for this operation indicates that Capers did not own a watch. He never mentioned a watch in his letters except for this single incident.
27. Steinmeyer diary, p. 26, SCL.
28. *OR*, Vol. XXXVIII, Part 3, p. 714; Steinmeyer diary, p. 26, SCL.

29. Makall memo, September 9, 1864, UNC; Steinmeyer diary, p. 26, SCL; *OR*, VOL XXXVIII, Part 3, pp. 615-616, 621-622.
30. Capers papers, NA.
31. *OR*, Vol. XXXVIII, Part 3, p. 716.
32. Steinmeyer diary, p. 27, SCL.
33. *Ibid.*
34. *OR*, Vol. XXXVIII, Part 3, p. 716; Manning letter, June 4, 1864, SCL.
35. Capers letter, June 4, 1864, Duke; Manning letter, June 4, 1864, SCL.
36. *The Charleston Mercury*, June 11, 1864.
37. *The Charleston Mercury*, May 26, 1864.
38. Capers letter, June 4, 1864, Duke.
39. Padgett letter, June 9, 1864, AWC; *OR*, Vol. XXXVIII, Part 3, p. 716.
40. Gale/Polk papers, Sewanee.
41. Capers letter, July, 4, 1874, Citadel; LaBree, p. 228; Capers letter, June 11, 1864, Sewanee; Manning letter, June 8, 1864, SCL.
42. Beckwith papers, note, June 15, 1864, UNC; *OR*, Vol. XXXVIII, Part 3, p. 716.
43. Padgett letter, June 9, 1864, AWC.
44. Gale/Polk papers, letter, June 15, 1864, Sewanee; Watkins, p. 154; LaBree, p. 228.
45. Steinmeyer diary, p. 27, SCL.
46. *Ibid.*
47. *Ibid.*
48. Steinmeyer diary, p. 28, SCL. Tipper died while a prisoner in a Northern prisoner of war camp.
49. Steinmeyer diary, p. 28, SCL.
50. *Ibid.*
51. LaBree, p. 228.
52. *OR*, Vol. XXXVIII, Part 3, p. 713.
53. *OR*, Vol. XXXVIII, Part 3, p. 716; LaBree, p. 229.
54. Capers letter, June 20, 1864, Duke.
55. *OR*, Vol. XXXVIII, Part 3, p. 716.
56. Steinmeyer diary, p. 28, SCL; *The Charleston Courier*, June 24, 1864.
57. *The Charleston Courier*, June 24, 1864.
58. Labree, p. 229.
59. *OR*, Vol. XXXVIII, Part 3, pp. 716-717; LaBree, p. 229.
60. *OR*, Vol. XXXVIII, Part 3, p. 717.
61. *Ibid.*
62. Capers letter, July 17, 1864, Duke; *OR*, Vol. XXXVIII, Part 3, p. 717.
63. *OR*, Vol. XXXVIII, Part 3, p. 679.
64. Manning letter, July 10, 1864, SCL.
65. OR, Vol. XXXVIII, Part 3, p. 717.
66. Julian letter, January 30, 1961, SCL. Many historians do not think General Johnston could have saved Atlanta from Sherman's Army. However, the *Charleston Mercury* thought he would have been successful. In his 1961

letter cited here, Colonel Julian of the Atlanta Historical Society opined, "Had General Johnston been left in command, I am convinced that Atlanta would never have fallen.....a matter which could well have led to the defeat for reelection of Mr. Lincoln and an arranged peace between the North and the South." General Clement Hoffman Stevens thought Johnston would have saved Atlanta, and Colonel (later general) Ellison Capers wrote that he never doubted a favorable outcome of the Atlanta Campaign until July 17, 1864. Every man assigned to the 24th Regiment who removed his hat to Ole Joe as a token of their love and respect thought he would have succeeded.

67. *OR*, VOL. XXXVIII, Part 3, p. 717.
68. Capers letter, July 4, 1874, Citadel.
69. *OR*, Vol. XXXVIII, Part 3, pp. 890-891.
70. Watkins, p. 178. If it took someone "who was there" 20 years to find that Old Joe made mistakes, the mistakes must have been hard to find. Certainly no one hid any of General Johnston's blunders. However, some historians consider Watkins' accounts as very questionable and independent confirmation is needed to verify that some men deserted because General Johnston was replaced. No one from the 24th deserted for that reason.
71. *The Charleston Mercury*, June 29, 1864.
72. Capers letter, July 4, 1874, Citadel.
73. *OR*, Vol. XXXVIII, Part 3, p. 718.
74. *OR*, Vol. XXXVIII, Part 3, p. 717.
75. Julian letter, January 30, 1961, SCL.
76. Capers letter, July 17, 1864, Duke. In this letter Capers did not mention General Johnston's removal. He probably learned about the removal after he posted the letter.

Chapter 8
1.   Dowdey and Manarin, p. 821.
2.   *The State*, May 11, 1893.
3.   Symond p. 97; *OR*, Vol. XXXVIII, Part 3, p. 630.
4.   Walthall letter containing extract of Walthall's report of July 20, 1864, SCL; *OR*, Vol. XXXVIII, Part 3, p. 925.
5.   Capers letter, June 11, 1889, SCHS; *OR*, Vol. XXXVIII, Part 3, p. 925. The only evidence of Capers receiving a wound on that day was found in a letter Capers penned in 1889. He gives no details of the circumstances or the extent. That same day, Capers walked 40 miles to his wife's side and after several days removed her to South Carolina, farther from the battle zone. Obviously his wound was slight.
6.   Stevenson letter, August 28, 1885, Duke; Gale/Polk papers, Sewanee.
7.   Stevenson letter, August 28, 1885, Duke.
8.   *Ibid.*
9.   R.J. Rivers letter, not dated, SCL.
10. *OR*, Vol. XXXVIII, Part 3, p. 941.
11. *Ibid.*; Stevenson letter, August 28, 1885, SCL; Manning letter, August 29,

1854, SCL. Freeman, Vol. 3, p. 222.

12. *Ibid.*

13. *Battles and Leaders*, Vol. IV, p. 314; *OR*, Vol. XXXVIII, Part 3, p. 631.

14. *The Savannah Republican*, July 24, 1864, Duke.

15. Hughes, p. 229; *OR*, Vol. XXXVIII, Part 3, p. 631.

16. Nesbit, p. 212.

17. Hughes, p. 229.

18. *Augusta Chronicle & Standard*, May 3, 1868, Duke.

19. *Ibid.* Roddey letter, August 13, 1879, SCL;. Private Bagley was also cited for heroic action during the Battle of Franklin.

20. *OR*, Vol. XXXVIII, Part 3, p. 476; *Augusta Chronicle & Standard*, May 3, 1868; W. L. Roddey letter, August 13, 1879, SCL; Steinmeyer diary, p. 29, SCL. There are numerous newspaper accounts and historian accounts, especially those filed with the Atlanta Historical Society, that allege that General Walker was killed with one shot fired by a picket or a sharpshooter. One historian discounts the report by Colonel Sheldon listed in the ORs, cited herein. The Atlanta Cyclorama announces that General Walker was killed by a Union picket. Another account indicates that Walker's body "fell into Union hands and was later recovered." Possibly the confusion that surrounds the death of General Walker is reflective of the conditions that existed during the Battle of Atlanta. However, this sequence of events concerning Walker's death as they are recorded here is gleaned from documents produced by people who were there or from documents written shortly after the War. Therefore, this information should receive due consideration.

21. *OR*, Vol. XXXVIII, Part 3, p. 502.

22. Smith letter, April 3, 1880, Citadel.

23. Smith letter, April 3, 1880, Citadel; Nisbet, pp. 212, 216.

24. RG 109, SC Records, Microcopy M267, NA. The letters of the McGee brothers definitely provided extensive information and insight about the conditions which confronted the soldiers of the 24th regiment.

25. *The Charleston Mercury*, August 20, 1864.

26. *OR*, Vol. XXXVIII, Part 3, p. 631.

27. *The Charleston Mercury*, July 27, 1864.

28. *OR*, Vol. XXXVIII, Part 3, pp. 631-632.

29. Smithe, pp. 236 - 243.

30. Smithe, p. 235. Kalmia was located near Aiken, SC. The town no longer exists.

31. Gale/Polk papers, Sewanee.

32. *Ibid.*

33. Polk/Gale papers, Sewanee.

34. Espey letter, August 27, 1864, UNC.

35. Espey letter, August 27, 1864, UNC; *The State*, August 28, 1888.

36. *The Charleston Mercury*, September 1, 1864.

37. Watson diary, p. 12, UNC.

38. *OR*, Vol. XXXVIII, Part 3, p. 717; Capers letter, August 11, 1864, Duke.

39. Examining Board report, August 12, 1864, Citadel.
40. Capers letter, August 12, 1864, Duke.
41. *OR*, Vol. XXXVIII, Part 3, p. 680.
42. *Ibid.*
43. Capers letter, August 12, 1864, Duke. The Honorable Dennis Kelly, Kennesaw National Military Park Historian, thinks that many of General Hood's wagons were burned by Sherman's forces during the Atlanta Campaign. He concludes that the wagons contained many records about the activities of the Army of Tennessee. Colonel Capers in this reference seems to give additional credence to that conclusion. He mentions in this letter to his wife that the wagons containing the men's "personal belongings were not among those burnt by the enemy."
44. Capers letter, August 12, 1864, Duke; Watson diary, p. 12.
45. Capers letter, August 12, 1864, Duke; Capers letter, August 16, 1864, NA.
46. Capers letter, August 18, 1864, Sewanee.
47. Capers letter, August 19, 1864, Duke.
48. RG 109, AGIG records, Microcopy M935, NA.
49. *Ibid.*
50. Capers letter, August 19, 1964, Duke.
51. *Ibid.*
52. Capers letter, August 22, 1864, Duke.
53. Capers letter, August 24, 1864, Citadel. Mr. Walter Capers indicated that Ellison's horse survived the war and lived a long life afterwards. He does not mention the horses name and it is unknown whether the horse he refers to was "Hardtimes." Two months later, Capers purchased a new horse and wrote Lottie that he had done so because "Hardtimes and his brown horse had given out."
54. *Ibid.*
55. Epsey letter, September 27, 1864, UNC.
56. *OR*, Vol. XXXVIII, Part 3, p. 693.
57. *OR* Vol. XXXVIII, Part 3, p. 694; Capers letter, September. 7, 1864.
58. *OR*, Vol. XXXVIII, Part 3, p. 668; Capers letter, September 28, 1898, SCL.
59. *OR*, Vol. XXXVIII, Part 3, pp. 710-711.
60. Capers letter, September 7, 1864, Citadel.
61. *OR*, Vol. XXXVIII, Part 3, p. 695; Capers letter, September 7, 1864, Citadel.
62. *Ibid.*
63. *OR*, Vol. XXXVIII, Part 3, p. 703; Capers letter, September 7, 1864, Citadel.
64. *OR*, Vol. XXXVIII, Part 5, p. 1021.
65. Capers letter, September 7, 1864, Citadel.
66. *Ibid.*
67. *OR*, Vol. XXXVIII, Part 3, p. 718. The report does not mention the 8th Georgia Battalion or the 65th Georgia Regiment at the battle of Jonesboro.
68. *OR*, Vol. XXXVIII, Part 3, p. 719.
69. *OR*, Vol. XXXVIII, Part 3, p. 719; Capers letter, September 7, 1864, Citadel.
70. *OR*, Vol. XXXVIII, Part 3, pp. 719-720.

71. *Ibid.*
72. *OR*, Vol. XXXVIII, Part 3, p. 720; Steinmeyer diary, p. 23, SCL.
73. *OR*, Vol. XXXVIII, Part 3, p. 720.
74. Capers letter, September 7, 1864, Citadel.
75. *OR*, Vol. XXXVIII, Part 3, p. 283.
76. Capers letter, September 4, 1864, Duke.
77. *Ibid.*
78. *OR*, Vol. XXXVIII, Part 3, p. 283.
79. Capers letter, September 4, 1864, Duke.
80. Evans, p. 340.
81. Tillman diary, September 6-7, 1864, Clemson.
82. *OR*, Vol. XXXVIII, Part 5, p. 1028; Capers letters, September 7, 9, 1864, Citadel; Tillman diary, September 6-7, 1864, Clemson.
83. Tillman diary, September 8, 1864, Clemson.
84. Capers memo, September 1864, NA.
85. Capers letter, September 9, 1864, Citadel.
86. *Ibid.*
87. *Ibid.*
88. *Ibid.*
89. Tillman diary, September 17, 1864, Clemson.
90. Tillman diary, September 19, 1964, Clemson.
91. *Ibid.*
92. Tillman diary, September 23, 1864, Clemson.
93. *Ibid.*
94. Capers, p. 188.
95. *The Charleston Mercury*, September 12, 1864.
96. *OR*, Vol. XXXIX, Part 3, p. 879; Tillman diary, September 28, 1864, Clemson.
97. *OR*, Vol. XXXVIII, Part 5, pp. 1018, 1021, 1030; *OR*, Vol. XXXVIII, Part 3, pp. 628-629, 633, 702.
98. *OR*, Vol. XXXVIII, Part 5, pp. 836, 846, 1021; *OR*, Vol. XXXVIII, Part 3, p. 782.
99. *OR*, Vol. XXXIX, Part 2, p. 830; *OR*, Vol. XXXIX, Part 1, p. 805.

Chapter 9
1. Symond, p. 99; *OR*, Vol. XXXIX, Part 1, p. 801.
2. Padgett letter, September 16, 1864, AWC.
3. *Ibid.*
4. Evans, p. 340; Capers notes, NA; Tillman Diary, September 13-14, 1864, Clemson.
5. Tillman diary, October 2, 1864, Clemson.
6. *The Edgefield Advertiser*, October 5. 1864.
7. Tillman diary, October 4-5, 1864, Clemson; RG 106, SC Records, Microcopy M267, NA. The quartermaster issued to the regiment, 44 pairs of pants, 22 pairs of shoes and 14 blankets. This was one of several issues of clothing the

men received during Hood's Tennessee campaign.

8. Capers notes, October 6, 1864, NA; Tillman diary, October 6, 1864; Steinmeyer diary, Page 30, SCL.
9. Capers letter, October 5, 1864, NA. General Gist told Capers that General Hardee would promote him (Gist) to major general and seek his transfer to Charleston as soon as Hood's Tennessee Campaign was completed. Gist thought that Capers would be promoted to brigadier general and assigned to command Gist's brigade.
10. Capers notes, NA; Tillman diary, October 7-9, 1864, Clemson.
11. *OR*, Vol. XXXIX, Part 3, pp. 785, 812; Capers Notes, October 9, 1864, NA.
12. Capers notes, October 9, 1864, NA.
13. Capers notes, October 10-12, 1864; Tillman diary, October 10-12, 1864.
14. Capers notes, October 13, 1864, NA; Tillman diary, October 13, 1864, Clemson; Steinmeyer diary, p. 30, SCL.
15. Capers notes, October 14, 1864, NA; Tillman diary, October 14, 1864, Clemson; Steinmeyer diary, p. 30, SCL.
16. *OR*, Vol. XXXIX, Part 3, p. 311; *The Daily Courier*, November 4, 1864; Capers notes, October 16, 1864, NA; Tillman diary, October 16, 1864, Clemson; Steinmeyer diary, page 31, SCL.
17. Capers notes, October 16, 1864, NA; *The Daily Courier* November 4, 1864.
18. *OR*, Vol. XLV, p. 734; Capers notes, Dec 16, 1864, NA; Steinmeyer diary, p. 31, SCL.
19. Steinmeyer diary, p. 3, SCL; *The Daily Courier*, November 4, 1864.
20. *OR*, Vol. XXXIX, Part 1, pp. 582, 742; *OR*, Vol. XLV, Part 1, p. 734; Steinmeyer diary, p. 32, SCL; *The Daily Courier*, November 4, 1864.
21. *OR*, Vol. XXXIX, Part 1, pp. 807, 809; Capers notes, October 17, 1864, NA; Tillman diary, October 17, 1864, Clemson.
22. *OR*, Vol. XXXIX, Part 3, p. 421.
23. *OR*, Vol. XXXIX, Part 3, p. 335.
24. *OR*, Vol. XXXIX, Part 3, p.358.
25. *OR*, Vol. XXXIX, Part 3, pp. 335, 358, 421.
26. Capers notes, October 18, 1864, NA; Tillman diary, October 18, 1864, Clemson.
27. Capers notes, October 19, 20, NA; Tillman diary, October 19, 20, Clemson. The men were issued 60 pair of pants, 52 pairs of shoes, 44 jackets, 32 pairs of socks, 37 shirts and 46 pairs of drawers. This was another issue of clothing the men received during Hood's Tennessee campaign.
28. Capers letter, October 21, 1864, Citadel.
29. Capers notes, October 21-23, 1864, NA; Tillman diary, October 21-23, 1864, Clemson.
30. *OR*, Vol. XXXIX, Part 1, p. 439; Capers notes, October 24-24, 1864, NA; Tillman diary, October 24-25, 1864, Clemson.
31. *OR*, Vol. XLV, Part 1, p. 735; Capers notes, October 24-25, 1864, NA; Tillman diary, October 24-25, 1864, Clemson.
32. *OR*, Vol. XLV, Part 1, p. 735.

33. Capers letter, November 1-2, 1864, Citadel.
34. *OR*, Vol. XLV, p. 735; Capers notes, October 27-28, 1864, NA; Tillman diary, October 27-28, 1864, Clemson; Capers letter, November 5, 1862, Citadel. The regiment was issued 16 pairs of trousers, 28 pairs of shoes, 30 pairs of socks, 64 jackets, and 24 blankets. This was yet another issue of clothing received by the men during Hood's Tennessee campaign.
35. Capers letters, November 5-6, 1864, Citadel. The "little dashed with crazy" comment must have been a private joke between the deeply in love couple.
36. *OR*, Vol. XLV, Part 1, p. 735; Capers letter, November 9, 1864, Citadel.
37. RG 109, SC Records, Microcopy M267, NA; Capers journal, November 1-11, 1864, NA; Tillman diary, November 1-11, 1864, Clemson.
38. *OR*, Vol. XLV, Part 1, p. 735; Capers journal, November 13-30, 1864, Citadel; Tillman diary, November 13-20, 1864, Clemson. The regiment received 16 pairs of shoes, 45 pairs of pants, 50 pairs of socks, 34 pairs of drawers, and 26 shirts. This was yet another issue to the men during Hood's Tennessee campaign.
39. *Ibid.*
40. Capers letters, November 18-19, 1864, Duke.
41. Capers letter, November 20, 1864, Duke.
42. Capers papers, Examining board report, November 15, 1864, NA.
43. Capers letter, November 18, 1864, Duke.
44. Capers notes, November 21-22, 1864; Tillman diary, November 21-22, 1864, Clemson.
45. Capers journal, November 22-23, 1864, NA; Tillman diary, November 22-23, 1864, Clemson.
46. Capers notes, November 25-27, 1864, NA; Tillman diary, November 25-27, 1864, Clemson.
47. Tillman diary, November 27, 1864, Clemson.
48. Capers notes, November 28, 1864, NA; Capers diary, November 27-28, 1864, Citadel; Tillman diary, November 28, 1864, Clemson.
49. Moire letter, Nov 26, 1864, Duke.
50. *Ibid.*
51. J. P. Young letter, June 19, 1899, SCL; Tillman diary, November 29, 1864, Clemson; *OR*, Vol. XLV, Part I, p. 736.
52. Young letters, June 10, and July 13, 1899, SCL.
53. Young letter, June 10 and July 13, 1899, SCL; Capers journal, p. 10, Duke.
54. *OR*, Vol. XLV, Part 1, p. 736; Capers journal, Duke; Capers journal, SCL; Tillman diary, November 29, 30, 1864, Clemson; J. P. Young letter, June 10, 1899, SCL.
55. Capers journal, p. 12, Duke.
56. Young letter, July 13, 1899, SCL.
57. Capers journal, Duke.
58. Tillman diary, November 30, 1864, Clemson.
59. *OR*, Vol. XLV, Part 1, p. 736.
60. *OR*, Vol. XLV, Part 1, p. 736; Microcopy, Reel 1, TSLA.

61. Lossom, p. 218.
62. Taylor, p. 24. Immediately prior to the battle of Franklin, Private Perry Taylor, a member of the 16th Regiment, South Carolina Volunteers, Infantry, was on sentry duty guarding Hood's headquarters and reported that he overheard the conversation between Generals Forrest and Hood.
63. Chapman, p. 372.
64. Capers journal, p. 13, Duke.
65. *Ibid.*
66. *Ibid.*
67. *OR*, Vol. XLV, Part 1, pp. 736-737.
68. *Ibid.*
69. *Ibid.*
70. *Ibid.* Colonel Capers did not see Brigadier General Gist again after Gist gave the order for the charge. The story in his journal probably was repeated from the report of another soldier, who, no doubt, did think Gist was shot "through the heart and died at 5:30 P.M."
71. Chapman, p. 372.
72. *Ibid.*
73. Capers journal, Duke.
74. *Ibid.*
75. *Ibid.*
76. Blackwell letter, August 15, 1885, SCL; Capers journal, Duke.
77. *Ibid.*
78. *Ibid.*
79. *Ibid.*
80. Roddey letter, August 13, 1879, SCL.
81. Capers journal, Duke.
82. *Ibid.*
83. *Ibid.*
84. *Ibid.*
85. Capers journal, Duke; Jackson letter, December 10, 1864, TSLA.
86. Capers journal, Duke; Pamphlet, "The Battle of Franklin," July 18, 1883, Sewanee.
87. Noll, pp. 118-119; Capers journal, Duke; *OR*, Vol. XLV, Part 1, p. 737. Bryan, pp. 109, 309, 552. RG 109, SC Records, Microcopy M267; Jones' family oral history.
88. *OR*, Vol. XLV, Part 1, p. 738.
89. *The State*, newspaper clipping, not dated, SCL; RG 109, SC records, Microcopy M267. The only captain killed in battle from the 24th SCV was killed at Franklin. There is no independent confirmation that such a grave existed with soldiers from the 24th regiment.
90. *Ibid.*
91. *OR*, Vol. XLV, Part 1, p. 738.
92. Capers journal, Duke.
93. Capers papers, SCL.

94. *OR*, Vol. XLV, Part 1, pp. 738-739; Capers journal, Duke.
95. Tillman diary, December 1, 1864, Clemson.
96. Gottschalk, p. 489.
97. *OR*, Vol. XLV, Part 1, p. 739; Tillman diary, December 2, 1864, Clemson.
98. Gale letter, January 19, 1865, TSLA.
99. *OR*, Vol. XLV, Part 1, p. 731; Tillman diary, December 2, 1864, Clemson; Capers diary, December 3, 1864, SCL.
100. Tillman diary, December 3, 4, 1864, Clemson.
101. *OR*, Vol. XLV, Part 1, p. 731; Tillman diary, December 4, 1864, Clemson; Capers journal, Duke.
102. *OR*, Vol. XLV, Part 1, p. 731; Tillman diary, December 6, 1864; Capers journal, SCL.
103. Tillman diary, December 9, 1864, Clemson; Capers journal, December 9, 1864, SCL.
104. Tillman diary, December 11-15, 1864; Capers journal, December 11-15, 1864, SCL.
105. *Ibid.*
106. Gale/Polk papers, TSLA.
107. *Ibid.*
108. Watkins, p. 227; Tillman diary, December 16, 1864, Clemson; Capers journal, December 16, 1864, Citadel.
109. Gale letter, January 19, 1865, TSLA.
110. Hood, p. 304; Gale/Polk papers, TSLA.
111. Sanders note, n.d., SCL.
112. Watkins, p. 224; Gale/Polk papers, Sewanee. Neither Lieutenant James Tillman nor Private S. C. Cartledge recorded the event in their diaries. Cartledge's diary, not held by this writer, is the primary basis for Colonel Capers' journal for the period.
113. The estimate of losses at Nashville is modest on the part of Capers. If the regiment lost one third at Franklin, they had less than 175 soldiers at Nashville. One third of the 175 is less than the number known captured at Nashville. There is no record of the number of soldiers killed or missing, or their identities.
114. Watkins, p. 224; Gale/Polk papers, Sewanee; *The Charleston Mercury*, January 20, 1865.
115. Lossom, p. 239; Gale/Polk papers, Sewanee; Cheatham papers, TSLA.
116. RG 109, SC Records, Microcopy M267, NA.
117. *Ibid.*
118. Lossom, p. 228.
119. Lossom, p. 228; Tillman diary, December 19, 1864, Clemson; Capers journal, December 19, 1864, SCL; Cheatham papers, TSLA.
120. *OR*, Vol. XLV, Part 1, p. 757, 759.
121. Capers journal, SCL; Tillman diary, December 20, 1864, Clemson; Gale/Polk papers, Sewanee.
122. Tillman diary, December 21, 1864, Clemson; Capers journal, SCL; Gale/Polk

papers, TSLA.

123. Tilman diary, December, 22, 1864, Clemson; Capers journal, SCL; Gale/Polk papers, Sewanee.
124. Tillman diary, December 24-28, 1864, Clemson; Capers journal, SCL.
125. *Ibid.*
126. *Ibid.*
127. Smith letter, October 17, 1878, Citadel.
128. Tillman diary, December 29, 1864, Clemson; Capers journal, SCL.
129. Tillman diary, December 30-31, 1864, January 1, 1865, Clemson; Capers journal, SCL.

Chapter 10

1. Tillman Diary, January 2-3, 1865, Clemson.
2. Capers journal, SCL; Tillman diary, January 2-9, 1865, Clemson.
3. Tillman, diary, January 10, 1865, Clemson.
4. Capers journal, SCL; Tillman diary, January 11-12, 1865, Clemson.
5. Capers journal, SCL; Tillman diary, January 12, 1865, Clemson. The Tillman diary stopped on January 12, 1865. It starts up again on April 1, 1865. Family history indicates that the missing diaries were in the possession of a sister and destroyed during a house fire.
6. *OR*, Vol. XLIX, Part 1, p. 929.
7. *The Charleston Courier*, February 7, 1865.
8. Capers journal, SCL.
9. Hardee letter, January 26, 1865, NA.
10. Johnson telegram to General S. Cooper, 1965, NA.
11. Capers journal, SCL. On this date Capers' journal, based on the diary of Private S. C. Cartledge, Co. I, stops. Cartledge survived the war. Perhaps someday his diary will surface and promote added insight into the activities of the gallant regiment during the last days of the war. Records documenting regimental movements from February 2 - April 1, 1865 are practically non-existent. However, a record of the move of Cheatham's corps to North Carolina, via Georgia and South Carolina, does exist.
12. *OR*, Vol. XLVII, Part 1, pp. 1081-1082. This writer has turned up no independent record of the gallant regiment's moves from Montgomery to Bentonville. Lieutenant Tillman received a furlough during this period and possibly did not travel with the regiment.
13. *Ibid.*
14. *OR*, Vol. XLVII, Part 1, p. 1082.
15. *Ibid.*
16. *OR*, Vol. XLVII, Part 2, p. 1441.
17. Smith letter, October 17, 1866, Citadel; *OR*, Vol. XLVII, Part 1, p. 1083.
18. *OR*, Vol. XLVII, Part 1, p. 1083.
19. Tillman diary, April 1-4, 1865, Clemson.
20. Tillman diary, April 3-9, 1865, Clemson.

21. RG 109, SC Records, Microcopy M267, NA. A roster of the consolidated regiment is at Appendix II.
22. Smith letter, October 17, 1866, Citadel; Tillman diary, April 9, 1865, Clemson.
23. J. B. Cummings papers, UNC; RG 109, SC records, Microcopy M267, NA.
24. Tillman diary, April 10-12, 1865, Clemson.
25. Tillman diary, April 14-15, 1865, Clemson.
26. Tillman diary, April 16, 1865, Clemson.
27. J. B. Cummings papers, UNC; *OR*, Vol. XLVII, part 3, p. 790. The South Carolina soldier under the death sentence could not have been from Gist's brigade or the 24th Regiment. The individual was apparently assigned to Stewart's corps. There is no record of any soldier from the 24th Regiment having been sentenced to death as a result of a court-martial sentence.
28. J. B. Cummings papers, UNC.
29. Tillman diary, April 17, 1865, Clemson.
30. Tillman diary, April 18-20, 1865, Clemson.
31. *OR*, Vol. XLV, Part 1, p. 1083.
32. Smith letter, October 17, 1866, Citadel.
33. *OR*, Vol. XLVII, Part 1, p. 1084.
34. Tillman diary, April 26-29, 1865, Clemson; Smith letter, October 17, 1866, Citadel.
35. Tillman diary, April 29, 1865, Clemson.
36. Tillman diary, May 1-5, 1865, Clemson.
37. Tillman diary, May 6-12, 1865, Clemson.
38. Tillman diary, July 1, 1865, Clemson.

STATE OF SOUTH CAROLINA.

HEADQUARTERS ADJ'T AND INSP'T GENL'S OFFICE,
Charleston, November 15, 1861.

ORDER NO—

I. * * * DESIROUS OF FORMING AN EFFECTIVE Volunteer Force, for the defence of the State, under the authority of a resolution of the State Legislature, His Excellency the Governor, hereby orders that portion of the State Militia, now under orders or in service, be remanded at once to their homes, except troops of the City of Charleston, S. C., and those Companies guarding bridges, or other important posts, who will be retained, for the present, in service.

II. All arms, supplies, camp and garrison equipage, that may have been drawn from the State or Confederate States stores, for the troops remanded by this order, are ordered to be returned to the proper Departments by the officers receipting for them.

III. All persons of the State Militia, capable of bearing arms, are earnestly requested and urged to form themselves into effective Volunteer organizations, for the purpose of being mustered into the State or Confederate service for the defence of South Carolina. Companies, Battalions and Regiments thus formed, will be accepted by the Commander-in-Chief.

IV. Generals of Division, of the S. C. M., are charged with the prompt extension of this order.

By command of the Governor.

S. R. GIST,
Adj't and Insp't Gen. of South Carolina.

November 18

478

BIBLIOGRAPHY

BOOKS

Bearss, Edwin C., and Warren Grabau. *The Battle of Jackson May 14, 1863*. Baltimore, Gateway Press, Inc., 1981.

Bearss, Edwin C.. *The Siege of Jackson July 10-17, 1863*. Baltimore, Gateway Press, Inc., 1981.

Bearss, Edwin C.. *Three Other Post-Vicksburg Actions*. Baltimore, Gateway Press, 1981.

Beers, Henry Putney. *The Confederacy - A Guide to the Archives of the Government of the Confederate States of American*. Washington, National Archives and Records Administration, 1986.

Blackburn, John. *A Hundred Miles A Hundred Heartbreaks*. Detroit, Reed Printing Co., 1961.

Bryan, Evelyn M. F., and Gibson Howard Bryan. *Cemeteries of Upper Colleton County South Carolina*. Jacksonville, The Florentine Press, 1969.

Buck, Irving A.. *Cleburne and His Command*. Wilmington, Broadfoot Publishing Company, 1982.

Burton, E. Milby. *The Siege of Charleston*. Columbia, University of South Carolina Press, 1970.

Capers, Walter B.. *The Soldier-Bishop Ellison Capers*. New York, The Neale Publishing Co., 1912.

Chapman, John A.. *History of Edgefield County*. Newberry, Elbert H. Aull, Publisher and Printer, 1897.

Collins, Ann Pickens, and Louise Gill Knox. *Chester County Heritage History*. Chester, Taylor Publishing Co., 1982.

Connelly, Thomas Lawrence. *Autumn of Glory*. Baton Rouge, Lousiana State University Press, 1971.

Connelly, Thomas Lawrence. *Army of the Heartland*. Baton Rouge, Lousiana State University Press, 1967.

Cross, J. Russell. *Historic Ramblin's Through Berkeley*. Columbia, R. L. Bryan Co., not dated.

Dowdy, Clifford, and Louis H. Manarin. *The Wartime Papers of R. E. Lee*. New York, Bramhall House, not dated.

Evans, Clement A.. *Confederate Military History, Vol. V, South Carolina*. Secaucus, The Blue and Grey Press, not dated.

Gavin, William Gilfillan. *Campaigning with the Roundheads*. Dayton, Morningside Publishing Co., 1989.

Hagood, Johnson. *Memoirs of the War of Secession*. Columbia, The State Co., 1910.

Henderson, William D.. *41st Virginia Infantry*. Lynchburg, H. E. Howard, Inc., 1986.

Hood, J. B.. *Advance and Retreat*. Secaucus, Blue and Grey Press, 1985.

Hughes, Nathaniel C. Jr.. *General William J. Hardee: Old Reliable*. Wilmington, Broadfoot Publishing Co., 1987.

Johnson, John. *The Defense of Charleston Harbor*. Charleston, Walker, Evans &

Cogswell Co., 1890.

Johnson, Robert U.. and Clarence C. Buel. *Battles and Leaders of the Civil War of the Civil War, Volume I - IV*. Secacus, 1987 (Reprint).

LaBree, Ben. *The Confederate Soldier in the Civil War*. Louisville, The Courier Journal Job Printing Co., 1895.

LaBree, Ben. *Camp Fires of the Confederacy*. Louisville, The Courier Journal Job Printing Co., 1898

Law, Tom. *Citadel Cadets: The Journal of Tom Law*. Clinton: P C Press, not dated.

Lossom, Christopher. *Tennessee's Forgotten Warriors, Frank Cheatham and his Confederate Division*. Knoxville, University of Tennessee Press, 1989.

Malone, Dumas. *Dictionary of American Biography*. New York, Charles Schribner's Sons, 1964.

McDonough, James Lee, and Thomas L. Connelly. *Five Tragic Hours*. Knoxville, University of Tennessee Press, 1983.

McDonough, James Lee. *Chattanooga: A Death Grip on the Confederacy*. Knoxville, University of Tennessee Press, 1984.

McMurray, Richard M.. *John Bell Hood*. Lexington, The University Press of Kentucky, 1982.

Meredith, Roy. *Storm Over Sumter*. New York, Simon and Schuster, 1957.

Nesbit, James Cooper, edited by Bill Erwin Wiley. *4 Years on the Firing Line*. Wilmington, Broadfoot Publishing Co., 1989.

Noll, Arthur Howard. *Doctor Quintard*. Sewanee, The University Press, not dated.

Rosengarten, Theodore. *Tombee*. New York, William Morrow and Company, Inc., 1986.

Scaife, William R.. *The Campaign for Atlanta*. Atlanta, William R. Scaife, 1985.

Simkins, Francis Butler. *The Election of 1890 - The Tillman Movement in S.C.* Durham, Durham University Press, 1926.

Smithe, Mrs. A. T., Miss M. B. Poppenheim, and Mrs. Thomas Taylor. *South Carolina Women in the Confederacy*. Columbia, The State Company, 1903.

Sterling, Dorothy. *Captain of the Planter*. Garden City, Doubleday & INC., 1958.

Stern, Philip Van Doren. *Prologue to Sumter*. Greenwich, Fawcett Publications, Inc., 1961

Stevens, Robert J.. *Captain Bill, Book 1*. Richburg, The Chester District Genealogical Society, 1985.

Stevens, Robert J.. *Captain Bill, Book 2*. Richburg, The Chester District Genealogical Society, 1985.

Symonds, Craig L.. *A Battlefield Atlas*. Baltimore, The Nautical and Aviation Publishing Company of America, 1985.

Swanberg, W. A.. *First Blood*. New York, Charles Scribner's Sons, 1957

Thomas, J. A. W.. *A History of Marlboro*. Baltimore, Regional Publishing Company, 1978.

Taylor, John S.. *Sixteenth South Carolina Regiment CSA from Greenville County, S.C.* Greenville, Greenville County Confederate Centennial Commission, 1964.

Thomas, John P.. *History of the South Carolina Military Academy*. Charleston, 1893.

Tillman, S. F.. *The Tillman Family*. Richmond, The William Byrd Prss, Inc., 1930.

Tucker, Glenn. *Chickamauga: Bloody Battle in the West*. Dayton, Morningside Bookshop, 1984.

Warner, Ezra J.. *Generals in Gray*. Baton Rouge, Lousiana State University Press, 1959.

Warner, Ezra J.. *Generals in Blue*. Baton Rouge, Lousiana State University Press, 1964.

Watkins, Sam. *"Co. Aytch."* Wilmington, Broadfoot Publishing Co., 1987.

Woodward, C. Vann. *Mary Chestnut's Civil War*. New Haven, Yale University Press, 1981.

Yeary, Mamie. *Reminiscences of the Boys in Gray 1861-1865*. Dayton, Broadfoot Publishing Co., 1986.

NEWSPAPERS

The *Charleston Mercury*
The *Daily Courier*
The *Edgefield Advertiser*
The *Guardian*
The *News and Courier*
The *Charleston Evening Post*
The *State*
The *Augusta Chronicle & Sentinel*

BOOKLETS/PAMPHLETS

Appleby, J. Gavin and Yvonne Maxey. *History of Appleby Church and Hagerman Cemetery*. Not published, 1987.

_____. *United Daughters of the Confederacy Pamphlet: Confederate Dead Buried in Charleston*. Charleston, 1888.

Capers, Ellison. *Captain Francis Huger Harleston*. Suffolk, not dated.

Luvaas, Jay. *The Battle of Bentonville: Johnston's Last Stand*. Smithfield, not dated.

Wilcox, Arthur M., and Warren Ripley. *The Civil War at Charleston*. Charleston, The News and Courier, 1980.

GOVERNMENT DOCUMENTS

South Carolina State Archives (SA). Microcopy Number AO 700, Roll PEP.

U. S. Government. *Official Records of the War of the Rebellion, 128 Vol.* Harrisburg, The National Historical Society, 1971.

U. S. Government. *Official Records of the Union and Confederate Navies, 30 Vols.* Washington, 1894-1922.

The National Archives of the United States (NA). RG 109, Compiled Service Records, Microcopy, M267.

The National Archives of the United States. RG 109, Compiled Records of Confederate Organizations, Microcopy M861.

The National Archives of the United States. RG 109, The Ainsworth File, Microcopy T816.

The National Archives of the United States. RG 109, Letters Received by the Confederate Secretary of the Treasury, Microcopy M499.

The National Archives of the United States. RG 109, Letters sent by the Confederate Secretary of the Treasury. Microcopy M500.

The National Archives of the United States. RG 109, Index to Letters Received by the Confederate Secretary of War, Microcopy M4098.

The National Archives of the United States. RG 109, Index to the Letters Received by the Confederate Adjutant and Inspector General and by the Confederate Quartermaster General, Microcopy M410.

The National Archives of the United States. RG 109, Letters Received by the Confederate Adjutant and Inspector General, Microcopy M474.

THESES

Stark, William C., *History of the 103rd Ohio Volunteer Infantry Regiment, 1862-1865.* Ann Arbor, William C. Stark, 1986.

MANUSCRIPTS

Army War College
    J. D. Padgett Papers
Atlanta Historical Society
    Wilbur G. Kurtz Papers
The Citadel
    Ellison Capers Papers
    J. D. Padgett Papers
    J. H. Steinmeyer Papers
Chickamauga National Battlefield Park
    Ellison Capers Journal
Clemson University
    Tillman Papers
Duke University
    Braxton Bragg Papers
    Ellison Capers Papers
    Confederate States of America Archives
    W. H. T. Walker Papers
Emory University
    Confederate Miscellaneous
    Albert Quincy Porter Diary
Georgia Department of Archives and History
    Purvis Papers
    Cayman Papers
Georgia Historical Society
    W. P. Burt Diary
    A. E. Sinks Papers

Kennesaw Mountain National Battlefield Park
    Bears Maps
National Archives
    Ellison Capers Papers
Rice University
    W. M. Brooker Diary
South Carolina Archives and History
    Memory Rolls
South Carolina Historical Society
    Teague Papers
    Augustine T. Smythe Papers
    J. H. Steinmeyer Papers
    Stevens Family Papers
University of North Carolina
    Beckwith Papers
    Bragg Papers
    Ellison Capers Papers
    J. B. Cummings Papers
    Joseph Espey Papers
    Gale/Polk Papers
    Govan Papers
    R. M. Gray Papers
    Hall Papers
    Makall Papers
    Marcus J. Wright Papers
    Watson Diary
University of South Carolina
    Ellison Capers Papers
    Charles Cronenberg Papers
    Alfred Gailey Papers
    States Rights Gist Papers
    Manning/Chestnut/Miller Papers
    McGee Papers
    Sheppard Family Papers
    J. H. Steinmeyer Papers
    Clement Hoffman Stevens Papers
    Lawrence Whitaker Taylor Papers
    Waites Parker Family Papers
University of the South
    Ellison Capers Papers
    Gale/Polk Papers
Tennessee State Library and Archives
    Cheatham Papers
    Pictures

PRIVATE COLLECTIONS

Hills, Parker, Jackson, MS
    Confederate Deaths, Jackson, MS
    Battle of Jackson Maps
    Sketch of battle field
Kirkland, Randolph W., Pawleys Island, S.C.
    Roster at Surrender
Moseley, Cynthia, Spartanburg, SC
    Papers concerning General Clement Hoffman Stevens
Warren, Otto J., Orangeburg, SC
    J. K. Risher Papers
    Pictures of Capt. Joe K. Risher and survivors
Jones, Eugene W., Jr., Goose Creek, SC
    Jones Family oral history

INTERVIEWS

Bigham, John, South Carolina Relic Room. 1989.
Rivers, Mildred, Hampton County Museum. 1989.
Timmerman, Diane, Edgefield County Archives. 1989.
Wells, June, Confederate Museum, Charleston, S.C. 1989.

INDEX

Note: Does not include names on alphabetical roster.

486

Davis, Gen. Jeff C., 136, 194.

Davis, Maj. Henry C., 96-97.

Davis, President Jefferson, 7, 17-18, 74-75, 79-80, 84, 102, 108, 148, 152, 184, 186, 189,198-199, 201, 245-246.

Davis' Ford, 216.

Department of S.C., Ga., and Fla., 17.

Department of the South, 26.

Dodge's Corps, 180.

Dotterer, Sgt. Maj. James B., 99, 124, 162.

Duck River, 216, 235, 237-238.

East Point, Ga., 191.

Ector, Gen. M. D., 103, 122.

Edgefield Advertiser, 133.

Edgefield District, S. C., 14-15, 109, 247, 253.

Edgefield Light Infantry, 14, 35, 102, 134, 147, 157, 170, 253.

Edisto River (Island), S. C., 73-75.

Etowah River, 164, 203.

Eutaw Bn., 17, 21, 34, 41.

Evans, Gen. Nathan G. "Shanks," 26, 33, 38-39, 42, 80.

Evans Guard, 13, 27-28, 35.

Ezra Church, 184.

Feehan, Sgt. F. P., 87.

Ferguson's Light Battery, 80, 87, 151.

Flint River, 191.

Florence, Ala., 212-213, 215.

Florence, S. C., 206.

Folly Island, S. C., 11, 19, 22, 24, 74, 75.

Folly River, S. C., 26, 39.

Forrest, Gen. Nathan B., 219, 232, 238.

Forrest's Cavalry, 217, 232, 238.

Fort Delaware, 25.

Fort Johnson, S. C., 17-18, 22, 34, 45.

Fort Ripley, S. C., 18.

Foster, Col. W. G., 215.

Franklin, Tenn., 218-219, 222, 227-233, 235-237, 249, 252.

French, Gen. Samuel C., 169-170, 172, 236.

French's Div., 103, 169.

Gadsden, Ala., 111, 210.

Gaillard, Lt. Col. P. C., 28-29.

Garden, Capt. D. S., 223, 227, 243.

Georgia, State of, 201-202, 209-210, 225, 239-240, 244-245.

Georgia Troops, 63, 66, 86, 102, 160.
>   1st Confederate Georgia Bn., 250.
>   1st Georgia Regt., 150.
>   1st Bn., Georgia Sharpshooters, 86, 161-162.
>   2nd Bn., Georgia Sharpshooters, 173, 193-194, 233.

(Georgia Troops)

Hardtimes, 28-29, 89, 91, 107, 117, 121, 162, 191.
Harpeth River, 219, 225.
Harris, Sgt. Morris, 124.
Harrison House, 223, 229, 231-232, 237.
Hartford, Conn., 31.
Hartford Courant, 31
Hawkins, Lt. William G., 23-24, 30, 169, 244.
Helm, Gen. Benjamin H., 119, 122.
Helms' Brigade, 116-117, 119, 122.
Hill, Maj. D. F., 14, 106, 121-122, 124-127, 134, 150-151, 169, 189, 194-195.
Hill, Gen. D. H., 73, 116-117, 119, 122-123.
Hilton Head, S. C., 5, 7, 15, 26, 34, 50, 55, 67, 73.
Holmes, Lt. Alfred, 9, 75, 83, 151, 189, 194-195, 212, 214, 249.
Holmes' Brigade, 86-87.
Hood, Gen. John Bell, 3, 148, 160, 163, 165, 167, 173, 174, 177-178, 180, 184, 186-187, 189, 191-193, 195, 198-201, 204, 209-210, 212-214, 216, 219, 221, 227, 231-232, 235, 237-238, 244-245, 250.
Hoskins' Battery, 85, 87, 91.
Howard's (Eleventh) Corps, 136.
Hudson, Pvt. Andrew, 25.
Hudson, Pvt. B. C., 25-26.
Hundred Day Battle, 155, 175, 100.
Hunter, Gen. David, 26, 33-34, 42-43, 73.
Iowa Troops, 86, 207.
Irish Volunteers, 29.
Ironclad Battery, 4.
Jackson, Gen. H. R., 150-151, 227, 229, 236.
Jackson, Miss., 80-86, 88-96, 98, 101-104, 106-107, 117, 151, 191.
James Island, S. C., 17, 19, 21-22, 24-27, 31-32, 39, 43-45, 47, 49, 53, 66, 74-75, 77.
Jenkins' Brigade, 132-133.
Johns Island, 26.
Johnson Island, 138, 162.
Johnson, Capt. John, 27.
Johnson, Col. L., 204.
Johnson, Capt. Robert, 13, 122, 124, 126-127.
Johnson, Gen. Ed, 217, 229.
Johnston, Gen. Albert S., 14, 16.
Johnston, Gen. Joseph Eggleston, 70, 84-85, 91-93, 97-98, 100-103, 106-108, 115, 141-146, 148-151, 155, 157, 160-161, 163, 165-168, 171-176, 186, 198-200, 244-246, 248-252.
Johnston's Army, 85, 98, 100-103, 106, 108, 143, 251.
Jones, Lt. Col. Jesse Stancel, 11, 14, 25, 28, 61, 100, 117, 119-120, 122, 124, 126, 143, 150,117, 179, 184, 189, 192-193, 214, 223, 227-230, 233.
Jonesboro, Ga., 191-193, 195-198, 205, 210-211, 216, 219.
Kalmia, S. C., 186-187, 191.
Kelly's Farmhouse, 116-117.

Kennesaw Mountain, Ga., 168-172, 176.
Kershaw, Gen. Joseph B., 115.
Kinard, 1st. Sgt. Melvin L., 77, 79.
King, Gen. John H., 117.
King's Brigade, 117, 119.
Kingman, Maj. Robert H., 15, 43, 49.
Kingston, Ga., 111-112, 115, 126, 163.
Lane, John Q., 161.
Lane's Brigade, 218, 223.
Lay's Ferry, 161.
Lee, Gen. G. W. C., 75.
Lee, Gen. Robert E., 17, 57, 70, 107, 115, 144, 152, 177, 199, 244, 249, 251.
Lee, Gen. Stephen D., 107, 186, 216-217, 237-238.
Lee's Corps, 192-193, 195, 216, 229, 235, 237-238.
Legare Place, 26, 28-29.
Lewis, Gen. Joseph C., 194.
Lightwood Knot Springs, 15, 17.
Lincoln, President Abraham, 73.
Longstreet, Gen. James, 116, 123, 127, 141.
Longstreet's Corps, 112, 115, 127, 132, 134-135.
Lookout Creek, Tenn., 132-133.
Lookout Mountain, Tenn., 111, 128-129, 132, 136-137, 141, 209-210.
Loring, Gen. William W., 103, 170, 248
Loring's Division, 115.
Louisiana Troops, 33-36, 168.
Lovejoy Station, 195, 200.
Lucas Battery, 17.
Macon, Ga., 184, 190-191, 195, 214, 246.
Magnolia Cemetery, S. C., 3, 162.
Maney, Gen. George, 138, 188, 191-192.
Maney's Brigade, 138-139.
Manigault's Brigade, 137.
Marietta, Ga., 165-167, 170, 172, 203.
Marion Rifles, 5, 13, 28-30, 56, 64-68, 87, 164, 171, 244.
Marion Rifles Glee Club, 65, 83.
Marlboro District, 5, 13.
Martin, Pvt.. James B., 64.
Massachusetts Troops, 29.
McCollough, Col. James, 101, 127, 137, 188-189, 192.
McGee, Sgt. John Lewis (Buddy), 44, 46-48, 50, 53-54, 63, 65, 73-74, 99, 101-102, 104, 107, 111, 127, 129-130, 134-135, 140, 145, 184.
McGee, Lt. G. L., 53-54, 68.
McGee, Pvt. Silvester (Vessie), 46, 53-54, 59, 65-66, 68, 72-74, 101, 104, 106-107, 109, 126-127, 130-131, 134-135, 145, 153, 184, 209, 251, 255.
McGinnis' Ferry, 158, 161.
McPherson, Gen. James B., 86-87, 157-158, 177, 180.
Mercer's Brigade, 151, 157, 161, 188.

Michigan Troops, 29.

Miles, Congressman W. Porcher, 96-97, 246.

Mill Creek Gap, 155, 157, 205

Missionary Ridge, 127-129, 135-137, 140-141, 143, 145, 148.

Mississippi, State of, 81, 83, 88, 90, 92, 94, 97-100, 102, 107-109.

Mississippi Troops, 86, 96, 151, 160.
  5th Miss. Regt., 173.
  8th Miss. Regt., 150, 173.
  14th Miss. Bn., 85-89.

Missouri Troops, 87, 181, 183, 221, 267.
  10th Missouri Regt., 86, 88.

Morgan, Lt. Col. Thomas C., 15, 35, 127, 129, 134, 137-139, 143, 162, 235, 249, 253.

Morgan, Lt. Joseph E., 124, 127.

Morton, Miss., 106-107, 109.

Murfreesboro, Tenn., 232-233.

Napier, Lt. Col. Leroy, 121.

Nashville, Tenn., 196, 235-237, 240-241, 244, 252.

New Bern, N. C., 56-57, 63, 73.

New Hope Church, Ga., 165.

New Hampshire Troops, 35, 38, 40, 69.

New York Troops, 25.

Nisbet, Col. James C., 149, 152, 181, 184.

Northeast River, 56.

Ohio Troops, 163, 171.
  80th Ohio Regt., 86-87, 92, 95.
  97th Ohio Regt., 218, 226-227, 230-231.

O'Neal, Col. Edward A., 177, 179-180.

Ogier, Maj. Thomas S., Jr., 15, 57, 62, 93, 100, 109-110.

Old City Cemetery or Burial Grounds, 103.

Oostanaula River, 158, 160-161, 163.

Oothkaloga Creek, 161.

Overton House, 235.

Oxford, Ga., 126, 153, 176, 185-186.

Padgett, Lt. James D., 19, 21, 71, 167-168, 202.

Palmer, 1st Lt. J. Clarence, 15, 17, 41, 83, 89, 106, 110, 117, 119-121, 124, 151.

Palmetto, Ga., 198, 201.

Palmetto Sharpshooters, 48.

Paroled Prisoners Camp, 96-97.

Peachtree Creek, 3, 173-174, 177, 179-180, 184.

Pearson, Capt. John H., 14, 35, 50.

Pee Dee Rifles, 5, 13, 18.

Pemberton, Gen. John C., 17-18, 21-22, 26-27, 32-33, 39, 42, 65, 79, 84, 98, 100.

Pemberton's Army, 97-98, 100.

Pendleton, S. C., 4, 7, 18, 51-52.

Pennsylvania Troops, 28-30, 35.

Phillips Ferry, 202.
Pickens, Gov. F. W., 3, 11, 18, 49.
Pickett's Mill, 165.
Pine Mountain, 167-168.
Planter, 18, 23.
Pocotaligo, S. C., 49-50, 55, 66-68, 70-75.
Polk, Gen. Leonidas, 97, 116, 123, 160, 163, 166, 168, 175.
Polk, Gen. Lucius E., 119, 123, 141.
Polk's Corps, 170.
Porter, Gen. George C., 191.
Preston's Light Battery, 55-56, 74.
Pumpkin Vine Creek, 165.
Quintard, Bishop, 229.
Raccoon Mountain, 132.
Ravenel, Maj. St. Julian, 13.
Resaca, 157-158, 160-161, 204.
Rhett, Maj. Alfred, 50, 52.
Rhett, Robert Barnwell, 16, 51, 70, 73.
Rhode Island Troops, 35-36, 38.
Richland District, S. C., 14, 50.
Richmond, 17, 26, 47, 50, 55, 99, 148, 167, 193, 196, 244-245, 249.
Ringgold, Ga., 138-140, 155.
Ripley, Gen. Roswell S., 11-12, 18, 22, 27, 70.
Risher, Capt. Joseph K., 11, 14, 101, 124, 213, 227, 253.
Rivers' Place, 22, 26, 28.
Robinson, Sgt. B. E., 24.
Rockwell's Battery, 34.
Roddey, Capt. W. Lyle, 14, 134, 163, 205, 207.
Rome, Ga., 110-111, 115, 125-126, 129.
Rosecrans, Gen. William 108, 111, 115-116.
Roswell, Ga., 173, 175.
Rough and Ready, Ga., 200.
Rowlinski, Pvt. William, 126.
Rutherford Creek, 216, 238.
Savannah and Charleston Railroad, 9, 63-67, 73.
Schofield, Gen. John M., 163, 177, 209, 227, 231.
Scribner, Col. Benjamin F., 117.
Scribner's Brigade, 119.
Seabrook Island, S. C., 73, 75.
Secessionville, Battle of, 39, 43, 71.
Secessionville, S. C., 17, 21-22, 27, 32-33, 41, 43-45, 47-51, 55, 72, 74-75, 81,
    87.
Seddon, Secretary James., 84, 97, 108.
Sherard, Capt. Samuel W., 14, 54, 205.
Sherman, Gen. William T., 86, 95-96, 104, 135-136, 155, 157, 160-161, 163,
    165-168, 170, 172-175, 177, 187, 190-196, 200-201, 204, 207,209-210,
    212, 214, 233, 239-240, 245, 247, 250-252.

EUGENE WALTER JONES, JR.

The author is a retired federal employee and a resident of Goose Creek, South Carolina after serving over 40 years Federal government service. He holds a Master of Arts degree. While making his retirement plans, he attended a Civil War seminar at Fort Ward in Alexandria, Virginia, and purchased the book which informed how to trace one's Civil War ancestors. That book mentioned that there had been little written about the 24th Regiment, South Carolina Volunteers Infantry. He decided then and there that he would pursue the activities of the 24th as his retirement vocation. Later he discovered that some of his ancestors had indeed served in the regiment. After nearly eight years, his efforts have culminated in publication of this book.

Gene Jones is a member of the Sons of Confederate Veterans and various other Civil War organizations. Although this is his first book, he is working on other aspects of the Civil War and expects to offer them soon.

GETTYSBURG TITLES

These Honored Dead: The Union Casualties at Gettysburg, **REVISED EDITION**, by John W. Busey. Full listing of all 5101 killed and mortally wounded, listed by state and regiment, plus complete alphabetical index. A definitive study that gives age, enlistment data, nature of wound, and burial data. New edition contains 100 extra pages and over 20 new photographs of casualties. 508 pages, over 40 illustrations. Hard bound. Published 1996. $30.00.

The Last Full Measure: Burials in the Soldiers' National Cemetery at Gettysburg, by John Busey. The only published index to the cemetery; contains corrected name listings. 277 pages, 7 illustrations, map. Hard bound. Published 1988. $20.00.

Regimental Strengths and Losses at Gettysburg, **THIRD EDITION**, by John Busey and Dr. David Martin. Revised and Corrected edition of this highly respected study. Contains order of battle and strength information not available elsewhere. Detailed comparative strength and loss tables. 360 pages, indices. Hard bound. Published 1994. $20.00.

Final Report of the New Jersey Gettysburg Battlefield Monument Commission. Reprint of scarce 1891 government report. Gives excellent background on the erection of the monuments and their dedication ceremonies. 194 pages, numerous illustrations, index; 1 new map added. Published 1997. $20.00.

New Jersey Troops in the Gettysburg Campaign, by Samuel Toombs, Reprint of 1888 edition, with new introduction and index by Dr. David Martin. 440 pages. Hard bound. Published 1988. $30.00.

Address Delivered at the Rededication of the Monument to the First New Jersey Brigade at Gettysburg, October 9, 1982, by Dr. David Martin. 12 page booklet. Published 1992. $3.50.

A Casualty at Gettysburg and Andersonville: Selections from the Civil War Diary of Private Austin A. Carr of the 82nd New York Infantry, edited by Dr. David G. Martin. 22 page booklet. Published 1990. $6.00.

Holding the Left at Gettysburg: The 20th N.Y.S.M. on July 1, 1863, by Seward Osborne. A well received original booklet. 36 pages, 2 maps, 6 photographs. Published 1990. $6.00.

Order from Longstreet House, PO Box 730, Hightstown, NJ 08520
Postage $3.00 per order. N.J. residents kindly include tax.